Legacies of the
Permanent Court of International Justice

Queen Mary Studies in International Law

Edited by

Malgosia Fitzmaurice
Panos Merkouris
Phoebe Okowa

VOLUME 13

The titles published in this series are listed at brill.com/qmil

Legacies of the Permanent Court of International Justice

Edited by

Christian J. Tams
Malgosia Fitzmaurice

Assistant editor

Panos Merkouris

MARTINUS NIJHOFF PUBLISHERS

LEIDEN · BOSTON
2013

Library of Congress Cataloging-in-Publication Data

Legacies of the Permanent Court of International Justice / edited by Christian J. Tams, Malgosia Fitzmaurice.
pages cm. -- (Queen Mary studies in international law ; v. 13)
ISBN 978-90-04-24493-1 (hardback : alk. paper) -- ISBN 978-90-04-24494-8 (e-book) 1. Permanent Court of International Justice. 2. Jurisdiction (International law) 3. Arbitration (International law) 4. International courts. I. Tams, Christian J. II. Fitzmaurice, M.
KZ6260.L44 2013
341.5'52--dc23

2012044132

This publication has been typeset in the multilingual "Brill" typeface. With over 5,100 characters covering Latin, IPA, Greek, and Cyrillic, this typeface is especially suitable for use in the humanities. For more information, please see www.brill.com/brill-typeface.

ISSN 1877-4822
ISBN 978-90-04-24493-1 (hardback)
ISBN 978-90-04-24494-8 (e-book)

This book is printed on acid-free paper.

FSC www.fsc.org MIX Paper from responsible sources FSC® C109576

Printed by Printforce, the Netherlands

CONTENTS

PART THREE

THE PCIJ AND OTHER FORA OF DISPUTE RESOLUTION

PART FOUR

METHOD AND SOURCES

PART FIVE

CONSTITUTIONAL INTERNATIONAL LAW

CONCLUSIONS

PREFACE

The present book brings together papers presented at a conference on 'The Permanent Court and Modern International Law', co-organized by Queen Mary University of London, the University of Glasgow, the British Institute for International and Comparative Law, and the Embassy of the Republic of Poland in London. To these, a number of 'commissioned' contributions have been added.

The editors gratefully acknowledge the support received from the Modern Law Review Seminar Fund and the Polish Ministry for Foreign Affairs, and in particular Dr Maciej Szpunar, Under-Secretary of State in the Ministry of Foreign Affairs of the Republic of Poland, and Mr Emil Pietras, formerly of the Embassy of the Republic of Poland in London. During the various stages of planning, organizing and editing, Dr Panos Merkouris (London), Ms Athene Richford (Glasgow) and, at Brill, Ms Ingeborg van der Laan, have been of great assistance, and we are grateful to them.

August 2012
Glasgow and London

Malgosia Fitzmaurice
Christian J. Tams

LIST OF CONTRIBUTORS

JEAN D'ASPREMONT is Professor of Public International Law, University of Manchester.

CATHERINE BRÖLMANN is Associate Professor of International Law at the University of Amsterdam, Department of International Law and Research Fellow at the Amsterdam Centre for International Law.

MALGOSIA FITZMAURICE is Professor of Public International Law in the Department of Law, Queen Mary, University of London.

MARIKA GILES SAMSON is O'Brien Doctoral Fellow at the Centre for Human Rights and Legal Pluralism, Faculty of Law, McGill University.

JOANNA GOMULA is Visiting Reader at the Centre for Commercial Law Studies, Queen Mary College, University of London, and a Fellow at the Lauterpacht Centre for International Law, Cambridge.

DOUGLAS GUILFOYLE is Reader in Law at the Faculty of Laws, University College London.

URSULA KRIEBAUM is Professor for Public International Law at the University of Vienna, Department of European, International and Comparative Law.

ROMAN KWIECIEŃ is Associate Professor of Law at Maria Curie-Sklodowska University in Lublin (Poland).

PANOS MERKOURIS is Post-Graduate Teaching Associate at Queen Mary, University of London.

PHOTINI PAZARTZIS is Associate Professor of International Law, National and Capodistrian University of Athens, Faculty of Law.

ANNELIESE QUAST MERTSCH is Special Assistant to the Executive Head, UNCC Secretariat, Geneva.

AKBAR RASULOV is Lecturer in Public International Law, University of Glasgow.

IAIN SCOBBIE is the Sir Joseph Hotung Research Professor in Law, Human Rights and Peace Building in the Middle East at SOAS, University of London.

OLE SPIERMANN is a Partner at Bruun & Hjejle Law Firm, Copenhagen and a former Professor in International Law at the University of Copenhagen.

CHRISTIAN J. TAMS is Professor of International Law, University of Glasgow.

ANTONIOS TZANAKOPOULOS is University Lecturer in Public International Law at the University of Oxford and Fellow of St Anne's College. He also teaches at the University of Glasgow.

STEPHAN WITTICH is Associate Professor of International Law, University of Vienna.

INTRODUCTION

Malgosia Fitzmaurice and Christian J. Tams

> The PRESIDENT in opening the sitting, stated that it marked the commencement of the work for which the Court had been established. In fact, it was the opening of the first ordinary session of the Court, fixed by the Statute for June 15th of each year.[1]

In these rather matter-of-factly words, the minutes record the beginning of the PCIJ's 'operative life' on 15 June 1922, almost ninety years ago to the day.[2] The Court's first proceedings dealt with rather mundane issues;[3] but to most participants and many observers, the establishment of the PCIJ was anything but a mundane matter. The British Attorney-General, Sir Ernest Pollock, expressed his hope that

> each case here decided [by the newly-established Court] may light a beacon over the shoals and rocks of misunderstandings, by which they can be avoided in the future, that gradually step by step, a causeway may be built, by reverence and respect for public law, for international rights and international aims, that will lead to enduring peace worthy of the great lawyers before whom I stand, worthy of the great nations which are here represented.[4]

Four months earlier, at the Permanent Court's inaugural ceremony, the Secretary-General of the League of Nations, Sir Eric Drummond, had praised the Court's establishment as 'the greatest and ... most important creative act of the League' and had gone on to observe:

> There have been various well-distinguished marks in the progress of mankind. The opening of the Court is not the least of these. Indeed, we believe and hope that it will prove the greatest. After all, the ideal to which

---

[1] [1922] PCIJ Ser C No 1, vol I (Public Sittings), at 1. (These and all other official documents relating to the Permanent Court are available at <www.icj-cij.org/pcij/>).

[2] Four months earlier, the PCIJ had held its preliminary and inaugural sittings, devoted notably to the elaboration of the first Rules of Court. For details see [1922] PCIJ Ser D No 2.

[3] Namely issues arising from the *Designation of the Workers' Delegate for the Netherlands at the Third Session of the International Labour Conference*, the PCIJ's first Advisory Opinion ([1922] PCIJ Ser B No 1).

[4] [1922] PCIJ Ser C No 1, vol II (Speeches and Documents), at 42.

> I presume all men of goodwill look forward is that not only individual nations but the whole world shall be ruled by law.[5]

Twenty-four years, sixty-five proceedings, thirty-two judgments and twenty-seven Advisory Opinions later, the 'great [land]mark in the progress of mankind' was displaced rather quietly—but, perhaps fittingly for a judicial institution, in an orderly way. Judges tendered their resignations in early 1946, following which the Assembly of the League of Nations (after deliberations in the First Committee) decided that the PCIJ could be terminated by agreement; and after this had been effected through a resolution of 18 April 1946;[6] the PCIJ's registry oversaw the transfer of archives and property to the ICJ. The Court's active life of course had effectively ceased in 1940, when German troops had invaded the Netherlands.[7]

***

The decision to dissolve the PCIJ after World War II was taken deliberately, and after considerable debate.[8] Most agreed that—just as the League—so the new world order of the United Nations should include a court. Yet a majority felt that a fresh start required new players, and the PCIJ, while not one of its organs, was too closely linked to the League, whose structural deficiencies the United Nations sought to overcome.[9] And so, on one view,

---

[5] [1922] PCIJ Ser D No 2, at 320.

[6] [1946] LNOJ Spec Suppl 194, 256; and also reproduced in *ICJ Yearbook 1946–1947*, 28–29, fn 2. The operative paragraph provided that "the Permanent Court of International Justice is for all purposes to be regarded as dissolved with effect from the day following the close of the present session of the Assembly" (ie 19 April 1946). A concise summary can be found in S Rosenne, *The Law and Practice of the International Court, 1920–2005* (Vol 1, Nijhoff, Leiden/Boston 2006) 14–16.

[7] From 1940, the PCIJ's President and the Registrar were based in Geneva, at the seat of the League, while 'Judge Jonkheer van Eysinga sought to defend the rights of the PCIJ at The Hague'. See Ole Spiermann, Historical Introduction, in A Zimmermann, C Tomuschat, K Oellers-Frahm, and CJ Tams (eds), *The Statute of the International Court of Justice. A Commentary* (2nd edn, OUP, Oxford 2012) 68–69.

[8] The matter had notably been left open in the influential report of the Informal Inter-Allied Committee (the 'London Committee': see (1945) 39 AJIL (Supplement) 1–42); and at Dumbarton Oaks. The decision in favour of a new court was reached at the San Francisco Conference: see the reports of Subcommittee IV/1/A and Subcommittee IV/1, both in *United Nations Conference on International Organization*, vol 13, at 524 and 381. Drawing on informal accounts, Rosenne states that the decision to dissolve the PCIJ was reached with a majority of 7:3 (with Brazil, France and the United Kingdom against) (n 6, 66).

[9] To quote again Rosenne (n 6, 66): 'Both Powers [the USSR and the United States], it seems, shared a general belief that the previous association of the Permanent Court with the League of Nations would be an inauspicious augury for the reconstruction of the judicial arm of the organized international community.'

the PCIJ has been history for six-and-a-half decades and the active PCIJ for more than seven. It could be said to belong to the past, in fact an increasingly distant one.

Yet the organizational rupture between the old and the new was merely superficial. True, the new Court was a novel entity, was given a new name; it was to hold its own inaugural session; and in some ways it differed from the old.[10] But in most respects, it was supposed to follow in the PCIJ's footsteps:[11] formally a new institution, it was closely modelled on the PCIJ; led initially by the same President;[12] and for the first 25 years of its existence, it effectively applied the PCIJ's Rules of Court.[13] Having advocated the establishment of a new court, Subcommittee IV/1 of the San Francisco Conference confidently observed that this would

> not break the chain of continuity with the past. ... [T]he 1945 Statute will garner what has come down from the past ... [and] continuity in the progressive development of the judicial process will be amply safeguarded.[14]

Indeed, the new Court quickly made clear that it had no intention to break the 'chain of continuity'. From early on, its jurisprudence built on that of the PCIJ, to which ICJ judgments and opinions refer frequently. In short, the organizational break notwithstanding, there was, and there remains,

---

10 Among them, the organic link with the United Nations (cf Articles 7 and 92–96 of the Charter); and the decision to move away from the system of general elections of judges.

11 In the opening paragraphs of their 'General Introduction' to the ICJ Statute, Robert Jennings and Rosalyn Higgins note that '[t]he intention in 1946 was that there should be continuity between the new Court and the old Court, the PCIJ' (in Zimmermann, Tomuschat, Oellers-Frahm, and Tams, n 7, 4). In October 1945, the PCIJ had equally passed resolutions seeking to ensure 'continuity in international justice': cf *ICJ Yearbook 1946–1947*, 26.

12 Namely José Gustavo Guerrero, elected President of the PCIJ in late 1936 (in office 1937–1946) and President of the ICJ from 1946–1949. With Charles de Visscher, another serving PCIJ judge (1937–1946) was elected to the ICJ's first bench.

13 In 1946, the ICJ took over the 1936 version of the PCIJ's Rules of Court with only minimal amendments. These were not revised until 1972 and again, comprehensively, in 1978.

14 *United Nations Conference on International Organization*, vol 13, 381, at 383.

A very similar point was made in one of the earliest retrospective studies of the PCIJ, JP Fockema Andreae's *An Important Chapter from the History of Legal Interpretation: The Jurisprudence of the First Permanent Court of International Justice* (Sijthoff, Leyden 1948), in which the author observed on p 141: 'But in any case it is to be expected that much of the present legal material, i.e. as far as laid down in treaties, conventions, declarations etc. from the first years after the world war of 1914, shall have lost its importance and that the judgments of the Court based on it shall have lost their practical value.' Yet this did not 'in the least mean that the great pains which the Court has taken, will have been in vain. The judgments and advisory opinions keep their full value as instructive examples, as precious specimens of the thorough, sagacious and noble way in which the Court has considered the legal questions put before it and which it has brought to a solution.'

'functional continuity between the two Courts',[15] and this has been the dominant narrative: in fact, in Manley O Hudson's influential '*annuaire*', the year 1946 was not primarily a new beginning, but 'the twenty-fourth year of the world court',[16] and without much ado, comprehensive works treat the jurisprudence of the World Court's 'two incarnations'—notwithstanding changing in circumstances and perceptions over time—in principle as one joint *acquis*.[17]

***

Against that background, the contributions to the present book assess legacies of the Permanent Court. 'Organizational rupture' and 'functional unity/continuity' are taken as premises; and an attempt is made to bring to light choices and challenges that faced the PCIJ. As the term 'legacy' implies, this is retrospection, but one that appreciates the PCIJ in its own right rather than reducing it to the role of a precursor that would morph into the ICJ. The focus of the inquiry is on the legal and institutional framework within which the PCIJ operated, and on the law that it applied and shaped. More specifically, the contributions are organized in five parts: (i) A first cluster of pieces explores the PCIJ's regime of jurisdiction: Marika Giles Samson and Douglas Guilfoyle, as well as Panos Merkouris trace the Court's invention and application of advisory proceedings at the international level; while Christian J Tams assesses the different bases of contentious jurisdiction and highlights how in the 1920s, the modern understanding of contentious jurisdiction was shaped. (ii) Four further contributions—by Stephan Wittich, Catherine Brölmann, Ursula Kriebaum and Joanna Gomula—analyse the PCIJ's influence on selected areas of substantive law: the law of treaties, minority and human rights law, rules of international trade, and those designed to protect foreign investments.

Three further clusters of contributions are devoted to more specific sets of questions: (iii) Anneliese Quast, Iain Scobbie and Jean d'Aspremont address the relationship between the PCIJ and other judicial and arbitral bodies of the inter-War period—an early, sometimes overlooked,

15 Rosenne (n 6) 73.

16 MO Hudson, 'The Twenty-Fourth Year of the World Court' (1946) 40 AJIL 1.

17 Rosenne's *Law and Practice of the International Court (1920–2005)* (n 6) is a prominent example; on p 16 of that book, the author speaks of the two Courts' 'joint history', which he suggests can be divided into five periods. See also JHW Verzijl, *The Jurisprudence of the World Court* (2 vols., Sijthoff, Leyden 1965/1966) whose two volumes address the work of the PCIJ and ICJ respectively.

variation on the theme of 'proliferation'. (iv) In two very different pieces, Photini Pazartzis and Akbar Rasulov deal with fundamental aspects of legal method: the former revisiting the Court's *Lotus* judgment, the latter scrutinizing the PCIJ's conception of sources and the role of a contractual paradigm in particular. (v) Antonios Tzanakopoulos and Roman Kwiecień use the PCIJ's jurisprudence to reflect on 'constitutional' issues, namely the Permanent Court's perception of the international community (a notion subsequently popularized by its successor) and its contribution to what might be termed international constitutional law more generally. The book concludes with Ole Spiermann's general assessment of the Court, whose work, in Spiermann's words, 'brought not only the Peace Palace but also international law to life.'[18]

***

As readers will quickly realize, the approaches adopted in the contributions vary, and contributors do not necessarily agree on the relevance of the PCIJ's legacy in 'their' respective area. However, while reaching different conclusions, the contributions share two characteristics. First, throughout, the PCIJ is—to adapt an expression coined by Richard Falk—assessed as 'fact', not as 'dream'.[19] This may be obvious, but it seems worth mentioning: With the establishment of a permanent international court, the dream of organised and regular adjudication by an international court—giving effect to 'the ideal [of] the whole world ... ruled by law'[20]—had become a possibility. However, the newly-established Court that many had dreamt of had to grapple with realities, practical as well as political; had to attract and persuade its clients; and had to find its place in the legal system of the day and within the organised international community. The contributions to the book provide much evidence of the difficulties encountered in the process.

Second, throughout, an attempt is made to appreciate the PCIJ not merely as a precursor to the ICJ, but as an institution in its own right. Of course, in order to assess legacies, one has to identify what has remained; and typically, contributions conclude with reflections on developments post-1945. However, the PCIJ is not treated as a prequel; instead, the

18 O Spiermann (in this volume), at 400.

19 See R Falk, *Reviving the World Court* (Univ Press of Virgina, Charlottesville 1986), chapter 1.

20 Cf Drummond (n 5).

different contributions revisit debates of the day, occasionally unearth forgotten evidence, and often provide fresh perspectives.

The perspectives offered in the following are diverse, and no one single view on the PCIJ is presented. Yet two recurring 'themes' can be made out: The first is that of the *PCIJ as a pioneer*. This is well-known aspect of our retrospective assessment of the Permanent Court: '[w]hat remains so particularly attractive about the Permanent Court and its decisions is that they were pioneers' writes Ole Spiermann early on in his *International Legal Argument*.[21] Pioneering was the 'invention' of advisory proceedings;[22] pioneering was the Court's 'judicial legislation' in the field of minorities law, 'a new body of law, without much doctrine or precedent to rely on';[23] and a pioneering spirit was required where the Court, in handling questions of jurisdiction, admissibility and procedure, 'had to determine how it would discharge its judicial function, and had to do so more or less from scratch'.[24] These are but a handful of examples, of course, and the subsequent contributions provide much further evidence of the Permanent Court's pioneering work, which indeed 'remains so particularly attractive'[25] and which retains its relevance (as Ursula Kriebaum and Joanna Gomula show) even in areas of international law that have undergone substantial reform.[26]

A common association is that pioneers not only venture into new terrain, but that they march boldly, oblivious to threat and danger. The chapters provide evidence of that, no doubt; but they also show the *PCIJ as a pragmatic institution*. This second theme, does not immediately fit in with idealistic views of a world court supervising a world order based on law; but it is a recurring feature of many of the subsequent chapters. Roman Kwiecień emphasises the Court's willingness to rely on a consensual model of international law, which could be said to be a pragmatic strategy

---

21 O Spiermann, *International Legal Argument in the Permanent Court of International Justice* (Cambridge, CUP 2005), 19.

22 See M Giles Samson and D Guilfoyle (in this volume), at 42–43, for brief comment on the background.

23 C Brölmann (in this volume), at 142.

24 I Scobbie (in this volume), at 208, (where the process is aptly described as one of 'role-negotiation'). Aspects of this role-negotiation are addressed in the chapters on advisory proceedings, as well as the contributions by Tams, Quast and d'Aspremont.

25 Cf Spiermann (n 21).

26 See the contributions by U Kriebaum (on foreign investment) and J Gomula (on world trade law) to this volume.

designed not to frighten its 'customers'.[27] Jean d'Aspremont points to PCIJ cases in which the Court drew a clear line between international law and domestic legal orders (which were famously said to be 'merely facts'[28]), but also notes that the PCIJ, unlike its successor, 'had no qualms endorsing the role of domestic courts and independently acting as a domestic court'.[29] In matters of jurisdiction and procedure as well, the Court, in 'mapp[ing] out the contours of the international judicial function',[30] was certainly not oblivious to the dangers of judicial activism, but typically moved cautiously.[31] In fact, even in respect of advisory jurisdiction (which certainly was pioneering or 'innovative in conception') Marika Giles Samson and Douglas Guilfoyle observe that it 'did not prove groundbreaking in design or execution'.[32] In short, while the PCIJ was a pioneer, it typically moved carefully, and the general picture emerging may perhaps be said to be that of 'pragmatic pioneer'.

***

As the subsequent contributions show, this 'pragmatic pioneer' was in many respects more than just the ICJ's precursor, or its 'previous incarnation'. It faced particular challenges, and as many contributors note, it operated in a different era. A retrospective assessment cannot ignore these differences; they concern, amongst other things, the institutional setting, the density of international rules, and the different priorities of participants in international dispute resolution.[33] However, even though the conditions of international adjudication have changed, the 'pragmatic pioneer' remains relevant: In many fields, the PCIJ's 'accepted success [has

[27] R Kwiecien (in this volume), at 392–393.
Akbar Rasulov challenges the dominance of a consensualist/contractualist paradigm in PCIJ jurisprudence and pointedly describes the Court as a 'committed practitioner of conceptualist reasoning'; however he would not seem to rule out that the Court (pragmatically) might have felt the need to use consensualist arguments so to maintain its position. See A Rasulov (in this volume) at 308.
[28] Cf *Upper Silesia Case*, [1926] PCIJ Ser A No 7 at 19.
[29] J d'Aspremont (in this volume), at 236.
[30] I Scobbie (in this volume), at 203.
[31] See also CJ Tams (in this volume) especially at 29–33.
[32] M Giles Samson and D Guilfoyle (in this volume), at 67–68.
[33] To give just two examples, explored by Stephan Wittich and Antonios Tzanakopoulos in their contributions, when the PCIJ pronounced on the law of treaties or began to deal with issues of community interest, it could not draw on developed sets of rules, but needed to map the ground itself.

indeed] ensured the constitution of its successor';[34] in others, the Court may have missed opportunities or taken wrong directions. Yet one thing seems clear: the PCIJ's legacies are manifold. The subsequent contributions identify and assess many of them. They are an invitation to reacquaint ourselves with a pragmatic pioneer that began to operate ninety years ago and that, for better or worse, has shaped our thinking about binding legal dispute resolution.

34 Sir R Y Jennings, 'The International Court of Justice after Fifty Years' (1995) 89 AJIL 493.

PART ONE

JURISDICTION

THE CONTENTIOUS JURISDICTION OF THE PERMANENT COURT

Christian J. Tams

I. Introduction

Like its successor, the International Court of Justice (ICJ), the Permanent Court of International Justice (PCIJ) possessed a dual jurisdiction comprising contentious and advisory proceedings. While the concept of advisory jurisdiction had to be 'invented',[1] contentious proceedings are the natural province of courts, including those established at the international level: courts settle disputes between parties, in proceedings submitted by one or both of them. The PCIJ formed no exception, and yet its approach to contentious jurisdiction displays peculiar features, which contemporary debate risks overlooking. International lawyers have become so used to the jurisdictional regime of the 'World Court'[2] that its basic aspects are simply taken for granted. Against that background, the initial purpose of the present contribution is to raise awareness of the fact that our understanding of the contentious jurisdiction of the World Court is by no means natural, but the result of decisions taken during the establishment of the PCIJ (Section II). On that basis, Sections III and IV assess how the PCIJ's regime of contentious jurisdiction fared in practice, notably by looking at the practice of States as the main 'clients' of the Court, and at the Court's approach to issues of contentious jurisdiction. Section V concludes.

---

[1] For comments on this successful 'invention' see the contribution from D Guilfoyle and M Giles Samson to the present volume.

[2] The term 'World Court' is used here to refer collectively to the PCIJ and the ICJ as the two standing international courts of potentially general jurisdiction. The term is used for reasons of convenience, and as it has become common shorthand parlance. As will be shown below, in section II, it is not without problems, as it may raise expectations that the PCIJ was, and the ICJ is, unable to fulfill. For much more on the point see G Abi-Saab, 'The International Court as a World Court' in M Fitzmaurice and V Lowe (eds), *Fifty Years of the International Court of Justice: Essays in Honour of Sir Robert Jennings* (CUP, Cambridge 1996), 3.

II. The Framework: Contentious Jurisdiction in the Statute

The Statute of the Permanent Court regulated contentious proceedings in Chapters II and III (Articles 34–64).[3] The majority of these provisions addressed the procedural regime to be followed—the languages to be used, the role of counsel and agents, the interaction between the bar and the bench etc.[4] By contrast, only four provisions, Articles 34–37, dealt with the *contentious jurisdiction proper* of the Court. These four provisions—set in the chapter on the Court's 'competence'[5]—were the product of long deliberations, within the Advisory Commission of Jurists and, subsequently, the League Council and Assembly.[6] It was clear to contemporary observers that the regime they laid down was a "central and vital point in the constitution of the Court", as it predetermined "the Court's sphere of action, and to a great extent, therefore, its usefulness and value".[7]

For nine decades, these "central and vital"[8] provisions have determined the scope of the World Court's contentious jurisdiction. As neither the

---

[3] See [1926] 1st edn PCIJ Ser D No 1 at 7, for the initial PCIJ Statute of 1922, and [1940] 4th edn Ser D No 1 for the revised Statute (as modified by the Protocol of 1929). The latter document is largely identical to the present ICJ Statute.

Both versions of the Statute, as well as all other PCIJ publications referred to in the following, are available online at http://www.icj-cij.org/pcij/index.php?p1=9.

[4] See Articles 39, 40 and 43–45 of the PCIJ Statute.

[5] Then as now comprising Articles 34–38, ie provisions on the scope of the Court's contentious jurisdiction and the law to be applied by the Court.

[6] See notably the following documents published by the PCIJ (all available at http://www.icj-cij.org/pcij/other-documents.php?p1=9&p2=8): (i) Advisory Committee of Jurists, Documents presented to the Committee relating to existing plans for the establishment of a Permanent Court of International Justice, 1920; (ii) Advisory Committee of Jurists, Procès-verbaux, 1920; (iii) Documents concerning the action taken by the Council of the League of Nations under Article 14 of the Covenant and the adoption by the Assembly of the Statute of the Permanent Court, 1921. Insightful summaries are provided by B Schenk Graf Stauffenberg, *Statut et Règlement de la Cour Permanente de Justice internationale* (Carl Heymann, Berlin 1934) 2 et seq; RP Anand, *Compulsory Jurisdiction of the International Court of Justice* (1961) 18–25; O Spiermann, *International Legal Argument in the Permanent Court of International Justice* (CUP, Cambridge 2005) 3–22; idem, 'Historical Introduction' in A Zimmermann, C Tomuschat, K Oellers-Frahm, and CJ Tams (eds), *The Statute of the International Court of Justice: A Commentary* (OUP, Oxford/ New York 2nd edn 2012); J Kammerhofer, 'Introduction' in *League of Nations, Advisory Committee of Jurists for the Establishment of a Permanent Court of International Justice* (reprint: 2006); S Rosenne, 'Permanent Court of International Justice' in R Wolfrum (ed) *Max Planck Encyclopedia of Public International Law* (OUP 2006) online edition <www.mpepil.com> [4]-[9].

[7] AP Fachiri, *The Permanent Court of International Justice: Its Constitution, Procedure and Work* (OUP, Oxford 1925) 53.

[8] Ibid.

Protocol of 1929 nor the debates of 1944–45 introduced substantial changes to Articles 34–37,[9] it is no surprise that international lawyers should have grown so accustomed to it. Yet, upon reflection, the Statute's approach to contentious jurisdiction was by no means "natural" or obvious. Quite to the contrary, it was the consequence of three important decisions taken in 1920, during the preparation of the initial PCIJ Statute, which shaped three essential features of the World Court's regime of contentious jurisdiction:

(i) State-centrism: Article 34 clarified that the World Court would handle inter-State disputes only (plus those involving dominions admitted to the League).
(ii) Derivative jurisdiction: While linked in some way to the respective world organisation of the time, the World Court would not be integrated into that organisation's constitutional regime. It would be an agency for settling disputes arising under *other* treaties or general international law rather than (like the ECHR, the WTO Appellate Body, or the ECJ) an institution supervising a substantive regime of international law; in this respect, its contentious jurisdiction was derivative.
(iii) Lack of automatic jurisdiction: The World Court would not possess automatic jurisdiction (or 'compulsory jurisdiction' in the proper sense of the word), but depend on the consent of parties, typically expressed in special agreements (*compromis*), compromissory clauses or unilateral declarations.

It is worth noting that on all of these issues, one might have opted for a different approach. It would have been perfectly possible (and indeed perhaps even more desirable for a World Court) to adopt a different a concept of contentious jurisdiction, to define "the Court's sphere of action"[10] differently. A World Court could very well possess automatic jurisdiction—and indeed, one of the common misconceptions about the Court is that it does.[11] It could be open to parties other than States. It could be closely

---

[9] The main textual changes adopted in 1945–46 are the following: (i) the modification of Article 37, which in the ICJ Statute has become a 'renvoi clause' transferring PCIJ jurisdiction to the ICJ; and (ii) the addition, in Article 36(1), of a reference to "matters specially provided for in the Charter of the United Nations", which—as explored below—is of no practical relevance.

[10] Fachiri (n 7) 53.

[11] It is telling that in recent years, the ICJ has gone out of its way to stress the limits of its jurisdiction—as if to avoid being criticized for failing to render justice to the world: see e.g. the following statement to the press by Judge Rosalyn Higgins, the Court's (then) President, made immediately after the reading of the Court's judgment in the *Bosnian Genocide case*

linked to a 'World Order treaty' like the UN Charter or the League Covenant and charged to supervise compliance with it. And yet, for ninety years, the PCIJ and ICJ have followed the model devised in 1920: they are State-centred, their jurisdiction is derivative, and it is consensual, not automatic. Before assessing how the regime of contentious jurisdiction has fared in practice, each of these aspects merits some further comment:

1. *State-Centrism*

Since the inauguration of the PCIJ in 1922, Article 34 of the PCIJ and ICJ Statute has meant that the World Court's contentious jurisdiction would effectively be limited to inter-State disputes. It is worth noting that the PCIJ Statute was slightly less strict than the ICJ Statute: whereas the latter provides that "[o]nly States can be parties in cases before the Court"; the former also mentioned "Members of the League of Nations". This was meant to give access to the Court to those Dominions of the British Empire and India that had joined the League even though their statehood was disputed.[12] For practical purposes, though, requiring either statehood or membership in the League ensured that the parties in contentious proceedings were a relatively homogeneous group of States, complemented by a small number of 'quasi-States' or 'would-be-States'. It notably excluded the direct participation, in contentious proceedings, by individuals, groups, peoples, and international organisations, whose concerns either had to be represented by States of nationality under the concept of diplomatic protection, or raised in advisory proceedings.

(26 February 2007) <www.icj-cij.org/court/index.php?pr=1898&;pt=3&p1=1&p2=3&p3=1>: "In this case, the Court's jurisdiction is solely based on Article IX of the Genocide Convention. This means that the Court has no authority to rule on alleged breaches of obligations under international law other than genocide, as defined by the Genocide Convention. This is important to understand because in this case we were confronted with substantial evidence of events in Bosnia and Herzegovina that may amount to war crimes or crimes against humanity—but we had no jurisdiction to make findings in that regard. We have been concerned *only* with genocide—and, I may add, genocide in the legal sense of that term, not in the broad use of that term that is sometimes made."

[12] For brief comment see Fachiri (n 7) 54 et seq; Shabtai Rosenne, *The Law and Practice of the International Court, 1920–2005* (Martinus Nijhoff, The Hague 2006) 591; and idem, 'Permanent Court of International Justice' (n 6) [28]. Article 34 was supplemented by Article 35, pursuant to which the Court was "open to the Members of the League and also to States mentioned in the Annex to the Covenant"; other States could participate in proceedings if they accepted the jurisdiction of the Court in accordance with the Covenant and the Statute—as clarified in the League Council's resolution of 17 May 1922, reproduced in MO Hudson, *The Permanent Court of International Justice 1920–1942: A Treatise* (Macmillan, New York 1943) 755–756.

During the drafting of the PCIJ Statute, Article 34 gave rise to some debates, but was not a major issue. The Committee of Jurists was cautious to note that the provision would be "without prejudice to any subsequent development of the Permanent Court of International Justice", but—having mentioned potential direct claims by individuals against States—"was unanimously of opinion that ... for the moment [the Court's jurisdiction *ratione personae*] must be given a basis which, though restricted, would, for that very reason, be firmer and more substantial."[13] Accordingly, the Committee's draft (which otherwise put forward far-reaching proposals for the Court's jurisdiction) envisaged the PCIJ as a court competent to address "suits between States".[14] While this was no doubt a plausible approach and in line with the State-centred approach of international law at the time, it should be noted that other early standing courts like the Central American Court of Justice (the Court of Cartago)[15] or the abortive International Prize Court[16] had been more inclusive. From today's perspective, Article 34 may still be a useful 'filter' shielding the World Court from mass litigation; however, it is increasingly seen as "out of tune with modern international requirements".[17]

---

[13] Advisory Committee of Jurists, Procès-verbaux (n 6) 723.

[14] This expression was used in the Draft Article 31 of the Advisory Committee's text (reproduced in Advisory Committee of Jurists, Procès-verbaux; *supra* n 6).

[15] See Article II of the Statute of the Central American Court of Justice (100 BFSP 841), which authorized the Court to "take cognizance of the questions which individuals of one Central American country may raise against any of the other contracting Governments, because of the violation of treaties or conventions, and other cases of an international character; no matter whether their own Government supports said claim or not; and provided that the remedies which the laws of the respective country provide against such violation shall have been exhausted or that denial of justice shall have been shown". For details see MO Hudson, 'The Central American Court of Justice' (1932) 26 AJIL 759; SM Jordison, 'The Central American Court of Justice: Yesterday, Today and Tomorrow?' (2009) 25 Conn. J Intl L 183, 194 et seq. In his Hague lectures, Lucius Caflisch offers the following assessment of the Central American Court of Justice: "une experience qui aurait pu être exaltante et qui, dans l'histoire du RPD [règlement pacifique des différends], n'a guère trouvé son pareil" ('Cent ans de règlement pacifique des différends interétatiques', (2001) 288 Receuil des Cours 245, 314).

[16] See Article 4 of the Convention on the Establishment of an International Prize Court, which envisaged claims by individuals against judgment of national prize courts (in Deuxième Conférence internationale de la Paix. Actes et documents, vol I, 668). On the Prize Court (and the reasons for its failure) see U Scheuner, 'International Prize Court', in EPIL II, 1346; Brown, 'The Proposed International Prize Court' (1908) 2 AJIL 458; Scott, 'The International Court of Prize' (1911) 5 AJIL 302.

[17] Rosenne, *Law and Practice* (n 12) 591. For a comparative perspective see F Orrego Vicuña, 'Individuals and Non-State Entities before International Courts and Tribunals' in JA Frowein, R Wolfrum and CE Philipp (eds), 5 *Max Planck Yearbook of United Nations Law*

2. *Derivative Jurisdiction*

A second aspect may be less obvious, but is equally fundamental to our thinking about the contentious jurisdiction of the World Court. It concerns the way by which the Court's jurisdiction is established. This matter was addressed in Article 36 of the PCIJ Statute which—in near-identical terms to the present provision—provided in relevant part:

> The jurisdiction of the Court comprises all cases which the parties refer to it and all matters specially provided for in treaties and conventions in force.
>
> The Members of the League of Nations and the States mentioned in the Annex to the Covenant may ... declare that they recognize as compulsory ipso facto and without special agreement, in relation to any other Member or State accepting the same obligation, the jurisdiction of the Court.

As was soon appreciated, this meant that the Court's jurisdiction could be established in three main ways: through special agreements ("cases which the parties refer to it"), through compromissory clauses ("matters specially provided for in treaties and conventions in force") and through matching unilateral declarations submitted under the 'optional clause' of Article 36(2). As is well-known, these three modes of conferring jurisdiction shape the World Court's contentious jurisdiction to this day.[18] For present purposes, Article 36 is crucial not only for what it states expressly, but also for what it implies. As is clear from the provision, the Statute itself—with the exception of instances of mandatory jurisdiction over incidental matters—did not provide the Court with jurisdiction in contentious proceedings. It was an invitation to provide the Court with jurisdiction: a vessel waiting to be filled with life.

This may seem obvious, as this is how the World Court has functioned for nine decades.[19] However, it is worth noting that the approach followed

(Martinus Nijhoff, The Hague 2001), 53. For broader perspectives on non-State actors and the ICJ see the contributions in *International Community Law Review* 9/2 (2007); especially Martin Scheinin 'The ICJ and the Individual', ibid at 123.

18 See below, section IV(2), for brief comments on *forum prorogatum*, which is sometimes viewed as a fourth basis of jurisdiction.

19 It is important to note that the approach adopted in 1920 was continued in 1944–45, notwithstanding the fact that the ICJ was to be the UN's 'principal judicial organ' (cf Article 92 of the UN Charter). While integrated into the institutional structure of the new world organization, the ICJ's contentious jurisdiction continues to depend on other treaties and other expressions of consent. In particular, the reference, in Article 36(1) of the ICJ Statute, to "all matters specially provided for in the Charter of the United Nations" is not an autonomous head of jurisdiction, as the Charter (notwithstanding the Security Council's power to recommend recourse to the Court, as per Article 36(3) of the Charter) does not provide the Court with compulsory jurisdiction. For details see the joint separate opinion of seven

in 1920, and confirmed after World War II, has lost appeal over time. Courts established since World War II have typically followed a different 'jurisdictional structure'.[20] Rather than setting up an institution and waiting for it to be vested with competence, States more recently have preferred to set up courts—as well as other dispute settlement mechanisms—as parts of comprehensive sectoral regimes. Institutions like the ECJ, SADC, regional human rights courts, the WTO Appellate Body, but also ITLOS and its alternatives under Part XV LOSC follow a jurisdictional 'design' very different from that of the World Court: they are part and parcel of a comprehensive regulatory regime that lays down substantive rules and establishes dispute settlement institutions as the 'guardian' of a treaty, typically with compulsory jurisdiction to address disputes.[21] This in turn has important consequences for our understanding of dispute settlement.[22] It may result in courts acquiring specialised expertise; it allows for tailor-made dispute settlement reflecting the demands of a given subject-area; in the long run, it may result in courts developing a sense of 'ownership' of 'their' regime.

None of these concerns was felt very strongly in 1920. Rather than specialised, the World Court was designed to possess potentially general competence. Accordingly, the PCIJ was not set up as the 'guardian' of a specific treaty; it was not limited to dispute settlement in a particular area. And as it depended on the willingness of States to 'opt in', to realise the potential of Article 36, its jurisdiction was always going to be a patchwork. At the time, this indeed seemed the normal way to proceed. Multilateral law-making was still in its infancy:[23] law-making treaties agreed at major international conferences were becoming a common method of regulating international affairs, most visibly at the Hague Conferences of 1899 and 1907; however, treaties typically focused either on substantive rules *or* on dispute settlement procedures—rather than combining substantive

judges in the *Corfu Channel Case*, ICJ Rep [1948] 15, 31; and Rosenne, *Law and Practice* (n 12) 669 et seq. For suggestions as to the potential use of the phrase "all matters specially provided for in the Charter of the United Nations" cf C Tomuschat, in Zimmermann, Tomuschat, Oellers-Frahm and Tams (n 6) at 664–665.

20 See Y Shany, 'No Longer a Weak Department of Power? Reflections on the Emergence of a New International Judiciary' (2009) 20 EJIL 73, 79–80.

21 The move towards a 'compulsory paradigm' is explored (and perhaps overstated) in CP Romano, 'The Shift from the Consensual to the Compulsory Paradigm in International Adjudication: Elements for a Theory of Consent' (2007) 39 NYU J Intl L & Politics 791, especially at 808 et seq.

22 Shany (n 20), 80, argues that "the new courts seem to be committed to a different ethos from that which had underlain the PCIJ and ICJ".

23 For much more on this see James Crawford, 'Multilateral Rights and Obligations in International Law' (2006) 319 Recueil des Cours 325.

regulation and dispute settlement in a comprehensive normative framework.[24] The idea that a major regulatory instrument would include a specialised enforcement mechanism—absolutely common today, and tried out in fields as diverse as the law of the sea, investment protection, arms control (typically side-stepping binding dispute resolution) and environmental law—had not been fully accepted. And conversely, the need for tailor-made dispute settlement procedures reflecting the particular demands of specialised areas of international law was felt less acutely: with the potential carve-out for questions of national honour,[25] arbitration and adjudication were held to be *generally* useful methods of dispute resolution, not context-specific.

Consequently, the Hague Conferences had established the Permanent Court of Arbitration as an agency for dispute settlement that would become active when (and only when) States decided to avail themselves of it.[26] And the drafters of the PCIJ, while moving from 'permanency in name' to permanency proper,[27] followed the same approach that required an 'opt-in'. With the benefit of hindsight, it seems clear that in so doing, they designed a particular type of World Court: one that (in terms of its jurisdictional regime) increasingly stands out from the mass of specialised courts supervising 'their' respective treaties.

---

24 The 'dispute settlement movement' of the late 19th and early 20th century provides a good example: 'peace through law' was to be attained on the basis of general dispute settlement conventions of a bilateral or (preferably) multilateral type; not through establishing comprehensive, but sector-specific, regimes. For a clear illustration see e.g. H Kelsen, *Peace Through Law* (The University of North Carolina Press, Chapel Hill 1944) 13 et seq.

25 Cf the typical caveat, in bilateral dispute settlement conventions, exempting disputes affecting 'vital interests' or 'national honour' of parties, which became "a stock formula for bilateral arbitration treaties of the late 19th and early 20th century]" (JL Simpson and H Fox, *International Arbitration: Law and Practice* (Stevens, London 1959) 16).

26 See Article 38 of the 1907 Hague Convention for the Pacific Settlement of International Disputes, which provided: "In questions of a legal nature, and especially in the interpretation or application of International Conventions, arbitration is recognized by the Contracting Powers as the most effective, and, at the same time, the most equitable means of settling disputes which diplomacy has failed to settle. Consequently, it would be desirable that, in disputes about the above-mentioned questions, the Contracting Powers should, if the case arose, have recourse to arbitration, in so far as circumstances permit." For brief comment see Caflisch (n 15) 309; and further CJ Tams, 'Die Zweite Haager Konferenz und das Recht der friedlichen Streitbeilegung' (2007) 82 *Die Friedens-Warte* 119, 126–127.

27 As is often observed, the Permanent Court of Arbitration "is neither a court nor permanent" (R Mackenzie et al, *Manual on International Courts and Tribunals* (2nd edn, OUP, Oxford 2010) 102; similarly Caflisch, (n 15) at 309). One might add that it has stopped arbitrating under the Hague Conventions long ago, and since focuses on the administration of arbitration proceedings instituted under other agreements (Tams (n 26) 131–132).

3. *No Automatic Jurisdiction*

Article 36 yields another lesson. By requiring States to opt into the jurisdictional regime, the drafters accepted that the World Court would not possess automatic jurisdiction.[28] In this respect as well, the Statute has shaped our thinking about the World Court's contentious jurisdiction. Unlike with respect to the previous point, the decision taken in 1920 (against automatic jurisdiction) was the result of heated debate, but after the Court's inauguration in 1922 seems to have become quickly accepted.[29] A quick glance at the drafting of the PCIJ Statute is sufficient to appreciate how decisively contemporary international lawyers have moved on.

In fact, in 1920, the international community came very close to accepting the principle of general compulsory jurisdiction on the universal level. Pursuant to Article 33 of the Advisory Committee Draft, each State would have been able to bring before the PCIJ any dispute that had been found "impossible to settle ... by diplomatic means".[30] As the Committee made clear in its explanatory commentary, jurisdiction would still have been consensual—however consent to the Statute would have been sufficient to establish jurisdiction. This approach, the Committee felt, "followed the spirit" of the Hague Conferences and Article 13 of the League Covenant to an extent that it would have been "a great pity, now that the Court is being definitely organized, *not* to complete the progress made" so far.[31]

As is well-known, intervention by the Great Powers within the League Council, precluded this dispute settlement revolution.[32] After much

---

[28] Admittedly, this may be but another way of looking at the distinction between courts with derivative jurisdiction and courts set up as guardians of treaties: in fact, the rise of the latter is seen as evidence of a new trend towards the 'compulsory paradigm' in binding dispute settlement: see notably Romano (n 21). However, it is clear that even this new form of sectoral compulsory jurisdiction remains premised on consent; what has increased is the cost of remaining out of the dispute settlement framework.

[29] For details on the Court's 'internalization' see below, section IV.

[30] Advisory Committee of Jurists, Procès-verbaux (n 6) 726. Pursuant to Hudson, this provision 'was the outstanding feature of the draft scheme to occupy the attention of the Council and the Assembly' (n 12) 191).

[31] Advisory Committee of Jurists, Procès-verbaux (n 12) 727. The Japanese member, Minéitciro Adatci, was the 'lone dissenter' at this stage. The Committee was not persuaded by his view that Draft Article 33 was at odds with the voluntarist approach underlying Article 13 of the League Covenant, pursuant to which the Members of the League had agreed that "whenever any dispute shall arise between them which they recognise to be suitable for submission to arbitration or judicial settlement and which cannot be satisfactorily settled by diplomacy, they will submit the whole subject-matter to arbitration or judicial settlement".

[32] The various amendments to the Draft Scheme are published in Documents concerning the action taken by the Council of the League of Nations (n 6). A useful summary is provided by Anand (n 6) 34–37.

debate,[33] the Council abandoned Draft Article 33 in favour of the more modest scheme of Article 36, arguing that the Committee's approach could not be brought in line with the principle of voluntary adjudication underlying Articles 12 and 13 of the League Covenant.[34] Both in the Council, and in the ensuing debate in the League Assembly, Great Power delegates were careful to emphasise their support for the principle of compulsory jurisdiction, but "felt" that if these things are to be successful, they must be allowed to grow".[35] A dispute settlement 'reform' was to be preferred to 'revolution'—much to the chagrin of delegates of smaller powers and commentators who criticised the Great Powers' lack of inspiration,[36] just as an earlier generation of commentators had chided Germany and its allies for blocking the principle of compulsory arbitration at The Hague, in 1907. The curious 'optional clause system', enabling States to accept the Court's jurisdiction "as compulsory *ipso facto* and without special agreement" eventually was to prove an "ingenious compromise"[37] allowing everyone to save face.

Since 1920, things have taken a different turn. Rather than gradually grow (as predicted by the 'reformists'), the idea of general compulsory jurisdiction—at least at universal level—has lost momentum. As will be shown below, the PCIJ almost immediately embraced the principle of consensualism.[38] The General Act for the Pacific Settlement of International Disputes[39] marked the last major attempt to introduce compulsory arbitration or adjudication through a universal dispute settlement treaty, yet limited ratification and far-reaching reservations affected its relevance.[40] In 1945 at San Francisco and 1948/49 (when the General Act

33 In the words of Manley Hudson, Article 36 had been "the result of the greatest contest waged in the creation of the Court" (n 12) 190).

34 See notably the report by Léon Bourgeois, in Documents concerning the Action taken by the Council of the League of Nations (n 6) 47.

35 As noted by Mr. Balfour, the British representative in the League Assembly (in League of Nations, Records of the First Assembly, Plenary Meetings, 243). For further references see Anand (n 6) 34–35.

36 See e.g. the statements of Mr Urrutia (Colombia) (in Documents concerning the Action taken by the Council of the League of Nations (n 6) 241), Mr Costa (Portugal) (ibid at 245), and Mr Fernandez (Brazil) (ibid at 234).

37 Anand (n 6) 35.

38 See below, section IV.

39 LNTS, vol 93 344.

40 Caflisch (n 15) 317–318. For a contemporary perspective on the 1928 General Act see JL Brierly, 'The General Act of Geneva, 1928' (1930) 11 BYIL 119; for a clear summary cf F Freiherr von der Heydte, 'General Act for the Pacific Settlement of International Disputes, 1928' in EPIL II, 499.

was revised), history was to repeat itself, if not as a farce, then certainly in a much less dramatic way: In the Washington Committee of Jurists set up in 1945, a majority of members favoured the principle of compulsory jurisdiction, but felt unable to recommend a move towards it because of staunch opposition from the United States and the Soviet Union.[41] In San Francisco, Committee IV/1 opted to retain the status quo.[42] Soon afterwards, the General Assembly, attempted to revise the 1928 General Act, but failed to garner real support. Since then, for all intents and purposes, the idea of a World Court possessing general compulsory jurisdiction has been abandoned. To be fair, it continues to inform dispute settlement conventions agreed at the regional level;[43] and (as mentioned already[44]) it is being implemented in special, sectoral, areas of international relations such as investment, trade, and the law of the sea. Yet even among the more idealist international lawyers, the proposition that a World Court should have compulsory jurisdiction over all types of inter-State disputes is unlikely to find acceptance.[45] The modern approach to adjudication has become (depending on one's perspective) 'realistic', or 'technical/cynical': dispute settlement has been successfully de-coupled from war-prevention; it is useful, no doubt, but no longer seen as a cure-all. Re-reading the debates of 1920 (or 1907, for that matter) illustrates the difference in perception.

III. Contentious Jurisdiction in Practice

A second set of observations relates to the attitude of States vis-à-vis the PCIJ's regime of contentious jurisdiction. As Articles 34–37 of the Statute in essence were an invitation to confer jurisdiction, the attitude of States was decisive. In assessing it, two main questions may be asked: Did States

---

41 For details see Anand (n 6) 39–41. The report of the Washington Committee, by Professor Basdevant, is at UNCIO, vol XIV, 840.

42 See UNCIO, vol XIII, 391; and further Anand (n 6) 42–44.

43 See the 1948 American Treaty on Pacific Settlement, UNTS vol 30, 55; and the 1957 European Convention for the Peaceful Settlement of Disputes, UNTS vol 329, 243.

44 Section II(2).

45 See Rosenne, *Law and Practice* (n 12) 16 et seq. More generally, Caflisch speaks of the decline of (binding) peaceful dispute settlement (n 15) 318 et seq.). Pursuant to Shany, the World Court—initially 'established as a dispute-settlement body primarily designed to offer states an attractive alternative to international violence'—'over time, effectively redefined [its] role and assumed the more mundane tasks of defusing low-level and mid-level tensions before they escalate further ... [T]he PCIJ and ICJ seem to have transformed themselves from providers of heroic and life-saving emergency treatment into providers of preventive health care and quality-of-life related treatment': Shany (n 20) 80.

accept the invitation and establish the Court's jurisdiction over relevant aspects of their international relations? And if so, did they actually use the Court's jurisdictional potential by instituting contentious proceedings?[46] With respect to both questions, a closer look at the PCIJ's record yields an interesting answer.[47]

1. *The Court's Jurisdictional Potential*

The Court's jurisdictional potential depended on the extent to which States were prepared to confer jurisdictional competence upon it. As has been noted above,[48] Article 36 of the Statute envisaged three main heads of jurisdiction: dispute-specific special agreements, treaty-based compromissory clauses and unilateral declarations under the optional clause. When seeking to evaluate the PCIJ's potential, the latter two forms of consent to jurisdiction *ante hoc* are of particular relevance. An analysis of States' practice under these two bases of jurisdiction suggests a surprisingly clear result. The PCIJ had a huge jurisdictional potential; even though the Statute had rejected the notion of compulsory/automatic jurisdiction, States, almost enthusiastically, recognised the Court's jurisdiction to decide disputes in contentious proceedings. This result can be verified with respect to treaty-based compromissory clauses as well as unilateral declarations under the optional clause.

Compromissory clauses are the most obvious indicator. Judged by present-day standards, the number of treaties envisaging unilateral recourse to the PCIJ as an agency of dispute settlement is remarkable. Even today, it seems fair to say that the potential for unilateral proceedings under compromissory clauses is under-appreciated. Yet, it was during the inter-War era that compromissory clauses were most common. While

---

For a more ambitious approach asserting the continuing relevance of general compulsory jurisdiction see AA Cançado Trindade, 'The Relevance of International Adjudication Revisited: Reflections on the Need and Quest for International Compulsory Jurisdiction' in R St. John Macdonald and D Johnston (eds), *Towards World Constitutionalism* (Martinus Nijhoff, Leiden/Boston 2005) 515. A similar approach is advocated in his dissenting opinion appended to the ICJ's judgment in the *Georgian-Russian Racial Discrimination* case (Judgment of 1 April 2011, at www.icj-cij.org).

46 See Rosenne, *Law and Practice* (n 12) 797.

47 The subsequent section draws on, and develops, arguments set out in more detail in CJ Tams, 'The Continued Relevance of Compromissory Clauses as a Source of ICJ Jurisdiction' in T Giegerich (ed), *A Wiser Century?—Judicial Dispute Settlement, Disarmament and the Laws of War 100 Years after the Second Hague Peace Conference* (Duncker & Humblot, Berlin 2009) 461.

48 Section II(2).

precise figures are difficult to establish,[49] estimates suggest that in the two decades of the PCIJ's existence, as many as 500 compromissory clauses were concluded, ie roughly twenty-five per year.[50] To help put this figure in perspective, it is useful to compare it to developments since 1946. These in fact are revealing: the ICJ has seen roughly 300 clauses in sixty-five years, ie less than five per year, and very few at all since the 1970s.[51] Compared to that, the PCIJ was much more successful in 'attracting' compromissory clauses.

Admittedly, the absolute figure of compromissory clauses is just the starting point of the analysis: the true jurisdictional potential of a Court depends not just on the number of treaty-based compromissory clauses, but also on their substantive and personal scope. As regards the latter, it seems fair to say that the rise of multilateral treaty-drafting since World War II has seen a shift from bilateral clauses to multilateral ones.[52] Yet it is a gradual shift, and even in the inter-War period, multilateral treaties were by no means uncommon. As regards their substantive scope, the picture is mixed. Some treaties were clearly limited in scope, others covered relevant aspects of international relations. To give just a handful of examples, the PCIJ was competent to address disputes under most of the minority protection treaties and mandate agreements,[53] under the 1944 ICAO Convention[54] and under the 1926 Anti-Slavery Convention.[55] Beyond

[49] A list of compromissory clauses referring to the PCIJ agreed before 1932 can be found in [1932] PCIJ Series D No 6 (4th edn). After 1932, the PCIJ no longer produced a consolidated list, but included information on new clauses in the respective Chapter X of its Annual Reports (published as Series E No 8, 9, 10 etc). The most reliable source is LB. Sohns (ed) *Systematic Survey of Treaties for the Pacific Settlement of International* Disputes, *1928–1948* (United Nations 1949).

[50] FL Morrison, 'Treaties as a Source of Jurisdiction' in L F Damrosch (ed), *The International Court of Justice at Crossroads* (Transnational Publishers, Dobbs Ferry, NY 1987) 58, 69. Anand (n 6) gives a figure of 400 (at 38). The PCIJ itself, in its last annual report, takes a middle way, noting that '[s]ome four or five hundred international instruments are in force, providing for the Court's jurisdiction' (Series E No 16, 11).

[51] See the list of clauses available at <http://www.icj-cij.org/jurisdiction/index.php?p1=5&p2=1&p3=4>. The Court itself has added the following disclaimer: "The fact that a treaty is or is not included in this section is without prejudice to its possible application by the Court in a particular case."

[52] Developments in consular relations illustrate the point: acceptance of the ICJ's jurisdiction under Article I of the (multilateral) Optional Protocol to the Vienna Convention on Consular Relations has rendered obsolete many PCIJ compromissory clauses found in bilateral treaties on consular relations.

[53] For details see Nathan Feinberg, 'La jurisdiction et la jurisprudence de la Cour permanente de Justice internationale en matière de mandates et de minorités' (1937 I) 59 Receuil des Cours 591.

[54] UNTS, vol 15, 293 (Article 84, requiring a prior decision by the ICAO Council).

[55] LNTS, vol 60, 253 (Article 8).

these agreements regulating substantive questions of international law, to which an ancillary dispute settlement clause was added, it is worth noting that—unlike in the ICJ era[56]—States during the inter-War period entered into (bilateral or plurilateral) dispute settlement conventions on a regular basis, which established the PCIJ's jurisdiction over all kinds of disputes between the relevant State parties.

Finally, it is worth noting that compromissory clauses agreed during the PCIJ's times, as a general rule bound all States parties to the relevant treaty. The many subtle and not-so-subtle avoidance techniques invented since World War II did not yet feature. Reservations—now commonly used to avoid the possibility of contentious proceedings before the ICJ—were rare and their effects controversial.[57] As importantly, treaty drafters did not at the time make regular use of flexibility mechanisms that in subsequent decades would be deployed to permit the establishment of contentious jurisdiction *à la carte*: optional protocols 'outsourcing' dispute settlement into separate treaties[58] (which participating States could elect to join, but did not have to) were rather uncommon; opt-in or opt-out models of dispute settlement clauses were unheard of.[59] In sum, and at the risk of overgeneralisation, compromissory clauses of the inter-War years tended to be straightforward. Given their number and scope, it is no exaggeration to say that the PCIJ's jurisdictional potential was enormous.

---

[56] Since 1946, dispute settlement conventions have gradually lost relevance. Two regional conventions have been mentioned already (*supra* n 43); in recent years, States have begun to make use of them. However, the number of bilateral dispute settlement treaties has dropped dramatically, the last one having been concluded in 1965.

[57] The modern regime of reservation, recognizing the permissibility of reservations as long as these are compatible with a treaty's object and purpose, only became accepted when the ILC's, in its work on treaty law and after considerable hesitation, accepted the approach adopted in the ICJ's *Genocide* opinion ([1951] ICJ Rep 15) for details see [1]-[16] of the ILC's explanatory commentary to Draft Articles 16 and 17 of its Draft Text on the Law of Treaties (Yearbook ILC 1966, vol. II, 203–207).

[58] See e.g. the Optional Protocols to the Vienna Conventions on Diplomatic and Consular Relations (UNTS, vol. 500, 241, and vol 596, 487) or to the four 1958 Geneva Conventions on the Law of the Sea (UNTS, vol. 450, 169).

[59] Article 27(3) of the 2004 UN Convention on Jurisdictional Immunities (not yet in force, annexed to GA Res 59/38 [2004]) provides an example of an 'opt-out mechanism': it allows State parties to declare that they do 'not consider [themselves] bound by [the compromissory clause of] paragraph 2'.

As regards 'opt-in mechanisms' see e.g. Art 15(2) of the Espoo Convention (UNTS, vol. 1989, 309), which provides that 'a Party may declare in writing to the Depositary that for a dispute not resolved in accordance with paragraph 1 of this Article [i.e. through negotiation], it accepts one or both of the following means of dispute settlement as compulsory in relation to any Party accepting the same obligations: (a) Submission of the dispute to the International Court of Justice; (b) Arbitration in accordance with the procedure set out in Appendix VII.' A similar approach has been adopted in many environmental agreements.

Crucially, the willingness of States to submit unilateral declarations under the optional clause confirmed this impression. A curious compromise formula devised in 1920, the optional clause system, at least from the late 1920s onwards, proved to be surprisingly popular.[60] This in fact is implicit in the popular comments about the 'decline of the optional clause'[61] since the 1950s: whether or not these comments remain justified today, at a time of gradual increase in the number of declarations,[62] may be open to doubt. However, at least initially, a feeling of 'decline' was hard to avoid, as the ICJ's jurisdictional potential under Article 36(2) had to be compared to that of the PCIJ. And in this respect, one cannot fail to notice that indeed, States parties to the PCIJ Statute made use of the 'option' of Article 36(2) in large number: after a modestly successful start, the figure of States recognising the PCIJ's jurisdiction rose quickly: In 1939, of the fifty-two States parties to the Statute or otherwise entitled to appear before the PCIJ, forty had submitted an optional clause declaration; this amounted to roughly 75%.[63] A quick glance at present-day statistics underlines the relevance of these figures: at the time of writing, sixty-eight of the 193 parties to the Statute have submitted an optional clause declaration; the relative figure has dropped from nearly 75% to approximately 35%.

A closer look would seem to confirm this impression. For once, the optional clause was popular among States of political influence. In the early 1930s, four of the permanent members of the League Council (the United Kingdom, France, Germany and Italy) had submitted optional clause declarations[64]—whereas today, only one of the P-5 (the United Kingdom) has availed itself of that possibility.[65] To move to individual instances, even the Nazi German government, soon after having assumed power in 1933, chose to re-affirm the German declaration for a further five years.[66] Finally, and in line with what has been stated already in the

---

60 It is widely assumed that the British declaration of 19 September 1929 was responsible for the subsequent rise of the optional clause: see Rosenne, 'Permanent Court of International Justice' (n 6) [30].

61 Cf CHM Waldock, 'Decline of the Optional Clause' (1955–56) 32 BYIL 244.

62 For a list of optional clause declaration see <http://www.icj-cij.org/jurisdiction/index.php?p1=5&p2=1&p3=3>.

63 Cf Rosenne, *Law and Practice* (n 12) 797–798. In total, the number of States that at some point submitted a declaration amounted to 45: see MO Hudson, *International Tribunals: Past and Future* (Carnegie Endowment for International Peace and Brookings Institution, Washington DC 1944) 76–78.

64 See PCIJ Series D (n 49), at 55 et seq.

65 Two other permanent members, France and the United States, withdrew their declarations in 1974 and 1984 respectively.

66 See PCIJ Series E No 10, 274.

context of compromissory clauses, it deserves to be noted that declarations of the inter-War period typically were short and straightforward; while they often included reservations, these—on average—tended to be not as far-reaching as those attached to modern-day declarations.[67]

In short, just as compromissory clauses were very common, optional clause declarations meant that a huge range of inter-State disputes could be brought before the PCIJ by way of unilateral application. As a result of both factors, and notwithstanding the decision against compulsory jurisdiction in the proper sense of the term, the PCIJ's jurisdictional potential was enormous.

2. *States' Reluctance to Make Use of the Court*

Against that background, it may be asked whether States made use of their jurisdictional options. Did they actualize the Court's potential by instituting contentious proceedings? On this count, the PCIJ's record is equally revealing. Whereas States established the Court's jurisdiction with surprising regularity (and in fact much more regularly than States today), they hardly ever submitted actual disputes to the Court. On the basis of the manifold optional and compromissory clauses, the PCIJ could have been seized with a whole range of high-profile or everyday cases; yet States decided to use the Court only exceptionally. The Court's enormous jurisdictional potential therefore was not 'translated' into real cases. Four points may serve to support this general assessment:

First, the number of contentious cases litigated before the PCIJ remained very limited. Between 1922 and 1946, thirty-three contentious cases were brought before the Court (ie less than one-and-a-half per year).[68] Of these, eleven were based on a special agreement, and twenty-two (ie one per year) on consent expressed *ante hoc*, whether in the form of optional clause declaration or a compromissory clause. Even compared to the ICJ, these figures are very limited indeed;[69] they make very clear that States considered recourse to the World Court to be a highly exceptional form of dispute settlement.

---

67 For much more on this see Hudson (n 12) 449 et seq. Cf further Rosenne, *Law and Practice* (n 12) 739, who notes that until the late 1920s, 'the admissibility of reservations to declarations accepting the optional clause was controversial'.

68 See the list of contentious cases in PCIJ Series E (n 50) 43–44 and 51–54; and H Lauterpacht (ed), *Oppenheim's International Law* (vol II, 7th edn, D McKay, New York 1952) 80–83. Cf further CW Jenks, *The Prospects of International Adjudication* (Stevens, London 1964) 71.

69 Between 1946 and 2011, 126 contentious cases have been brought before the Court: for a list see <http://www.icj-cij.org/docket/index.php?p1=3>.

Second, the small number of cases was brought by an even smaller number of States. Most States parties to the Statute never appeared before the Court in contentious proceedings. The thirty-three cases involved a total of twenty-four States.[70] More specifically, the widespread recognition, by States from all continents and regions, of the Court's jurisdiction did not result in widespread use of the Court. Only in *four* cases did non-European States appear, and in only *one* single case did a non-European State (Brazil) play a decisive role.[71] The PCIJ therefore essentially remained an institution for European 'clients'.[72]

Third, and perhaps most tellingly, only the smallest proportion of the many jurisdiction-conferring instruments was ever invoked before the Court. The point may be best illustrated by looking at the approximately 500 compromissory clauses[73] establishing the Court's jurisdiction. Of course, with only fourteen cases based on Article 36(1) of the Statute, it is no surprise that the number of compromissory clauses actually invoked would remain small. However, it was really very small: only eight out of approx 500 compromissory clauses were ever invoked.[74] Beyond the mere statistics, it is interesting to note that of the fourteen compromissory clause cases, twelve were based on agreements concluded as part of the political settlement following World War I, such as the Treaties of Versailles and Trianon, Mandate Agreements, Minority Treaties, and the German-Polish Convention on Upper Silesia. This meant that while the Court had been founded to inaugurate a new era, in practice—at least in cases based on compromissory clauses—it was busy addressing the 'follow up' of the previous War. By contrast, there was "little reflection in the business of the Court of the widespread network of bilateral treaties of conciliation, arbitration and judicial settlement",[75] and none of the sectoral agreements of a multilateral character were ever invoked.

---

[70] Cf the information in PCIJ Series E (n 50) 43–44 and 51–54; Lauterpacht (n 68) 80–83.

[71] See Jenks (n 68) 75–76, for further details on the geographical distribution of cases. The one case with relevant 'input' by a non-European State was *Brazilian Loans*, [1929] PCIJ Ser A No 21. Other non-European States participating in contentious proceedings were Japan (as joint applicant in *SS 'Wimbledon'* [1923] PCIJ Ser A No 1, and *Statute of Memel*, [1932] PCIJ Ser A/B No 47) and China (in *Denunciation of the Sino-Belgian Treaty of 2 November 1865*, [1929] PCIJ Ser A No 18).

[72] Pursuant to Abi-Saab (n 2) 4, 'the Court faithfully reflected in its stance and its jurisprudence the legal outlook of this Eurocentric community'.

[73] For comment on the reliability of the figure see above, n 49–50.

[74] Jenks (n 68) 72–73.

[75] Ibid at 73.

Fourth, and finally, even though States occasionally did invoke treaty provisions relating to the political settlement of World War I, on balance, the bulk of contentious cases submitted to the Court were of a technical character. With the exception of the *Customs Union* opinion[76] (not a contentious case to begin with), the PCIJ had to deal with disputes of limited political significance. Whereas the debates of 1899/1907 and 1920 had viewed binding dispute resolution as an alternative to war, in reality States saw it as a useful means of solving small-scale disputes.[77] As the preceding comments on the Court's jurisdictional potential indicate, this need not have been so: the many dispute settlement conventions in particular would have allowed States to bring before the Court high-profile disputes on the basis of unilateral applications.[78] However, for a range of reasons, States chose to not to use the PCIJ as a means of addressing (or mounting pressure in) highly contentious disputes: there was, in the inter-War period, no equivalent to contentious cases like *Nicaragua* or *Bosnian Genocide,* which, in recent decades, have clearly brought out the chances and limits of adjudication in major political conflicts.[79]

To sum up, States' attitudes to the PCIJ's contentious jurisdiction were characterised by a certain degree of ambivalence: without much debate, and much more willingly than today, States established the Court's jurisdiction over important areas of international relations. By contrast, they hardly ever made use of the Court's jurisdictional potential. The PCIJ seems to have been seen as a useful institution that could help settle disputes of limited political significance. However, States did not provide the PCIJ with an opportunity to address significant disputes of a sensitive character.

---

[76] [1931] PCIJ Ser A/B No 41.

[77] In the words of Shany, 'the PCIJ and ICJ have typically been utilized in cases of low-level and mid-level importance, where both parties have believed that the prolongation of their disputes entailed more costs than the risks that might be associated with losing the subject matter of the dispute' (n 20, 78). Whether—notwithstanding recent 'high-profile' cases such as the Georgian-Russian case about Racial Discrimination or the Genocide litigation between Bosnia, Croatia and Serbia—this statement remains true for the ICJ, may be a matter for debate. For the PCIJ, it is shared by Rosenne, *Law and Practice* (n 12) 16 et seq.

[78] To give just one example, pursuant to the information on the UN treaty website (<http://treaties.un.org/doc/Publication/MTDSG/Volume%20II/LON/PARTII-29.en.pdf>), in 1935/1936, both Italy and Abyssinia were parties to the 1928 General Act, as were a majority of European powers who considered the invasion to be in violation of international law. No State seems to have contemplated recourse to the PCIJ.

[79] For more on the underlying problems see C Gray, 'The Use and Abuse of the International Court of Justice: Cases concerning the Use of Force after Nicaragua' (2003) 14 EJIL 867.

IV. The Court's Handling of Contentious Cases

A third and final set of observations concerns the PCIJ's approach to questions of contentious jurisdiction. How did the Court handle contentious cases, and how did it interpret its role as defined by the Statute? More than the first two aspects, these questions eschew a clear-cut answer. A detailed assessment would have to look at the role of individual judges and their influence on the work of the Court, and take into account of developments in the Court's self-perception.[80] Neither approach will be pursued here. Instead, the following considerations draw on jurisprudence and the Court's attempt at self-regulation (notably the drafting of Rules of Court) to present a fairly general sketch of the role questions of contentious jurisdiction came to play in the PCIJ's jurisprudence.

1. *The Overriding Importance of Jurisdiction*

The most important observation concerns the relevance of jurisdictional issues in contentious proceedings. From the very beginning of the World Court era, questions of jurisdiction came to be of "overriding importance"[81] in the work of the Court—and remain so until today. To some extent, this was but a consequence of Articles 34–37 of the Statute, and notably of two decisions taken in 1920: (i) the rejection of automatic jurisdiction (which meant that jurisdiction would have to be established) and (ii) the acceptance of generalised forms of consent (which meant that proceedings could be instituted against States that, at the time of the application, would rather have avoided recourse to the Court and thus were likely to contest jurisdiction). The Statute, however, left considerable room for development; and it was through interpreting and applying its provisions that the PCIJ shaped the World Court's approach which, in large measure, remains valid to date.

The main feature of the World Court's approach, as shaped by the PCIJ, is the conscientiousness with which jurisdiction is assessed. There are three related aspects to this:

(i) Although the matter had been highly controversial in 1920,[82] the PCIJ never considered re-opening debates about compulsory

[80] See notably Spiermann's distinction between three 'eras' of the PCIJ: 'the foundational period' (n 6, chapter 5); 'an international lawyer's approach' (chapter 6); and 'a national lawyer's approach' (chapter 7).

[81] Rosenne, *Law and Practice* (n 12) 808.

[82] See above, section II(2).

jurisdiction—or a move towards at least a presumption in favour of jurisdiction. Instead, beginning with its second contentious case, *Mavrommatis,* it began to emphasise the consensual basis of jurisdiction[83] and clarified that a State availing itself of a compromissory clause "must be prepared for the contingency that the other Party may cite agreements entered into between the opposing Parties which may prevent the exercise of the Court's jurisdiction."[84] There is very little jurisdictional activism in its jurisprudence, and nothing approaching jurisdictional 'bombshells' of the '*Marbury v Madison*' or '*Tadić*' categories.[85] If anything, the PCIJ's approach to jurisdiction seemed to be inspired by judicial caution: In a well-known passage in the *Chórzow Factory case,* the Court observed that its jurisdiction "is always a limited one, existing only in so far as States have accepted it; consequently, the Court will, in the event of an objection—or when it has automatically to consider the question—only affirm its jurisdiction provided that the force of the arguments militating in favour of it is preponderant."[86] In fact, a short passage from the *Phosphates in Morocco* judgment could be said to go even further: as the French optional clause declaration in that case was clear, the Court found "no occasion to resort to a restrictive interpretation that, this is a truism in case of doubt, might be advisable in regard to a clause which must on no account be interpreted in such a way as to exceed the intention of the States that subscribed to it".[87]

The two statements have at times been interpreted as endorsing a principle of restrictive interpretation of jurisdictional titles; and while that may be overstating their relevance, they provide clear evidence of the PCIJ's cautious approach.[88] Jurisdiction is not to be taken for granted, but must be carefully established. It may not be a "truism" to revert to restrictive interpretations in case of doubt, since both PCIJ and ICJ have, on

83 [1924] PCIJ Ser A No 2 at 16 ("bearing in mind the fact that its jurisdiction is limited").

84 Ibid, at 29–30.

85 Cf 5 US (1 Cranch) 137 (1803) (asserting a power to review the constitutionality of statutes); and ICTY, IT-94-1-AR72 (extending the jurisdiction of the Tribunal by asserting the criminality of violations of the law of internal armed conflict).

86 [1927] PCIJ Ser A No 9, at 32.

87 [1938] PCIJ Ser A/B No 74, at 24.

88 In the words of CF Amerasinghe, "[w]hile interpretation of jurisdictional clauses is not restrictive, it is equally not excessively liberal. While a functional or teleological approach may be warranted in the appropriate circumstances, generally there are limits to functionalism which turn on the avoidance of legislating": *The Jurisdiction of Specific International Tribunals* (Martinus Nijhoff, The Hague 2009) 34.

occasion, construed jurisdictional titles rather broadly.[89] Yet beginning with *Mavrommatis*, both courts have most certainly considered it "advisable" to avoid the impression that they were "exceed[ing] the intention of the States"[90] in accepting jurisdiction. By way of illustration, suffice it to mention the PCIJ's careful approach in determining whether jurisdictional titles applied *ratione temporis*.[91]

Since the end of World War II, references to the consensual character of the Court's jurisdiction have remained common.[92] More recently, members of the ICJ have begun to express discontent at the frequency of 'cases within cases'.[93] However, the ICJ has regularly emphasised the principle of consensual jurisdiction, including in the face of challenges: notably, it has expressly affirmed that 'higher law' concepts like *jus cogens* and obligations *erga omnes* do not provide autonomous titles of jurisdiction, but follow the regular rules.[94] And perhaps most importantly, the present Court has embraced the principle of 'indispensable third party', deciding that even where jurisdiction between the litigants was established, it would not entertain claims implicating an absent third State.[95] This doctrine should not be seen as a necessary implication of consensualism, but as a

---

89 To give but one example, in his dissent in *Nicaragua*, Judge Oda stressed the importance of founding the Court's jurisdiction on the consent of States, and went on to observe: "I doubt whether this particular point has been given all the weight due to it" [1986] ICJ Rep 14 [125].

90 Cf (n 87) at 24.

91 See e.g. *Pajzs, Csáky, Esterházy case*, [1938] PCIJ Ser A/B No 66 at 5 (lapse of an optional clause declaration prior to institution of proceedings); *Phosphates in Morroco*, [1938] PCIJ Ser A/B No 74 at 23–29 (finding a dispute to have its 'real source' in "facts and situations" preceding an optional clause declaration).

92 See e.g. *Interpretation of Peace Treaties Case*, [1950] ICJ Rep 65, 71 ("[t]he consent of States, parties to a dispute, is the basis of the Court's jurisdiction in contentious cases"); *Monetary Gold Removed from Rome in 1943*, [1954] ICJ Reports 19, 32 ("a well-established principle of international law embodied in the Court's Statute, namely, that the Court can only exercise jurisdiction over a State with its consent"); *Application for Revision and Interpretation of the Judgment of 24 February 1982 in the Case concerning the Continental Shelf (Tunisia/Libyan Arab Jamahiriya) (Tunisia v. Libyan Arab Jamahiriya)*; [1985] ICJ Rep 192 [216].

93 See e.g. the Speech by HE Judge Rosalyn Higgins, (then) President of the International Court of Justice, to the Sixth Committee of the General Assembly (31 October 2008, <http://www.icj-cij.org/presscom/files/1/14841.pdf>), where attention is drawn to the large number of 'cases within cases'. In the words of President Higgins, "[t]his is hardly a model for efficiency in the substantive resolution of disputes."

94 See *East Timor*, [1995] ICJ Rep 90 [29]; *Armed Activities (Congo v. Rwanda)*, [2006] ICJ Rep 6 [64].

95 See *Monetary Gold Removed from Rome* (n 92) 19; *Phosphate Lands in Nauru*, [1992] ICJ Rep 240; *East Timor* (n 94) 90. The Court's jurisprudence is summarized by Caflisch (n 15) 406 et seq, and Amerasinghe (n 88) 13–14 and 50 et seq.

deliberate extension; its acceptance by the ICJ testifies to the strength of the consensual paradigm and 'rounds off' the conscientious approach to jurisdiction.[96]

(ii) In terms of 'controlling' jurisdiction, the PCIJ from early on clarified that questions of jurisdiction would be a matter for objective determination. This indeed was indicated by (then) Article 36(4) [now Article 36(6)] of the Statute, pursuant to which, "[i]n the event of a dispute as to whether the Court has jurisdiction, the matter shall be settled by the decision of the Court." The PCIJ read the affirmation of its *Kompetenzkompetenz* to mean that it would have to consider questions of jurisdiction *ex officio*: "the raising of an objection by one Party merely draws the attention of the Court to [it]".[97] While generally, the attitude of parties would be indicative, it is clear from its record that the PCIJ would take this task seriously: Hence in the *Prince von Pless case,* the PCIJ upon its own initiative raised a preliminary matter (though perhaps one going to admissibility as well as jurisdiction[98]) that had not been pleaded by the respondent. While this has remained unusual, it shows the relevance of treating jurisdiction as an objective condition.[99]

(iii) It is with respect to the process of addressing the question of jurisdiction that the PCIJ has most obviously shaped the approach of later courts and tribunals. It did so by 'introducing' a special procedure for preliminary objections, which—notwithstanding refinements and adjustments—is largely applied to this date. As the Statute and the 1922 Rules were silent on the matter,[100] the PCIJ in fact had considerable room for judicial creativity, and was required to display it already in its second contentious case, ie *Mavrommatis*. In response to Britain's "objection *in limine litis* to ... jurisdiction", the Court drew attention to the lack of regulation and declared itself "at liberty to adopt the principle which it considers best calculated to ensure the administration of justice, most suited to procedure before an international tribunal and most in conformity with the

96 See Amerasinghe (n 88) 13.

97 *Minority Schools in Albania*, [1928] PCIJ Ser A No 15 at 23.

98 See [1933] PCIJ Ser A/B No 52 at 15: "Whereas the claim thus made raises a question regarding the Court's jurisdiction, ... namely, whether, on the basis of Article 72, paragraph 3, of the Geneva Convention, a State, in its capacity as a Member of the Council, may claim that an indemnity be awarded to a national of the respondent State, who is a member of a minority; ... which the Court feels called upon to raise proprio motu".

99 While the present Court has continued to emphasise the objective character of jurisdiction, it does not seem to have raised jurisdictional matters directly.

100 See Rosenne, *Law and Practice* (n 12) 834. The 1922 Rules are reproduced in [1926] PCIJ Ser D No 1.

fundamental principles of international law."[101] Without much debate, it decided to treat the British objection as a separate, preliminary matter and to address it in a distinct phase of the proceedings, during which proceedings on the merits would be suspended.[102] Both aspects would be confirmed in the subsequent jurisprudence and 'ratified' in later versions of the Court's Rules.[103] In the *Prince von Pless case,* the Court refined the previous approach by asserting a competence to join a preliminary objection, which "concern[ed] the merits";[104] this in turn was later rephrased to permit joinders of objections where a decision "would run the risk of adjudicating on questions which appertain to the merits of the case or of prejudging their solution",[105] and from 1936 formed part of the Rules of Court.[106] In subsequent rounds of revision, the provision on preliminary objections would assume an ever-greater relevance and detail, culminating in present Article 79, which runs to just under 500 words.[107]

These considerations indicate the immense relevance that questions of jurisdiction played in the jurisprudence of the PCIJ, and the lasting impact of its approach. The general impression is one of a World Court that, from its establishment, had fully 'internalized' the limited scope of its jurisdiction and accepted the need to be treading carefully (or at least: to be seen to be treading carefully), so not to upset its clients.[108]

2. *Occasional Jurisdictional Liberties*

While the general picture is one of jurisdictional caution, it is worth mentioning a number of "jurisdictional liberties" that the PCIJ has taken and which remain influential. They accentuate the general picture of a World

---

101 *Mavrommatis* (n 83) at 16.

102 See Rosenne, *Law and Practice* (n 12) 834–835 and 862, for an account of the procedural history.

103 See e.g. Article 38 of the revised Rules of 1931 (in [1931] 2nd edn PCIJ Ser D No 1) and Article 62 of the 1936 Rules (3rd edn, 1940).

104 *Prince von Pless* (n 98) at 15.

105 *Panevezys-Saldutiskis Railway*, [1938] PCIJ Ser A/B No 75 at 56; and further *Electricity Company of Sofia*, [1939] PCIJ Ser A/B No 77 at 83.

106 Article 62(5) of the 1936 Rules.

107 See Rosenne, *Law and Practice* (n 12) 836 et seq, for much more on the subsequent development. For a comprehensive assessment of the applicable procedure cf Stefan Talmon, in Zimmermann, Tomuschat, Oellers-Frahm and Tams (n 6), at 1158–1169.

108 Judge Koroma (writing extrajudicially) has aptly spoken of "the careful and strict approach of the Court to asserting jurisdiction"(in Capps et al [eds], *Asserting Jurisdiction: International and European Legal Perspectives* [Hart 2003] 189, 191).

Court emphasising the need carefully to establish its jurisdiction. To illustrate the point, three such 'liberties' may be briefly mentioned.

(i) First, while approaching questions of jurisdiction carefully, the PCIJ opted to define the notion of a 'legal dispute'—as "the primary condition for the Court to exercise its judicial function"—in a rather broad way. Since *Mavrommatis*, a 'legal dispute' has been understood to mean "a disagreement on a point of law or fact, a conflict of legal views or of interests between two persons".[109] As this statement continues to be referred regularly,[110] it has become a standard phrase and commonplace; yet it is worth noting that the Court could have adopted a more demanding approach and have 'used' the notion of a 'legal dispute' as a relevant 'filter mechanism'. As it has not usually done so, the "primary condition for the Court to exercise its judicial function"[111] can be fulfilled fairly easily; typically, the Court's discussion of it is no more than a formality.[112] It may be added that the PCIJ and the ICJ have been unwilling to read much into the requirement that the dispute be "legal"—and notably have not heeded invitations to draw categorical distinctions between 'political' and 'legal' disputes,[113]

109 *Mavrommatis* (n 83) at 11.

110 See e.g.—with slight variations, but generally in line with, and referring to, *Mavrommatis—Certain Property*, [2005] ICJ Rep 6 [24]; *East Timor* (n 94) 90 [22]; *South West Africa*, [1962] ICJ Rep 319 at 328. As noted by Merrills, the *Mavrommatis* statement "has stood the test of time" ('The Role and Limits of International Adjudication' in WE Butler [ed], *International Law and the International System* [Martinus Nijhoff, The Hague 1987] 169, 170). In the words of Judge Koroma, "[t]he [ICJ's] jurisprudence is quite consistent on this issue in referring to the Permanent Court's decision in the Mavrommatis": (n 108) at 193.

For details see C Schreuer, 'What is a Legal Dispute?' in: I Buffard et al (eds), *International Law between Universalism and Fragmentation: Festschrift in Honour of Gerhard Hafner* (Martinus Nijhoff, The Hague 2008), 959; R Jennings, "Reflections on the Term 'Dispute'", in: R St. John MacDonald (ed), *Essays in Honour of Wang Tieya* (Martinus Nijhoff, The Hague 1994) 401.

111 *Mavrommatis* (n 83) at 11.

112 Schreuer (n 110) concludes his analysis by noting that "[a]rguments attempting to deny the existence of a dispute have hardly ever succeeded".

113 See notably *Tehran Hostages*, [1980] ICJ Rep 3, where the ICJ noted at [35]: "[L]egal disputes between sovereign States by their very nature are likely to occur in political contexts, and often form only one element in a wider and long-standing political dispute between the States concerned. Yet never has the view been put forward before that, because a legal dispute submitted to the Court is only one aspect of a political dispute, the Court should decline to resolve for the parties the legal questions at issue between them". For much more on this point, including references to PCIJ cases, see H Lauterpacht, *The Function of Law in the International Community* (Clarendon, Oxford 1933) 161 et seq.; Merrills in Butler (n 110) 171–174.

or to differentiate between disputes suitable for judicial, as opposed to arbitral, settlement.[114]

(ii) While generally cautious in its interpretation and application of jurisdictional titles, the PCIJ did accept the idea of *forum prorogatum*—ie the establishment of consent to jurisdiction *post hoc,* if the parties so agreed implicitly. The Court's approach seems to have been shaped by the proceedings in the *Minority Schools case,* in which it held that "the consent of a State ... may not only result from an express declaration, but may also be inferred from acts conclusively establishing it".[115] Subsequently, the concept was discussed at length during the revision of the Court's Rules; in the 1936 version, these accepted the notion of *forum prorogatum* by merely requiring applicants to state, "*as far as possible,* ... the provision on which they found the jurisdiction of the Court".[116]

In retrospect, the relevance attached to the matter may seem surprising: after all, even though the concept required the PCIJ to apply Article 36 flexibly, *forum progatum* "ultimately rests on the same consensual basis as do special agreements and treaties in force; essentially it is a particular form of special agreement without its formalities."[117] As such—a form of tacit *compromis*—it has been applied ever since: a conceptually interesting variation on the theme of consensualism; a 'jurisdictional liberty' that is useful on occasion, but that remains of limited practical relevance.

(iii) Perhaps most importantly, in at least one respect, the PCIJ adopted a broad reading of jurisdictional clauses.[118] Already in its first contentious case, *Wimbledon,* the Court implicitly accepted that where it had jurisdiction over substantive matters, this jurisdiction would cover consequential disputes about reparation/remedies: hence France successfully obtained a damages judgement even though the jurisdictional title, Article 386 of the Treaty of Versailles, had not mentioned remedies expressly.[119] Some years

---

114 It is worth noting that this distinction underlies a number of dispute settlement conventions, most importantly the 1928 General Act: cf Articles 17 and 21.

115 *Minority Schools* (n 97) at 24. Judges Huber, Nyholm, and Negulesco appended 'robust' dissents: see ibid, especially at 48 et seq; 57 et seq, 69.

116 Article 32(2) of the 1936 Rules (emphasis added). The present version of the Rules is much clearer: see Article 38(5). For a detailed discussion of the concept see Sienho Yee, 'Forum prorogatum in the International Court' (2000) 42 GYIL, 145; idem, 'Forum prorogatum Returns to the International Court of Justice' (2003) 16 Leiden JIL 701.

117 Yee, Leiden JIL (n 116) 705. He goes on to note that "Only when the Court is satisfied that there is an agreement to have it decide the dispute does it proceed to adjudicate upon the matter."

118 For more on the following see Amerasinghe (n 88) 164 seq.

119 See *Wimbledon* (n 71) at 33 (operative clause 5). Article 386 had recognized the right of parties "to appeal to the jurisdiction instituted ... by the League of Nations" if the Kiel

later, the matter was argued more fully, and settled, in *Chorzów Factory*, where Poland questioned the Court's jurisdiction to award damages (as claimed by Germany). Article 23(1) of the Upper Silesia ('Geneva') Convention had established the Court's jurisdiction over "[d]ifferences of opinion resulting from the interpretation and the application of Articles 6 to 22", which in Poland's reading did not comprise the competence to determine and award damages.[120] Judge Ehrlich in principle accepted this argument, holding that

> in international law jurisdiction to decide ... that a violation of an international engagement has taken place and that, consequently, reparation is due, is distinct from jurisdiction to determine the nature and extent of reparation in general and the amount of a pecuniary indemnity in particular.[121]

The majority judgment of the Court adopted a much more robust approach; it considered the duty to make reparation to be an integral part of the treaty rule:

> It is a principle of international law that the breach of an engagement involves an obligation to make reparation in an adequate form. Reparation therefore is the indispensable complement of a failure to apply a convention and there is no necessity for this to be stated in the convention itself. Differences relating to reparations which may be due by reason of failure to apply a convention are consequently differences relating to its application.[122]

And further:

> An interpretation which would confine the Court simply to recording that the Convention had been incorrectly applied or that it had not been applied, without being able to lay down the conditions for the re-establishment of the treaty rights affected would be contrary to what would, prima facie, be the natural object of the clause; for a jurisdiction of this kind, instead of settling a dispute once and for all, would leave open the possibility of further disputes.[123]

Ever since then, the PCIJ and ICJ have pronounced on the availability of remedies for wrongful conduct. Versions of the 'Polish objection' were raised by Albania, in *Corfu Channel*, and Iceland, in *Fisheries*, but proved

---

Canal regime laid down in Articles 380–386 of the Treaty had been infringed, or in the event "of disputes as to the interpretation of these Articles".

120 *Chorzów Factory* (n 86) at 20.

121 Ibid (Diss Op Ehrlich) at 37.

122 Ibid (majority judgment) at 21.

123 Ibid at 25.

unsuccessful.[124] In *Nicaragua,* the ICJ almost laconically stated that "[i]n general, jurisdiction to determine the merits of a dispute entails jurisdiction to determine reparation".[125] Since then, the matter seems to have been settled: by broadly construing jurisdictional titles to comprise questions of reparation both the PCIJ and ICJ have avoided undesirable implications of the curious practice, by treaty-makers, of omitting from international conventions rules on remedies. The ICJ's subsequent holding, in *LaGrand,* that jurisdictional titles would comprise the power to order interim measures,[126] may perhaps be seen as a coda.

V. Concluding Observations

The preceding considerations suggest that in many respects, the PCIJ Statute and jurisprudence has shaped the contemporary understanding of contentious jurisdiction. In this respect, the PCIJ's legacy is very obvious and can be felt to this day. To some extent, this may be natural: after all, the essential features of the World Court's regime of contentious jurisdiction depended on decisions taken in Articles 34–37 of the PCIJ's Statute, which were effectively copied into the Statute of the present Court. The discussion in Section II suggests that—as much as we have become used to these provisions and the implications that follow from them: State-centrism; derivative and optional jurisdiction—we should appreciate that they were agreed upon after considerable debate. There is nothing 'natural' or 'God-given' about the regime of contentious jurisdiction devised in 1920; there would have been, and there remain, alternative ways of setting up a World Court.

The jurisdictional design adopted in 1920 was merely a framework waiting to be activated by States conferring jurisdiction upon the World Court and instituting proceedings before it. Section III highlights continuity and change in the perception of the World Court, and in the willingness of its clients to 'unlock' its jurisdictional potential. As regards jurisdictional titles, the PCIJ's jurisdictional potential was far greater than that of the ICJ (which is still considerable). The PCIJ's legal community was far more willing to agree on compromissory clauses establishing the World Court's jurisdiction, and to a much greater degree submitted declarations under

---

124 See [1949] ICJ Rep 4, 26; [1974] ICJ Rep 175 [72].
125 [1986] ICJ Rep 14 [283].
126 [2001] ICJ Rep 466 [45].

the optional clause. In this respect, the PCIJ's era, in retrospect, may almost seem like a golden age—when the possibility of binding dispute settlement by a standing court was seen as the norm. Yet, even in the 'good old days', the PCIJ's enormous jurisdictional potential was hardly ever translated into actual cases. The preceding discussion has drawn attention to the huge gap between potential and real cases. Since 1945, this gap may have closed a little, but it remains wide: then as now, World Court litigation is a rare phenomenon, an exceptional step taken only after serious contemplation. In this respect, the lasting legacy of the PCIJ's era is that of an international legal community not even beginning to realise the jurisdictional potential of 'its' World Court.

Given the cautious approach of its clients, the World Court was probably well-advised to recognise the "overriding importance"[127] of questions of jurisdiction. As shown in Section IV, jurisdictional titles were not necessarily read restrictively; yet from the start, the PCIJ expressly recognised that its jurisdiction would be limited and would have to be tied back carefully to State consent. In this respect, the PCIJ, notwithstanding occasional 'jurisdictional liberties', has left us with a culture of caution and conscientiousness in addressing jurisdictional matters—a culture that remains influential.

The general impression emerging from these considerations may perhaps best be characterised as one of pragmatism, or gradualism. The establishment of a permanent international court may have been a giant leap, but since 1920, international adjudication has at best evolved in small steps—presumably rather smaller than the drafters of the PCIJ Statute would have anticipated. In fact, all relevant actors responsible for setting up the PCIJ's regime of contentious jurisdiction seemed to opt for pragmatic approaches. The drafters of the PCIJ Statute in the end preferred reform over revolutionary schemes; the Court's clients established the PCIJ's jurisdiction over broad and important aspects of international relations, but did not institute many cases; the Court itself fully accepted that it would need to tread carefully in matters of jurisdiction. As a result, by 1945, idealistic visions of a World Court presiding over a world order based on law—clearly articulated in 1907 and 1920—had given way to a much more realistic, and unambitious, assessment: international adjudication by a standing international court was no longer perceived as

127 Rosenne, *Law and Practice* (n 12) 808.

a decisive tool for the prevention of wars, but seen as one among many techniques that could contribute to the gradual regularisation of international relations—useful, but with obvious limitations. This may be the most important legacy of the inter-War approach to contentious jurisdiction.

THE PERMANENT COURT OF INTERNATIONAL JUSTICE AND THE "INVENTION" OF INTERNATIONAL ADVISORY JURISDICTION

Marika Giles Samson and Douglas Guilfoyle

I. Introduction

Idealistic visions of a new and more rational system of international relations following the horrors of World War I were undoubtedly the immediate impetus behind the founding of both the League of Nations and the Permanent Court of International Justice (PCIJ). Nonetheless, there had been repeated calls for a permanent world court since the establishment of the Permanent Court of Arbitration in 1899. While the PCIJ was not an organ of the League, the two were institutionally interlinked, with Article 14 of the League Covenant calling for its executive body, the League Council, to:

> formulate and submit to the Members of the League for adoption plans for the establishment of a Permanent Court of International Justice. The Court shall be competent to hear and determine any dispute of an international character which the parties thereto submit to it. *The Court may also give an advisory opinion upon any dispute or question referred to it by the Council or by the Assembly* (emphasis added).

This last sentence settled in advance the question of the PCIJ's advisory jurisdiction, effectively expanding its role to encompass both being a legal arbiter of disputes between States and an expert counsel to the League. The purpose of an advisory jurisdiction would be, as Pratap put it, to "assist the Council and the Assembly of the League in the discharge of their duties of conciliation and mediation by clarifying the legal issues involved in disputes between States that were brought before the organs of the League."[1] This was the first time that an international court was given an advisory role,[2] and it is worth reflecting upon what an extraordinary innovation this was at the time. How the PCIJ chose to define and fulfil that

[1] D Pratap, *The Advisory Jurisdiction of the International Court* (Clarendon Press, Oxford 1972) 229.

[2] C F Amerasinghe, *Jurisdiction of International Tribunals* (Kluwer Law International, The Hague 2003) 503.

role has become a source of both influence upon the International Court of Justice (ICJ) and considerable scholarly controversy.

At the time, some jurists saw in the advisory jurisdiction an extraordinary opportunity for legal innovation. Thus Harvard professor and later PCIJ judge, Manley O Hudson, said in 1925:

> The Court is principally a *sui generis* institution and we should be willing to employ it as such. It may be necessary to travel new paths, use unfamiliar tools; our old ideas about judicial function may have to be reconsidered. It is in this spirit that the advisory activities of the Permanent Court of International Justice must be examined.[3]

Others, however, were less inclined to reconsider "old ideas about judicial function" and were more disposed to criticise the inclusion of advisory jurisdiction on the basis of perceived conflicts between advisory and judicial functions. In this vein, some were profoundly concerned about the effect such an expansive jurisdiction might have on the credibility of the Court, and would have preferred that the Court's work be confined to the traditional role of adjudicating actual disputes between specific parties. This debate was driven most prominently by American jurists and politicians, and was to have a disproportionate effect on the Court's decisions as to how to fulfil its advisory role.

This chapter thus reflects on the evolution of the advisory jurisdiction over the life of the PCIJ, and some of the implications of that development. Given that the advisory procedure of the PCIJ as it stood at 1940 was reproduced almost verbatim in the Statute and Rules of its successor, the ICJ, the history of the PCIJ's advisory jurisdiction is a question of more than purely historic interest. Indeed, that the ICJ should have an advisory jurisdiction was accepted largely without controversy. As such, the PCIJ stands as the pioneer in a successful experiment in the international judicial function.

II. The Origins of the Advisory Jurisdiction

Little is known about the source of inspiration for granting the PCIJ an advisory jurisdiction in 1919. Certainly, some national justice systems furnished precedents. In Britain, the Judicial Committee of the Privy Council

---

[3] MO Hudson, 'Les avis consultatifs de la cour permanente de justice internationale' (1925) 8 Recueil des cours 349. (Note: all translations of French texts are those of the co-authors.)

had, from time to time, furnished opinions to the Crown or the House of Lords on legal questions. By 1872, the French Conseil d'État, long an executive body of legal advisors with a quasi-judicial function, had been formally reconstituted as a court exercising sovereign authority while retaining its advisory role.[4] Legal questions could be referred to the Supreme Court of the Dominion of Canada, the Supreme Court of Ireland, as well as courts in Europe (Bulgaria, Norway, Sweden, Austria, Finland, Poland), Central and South America (Colombia, Ecuador Honduras, Nicaragua, Panama and El Salvador), and to state courts in some American states.[5]

However, such national law experiences may not have had any particularly decisive role or influence. Certainly, there is not much evidence they were studied systematically in the course of drafting the PCIJ statute. Charles de Visscher, later a PCIJ judge, observed in 1929 that "it must be recognised, albeit without too much regret, that the issue of advisory opinions was not studied deeply by the Committee of Jurists".[6] The original text put forward by President Wilson and Lord Robert Cecil would have given the court the power to "hear and determine" both arbitrations submitted by State parties and any "issue" submitted by the Council or by the Assembly. Dealing with these two functions in a single sentence tended to suggest that the Council could impose an obligation upon parties to submit to binding arbitration by referring a dispute to the Court as an "issue".[7] Unsurprisingly, other language was sought.

The final language chosen to avoid this result appears to have emerged in the drafting committee, which preferred to give the Court the power to "give advisory opinions" rather than the power to "to advise upon" issues or questions.[8] Given the contentious drafting history, at least one contemporary observer has suggested that it is unlikely that national experiences

---

[4] Albeit one quite different from the issuance of Advisory Opinions. See e.g. S Riesenfeld, 'The French System of Administrative Justice: A Model for America (Part I)' (1938) 18 Boston University Law Review 52 n 33 (quoting Wade); J-M Sauvé, 'The French administrative jurisdictional system', *Conseil d'État,* 4 March 2010, <http://www.conseil-etat.fr/cde/node.php?articleid=1992>.

[5] MO Hudson, *The Permanent Court of International Justice 1920–1942: A Treatise* (The MacMillan Company, New York 1943) 485–86.

[6] C de Visscher, 'Les avis consultatifs de la Cour permanente de justice internationale' (1929) 26 Recueil des cours 18.

[7] D Négulesco, 'L'évolution de la procédure des avis consultatifs de la Cour permanente de justice internationale' (1936) 57 Recueil des cours 10–11; M Pomerance, *The Advisory Function of the International Court in the League and UN Eras* (The Johns Hopkins University Press, Baltimore, London: 1973) 16–18.

[8] Négulesco (n 7) 10–11.

had much impact on the precise formulation of the provision for advisory jurisdiction.[9] Indeed, as it developed, the PCIJ's advisory practice tended to be quite different from that of domestic courts.[10]

III. US Opposition

For many, advisory jurisdiction was an oddity,[11] if not an abomination. There was no mechanism for Advisory Opinions in many civil law jurisdictions. The US federal system had specifically rejected such a power. In 1793, a request from President Washington for an opinion from the United States Supreme Court in the Citizen Genêt affair had been rebuffed as being an executive, and not a judicial, function.[12] In the same year, an effort to seek opinions on the assessment of pensions was rejected by a series of US circuit courts on the basis that this task was not "of a judicial nature" and that decisions of the Court in such matters could be reviewed and overturned by cabinet or the legislature, thus threatening the independence of the judiciary.[13] This US jurisprudence seems to have laid the foundations for much of the spirited, often vitriolic, American opposition to the PCIJ's advisory jurisdiction.[14] When first considered by the Advisory Committee of Jurists during the process of drafting the Court's Statute in 1920, the advisory function was described by the eminent American jurist, Elihu Root, as a "violation of all juridical principles".[15] Two years later, the American judge of the PCIJ, John Bassett Moore, urged the Court to ignore its advisory jurisdiction, stating in a well-known memorandum to the members of the PCIJ Rules Committee:

---

[9] Hudson (n 5) 485. See also M Pomerance, 'The Advisory Role of the International Court of Justice and Its 'Judicial' Character: Past and Future Prisms' in Muller et al (ed), *The International Court of Justice: Its Future Role After Fifty Years* (Kluwer Law International, The Hague 1997) 272.

[10] Pomerance (n 7) 9.

[11] E Remlinger, *Les avis consultatifs de la cour permanent de justice* (Éditions A Pedone, Paris 1938) 2, uses the term 'bizarrerie'.

[12] M Pomerance, 'The United States and the Advisory Function of the Permanent Court of International Justice' in Y Dinstein (ed), *International Law at a Time of Perplexity: Essays in Honour of Shabtai Rosenne* (Martinus Nijhoff, Dordrecht 1989) 567.

[13] *Hayburn's Case* 2 US 409 (1792), 411–414.

[14] Spiermann makes a similar observation: "The notion of a court of justice to which Judge Moore repeatedly compared the Permanent Court was just his notion of a national court." O Spiermann, *International Legal Argument in the Permanent Court of International Justice: The Rise of the International Judiciary* (CUP, Cambridge 2005) 165.

[15] Advisory Committee of Jurists, *Procès-Verbaux of the Proceedings of the Committee, 16 June-24 July 1920* (League of Nations Doc V Legal, 1920, Vol 2) 584.

> A Court of Justice, whether national or international, is essentially a judicial body, whose function it is to end disputes by deciding them. The maintenance of the character, reputation and usefulness of such a Court is inextricably bound up with the obligatory force and the effective performance of its decisions or judgments. The advisory function, as between private parties, is appropriately exercised by private counsel, and in the case of Governments, by tribunals or law officers duly established for that purpose.
>
> It is evident that, to impose upon a court of justice the duty of giving advice, which those requesting it were wholly at liberty to reject, would reduce the Court to a position inferior to that of a tribunal of conciliation ...[16]

While Judge Moore ostensibly lost the argument that an advisory function was incompatible with the Court's institutional identity[17] that view was nonetheless influential in how the Permanent Court perceived and performed its advisory role. The Court's emphasis in early proceedings was clearly upon establishing a reputation for legal rigour and procedural propriety, perhaps precisely to counter such scepticism.

Nonetheless, the advisory function was seized upon by those in the US Senate opposed to the Court as being the great danger of adherence, allowing them to argue that the Court was "political".[18] Of course, American opposition to the Court was by no means exclusively based on advisory jurisdiction. The Senate debates reveal deep-seated misgivings about the Court's institutional relationship with the League of Nations (membership of which the United States had rejected in 1920) and many found it objectionable that the US might be judged by a Court made up almost entirely of foreigners, the tone of the Senate debates being often overtly xenophobic.[19] Ultimately, however, the paramount concern was that "[t]he Court ... might pronounce itself, by means of advisory opinions, on questions which the United States did not wish to have adjudicated in any manner."[20] In effect, the fear was that the advisory jurisdiction could be used to create a form of compulsory jurisdiction, circumventing the US's desire (and right) not to be subjected to adjudication without its

---

16 JB Moore, 'The Question of Advisory Opinions' (18 February 1922), *Publications of the Permanent Court of International Justice*, Ser D No 2, 383.

17 Moore carried the fight to other fora and was notably not above privately briefing US Senators on the potential evils of the advisory function: DF Fleming, *The United States and the World Court 1920–1966* (Russell & Russell, New York 1968) 60–61.

18 Ibid at 52–53. Compare: M Dunne, *The United States and the World Court 1920–35* (Pinter Publishers, London 1988), 104 (noting the advisory function "brought the League and the Court into intimate contact; indeed it was the point at which the two bodies were most closely joined").

19 Ibid at 58–59.

20 Pomerance (n 12) 568.

consent.[21] This was sometimes put on the basis that members of the League (or at least members of the Council) were procedurally in a position to prevent the Council referring questions to the Court which affected their interests; whether this was a correct interpretation of the Covenant, however, was disputed at the time.[22] These concerns were evident in the fifth reservation included in the Senate's 1926 Resolution of Adherence to the Court Protocols:[23]

> That the Court shall not render any advisory opinion except publicly after due notice to all states adhering to the Court and to all interested states and after public hearing or opportunity for hearing given to any state concerned; nor shall it, without the consent of the United States, entertain any request for an advisory opinion touching any dispute or question in which the United States has or claims an interest.

This Fifth Reservation ultimately scuppered efforts to have the United States join the Court, as it was unacceptable to the existing parties. The Fifth Reservation in particular would, if accepted, have effectively both amended the Court Statute and created special privileges for one member that would necessarily have affected the work of the League (an institution of which the US was not a member). This was viewed as unacceptable in principle and unworkable in practice. The posture of the US Senate, and the process of trying to bring the US on board, appears to have had a profound institutional influence on the PCIJ: both the assimilation of the Court's advisory procedure to its contentious procedure and the ultimate inclusion of strong procedural safeguards in the Court Statute for States potentially affected by advisory proceedings appear prompted, in large measure, by the desire to assuage US concerns.[24] Indeed, as the Court's

---

[21] See e.g. the extracts from President Coolidge's 1925 Annual Message to Congress, reproduced in (1926) 20 AJIL 146–7. Curiously, the *Eastern Carelia* Case did nothing to assuage US concerns despite the fact that it seemed designed to do so; "apparently the Senate wished to give this jurisprudence the additional sanction of a treaty": Q Wright, 'The United States and the Permanent Court of International Justice', (1927) 21 AJIL 21.

[22] MO Hudson, 'The United States Senate and the Permanent Court of International Justice' (1926) 20 AJIL 332; Wright (n 21) 14.

[23] Senate Resolution No 5 (1926), as reproduced in: (1926) 20 AJIL 150.

[24] Excellent histories of the relationship between the United States and the PCIJ can be found in both Dunne, *The United States and the World Court* (n 18) and M Pomerance, *The United States and the World Court as a 'Supreme Court of the Nations': Dreams, Illusions and Disillusion* (Martinus Nijhoff, The Hague, London, 1996). Négulesco (n 7) 26–37 is also very good on the subject of US/PCIJ relations.

advisory procedure and jurisprudence developed, Judge Moore and other early critics of the jurisdiction were in fact considerably appeased.[25]

It is also perhaps significant that there was no comparable controversy when the US became a party to the International Court of Justice, which had a virtually identical advisory jurisdiction. This could be explained at least in part on the basis of the generally positive experience of the PCIJ's advisory jurisdiction, although it may have had more to do with the political perception that the ICJ would be the court of an institution that was itself an American project. As one commentator put it: "the US had failed to join the Court of the League it had rejected, but was happy to endorse the Court of the United Nations that it had created."[26]

IV. The Question of the PCIJ's Judicial Nature

It was not a uniquely American argument that to issue Advisory Opinions having no binding force was incompatible with a court's judicial function. In 1929 Judge de Visscher, a Belgian national, noted that the Court's advisory jurisdiction would have struck the continental jurist as unusual due to its non-binding character.[27] This led both the Court and commentators to consider the extent to which the binding quality of decisions is an essential component of the judicial function.

Certainly, Hudson considered in 1925 that "judicial function" is not a term of art capable of precise definition, and he noted that the assertion that judicial activity necessarily excludes an advisory role would be inaccurate for a large number of countries: "in truth, it is limiting judicial power to litigation that would be contrary to a long tradition of judicial history."[28] He set out the following "essential conditions" that he considered part of the judicial function in a cross-section of legal systems: public decision-making; the right of interested persons to be heard; the detailed and evidence-based examination of legal issues (whether through the adversarial system or otherwise); and objective and unbiased judges.[29] In a book published in the same year, he concluded that "…it is difficult to see

---

25 Dunne (n 18) 104 (noting that the assimilation of advisory to contentious proceedings played a large role in this result).

26 Dunne (n 18) 265 (see also 264 on the lessons learned in the "lost campaign of 1920–35" for US involvement).

27 de Visscher (n 6) 8.

28 Hudson (n 3) 408.

29 Ibid.

what the advisory opinions of the Permanent Court of International Justice lack to give them the quality of judiciality in the full sense of that term."[30] The question is, of course, one of definition. The greater conformity one requires with a given national conception of judicial institutions, the more defective an international institution will almost invariably appear.[31] The more one focuses on the general characteristics of a legal system, or conformity with basic rule of law principles, the greater the chance an international court will seem adequately judicial.[32]

The issue was not purely academic: the Court's conception of its own status affected the manner in which it exercised its advisory function. In its refusal to provide an opinion in the *Eastern Carelia* case, the Court held that it was bound by certain fundamental rules of conduct stemming from its character as a judicial institution. We return to the decision of the Court in *Eastern Carelia* below.

V. A Deliberately Conservative Approach

Rather than "travel new paths" or "use unfamiliar tools" as urged by Professor (and later Judge) Hudson, the Court chose to apply a conservative judicial method and procedure in exercising the advisory function. A number of commentators, many of them critics, believe that this was at odds with the role originally conceived in Article 14 of the League Covenant which appeared more akin to that of a legal advisor. There are certainly *indicia* of such an intention: that the request comes from a designated body, that the scope of the request is specifically defined, that it is to be accompanied by whatever materials are deemed to be relevant, and that the response sought is in the nature of opinion on the particular question asked. Legal practitioners would recognise this exchange as quite familiar, and would respond to such a request with an opinion letter. Pomerance describes this as a tension between the "lawyer-client" and "quasicontentious" views of the advisory function,[33] and it had practical implications that came into sharp relief in the *Eastern Carelia* case.

Indeed, when the Court was formulating the rules governing its advisory jurisdiction an issue arose over Rule 73. This required the Registrar,

30 Manley O Hudson, *The Permanent Court of International Justice and the Question of American Participation, with a collection of documents* (Harvard UP, Cambridge 1925) 168.
31 See especially n 14, above.
32 E.g. HLA Hart, *The Concept of Law* (Clarendon Press, Oxford 1965) 231.
33 Pomerance (n 7) 287.

upon receipt of a request for an Advisory Opinion, to notify a wide range of specified States and organisations. As PCIJ Judge De Bustamente y Sirvén describes: "M. Beichmann asserted that the request should not be communicated to anyone, other than the judges, … because it is for the person seeking advice and not the one from whom it is sought to decide how widely the request should be publicised."[34] Again, this sounds, to the practitioner's ear, like a defence of solicitor-client privilege. The idea, however, that requests or the resulting opinions would be kept secret was rejected by the Court. The Rules clearly reflected that requests and opinions would be made public, for reasons both of principle and practicality. In principle, it was felt that operating publicly, including in giving notice to potentially interested parties, was more consistent with the exercise of a judicial function. Practically, wide notice also ensured that the Court had access to the information that it needed to form an accurate view.

Considerable energy has been spent discussing whether the Court was, in general, compelled to comply with requests for Advisory Opinions or whether it could choose not to do so.[35] The debate follows in part from an apparent conflict between the English and French texts of Article 14 (the wording of the former appeared permissive while the latter seemed more imperative);[36] it also followed from the broader principle that a Court be able to control its own jurisdiction. The Court itself seems to have assumed that it could refuse to give an opinion, and did just that in *Eastern Carelia*.

The case concerned a treaty between Finland and Russia and the rights of certain people living in an autonomous region within Russia. Finland alleged that Russia was in breach of its obligations under the treaty; Russia responded that the concerns raised were unrelated to the terms of the treaty and were a matter of domestic jurisdiction. Finland sought first the intervention of the League Council, which refused to intervene given Russia's position that this was an internal matter. Finland then successfully petitioned the Council to refer the threshold question of whether the issue was of an international nature to the PCIJ. Russia refused to participate, save to send a telegram to the Court confirming its position that the issue was domestic and, further, that given the refusal of many members

---

[34] Antonio Sánchez de Bustamente y Sirvén, *La cour permanente de justice internationale* (Recueil Sirey, Paris 1925) 253.

[35] See, for example: Hudson (n 3) 356–357; de Bustamente y Sirvén (n 34) 246–247; Négulesco (n 7) 67–68; Hudson (n 5) 498–501.

[36] Specifically: "The Court may also give an advisory opinion …"; as opposed to: "[la Cour] donnera aussi des avis consultatifs …"(literally, "the Court will also give advisory opinions", although the exact effect of the future tense here is debateable).

of the League of Nations to recognise the Soviet government, neither the League nor the PCIJ could be seen as impartial.

The Court declined to provide an opinion on the stated question on the basis that, given that Russia was not a member of the League of Nations, the matter was not properly before the Council and thus the Council lacked jurisdiction to request an Advisory Opinion. While this was the primary reason for the Court's decision, subsidiary reasons included the inability of the Court to obtain the information it required without Russia's participation and the Court's view that "[a]nswering the question would be substantially equivalent to deciding the dispute between the parties."[37] In the next sentence the Court confirmed that "being a Court of Justice, [its judges] cannot, even in giving its advisory opinions, depart from the essential rules guiding their activity as a Court."[38] This somewhat tautological passage does little to illuminate what those "essential rules" might be, but from the evolution of the Court's practice (and consequential amendments to its Rules and Statute), its list would seem to coincide with Judge Hudson's essential criteria above. In particular, given the context, it seems that one of these essential rules was the principle of fairness. The Court was loath to issue an opinion that would effectively define the rights of Finland and Russia without hearing from Russia, which had (as was its right) refused to consent to the Court's jurisdiction. On one view, then, the essential reason for the Court's refusal to give the requested opinion was a desire to protect its "judicial character".[39] For Pomerance, the decision reflects an emerging institutional identity in which "quasicontentious" questions without the implicit or explicit consent of one of the disputants would justify the Court eschewing its "lawyer-client'" function in "rendering to its 'client', the requesting organ, the elucidation it desires".[40]

The decision to conduct all of the Court's activities in public clearly had a defining effect. One need only imagine that, instead of opinions being rendered after broad notice, wide submissions and argument and the result being read out in open Court, the process had instead been conducted in private. The Court would have had quite a different look and feel, and the contentious and advisory roles would have been truly distinct. Rather than accept the advisory jurisdiction as creating a separate role in which it would act as a private advisor, the Court's conception its

---

37 *The Status of the Eastern Carelia* [1923] PCIJ Ser B No 5 at 29.
38 Ibid at 29.
39 Pomerance (n 7) 280.
40 Ibid at 287.

judicial character (and the essential requirements of that function) led its Advisory Opinions to become part of its public jurisprudence. The desire to apply the same standards of judicial conduct and decision-making to both jurisdictions would also lead, over time, to a convergence at the level of procedure.

One other early, procedural decision bears consideration here: the Rule requiring all opinions to be rendered by the full court. In 1920, the Advisory Committee of Jurists' draft Statute for the PCIJ had included a draft Article 36 on Advisory Opinions. This draft article had distinguished between requests that were theoretical in nature, so-called 'questions', and those that arose from actual inter-State disputes. In the case of theoretical questions, it was proposed that a chamber of between three and five judges be convened to issue an opinion. This seems to be consistent with the practice of some US states where a procedural distinction is drawn between judges acting as legal experts and members of the court. A contemporary example could have been found in the form of the Massachusetts Supreme Court, where Advisory Opinions were considered as being offered by the judges, not by the Court as an institution.[41] Where an Advisory Opinion is offered by a full court as an institution, that court is obviously much less likely to depart from its stated views on abstract questions when it comes time to apply the same law in contentious cases.

When the draft scheme was submitted to the Assembly of the League of Nations for approval, the whole of draft Article 36 was deleted. For the most part, it was felt that the matters outlined there were more properly left to the Court to elaborate in its Rules, but it was clear from the report recommending deletion that there was no appetite for opinions being rendered by panels composed of less than the full Court. The effect of this was, as Judge Hudson puts it, to provide "advisory opinions with the full grant of prestige of the whole Court".[42]

VI. The Legal Effect of Opinions

1. *Introduction*

The effect of the procedural safeguards imposed on the advisory jurisdiction was to imbue the opinions given with a high degree of persuasive

---

[41] Hudson (n 30) 82 (though noting that the judges of that court in giving Advisory Opinions acted "without the benefit of argument" and "it is not clear that briefs may be filed by interested persons").

[42] Hudson (n 3) 362.

authority; but this perceived authority was obviously at odds with their strict legal effect. Formally, the Advisory Opinions of the PCIJ were not binding: not on the League, nor on the interested parties, nor even on the Court itself as precedent. As noted above, this lack of mandatory force lay at the heart of some concerns, especially those of Judge Moore, about the advisory jurisdiction.[43]

It is hardly surprising, then, that the question of the force of Advisory Opinions has attracted much debate and comment. It is not a question, however, susceptible of a purely formal answer. Given the procedural safeguards involved and the fact that opinions were rendered by the full Court (thus bringing to bear all its prestige and intellectual power), Advisory Opinions had sufficient judicial heft to 'feel' like judgments and were certainly at least as authoritative. Thus whether or not they were formally binding came to be viewed as a somewhat secondary concern. As Pratap noted, while "advisory opinions are not binding ... 'their persuasive character and substantive authority' is great."[44] Pratap further observes that in a system of law where compliance with a court's decision will, as a matter of fact, essentially be voluntary the ultimate "authority of [judicial] pronouncements ... depends on their intrinsic merit".[45] Others saw the authority of the opinions emanating from the process through which they were reached. Judge Négulesco noted that "[a]ll of the judicial guarantees provided to interested states lead to render illusory the non-binding character of the advisory opinion."[46] Eleven years earlier, his future colleague, Professor Hudson, had opined that whether a Court's opinion was binding was a matter of degree. While an Advisory Opinion may have less weight than a judgment, and may not cause a matter to be *res judicata*, it should surely be entitled to "serious consideration". In his mind, the central question bearing on the weight to be accorded to an opinion was whether it was rendered after a "full opportunity for counsel to be heard and for all questions to be fully argued".[47]

---

43 See especially n 16, above.

44 Pratap (n 1) 231, quoting Fitzmaurice.

45 Ibid 233. Similarly, Judge de Bustamente y Sirvén opined that the value of an advisory opinion was a direct result of its reasoning: de Bustamente y Sirvén (n 34) 255.

46 Négulesco (n 7) 80. Similarly, Professor Leland Goodrich cited judicial safeguards as the source of an Advisory Opinion's precedential value, observing that most Advisory Opinions are akin to declaratory judgments: LM Goodrich, 'The Nature of the Advisory Opinions of the Permanent Court of International Justice' (1938) 32 AJIL 756. Similar analogies have been drawn between Advisory Opinions and declaratory judgments by, among others, C Gray, *Judicial Remedies in International Law* (Clarendon Press, Oxford 1990) 112–116.

47 Hudson (n 30) 150.

At two levels, then, it is unsurprising that Advisory Opinions came to be seen to have much the same force as judgments, given the ultimately voluntarist nature of compliance with international law. First, the procedure adopted clearly met the criteria of legality/basic rule of law standards commonly accepted as giving rise to procedural legitimacy: judgments or Advisory Opinions alike were delivered publically, after a full and fair hearing on the issues, the standards applied were legal, and both contained detailed reasons for decisions (which attempted to be clear, persuasive, and consistent with the pre-existing law as then understood). Second, to the extent that pronouncements of the court complied with these essential criteria of legality and reflected generally shared understandings of international law, they were highly likely to be viewed as legitimate in substance by international actors and therefore to attract compliance.[48] In this sense of substantive legitimacy, the form in which a judicial pronouncement is initially delivered is likely to be irrelevant.

2. *Reception by the League Council*

Whether or not Advisory Opinions were formally binding, the Council (which was the only body, ultimately, that ever requested opinions from the PCIJ) certainly accorded them a high degree of respect. While it was under no formal obligation to follow an opinion, Judge de Bustamente y Sirvén observed that the Council "would be in an awkward position on the world stage"[49] if it did not. Judge Négulesco similarly commented:

> Theoretically, [the Council] is not obliged to [adopt the advisory opinion of the Court], but, morally, it must follow the Court's opinion, as what will the Court's authority be if the Council, after having received the opinion and wanting to keep matters on a legal plane, adopted a solution contrary to the Court's view, and what would be the Council's authority ... if it wanted to impose that solution on the parties despite the contrary opinion of the Court?[50]

This sense of 'moral obligation' would now probably be described as embodying questions of the legitimacy and 'compliance pull' of the Court's legal pronouncements. A number of other contemporary commentators

---

[48] In an obviously wide literature, see: J Brunnée and SJ Toope, *Legitimacy and Legality in International Law: An Interactional Account* (CUP, Cambridge 2010) especially at 6, 26–7; compare *passim* TM Franck, *The Power of Legitimacy among Nations* (OUP, Oxford 1990).

[49] de Bustamente y Sirvén (n 34) 256.

[50] Négulesco (n 7) 80.

endorsed the view that the Council was under a moral obligation to accept the Court's opinion, at least one observing that it would have been "impossible" for the Council to disregard the Court's opinion.[51] Studies of the subsequent minutes of the Council have shown that the Council did accept and, wherever it was within its power to do so, apply the opinions of the Court.[52]

3. *Treatment of Advisory Opinions by the Court Itself*

Was the Court, too, persuasively bound by the legitimacy or moral authority of its own Advisory Opinions? Clearly, it had a vested interest in assigning its opinions the highest possible value. Undoubtedly, they would at the very least, as Judge de Visscher put it, "inspire the Court in later decisions".[53] Fachiri (writing in 1932) went considerably further:

> It can be confidently stated that the principles laid down ... in advisory opinions have the same effect by way of precedent as the judgements of the Court, and are of equal importance in the development of international law. The Court being bound, in formulating opinions, to apply legal rules and principles, is, by the nature of things, constrained to follow in subsequent cases, be they contentious or advisory, the decisions of law arrived at in earlier ones ... Further, these opinions, in so far as they relate to questions of international law, necessarily tend to become recognized as authoritative statements of the law by the community of nations.[54]

However, the possibility that in practice the 'bindingness' of Advisory Opinions and judgments in contentious cases would be effectively the same was itself cause for concern. From the outset, jurists were troubled by the possibility of conflicts between the advisory and contentious jurisdictions of the Court. Of particular concern was the possibility that the Court might be requested by the Council to give an opinion *in abstracto* on a legal issue relating to a concrete dispute and then later be faced with the affected States themselves bringing the same question before the Court as part of a contentious proceeding. It was always clear that such cases would

---

[51] AP Fachiri, *The Permanent Court of International Justice: Its Constitution, Procedure and Work* (2nd edn, OUP, London 1932) 80–81. The reception of Advisory Opinions by States is addressed below.

[52] Goodrich (n 46) 748; E Hambro, 'The authority of the advisory opinions of the International Court of Justice' (1954) 3 ICLQ 8. A somewhat more nuanced review is found in Pratap (n 1) 235–244 (especially at 235 n 3). Judge Hudson also reviews the response to each opinion, (n 5) 513–522.

[53] de Visscher (n 6) 60.

[54] Fachiri (n 51) 81–82.

not be *res judicata* as such, but it was feared that the possibility that the Court might be in a position to contradict an earlier pronouncement on the same question might prove paralysing. Judge de Bustamente y Sirvén considered this concern exaggerated: "Courts always judge cases based on the evidence called and proven, and if in a later case information or issues of fact or law are argued that were absent in the earlier case, the results could be contradictory without scandal or injustice."[55] His answer, though undoubtedly technically correct, may not strike all readers as wholly satisfactory. In the end, though, the question of conflicting results did not arise. This may be taken either as a sign of good fortune or that Advisory Opinions tended, in fact, to be rather successful at resolving underlying disputes.

4. *The Behaviour of Interested States*

Of the twenty-seven Advisory Opinions rendered by the PCIJ, seventeen addressed existing disputes between States.[56] A detailed study in 1938 found that, of those seventeen, in only one case, the *Mosul* matter, did one of the States concerned reject the Court's opinion outright.[57] Indeed, there were at least two cases in which the States concerned had agreed, in advance and as between themselves, to abide by the Court's pronouncement in advisory proceedings.[58] Conversely, it is notable that in the one case where a State rejected the opinion delivered, that State (Turkey) had objected from the outset to the request for an opinion put to the Court.

However, in his 1943 treatise, Judge Hudson cautioned against drawing too strong a conclusion from the popularity of the advisory mechanism. Responding to a comment made by a Greek representative in the Assembly of the League that Advisory Opinions were "equivalent in the eyes of the Council, of public opinion and of the interested parties to a judgment", Hudson contended: "[t]he history of the opinions given by the Court lends no support to the view that the character of the opinions has been changed by the reception accorded to them."[59] This may, though, have been putting questions of form ahead of substance.

---

[55] de Bustamente y Sirvén (n 34) 257.
[56] Goodrich (n 46) 744–745.
[57] Ibid at 751.
[58] Ibid at 751–752; de Bustamente y Sirvén (n 34) 256; Négulesco (n 7) 84–85.
[59] Hudson (n 5) 513.

However, the very fact that the resulting opinions were not formally binding may have contributed to the popularity of the advisory jurisdiction. While all requests heard by the Court were routed through the Council, ten came before the Court with the consent, or at the behest, of interested States effectively in a form of 'self-referral'.[60] All of these were matters where, presumably, the States could have opted to initiate contentious proceedings. Seeking Advisory Opinions instead gave States the ability to obtain authoritative opinions on legal points at issue without having the entire matter adjudicated, especially in the inevitable context of disputes having both legal and non-legal dimensions.[61] As Judge Hudson observed:

> Even though agreements in force may provide for the compulsory jurisdiction of the Court, the States interested in a dispute may prefer to have an advisory opinion which by clarification of legal questions will aid them in reaching a settlement on broader grounds and which will not have the binding effect of a judgment.[62]

The original reason for having a mechanism permitting non-binding Advisory Opinions to be given was to enable them to "assist the Council and the Assembly ... in the discharge of their duties of conciliation and mediation by clarifying the legal issues involved in disputes" brought before the League.[63] In practice, it was not only the League organs which were assisted in this manner: in effect, legal issues between States could be addressed without initiating full-blown adversarial proceedings which might be seen as (or have the effect of) escalating a dispute.[64]

The advisory jurisdiction was thus able to fulfil something of a 'preventative law' function, which was regarded as particularly beneficial in a post-World War I world. In 1929, US Secretary of State Henry Stimson observed that Advisory Opinions "rendered on questions before they have ripened into bitter quarrels and wounded pride, can play a most useful part" especially where "rendered with all the advantages of full argument

[60] SM Schwebel, 'Was the capacity to request an advisory opinion wider in the Permanent Court of International Justice than it is in the International Court of Justice?' (1992) 62 British Ybk of Intl L 82. This number does, however, include those referred by the Mixed Commission for the Exchange of Greek and Turkish Populations and the Greco-Bulgarian Mixed Emigration Commission.

[61] See Hudson (n 3) 410; de Visscher (n 6) 61.

[62] Hudson, (n 5) 524.

[63] Pratap (n 1) 229.

[64] J Hostie, 'The Statute of the Permanent Court of International Justice' (1944) 38 AJIL 429–430.

from opposing interests but before those interests have settled into dangerous international grievances."[65] Thus, "[t]he fact that so many requests for advisory opinions … [were] made seems to be some proof of the need for a jurisdiction of this kind in the post-war world."[66] The use of the PCIJ's advisory function as an alternative to contentious proceedings came to be a sufficiently well-worn path that the term "advisory arbitration" was coined and applied by a number of commentators.[67]

Judge de Visscher notes that it was not only the authoritative nature of its opinions that made the Court's advisory jurisdiction popular, but also "its great flexibility, its ability to adapt to situations that might be amenable neither to mediation, nor to the external mechanisms of arbitral or judicial ruling".[68] Thus the advisory jurisdiction was sometimes used by governments where public opinion would have been against binding arbitration, but the moral authority of the Court's Advisory Opinion on a question of law allowed them more easily to make concessions they knew to be necessary.[69] Others have referred to it as an indirect judicial settlement mechanism for legal aspects of larger questions "in dispute between Governments and [which] would not, or could not, have come before the Court in any other way."[70]

Crucially, access to such a facility encouraged States and the Council to identify and isolate the legal issues in larger debates as they could then be referred for an authoritative opinion.[71] This, in turn, gave law, and the legal method, a critical position within international dispute resolution. "Advisory arbitration" would thus seem to have been quite a successful instrument for the peaceful settlement of international disputes.

---

65 As cited in Pomerance (n 24) 115.

66 Hudson (n 30) 160.

67 It seems that the term was first used by Judge Négulesco and Albert de Lapradelle in their 1928 *Rapport sur la nature juridique des avis consultatifs de la Cour permanente de Jutice internationale, leur valeur at leur portée positive en droit international* to the Institute of International Law. It was subsequently picked up and used by Remlinger (n 11) 3; cf Hambro (n 52) 8.

68 de Visscher (n 6) 61.

69 Ibid at 62 ("L'avis de la Court comporte une autorité morale qui souvent permettra aux Gouvernements de se prêter plus facilement à des concessions dont ils sentent eux-mêmes la nécessité, mais qu'ils ne sentent pas la force d'imposer à leur pays.").

70 Hostie (n 64) 429. See also Remlinger (n 11) 3.

71 Hudson comments: "This role for the Court cannot be too highly valued. … If the legal issues could be isolated and addressed separately, with the political side examined elsewhere, we would have a greater chance of successfully resolving both sides of a dispute." Hudson (n 3) 410. Similarly, Remlinger, citing Lapradelle, notes that the advisory jurisdiction allowed the Council to return to the legal arena those issues that the parties to a dispute had inaccurately characterised as political: (n 11) 3.

VIII. The Line between Contentious and Non-Contentious Proceedings

The use of the advisory jurisdiction as an alternative to contentious proceedings led to obvious questions about the relative merits and procedural differences between the two. Over time, these questions would largely be resolved by a procedural assimilation of the advisory jurisdiction to the contentious jurisdiction. However, this process was by no means inevitable, or even foreseen at the outset.

1. *The Distinction between Questions and Disputes*

When, in 1920, the Advisory Committee of Jurists drafted the Court's Statute, they noted that requests for Advisory Opinions could be made either on "questions" or "disputes" and proposed in draft Article 36 a different procedure for each type of request. As noted above, at the time, it was thought that "questions" would be of an abstract or theoretical nature and could perhaps be answered by a chamber of the Court. (As it turned out, the Court was never asked to opine on a purely abstract question.[72]) On the other hand, it was suggested that requests for an Advisory Opinion arising from "disputes" should be addressed in a very similar manner to contentious proceedings.

In recommending the deletion of this draft Article, the Committee of the League Assembly opined that "[t]his distinction seemed lacking in clearness and likely to give rise to practical difficulties".[73] Nonetheless, the instinct to distinguish between the two types of Advisory Opinions was sound. The nature of an opinion may be quite different as between the two, as Judge Négulesco observed. Where the Advisory Opinion is rendered on an abstract "question", this opinion would be in the nature of legal advice, with no mandatory nature.[74] Where, on the other hand, it arises from a live dispute, the opinion has the characteristics of a declaratory judgment (and even the "declaratory" aspect tended to disappear in

---

[72] Hudson (n 5) 496; Pomerance (n 7) 308. But see Goodrich, who, referring to the *Memel* and *Danzig Postal Service* cases, says that these were cases "where the formulation of questions purely *in abstracto* without any reference to the facts of the dispute which had arisen, has caused inconvenience and embarrassment to the Court: (n 46) 430.

[73] Records of First Assembly, Committees, I, 534. See (3rd add) Ser D No 2 at 838. Cited in Hudson (n 5) 494, fn 66.

[74] Négulesco, (n 7) 8–9, 65. Remlinger also considers that the 'declaratory' nature of the judgment is somewhat ethereal: (n 11) 3; Gray considers that there is little practical difference between Advisory Opinions and declaratory judgments: (n 46) 112.

some cases).[75] As a matter of substance, while the formal relationship created by the advisory jurisdiction was a straightforward one between the Court and the Council, where an opinion was sought on a live dispute there was surely also some relationship created between the Court and the States concerned.[76]

If a practical distinction exists, where was the line between mere questions and actual disputes to be drawn? As Hudson noted:

> one cannot establish a precise boundary between *disputes* and *questions* as referred to in Article 14, ... both words must relate to the current conduct of international affairs. [However, in] some cases, it may not only be difficult, it may be specious to categorise a situation between states in which a legal question arises as a dispute. This is even more evident if one recalls the use of the term *dispute* elsewhere in the Covenant, where it implies elements of severity or hostility that may not be present in each case.[77]

Even if Hudson's dividing line is less than precise, the intent is reasonably plain: one must be careful not to upgrade a legal question into an international incident, particularly given that some cases had come before the Court under its advisory jurisdiction specifically to avoid full adversarial proceedings. Judge Négulesco's pragmatic approach to the issue was, perhaps, the most sensible: not to attempt to distinguish types of dispute at the level of abstract characterisation but rather consider whether there was an existing, live dispute or disagreement between States at the time that the request was transmitted by the Council.[78]

2. *Procedural Assimilation*

In the event, and in the absence of abstract "questions" being referred to the Court, the tendency was to apply the judicial safeguards applicable in live disputes to Advisory Opinions in order to do justice to interested or affected States. This required: formal notice to interested parties, the opportunity for them to participate in the proceedings, the ability to file responsive memorials, and, perhaps most notably, the appointment of *ad hoc* judges, all mechanisms which had traditionally been reserved to contentious proceedings.

---

75 Ibid (Négulesco).

76 Négulesco (n 7) 64–65.

77 Hudson (n 3) 358 (emphasis in original).

78 Négulesco (n 7) 70. In this respect, Judge Négulesco cites the definition of "dispute" as provided by the Court in the *Mavrommatis* case: "A dispute is a disagreement on a point of law or fact, a conflict of legal views or of interests between two persons": *Mavrommatis Palestine Concessions Case* (Judgment on Jurisdiction) [1924] PCIJ Ser A No 2, 5 at 11.

This procedural assimilation between contentious and advisory proceedings was seen by Judge Négulesco as a turning point in the Court's history, dividing it into two phases.[79] In the first phase (1922–27) the Court's Rules made no formal distinction in the Rules between Advisory Opinions rendered on "questions" and those rendered on "disputes". However, from 1923 onward, the Court progressively recognised that at least some of the cases that came before it under the advisory jurisdiction were live disputes, and that by giving its opinion, it was effectively deciding the issue between the parties (as in *Eastern Carelia*). Nonetheless, it did not permit interested States to appoint *ad hoc* judges during this phase, although in other respects there was a gradual *rapprochement* of advisory and contentious procedure. This refusal to allow directly affected parties to appoint *ad hoc* judges had the potential to lead to flagrant inequalities, as highlighted in the 1927 *Danube Commission* case. In that case of four interested States, three already had judges on the Court; the fourth, which was, for all practical purposes, in opposition to the other three, did not. This led to Négulesco's second phase (1927–1936), which began with the amendment of Rule 71 to allow for the appointment of *ad hoc* judges in advisory proceedings arising from an existing inter-State dispute.

Subsequently, the 1929 Committee of Jurists appointed to revise the Statute copied the Rules pertaining to Advisory Opinions into the Statute itself. A new Article 68 was also included, which read:

> In the exercise of its advisory functions, the Court shall further be guided by the provisions of the Statute which apply in contentious cases to the extent to which it recognizes them to be applicable.

These suggested amendments were adopted, and subsequently came into force in 1936. However, this was merely to formalise what was by then the Court's established practice, which had been since 1927 to apply the contentious procedure to relevant advisory proceedings. This process of assimilation was largely welcomed. Hudson's comments capture the general tone:

> The policy of assimilation is undoubtedly sound; the judicial character of the Court should be safeguarded in the rendering of advisory opinions, and the opinions themselves will be more authoritative, the prestige of the Court will be better protected, if they are preceded by the thorough explorations which contentious procedure is designed to facilitate.[80]

[79] Négulesco (n 7) 17, 37.
[80] Hudson (n 5) 509. See also Goodrich (n 46) 743 and Pratap (n 1) 230.

Judge Hudson’s latter-day support of assimilation may seem somewhat at odds with his early calls to reconsider existing and overly conservative ideas about judicial function.[81] He had even previously observed that “Courts have often hedged themselves with self-imposed limitations, and have readily accepted such limitations as inherent”; a tendency he felt was related to a general unwillingness on the part of the legal profession to experiment, especially with judicial methods.[82] His curious failure to mourn a lack of innovation in the advisory jurisdiction may suggest that his favourable assessment of the advisory jurisdiction was intended more as a direct riposte to Moore’s line of criticism, than a judgment that the ideal state of affairs had been reached. Judge de Visscher, however, did explicitly query whether the Court had missed an opportunity to create a unique mechanism:

> Despite initial misgivings, no one would dare say that the advisory jurisdiction has tarnished the reputation of the PCIJ as a court of justice, but this is largely because the Court has subordinated all to the preservation of its judicial character. It has rebuffed all proposals that would have given its advisory role a distinct physiognomy, all the while amending its advisory procedure to mimic the contentious procedure, to the point of almost complete assimilation. No one could cite a single example for which the Court could be reproached for not putting the absolute integrity of the judicial function first. But hasn’t this caused the Court to dissipate little by little the particular advantages of the advisory function?[83]

Judge de Visscher went further still, asking whether assimilation had not “more or less transformed an advisory opinion into a judgment”.[84] The same point had been made by the Rules Committee in 1927: “[i]n reality, where there are in fact contending parties, the difference between contentious cases and advisory cases is only nominal. The main difference is the way in which the cases come before the Court. … So the view that advisory opinions are not binding is more theoretical than real.”[85] Perhaps such a result could, in any event, have been expected in a system of law where, as noted above, the “bindingness” of judgments may be largely a function of

81 See text accompanying n 3, above.
82 Hudson (n 30) 137.
83 de Visscher (n 6) 58–59.
84 Ibid 60.
85 PCIJ Ser E No 4 at 76. See in accord: Hambro (n 52) 6; and Goodrich (n 46) 740. Hudson (n 5: 509), however, was concerned that: “too complete assimilation might encourage a view that an advisory opinion is a species of judgment, that because of the procedure followed before the Court it attains an obligatory character; advisory jurisdiction might then come to be looked upon as an alternative to obligatory jurisdiction, and this might result in diminishing the frequency of requests for advisory opinions.”

procedural and substantive legitimacy and distinctions of form are less likely to be of significance.

In any event, by the time the Court issued its last Advisory Opinion in December 1935, it had undoubtedly allayed the worst fears of the early critics of the jurisdiction. In the process, it had secured a large measure of authority, if not substantial binding effect, for its Advisory Opinions. As one early observer put it:

> No one can read these utterances of the court without being impressed by the fact that they constitute a notable contribution to international jurisprudence, that they have been given in the exercise of a very high judicial function and that they have contributed to the maintenance of peaceful relations among nations.[86]

IX. Advisory Jurisdiction in the Post-League Era

1. *The Advisory Jurisdiction of the International Court of Justice*

Whatever controversies surrounded the creation of the PCIJ and vesting it with an advisory jurisdiction, it is notable that, when the League of Nations was replaced with the United Nations, and PCIJ was succeeded by the International Court of Justice, the structure of the advisory jurisdiction remained not only intact, but virtually identical. That said, there are two minor differences in the wording of the relevant statutory provision (Articles 65 in both cases), but they have perhaps proved significant in practice.

The first is that the ICJ Statute specifies that Advisory Opinions can only be rendered on "legal" questions. While this qualification was implicit in the PCIJ era (identical wording having been abandoned for other reasons), whether a particular question is truly legal has attracted considerable argument before the ICJ.[87] Such arguments, however, have generally been rebuffed by the ICJ, which has developed a strong "presumption of

[86] DH Miller, 'The Senate Reservations and the Advisory Opinions of the Permanent Court of International Justice' (1926) 26 ColumbiaLRev 668–669.

[87] In *Legal Consequences of the Construction of a Wall in the Occupied Palestinian Territory*, Israel raised the interesting argument that the question posed was so imprecisely worded as to be incapable of a legal answer. See: Letter dated 29 January 2004 from the Deputy Director General and Legal Advisor of the Ministry of Foreign Affairs, together with the Written Statement of the Government of Israel, available at: <http://www.icj-cij.org/docket/index.php?p1=3&p2=4&k=5a&case=131&code=mwp&p3=1>.

jurisdiction in the exercise of the advisory function."[88] This difference in practice has given the modern ICJ's advisory jurisdiction, for better or worse, a greater scope than the consent-based "advisory arbitrations" of the PCIJ and as a consequence the "general rule expressed in the *Eastern Carelia* case has to a very large extent been weakened."[89]

The second difference is the wider range of bodies which may seek Advisory Opinions. Under the PCIJ Statute, only the League Council and the Assembly had that prerogative. In fact, only the League Council ever submitted such requests, and generally had a self-imposed requirement of unanimity for doing so. By contrast, the ICJ can hear requests not only from the Security Council and the General Assembly but also, "other organs of the United Nations and specialized agencies" that have been granted the power to make such requests, with respect to "questions arising within the scope of their activities".[90] Interestingly, by contrast to the League of Nations, the UN Security Council has only once submitted a request for an Advisory Opinion to the ICJ, with all other requests emanating from the General Assembly and other authorised bodies, and such requests have certainly not always involved a unanimous resolution of the body concerned. In this context, the emphasis in the ICJ's jurisprudence has shifted from the question of consent that dominated *Eastern Carelia*, to question of sufficiency of evidence and identifying whether the question posed falls within the "scope" of the requesting body's "activities".[91]

Despite the increase in the number of bodies which can request Advisory Opinions, this has notably not led to a higher demand for Advisory Opinions. Indeed, the PCIJ's advisory jurisdiction proved more popular than the ICJ's: in the eighteen years of its operation, the PCIJ delivered twenty-seven Advisory Opinions; in the ICJ's sixty-five years, it has delivered only twenty-five (a twenty-sixth is pending at time of writing). Such a disparity calls for some explanation.[92] The League Council certainly embraced its ability to refer to the PCIJ discrete legal questions forming part of a broader dispute. As noted, this "advisory arbitration"

---

88 IFI Shihata, *The Power of the International Court to Determine Its Own Jurisdiction: Compétence de la Compétence* (Martinus Nijhoff, The Hague 1965) 46. Shihata notes that six of the first thirteen Advisory Opinions rendered by the ICJ included explicit affirmations of the Court's jurisdiction.

89 MN Shaw, *International Law* (6th ed, CUP, Cambridge 2008) 1111.

90 Art 96(2), Charter of the United Nations 1945 (as amended), 9 Hudson 327; UKTS (1946), Cmd 7015.

91 Shaw (n 89) 1111; see for example, *Legality of the Use by a State of Nuclear Weapons in Armed Conflict* (Advisory Opinion) [1996] ICJ Rep 66, especially [25]-[26].

92 On the lesser popularity of the ICJ's advisory procedure see Pomerance (n 9) 290 ff.

mechanism clearly proved useful to States, and having an issue placed before the Court seems to have been a rather straightforward matter of asking the Council to refer it.[93] Such a mechanism has simply not been a part of UN-era practice.

Further, the sheer speed of the PCIJ in rendering Advisory Opinions must have been attractive to the League and to States. Delivering twenty-seven opinions in thirteen years suggests that about two opinions were delivered per year, but in fact five were delivered in 1923 alone. Eighteen of the opinions were issued within four months of the request being submitted, most of those within two months or so; indeed, one came out within twenty-five days.[94] Only six took more than six months and not one took as long as a year. All of this was accomplished in an era before word processing or jet travel, and without cutting procedural corners—the Court consulted widely and interested parties often made both written and oral submissions.

By contrast, the most recently concluded advisory proceedings at the ICJ, the *Kosovo* case, took twenty-one months from request to opinion.[95] This is not slow by either contemporary standards of national or international litigation. However, whether the PCIJ, with its emphasis on delivering opinions fast enough for them to have a practical impact on current international disputes, would have considered this swift is open to question. At the very least, delay has likely limited the ICJ's potential to provide 'advisory arbitration.' By being so efficient, and so responsive, the PCIJ may have encouraged parties to identify the discrete legal components of international disputes as separate questions capable of reasoned resolution.

It has also been widely observed that the PCIJ's primary 'client', the League Council, also showed prudence and even-handedness in its use of the mechanism:[96] the Council did not refer to the Court abstract or biased questions. By contrast, at least some of the referrals to the ICJ have been criticised for being overbroad, vaguely worded or advocating (or presuming) a particular result.[97] As Pomerance observes:

---

93 Schwebel (n 60) 90–99.

94 The *Competence of the ILO to Examine Proposal for the Organization and Development of the Methods of Agricultural Production* Advisory Opinion was requested on 18 July 1922 and delivered on 12 August 1922.

95 The decision in *Legality of the Use by a State of Nuclear Weapons in Armed Conflict* (n 91) 66, resulting in essentially a decision by the Court to declare the request inadmissible, took almost 3 years to be rendered.

96 See e.g. Pomerance (n 9) 284–285.

97 Israel, for example, raised a number of such objections in *Legal Consequences of the Construction of a Wall in the Occupied Palestinian Territory* (see n 87, above).

> In sum, the desire of the [PCIJ] not to permit the advisory function to adversely affect the judicial character, prestige, and general standing of the Court in the world community, was powerfully buttressed (save in the *Eastern Carelia* and *Customs Union* aberrations) by the steady practice of the League Council and the organs whose legal questions it transmitted.[98]

It is hard to conclude that United Nations organs have, in the contemporary, era been quite as interested in 'buttressing' the Court's position.

Thirdly, referrals by the League Council were generally made on the basis of consensus (requiring in practice unanimity in Council as well as in the views of the affected States), thereby significantly increasing the likelihood of compliance.[99] Elimination of any such unanimity requirement may prove effective in allowing greater recourse to Advisory Opinions, but it is not necessarily "a procedure for effective advisory opinions."[100] It is frequently those States that would be most affected by opinions that oppose or abstain from voting to refer a question to the ICJ.[101] Thus, unlike the PCIJ era, when the non-binding character of Advisory Opinions was perceived as somewhat illusory, some ICJ opinions have suffered from an entirely predictable lack of compliance by directly affected States such as South Africa and Israel.[102] Where it appears that the Court has been turned to for "propaganda purposes" or to endorse "positions already firmly taken by political organs" rather than for genuine "problem-solving", this risks damaging the Court's reputation and authority.[103] Such concerns date back to the inception of the PCIJ itself. PCIJ judges recognized that "[t]echnically, the post-adjudicative phase is of no concern to the Court, but the attenuation of the practical authority of the Court's opinion ... tends to degrade the Court and destroy its judicial character."[104]

2. *The Advisory Jurisdiction of Other Courts and Tribunals*

Numerous contemporary international courts and tribunals have some form of advisory jurisdiction.[105] However, such grants of jurisdiction have

---

98 Pomerance (n 9) 285.

99 Schwebel (n 60) 108.

100 Pomerance (n 9) 290 quoting L Gross, 'The International Court of Justice and the United Nations' (1967-I) 120 Recueil des cours 369.

101 Pomerance (n 9) 294–295.

102 D Harris, *Cases and Materials on International Law* (7th ed Sweet & Maxwell, London 2010), 875; and cf Pomerance, ibid.

103 Pomerance (n 9) 323; compare Hambro (n 52) 19.

104 Pomerance (n 9) 318–319.

105 P Sands, R Mackenzie, and Y Shany (eds), *Manual on International Courts and Tribunals* (Tottel Publishing, Haywards Heath 2006) list, for example: the African

often been quite limited in character and it is hard to draw any direct line from the practice of the PCIJ through the ICJ to these newer institutions. In particular, a power to issue Advisory Opinions was conferred on the European Court of Human Rights (ECHR) in 1963 by the Second Protocol to the European Convention on Human Rights.[106] The question had, in fact, been debated among the Judges of the ECHR in their first session, whether the Court's Statute could (or should) be interpreted as allowing it to exercise an advisory jurisdiction in any event. Without any reference to PCIJ or ICJ practice, it appears the general sense among the judges was negative: they thought the Court already too radical experiment to proceed other than cautiously; if it were to have an advisory jurisdiction they felt it should be left to the member States to amend the Convention.[107] Under the power conferred on precisely this basis in 1963, however, opinions may only be requested by the Council of Ministers and "can only deal with procedural questions and may not deal with matters concerning the scope of the substantive rights and freedoms enumerated in the Convention and Protocols".[108] This limited grant of power has long been seen as disappointingly narrow.[109]

Similarly, The International Tribunal for the Law of the Sea (ITLOS) has no general advisory jurisdiction under the United Nations Convention on the Law of the Sea (UNCLOS).[110] Instead, a rather narrow advisory jurisdiction is conferred on its Seabed Disputes Chamber[111] which "is limited to legal questions that may be referred to it only by the Assembly or Council of the [International Seabed Authority] within the scope of their

Commission on Human and Peoples' Rights [20.17]; the Central American Court of Justice [11.8]; the European Court of Justice [8.22]; the European Free Trade Association Court of Justice [9.5]; the European Court of Human Rights [18.14]; the Inter-American Court of Human Rights [19.17]; the International Court of Justice [1.21]; and the International Tribunal for the Law of the Sea [3.14].

106 Art 47, Protocol No 2 to the Convention for the Protection for the Protection of Human Rights and Fundamental Freedoms 1963, (1963) ETS 44.

107 See: Summary Report of the sitting held by the Court, 23 February 1959, Council of Europe Document CDH/Misc (59) 23, <http://www.echr.coe.int/ECHR/EN/Header/The+Court/How+the+Court+works/Archives/Historical.htm>.

108 Sands, Mackenzie and Shany (n 105) 204.

109 R Beddard, 'The Second Protocol to the European Convention of Human Rights' (1964) 13 ICLQ 256, 259. The reasons for this were cryptically described as "self-evident": see the Council of Europe Explanatory Report: <http://conventions.coe.int/Treaty/Commun/QueVoulezVous.asp?NT=044&CM=8&DF=24/11/2011&CL=ENG>.

110 Although other treaties may confer an advisory jurisdiction upon it.

111 Arts 159(10) and 191, United Nations Convention on the Law of the Sea 1982 (UNCLOS), 1833 UNTS 3.

activities".[112] It is a jurisdiction which does not "involve disputes between States",[113] but which is intended to allow the Chamber to "assist the Council [and Assembly] in the performance of [their] activities and contribute to the implementation of the Convention's regime" governing deep seabed mining.[114] This peculiarly circumscribed jurisdiction has its origin in the 1970 US draft UN Convention on the International Seabed Area, where it was proposed that an International Seabed Resource Authority should have as one of its principal organs a Tribunal capable of giving Advisory Opinions.[115] With little discussion this function was transferred to ITLOS in the drafting of UNCLOS in 1976.[116] The precise historic reasons this jurisdiction was thought necessary are somewhat obscure, but it has now been used for the first time in order to render an Advisory Opinion on questions of the responsibility of States for the activities of sponsored "entities" (prospecting and mining corporations) in the seabed area beyond national jurisdiction.[117]

Overall, there appears something of a reluctance to confer on more recent dispute settlement bodies a power to grant Advisory Opinions comparable to that enjoyed by the PCIJ. Conversely, however, it has clearly been thought a desirable function to have—at least in some limited cases. One can perhaps, tentatively, conclude that part of the legacy of the PCIJ's advisory jurisdiction is that such a jurisdiction now forms part of the standard intellectual furniture available to negotiating States when faced with new exercises in institutional design.

X. Conclusion

In coming to maturity, the advisory jurisdiction of the PCIJ, like so many bright young things looking for respectability, had to make a number of compromises in light of the realities of the day. While the jurisdiction was

112 MH Nordquist et al (eds), *United Nations Convention on the Law of the Sea, 1982: A Commentary* (vol 5, Martinus Nijhoff, London 1989) 401; see further, SN Nandan et al (eds), *United Nations Convention on the Law of the Sea, 1982: A Commentary* (vol 6, Martinus Nijhoff, London 2002) 641–44.

113 Ibid.

114 *Responsibilities and Obligations of States Sponsoring Persons and Entities with respect to Activities in the Area* (Advisory Opinion) 1 February 2011, Seabed Disputes Chamber of the International Tribunal for the Law of the Sea (Case No 17) [30] <http://www.itlos.org/>.

115 See: Art 46, Draft United Nations Convention on the International Seabed Area 1970, 9 ILM 1046, UN Doc A/AC 138/25.

116 Nandan (n 112) 643.

117 See n 114, above.

innovative in conception, it did not prove groundbreaking in design or execution. At the very least, however, the Court did a good and solid job, as evidenced by the continued faith placed in the advisory mechanism at the founding of the ICJ. More importantly, the PCIJ's practice in its early advisory jurisdiction served to build the confidence of States in it as an institution. The withering away of 'advisory arbitration' was probably a direct consequence of States' increasing resort to (and obvious comfort with) its contentious jurisdiction.

Overall, the PCIJ was not radical or particularly experimental when confronted with this novel jurisdiction. That may represent a missed opportunity, but perhaps the most important thing that the Court did was to choose not to innovate. By following a conservative path perhaps the court did the better job of engaging States and international organisations with its processes and of promoting as best it could the rule of law in international dispute resolution. If anything, there would be some virtue in returning to the better features of the PCIJ model of Advisory Opinions: one of a broad jurisdiction, based on political organs furnishing unbiased questions, referred by consent or consensus, and rendered speedily enough to affect the resolution of live disputes.

THE ADVISORY JURISDICTION OF THE PERMANENT COURT OF INTERNATIONAL JUSTICE IN PRACTICE: A TALE OF TWO SCOPES

Panos Merkouris*

I. Introduction

The present contribution addresses the antithetical notions of success and failure, hope and despair, tradition and innovation in relation to the PCIJ's advisory jurisdiction. It aims to complement the analysis provided by Marika Giles Samson and Douglas Guilfoyle in their contribution[1] by focusing on specific features arising in the exercise of the Court's advisory jurisdiction.

In so doing, it approaches the PCIJ from the perspective of two scopes. The first scope is one of *ratione personae*, ie which organs had the competence to request Advisory Opinions. The second scope is one of *ratione materiae*, focusing on the questions themselves. This analysis is further subdivided into two parts: firstly, as to the nature of the issues that could be brought before the PCIJ; and secondly, as to the extent that the PCIJ could deviate from, or "reformulate", the question put to it. Both inquiries yield insights into the practice of the PCIJ's advisory jurisdiction and allow us to gauge commonalities and differences between the ICJ and its predecessor.

II. Scope *Ratione Personae*: The Bodies Permitted to Ask the PCIJ for an Advisory Opinion

What is immediately striking is the identity of the bodies that could request an Advisory Opinion. In the case of the PCIJ, only the Council of the League of Nations and the Assembly had that right.[2] At this point one needs to refer to the somewhat bizarre representation of the advisory

[1] See M Giles Samson and D Guilfoyle (in this volume).

[2] Article 14 of the Covenant and Article 65 of the Statute (as amended by the Protocol of September 14, 1929).

jurisdiction in the relevant documents. Whereas Article 14 of the Covenant referred to the Council and the Assembly as the two bodies permitted to request an Advisory Opinion, this was not also reflected in the original Statute of the PCIJ. In fact, no provision relating to the advisory jurisdiction of the Court was included in that document. As a result, the advisory jurisdiction envisaged in Article 14 of the Covenant, was expounded upon only in 1922 in Articles 71–74 of the Rules of Procedure of the PCIJ. This led, as Forwein and Oellers-Frahm correctly point out, to the somewhat paradoxical situation that these rules came into effect *after* the PCIJ had already given two Advisory Opinions.[3] Despite this, the 1922 Rules[4] referred to Article 14, and confirmed that only those two bodies were permitted to ask for an Advisory Opinion.[5] This solution was eventually reflected in the Statute when it was revised in 1929 and a new Chapter, Chapter IV, was introduced dedicated to Advisory Opinions.[6]

It goes without saying that the power to request an Advisory Opinion was not limitless. As the PCIJ made clear in the *German Settlers in Poland* Advisory Opinion: "If ... the subject-matter of the controversy is not within the competence of the League, the Court would not be justified in rendering an opinion as to the rights of the settlers. The Court therefore will first consider the question of competency."[7]

---

3 ie *Designation of the Workers' Delegate for the Netherlands at the Third Session of the International Labour Conference* (Advisory Opinion) [1922] PCIJ Ser B No 1, at 9 seq; *Competence of the International Labour Organization* (Advisory Opinion) [1922] PCIJ Ser B Nos 2–3, at 9 seq.

4 And all its consecutive amendments in 1926, 1927, 1931 and 1936.

5 In more detail see: J Frowein and K Oellers-Frahm, 'Chapter IV Advisory Opinions: Article 65', in A Zimmermann, C Tomuschat, and K Oellers-Frahm (eds), *The Statute of the International Court of Justice: A Commentary* (OUP, Oxford 2006) 1404; G Guyomar, *Commentaire du Règlement de la Cour Internationale de Justice: Adopté le 14 Avril 1978 : Interprétation et Pratique* (Pedone, Paris 1983) 644 seq; MO Hudson, 'Les Avis Consultatifs de la Cour Permanente de Justice Internationale' (1925) 8 Recueil des Cours 341 seq.

6 Pursuant to Article 65, as introduced in 1929, "[q]uestions upon which the Advisory Opinion of the Court is asked shall be laid before the Court by means of a written request, *signed either by the President of the Assembly or the President of the Council of the League of Nations, or by the Secretary-General of the League under instructions from the Assembly or the Council*." (emphasis added).

7 *German Settlers in Poland* (Advisory Opinion) [1923] PCIJ Ser B No 6, at 19; see also Individual Opinion of Judge Anzilotti in the *Free City of Danzig and ILO* Advisory Opinion where he comments on the fact that only the body which had *exclusive* competence over certain matters had the corresponding authority to request an Advisory Opinion on those matters; *Free City of Danzig and ILO* (Advisory Opinion) [1930] PCIJ Series B No 18, Individual Opinion of Judge Anzilotti, at 20; and Hudson, who argues that any attempt by any of the two bodies of the League to delegate their authority to request an Advisory Opinion would be *ultra vires;* MO Hudson, 'The Two Problems of Approach to the Permanent Court of International Justice' (1935) 29 AJIL 636, 642–643.

For the same reason, if a dispute fell within the domestic jurisdiction of a State, both the Council and the Assembly were barred from asking for an Advisory Opinion, unless the States gave their consent either explicitly[8] or through their conduct, as an expression of the principle of *forum prorogatum*.[9]

The fact that a request for an Advisory Opinion had been rejected by one of the two bodies did not preclude the other from considering whether or not it should give its own approval. This is what happened in the Vilna dispute, in 1923, when the Council refused the request made by the Lithuanian Government for a request for an Advisory Opinion. This led Lithuania to submit an identical request for consideration by the Assembly.[10]

While Article 14 of the Covenant and Article 65 of the Statute (post 1929) put the Council and Assembly on the same footing, in practice their roles were rather different. All of the twenty-seven Advisory Opinions rendered by the PCIJ had been requested by the Council, and none by the Assembly. However, this statistical fact may be somewhat misleading,[11] since what actually happened was that the Council quite often functioned as intermediary transmitting requests for Advisory Opinions

---

[8] Which stems from Article 15 of the Covenant. See also D Pratap, *The Advisory Jurisdiction of the International Court* (Clarendon Press, Oxford 1972) 52.

[9] On this issue *see*: *Mosul Case*, PCIJ Ser E No 2 at 164; *see also Interpretation of Peace Treaties with Bulgaria, Hungary and Romania* (Advisory Opinion) [1950] ICJ Rep Dissenting Opinion of Judge Winiarski, at 96 and Dissenting Opinion of Judge Krylov, at 107; Advisory Opinions that are considered to have been applications of the principle of *forum prorogatum* are: *Nationality Decrees Issued in Tunis and Morocco* (Advisory Opinion) [1923] PCIJ Ser B No 4; *Delimitation of the Polish- Czechoslovakian Frontier* (Advisory Opinion) [1923] PCIJ Ser B No 8 (hereafter *Jaworzina Case*); *Interpretation of the Greco-Bulgarian Agreement of 9 December 1927* (Advisory Opinion) [1932] PCIJ Ser A/B No 45.

[10] Pratap (n 9) 52.

[11] Actually the requests for Advisory Opinions that were submitted at the initiative of the Council itself were the following: *German Settlers in Poland* (n 8); *Acquisition of Polish Nationality* (Advisory Opinion) [1923] PCIJ Ser B No 7; *Polish Postal Service in Danzig* (Advisory Opinion) [1925] PCIJ Ser No 11; *Article 3, Paragraph 2, of the Treaty of Lausanne (Frontier between Turkey and Iraq)* (Advisory Opinion) [1925] PCIJ Ser B No 12; *Jurisdiction of the Courts of Danzig* (Advisory Opinion) [1928] PCIJ Ser B No 15; *Customs Regime between Germany and Austria* (Advisory Opinion) [1931] PCIJ Ser A/B No 41; *Railway Traffic between Lithuania and Poland* (Advisory Opinion) [1931] PCIJ Ser A/B No 42; *Access to, or Anchorage in, the Port of Danzig, of Polish War Vessels* (Advisory Opinion) [1931] PCIJ Ser A/B No 43; *Interpretation of the Greco-Bulgarian Agreement of 9 December 1927* (n 10); *Minority Schools in Albania* (Advisory Opinion) [1935] PCIJ Series A/B No 64; *Consistency of Certain Danzig Legislative Decrees with the Constitution of the Free City* (Advisory Opinion) [1935] PCIJ Ser A/B No 65 (hereafter *Danzig Legislative Decrees*); and the *Expulsion of the Oecumenical Patriarch* PCIJ Ser C No 09/2.

to the PCIJ either on behalf of two or more States[12] or emanating from other international organizations. In the latter scenario, the Council had requested the PCIJ to render Advisory Opinions for the benefit of: i) the ILO,[13] ii) the Conference of Ambassadors,[14] iii) the Mixed Commission for the Exchange of Greek and Turkish Populations,[15] iv) the President of the Greco-Bulgarian Mixed Commission with the agreement of the Greek and Bulgarian Governments,[16] and v) the High Commissioner for the League of Nations for Danzig in agreement with Poland and Danzig.[17]

The brief survey reveals that while indeed, after 1945, "the structure of the advisory jurisdiction remained ... intact",[18] the circle of actors was broadened. According to the ICJ Statute and the UN Charter, not only the General Assembly and the Security Council, but also "[o]ther organs of the United Nations and specialized agencies, which may at any time be so authorized by the General Assembly, may ... request Advisory Opinions of the Court on legal questions arising within the scope of their activities".[19]

---

12 In more detail: i) on behalf of France: *Competence of the International Labour Organization* (n 4); ii) on behalf of Great Britain and France: *Nationality Decrees Issued in Tunis and Morocco* (n 10); iii) on behalf of Finland: *Status of Eastern Carelia* (Advisory Opinion) [1923] PCIJ Ser B No 5; iv) on behalf of Great Britain, France, Italy, and Romania: *Jurisdiction of the European Commission of the Danube* (Advisory Opinion) [1927] PCIJ Ser B No 14; and v) on behalf of Germany and Poland: *Access to German Minority Schools in Upper Silesia* (Advisory Opinion) [1931] PCIJ Ser A/B No 40.

13 *Designation of the Workers' Delegate for the Netherlands* (n 4); *Competence of the ILO to Regulate Incidentally the Personal Work of the Employer* (Advisory Opinion) [1926] PCIJ Ser B No 13 (hereafter *Competence of the ILO Advisory Opinion*); *Free City of Danzig and ILO* (n 8).

14 *Jaworzina Case* (n 10); *Monastery of Saint-Naoum* (Advisory Opinion) [1924] PCIJ Ser B No 9.

15 *Exchange of Greek and Turkish Populations* (Advisory Opinion) [1925] PCIJ Ser B No 10; *Interpretation of the Greco-Turkish Agreement of December 1st, 1926 (Final Protocol, Article IV)* (Advisory Opinion) [1928] PCIJ Ser B No 16 (hereafter *Interpretation of Greco-Turkish Agreement*).

16 *The Greco-Bulgarian "Communities"* (Advisory Opinion) [1930] PCIJ Ser B No 17.

17 *Treatment of Polish Nationals and Other Persons of Polish Origin or Speech in the Danzig Territory* (Advisory Opinion) [1932] PCIJ Series A/B No 44.

18 See Giles Samson and Guilfoyle, (in this volume) at 62.

19 Article 65(1) of the ICJ Statute in combination with Article 96(1) & (2) of the UN Charter; at present apart from the Security Council and the General Assembly there are three more organs of the United Nations and 16 specialized agencies and/or related organizations, which have the right to request an Advisory Opinion from the ICJ. These are: the Economic and Social Council, the Trusteeship Council, the Interim Committee of the General Assembly, the International Labour Organization (ILO); the Food and Agriculture Organization of the United Nations (FAO); the United Nations Educational, Scientific and Cultural Organization (UNESCO); the World Health Organization (WHO); the International Bank for Reconstruction and Development (IBRD); the International Finance Corporation (IFC); the International Development Association (IDA); the International Monetary Fund

To make this contrast starker, unlike its counterpart in the League of Nations, the Security Council has only once submitted a request for an Advisory Opinion to the ICJ.[20] All the other Advisory Opinions have emerged from the initiative of either the General Assembly or other specialized agencies.[21]

III. Scope *Ratione Materiae* of the Advisory Jurisdiction of the PCIJ (I): The Nature of the Question/Dispute

In the majority of the Advisory Opinions given by the ICJ, the structure of the Court's judicial reasoning begins with a consideration of the jurisdiction and discretion of the Court, and then the scope of the question. In the first leg apart from examining whether the body submitting a question to the ICJ has the authority to do so, the ICJ examines also whether the question submitted is of a "legal nature" an element required by Article 96 of the UN Charter and Article 65 of the ICJ Statute. According to the consistent jurisprudence of the ICJ on this matter, a question "framed in terms of law and rais[ing] problems of international law ... are by their very nature susceptible of a reply based on law".[22] The fact that a question may have certain political aspects,[23] or that it may be motivated by political reasons

(IMF); the International Civil Aviation Organization (ICAO); the International Telecommunication Union (ITU); the International Fund for Agricultural Development (IFAD); the World Meteorological Organization (WMO); the International Maritime Organization (IMO); the World Intellectual Property Organization (WIPO); the United Nations Industrial Development Organization (UNIDO) and the International Atomic Energy Agency (IAEA). Information available at: ICJ, <http://www.icj-cij.org/jurisdiction/index.php?p1=5&p2=2&p3=1>. Some authors have also argued whether the UN Secretary-General should also be given the authority to request an Advisory Opinion; see R Higgins, 'A Comment on the Current Health of Advisory Opinions' in V Lowe and M Fitzmaurice (eds), *Fifty Years of the International Court of Justice: Essays in Honour of Sir Robert Jennings* (CUP, Cambridge 1996) 569–570.

20 Namely *Legal Consequences for States of the Continued Presence of South Africa in Namibia (South West Africa) notwithstanding Security Council Resolution 276 (1970)* [1971] ICJ Rep at 16.

21 And in the case of the latter, the ICJ is always preoccupied in its Opinion to establish that the request falls within the scope of activities of the relevant agencies; see for instance, *Legality of the Use by a State of Nuclear Weapons in Armed Conflict* (Advisory Opinion) [1996] ICJ Rep [25]-[26] (hereafter *Nuclear Weapons Advisory Opinion*).

22 *Western Sahara* (Advisory Opinion) [1975] ICJ Rep [15]; see also *Accordance with International Law of the Unilateral Declaration of Independence in Respect with Kosovo*, Advisory Opinion of 22 July 2010, ICJ, available online at: <http://www.icj-cij.org/docket/files/141/15987.pdf> [25] (hereafter *Kosovo Advisory Opinion*); *Nuclear Weapons Advisory Opinion* (n 22) [13].

23 *Application for Review of Judgement No 158 of the United Nations Administrative Tribunal* (Advisory Opinion) [1973] ICJ Rep [14] (hereafter *Review of Judgment No 158*).

or have political implications, does not suffice to deprive it of its legal nature.[24] Again, this presents a stark contrast to the approach of the PCIJ. Contrary to ICJ practice, the number of PCIJ Advisory Opinions that addressed the 'legal nature' of a question amounted to a resounding zero. This, however, should not strike us as bizarre. Whereas the requirement of a "legal question" is explicitly provided for in the text of Article 96 of the UN Charter and Article 65 of the ICJ Statute, no such requirement existed either in Article 14 of the Covenant of the League of Nations or Chapter IV of the PCIJ Statute. Article 65 of the PCIJ Statute only talks about "questions" without attaching any distinguishing adjective to this term, whereas Article 14 of the Covenant uses the terms "any dispute or question" again without any further qualification. As was observed, in both instances their nature should have been a "legal" one.[25]

During the inter-War era, debates about the scope of the Court's advisory jurisdiction instead centred on the curious two-pronged terminology adopted in the text of Article 14 of the Covenant, ie "dispute" and "question". As Pratap mentions, it is not quite evident why this formulation found its way into the official text of the Covenant but the "original idea was to refer to the Court legal issues arising out of certain classes of disputes ... and the idea seems to have been to refer either the whole dispute to the Court, or only the legal elements involved which alone required clarification".[26] In essence, "dispute" referred to an *actual* dispute between States members of the League of Nations as to their rights and interests, but which wanted, for whatever reasons, to take advantage of the option of the advisory function of the Court rather than submitting it for adjudication.[27] On the other hand, the Advisory Committee of Jurists

[24] *Conditions of Admission of a State to Membership in the United Nations* (Advisory Opinion) [1948] ICJ Rep at 61, and *Nuclear Weapons Advisory Opinion* (n 22) [13]; *Interpretation of the Agreement of 25 March 1951 between the WHO and Egypt* (Advisory Opinion) [1980] ICJ Rep [33] (hereafter *WHO-Egypt Advisory Opinion*).

[25] Pratap (n 9) 86 seq. Pratap also examines whether the bodies had the power to submit "political", "abstract" and/or "hypothetical" questions; ibid, 90–93. The PCIJ was never asked to give an Opinion on a purely abstract question; *see* M Pomerance, *The Advisory Function of the International Court in the League and UN Eras* (The Johns Hopkins UP, London 1973) 308.

[26] Pratap (n 9) 86.

[27] LM Goodrich, 'The Nature of the Advisory Opinions of the Permanent Court of International Justice' (1938) 32 AJIL 738, 744; MO Hudson, *The Permanent Court of International Justice 1920–1942: A Treatise* (The MacMillan Company, New York 1943) 495; Pratap (n 9) at 86.

saw the "question" as having a more abstract/theoretical nature. Whereas "dispute" referred to a particular situation at hand, "question" did not.[28]

But was this sufficient to require different procedures and solutions to be adopted by the PCIJ in each instance? Judge Anzilotti felt that the distinction between the two terms was merely semantic.[29] Originally, however, the Advisory Committee of Jurists had played with the idea of giving substance to this terminological difference. One of the original drafts of the article referring to the advisory jurisdiction of the PCIJ (then Draft Article 32) went as follows:

> The Court shall give an advisory opinion upon any question or dispute of an international nature referred to it by the Council or Assembly.
>
> When the Court shall give an opinion on a question of an international nature which does not refer to any dispute that may have arisen, it shall appoint a special Commission of from three to five members.
>
> When it shall give an opinion upon a question which forms the subject of an existing dispute it shall do so under the same conditions as if the case had been actually submitted to it for decision.[30]

This draft envisaged two different procedures: one (for 'questions') involved the establishment of a Commission; the other (for 'disputes') was similar to those governing contentious proceedings. De la Pradelle considered that this was the correct approach due to the *sui generis* nature of the advisory procedure relating to "disputes".[31] Hudson, on the other hand, was of the opinion that the Court should not have the right to give an Advisory Opinion with reference to an existing dispute as this would be "a violation of all judicial principles".[32] Eventually, the Committee of the Assembly of the League of Nations recommended the deletion of Draft Article 32 because it seemed "lacking in clearness and likely to give rise to

---

[28] Although it was possible that at a later date the issues raised by the "question" could arise in an actual dispute brought before the PCIJ; *Minutes of the 1920 Committee of Jurists*, available online at: <http://www.icj-cij.org/pcij/serie_D/D_proceedings_of_committee_annexes_16june_24july_1920.pdf> 548 seq.

[29] *Danzig Legislative Decrees* (n 12), Dissenting Opinion of Judge Anzilotti, at 64; see also Hudson (n 8) 358.

[30] *Minutes of the 1920 Committee of Jurists* (n 29) 567.

[31] Ibid, 584; see also D Négulesco, 'L'évolution de la procédure des avis consultatives de la Cour permanente de justice internationale' (1936) 57 Recueil des Cours 1, 12; de la Pradelle also upheld the aforementioned understanding of the difference between the terms "question" and "dispute".

[32] Ibid, 584. He was later convinced by de la Pradelle that this was not the case as there was a legal basis for it in the form of Article 13 of the Covenant.

practical difficulties".[33] For instance, as Pratap points out, one such difficulty could have arisen with respect to Article 15 para 8 of the Covenant according to which "[i]f the dispute between the parties is claimed by one of them, and is found by the Council, to arise out of a matter which by international law is solely within the domestic jurisdiction of that party, the Council shall so report, and shall make no recommendation as to its settlement." In such a situation the Council would not have had the right to seek an Advisory Opinion from the PCIJ and the latter would equally have to refuse such a request were it to be made. In two cases, a State objected to the Council's action of requesting an Advisory Opinion.[34] In both these cases, the objecting State refused to participate in the proceedings.[35] However, in both of these cases the possible legal implications of Article 15 para 8, identified by Pratap above, never came to the forefront as the issue was resolved through different means. In the first of these cases, the *Eastern Carelia* case the PCIJ refused to give the opinion but on different grounds than the ones objected to, and in the second one, the *Expulsion of the Oecumenical Patriarch*, the Council withdrew the request.

Despite this, the practice of both the Council and the PCIJ is peppered with requests for Advisory Opinions on issues pertaining to actual disputes, sometimes even on the request of the States themselves.[36] In submitting these requests, e.g. in the *Nationality Decrees* and *Danube Commission* proceedings, the Council gave effect to the preference of disputing States to have 'their dispute' settled by means of an Advisory Opinion (which they undertook to accept) rather than by means of a judgment. In *Nationality Decrees*, Great Britain and France agreed that if the issue did not fall within the domestic jurisdiction of one of the States, the whole dispute would

---

33 *Documents Concerning the Action Taken by the Council of the League of Nations under Article 14 of the Covenant and the Adoption by the Assembly of the Statute of the Permanent Court* (1921), available online at: <http://www.icj-cij.org/pcij/serie_D/D_documents_conseil_de_la_societe_des_nations.pdf>.

34 *Eastern Carelia* (n 13) at 13, 15; *Expulsion of the Oecumenical Patriarch* (n 13) at 107–108.

35 Consequently, the principle of *forum prorogatum* did not come into play.

36 For a detailed analysis of the relevant Advisory Opinions and the States that were connected to them, see (n 13). There were also a few other Advisory Opinions where the agreement of the States was secured but the request to the Council was submitted through another organ, e.g. *the Greco-Bulgarian "Communities"* (n 17), with the agreement of Greece and Bulgaria, on the request of the President of the Greco-Bulgarian Mixed Commission; *Treatment of Polish Nationals and Other Persons of Polish Origin or Speech in the Danzig Territory* (n 18), with the agreement of Poland and Danzig on the request of the High Commissioner for the League of Nations for Danzig.

then be referred to arbitration or the PCIJ for judicial settlement.[37] In *Danube Commission*, France, Great Britain, Italy and Romania agreed to use the Advisory Opinion as a basis for future negotiations and for the final resolution of the dispute.[38] The fact that in a great number of instances where the PCIJ was seized in its advisory function the issue was a "dispute" rather than a "question" can be attributed to the officially non-binding character of the Advisory Opinions, which made this procedure more appealing to States and explains why the "self-referral" of existing disputes to this process was a common feature in the jurisprudence of the PCIJ.[39] States tended to use the advisory procedure of the PCIJ as a springboard for the eventual resolution of an existing dispute. In fact, such was the plethora of these "self-referral" cases and such was the similarity of "disputes" in advisory proceedings with "disputes" in contentious proceedings that when the Statute of the PCIJ was amended through the Protocol of 14 September 1929, a new Article was introduced, Article 68 that provided that "[i]n the exercise of its advisory functions, the Court shall further be guided by the provisions of the Statute which apply in contentious cases *to the extent to which it recognizes them to be applicable*." (emphasis added).

IV. Scope *Ratione Materiae* of the Advisory Jurisdiction of the PCIJ (II): The Possibility of Reformulation of the Questions Submitted to the PCIJ

One final issue to be taken into account concerns the discretion of the Court in dealing with a request: is it required to address the question (or the 'dispute') as put by the requesting body, or is it entitled to reformulate it? As the ICJ's recent Advisory Opinion on the *Accordance with International Law of the Unilateral Declaration of Independence in Respect with Kosovo*[40] suggests, the matter is of current relevance. In it, the ICJ felt it necessary to explain why it *would not* reformulate the question. In more detail:

37 PCIJ Ser E No 4, at 7–8.

38 *Jurisdiction of the European Commission of the Danube between Galatz and Braila,* PCIJ Ser C No 13/IV, Vol 2, at 326–327.

39 SM Schwebel, 'Was the Capacity to Request an Advisory Opinion Wider in the Permanent Court of International Justice than it is in the International Court of Justice' (1992) 62 British Ybk of Intl L 82.

40 *Kosovo Advisory Opinion* (n 23).

51. In the present case, the question posed by the General Assembly is clearly formulated. The question is narrow and specific; it asks for the Court's opinion on whether or not the declaration of independence is in accordance with international law. It does not ask about the legal consequences of that declaration. In particular, it does not ask whether or not Kosovo has achieved statehood. Nor does it ask about the validity or legal effects of the recognition of Kosovo by those States which have recognized it as an independent State. The Court notes that, in past requests for advisory opinions, the General Assembly and the Security Council, when they have wanted the Court's opinion on the legal consequences of an action, have framed the question in such a way that this aspect is expressly stated (see, for example, *Legal Consequences for States of the Continued Presence of South Africa in Namibia (South West Africa) notwithstanding Security Council Resolution 276 (1970), Advisory Opinion, I.C.J. Reports 1971*, p. 16 and *Legal Consequences of the Construction of a Wall in the Occupied Palestinian Territory, Advisory Opinion, I.C.J. Reports 2004 (I)*, p. 136). Accordingly, the Court does not consider that it is necessary to address such issues as whether or not the declaration has led to the creation of a State or the status of the acts of recognition in order to answer the question put by the General Assembly. The Court accordingly sees no reason to reformulate the scope of the question.

Of the twenty-seven Advisory Opinions rendered by the PCIJ, one—and only one—was a clear-cut case of reformulation.[41] Two other cases are borderline,[42] in that some authors consider the PCIJ to have reformulated the question, while others argue it had merely interpreted them. These numbers clearly suggest that reformulation was far from a common practice in the jurisprudence of the PCIJ.[43] But even if it was not common, it needs to be asked whether the Court was permitted to reformulate questions.

Kammerhofer, when examining this issue from the perspective of the ICJ, begins by examining Article 96 of the UN Charter and Article 65 of the ICJ Statute but finds both of them to be "relatively open-textured" and that

41 *Interpretation of Greco-Turkish Agreement* (n 16).

42 *Article 3, Paragraph 2, of the Treaty of Lausanne (Frontier between Turkey and Iraq)* (n 12); *The Greco-Bulgarian "Communities"* (n 17).

43 This preliminary conclusion is reinforced by the jurisprudence of the ICJ. Out of twenty-six Advisory Opinions, only four are clearly cases of reformulation: *Admissibility of Hearings of Petitioners by the Committee on South West Africa* (Advisory Opinion) [1956] ICJ Rep (hereafter *Hearings of Petitioners Advisory Opinion*); *WHO-Egypt Advisory Opinion* (n 25); *Application for Review of Judgement No 273 of the United Nations Administrative Tribunal* (Advisory Opinion) [1982] ICJ Rep (hereafter *Review of Judgment No 273 Advisory Opinion*); *Nuclear Weapons Advisory Opinion* (n 22). Similarly to the PCIJ there are two cases that are borderline: *Application for Review of Judgment No 333 of the United Nations Administrative Tribunal* (Advisory Opinion) [1987], ICJ Rep (hereafter *Review of Judgment No 333 Advisory Opinion*); *Kosovo Advisory Opinion* (n 23).

the text of neither of them "can establish an exclusive logical connection between the content of the request (the form of the question asked) and the answer given".[44] According to Kammerhofer, the necessity to adhere to a certain extent to the form of the question would seem to emanate somewhat more strongly, but in no way imperatively, from the 1978 Rules of the Court and Article 107(2): "The advisory opinion *shall contain*: ... the reply *to the question put to the Court*".[45] Irrespective of the conclusions one may draw from these provisions, one has to look at their counterparts in the PCIJ. Article 14 of the Covenant seems to be equally "open-textured" as Article 96(1) of the UN Charter; the former stating that "... The Court may also give *an advisory opinion upon any dispute or question* referred to it by the Council or by the Assembly",[46] while the latter: "The General Assembly or the Security Council may request the International Court of Justice to give *an advisory opinion on any legal question*".[47] As has been noted, the Statute itself originally did not regulate advisory proceedings, and Article 65 introduced during the 1929 revision[48] in this respect is almost identical with that of the ICJ Statute.[49] Finally, no counterpart to Article 107(2) of the Rules of the ICJ existed in the Rules of the PCIJ. While Article 74 of the Rules in their 1936 version listed elements to be included in a judgment, no comparable provision was included in Articles 82–85 dealing with Advisory Opinions.[50] Consequently, the relevant texts governing the work of PCIJ did not seem to impose upon the Court an obligation to adhere in the strictest sense to the text of the question, but rather reply to what was actually being asked. This, in turn, could be read as permitting some element of reformulation.

The reasons supporting such a *pouvoir de reformuler* were set out by the PCIJ's successor, in its Opinion on the *Interpretation of the Agreement of*

---

44 J Kammerhofer, 'Begging the Question? The *Kosovo* Opinion and the Reformulation of Advisory Requests' available at: <http://papers.ssrn.com/sol3/papers.cfm?abstract_id=1684539>, 10.

45 Rules of the ICJ, Article 107(2), (emphasis added).

46 (emphasis added).

47 (emphasis added).

48 With Chapter IV dedicated to advisory proceedings.

49 "Article 65 [PCIJ Statute] ... Questions upon which the advisory opinion of the Court is asked shall be laid before the Court by means of a written request, signed either by the President of the Assembly or the President of the Council of the League of Nations, or by the Secretary-General of the League under instructions from the Assembly or the Council. The request shall contain an exact statement of the question upon which an opinion is required, and shall be accompanied by all documents likely to throw light upon the question."

50 In a fashion similar to Article 95 of the ICJ Statute.

25 March 1951 between the WHO and Egypt, but equally apply to the PCIJ. In more detail, the Court in the *WHO-Egypt Advisory Opinion* said: "... if it [the Court] is to remain faithful to the requirements of its judicial character in the exercise of its advisory jurisdiction, it must ascertain *what are the legal questions really in issue* in questions formulated in a request ... [and] a reply to questions of the kind posed in the present request may, if incomplete, be not only ineffectual but actually misleading as to the legal rules applicable to the matter under consideration by the requesting Organization."[51] What the Court is advocating, is that reformulation may be necessary in certain circumstances as otherwise the Court would not be able to dispense with its duty to render a reasonable, meaningful and effective Advisory Opinion. Ascertaining the *actual legal question* is a *sine qua non* during any advisory proceeding.

The question remains whether the jurisprudence of the PCIJ affirms the existence of such a *pouvoir de reformuler*. As mentioned at the outset, in only one Advisory Opinion did the PCIJ clearly reformulate the question posed, namely in the *Interpretation of the Greco-Turkish Agreement of December 1st, 1926 (Final Protocol, Article IV)*. This Opinion was unique in that in fact *no question* had been submitted to the Court. Instead, the request referred to a letter addressed by the President of the Mixed Commission for the Exchange of Greek and Turkish Populations to the Secretary-General of the League of Nations.[52] Clearly, therefore, the PCIJ had to engage with the request in order to be able to reply to it. At this point it is apposite to reproduce the relevant passage of the reasoning of the PCIJ:

> Article 72, paragraph 2, of the Rules of Court, lays down that "the request shall contain an exact statement of the question upon which an opinion is required". But the Request transmitted to the Court in pursuance of the Resolution of the Council of the League of Nations of June 5th, 1928, simply refers to the letter addressed by the President of the Mixed Commission for the Exchange of Greek and Turkish Populations on February 4th, 1928, to the Secretary-General of the League of Nations, with a view to obtaining an advisory opinion from the Permanent Court of International Justice upon the interpretation of Article IV of the Final Protocol of the Greco-Turkish Agreement of December 1st, 1926, concerning "the conditions for appeals to the arbitrator" contemplated in this article. The Court, however, considers that, as the letter referred to does not exactly state the question upon which its opinion is sought, *it is essential that it should determine what this question*

[51] *WHO-Egypt Advisory Opinion* (n 25) [35] (emphasis added).
[52] *Interpretation of Greco-Turkish Agreement* (n 16) at 14.

> *is and formulate an exact statement of it,* in order more particularly to avoid dealing with points of law upon which *it was not the intention of the Council or the Commission to obtain its opinion.*[53]

The Court, in essence, felt that the lack of any actual question in the request by the Council was of no consequence. The question that the Council had *intended* to ask could be easily identified through the relevant documents that accompanied the request, and in particular the letter addressed by the President of the Mixed Commission to the Secretary-General of the League of Nations, to which the request referred to as its basis. All these elements allowed it to "determine what this question is and formulate an exact statement of it".[54]

Apart from this case, two more Advisory Opinions of the PCIJ may stake a claim at being instances of reformulation. In *Article 3, Paragraph 2, of the Treaty of Lausanne* (*Frontier between Turkey and Iraq*) the PCIJ stated that "it intends strictly to confine itself to considerations of [the questions put to it by the Council], without in any way prejudging the merits of the problem before the Council".[55] Of import for the present analysis is the fact that although the request for the Advisory Opinion related to the determination of the character of the decision of the Council, ie whether it was "an arbitral award, a recommendation or a simple mediation",[56] the PCIJ felt it was not restricted to the given alternatives but stated that the decision "will be binding on the Parties and constitute a definitive determination of the frontier between Turkey and Iraq".[57] This point is what makes this Opinion a borderline one, between "reformulation" and "classical interpretation". The answer may vary depending, as Kammerhofer argues, on whether the "alternatives provided are understood as contravalence rather than as mere disjunction".[58]

The final case, where the PCIJ can be argued to have reformulated the question is the *Greco-Bulgarian "Communities"*. In this Opinion the PCIJ held that question No 2 drawn up by the Mixed Commission—namely "2. What conditions must be satisfied in order to cause the Mixed Commission provided for in the Convention to dissolve a community such as is meant by the Convention?"—was wrong because it was based on the premise

---

53 Ibid.
54 Ibid.
55 *Article 3, Paragraph 2, of the Treaty of Lausanne* (*Frontier between Turkey and Iraq*) (n 12) at 18, 33.
56 Ibid, 6.
57 Ibid, 33.
58 Kammerhofer (n 46).

that the Commission could itself dissolve communities. However, the PCIJ held that such dissolution is "a question of fact and not of law". For this reason, the PCIJ not only did not answer the question posed, but rather provided a set of factual criteria that it felt may assist the Commission in its task of verifying whether dissolution has taken place.[59]

The afore-analysed jurisprudence of the PCIJ on the issue of reformulation may be somewhat scarce, but nonetheless provides us with some useful insights. First of all, it demonstrates beyond the shadow of a doubt that reformulation was not only not considered *contra legem* but on the contrary an integral part of the competence of the Court in exercising its advisory function.[60] Furthermore, according to the same cases, such reformulation was to be guided by a variety of elements such as *the intention* of the requesting body,[61] the nature and/or purpose of the question[62] as well as other documents that may reveal the actual question that was intended to be asked.[63] These elements, which have been reaffirmed and expounded in more detail in the jurisprudence of the ICJ,[64] are of course familiar, as they are constantly resorted to in the process of interpretation. This, as well as the relatively minor number of cases of reformulation, suggests that reformulation is nothing more than an extreme form of interpretation. A form of interpretation, which may deviate from the actual text but only under specific conditions and insofar as this is based on the intention of the parties, the object and purpose of the question and or other surrounding documents or *travaux préparatoires*.

The exceptional nature of reformulation is reaffirmed by the *Exchange of Greek and Turkish Populations*, where the PCIJ focused on the text and refused to take cognizance of the question relating to the special position of the Ecumenical Patriarchate of Constantinople on the basis that, "... [the] Council, if it *had wished* also to obtain the Court's opinion on this point, which was the subject of discussion at Lausanne, would not have failed to say so *in terms*. In these circumstances the Court does not consider that it has cognizance of this question."[65]

59 *The Greco-Bulgarian "Communities"* (n 17) at 23, 33–34; *see* Kammerhofer (n 46).

60 This was explicitly stated, much later, by the ICJ in the *WHO-Egypt Advisory Opinion* (n 25) [35].

61 *Interpretation of Greco-Turkish Agreement* (n 16) at 14.

62 *The Greco-Bulgarian "Communities"* (n 17) at 23, 33–34.

63 The letter addressed by the President of the Mixed Commission to the Secretary—General of the League of Nations, in *Interpretation of Greco-Turkish Agreement* (n 16) at 14.

64 See the "reformulation" Advisory Opinions of the ICJ, mentioned at (n 45).

65 *Exchange of Greek and Turkish Populations* (n 16) at 17 (emphasis added).

In this case, text and intention were the main driving forces behind the PCIJ's refusal to reformulate the question as there was no friction between the two. The text was a clear reflection of the intention of the requesting body. The *travaux préparatoires* or other relevant documents have also had bearing in the reformulation/interpretation of Advisory Opinions. Apart from the letter (mentioned above) of the President of the Mixed Commission for the Exchange of Greek and Turkish Populations in the *Interpretation of Greco-Turkish Agreement Advisory Opinion*[66] such documents influenced the interpretation of questions in the *Access to, or Anchorage in, the Port of Danzig, of Polish War Vessels*,[67] and the *Jaworzina* case;[68] while the object and purpose of the question guided the interpretation in the *Exchange of Greek and Turkish Populations* where the PCIJ held that: "The Court is of the opinion that the *chief aim of this question* is to develop and obtain a statement of the precise practical effect of certain aspects of the reply given to it ...".[69] Finally, the existence of multiple authentic texts, an issue eventually to be addressed in Article 33 of the VCLT, has also had "its day in Court" in *Competence of the ILO*[70] and *Nationality Decrees Issued in Tunis and Morocco*.[71]

In conclusion, the PCIJ had the power to reformulate questions put to it by the Council or the Assembly. In doing so it applied *mutatis mutandis* the customary rules on the interpretation of treaties, but with a somewhat heightened emphasis on the intention of the requesting body. This characteristic emphasis on the intention of the submitting body seems to be a common denominator throughout the interpretative process when the courts are dealing with interpretation of unilateral acts, irrespective of whether they are acts of States,[72] or of international organizations.[73]

---

66 *Interpretation of Greco-Turkish Agreement* (n 16) at 14.

67 *Access to, or Anchorage in, the Port of Danzig, of Polish War Vessels*, (n 12) at 140.

68 *Jaworzina Case* (n 10) at 50.

69 *Exchange of Greek and Turkish Populations* (n 16) at 17 (emphasis added).

70 *Competence of the ILO Advisory Opinion* (n 14) at 13.

71 *Nationality Decrees Issued in Tunis and Morocco* (n 10) at 21–22.

72 V Rodríquez Cedeño, *ILC Fourth Report on Unilateral Acts of States* (A/CN4/519, 30 May 2001). Optional clause declarations are a *sui generis* category of acts, which may fall under the category of unilateral acts of States as well. In the interpretation of these declarations intention is also of crucial importance. M Fitzmaurice, 'The Optional Clause System and the Law of Treaties: Issues of Interpretation in Recent Jurisprudence of the International Court of Justice' (1999) 20 Australian Ybk of Intl L 127–59.

73 E Papastavridis, 'Interpretation of Security Council Resolutions under Chapter VII in the Aftermath of the Iraqi Crisis' (2007) 56 ICLQ 83–118; see also Sir MC Wood, 'The Interpretation of Security Council Resolutions' (1998) 2 Max Planck Ybk of UN L 73–95.

However, the PCIJ made use of its power in exceptional circumstances only, when it was absolutely clear from all of the interpretative elements taken into consideration that the actual question to be answered was different from the one put down in black ink.

VI. Concluding Remarks

In the present submission the advisory jurisdiction of the PCIJ was examined from its scope *ratione personae* and *ratione materiae*. As was demonstrated, even though the Assembly and the Council could request Advisory Opinions of the Court, only the Council made use of this option. Its practice was not without problems, as the debate about 'question vs dispute' illustrates in particular. However, despite the peculiarities and particularities of the advisory process of the PCIJ, which could result in the procedure at times functioning effectively and at others not, practice indicates that it appealed to States, who did not wish a binding judicial settlement of actual disputes, to such a degree, in fact, that such Advisory Opinions have become known as "advisory arbitrations".

In addressing requests, the PCIJ was not strictly bound by the text of the question asked, but enjoyed a measure of discretion. As has been shown, the PCIJ's interpretation of questions was based on a *mutatis mutandis* application of the customary rules of interpretation as they were to be enshrined in Articles 31–33 of the VCLT. Strong emphasis was placed on the intention of the requesting body, in fact to the point where intention was seen as an absolute limit to the Court's discretion. If the requesting body did not 'say what it meant' the Court could 'correct' this oversight, but it could not do more than that.

The ICJ has, for better or worse, taken the torch from the PCIJ and today continues its 'legacy'. Not only have its Statute and Rules been heavily influenced by its predecessor but in its judgments and Advisory Opinions reference is made to the jurisprudence of both the PCIJ and the ICJ in the same breath, which goes to demonstrate a sense of continuity. That is not to say that the ICJ has followed blindly the practice of the PCIJ as to the advisory proceedings, as is demonstrated by the expansion of the number of bodies capable of requesting an Advisory Opinion and the abandonment of the "dispute", "question" dichotomy. However, such changes are only to be expected in an evolutionary process and thus following the 'legacy' of the PCIJ is not to be equated with blindly sticking to solutions and ideas of the past.

In summation, the PCIJ's approach to the exercise of, inter alia, its advisory jurisdiction contained success and failure, progressiveness and conservatism, idealism and practicality. These influences and experiences have found their way into the structure and essence of the ICJ and continue to influence its work; so the PCIJ and its 'legacy' keeps living on through the functioning of the ICJ. Thus the relationship of the PCIJ to the ICJ could be described as that of parent and child; these institutions share many similar characteristics but are also distinct and whilst the legacy of the PCIJ lives on in the ICJ the latter is free to continue its own journey.

PART TWO

SHAPING SUBSTANTIVE INTERNATIONAL LAW

THE PCIJ AND THE MODERN INTERNATIONAL LAW OF TREATIES

Stephan Wittich

I. Introduction and Overview

Assessing the impact which the Permanent Court had on the international law of treaties as we know it today requires determining what the modern international law of treaties itself is. It may well be assumed to be common ground that the relevant reference point is the Vienna Convention on the Law of Treaties (in the following 'Vienna Convention' or 'VCLT') in the first place; for not only is the Vienna Convention in a formal sense the 'treaty of treaties' and thus governs the subject matter of this survey, but it is also largely and rightly considered to be the authoritative expression of the modern law of treaties and even is applied in practice to treaties not coming within its scope. The second reference point against which to measure the influence of the Permanent Court is arbitral and judicial practice in general and the case law of the present Court in particular. The International Court has on occasion invoked the case law of the Permanent Court on matters of treaty law, especially prior to the adoption and entry into force of the Vienna Convention. But there are also a number of cases where the International Court has not expressly referred to its predecessor but where it has applied treaty rules in a similar or even the same manner. Unlike the International Court, that was and still is 'privileged' in this regard because it usually has the Vienna Convention at its disposal, the Permanent Court, when dealing with issues of treaty law, was faced with the problem that it could not resort to pre-existing rules on the matter. It could not apply a received stock of legal concepts and techniques on treaty law, but it simply had to deduce them as some kind of general principles or even to invent them. This problem was succinctly described by Lord McNair who, in relation to the principle *pacta sunt servanda*, said: 'In every uncodified legal system there are certain elementary and universally agreed principles for which it is almost impossible to find specific authority.'[1] Of course the need of 'creating' law in the absence of clearly

[1] AD McNair, *Law of Treaties* (Clarendon Press, Oxford 1961) 493.

determined and codified rules held true for virtually any area of international law of the time, but I think it is particularly perceptible in the law of treaties where we nowadays have the rules of treaty law widely recognized and largely codified in the VCLT. The example of the *pacta sunt servanda* rule may also serve as a useful starting point for our analysis as the Court has, together with the principle of good faith, repeatedly invoked it, without however mentioning it *eo nomine*.[2] The *pacta sunt servanda* rule probably is the paradigmatic example for a rule of treaty law whose existence has been beyond doubt ever since, but whose source is far from clear.[3]

While the VCLT, as the codification of international treaty law, is the authoritative reference point for assessing the impact of the Permanent Court's judicial practice on matters of treaty law, it is at the same time an 'unreliable' yardstick for engaging in this task. For it is not easy to trace the marks left by the Permanent Court, the more so as the preparatory works and the commentary to the Convention only occasionally refer to it. There are a number of reasons for this, one being that, at the time of codification, the International Court had already absorbed a lot of the Permanent Court's practice on treaty law; incorporated it into its own body of case law and developed it further. The International Court's refined case law was then taken up by the International Law Commission in its elaboration of what was to result in the Vienna Convention. Furthermore, with particular focus on the rules of interpretation, the fact that Articles 31 and 32 (and probably also Article 33) of the Vienna Convention have come to reflect customary international law has reduced the frequency with which the numerous relevant propositions made by the Permanent Court on treaty interpretation are invoked in practice today.[4]

Speaking of interpretation, I think it is no exaggeration to state that the single most significant influence of the Permanent Court on the law of treaties was its contribution to the elaboration of the rules of interpretation. And it is particularly in the context of interpretation that the absence of codified rules required the Permanent Court to resort to rules of logic

---

[2] In fact, the reference to *pacta sunt servanda* has been a leitmotif of the Court, see MO Hudson, *The Permanent Court of International Justice, 1920–1942* (The Macmillan Company, New York 1943) 636–638 and below III.D.

[3] For an overview of the various theories on the foundation of *pacta sunt servande* see; J Salmon, 'Commentary on Art 26' in O Corten and P Klein (eds), The Vienna Conventions on the Law of Treaties. A Commentary, vol I (OUP, Oxford 2011) 659–663; K Schmalenbach, 'Commentary on Art 26' in O Dörr and K Schmalenbach (eds), *Vienna Convention on the Law of Treaties. A Commentary* (Springer-Verlag, Berlin/Heidelberg/New York 2012) 433–437.

[4] RK Gardiner, *Treaty Interpretation* (OUP, Oxford/New York 2008) 59.

and common sense,[5] and considerations of good faith. Also the fact cannot be concealed that some members of the Court were also guided by concepts of interpretation derived from their legal background and education shaped by the respective municipal legal orders. This becomes apparent especially in the Court's varying approaches to treaty interpretation in the different periods of its work.[6]

With all these considerations in mind let me now explain in some more detail what could be considered to be the lasting influence of the Permanent Court on the modern international law of treaties. I will do so in a very selective manner, which of course does not claim to be exhaustive. In particular, issues that more properly fall within the subject matter of other contributions to the conference, which originally inspired this book, will not be dealt with here, even though they have strong implications for treaty law.[7] The major part of this brief study is devoted to different aspects of treaty interpretation that were raised and applied by the Permanent Court. The remainder deals with individual issues such as the existence of a treaty, treaties and third parties, or the duty of a signatory. The study is conducted in the form of a descriptive analysis that attempts to identify the influence of the Permanent Court by way of comparison with relevant decisions of the present Court—or other international tribunals, as the case may be—as well as with the rules of the Vienna Convention.

II. Treaty Interpretation

A. *The General Rule: Ordinary Meaning, Context, and Object and Purpose*

1. *The PCIJ and Article 31(1) VCLT*

As already stated, treaty interpretation no doubt is *the* area of international treaty law where the Court left its most visible mark. This is not

---

[5] A Orakhelashvili, *The Interpretation of Acts and Rules in Public International Law* (OUP, Oxford 2008) 301.

[6] The move between international and national laywer's approaches which was largely due to a change in the Court's composition after 1930, was wonderfully demonstrated by Ole Spiermann in his masterly thesis *International Legal Argument in the Permanent Court of International Justice: The Rise of the International Judiciary* (CUP, Cambridge 2005) esp chapters 6 and 7. For comment on the pertinence of individual Judges' backgrounds to the character of PCIJ judgments see J d'Aspremont (in this volume), at 227–228.

[7] This for instance concerns the treatment of the Court of the position of individuals under international law, including treaty law. For more on this point see generally C Brölmann (in this volume); 123, also see CJ Tams (in this volume), at 13–15, A Tzanakopoulos (in this volume), at 344–346. and I Scobbie (in this volume), at 218–220.

surprising as the application of treaties almost invariably calls for prior interpretation of its provisions. Furthermore, and this is a historical peculiarity of the Permanent Court, the vast majority of the cases in both contentious and advisory proceedings not only concerned the interpretation of treaties, but interpretation itself was, often, the very subject-matter of the entire case. The treaties at issue were mainly the Peace Treaties concluded after World War I and treaties that were in some way connected to them.[8] In many cases, these treaties also provided for the basis of jurisdiction of the Court.

Probably the most important aspect of its exercises in treaty interpretation is the fact that the Court did not formulate any rigid rules; rather its statements were made in such guarded form as to allow the Court to remain flexible in interpreting treaties. Again, in finding the source of the rules of interpretation to be applied, the Court lacked any kind of codified rules and had thus to proceed 'in accordance with the rules of law'.[9] This general attitude paved the way for the all-embracing provisions of the Vienna Convention laying down the 'canons' of treaty interpretation. The totally unclear state of the law as regards both the source and the precise content of the rules of interpretation, with which the Permanent Court was faced, was in a sense recognized by the ILC in drafting the Vienna Convention. It is in this light that one has to read the introductory commentary to what are now Articles 31 and 32 where the Commission conceded that there were only 'comparatively few general principles which appear to constitute general rules for the interpretation of treaties'.[10]

A perusal of the Permanent Court's case law on interpretation yields a number of examples where the Court's pronouncements contained

[8] Thus, no less than seven judgments or Advisory Opinions contain the word 'interpretation' (referring to treaty interpretation) in their title. These are *Treaty of Neuilly, Article 179, Annex, Paragraph 4 (Interpretation)*, [1924] PCIJ Ser A No 3; *Interpretation of Article 3, Paragraph 2, of the Treaty of Lausanne*, [1925] PCIJ Ser B No 12; *Interpretation of the Greco-Turkish Agreement of 1 December 1926 (Final Protocol, Article IV)*, [1928] PCIJ Ser B No 16; *Interpretation of the Greco-Bulgarian Agreement of 9 December 1927*, [1923] PCIJ Ser A/B No 45; *Interpretation of the Statute of the Memel Territory*, [1932] PCIJ Ser A/B No 47; *Interpretation of the Statute of the Memel Territory*, [1932] PCIJ Ser A/B No 49; *Interpretation of the Convention of 1919 concerning Employment of Women during the Night*, [1932] PCIJ Ser A/B No 50. Not included in this list are decisions concerning interpretation of the Court's own judgments. On the other hand, there are other cases whose subject-matter exclusively concerned treaty interpretation without that being expressed in the title of the case or opinion, see e.g. *Exchange of Greek and Turkish Populations (Lausanne Convention VI, January 30th, 1923, Art. 2)*, [1925] PCIJ Ser B No 10.

[9] *Access to German Minority Schools in Upper Silesia*, [1931] PCIJ Ser A/B No 40 at 19.

[10] *Yearbook of the International Law Commission* 1966, vol. II, 218–219 [5].

aspects of interpretation that are of continuing validity. In particular the essence of the general rule of interpretation as now contained in Article 31 VCLT was already foreshadowed by the Permanent Court. The *Chorzów* case is a good example of this. There the Court enunciated a formula of interpretation that bears great resemblance to the rule we have now in Article 31(1) of the Vienna Convention. In the words of the Court:

> For the interpretation of Article 23 of the Geneva Convention between Germany and Poland, account must be taken not only of the historical development of arbitration treaties, as well as of the terminology of such treaties, and of the grammatical and logical meaning of the words used, but also ... of the function which, in the intention of the contracting parties, is to be attributed to this provision.[11]

Leaving aside for the moment the fact that the Court emphasized the development of treaties—and thereby alluded to some kind of historical interpretation—the Court referred to the grammatical and logical meaning, that is, the ordinary meaning the terms of the treaty have in their context and in light of their function or purpose. Thus almost everything contained in Article 31(1) VCLT was already part of the Permanent Court's repertoire of treaty interpretation. Similarly, in *Polish Postal Service in Danzig* the Court emphasized the paramount importance for treaty interpretation of the ordinary meaning of the words used in their context[12]—a statement gratefully raised by the current Court in its closely related first two Advisory Opinions concerning admission to the United Nations.[13]

Where the wording is clear and raises no doubt, there remains little room for interpretation or even speculation as to how the drafting could have been carried out differently. Thus in *Acquisition of Polish Nationality*, the Permanent Court gave clear guidance on this in a dictum frequently invoked by the present Court:[14] 'The Court's task is clearly defined. Having before it a clause which leaves little to be desired in the nature of clearness, it is bound to apply this clause as it stands, without considering

[11] *Factory at Chorzów* (Jurisdiction) [1927] PCIJ Ser A No 9 at 24.

[12] *Polish Postal Service in Danzig*, [1925] PCIJ Ser B No 11 at 39: 'It is a cardinal principle of interpretation that words must be interpreted in the sense which they would normally have in their context, unless such interpretation would lead to something unreasonable or absurd.' For some other interesting comments on the PCIJ's mode of interpretation see J d' Aspremont (in this volume), at 226 and A Tzanakopoulos (in this volume), at 343, 356–357.

[13] *Competence of the General Assembly for the Admission of a State to the United Nations*, [1950] ICJ Rep 4, 8.

[14] E.g. *Territorial Dispute* (*Libyan Arab Jamahiriya v Chad*), [1994] ICJ Rep 6, 25 [51]; *LaGrand*, [2001] ICJ Rep 466, 494 [77].

whether other provisions might with advantage have been added to or substituted for it.'[15]

As to the meaning of meaning itself, the Court referred to a number of adjectives, such as 'ordinary', 'natural', 'plain', 'normal', 'reasonable', 'grammatical', 'literal', 'logical', or 'clear',[16] without however clarifying the relation among these qualifiers, whether they are meant to be synonyms or whether each have distinct meanings. To establish the ordinary meaning, the Permanent Court referred to the etymology of the relevant term as well as to the 'current practice of the language'[17] and looked at ordinary language dictionaries.[18] This valid method of discerning the ordinary meaning has been applied by international courts and tribunals ever since.[19]

2. *The Importance of the Context*

Already in its second Advisory Opinion, the Court emphasized the importance of the context of treaty terms when it made it clear that in determining the ordinary meaning of the terms, 'the context is the final test'.[20] The contextual approach was a constant feature of the Court's case law on interpretation,[21] and it was never disputed in principle; but there was much less clarity or consistency as to what exactly the context is or may be in a given case. On the whole, the varieties or manifestations of context as applied by the Court were manifold, and the general abstract rule is that it is not necessarily a particular phrase, sentence, or paragraph in which the word or term to be interpreted appears. Even so the Court did not confine the context to the particular treaty instrument at issue but also consulted other treaties and instruments—either related and interdependent or totally detached from the original instrument—as part of the relevant

---

15 *Acquisition of Polish Nationality*, [1923] PCIJ Ser B No 7 at 20.

16 See the ample references in Hudson (n 2) 645–646.

17 *Exchange of Greek and Turkish Populations* (n 8) 18.

18 *Competence of the ILO in regard to International Regulation of the Conditions of the Labour of Persons Employed in Agriculture*, [1922] PCIJ Ser B No 2 at 33 and 35.

19 See e.g. *Golder v UK* App no 4451/70 (ECHR, 21 February 1975) [32]; *Kasikili/Sedudu Island (Botswana/Namibia)*, [1999] ICJ Rep 1045, 1064 [30]; *Canada—Measures Affecting the Export of Civilian Aircraft*, WTO Appellate Body Rep AB-1999–2 (2 August 1999) WT/DS70/AB/R at 39 [154]; *Marvin Feldman v Mexico* ICSID Case No ARB(AF)/99/133–34, [96].

20 (n 18) 35.

21 For instance, throughout its Opinion in *Interpretation of the Convention of 1919 concerning Employment of Women during the Night* (n 8) the Court was concerned with and applied a textual interpretation. See also *Interpretation of the Statute of the Memel Territory*, No 47 (n 8) at 249; *SS 'Wimbledon'*, [1923] PCIJ Ser A No 1 at 23 (comparing the wording of the provision to be interpreted with that of other provisions of the treaty).

context. In the latter case, the context of the terms would be totally extrinsic to the treaty to be interpreted, thus stretching the notion quite far beyond what the Vienna Convention considers as relevant context.[22]

There are a number of cases in the Permanent Court that illustrate the diversity which context may assume. With regard to the 'easier' situation of context intrinsic to the treaty two approaches taken by the Court are discernible. For one, the context may be confined to a particular paragraph, section or part of a treaty. A good example of this approach towards context is provided by the very first case decided by the Court, the *Wimbledon* case. There the Court held the provisions of the Treaty of Versailles relating to the Kiel Canal to be 'self-contained' and that 'if they had to be supplemented and interpreted by the aid of those referring to the inland navigable waterways of Germany in the previous Sections of Part XII, they would lose their "raison d'être"'.[23] In the *Free Zones* case where the Court similarly read a specific provision of the Treaty of Versailles as forming 'a complete whole', the relevant context being confined to the particular article. Accordingly, the Court stated that 'it would therefore be impossible to interpret the second paragraph without regard to the first paragraph'.[24]

There are other examples where the Court considered particular parts of the Treaty of Versailles 'as a whole'[25] or as forming an 'entire framework'.[26] Such restricted understanding of context is the exception rather than the rule and most likely due to the peculiarities of the particular regime established by the relevant provisions of the Treaty of Versailles—or, for that matter, to a peculiar reading of them by the Court.[27] This is also

22 According to Art 31(2) VCLT, context 'shall comprise, in addition to the text, including its preamble and annexes: (a) any agreement relating to the treaty which was made between all the parties in connexion with the conclusion of the treaty; (b) any instrument which was made by one or more parties in connexion with the conclusion of the treaty and accepted by the other parties as an instrument related to the treaty'.

23 *SS 'Wimbledon'*, (n 21) at 23–24.

24 *Case of the Free Zones of Upper Savoy and the District of Gex*, [1932] PCIJ Ser A/B No 46 at 140. Note however that the Court reached this conclusion on restricted context after having applied a broader contextual approach by invoking the position of the relevant provision in the treaty (ibid).

25 (n 18) 33, 39. Note however the inconsistency of the Court's position given the fact that in this opinion it also stated that the Treaty—and not just a particular part of it—must be read as a whole, ibid 23, 35. See below, text accompanied by n 32.

26 *Competence of the ILO to Regulate Incidentally the Personal Work of the Employer*, [1926] PCIJ Ser B No 13 at 18.

27 See however the Court's findings in *Certain German Interests in Polish Upper Silesia* (Merits) [1926] PCIJ Ser A No 7, at 48–49, and in *Rights of Minorities in Upper Silesia*, [1928] PCIJ Ser A No 15 at 31.

borne out by the fact that in a number of other cases concerning interpretation of treaties establishing a specific regime, the Court viewed the context as covering the entire treaty instrument. Thus in *Diversion of Water from the Meuse,* the Court held that the relevant treaty 'brought into existence a certain regime which results from all of its provisions in conjunction. It forms a complete whole, the different provisions of which cannot be ... considered apart by themselves'.[28]

Other examples are the *Statute of Memel* case, where the Court said that 'the Convention of Paris of 1924 and the Statute annexed to it must be considered as a whole in order to understand the *régime* ... for the Memel Territory';[29] or the *Postal Service in Danzig* case in which the Court held that 'the construction which the Court has placed on the various treaty stipulations is ... also supported by reference to the various articles taken by themselves and in their relation one to another';[30] or the *Treaty of Lausanne* case where the Court read the provision to be interpreted against the background of other articles in order to assess whether these were 'calculated to throw any light upon the scope of Article 3'.[31] Similarly, in *Labour of Persons Employed in Agriculture,* the Court made it clear that the regular reference point for the context is the entire treaty and that this is of course not limited to specific treaties establishing a regime: 'In considering the question before the Court upon the language of the Treaty, it is obvious that the Treaty must be read as a whole, and that its meaning is not to be determined merely upon particular phrases which, if detached from the context, may be interpreted in more than one sense.'[32]

Yet, while this position is clearly reflected in the perception of the context in Article 31(2) VCLT, the Permanent Court, in determining what the context is for the purpose of interpretation, seems to have gone beyond the treaty instrument and also included treaties, instruments, and other documents extrinsic to the particular treaty under construction. In some cases the need for such a broad reading of the relevant context was not only reasonable but even warranted on the basis that the instruments concerned were closely related or interdependent. For instance in *German Interests in Upper Silesia,* the Court stated in a general way that 'the interpretation of other international agreements is indisputably within the

---

[28] *Diversion of Water from the Meuse,* [1937] PCIJ Ser A/B No 70 at 21 and 23.

[29] *Interpretation of the Statute of the Memel Territory,* No 49 (n 8) at 312. The Court also rejected an interpretation that 'would destroy the general scheme of the Convention of Paris of 1924 and the Statute annexed to it' (ibid 317).

[30] (n 12) at 40.

[31] *Interpretation of Treaty of Lausanne* (n 8) at 21.

[32] (n 18) 23.

competence of the Court if such interpretation must be regarded as incidental to a decision on a point in regard to which it has jurisdiction'. In particular it said 'that the application of the Geneva Convention [was] hardly possible without giving an interpretation of Article 256 of the Treaty of Versailles and the other international stipulations cited by Poland'.[33] In the *Danube Commission* case the Court invoked 'the whole system of the international acts applicable before the war to the maritime Danube'.[34]

The significance of this broad use of the context is difficult to assess, especially because the Court was not coherent and consistent in applying this approach, nor did it make it clear that it considered this extensive context as coming within the 'rules' of interpretation properly speaking. It is striking—and it certainly testifies to the at times contradictory approach by the Court—that in other cases the Court not only shied away from looking at related instruments, but even expressly denied to do so. Thus in *Diversion of Water from the Meuse*, a previously achieved arrangement was implemented by three treaties concluded on the same day, the exchange of ratifications taking place on the same date, and that exchange having been recorded in a single instrument—and yet the Court, without giving any explanation, considered each of these treaties to be 'entirely independent of the others' and said that, in its application and interpretation, the treaty under construction stood 'entirely by itself'.[35]

On the other hand, when a treaty to be interpreted forms part of a broader system of treaties, it is generally considered permissible to interpret it in the light of the other treaties of that system. This principle is well-known under the term *pari materia* which, in its broad sense, also extends to treaties not part of a 'system', but whose subject matter is identical with, or very similar to, the subject matter covered by the treaty to be

---

[33] *Certain German Interests in Polish Upper Silesia* (Preliminary Objections) [1925] PCIJ Ser A No 6 at 18. It remains however unclear whether the Court's concerns related to issues of competence and jurisdiction under the precise terms of the constituent instrument or to matters of interpretation under general international law to determine the applicable rules. The former aspect was raised by the International Court in the *Arbitral Award* case between Guinea-Bissau and Senegal, when it considered that a possible failure of an arbitral tribunal 'properly to apply the relevant rules of interpretation to the provisions of the Arbitration Agreement which govern [the tribunal's] competence' to constitute a manifest breach of competence. See *Arbitral Award of 31 July 1989*, [1991] ICJ Rep 53, 69 [48].

[34] *Jurisdiction of the European Commission of the Danube*, [1927] PCIJ Ser B No 14 at 55.

[35] (n 28) at 13. The Court only admitted an interdependence among these treaties in so far as the concessions made by each government in one of the treaties would not have been made without the concessions made by the other government in the other treaties (ibid), and thus insinuated some kind of integral obligations contained in different treaties.

interpreted.[36] Resort to treaties *in pari materia* seems to have been an issue in several cases of the Permanent Court,[37] and it is also discernible in the present Court's case law[38] as well as that of arbitral tribunals.[39] It must however be added that what is often subsumed under the term *pari materia* involves instruments that are different in nature or character, and that it is not easy to see what the value of this principle is under current international treaty law. This can be shown by examining whether the principle of *pari materia* finds support at all in the VCLT. Any answer depends on the relationship between the treaty to be interpreted and the treaties or instruments resorted to.[40] Thus similar treaties may be considered part of the circumstances of the conclusion of the relevant treaty. In the *Jaworzina* case for example, the Court compared the treaty under discussion with 'a treaty concluded only a few days after' the former and 'signed by the same persons'.[41]

Second, the instruments resorted to may form part of 'relevant rules of international law applicable in the relations between the parties' pursuant to Article 31(3)(c) VCLT. This of course requires that the parties to the treaty under construction are also parties to the similar treaties resorted to unless reference is made to rules of general international law (customary law and general principles, that is). In the *Oder Commission* case, the Permanent Court, for instance, deemed it appropriate to refer to 'the principles underlying the matter to which the text refers', those being 'the principles governing international fluvial law in general',[42] and the relevant treaty provision was then 'interpreted in the light of these

36 See DP O'Connell, *International Law*, (vol 1, Stevens and Sons, London 1965) 279; U Linderfalk, *On the Interpretation of Treaties* (Springer, Dordrecht 2007) 255.

37 *Chorzów Factory* (Preliminary Objections) (n 11) at 22; *Polish Nationals in Danzig*, [1932] PCIJ Ser A/B No 44 at 32; *Interpretation of the Convention of 1919 concerning the Employment of Women During the Night* (n 8) at 380–381 (where the Court was prepared to attach some importance to provisions of another ILO convention because of its 'similarity both in structure and in expression'); *Question of Jaworzina* (*Polish-Czechoslovakian Frontier*), [1923] PCIJ Ser B No 8 at 38.

38 For example, see *Arbitral Award of 31 July 1989* (n 33).

39 See the references in O'Connell (n 36) 279 fn 88. For a more recent example see *United States—Import Prohibition of Certain Shrimp and Shrimp Products* WTO Appellate Body Rep AB-1998-4 (12 October 1998) WT/DS58/AB/R, [127]-[132]. For a further discussion of the on-going legacy of the PCIJ in WTO jurisprudence see generally J Gomula (in this volume), 175.

40 Linderfalk (n 36) 255.

41 *Question of Jaworzina* (n 37) at 38.

42 *Territorial Jurisdiction of the International Commission of the River Oder*, [1929] PCIJ Ser A No 23 at 26.

principles'.[43] Finally—and this will not be an unusual case of *pari materia*—it may be the case that there is no relation at all between the treaties except for the similarity in their subject matter. It is not easy to see how this constellation is governed by the VCLT.[44]

3. *Object and Purpose*

As a final point in discussing the general rule of interpretation, it remains to be recalled that the Permanent Court further considered it necessary to look at and assess the function to be performed by the provision to be interpreted. In this clear stand of the Court are several aspects concerning teleological interpretation worthy of consideration. First of all, this functional approach no doubt indicates the need to have regard to considerations of effectiveness in a broad sense as distinct from the principle of effectiveness as strictly understood.[45] Furthermore, it does not only include the purpose of the particular provision at issue, but of course also the object, nature and overall purpose of the treaty as a whole—which in fact is the third component of the general rule of interpretation of Article 31(1) VCLT. Throughout its activity, the Permanent Court regularly referred to the object and purpose using a plethora of different words.[46] Also it is no exaggeration to say that the Court's early acceptance of the distinct function and purpose of different treaties allowed it to adapt its interpretation in a flexible way to the needs of the individual instruments according to their different character and nature. This may be illustrated by the treaties concerning protection of the rights of minorities which were the subject matter of a great many cases in the Permanent Court.

Thus in the *German Settlers* case, the Court emphasized the 'main object' of a minority protection treaty and sought to prevent that the Minority Treaty is 'to a great extent ... deprived of value' and to ensure that 'the pledged protection may be certain and effective'.[47] Similarly, in *Acquisition of Polish Nationality*, it held that 'an interpretation which would deprive the Minorities Treaty of a great part of its value is inadmissible'.[48] In *Minority Schools in Albania* the Court invoked the 'object and

---

[43] Ibid 29. In *Certain German Interests in* (n 26) 42, the Court similarly viewed the 'generally accepted international law' as constituting a basis of the treaty to be interpreted.

[44] Linderfalk (n 36) 255–259 argues that this use of *pari materia* is 'a means of interpretation in and of itself'.

[45] See below II.B.2.b.

[46] Hudson (n 2) 650.

[47] *German Settlers in Poland*, [1923] PCIJ Ser B No 6 at 25.

[48] (n 15) at 17.

effect' of a minority protection provision.[49] Where the initial motive of a provision cannot be made out, the Court seems to have preferred to look at the practical effect of that provision rather than to conjecture on the intention behind that provision.[50] It may perhaps validly be said—even though the Permanent Court might itself have rejected this assertion as pure conjecture—that similar ideas and considerations play a role in the case law of the European Court of Human Rights concerning the dynamic and evolutionary interpretation of the European Convention as a 'living instrument' that must be interpreted in the light of present-day conditions.[51] That the Permanent Court identified in a number of cases other treaties which, according to their nature, object and purpose, have to be interpreted according to the terminological and, if the case may be, political and social background at the time of the conclusion of the treaty, will be discussed in the following section, which deals with some specific variations to the general rule of interpretation.

B. *Specific Variants of the General Rule*

1. *Territorial Regimes and the Temporal Element in Interpretation*

In relation to territorial regimes of various kinds, the Permanent Court has applied a static approach to interpretation that rests upon the political and social background that existed at the time the treaty was entered into and upon all other circumstances that have resulted in the conclusion of the treaty. An example of this is the opinion in the *Austro-German Customs Régime*. There the interpretation by the Court of the treaties concerning the proposed regime was based on 'the existing political settlement which has laid down in Europe the consequences of the break-up of the Austro-Hungarian monarchy' as well as the 'profound political changes' resulting from World War I.[52] In *Polish Nationals in Danzig*, the Court interpreted treaty provisions 'in the light of the circumstances which led to the creation of Danzig as a Free City'.[53] The Definitive Statute of the Danube was viewed by the Court against the background of 'the historical facts upon which it rests'.[54]

---

[49] *Minority Schools in Albania*, [1935] PCIJ Ser A/B No 64 at 20.
[50] (n 26) at 19, *Interpretation of the Convention of 1919 concerning Employment of Women during the Night* (n 8) at 374.
[51] See *Tyrer v UK* Appl no 5856/72 (ECHR, 25 April 1978; Series A No 26), at [31].
[52] *Customs Régime between Germany and Austria* [1931] PCIJ Ser A/B No 41 at 42.
[53] *Treatment of Polish Nationals and Other Persons of Polish Origin or Speech in the Danzig Territory* [1932] PCIJ Ser A/B No 44 at 27.
[54] (n 34) at 28.

As a specific variant of the static approach developed in the context of boundary treaties, the Court established the rule of strict teleological interpretation according to which such treaties must be considered to be definite. In the *Treaty of Lausanne* opinion the Court stated that 'the very nature of a frontier and of any convention designed to establish frontiers between two countries imports that a frontier must constitute a definite boundary line' and that '[i]t is … natural that any article designed to fix a frontier should, if possible, be so interpreted that the result of the application of its provisions in their entirety should be the establishment of a precise, complete and definitive frontier'.[55] In the *Jaworzina* opinion concerning the Polish-Czechoslovakian border, the Permanent Court not only made a lengthy historical and political argument as to the basis for the delimitation of the disputed boundary;[56] it also viewed the purpose of a boundary treaty agreement to determine 'once and for all the territories in dispute'.[57]

The present Court literally invoked that decision of the Permanent Court in the *Territorial Dispute between Libya and Chad*.[58] Already in the *Temple* case the International Court, while not directly referring to the Permanent Court, applied the same considerations when it stated that '[i] n general, when two countries establish a frontier between them, one of the primary objects is to achieve stability and finality'.[59] The Eritrea-Ethiopia Boundary Commission also followed the Permanent Court's approach of contemporaneity which it described as requiring 'that a treaty should be interpreted by reference to the circumstances prevailing when the treaty was concluded'.[60] These considerations also imply that expressions, including names, used in the treaty must be given the meaning they would have possessed at that time as well.[61]

However, there is an important exception to this rule, and this concerns conceptual or generic terms that are generally considered to change through the course of time alongside the transformation of political, social and other conditions. In this sense, the Court held in *Nationality Decrees Issued in Tunis and Morocco* that the term '*matter which by international*

55 (n 8) at 20.
56 *Question of Jaworzina* (n 37) at 20–22.
57 Ibid at 23.
58 *Territorial Dispute* (n 14) 23–24 [47].
59 *Temple of Preah Vihear* (*Cambodia v Thailand*), [1962] ICJ Rep 34.
60 Reports of International Arbitral Awards, *Eritrea-Ethiopia Boundary Commission, Delimitation of the Border between Eritrea and Ethiopia* (25 RIAA, 2002) 83, 110.
61 Ibid. See also *Dispute Regarding Navigational and Related Rights* (*Costa Rica v Nicaragua*), Judgment of 13 July 2009 [63] <at www.icj-cij.org>.

law is solely within the domestic jurisdiction' is 'an essentially relative question [that] depends upon the development of international relations'.[62] As is well known, this concept of inter-temporal interpretation played a key role in the *Namibia* opinion[63] and was subsequently applied in a number of other cases decided by the International Court,[64] arbitral tribunals,[65] and the WTO Appellate Body.[66]

2. *Rules of Doubt: The Principle of Effectiveness and Restrictive Interpretation*

a. *Supplementation and Mutual Incompatibility*

In the following I will briefly address two approaches that have developed in the jurisprudence of the Permanent Court in a somewhat loose sense, but which clearly assume the role of supplementary means of interpretation if the indeterminacy or ambiguity of terms cannot be resolved and clarified by literal and grammatical interpretation. These are the principles of effectiveness and that of restrictive interpretation. The residual character of these was made clear by the Court in *Postal Service in Danzig* where it held that 'rules as to a strict or liberal construction of treaty stipulations can be applied only in cases where ordinary methods of interpretation have failed'.[67] In principle, this may well be correct, but as Lauterpacht

---

62 *Nationality Decrees Issued in Tunis and Morocco*, [1923] PCIJ Ser B No 4 at 24.

63 *Legal Consequences for States of the Continued Presence of South Africa in Namibia (South West Africa) notwithstanding Security Council Resolution 276 (1970)*, [1971] ICJ Rep 16, 31 [53] (concerning the term 'sacred trust').

64 See e.g. *Aegean Sea Continental Shelf (Greece v Turkey)*, [1978] ICJ Rep 3, 33 [77], where the Court referred to *Nationality Decrees* (n 62). See also *Navigational and Related Rights* (n 61) 242 [64]. The Court described the principle of dynamic interpretation as follows:

> It is founded on the idea that, where the parties have used generic terms in a treaty, the parties necessarily having been aware that the meaning of the terms was likely to evolve over time, and where the treaty has been entered into for a very long period or is "of continuing duration", the parties must be presumed, as a general rule, to have intended those terms to have an evolving meaning.

Ibid 243 [66].

65 Reports of International Arbitral Awards, *Arbitration regarding the Iron Rhine ('Ijzeren Rijn') Railway (Belgium/Netherlands)* (Award of 24 May 2005) 36 [79], again with reference to *Nationality Decrees* (n 62).

66 *United States—Import Prohibition of Certain Shrimp and Shrimp Products* (n 39) [130]; *China—Measures Affecting Trading Rights and Distribution Services for Certain Publications and Audiovisual Entertainment Products* WTO Appellate Body Rep AB-2009-3 (21 December 2009) WT/DS363/AB/R, [369].

67 (n 12) at 39.

has convincingly argued,[68] there not only is a certain tension between these two principles, but in reality they are mutually incompatible. For where it is said that treaty obligations must be interpreted so as to impose the minimum extent of obligation upon the party bound by it, it cannot at the same time be argued that treaty provisions (including obligations) ought to be construed so as to yield the appropriate—probably the utmost—degree of effectiveness. As will be seen, this tension has also been visible in the case law of the Permanent Court. And yet, the analysis quite clearly demonstrates that the case law of the Court has resolved it without however expressly raising it. This will be shown in the following two subsections.

b. *The Principle of Effectiveness*

The principle of effectiveness is a generic description of an idea that covers several closely connected ways of adapting and fine-tuning individual aspects of the general rule of interpretation. According to the ILC, the principle of effectiveness is a logical corollary of good faith as well as object and purpose: 'When a treaty is open to two interpretations one of which does and the other does not enable the treaty to have appropriate effects, good faith and the objects and purposes of the treaty demand that the former interpretation should be adopted.'[69]

According to this view, the principle of effectiveness forms part and parcel of the general rule of interpretation, and its scope and application depend on the particulars of the case. Thus it is usually resorted to in case of doubt and plays an important role in the context of specific types of treaties. We have touched upon this aspect already above.[70] A similar approach was taken by the Court when it had to interpret jurisdictional clauses. As I will discuss below,[71] the Court has applied the rule of effectiveness rather than gone for a restrictive approach.

The principle of effectiveness further means that not only individual, but all the terms and provisions of a treaty shall be interpreted so as to produce the intended effect. The Permanent Court has repeatedly rejected as 'inadmissible' proposed interpretations that would deprive a provision,

---

[68] H Lauterpacht, 'Restrictive Interpretation and the Principle of Effectiveness in the Interpretation of Treaties' (1949) 26 BYIL 48, 67.

[69] See ILC Yearbook (n 10) 219 [6]. The Commission concluded: 'Accordingly, it did not seem to the Commission that there was any need to include a separate provision on this point' (ibid).

[70] See above II.A.3.

[71] II.B.2.c.

or even the treaty, of its (practical) value and render it ineffective.[72] This was affirmed by the present Court in the *Corfu Channel* case when it said: 'It would indeed be incompatible with the generally accepted rules of interpretation to admit that a provision of this sort occurring in a special agreement should be devoid of purport or effect.'[73] Other tribunals or dispute settlement bodies have also upheld and confirmed this key aspect of effectiveness repeatedly. A striking example is provided by the WTO Appellate Body which has

> recognized, on several occasions, the principle of effectiveness in the interpretation of treaties (*ut res magis valeat quam pereat*) which requires that a treaty interpreter:
>
> ... must give meaning and effect to all the terms of a treaty. An interpreter is not free to adopt a reading that would result in reducing whole clauses or paragraphs of a treaty to redundancy or inutility.
>
> In light of the interpretive principle of effectiveness, it is the *duty* of any treaty interpreter to 'read all applicable provisions of a treaty in a way that gives meaning to *all* of them, harmoniously.'[74]

Since the principle of effectiveness is one of interpretation, it cannot yield a result that is not only unsupported by the text, but that would even be contrary to the actual terms of the treaty. This obvious, yet still important limitation of the operation of effectiveness was already pointed out by the Permanent Court[75] and later coined by the present Court in the often-quoted words: 'The principle of interpretation expressed in the maxim: *ut res magis valeat quam pereat*, often referred to as the rule of effectiveness, cannot justify the Court in attributing to the provisions for the settlement of disputes in the Peace Treaties a meaning which... would be contrary to their letter and spirit.'[76]

c. *The Principle of Restrictive Interpretation*

The principle of restrictive interpretation means that treaty provisions, especially those containing obligations for the parties, ought to be

---

72 See the decisions in notes 43 and 44 above. See also *Exchange of Greek and Turkish Populations* (n8) 25.

73 *Corfu Channel Case*, [1949] ICJ Rep 4, 24. The Court also quoted the *Competence of the ILO to Regulate Incidentally the Personal Work of the Employer*, (n 26) at 19 ('But, so far as concerns the specific question of competence now pending, it may suffice to observe that the Court, in determining the nature and scope of a measure, must look to its practical effect rather than to the predominant motive that may be conjectured to have inspired it.').

74 *Korea—Definitive Safeguard Measure on Imports of Certain Dairy Products* WTO Appellate Body Rep AB-1999-8 (14 December 1999) WT/DS98/AB/R, 24 [80]-[81] (emphases in the original, references suppressed).

75 (n 15) at 17.

76 *Interpretation of Peace Treaties*, [1950] ICJ Rep at 229.

interpreted so as to produce the minimum degree of obligation towards the individual party. It certainly owes its prominence to the fact that it is grounded in the theoretical or conceptual roots of the sovereignty and independence of States. It is certainly for this reason that the resort to restrictive interpretation is so appealing, and the Permanent Court's famous dictum in the *Lotus* case bears witness to the seemingly warranted caution towards taking 'presumed' obligations of States too seriously.[77] Already in its very first judgment the Permanent Court adopted the principle of restrictive interpretation, in case of doubt, of clauses which produce a limitation upon the exercise of State sovereignty.[78] It was followed by other judgments of similar kind, the most detailed description of restrictive interpretation being that in the *River Oder* case:

> This argument [on restrictive interpretation], though sound in itself, must be employed only with the greatest caution. To rely upon it, it is not sufficient that the purely grammatical analysis of a text should not lead to definite results; there are many other methods of interpretation, in particular, reference is properly had to the principles underlying the matter to which the text refers; it will be only when, in spite of all pertinent considerations, the intention of the Parties still remains doubtful, that that interpretation should be adopted which is most favourable to the freedom of States.[79]

In view of the prolific reference by the Court to restrictive interpretation, it is astonishing that in fact it never applied it in a case. Paradigmatic in this respect is its statement in the *Treaty of Lausanne* opinion where the Court said:

---

[77] *'Lotus'*, [1927] PCIJ Ser A No 10 at 18, where the Court stated: 'International Law governs relations between independent States. The rules of law binding upon States therefore emanate from their own free will. … Restrictions upon the sovereignty of States cannot therefore be presumed.' Although the Court made this statement in relation to a rule of customary law whose existence is often more difficult to assess, there is no reason to deny a transposition of these considerations to unclear, hence 'difficult' treaty provisions. See also the echo of the *Lotus* 'principle' in the *Kosovo* opinion, *Accordance with International Law of the Unilateral Declaration of Independence in Respect of Kosovo* (Advisory Opinion) [2010] ICJ Rep [84], concluding that 'general international law contains no applicable prohibition of declarations of independence' and that accordingly 'the declaration of independence [in respect of Kosovo] did not violate general international law'. See the criticism of such echo from an empty Lotus shell by Judge Simma in his Separate Opinion.

[78] *SS 'Wimbledon'*, (n 21) at 24. The Court added the following warning: 'But the Court feels obliged to stop at the point where the so-called restrictive interpretation would be contrary to the plain terms of the article and would destroy what has been clearly granted.' (Ibid 24–25).

[79] (n 42) at 26. See also (n 12) at 39 (quote accompanied by n 63); also (n 24) 167.

> This argument [on restrictive interpretation] appears to rest on the following principle: if the wording of a treaty provision is not clear, in choosing between several admissible interpretations, the one which involves the minimum of obligations for the Parties should be adopted. This principle may be admitted to be sound. In the present case, however, the argument is valueless, because, in the Court's opinion, the wording of Article 3 is clear.[80]

It is even more striking to realize that while the Court had endorsed the principle of restrictive interpretation with specific reference to clauses conferring jurisdiction upon itself, its actual case law clearly—and virtually systematically—contradicted the repeated propositions. In other words, contrary to what it occasionally said in theory concerning interpretation of jurisdictional clauses,[81] the Court, when in fact interpreting them, clearly preferred the rule of effectiveness over that of restrictive interpretation. Thus in the *Chorzów Factory* case, it was disputed that the Court had jurisdiction to assess the nature or extent of reparation. The Court argued that since the decision whether there has been a breach of international law involved no doubt 'a more important jurisdiction' than a decision as to the nature or extent of reparation due for such a breach, and since furthermore it had in its previous judgments decided that it had jurisdiction to decide whether a breach had taken place, it would be difficult to understand why—failing an express provision to that effect—it should not cover the less important disputes concerning reparation. The Court concluded: 'To say, therefore, that the *clause compromissoire*, while confessedly providing for the submission of questions of right and obligation, must now be restrictively interpreted as excluding pecuniary reparation, would be contrary to the fundamental conceptions by which the movement in favour of general arbitration has been characterized.'[82] The Court thus interpreted the relevant jurisdictional clause quite extensively and assumed implied jurisdiction. In the *Borchgrave* case the Court likewise interpreted the special agreement quite extensively by resorting to the subsequent practice of the parties themselves.[83] The inconsistency of the Court's attitude towards interpretation of jurisdictional clauses is strikingly illustrated by the *Free Zones* case where the Court came to completely opposite conclusions. Thus on the one hand it stated that 'every Special Agreement, like every clause conferring jurisdiction upon the

80 *Interpretation of Treaty of Lausanne* (n 8) at 25.
81 *Phosphates in Morocco*, [1938] PCIJ Ser A/B No 74 at 23–24.
82 *Factory at Chorzów* (n 11), at 22.
83 *The Borchgrave Case* (Preliminary Objections) [1937] PCIJ Ser A/B No 72 at 168.

Court, must be interpreted strictly';[84] in a different phase of the proceedings it however said that 'in case of doubt, the clauses of a special agreement by which a dispute is referred to the Court must, if it does not involve doing violence to their terms, be construed in a manner enabling the clauses themselves to have appropriate effects'.[85]

Given the overall weakness of the restrictive approach—irrespective of its context—it is not surprising that it has neither been incorporated into the VCLT, nor affirmed or taken up by the present Court. It is also very telling that in the *Corfu Channel* case, in which the existence and extent of the present Court's jurisdiction in relation to the assessment of the amount of compensation was disputed, the Court invoked and quoted the second statement in the *Free Zones* case quoted above, but ignored the first one.[86] It thereby indirectly applied and affirmed the decision in the *Chorzów Factory* case also quoted above in which the Permanent Court had to resolve substantially the same question.

A last word must however be said in favour of the principle of restrictive interpretation. There is some support in practice for the contention that in a very limited sense it does exist and is indeed applicable in specific circumstances. Thus in *Nationality Decrees*, the Permanent Court interpreted a paragraph of an Article of the Covenant restrictively on the ground that it 'is an exception to the principles affirmed in the preceding paragraphs and does not therefore lend itself to an extensive interpretation'.[87] Accordingly, exceptions to a rule must be interpreted restrictively, which is quite the opposite of restrictive interpretation and in the end leads to an extensive interpretation of the rule itself. There is some support for this also in subsequent international case law.[88]

C. *Intention of the Parties, Subsequent Practice, and the Relevance of the Travaux*

1. *Subsequent Practice*

As regards the long-lived dispute between 'subjective' and 'objective' approaches to interpretation, it is fair to say that the Permanent Court settled the question by giving preference to the objective textual approach. This is not to say that the Court ignored the common intention of the

84 *Free Zones* (n 24) 138–139.
85 *Free Zones of Upper Savoy and the District of Gex*, [1929] PCIJ Ser A No 22, at 13.
86 *Corfu Channel Case* (n 73) 4, 24.
87 *Nationality Decrees* (n 62) 25.
88 See e.g. *Litwa v Poland* App no 26629/95 (ECHR 2000-III) [59].

parties. But first of all, such intention must in any event be reflected in the terms of the treaty. Indeed, the Permanent Court invoked the parties' intention on several occasions, and it usually did so in relation to subsequent practice indicating the parties' intention as to the meaning of particular terms. Thus, in *Interpretation of the Treaty of Lausanne* the Court observed: 'The facts subsequent to the conclusion of the Treaty of Lausanne can only concern the Court in so far as they are calculated to throw light on the intention of the Parties at the time of the conclusion of that Treaty.'[89]

Similarly, in *Jurisdiction of the Courts of Danzig*, the Court, among other criteria, drew on the subsequent practice as a manifestation of the intention of the parties: 'The intention of the Parties, which is to be ascertained from the contents of the Agreement, taking into consideration the manner in which the Agreement has been applied, is decisive. This principle of interpretation should be applied by the Court in the present case.'[90]

In the *Borchgrave* case, the Court looked at subsequent practice and construction by the parties in order to interpret a special agreement.[91] In its opinion in *Labour of Persons Employed in Agriculture*, the Court put the matter very succinctly when it stated: 'If there were any ambiguity, the Court might, for the purpose of arriving at the true meaning, consider the action which has been taken under the Treaty.'[92]

Taken out of their context, these statements might be misleading and be read so as to imply that the Court generally advocated a 'subjective' interpretation with the intention of the parties as the prime guide in clarifying treaty provisions. But there are several considerations that support a cautious reading of this case law. The *Interpretation of the Treaty of Lausanne*, especially, is quite distinct, since the facts and the questions the Court was asked to answer in this case left the Court no other option than to apply a 'historicizing' interpretation.[93] In any event, it must be recalled

89 *Interpretation of Treaty of Lausanne* (n 8) at 24.

90 *Jurisdiction of the Courts of Danzig*, [1928] PCIJ Ser B No 15 at 18. In the *Serbian Loans* and *Brazilian Loans* cases, the Court addressed the relevance of the intention of the parties (as expressed by the subsequent conduct) to private law contracts concerning the issuance of bonds. In *Brazilian Loans*, it had to deal with the argument 'that where a contract is ambiguous, resort may be had to the manner of performance in order to ascertain the intention of the Parties', which it however denied as it did not see any ambiguity in the terms of the contracts [1929] PCIJ Ser A No 21 at 119. The Court held the same in *Serbian Loans* [1929] PCIJ Ser A No 20 at 38.

91 *Borchgrave* (n 83).

92 *Competence of the ILO to Regulate Agricultural Labour*, [1922] PCIJ Ser B No 2 at 39.

93 This becomes clear by what the Court added:

> The question put to the Council seems to refer solely to the interpretation of Article 3 of the Treaty; obligations which may have been assumed after the conclusion of the Treaty, or facts which may have had some influence in regard to the existence or

that interpretation always involves a text that—according to the ILC commentary to the Vienna Convention—'must be presumed to be the authentic expression of the intentions of the parties',[94] which in turn requires the clarification of that intention, whatever the mode used for such clarification may be. 'Intention of the parties' so understood is *declared* or *expressed* intention in the sense of the 'true' meaning of the treaty and its terms rather than the *real* or *true* intention in the sense of the 'true' will of the parties distinct from it.[95] It follows that the intention of the parties, apart from the difficult task of revealing this intention, does not carry any probative value unless, of course, it has somehow found its way into the text. This was put beyond any doubt by the Permanent Court itself. Indeed, the Court generally observed in *Port of Danzig and Polish War Vessels*: 'The Court is not prepared to adopt the view that the text of the Treaty of Versailles can be enlarged by reading into it stipulations which are said to result from the proclaimed intentions of the authors of the Treaty, but for which no provision is made in the text itself.'[96]

Essentially, this position has found its way into the Vienna Convention whose commentary on today's Article 31 states that 'the starting point of interpretation is the elucidation of the meaning of the text, not an investigation *ab initio* into the intention of the parties'.[97] The Permanent Court invoked subsequent practice of the parties only as a means subsidiary and residual to textual interpretation,[98] that is, only if the latter did not

---

> nature of engagements entered into under the Treaty, would therefore seem to be outside the scope of the question submitted by the Council.

Interpretation of Treaty of Lausanne (n 8) at 24. See W Karl, *Vertrag und spätere Praxis im Völkerrecht* (Springer, Berlin 1983), 130 and 232.

[94] (n 69) 220 [11]. See also *European Communities—Customs Classification of Certain Computer Equipment* WTO Appellate Body Rep AB-1998-2 (9 September 1997) WT/DS62/AB/R [93]: 'The purpose of treaty interpretation is to establish the *common* intention of the parties to the treaty.' (Emphasis in the original.)

[95] J-M Sorel and V Boré Eveno, 'Article 31' in O Corten and P Klein (eds), *The Vienna Conventions on the Law of Treaties: A Commentary*, vol I (OUP, Oxford 2011) 804, 809 [11].

[96] *Port of Danzig and Polish War Vessels*, [1931] PCIJ Ser A/B No 43 at 144. See also *Interpretation of the Statute of the Memel Territory*, No 47 (n 8) at 248:

> 'But it is to be observed that there is nothing in the text of Article 17 to show that it was the intention of the Parties to make proceedings before the Council a condition precedent to proceedings before the Court.'

[97] ILC Yearbook (n 10) 220 [11].

[98] See *Interpretation of the Treaty of Lausanne* (n 8), at 19:

> 'The Court must, therefore, in the first place, endeavour to ascertain from the wording of this clause what the intention of the contracting Parties was; subsequently, it may consider whether—and if so, to what extent—factors other than the wording of the Treaty must be taken into account for this purpose.'

produce a definite result, or in order to confirm a result already reached through textual interpretation.[99] Again, however, the Court's practice is not free from contradiction since, as we have seen, in *Labour of Persons Employed in Agriculture* the Court, while emphasizing the condition of ambiguity for considering subsequent practice, examined the subsequent action of the parties even without finding any ambiguity to exist in the text. This is a further example of the widespread inconsistency of the Court's practice already observed above and that makes it so difficult to provide a coherent overall assessment of its case law. At any rate, what remains of the Court's treatment of subsequent practice is that it has entered into the Vienna Convention, which in Article 31(3)(a) considers it on par with the context. Furthermore, the Permanent Court's handling of subsequent practice has also been adopted by the present Court, which, in order to confirm a result reached through textual interpretation, resorts to subsequent practice to confirm its earlier conclusion.[100]

To be sure, the relevance of the intention of the parties is to be assessed differently if it relates to unilateral declarations accepting the jurisdiction particularly of the Court itself, these declarations being, technically speaking, made under a treaty and hence governed by treaty law. However, since they are unilateral in nature, the weight to be given in interpreting such declarations to the intention of the party making the declaration is much higher than in the case of ordinary treaty interpretation. This distinct significance of the aspect of intention was clearly spelled out by the Permanent Court in several cases[101] and has subsequently found its way into the established case law of the present Court.[102]

2. *Authentic Interpretation*

A further aspect of subsequent practice is that it is relevant as a form of authentic interpretation to which a few thoughts will be devoted in the following. To begin with, authentic interpretation is of course not a form of interpretation in its strict sense as it usually goes beyond the limits of the terms agreed upon initially in the treaty by creating new law, whereas

---

99 (n 89) at 18 and 20; *Competence of the ILO* (n 92) 40–41.

100 See e.g. *Corfu Channel* (n 73) 25: 'The subsequent attitude of the Parties shows it has not been their intention, by entering into the Special Agreement, to preclude the Court from fixing the amount of compensation.'

101 See e.g. *Lighthouses Case between France and Greece*, [1934] PCIJ Ser A/B No 62 at 13. See also *Rights of Minorities in Upper Silesia*, (n 27) at 22; *Phosphates in Morocco* (n 81) at 22–24.

102 For instance *Anglo-Iranian Oil*, [1952] ICJ Rep 93 at 104; *Aegean Sea* (n 64) 29 [69].

interpretation must remain within the uttermost possible or reasonable meaning of a term. Indeed, in cases of authentic interpretation a distinction between 'mere' interpretation and revision or modification of the treaty is often difficult or even impossible to draw, even though it is important from both a conceptual and a pragmatic point of view.[103] This distinction was also expressed by the Permanent Court in the *Jaworzina* opinion, where it invoked the rule of authentic interpretation when it said that 'it is an established principle that the right of giving an authoritative interpretation of a legal rule belongs solely to the person or body who has power to modify or suppress it'.[104] This 'established principle', enunciated by the Court already in 1923, has become part of the Vienna Convention. Articles 31(2) and 31(3)(a) and (b) all are considered to include or indicate, in a very loose sense, forms of authentic interpretation.[105]

In practice a specific case of authentic interpretation has assumed a significance of its own. It concerns interpretation of resolutions of organs of international organizations, an issue that owes its distinctiveness to the fact that resolutions are not treaties, but legal acts made pursuant to a treaty, and thus 'only' secondary treaty law, if at all. This renders it highly doubtful whether the rules of treaty interpretation are applicable to such resolutions.[106] In this respect, two closely related questions arise: *who* is competent to interpret? And, *how* is the text to be interpreted? Quite surprisingly perhaps, both questions had already been addressed by the Permanent Court. In *Access to German Minority Schools in Upper Silesia* the Court had to determine the character, force, and scope of an arrangement adopted by the Council of the League of Nations in a Resolution of 12 March 1927. In doing so, the Court, in order to ascertain the Council's intention, mainly looked at a later resolution of the Council that was relevant to the earlier one, as it clarified some of the doubtful issues.[107] In other words, the Court looked at how the relevant organ itself interprets its own act.

---

103 Karl (n 93) 40–45.

104 *Question of Jaworzina* (n 37) at 37.

105 (n 69) [14]-[15]; ME Villiger, *Commentary on the 1969 Vienna Convention on the Law of Treaties* (Martinus Nijhoff, Leiden/Boston 2009) 429 Article 31 MN 16; Dörr (n 3) Article 31 MN 65.

106 For a convincing argument that the rules of the Vienna Convention are not applicable see E Papastavridis, 'Interpretation of Security Council Resolutions under Chapter VII in the Aftermath of the Iraqi Crisis' (2007) 56 ICLQ 83.

107 (n 9) at 18. See M Bos, 'The Interpretation of Decisions of International Organisations' (1981) 28 NILR 6.

As is well-known, the International Court in *Namibia* had to answer the question as to the binding effect of a Security Council resolution, and in providing an answer it did not refer to the VCLT that was adopted two years earlier. Rather it established four points to be taken into account in interpreting the effect of a resolution,[108] but unfortunately failed to justify its selection. More recently, the Court in its *Kosovo* opinion provided a somewhat different approach. It first said that Articles 31 and 32 VCLT 'may provide guidance' in interpreting a Council resolution, but emphasized that since resolutions significantly differed from treaties, their interpretation requires that other factors are to be taken into account. It then mentioned these other factors, however, again without providing any basis for this choice: 'The interpretation of Security Council resolutions may require the Court to analyse statements by representatives of members of the Security Council made at the time of their adoption, other resolutions of the Security Council on the same issue, as well as the subsequent practice of relevant United Nations organs and of States affected by those given resolutions.'[109] Also the Court did not say here—as it did not do in *Namibia* either—what the relationship among these criteria is, but it is interesting to see that two out of the four factors mentioned by the Court may be viewed as forms of authentic interpretation, that is, other resolutions of the Council and subsequent practice of relevant UN organs. It may validly be presumed that subsequent practice by the competent body, ie authentic interpretation in the true sense, may well enjoy priority over the other criteria.

This brings me to the second aspect of authentic interpretation, which concerns the question of *who* is competent to interpret a text. This is a general question that has not been dealt with by the VCLT.[110] Given the fact that interpretation is implied in any act of applying a treaty, a separate rule on this question would carry only little informative value.[111] Thus in principle it is up to each party to a treaty to apply and interpret its provisions, but there may be situations where specific persons or organs may enjoy a kind of 'preferential position' in the process of interpretation. In general treaty law, this may, for instance, be the case where the treaty

---

[108] *Namibia* Advisory Opinion (n 63) 53. These points are the terms of the resolution, the discussions leading to it, the Charter provisions invoked, and all circumstances that might assist in determining the legal consequences of the resolution.

[109] *Kosovo* Advisory Opinion (n 77) [94].

[110] Although the question was raised in the drafting of the Vienna Convention, see e.g. YILC 1964-I, 280 [72].

[111] O Dörr, 'Commentary to Article 31' in O Dörr and K Schmalenbach (n 3) MN 18.

bestows upon a treaty body or judicial organ the competence to apply and interpret its provisions, especially in the course of dispute settlement. The International Court has acknowledged that such interpretation enjoys special importance because it carries great weight for a number of reasons.[112] However, such interpretation, authoritative as it may be, is not authentic interpretation, and in case of conflicting results, the latter will prevail over the former. Authentic interpretation of a treaty means that it is interpreted by the treaty parties as a collective (and not the parties *uti singuli*), ie by those who have created the treaty. It plays an important role with regard to the interpretation by organs of international organizations of their own resolutions or decisions. In *Access to Minority Schools*, the Permanent Court impliedly restricted the possibility of authentic interpretation of a resolution by subsequent practice to the author of this resolution,[113] a logical rule that was explicitly affirmed by the Court in its *Jaworzina* opinion.[114]

In the practice of Security Council resolutions, it is clear that the only organ that is competent to give an authentic interpretation is the Council itself, and it may and will often be assisted by subsidiary organs, which then are 'relevant UN organs' within the meaning of the *Kosovo* opinion. Among those subsidiary organs Sanctions Committees of the Security Council play a key role in interpreting Council resolutions,[115] and once such an authentic interpretation has been passed it must, in line with the Permanent Court's *Jaworzina* statement, again be considered as prevailing over the other criteria of interpretation mentioned by the present Court in *Kosovo*.

3. *Travaux Préparatoires*

Now the fact that the Permanent Court viewed the textual and grammatical interpretation as the main and principal tool to clarify treaty terms

---

[112] This was argued in great detail in *Ahmadou Sadio Diallo* (*Republic of Guinea v Democratic Republic of the Congo*), Judgment of 30 November 2010 [66]-[67] <at www.icj-cij.org>.

[113] (n 9).

[114] *Question of Jaworzina* (n 37), at 37.

[115] MP Scharf and JL Dorosin, 'Interpreting UN Sanctions: The Rulings and Role of the Yugoslavia Sanctions Committee' (1993) 19 Brooklyn JIL 771, 814; P Conlon, 'Lessons from Iraq: The Functions of the Iraq Sanctions Committee as a Source of Sanctions Implementation Authority and Practice' (1995) 35 Virginia JIL 633, 650; MC Wood, 'The Interpretation of Security Council Resolutions' in JA Frowein, R Wolfrum and CE Philipp (eds), *Max Planck Yearbook of United Nations Law 2* (Martinus Nijhoff, The Hague 1998) 73, 85; Papastavridis (n 106) 90–91.

may also be inferred from its handling of the question of when it was permissible to look at the *travaux préparatoires*. The Court's treatment of the travaux was very similar to that of subsequent practice just discussed. In some cases, the Court resorted to the *travaux* where a text was found to be not 'absolutely clear'. Thus, in the *Polish Nationals in Danzig* case, it thought it 'useful, in order to ascertain its precise meaning, to recall here somewhat in detail the various drafts which existed prior to the adoption of the text now in force'.[116] It took a similar approach to the travaux in the *Borchgrave* case, where an interpretation according to the ordinary meaning in their context could not produce any clear result because the plain text of the treaty—a special agreement—was so rudimentary that it was open to many different interpretations. Therefore, the Court analysed at length and in great detail the various diplomatic notes exchanged prior to the conclusion of the special agreement and thus traced the history of the negotiations.[117] In the same vein, in the *Lighthouses case between France and Greece*, the Court, 'in accordance with its practice', explored the preparatory works in order to interpret the special agreement.[118]

On the other hand, and these are the much more frequent instances concerning the reference to the preparatory works of a treaty, the Court used the *travaux* to confirm conclusions already reached by interpreting the text according to its ordinary meaning in its context and in the light of its object and purpose. In the *Lotus* case, for example, after having arrived at a construction of an unclear term, the Court said that 'the records of the preparation of the Convention ... would not furnish anything calculated to overrule the construction indicated by the actual terms'[119] of the

---

116 *Interpretation of the 1919 Convention concerning Employment of Women during the Night* (n 8) at 380; See also *Lighthouses in Crete and Samos*, [1937] PCIJ Ser A/B No 71 at 125 (Individual Opinion Hudson).

117 *Borchgrave* (n 83) 164–167. It described the minimal content of the agreement as follows: 'So unlimited are its terms, so free is the text from qualifying expressions, that the Agreement may be said to be characterized by its generality.' Ibid 164. It may of course validly be doubted whether this is really a case of *travaux préparatoires* as the subject of the analysis were not preliminary drafts. Yet it should be recalled here that the ILC considered the *travaux* in a very broad sense and refrained from defining them. Thus in its commentary to Draft Article 28, it stated: 'The Commission did not think that anything would be gained by trying to define *travaux préparatoires*; indeed, to do so might only lead to the possible exclusion of relevant evidence.' (n 69) [20].

118 *Lighthouses case* (n 101) 13:

> Where the context does not suffice to show the precise sense in which the Parties to the dispute have employed these words in their Special Agreement, the Court, in accordance with its practice, has to consult the documents preparatory to the Special Agreement, in order to satisfy itself as to the true intention of the Parties.

119 *'Lotus'* (n 77) 17.

provision, and the *travaux* were gone into to justify this statement. In the *Treaty of Lausanne* opinion, the Court found a text to be 'sufficiently clear', and yet it proceeded to consider it 'in the light of the negotiations'.[120] In *Labour of Persons Employed in Agriculture*, on the other hand, the Court refused to go into the preparatory works of the relevant treaty 'as it ha[d] already on the construction of the text itself reached the conclusion' which yielded the answer it was asked for, but nevertheless added that 'there is certainly nothing in the preparatory work to disturb this conclusion'.[121]

The above mentioned two aspects of the place of the *travaux* in treaty interpretation, that is to say, that they may be resorted to where the textual interpretation does not yield a clear result, or in order to confirm a reasonable construction arrived at by the textual interpretation, are the essence of the conditions for the use of the preparatory work as a supplementary means of interpretation in Article 32 VCLT as well. And here again, the case law of the Permanent Court has been taken up by the International Court. The most prominent example no doubt is provided by its very first Advisory Opinion on *Admission of a State to the United Nations* where it stated: 'The Court considers that the text is sufficiently clear; consequently, it does not feel that it should deviate from the consistent practice of the Permanent Court of International Justice, according to which there is no occasion to resort to preparatory work if the text of a convention is sufficiently clear in itself.'[122]

III. Other Aspects of Treaty Law

While the Permanent Court's case law on the rules of interpretation no doubt are its most significant contribution to the modern international law of treaties, there are a number of other issues of treaty law in which the Court engaged and where it left clearly visible marks. I will mention some of them in a very cursory manner.

A. *Existence of a Treaty*

To begin with, the Court made some lasting pronouncements on the existence of a treaty.[123] In the first place, it put beyond doubt the fact that the

120 *Treaty of Lausanne* (n 8) 22.

121 (n 18) 41.

122 *Admission of a State to the United Nations (Charter, Art 4)*, [1948] ICJ Rep 57 at 63. See also (n 13) at 8.

123 See J Klabbers, *The Concept of Treaty in International Law* (Martinus Nijhoff, The Hague 1996) 166–182.

formal designation of an international instrument is without prejudice as to its binding character as a treaty under international law. In the *Austro-German Customs Union* case, the Court said that 'from the standpoint of the obligatory character of international engagements, it is well-known that such engagements may be taken in the form of treaties, conventions, declarations, agreements, protocols, or exchanges of notes'.[124] This approach that is so lenient towards formal requirements is now contained in the definition of 'treaty' in Article 2(1)(a) VCLT.[125] One may, with all due caution though, also draw a parallel here to the often-quoted passage in the *Mavrommatis* case that '[t]he Court, whose jurisdiction is international, is not bound to attach to matters of form the same degree of importance which they might possess in municipal law'.[126] This *dictum* was repeatedly invoked by the present Court in matters of procedure, and while it was made in the context of jurisdiction, it nevertheless concerned a question of treaty law. The Permanent Court applied this non-formalistic approach in several cases to examine whether documents and instruments concluded or adopted by States entailed treaty-like consequences.

Thus, in the *Jaworzina* case, the Court was faced with a declaration signed by the Polish and the Czechoslovak Foreign Ministers, in which they agreed to accept a decision of the Allied Powers regarding their frontier. Subsequently, the Powers entrusted the Conference of Ambassadors with the task of delimiting the boundary, which it did. Poland and Czechoslovakia declared to accept that delimitation but Poland subsequently regretted the solution arrived at by the Conference. In the proceedings, this change of position by Poland was not given any weight by the Court who considered the agreements concerned as having 'the force of a contractual obligation entered into by the parties'.[127] The Court was not hampered by any formalities, such as the powers of the acting State organs or the form of the agreement. This decision clearly foreshadowed the case law of the International Court with regard to the existence of an international treaty. Significant in this regard is the Court's decision in the delimitation case between Qatar and Bahrain, where it held that agreed minutes concluded between the parties constituted a legally binding

124 *Customs Régime* (n 52) 47.
125 ILC Yearbook 1966 (n 10) 188 [3].
126 *Mavrommatis Palestine Concessions*, 1924 PCIJ, Ser A No 2, at 34. *Corfu Channel Case* (n 73). For more on the Permanent Court's interaction with domestic courts see generally J d'Aspremont (in this volume), 221.
127 *Question of Jaworzina* (n 37) 30.

agreement under international law because they 'enumerate the commitments to which the Parties have consented. They thus create rights and obligations in international law for the Parties. They constitute an international agreement.'[128]

On the other hand, the Court also recognized oral agreements in bilateral negotiations that may well be considered as 'informal' treaties in a broad sense. In the *Free Zones* case, for instance, the Court said that the unilateral Manifesto of the Royal Sardinian Court of Accounts of 1829 embodied the consent of the King of Sardinia as a response to a claim made by the Canton of Valais. In the Court's view, this manifesto constituted a 'concord of wills' which conferred on the establishment of the particular zone 'the character of a treaty stipulation'.[129] And one could probably also include a reference to the often-cited *Eastern Greenland* case here that the actions and statements of the parties established some kind of international agreement based on the common intention of the otherwise opposing parties.[130]

B. *Status Treaties*

Another area of treaty law, albeit a minor one, where the Permanent Court has had a word to say that is of continuing validity today concerns the basic idea of status treaties. These are treaties which establish a specific territorial regime aimed at securing collective interests not limited to the State parties. Their distinctive feature is that they may be opposable also towards third States and that they have a specific structure of performance that bears on their enforceability. The Permanent Court was of course never concerned with such conceptual particulars, but in the *River Oder* case, for instance, it touched, at least peripherally, on the question of territorially based community interests concerning navigable rivers.[131]

---

128 *Maritime Delimitation and Territorial Questions between Qatar and Bahrain* (*Qatar v Bahrain*), *Jurisdiction and Admissibility*, [1994] ICJ Rep 112, at 121 [25].

129 *Free Zones of Upper Savoy and the District of Gex* (Second Phase) [1930] PCIJ Ser A No 24, at 17 and (n 24) at 145.

130 *Legal Status of Eastern Greenland*, [1933] PCIJ Ser A/B No 53 at 22–23. See also Hudson (n 2) 633; G Schwarzenberger, *International Law as Applied by International Courts and Tribunals* (vol 1, 3rd edn, Stevens, London 1957) 158; Klabbers (n 123) 178–181. The legal source of the so-called 'Ihlen Declaration' as an oral treaty is however contested, see O'Connell (n 36) 220; A Verdross and B Simma, *Universelles Völkerrecht* (Duncker and Humblot, Berlin 1984) 440 in fn 2.

131 (n 42) at 27.

This statement was prominently invoked by the present Court in the *Gabčíkovo-Nagymaros* case in the context of countermeasures.[132]

C. *Treaties and Third Parties*

It is one of the uncontested general principles of treaty law that a treaty is *res inter alios acta* and that it accordingly can neither create rights in favour of, nor impose obligations upon, third States (*pacta tertiis nec nocent nec prosunt*). This was also the firm position of the Permanent Court. In *German Interest in Polish Upper Silesia*, the Court denied to extend the application of the provisions of a treaty to third States: 'A treaty only creates law as between the States which are parties to it; in case of doubt, no rights can be deduced from it in favour of third States.'[133]

The Court invoked this general principle in a number of other cases,[134] and in the *Free Zones* case, it was quite clear in setting out in some detail the conditions on which a third State may be considered as entitled to a right under a treaty to which it is not a party:

> It cannot be lightly presumed that stipulations favourable to a third State have been adopted with the object of creating an actual right in its favour. There is however nothing to prevent the will of sovereign States from having this object and this effect. The question of the existence of a right acquired under an instrument drawn between other States is therefore one to be decided in each particular case: it must be ascertained whether the States which have stipulated in favour of a third State meant to create for that State an actual right which the latter has accepted as such.[135]

The similarity of this detailed rule to those in Articles 34 and 36 VCLT is evident, and the reference, however selective it may be, in the ILC commentary to cases of the Permanent Court clearly indicates that the latter has already 'codified' these two provisions in the case law presented above.

D. *Other Issues*

But there are many other general concepts of treaty law which are still important today and form an integral part of the Vienna Convention. These concern for example the general principles of *pacta sunt servanda*

[132] *Gabčíkovo-Nagymaros Project (Hungary/Slovakia)*, [1997] ICJ Rep 7, at 56 [85].
[133] *Certain German Interests in Polish Upper Silesia* (Merits) (n 27) at 30.
[134] *Customs Régime* (n 52) 48; *Interpretation of Judgments Nos 7 and 8 (Factory at Chorzów)*, Ser A No 13, at 45; *Free Zones* (n 85) at 20.
[135] *Free Zones* (n 24) 147–148.

and good faith[136] that we have already mentioned at the very beginning of this chapter. These principles imply the obligation of domestic implementation if the treaty so requires. Thus in *Exchange of Greek and Turkish Populations*, the Court '[laid] stress on a principle which is self-evident, according to which a State which has contracted valid international obligations is bound to make in its legislation such modifications as may be necessary to ensure the fulfilment of the obligations undertaken'.[137] Similarly, in the *Free Zones* case, the Court held that France could not 'rely on her own legislation to limit the scope of her international obligations'.[138] In *Greco-Bulgarian "Communities"*, it considered it to be 'a generally accepted principle of international law that in the relations between … contracting Parties to a treaty, the provisions of municipal law cannot prevail over those of a treaty',[139] and in *Polish Nationals in Danzig* it affirmed that 'a State cannot adduce as against another State its own Constitution with a view to evading obligations incumbent upon it under international law or treaties in force'.[140] In sum, the Permanent Court put the principles that were later embodied in Articles 26 and 27 VCLT beyond any doubt.

In *Certain German Interests* the Court, by way of implication, also said that a signatory's misuse of its rights under the as yet unratified treaty may amount to a violation of its general obligations concerning the treaty.[141] However, it later considered Germany's action as not constituting an 'infraction' of the principle of good faith concerning the subject matter of the treaty not yet ratified. It therefore concluded that '[i]n these circumstances, the Court need not consider the question whether, and if so how far, the signatories of a treaty are under an obligation to abstain from any action likely to interfere with its execution when ratification has taken place'.[142] Given the virtually identical content of Article 18 VCLT and the fact that the ILC commentary refers to that statement, one may reasonably assume that the latter had some impact on the drafting of Article 18 by the International Law Commission.[143]

---

136 See e.g. *Treatment of Polish Nationals* (n 53) 28; *Minority Schools in Albania* (n 49) 19–20.
137 *Exchange of Greek and Turkish Populations* (n 8) 20.
138 *Free Zones* (n 24) 167.
139 *Greco-Bulgarian 'Communities'*, [1930] PCIJ Ser B No 17 at 32.
140 *Polish Nationals in Danzig* (n 37) 24.
141 *Certain German Interests in Polish Upper Silesia* (n 27) at 30.
142 Ibid 39.
143 ILC Yearbook 1966 (n 10) 202 69) [1].

Still other examples include reasons for termination of treaties, such as impossibility of performance or the doctrine on fundamental change of circumstances. The latter doctrine was at issue in the *Free Zones* case and the Court said that the facts of the case did not require it to consider either the general status of the rule on fundamental change of circumstances in international law or the method by which it should be given effect.[144] However, a closer look reveals that the Court had in effect ruled that the considerations of the parties at the time of the conclusion of a treaty limit those circumstances which may subsequently bear upon the treaty obligations of the parties, an aspect essential to Article 62 VCLT.

IV. Assessment

In the course of this short chapter I have only covered some of the areas of treaty law as elaborated by the Permanent Court. And in doing so I have come to the conclusion that the experience of the Permanent Court in addressing matters of treaty law left clear marks on the modern law of treaties. The case law of the Permanent Court is very rich in rules, principles and concepts of treaty law, which the Court had to elaborate from scratch but which nevertheless found their way into both the Vienna Convention and the body of case law of the present International Court. However, the judicial development of treaty law by the Permanent Court took place in a rather organic, conceptually uncontrolled and uncoordinated manner. As we have seen on many occasions the case law of the Court was inconsistent and contradictory, and that makes a general, coherent assessment of the still continuing influence of the Court's work quite difficult.

Moreover, in the course of time, the Permanent Court's influence is diminishing gradually. Given the increasing case law of international courts in general, and the International Court of Justice in particular, we face a growing modern judicial practice on international treaty law that is largely guided by the VCLT and frequently takes on forms of self-reference. Also, treaty law itself is developing at an increasing rate, establishing subsystems in various distinct areas, reducing the provisions even of the VCLT to pure default rules. These factors severely limit the precedential value, not technically speaking of course, of the case law of the Permanent Court,

144 *Free Zones* (n 24) 156–158.

and references to it on the law of treaties have become very infrequent today.

However, Ole Spiermann wisely warned that while references to decisions of the Permanent Court may today indeed only be lingering on as echoes from a distant past, it would take a simplistic conception of history 'to conclude that international legal argument as used in the Permanent Court is no longer relevant'.[145] As the playground of treaty interpretation shows still today, many of the arguments made by the Permanent Court would adequately fit into the general repertoire of treaty-interpretation we may find in the work of the present Court. Whether this represents a good old tradition or mirrors obsolete rituals is not definitively settled.

145 Spiermann (n 6) 393.

THE PCIJ AND INTERNATIONAL RIGHTS OF GROUPS AND INDIVIDUALS

Catherine Brölmann

I. Introduction

The Permanent Court of International Justice (Permanent Court or PCIJ) was established in a period in which the position of the State as the 'natural' form of political organization had come under pressure, among others in academic-legal circles.[1] It was also the period in which international-legal concern for groups within the State became institutionalized, notably through the efforts of the League of Nations. And while the League brought institutional and procedural novelties, the Permanent Court contributed on significant points to the development of international law regarding non-State groups and—to a lesser degree—individuals.

Whether in that period international 'rights' or only 'benefits' were at issue, is a matter of debate,[2] but the Permanent Court's contribution to the legal emancipation of groups and individuals in international law is undisputed. This chapter aims to trace the contours of that contribution by addressing the international-legal context of the time (II.) and some hallmark decisions of the Permanent Court in which it considered the international-legal position of groups (III.) and individuals (IV.).

---

[1] C Tomuschat, *Human Rights: Between idealism and realism* (2nd edn, Oxford, OUP 2008) 17.

[2] Whether minorities enjoyed *rights* was linked to the question as to whether they were 'subjects' rather than 'objects' of international law. As to the *interbellum*, the debate on the minorities' status was (and is) undecided; see e.g. B Vukas, 'States, Peoples and Minorities as Subjects of International Law', (1991) 231 Receuil des Cours 231, at 499–501; A Mandelstam, 'La Protection des Minorités', (1923-I) 1 *Recueil des Cours* 362, at 475–477 and 511; F Ermacora, 'The Protection of Minorities before the United Nations' (1983-IV) 182 *Recueil des Cours* 249, at 310 and 346. A broadly shared view was that minorities enjoyed some sort of 'protected status' but no 'legal personality'; cf I Brownlie, *Principles of Public International Law* (7th ed, OUP, Oxford 2008), at 60; AK Meijknecht, *Towards International Personality: The Position of Minorities and Indigenous Peoples in International Law* (Antwerpen, Intersentia 2001). For a cautious assessment regarding the recognition of individual rights see K Parlett, *The Individual in the International Legal System* (CUP, Cambridge 2011) 65 et seq.

II. The PCIJ and the *Interbellum*

While being a Court for States in the State-oriented international system of the time, the Permanent Court did get to address issues of non-State entities. The context of the interwar period was specific, marked by the postwar arrangements and re-drawing of maps in Europe.[3] The Peace treaties, which sanctioned for example the independence of Poland and the territorial gains of Greece (see below III(1)), involved the creation of national States and the moving of boundaries, and had groups caught between newly drawn international borders.

The idea of nationality which had been on the rise following the birth of nation-States like Germany and Italy,[4] had also taken on *legal* relevance.[5] The protective clauses in treaties which in previous times had concerned the protection of religious minorities, now looked to national minorities. The 'national minorities' at issue were a direct result of the granting of self-determination to some peoples, which left sections of nations whose majority formed a State of their own, as a part of the population in another State in which the majority was of a different ethnic or linguistic structure to the minority.[6]

Thus, the relevant minority groups were specifically those linked to the majority population in another State. This link was one reason why, rising nationalism had the paradoxical effect of reinforcing both the State and the identity of minorities. The political concern of the time[7] was focused notably on the protection of minority groups with an independent 'kin-state', not on groups which may have constituted a minority without a link

---

[3] See e.g. IL Claude, *National Minorities: an International Problem* (Harvard UP, Cambridge 1955).

[4] HJ Steiner, P Alston and R Goodman, *International Human Rights in Context: Law, Politics, Morals: Text and Materials* (3rd edn, OUP, Oxford 2008) 87.

[5] See, e.g., JE Nijman, 'Minorities and Majorities' in B Fassbender and A Peters (eds), *The Oxford Handbook of the History of International Law* (OUP, Oxford 2012); H Wintgens, *Der Völkerrechtliche Schutz der nationalen, sprachlichen und religiösen Minderheiten* (W Kohlhammer, Stuttgart 1930); E Ruiz Vieytez, *The History of Legal Protection of Minorities in Europe* (The Univ of Derby, Derby 1999).

[6] Cf Ermacora (n 2) at 257; and, generally, Claude (n 3).

[7] P Thornberry, *International Law and the Rights of Minorities* (Clarendon Press, Oxford 1991); Claude (n 3) 1. Also, on the origins of the (national) minorities problem, CA Macartney, *National States and National Minorities* (Russell & Russell, New York 1934, 2nd edn 1968) 21–29; N Berman '"But the Alternative Is Despair": European Nationalism and the Modernist Renewal of International Law' (1993) 106 Harvard LRev 1792–1903; J Jackson Preece, *National Minorities and the European Nation-States System* (Clarendon Press, Oxford 1998).

to a majority population elsewhere, such as today for example the Inuit or the Kurds. These numerically inferior, distinct groups were perceived as a prominent factor in the post-Versailles political balance. The primary focus on inter-State interests (rather than for instance on 'fundamental rights') appears for example from the acclaimed treatment of international minority protection by Versailles participant Charles de Visscher in his lectures on "The Stabilization of Europe."[8]

While minorities figure prominently in the League system and the case law of the Court, such was not the case with 'peoples'. The difference between these two legal categories (which in most concrete cases are occupied by the same physical persons) was relevant as it is today, as they were already then part of different discourses, with self-determination being specifically linked to 'nations' or 'peoples' and not to 'minorities'.

Alongside the rise of the nationality principle and of nationalism, the principle of self-determination had played an important role in the political negotiations and ultimately the architecture of the post-War world. US President Wilson, after having introduced the principle of 'self-determination' in his Fourteen Points Speech, but "without the knowledge that nationalities existed," reportedly suffered "anxieties" over the powerful dynamic he had unleashed, in which many groups claimed independence.[9] 'Self-determination' has been said to have two manifestations - the classical or 'statist' one, which tends to legitimize existing States, and the revolutionary or 'anti-statist' one, which poses a challenge to the existing State-structures by concentrating on 'peoplehood' or "authentic communal feeling ... among the relevant group."[10] Once political solutions had been negotiated and effectuated, the statist version of 'self-determination' definitively prevailed and the principle did not enter the reasonings of the Permanent Court. Minorities were—as is the case today—as a legal category by definition part of a State

---

[8] Ch De Visscher, *The Stabilization of Europe* (Univ of Chicago Press, Chicago 1924), with I. "the problem of Nationalities" and II. "protection of Minorities" (3–50).

[9] According to De Visscher, describing his observations at the 1919 Paris Peace Conference (n 8) 18–19; also M Macmillan, *Paris 1919: Six Months That Changed the World* (Random House, New York 2002); and C Fink, 'The Minorities Question at the Paris Peace Conference: The Polish Minority Treaty', June 28, 1919, in MF Boemeke, G D Feldman, and E Gläser (eds) *The Treaty of Versailles: a Reassessment after 75 Years*, (CUP, Cambridge 1998) 263.

[10] M Koskenniemi, 'National Self-Determination Today: Problems of Legal Theory and Practice' (1994) 43 ICLQ 241, 246. Nathaniel Berman (n 7) points to a similar conceptual duality which permeated the inter-war debate on the meaning and definition of 'minority' and 'community'.

and in a legal sense emphatically *not* associated with the right to self-determination.

Part of the post-War legal scholarship challenged the State as the 'natural' entity in international law. Following the discredit brought by the Great War a number of international lawyers expressed hope and optimism about a 'new international law,' which would have an eye for the individual as the building block of international law. Scholars such as Brierly and Kelsen proposed a challenge to the State-centered international law of the nineteenth century proceeding from the individual as the vehicle.[11] Even if not consistently—when Feinberg in 1937 discusses the concept of equality as developed by the PCIJ (see below), for a frame of reference he mentions only the *Déclaration des Droits de l'Homme et du Citoyen* as found in "democratic states"[12]—the individual thus was present in the *international* law discourse of the interwar period. This said, no international framework or a 'system' for human rights was in place, nor a comprehensive discourse (proceeding from the individual as a logical point of departure for legal arrangements), as there would be in the United Nations era later on.

Meanwhile, the fact that minority protection was internationalized first of all in the cause of international peace and security made the context of the protection of groups different from that of today. Accordingly, while from the perspective of present day international law and human rights law it makes sense to take the legal position of individuals and groups together, at the time of the Permanent Court such conceptual unity may have been less self-evident. Otherwise, it is likely that for many international lawyers of the *interbellum* rights of the individual would be derived from rights of the group, rather than the other way around as it is most often construed today.[13]

---

[11] See e.g. JL Brierly, *Le Fondement du Caractère Obligatoire du Droit International,* (1928 III) 23 *Receuil des Cours* 463, at 511; H Kelsen, *Das Problem der Souveränität und die Theorie des Völkerrechts* (J.C.B. Mohr, Tübingen 1920), at 17 (the state as only "eine Menschen verpflichtende Ordnung"); and cf M Koskenniemi, *The Gentle Civilizer of Nations* (CUP, Cambridge 2002); JE Nijman, *The Concept of International Legal Personality: an Inquiry into the History and Theory of International Law* (TMC Asser, The Hague 2004).

[12] N Feinberg, *La Juridiction et la Jurisprudence de la Cour Permanente de Justice Internationale en Matière de Mandats et de Minorités*, (1937 I) 59 *Recueil des Cours* 587, 653.

[13] Cf e.g. G Triggs, 'The Rights of People and Individual Rights: Conflict or Harmony?' in J Crawford (ed), *The Rights of Peoples* (Clarendon Press, Oxford/New York 1988) 141, 146.

III. The PCIJ and the Protection of Minorities

1. *The Minorities Protection System*

The 'minorities protection system' in the framework of the League of Nations[14] was made up of commitments comprised in special "minorities treaties" (as with Poland, the Serb-Croat-Slovene State, Czechoslovakia, Romania and Greece, between 1919 and 1920);[15] in special chapters in peace treaties (as with Austria, Bulgaria, Hungary and Turkey, between 1919 and 1923);[16] in special provisions in the framework of other agreements (such as the—most elaborate—minority protection regime provided for in the Treaty between Germany and Poland on Upper Silesia);[17] and in unilateral declarations made to the Council of the League (as by Finland, Albania, Lithuania, Latvia and Estonia, between 1921 and 1923).[18] In substance these were similar provisions, all modeled on the Polish minority treaty. Generally they provided for three categories of rights: rights accruing to all citizens of a State, such as equal legal protection and a right to nationality; rights accruing to all inhabitants of a State, such as full protection of life and liberty; and rights of a minority group in particular, such as freedom of religion and freedom of education.[19]

---

[14] Cf Claude (n 3); Jackson Preece (n 7) 67–94; a concise treatment of the League system in CJ Tams, 'League of Nations' in R Wolfrum (ed) *Max Planck Encyclopedia of Public International Law* (OUP 2008) online edition <www.mpepil.com>.

[15] Treaty between the Principal Allied and Associated Powers and Poland (28 June 1919) 112 BSP 232 ("Polish Minority Treaty"or "Little Versailles"); Treaty between the Principal Allied and Associated Powers and the Serb-Croat-Slovene State (10 September 1919) 112 BSP 514; Treaty between the Principal Allied and Associated Powers and Czecho-Slovakia (10 September 1919) 112 BSP 502; Treaty between the Principal Allied and Associated Powers and Roumania (9 December 1919) 5 LNTS 336; Treaty concerning Thrace, between the Principal Allied and Associated Powers and Greece (10 August 1920) 28 LNTS 225.

[16] Treaty of Peace between the Allied and Associated Powers and Austria, Protocol, Declaration and special Declaration (10 September 1919, Part III, Chap V, 62 to 69) 112 BSP 317; Treaty of Peace between the Allied and Associated Powers and Bulgaria, and Protocol (27 November 1919, (Part III, Chap IV, 49 to 57) 112 BSP 781; Treaty of Peace between the Allied and Associated Powers and Hungary (4 June 1920, Part III, Chap VI, 54 to 60) 6 LNTS 187; Treaty of Peace with Turkey (24 July 1923, Part I, Chap Ill, 37 to 45) 28 LNTS 11.

[17] Treaty between Germany and Poland on Upper Silesia (15 May 1922, part III), 9 LNTS 466.

[18] See the list with primary source references in Ermacora (n 6) 249, 258–259; A Meijknecht, 'Minority Protection System between World War I and World War II' in R Wolfrum (ed) *The Max Planck Encyclopedia of Public International Law* (OUP 2008) online edition <www.mpepil.com>.

[19] Cf Article 2 Polish Minorities Treaty: 'Poland undertakes to assure full and complete protection of life and liberty to all inhabitants of Poland without distinction of birth, nationality, language, race or religion. All inhabitants of Poland shall be entitled to the free

The protection of named national minorities then was buttressed by a 'guarantee' of the League of Nations,[20] which had two components. It meant that the stipulations regarding minority protection could not be modified without approval (by majority) of the League Council. Secondly, it meant that the League had to ascertain that the provisions for the protection of minorities were always observed. This implied that the Council would have to take action in the event of any infraction, or danger of infraction, of any of the obligations with regard to the minorities in question.[21]

Taken together these stipulations are said to have constituted the first international system for minority protection. Importantly, that system did *not* set out general international rules. The League Covenant in its final version did not contain provisions generally ensuring the minorities' rights in all of the League's member States. Draft versions with obligations to this effect for all League of Nations members had been proposed by US President Wilson,[22] but in the end had been blocked by established States, generally for the reason that it 'assail[ed] the holy principle of 'full internal sovereignty".[23] Also, attempts to impose minority protection provisions upon Germany, Belgium, Denmark, France or Italy in the Peace Treaties had been unsuccessful.[24] The *system* thus embodied the maximum attainable solution of creating several individual regimes tailored to particular political situations and geographical areas. Minority protection would have been set as a condition for the recognition of independent Statehood (for example in case of Poland), for the recognition of territorial gains

---

exercise, whether public or private, of any creed, religion or belief, whose practices are not inconsistent with public order or public morals.' An overview in N Lerner, 'The Evolution of Minority Rights in International Law' in CM Brölmann, R Lefeber and MYA Zieck (eds) *Peoples and Minorities in International Law* (Martinus Nijhoff, Dordrecht 1993) 77, 83–84; A Mandelstam, 'La Protection des Minorités' in (1923 I) *Recueil des Cours* 362, 411–446; Feinberg (n 12) 634; Ermacora (n 6) 259.

20 Article 12 (1) of the Minorities Treaty between the Principal Allied and Associated Powers (the British Empire, France, Italy, Japan and the United States) and Poland, signed at Versailles, (28 June 1919) 225 CTS 412 (hereinafter: the Polish Minorities Treaty): "the stipulations ... shall be placed under the guarantee of the League of Nations." This provision was subsequently included in the treaties with Czechoslovakia, Yugoslavia, Romania, Greece, Austria, Bulgaria, and Hungary.

21 H Rosting, 'Protection of Minorities by the League of Nations', (1923) 17 AJIL 641–660; Meijknecht (n 18); cf Article 11 League Covenant.

22 See De Visscher (n 8), at 18–19.

23 Representative of Great Britain; see Nijman (n 5) section 5.5.3. See also C Fink, *Defending the Rights of Others: The Great Powers, the Jews, and International Minority Protection, 1878–1938* (CUP, Cambridge 2004) 152–4; and Thornberry (n 7) 38–40.

24 Claude (n 6) 35–36. Cf also Fink (n 23).

(for example in case of Greece) or for membership of the League (for example in case of the Baltic States).

Minority protection was therefore served by a non-general, non-reciprocal system imposed specifically on States of Central and Eastern Europe-with the seed of resentment sown.[25] From a positive law perspective, the selective scope of the rules and obligations certainly limited their potential for having "a fundamentally norm-creating character."[26] It is one reason why 'minority' did not become a general legal category with given legal implications. The *term* 'minority' is found occasionally, as in the Polish Minority Treaty;[27] but, for example, the Treaty of Versailles, in its provisions on the Czecho-Slovak and Polish State, referred to "inhabitants of that State who differ from the majority of the population in race, language, or religion".[28] If and when the term 'minority' was used, no legally relevant defintion would be added.

2. The Role of the PCIJ

This was the context in which several questions were put before the Permanent Court regarding the rights of minorities and State obligations in their regard. The Permanent Court dealt with these questions both in judgments and in Advisory Opinions.[29] Contentious procedures on

---

[25] See e.g. Fink (n 23).

[26] To borrow from the Permanent Court's successor; see *North Sea Continental Shelf* (Federal Republic of Germany v. Denmark and Federal Republic of Germany v. Netherlands), [1969] ICJ Rep 3 [72]: "that the provision concerned should ... be of a fundamentally norm-creating character such as could be regarded as forming the basis of a general rule of law".

[27] See e.g. Article 8 of the Treaty concerning the Recognition of the Independence of Poland and the Protection of Minorities 225 CTS 412.

[28] See Treaty of Peace at Versailles (28 June 1919) 225 CTS 188, Articles 86 and 93, respectively.

[29] For this chapter the following cases are taken do be directly concerned with the rights of groups or individuals: *Questions Relating to Settlers of German Origin in Poland* (Advisory Opinion), [1923] PCIJ Ser B No 6; *Question concerning the Acquisition of Polish Nationality* (Advisory Opinion), [1923] PCIJ Ser B No 7; *Jurisdiction of the Courts of Danzig (Pecuniary Claims of Danzig Railway Officials Who Have Passed into the Polish Service, Against the Polish Railways Administration)* (Advisory Opinion), [1928] PCIJ Ser B No 15; *Rights of Minorities in Upper Silesia (Minority Schools)* (Judgment), [1928] PCIJ Ser A No 15; *Interpretation of the Convention Between Greece and Bulgaria Respecting Reciprocal Emigration, Signed at Neuilly-Sur-Seine on November 27th, 1919 (Greco-Bulgarian Communities)* (Advisory Opinion), [1930] PCIJ Ser B No 17; *Access to German Minority Schools in Upper Silesia* (Advisory Opinion), [1931] PCIJ Ser A/B No 40; *Treatment of Polish Nationals and Other Persons of Polish Origin or Speech in the Danzig Territory* (Advisory Opinion), [1933] PCIJ Ser A/B No 44; *Minority Schools in Albania* (Advisory Opinion), [1935] PCIJ Ser A/B No 64.

minority issues at the time were less odd than they might seem today, because of the accepted role of kin-States. Advisory Opinions could be seen to serve, then as now,[30] as a vehicle for obtaining a legal pronouncement on the rights of non-State groups under international law, where they cannot assert these rights directly.

Although minority groups themselves had no *locus standi*, they did gain access to the mechanism via the petition system which the League developed early in the 1920s.[31] The filing of a petition with the League via the Secretary-General could on certain conditions lead to a formal request with the League Council, which in turn could ask the Permanent Court for an Advisory Opinion as per Article 14 of the League Covenant. In practice this happened only in a very few cases.[32] Ultimately the petition system proved too formal and burdensome, and fruitful negotiation and reconciliation would take place not on the basis of a formal petition but based on informal procedure or *procédure non-écrite.*[33]

3. *Points of Law*

This said, the Permanent Court had occasion to pronounce itself on some fundamental points of law. Arguably this was due also to the particular context of the minorities protection system, as reaffirmed, for example, by the comment of a contemporary observer that the "...système des droits, accordés aux minorités par les traités, ... en général, il est conforme aux exigences de l'heure actuelle. Il a seulement besoin d'être exposé avec plus de précision et de détail."[34] Precisely because the system was lacking 'precision and detail', the Court was faced with basic questions which it needed to address—without an existing body of case law or doctrine to rely on—before it could proceed to decide on the facts of a particular case.

---

30 See for example *Legal Consequences Of The Construction Of A Wall In The Occupied Palestinian Territory* (Advisory Opinion), [2004] ICJ Rep 151.; *Accordance With International Law Of The Unilateral Declaration Of Independence In Respect Of Kosovo* (Advisory Opinion), 22 July 2010, at http://www.icj-cij.org/docket/files/141/15987.pdf.

31 On the right to petition see e.g. J Robinson (ed), *Were the Minorities Treaties a Failure?* (Antin Press, New York 1943) 128.

32 Meijknecht (n 18) points out that between 1919 and 1939 "....only 16 petitions reached the agenda of the Council," while in total 950 petitions were filed, of which 758 were declared admissible.

33 These expressions were used by the League Secretariat; see C Gütermann, *Das Minderheitenschutzverfahren des Völkerbundes* (Duncker & Humblot, Berlin 1979) 149 et seq.

34 Mandelstam (n 18) 511.

The expression 'minority' came to be used—though not consistently—in legal doctrine notably with the creation of the minority protection system after the First World War,[35] but without a generally agreed definition. From the in depth analysis of the interwar debate by Nathaniel Berman emerges a highly political picture, in which the search for a definition of 'minority' moved along the lines of the tension between the 'statist' versus 'nationalist' interpretation of international law. Berman argues convincingly how, since in the end the question was decided by who had the power to define 'community' and 'minority', this debate was ultimately about international authority.[36] When it thus fell upon the Permanent Court to clarify the notion of 'minority' and the threshold for being (a member of) a minority for legal purposes, the impartial judicial authority (symbolically reinforced by the fact that the Court was not formally an organ of the League of Nations) was especially relevant.[37]

In an early case the Court was called upon to interpret a provision on the acquisition of nationality, which the new Polish State wished to apply restrictively with a view to limiting acquisition of Polish nationality by the German minority.[38] The Court in this occasion defined a minority as "inhabitants who differ from the population in race, language or religion"; it moreover adopted a famously 'broad' definition, contrary to Polish propositions: "that is to say ... inhabitants of this territory of non-Polish origin, *whether they are Polish nationals or not.*"[39]

Further elements were added to the definition in the *Greco-Bulgarian Communities* case, when the Court was asked for an Opinion on the consequences of liquidation of property of Greco-Bulgarian 'communities', such as churches, convents, schools, and on the dissolution of these communities when members voluntarily emigrated. By the interpretation of the 1919 *Convention Between Greece and Bulgaria Respecting Reciprocal Emigration* the Court in fact paralleled to some extent 'communities' and 'minorities.' In a well-known passage the Court then gave an intricate definition:

---

[35] Ermacora (n 6) 287.

[36] Berman (n 7).

[37] Cf H Lauterpacht, *The Development of International Law by the International Court* (Stevens & Son, London 1958) 261.

[38] Berman points out that "[t]he underlying political issue in the German Settlers and Polish Nationality cases was the same: to what extent would Poland have the right to take measures to reduce the size of its German minority?" (n 7) 1840 fn 201); see in general 1834–1842.

[39] *Acquisition of Polish Nationality* (n 29) 14–15, emphasis added.

> By tradition … the "community" is a group of persons living in a given country or locality, having a race, religion, language and traditions of their own and united by this identity of race, religion, language and traditions in a sentiment of solidarity, with a view to preserving their traditions, maintaining their form of worship, ensuring the instruction and upbringing of their children in accordance with the spirit and traditions of their race and rendering mutual assistance to each other.[40]

The definition in the *Greco-Bulgarian Communities* Opinion has several features which would prove foundational to the later doctrine regarding minority protection. First, it indicates that for a group to fall within the (legal) category of 'minority', recognition on the part of the minority State or 'host state' is not a constitutive element. This made the definition an essentially non-juridical exercise, which sometimes has been termed the 'sociological approach': [41] "[t]he existence of communities is a question of fact; it is not a question of law."[42] This, incidentally, was a delicate matter in view of the selective scope of the minorities protection obligations.[43] The factual approach also truly *internationalized* the position of minorities, as it followed that the existence of a minority would be given legal relevance independent from the consent of the individual States.

Furthermore, the definition of 'minority' proposed by the Court had both objective and subjective aspects. The objective and subjective 'theory' regarding the constitutive elements of a 'minority' had been the subject of intense debate in the 1920s.[44] Already in the 1928 *Minority Schools* case the Court had pointed to both objective signs, such as language or history, and subjective aspects of a minority identity, stating that, "the German-Polish Convention … concerning Upper Silesia bestow[s] upon every national the right freely to declare according to his conscience and on his personal responsibility…" whether or not his child "…belonged to a racial, linguistic or religious minority."[45]

---

40 *Greco-Bulgarian Communities* (n 29) at 21–22.

41 See the detailed analysis in Berman (n 7) 1855.

42 *Greco-Bulgarian Communities* (n 29) at 22.

43 Cf Mandelstam, in his brief *deuxieme partie* on ‚La reconnaissance de fait des minorités' (n 19, at 407–409).

44 Cf e.g. Nijman (n 5); Jackson Preece (n 7) 17. From contemporary writings see e.g. Redslob who, according to the subjective position, considers a nation not to be a given, but based on will and choice: R Redslob, *Histoire des Grands Principes du Droit des Gens Depuis l'Antiquité Jusqu'a la Veille de la Grande Guerre* (Rousseau, Paris 1923) 31–32).

45 *Rights of Minorities in Upper Silesia* (*Minority Schools*) (n 29) 46; see also Berman (n 7). A few years later the Court confirmed this stance in *Access to German Minority Schools in Upper Silesia* (n 29) at 20.

The case law of the Permanent Court, as in the *Greco-Bulgarian Communities* case, seemed to point to a combination of subjective and objective factors. At the time this was cause for criticism, suggesting the Court eschewed taking sides in a longstanding debate.[46] But precisely this combination would become a cornerstone of international law doctrine in regard of non-State groups later on. All contemporary definitions and criteria-of-belonging combine subjective and objective elements, and furthermore proceed from the 'sociological' approach, which does not require 'recognition' of the minority. The subjective factor in group identification for the purpose of international law—'self-identification' as it came to be named in the 1970s and 1980s - gained a firm place in the conceptualization of 'minorities', but also of 'peoples' and 'indigenous peoples' in the United Nations era.[47]

The legal definition of 'minority' commonly (though still not unanimously) used today,[48] which was proposed by Special Rapporteur Francesco Capotorti in the 1979 study for the UN Sub-Commission on Prevention of Discrimination and Protection of Minorities,[49] was directly based on the 1930 definition by the Permanent Court in the *Greco-Bulgarian Communities* case. It also includes non-dominance, another element which defines 'minority' in the sociological tradition.

In the context of minority protection the Permanent Court is perhaps best known for its development of the legal concept of 'equality'.[50] In an early case on the position of the German minority in Poland, the Court articulated the notion of equality both in law and in fact: "The fact that no racial discrimination appears in the text of the law ..., and that in a few instances the law applies to non-German Polish nationals ..., makes no substantial difference... There must be equality in fact as well as ostensible legal equality in the sense of the absence of discrimination in the words of the law."[51]

---

46 Cf Feinberg (n 12) 641.

47 See CM Brölmann and MYA Zieck, 'Indigenous Peoples', in Brölmann et al (eds) (n 19) 190–197.

48 Ermacora (n 6) 287.

49 F Capotorti, 'Study on the Rights of Persons Belonging to Ethnic, Religious and Linguistic Minorities' (United Nations, New York 1979) E/CN4/Sub2/384/Rev 1, at 96: 'A group numerically inferior to the rest of the population of a state, in a non-dominant position, whose members—being nationals of the state—possess ethnic, religious or linguistic characteristics differing from those of the rest of the population and show, if only implicitly, a sense of solidarity, directed towards preserving their culture, traditions, religion or language.'

50 Cf Lauterpacht (n 37).

51 *German Settlers in Poland* (n 29) 24.

Almost a decade later in relation to the treatment of a Polish minority, the Court specified the particular point of non-discrimination in law and in fact. In order to be effective the prohibition of discrimination should: "ensure the absence of discrimination in fact as well as in law. A measure which in terms is of general application, but in fact is directed against Polish nationals and other persons of Polish origin or speech, constitutes a violation of the prohibition."[52]

In the 1935 *Minority Schools in Albania* Opinion, following a decision of the Albanian government to close all private schools in Albania and a reaction by the Greek minority, the Court carried the concept of equality in law and in fact further by articulating the concept of positive discrimination. The passage merits quotation in full:

> The idea underlying the treaties for the protection of minorities is to secure for certain elements incorporated in a State, the population of which differs from them in race, language or religion, the possibility of living peaceably alongside that population and cooperating amicably with it, while at the same time preserving the characteristics which distinguish them from the majority, and satisfying the ensuing special needs. In order to attain this object, two things were regarded as particularly necessary, and have formed the subject of provisions in these treaties.
>
> The first is to ensure that nationals belonging to racial, religious or linguistic minorities shall be placed in every respect on a footing of perfect equality with the other nationals of the State.
>
> The second is to ensure for the minority elements suitable means for the preservation of their racial peculiarities, their traditions and their national characteristics. These two requirements are indeed closely interlocked, for there would be no true equality between a majority and a minority if the latter were deprived of its own institutions, and were consequently compelled to renounce that which constitutes the very essence of its being as a minority.[53]

As to "ensur[ing] suitable means" for the "minority elements", familiar objections were raised by dissenting judges: "This provision ... is intended to render the equality effective and real. There is nothing, however, in the wording of the provision to show that this equality in law may be disregarded and replaced by a system of different treatments for the minority and the majority so as to establish an equilibrium between them."[54]

---

[52] *Treatment of Polish Nationals and Other Persons of Polish Origin or Speech in Danzig Territory* (n 29) 28.

[53] *Minority Schools in Albania* (n 29) 17.

[54] *Minority Schools in Albania,* Dissenting Opinion by Sir Cecil Hurst, Count Rostworowski and M Negulesco (n 29) 24.

Yet, equality in law and in fact as well as the concept of 'positive discrimination' have since remained central concepts in human rights protection. Thus, in a speech to the UN General Assembly Sixth Committee in 2002 then President of the International Court of Justice Guillaume brought to mind how the 1935 Opinion by the Permanent Court "pav[ed] the way for the famous "affirmative action", so dear to American liberals in the 1970s."[55]

In the series of reasonings which culminated in the *Minority Schools in Albania* Opinion the Court thus developed what has been called the "two pillar structure" for minority protection, consisting of non-discrimination and the right of minorities to preserve their separate identity.[56] Arguably the latter can be considered a 'group right'[57] (borne by the collective as such), although group identity may also be seen as giving rise to 'collective rights' (individual rights enjoyed as member of a collective). Most of the *interbellum* minority rights are and were considered collective (thus individual) rights.[58] Article 8 of the Polish Minority Treaty for example contains the individualized formula we also find in Article 27 of the International Covenant on Civil and Political Rights: "Polish nationals who belong to racial, religious or linguistic minorities shall enjoy the same treatment and security in law and in fact as the other Polish nationals."[59]

Only some provisions have an unmistakable "group dimension", as is pointed out by Henrard; for instance the obligations towards the Jewish community as such set out in the Polish Minority Treaty.[60] Mandelstam, writing in 1923, has a similarly restrictive view of group rights (he calls them 'collective rights' using the reverse terminology) and identifies only "the right to proportional representation and the right to (forms of) autonomy".[61]

---

[55] Speech by President of the International Court of Justice Gilbert Guillaume, to the Sixth Committee of the General Assembly of the United Nations 30 October 2002 [2] <http://www.icj-cij.org/presscom/files/3/3123.pdf>.

[56] K Henrard, 'Minorities – International Protection' in R Wolfrum (ed), *Max Planck Encyclopedia of Public International Law* (OUP 2008) online edition <www.mpepil.com>.

[57] Ibid.

[58] Cf Henrard (n 56); Mandelstam (n 18) 436–442.

[59] Polish Treaty (n 16); and cf Art 27 CCPR (99 UNTS 171): "In those States in which ethnic, religious or linguistic minorities exist, persons belonging to such minorities shall not be denied the right, in community with the other members of their group, to enjoy their own culture, to profess and practise their own religion, or to use their own language".

[60] Henrard (n 36).

[61] Mandelstam (n 18) 436–442.

Two further features of the case law of the Permanent Court on minority rights must be mentioned. While these are not points of substantive law, but rather legal principles, they have set the tone for the protection of minority rights by the Court and have increased the impact of the Court's reasoning.

First, the Permanent Court has systematically confirmed the international character of minority rights and, by logical implication, their unconditional prevalence over the internal law of States. The breakdown of the old order of empires has been said to give way to "a murky situation[,] marked by a tangle of national and state identities, ... that called for increased *international* authority".[62] Indeed the Polish minority treaty and other treaties underscored the international character of minority protection obligations by referring to the guarantee of the League: "the stipulations ... so far as they affect persons belonging to racial, linguistic or religious minorities, constitute *obligations of international concern and shall be placed under the guarantee of the League of Nations.*"[63] Still, the internationalization of minority rights was a daring project which challenged the existing order. The Court, however, "in its determination to discourage evasion of international obligation"[64] reaffirmed it in the early case on *Acquisition of Polish Nationality.*[65] Once the Court decided on a—broad—definition of 'minority' (see above), the preliminary question of whether acquisition of nationality fell under the League guarantee stipulated in the Polish Minority Treaty, could be answered in the affirmative. The Court found that indeed international law determined who constitutes a minority in the sense of the Polish Minorities Treaty and the Versailles Peace Treaties, and not the Polish State, and said: "[t]hough, generally speaking, it is true that a sovereign State has the right to decide what persons shall be regarded as its nationals, it is no less true that this principle is applicable only subject to the Treaty obligations referred to above."

A second characteristic of the Court's decisions is the conspicuous role of *effet utile* in the interpretation of provisions on minority protection. In practically every pertinent case the Court referred to the principle of

62 Berman (n 7) 1841, emphasis added.

63 Article 12(1) the Polish Minorities Treaty (n 20) emphasis added. This provision was included in the treaties with Czechoslovakia, Yugoslavia, Romania, Greece, Austria, Bulgaria, and Hungary.

64 Lauterpacht (n 37) 262.

65 *Acquisition of Polish Nationality* (n 29) 13–17.

effectiveness and used an accordingly 'teleological approach' for the interpretation of provisions—which at the time was far from habitual in treaty interpretation.[66]

Thus in the *Aquisition of Polish Nationality* case the Court based its broad definition of 'minority' (see above) on the principle of effectiveness, lest the Article 4 of the Polish Minority Treaty would be deprived of meaning.[67] Also the aforementioned conceptualization of 'equality in law and in fact' in the *German Settlers* case and the *Polish Nationals in Danzig* case was inspired by the principle of effectiveness ("The prohibition against discrimination, in order to be effective…").[68]

Another example is the general statement of the Court in the *Greco-Bulgarian Communities* case: "the aim and object of the Convention, its connection with the measures relating to minorities, the desire of the signatory Powers … everything leads to the conclusion that the Convention regards the conception of a 'community' from the point of view of this exclusively minority character …".[69] When in the *Minority Schools in Albania* case the Court was called upon to interpret Albania's 1921 Minority Declaration, it held that in view of its objective the Minority Declaration should be interpreted in the same way as a minority treaty. The Court then proceeded from the Treaties' object and purpose ("the idea underlying…") to reach the 'two pillar' interpretation of 'equality' (see the text and quotation above).[70]

By taking minority protection as the ultimate objective and guiding principle in its interpretive practice, the Court to some extent gave minority protection provisions the standing of a regime of 'law', rather than a collection of 'obligations'.

IV. The PCIJ and the Rights of Individuals

The interwar period developed a 'system' for the protection of minorities, but no legal framework for the protection of rights of the individual. It is

[66] See the concise treatment of this point in Lauterpacht (n 37) 257–262; also A Spiliopoulou Åkermark, *Justifications of Minority Protection in International Law*, (Martinus Nijhoff, Dordrecht 1997) 110.

[67] Lauterpacht (n 37) 258.

[68] *Treatment of Polish Nationals and Other Persons of Polish Origin or Speech in Danzig Territory* (n 29) at 28; cf Lauterpacht (n 37) 257.

[69] *The Greco-Bulgarian "Communities"* (n 29) 21–22.

[70] *Minority Schools in Albania* (n 29) 17.

thus unsurprising that individuals figure less prominently than minority groups in the case law of the Permanent Court.

This said, the position of the individual was famously at issue in one of the Advisory Opinions delivered by the Court in relation to the newly established Free City of Danzig,[71] one of the post-War "experiments in internationalisation".[72] The case concerned the question whether Danzig railway employees could bring claims against the Polish Railway Association in Danzig Courts, based on the 1921 *Beamtenabkommen* between Poland and the Free City of Danzig; or in other words: whether the 1921 treaty was part of the legal relation between the Danzig railway employees who had become employees of the Polish Railway Association and Poland. An appeal by the Free City against the decision of the High Commissioner, who had answered this question in the negative, led to a request by the League Council for an Advisory Opinion with the Permanent Court. The 1928 Opinion on the *Jurisdiction of the Courts of Danzig* has entered literature as one of the first pronouncements on the individual as beneficiary of an international provision.[73] Meanwhile, scholarly debate on the precise meaning of the Opinion persists until today.[74] In the key passage of its 1928 Opinion the Court stated:

> It may be readily admitted that, according to a well established principle of international law, the *Beamtenabkommen*, being an international agreement, cannot, as such, create direct rights and obligations for private individuals. But it cannot be disputed that the very object of an international agreement, according to the intention of the contracting Parties, may be the adoption by the Parties of some definite rules creating individual rights and obligations and enforceable by the national courts. That there is such an intention in the present case can be established by reference to the terms of the Beamtenabkommen.[75]

According to Lauterpacht it was "difficult to exaggerate the bearing" of the Opinion,[76] which showed that "no considerations of theory can prevent the individual from becoming the subject of international rights if States so wish."[77] Lauterpacht's views on the legal position of the individual are

---

71 Feinberg (n 12).

72 Berman (n 7) 1874.

73 Cf CM Spofford, 'Third Party Judgment and International Economic Transactions' (1964 III) 113 *Recueil des Cours* 117, 172.

74 K Parlett, 'The PCIJ's Opinion in *Jurisdiction of the Courts of Danzig*. Individual Rights under Treaties' (2008) 10 J of the History of Intl L 119.

75 *Jurisdiction of the Courts of Danzig* (n 29) 17.

76 Lauterpacht (n 37) 175.

77 H Lauterpacht, 'The Subjects of the Law of Nations [Part II]' (1948) 64 LQR 97, 98.

reflected in his choice to discuss the case under the rubric of 'judicial legislation *by reference to parallel developments* in international law' rather than that of 'judicial legislation on account of absence of generally accepted law'.[78]

According to Anzilotti, on the other hand, the Court had said nothing more than that contracting parties could have the intention to adopt rules which create rights and obligations for individuals;[79] these could then be applied by domestic courts provided they had been incorporated into domestic law. The 'dualist' views of Anzilotti, who was at the time of this case serving as president of the PCIJ, have been well studied.[80]

A recent textual and contextual analysis of the *Danzig* Opinion traces the ambiguities in its wording, and convincingly argues how the conclusion must be that the Court said there is a possibility for individuals to obtain rights directly from international law (*in casu* a treaty) without adoption of rules in domestic law.[81]

Whichever reading one adopts, the Opinion undoubtedly broke new ground. The Court did perhaps not propose to accord international rights directly to individuals, but it did forward the idea of the individual as a beneficiary of rights that originated in international law. It seems fair to say that the Danzig Opinion, in its ambiguity, challenged the doctrinal premise that individuals could not be 'bearer' of rights under international law, and, implicitly, challenged also the separation between national and international law that was prevailing in doctrine at the time.[82]

It is worth noting that in the Court's reasoning, the 'human right' or 'fundamental right' discourse was absent. Rather, it revolved around a neutral 'individual right'—comparable to the individual right derived (in that case directly) from article 36(1) of the 1961 Convention on Consular Relations by the ICJ in the 2001 *LaGrand* case.[83] While in the latter case the international Court of Justice may have been "prudently avoiding a

---

78 Lauterpacht (n 37) 173–199 (emphasis added); see also, Lecture of Idelson and response by Lauterpacht in *Transactions of the Grotius Society*, Problems of Peace and War, Transactions for the Year 1944 (vol 30, CUP, Cambridge 1944), 50, 60–68, at <http://www.jstor.org/stable/743201>.

79 D Anzilotti, *Cours de droit International* (Librairie de Recueil Sirey, Paris 1929) 407.

80 Parlett (n 74). The different composition of the Court in different periods, and the possible effect on the decisions, is left out of account in the present chapter, but see the contributions by O Spiermann (at 401), and J d'Aspremont (227–228) to the present volume).

81 Parlett (n 74).

82 Parlett (n 74).

83 *LaGrand Case* (*Germany v United States Of America*) (Judgment—Merits) [2001] ICJ Rep 466 [77].

politicization of the dispute,"[84] it is likely that in the 1928 *Danzig* case the Permanent Court simply used the discourse prevalent at the time—that of a stable division of power between States. Interestingly, in *LaGrand* the International Court of Justice did not refer to the *Danzig* case, or any other possible precedent regarding individual rights, but to the PCIJ Opinion in the *Acquisition of Polish Nationality* case[85] as an authority for 'grammatical interpretation'.

V. The PCIJ and Legacy

The context of the PCIJ was quite different from that of its successor. The stated aim to prevent kin-States from intervening on behalf of their national minority in another State is evidence of the interest in inter-State stability underlying the minorites protection project. Furthermore, positive international law was much less diversified than it is today. Rules of minority protection were rather clear-cut; they had no generality of scope and were not embedded in a general human rights system or discourse. Today the generalization of human rights is an obvious influence on the legal position of minorities.[86] That minority protection in the United Nations era has come to be addressed within the human rights framework with its particular procedural remedies, and that 'kin-states' no longer have an accepted role to play in minority protection, are two possible reasons why questions concerning minorities have not come before the ICJ. Only in the 2011 *Georgia v Russian Federation* case—not adjudicated for lack of jurisdiction—did minority rights come up as part of the claim by Georgia that the Russian Federation, *inter alia,* had breached human rights including minority rights.[87] In contrast, questions of 'self-determination'—which had been kept outside the sphere of the Permanent

[84] CJ Tams, 'Consular Assistance: Rights, Remedies and Resposnibility', (2002) 13 EJIL 1257.

[85] *Acquisition of Polish Nationality* (n 29) 20.

[86] P Vuciri Ramaga, 'The Group Concept in Minority Protection' (1993) 15 Human Rights Q 575.

[87] *Case Concerning Application of the International Convention on the Elimination of All Forms of Racial Discrimination (Georgia v Russian Federation),* (Preliminary Objections), Judgment of 1 April 2012, at [32] (at <http://www.icj-cij.org/docket/files/140/16398.pdf>). The point is made by G Zyberi, 'The International Court of Justice and the Rights of Peoples and Minorities', in CJ Tams and J Sloan (eds), *The Development of International Law by the International Court of Justice,* (forthcoming OUP, Oxford 2013) (manuscript on file with the author).

Court—have come before the International Court of Justice, for example in the cases concerning *the Wall* and *Kosovo*.

The minority protection system ended with the demise of the League, but the holdings of the Court have kept their relevance, as appears from references in decisions by the International Court of Justice and commentaries from scholars, such as Lauterpacht, who straddled the two eras. Specifically the issues addressed by the Court have proven relevant in human rights law until this day. This holds for the notion of formal and substantive 'equality', and for the element of self-identification in the identity of a minority, to name two examples.[88] Bodies such as the UN Human Rights Committee have explicitly recognized the legacy of the Permanent Court, for instance on the 'factual approach' to the existence of minorities.[89] In the procedural sphere, the petition system—in which the Court was indirectly involved as a petition could ultimately trigger a request for an Advisory Opinion—according to several commentators can be seen as a precursor of the various complaint mechanisms linked to human rights regimes in the United Nations era.[90]

It is not certain whether the protection of rights of the individual was a stand-alone objective, for the League or for the Court. From the *Jurisdiction of the Courts of Danzig* case it appears the Court proceeded from a political perspective rather than from a premise of the individual's fundamental dignity. In fact, the impact of the judgment was not immediate; for example the *Jurisdiction of the Courts of Danzig* Opinion was not mentioned in the 1930 edition of Oppenheim's *International Law*.[91]

However, the *PCIJ can be said to have* "laid the groundwork for international concern of individual rights.[92] The decisions of the Court arguably have spurred on the visibility of individuals and groups in international law, identifying them as legally relevant categories. However, this did not mean they were construed as *Normadressat* or 'subjects' of international law according to the then prevailing doctrine. The subject-object

---

[88] Vuciri Ramaga (n 86); J Pejic, 'Minority Rights in International Law' (1997) 19 Human Rights Q 666, 671–672.

[89] See *General Comment No 23*, dealing specifically with minority issues (6 Apr 1994, 50 UNGA, Hum Rts Comm, 1314th mtg, UN Doc CCPR/C/21/Rev1/Add5, 1994) reprinted in (1994) 15 Human Rights LJ 234; and cf Pejic (n 88) 671–672.

[90] Vuciri Ramaga (n 86) 585 et seq.

[91] Parlett (n 2) 26: "the opinion did not have an immediately transformative effect on the position of the individual in the international legal system."

[92] LA Thio, *Managing Babel: The International Legal Protection of Minorities in the Twentieth Century*, (Martinus Nijhoff, Dordrecht 2005) 58.

dichotomy remained in place when it came to minorities and individuals.[93] This is perhaps the most fundamental difference with legal developments in the era of the International Court of Justice.

In the course of the 1920s, the optimism[94] about the League's system of minority protection turned to disenchantment.[95] For the perceived failure of the League system several explanations have been proposed: that 'the close link' between the League and the Peace Treaties made the defeated countries—notably Germany—consider the League to be part of an 'unjust' post-war settlement;[96] that the League and its Council suffered from general weakness due to the built-in inequality of States and the lack of full support of the Great Powers; that the protection system suffered from the reluctance of the League members to bring claims on behalf of minorities to the Council; the attitude of the new national States hosting minorities; the general political and economic context; and the fact that it was 'the inevitable concomitant of the disintegration of the moral foundations of international order'.[97] But commentators also mentioned the limited scope of the PCIJ's jurisdiction (disputes arising out of the Minorities Treaties and Declarations only) and the absence of a right of minorities themselves to bring a claim directly before the PCIJ.

Be that as it may, when it comes to the development of international law regarding minorities and individuals, the role of the Permanent Court was more important than that of the other law-making agents at the time. While the system was highly politicized, and "… the kin-states did not genuinely accept the internationalization of minority problems,"[98] the Permanent Court had occasion to clarify and contribute to a new body of law, without much doctrine or precedent to rely on. The PCIJ itself accepted this role, ostensibly engaging in 'judicial legislation' and increasingly referring to precedents from its own case law.[99] By virtue of its mission of applying general international law the Court could take a

93 Ibid.

94 See e.g. De Visscher (n 8) viii.

95 On the right to petition see e.g. Robinson (n 31) v; as well as Claude (n 6) 31–50; Jackson Preece (n 7).

96 Cf Tams (n 14), at [4].

97 Claude (n 6) 50.

98 Ibid 45.

99 O Spiermann, *International Legal Argument in the Permanent Court of International Justice: The Rise of the International Judiciary* (CUP, Cambridge 2005) 394; see also Ingo Venzke, 'The Role of International Courts as Interpreters and Developers of the Law: Working Out the Jurisgenerative Practice of Interpretation' (2011) 34 Loyola of Los Angeles International and Comparative Law Review 99.

broader view than the League and the Council. For this reason the PCIJ contributed more to the development of international law regarding minorities and individuals than can be said for example of the League. This was also the view of Lauterpacht, who found that especially "when compared with the parallel—negative—developments in the political sphere", the "important and progressive contributions" of the Court appeared in their "true significance."[100]

100 Lauterpacht (n 37) 262.

THE PCIJ AND THE PROTECTION OF FOREIGN INVESTMENTS

Ursula Kriebaum

I. Introduction

The list of issues on which investment tribunals have referred to the Permanent Court of International Justice's (PCIJ) case law is long. It includes jurisdictional issues, provisional measures, issues of substance such as whether contractual rights can be the object of an expropriation and the question of reparations, and a state of necessity.

Judgments and opinions in no less than thirteen cases[1] decided by the PCIJ have found their way into decisions and awards of investment tribunals. This runs from frequently quoted cases like *Factory at Chorzów* and *Mavrommatis* to the *Eastern Greenland* case on which only a few investment tribunals relied.

Two of the issues touched upon by the have PCIJ left important traces in the case law of investment tribunals: one is jurisdiction *ratione temporis*; the other is the standard of reparation for treaty violations. Other judgments of the PCIJ are mentioned in only very few awards of investment tribunals. The subsequent sections address four representative aspects of current investment law, as reflected in arbitral jurisprudence, with a view to tracing the PCIJ's legacy.

---

[1] *Losinger & Co (Switzerland v Yugoslavia)*, (Jurisdiction) [1936] PCIJ Ser C No 78; *Mavrommatis Palestine Concessions (Greece v UK)* (Jurisdiction) [1924] PCIJ Ser A No 2; *Case Concerning the Factory at Chorzów (Germany v Poland)* [1927] PCIJ Ser A No 9; *Case concerning Certain German Interests in Polish Upper Silesia (Germany v Poland)* [1928] PCIJ Ser A No 17; *Certain German Interests in Polish Upper Silesia (Germany v Poland)* (Jurisdiction) [1926] PCIJ Ser A No 7; *Electricity Company of Sofia and Bulgaria (Belgium v Bulgaria)* (Jurisdiction) [1939] PCIJ Ser A/B No 77; *SS Wimbledon (UK v Germany)* (Jurisdiction) [1923] PCIJ Ser A No 1; *Payment of Various Serbian Loans Issued in France (France v Yugoslavia)* (Jurisdiction) [1929] PCIJ Ser A No 20; *Phosphates in Morocco (Italy v France)* (Jurisdiction) [1938] PCIJ Ser A/B No 74; *Jurisdiction of the Courts of Danzig* (Advisory Opinion) [1928] PCIJ Ser B No 15; *Status of Eastern Carelia* (Advisory Opinion) [1923] PCIJ Ser B No 5; *Oscar Chinn* (Jurisdiction) [1934] PCIJ Ser A/B No 63; *Polish Postal Service in Danzig* (Advisory Opinion) [1925] PCIJ Ser B No 11; *Legal Status of Eastern Greenland (Denmark v Norway)* (Jurisdiction) [1933] PCIJ Ser A/B No 53.

II. The Jurisdiction of Investment Tribunals

1. *The Principle of Competence—Competence*

The ICSID Convention in Article 41 (1) contains the rule that 'The Tribunal shall be the judge of its own competence'.[2] Despite this clear rule on competence-competence ICSID tribunals have referred in this regard to the judgment of the PCIJ in *The Electricity Company of Sofia and Bulgaria*[3] case to confirm their finding that it is their task to decide upon the interpretation of the instrument of consent and thereby upon their own competence.

The approach of the Tribunal in *SPP* v *Egypt*[4] can serve as an example in this regard. The case concerned the cancellation of a hotel project by the Egyptian authorities. The basis for the jurisdiction of the ICSID Tribunal in *SPP* was Article 8 of the Egyptian Law No 43 of 1974. The Tribunal did not accept the contentions of the parties on how the Egyptian Law had to be interpreted. With regard to Egypt's contention that Egyptian law should be governing as far as the interpretation of its instrument of consent is concerned it said that it is for the Tribunal to decide upon its own competence:

> While Egypt's interpretation of its own legislation is unquestionably entitled to considerable weight, it cannot control the Tribunal's decision as to its own competence. The jurisprudence of the Permanent Court of International Justice and the International Court of Justice makes clear that a sovereign State's interpretation of its own unilateral consent to jurisdiction of an international tribunal is not binding on the tribunal or determinative of jurisdictional issues (...).[5]

It is not entirely clear why the Tribunal relied on the *The Electricity Company of Sofia and Bulgaria*[6] case in this context. The PCIJ had not announced openly in the *Electricity Company* that to exercise competence-competence was part of its judicial tasks. Furthermore, in the *Electricity Company of Sofia and Bulgaria* case, Belgium had invoked a Treaty of 1931 and Belgium's and Bulgaria's declaration of adherence to the Optional Clause of the PCIJ's statute as bases for consent. Therefore, in

[2] See C Schreuer et al, 'The ICSID Convention: A Commentary' (2nd ed, CUP, Cambridge 2009) 516 et seq.
[3] *The Electricity Company of Sofia and Bulgaria* (Judgment) (n 1) 64.
[4] *SPP* v *Egypt* (Decision on Jurisdiction, 14 April 1988), [1995] 3 ICSID Rep 131.
[5] Ibid [60].
[6] *The Electricity Company of Sofia and Bulgaria* (Judgment) (n 1) 64.

contrast to *SPP* in the *Electricity Company of Sofia and Bulgaria* case consent was not expressed in a national law. The PCIJ found that it was impossible to base its jurisdiction upon the Treaty of 1931 since one of the conditions laid down in this treaty had not been fulfilled, but the Court accepted jurisdiction under the Optional Clause.

It can generally be said that the PCIJ, like any other court, exercised its competence-competence in every case it decided. This is in particular so whenever the Court's or the Tribunal's jurisdiction was disputed. However, there is no specific finding on which the investment Tribunal in *SPP* was able to rely. This might explain why the PCIJ's judgment is only mentioned without reference to a specific paragraph.

The ad hoc Committee in *Soufraki* v *United Arab Emirates*[7] quoted the statement in *SPP* on the issue including the reference to the *Electricity Company of Sofia and Bulgaria* case. The Tribunals in *Cemex* v *Venezuela*[8] and *Brandes* v *Venezuela*[9] also refer to the *Electricity Company of Sofia and Bulgaria* case. None of the Tribunals indicated a specific paragraph of the judgment. The Tribunal in *Cemex* had to decide whether Venezuelan investment law did provide for consent to jurisdiction of an ICSID tribunal. The Respondent contended that '[a]part from the language of the statute itself, the Investment Law, as part of the law of Venezuela, must be interpreted in the light of Venezuelan legal principles' and, in particular, of Article 4 of its Civil Code. The Tribunal held that it was not bound by Venezuela's interpretation of its own law but that it had competence-competence with regard to its jurisdiction. It referred in this regard to the *Electricity Company of Sofia and Bulgaria* case and stated:

> 70. The Tribunal adds that the same solution has been adopted by the Permanent Court of International Justice and the International Court of Justice which have made clear that a sovereign State's interpretation of its own unilateral consent to the jurisdiction of an international tribunal is not binding on the tribunal or determinative of jurisdictional issues.[10]

---

7 *Soufraki* v *United Arab Emirates* (Decision on Annulment, 5 June 2007) ICSID Case No ARB/02/7.

8 *Cemex Caracas Investments BV and Cemex Caracas II Investments BV* v *Venezuela*, Decision on Jurisdiction, 30 December 2010 ICSID Case No ARB/08/15 [70].

9 *Brandes Investment Partners, LP* v *Venezuela* (Final award, 2 August 2011) ICSID Case No ARB/08/3.

10 *Cemex* (n 8) [70] (footnotes suppressed). Referencing *Electricity Company of Sofia and Bulgaria* (Preliminary Objections) [1939] PCIJ Ser A/B No 77; *Aegean Sea Continental Shelf* (Greece v. Turkey) [1978] ICJ Rep 3; *Fisheries Jurisdiction* (Spain v Canada) [1998] ICJ Rep 432.

The Tribunal in *Brandes* quoted paragraph 70 of the decision of jurisdiction of the *Cemex* Tribunal.[11]

Unlike in the *Electricity Company of Sofia and Bulgaria* case, the PCIJ did mention explicitly that it enjoyed competence-competence in other cases. An example is its 1928 *Advisory Opinion No 16 on the Interpretation of the Greco-Turkish Agreement of December 1st 1920* concerning the competence of the Greco-Turkish Commission when it said: '... as a general rule, any body possessing jurisdictional powers has the right in the first place itself to determine the extent of its jurisdiction ...'[12] However, none of the investment tribunals relied on this Advisory Opinion of the PCIJ in support of their competence-competence.

2. *Interpretation of Expressions of Consent*

In the *Factory at Chorzów* case Poland had argued that the PCIJ lacked jurisdiction concerning differences of opinion in respect of obligations arising out of a violation of the articles of the Upper Silesia Convention. The PCIJ stated in its judgment No 9 concerning this objection to its jurisdiction that it would only affirm its jurisdiction if the arguments in favour of the exercise of jurisdiction were preponderant:

> It is true that the Court's jurisdiction is always a limited one, existing only in so far as States have accepted it; consequently, the Court will, in the event of an objection—or when it has automatically to consider the question—only affirm its jurisdiction provided that the force of the arguments militating in favour of it is preponderant. The fact that weighty arguments can be advanced to support the contention that it has no jurisdiction cannot of itself create a doubt calculated to upset its jurisdiction. When considering whether it has jurisdiction or not, the Court's aim is always to ascertain whether an intention on the part of the Parties exists to confer jurisdiction upon it. The question as to the existence of a doubt nullifying its jurisdiction need not be considered when, as in the present case, this intention can be demonstrated in a manner convincing to the Court.[13]

The PCIJ affirmed its jurisdiction on this point and held Germany entitled to claim an indemnity for the illegal expropriation of the factory at Chorzów. Some investment tribunals have refered to this statement of the PCIJ when discussing guidelines to determine the scope of consent to be

[11] *Brandes* (n 9) [99] (footnotes suppressed). Referencing *Electricity Company of Sofia and Bulgaria* (Preliminary Objections) [1939] PCIJ Ser A/B No 77; *Aegean Sea Continental Shelf* (Greece v. Turkey) [1978] ICJ Rep 3; *Fisheries Jurisdiction* (Spain v Canada) [1998] ICJ Rep 432.

[12] *Interpretation of the Greco-Turkish Agreement* (1 December 1926, Final Protocol, Article IV) [1928] PCIJ Ser B No 16, at 20.

[13] *Factory at Chorzów* (Claim for Indemnity, Germany v Poland, Judgment No 9) (n 1) at 32.

found in instruments purporting to confer jurisdiction upon them. Relying on the PCIJ's dictum in *Chorzów*, the general assumption of these tribunals was that there is neither a presumption in favour of jurisdiction nor one against jurisdiction, but that the juridical instrument has to be interpreted objectively and in good faith and that the force of the arguments militating in favour of jurisdiction would have to be preponderant.[14]

3. *Jurisdiction Ratione Temporis*

Do facts, situations, and disputes that occur before the treaty containing the offer of jurisdiction of an investment tribunal had entered into force give rise to the jurisdiction of investment tribunals?

The distinction between jurisdiction *ratione temporis* and the temporal application of a treaty's (mostly bilateral investment treaties or BITs) substantive obligations is still controversial. Four distinct issues arise in the *ratione temporis* context:

(1) Are pre-BIT investments covered by the protection of the treaty or only post-BIT investments?
(2) Is pre-BIT conduct excluded from the jurisdiction of a tribunal?
(3) Are pre-BIT disputes excluded from the jurisdiction of a tribunal?[15]
(4) What substantive standards apply with regard to pre-BIT conduct/disputes if a tribunal has jurisdiction?

Sometimes the bilateral investment treaty offers answers to some of the above-mentioned questions. For example, Article 2 of the Peru-Chile BIT provides: 'This Treaty shall apply to investments made before or after its entry into force by investors of one Contracting Party, …' Therefore, under this provision pre-BIT investments are protected by the treaty. The same BIT also answers the question whether pre-BIT disputes are covered, this time in the negative. It provides: '… It shall not, however, apply to differences or disputes that arose prior to its entry into force.'

The definition of the term dispute by the PCIJ in the *Mavrommatis Palestine Concessions* case[16] has become widely accepted in the case law of

---

[14] See e.g. *SPP* v *Egypt* (n 4) 131 [63]; *Inceysa Vallisoletana SL* v *El Salvador* (Award, 2 August 2006) ICSID Case No ARB/03/26 [176]; *Sociedad Anónima Eduardo Vieira* v *Chile* (Award, 21 August 2007) ICSID Case No ARB/04/7 [191].

[15] See on the issue of disputes: C Schreuer, 'What is a Legal Dispute' in I Buffard et al (eds), *International Law Between Universalism and Fragmentation: Festschrift in Honour of Gerhard Hafner* (Martinus Nijhoff, Leiden/Boston 2008) 959.

[16] *Mavrommatis* (n 1) at 11; EM Borchard, 'The Mavrommatis Concessions Cases' (1925) 19 AJIL 728–38; N Bentwich, 'The Jurisdiction of the International Court of Justice Over Concessions in a Mandated Territory' (1928) 44 LQR 450–463; AK Kuhn, 'The Mavrommatis

investment tribunals. The case concerned concessions granted in Palestine by the Ottoman authorities to a Greek national relating to an electric tramway system. Great Britain became the Mandatory Power in 1920 and granted concessions which partly conflicted with the Mavrommatis concessions. Greece argued that this violated Protocol XII of the Lausanne Peace Treaty between Turkey and the Allied Powers and sued Great Britain before the PCIJ. The first judgment of the PCIJ in the *Mavrommatis* case concerned issues of jurisdiction, one of them being whether there was a dispute between Greece and Great Britain. The PCIJ said on the issue of a dispute: 'A dispute is a disagreement on a point of law or fact, a conflict of legal views or interests between two persons.'[17] Investment tribunals frequently refer to this definition.[18]

When assessing whether or not a particular dispute has arisen prior to the entry into force of the treaty, tribunals[19] as well as parties[20] refer to the judgment of the PCIJ in *The Electricity Company of Sofia and Bulgaria* case. The case concerned a Belgian electricity company which was taken over by the Municipality of Sofia in 1916 during World War I. After the War the Treaty of Neuilly provided for restitution and established

Case on Readaptation of the Jerusalem Concessions' (1928) 22 AJIL 383–385; N Feinberg, 'La Jurisdiction et la Jurisprudence de la Cour Permanente de Justice Internaitonale en Matière de Mandates et de Minorities' (1937) 59 Recueil des Cours 591–703; O Spiermann, *International Legal Argument in the Permanent Court of International Justice: The Rise of the International Judiciary* (CUP, Cambridge 2005) 191 et seq.; R Uerpmann-Wittzack, 'Mavrommatis Concessions Cases', in R Wolfrum (ed) *Max Planck Encyclopedia of Public International Law* (OUP 2011) online edition <www.mpepil.com>.

17 *Mavrommatis* (n 1) at 11.

18 See e.g. *El Paso* v *Argentina* (Decision on Jurisdiction, 14 January 2004) ICSID Case No ARB/03/15 [61]; *Tokios Tokelės* v *Ukraine* (Decision on Jurisdiction, 29 April 2004) ICSID Case No ARB/02/18 [106]; *Pan American Energy & BP* v *Argentina* (Decision on Preliminary Objections, 27 July 2006) ICSID Case No ARB/03/13 [80]; *Empresas Lucchetti SA and Lucchetti Peru SA* v *Peru* (Jurisdiction Award, 7 February 2005), ICSID Case No ARB/03/4 [48]; *Indústria Nacional de Alimentos SA and Indalsa Perú* v *Peru* (Decision on Annulment, 5 September 2007, Lucchetti) Ibid [90]; *Impregilo SpA* v *Pakistan* (Decision on Jurisdiction, 22 April 2005) ICSID Case No ARB/03/3 [302]; *Tokios Tokelės* v *Ukraine* (Decision on Jurisdiction and Dissent, 29 April 2004) idem [106]; *MCI Power Group LC and New Turbine Inc* v *Ecuador* (Award, 31 July 2007) ICSID Case No ARB/03/6 [63] fn 3; *MCI Power Group LC and New Turbine Inc* v *Ecuador* (Decision on Annulment, 19 October 2009) ibid [29], [52]; *Vieira* v *Chile* (Award, 21 August 2007) (n 14) [245].

19 See e.g. *Empresas Lucchetti SA and Lucchetti Peru SA* v *Peru* (n 18) [50]; *Grand River Enterprises Six Nations Ltd and ors* v *United States* (Decision on Objections to Jurisdiction, 20 July 2006) [86]; *Channel Tunnel Group Ltd and France-Manche SA* v *France and United Kingdom* (Partial Award on Jurisdiction, 30 January 2007) PCA [142].

20 See e.g. *Helnan International Hotels A/S* v *Egypt*, Decision of the Tribunal on Objection to Jurisdiction, 17 October 2006, para. 46; *Vieira* v *Chile* (n 14) [112]: *African Holding Company of America Inc (AHL) and the African Society of Contrauction in Congo (SARL)* v. *Congo*, Decision on Jurisdiction and Admissibility 29 July 2008 [112].

a Belgo-Bulgarian Mixed Arbitral Tribunal.[21] The Tribunal established in its award a formula for fixing the selling price of electric current.[22] A dispute arose concerning the application of this formula.[23] The Belgian Government instituted proceedings at the PCIJ against the Bulgarian Government. Bulgaria argued that the Court lacked jurisdiction since the dispute had arisen before the date of the Belgian acceptance of the Court's jurisdiction.[24] Belgium's consent was restricted to disputes arising after the acceptance of the Court's jurisdiction 'with regard to situations or facts subsequent' thereto, so limiting the area common to both declarations.[25] The Court held that the objection with respect to the declarations of acceptance failed because it was common ground between the parties that the dispute arose only in 1937, well after the dates of the two declarations.[26] The PCIJ observed: 'a dispute may presuppose the existence of some prior situation or fact ... it does [however] not follow that the dispute arises in regard to the situation or fact.'[27] The *Lucchetti* Tribunal[28] relied on this case to decide whether the dispute before it was the same as a dispute already settled before the entry into force of the Peru-Chile BIT.

The facts leading to a dispute typically occur sometime before the actual dispute. Under some treaties it is not just disputes that arose prior to the entry into force of the treaty but also facts or situations that occurred prior to its entry into force that are excepted from jurisdiction. The PCIJ found this to be the case in the *Phosphates in Morocco* case.[29] The case concerned certain alleged rights of Italian citizens to explore phosphate deposits in Morocco. Morocco was a French protectorate at that time. Italy's claim against France was rejected for lack of jurisdiction *ratione temporis*. France had limited the acceptance of the compulsory jurisdiction of the PCIJ to disputes arising after the declaration accepting the jurisdiction and only with regard to situations and facts subsequent to the declaration. The respondent in *Railroad Development Corporation*

---

21 *The Electricity Company of Sofia and Bulgaria* (Judgment) (n 1) 64 at 70.
22 Ibid 70.
23 Ibid 70.
24 Ibid 68.
25 Ibid 81.
26 Ibid 81, 82.
27 Ibid 81, 82.
28 *Empresas Lucchetti SA and Lucchetti Peru SA* v *Peru* (n 18) [50].
29 *Phosphates in Morocco* (Preliminary Objections) (n 1) at 25; Spiermann (n 16) 376 et seq; AP Fachiri, 'Note: Judgment Delivered June 14, 1938: Phosphates in Morocco', (1939) 20 BYIL 142; J Menzel, 'Phosphates in Morocco Case', in R Wolfrum (ed), *Max Planck Encyclopedia of Public International Law* (online edition, at www.mpepil.com).

v *Guatemala*[30] relied on the PCIJ's judgment in the *Phosphates in Morocco* case to argue that the tribunal lacked jurisdiction *ratione temporis*.[31] Article 10.1.3. CAFTA contains a wide exception in this regard. It reads as follows: 'For greater certainty, this Chapter does not bind any Party in relation to any act or fact that took place or any situation that ceased to exist before the date of entry into force of this Agreement.' Therefore, the CAFTA excludes pre-treaty conduct from the jurisdiction of a tribunal. The Tribunal in *Railroad Development* found, however, that the relevant facts had occurred after the CAFTA had entered into force and it therefore rejected the objection *ratione temporis* to its jurisdiction.[32]

In *Chevron* v *Ecuador*[33] certain of Ecuador's alleged acts or omissions supporting the claimants' denial of justice claim pre-dated the BIT's entry into force. Therefore, the issue arose whether claims relating to these acts or omissions were excluded *ratione temporis* from the jurisdiction of the tribunal. The Treaty protects investments existing at the time of its entry into force as well as investments made or acquired thereafter.[34] The Tribunal referred to the rule on non-retroactivity as contained in Article 28 Vienna Convention on the Law of Treaties (VCLT).[35] It pointed out that the PCIJ's judgment in the *Mavrommatis* case 'can be seen as applying Article 28 VCLT in view of the specific wording and intention of the respective treaties dealt with' in this case.

The Permanent Court in the *Mavrommatis Palestine Concessions* case had said with regard to jurisdiction *ratione temporis*:

> The Court is of opinion that, in cases of doubt, jurisdiction based on an international agreement embraces all disputes referred to it after its establishment ... The reservation made in many arbitration treaties regarding disputes arising out of events previous to the conclusion of the treaty seems

30 *Railroad Development Corporation v Republic of Guatemala* (Second Decision on Objections to Jurisdiction, 18 May 2010) ICSID Case No ARB/07/23.

31 Ibid [38].

32 Ibid [136], [137].

33 *Chevron* v *Ecuador*, (Interim Award, 1 December 2008) PCA.

34 Article XII: 1. This Treaty shall enter into force thirty days after the date of exchange of instruments of ratification. It shall remain in force for a period of ten years and shall continue in force unless terminated in accordance with paragraph 2 of this Article. It shall apply to investments existing at the time of entry into force as well as to investments made or acquired thereafter.

35 Unless a different intention appears from the treaty or is otherwise established, its provisions do not bind a party in relation to any act or fact which took place or any situation which ceased to exist before the date of the entry into force of the treaty with respect to that party.

to prove the necessity for an explicit limitation of jurisdiction and, consequently, the correctness of the rule of interpretation enunciated above.[36]

Therefore, according to *Mavrommatis*, pre-existing disputes must be specifically excluded by the treaty; otherwise they are covered. The *Chevron* Tribunal followed this approach. The Tribunal stated that the BIT's generally worded jurisdictional clause conferred jurisdiction also over customary international law claims and was not limited to causes of action based on the treaty.[37] The Tribunal therefore distinguished between the applicability *ratione temporis* of substantive obligations in a BIT and jurisdiction *ratione temporis*. The text of the relevant clause in the treaty which did not explicitly exclude pre-BIT disputes was decisive for its interpretation of the BIT.[38] The jurisdictional clause in *Walter Bau* v *Thailand*[39] was also broad, containing no explicit *ratione temporis* restrictions. It simply referred to '[d]isputes concerning investments'.[40] The Tribunal, however, questioned the *Mavrommatis* precedent and ultimately found that it had no jurisdiction to consider disputes that had arisen before the BIT's entry into force.[41]

Therefore, in investment case law the issue is still controversial. In my view the *Mavrommatis* approach is to be preferred: if the jurisdictional clause does not explicitly exclude pre-BIT disputes and is not limited

---

Article VI

> 1. For purposes of this Article, an investment dispute is a dispute between a Party and a national or company of the other Party arising out of or relating to (a) an investment agreement between that Party and such national or company; (b) an investment authorization granted by that Party's foreign investment authority to such national or company; or (c) an alleged breach of any right conferred or created by this Treaty with respect to an investment.

36 *Mavrommatis* (n 1) 6 at 35.

37 The *Chevron* Tribunal held that it had to interpret Article XII (1) of the BIT in accordance with Article 28 VCLT's "unless" clause to determine to what extent it makes an exception to non-retroactivity. The relevant part of Article XII(1) of the BIT states that the BIT "shall apply to investments existing at the time of entry into force as well as to investments made or acquired thereafter" [187]-[188]. The Tribunal found that the investments were existing at the time of entry into force of the BIT [189].

38 Ibid [265], [266].

39 *Walter Bau* v *Thailand* (Award, 1 July 2009).

40 Article 10.

> (1) Disputes concerning investments ... should as far as possible be settled amicably ...
> (2) If the dispute cannot be settled ... it shall ... be submitted for arbitration. ...

41 Ibid [9.93].

to BIT standards, the tribunal's jurisdiction extends to disputes that have arisen before the treaty's entry into force.

III. Liability

1. *Contractual Rights as Objects of Expropriation*

In international investment law it is well established that contractual rights are protected under investment protection treaties.[42] The judicial authority for the proposition that rights arising under contracts are protected against expropriation goes back for over a century.[43] In this context investment tribunals have often relied on the PCIJ's finding in the *Certain German Interests in Polish Upper Silesia* case.[44] The PCIJ had to decide whether the rights of the Bayerische to exploit the factory of Chorzów had been directly prejudiced by the taking over of the factory by Poland. It therefore had to decide whether contractual rights of the Bayerische had been expropriated. The PCIJ held that:

> [...] it is clear that the rights of the Bayerische to the exploitation of the factory and to the remuneration fixed by the contract for the management of the exploitation and for the use of its patents, licenses, experiments, etc., have been directly prejudiced by the taking over of the factory by Poland.

---

[42] See GC Christie, 'What Constitutes a Taking of Property Under International Law?' (1962) 38 BYIL 305, 311; BH Weston, '"Constructive Takings" Under International Law: A Modest Foray into the Problem of "Creeping Expropriation"', (1975) 16 Virginia JI L 103, 112–13; R Higgins, 'The Taking of Property by the State: Recent Developments in International Law' (1982-III) 176 Recueil des Cours 263, 271; G Sacerdoti, 'Bilateral Treaties and Multilateral Instruments on Investment Protection' (1997) 269 Recueil des Cours 251, 381; UNCTAD Series on issues in international investment agreements, 'Taking of Property' 36 (2000); T Waelde and A Kolo, "Environmental Regulation, Investment Protection and 'Regulatory Taking' in International Law" (2001) 50 ICLQ 811, 835; G H Sampliner, 'Arbitration of Expropriation Cases Under UP Investment Treaties - A Threat to Democracy or the Dog That Didn't Bark?' (2003) 18 ICSID Review-Foreign Investment Law Journal 1, 14; J Paulsson and Z Douglas, 'Indirect Expropriation in Investment Treaty Arbitrations' in N Horn and P Kröll (eds), *Arbitrating Foreign Investment Disputes* (Kluwer Law International, The Hague 2004) 145, 152; P Alexandrov, 'Breaches of Contract and Breaches of Treaty, The Jurisdiction of Treaty-based Arbitration Tribunals to Decide Breach of Contract Claims in SGS v Pakistan and SGS v Philippines' (2004) 5 The Journal of World Investment & Trade 555, 559; C Schreuer and U Kriebaum, 'The Concept of Property in Human Rights Law and International Investment Law' in S Breitenmoser et al (eds), *Human Rights, Democracy and the Rule of Law, Liber Amicorum Luzius Wildhaber* (Nomos, Baden-Baden 2007) 743, 750.

[43] *Rudloff Case,* Interlocutory Decision 1903 (9 RIAA, 1959) 244, 250; *Norwegian Shipowners' Claims (Norway* v *United States*), Award, (1 RIAA, 13 October 1922) 307, 318, 325; *Certain German Interests in Polish Upper Silesia* (n 1) 44.

[44] *Certain German Interests in Polish Upper Silesia* (n 1).

> As these rights related to the Chorzów factory and were, so to speak, concentrated in that factory, the prohibition contained in the last sentence of Article 6 of the Geneva Convention applies in all respects to them.[45]

The Tribunal in *SPP* v *Egypt*[46] serves as an example of a Tribunal that explicitly referred to this judgment of the PCIJ. The case concerned the cancellation of a hotel project by the Egyptian authorities. The Tribunal examined whether the measures by Egypt affecting rights under a contract to build hotels could amount to an expropriation. The Tribunal said:

> 165. Moreover, it has long been recognized that contractual rights may be indirectly expropriated. In the judgment of the Permanent Court of International Justice concerning *Certain German Interests in Polish Upper Silesia*, the Court ruled that, by taking possession of a factory, Poland had also "expropriated the contractual rights" of the operating company.[47]

Siemens v *Argentina*[48] concerned a project for the provision of an immigration control, personal identification and electoral information system. After the project's start, Argentina had taken a number of adverse measures, including postponements and suspensions of the profitable activities, fruitless renegotiations and ultimately the cancellation of the project. Argentina argued that unless a contract is internationalized through a stabilization clause, it is not susceptible of expropriation. The Claimant successfully invoked the provision in the applicable BIT protecting investors against uncompensated expropriations. The Tribunal held that a contract is covered by the definition of investment under the US–Argentina BIT which protects against uncompensated expropriations. It found that there is a long judicial practice that contracts can be expropriated and referred among other decisions to the PCIJ's Judgment in the *Certain German Interests in Polish Upper Silesia* case:

> 267. ... There is a long judicial practice that recognizes that expropriation is not limited to tangible property. The Tribunal will refer, for the sake of brevity, to the findings of the Permanent Court of Arbitration ("PCA") in the case of the *Norwegian Shipowners' Claims* and the Permanent Court of International Justice ("PCIJ") in the *Factory at Chorzów* Case.
>
> 268. ... The PCIJ found that: "[...] it is clear that the rights of the Bayerische to the exploitation of the factory and to the remuneration fixed by the

---

45 Ibid 44.

46 *SPP* v. *Egypt*, (Award, 20 May 1992), 3 ICSID Reports 189. Referencing *Certain German Interests in Polish Upper Silesia* (n 1) at 44.

47 *Certain German Interests in Polish Upper Silesia* (n 1) 228–229. See also *Wena Hotels Ltd* v *Arab Republic of Egypt* (Award, 8 December 2000) 6 ICSID Reports 89 [98].

48 *Siemens* v *Argentina* (Award, 6 February 2007) ICSID Case No ARB/02/8.

> contract for the management of the exploitation and for the use of its patents, licenses, experiments, etc., have been directly prejudiced by the taking over of the factory by Poland. As these rights related to the Chorzów factory and were, so to speak, concentrated in that factory, the prohibition contained in the last sentence of Article 6 of the Geneva Convention applies in all respects to them."
>
> 269. These findings on the issue are conclusive and have been followed by ICSID and NAFTA tribunals, and the Iran-US Claims Tribunal.[49]

The Tribunal in *Suez and others* v *Argentina*[50] had to decide whether the termination of a concession contract for a water concession was an expropriation. It stated that the possibility of an expropriation of contractual rights is long established in international law and referred to the *Norwegian Shipowners' Claims* case and the *Chorzów Factory* case. It said:

> 140. 'International law has recognized that contractual rights may be the subject of expropriation at least since the *Norwegian Shipowners' Claims case*. The *Chorzów Factory* case would come to a similar conclusion.'

The PCIJ's approach is reflected in many decisions of investment tribunals only some of which explicitly referred to the PCIJ. Furthermore, the definitions of 'investment' in BITs are in line with this tradition.[51]

2. *Indirect Expropriation*

Today indirect interferences with investments, often in the form of regulations, are the prevalent form of interference with foreign investors' property rights. Bilateral as well as multilateral investment protection treaties typically provide that direct as well as indirect expropriations or measures having equivalent effect require compensation.[52] Where to draw the line

---

[49] Ibid [267]-[269] (footnotes suppressed). Referencing *Certain German Interests in Polish Upper Silesia* (n 1) at 44.

[50] *Suez and others* v *Argentina* (Decision on Liability, 30 July 2010) ICSID Case No ARB/03/17 (footnotes suppressed). Referencing *Norwegian Shipowners' Claims* (n 43) 307; and, *Factory at Chorzów* (n 1).

[51] See e.g. the definition contained in the BIT between Argentina and the United States:

> 'investment' means every kind of investment in the territory of one Party owned or controlled directly or indirectly by nationals or companies of the other Party, such as equity, debt, and service and investment contracts; and includes without limitation:
>
> ...
>
> (v) *any right conferred by* law or *contract*, and any licenses and permits pursuant to law; (emphases added).

[52] See e.g. Treaty between United States of America and the Argentine Republic Concerning the Reciprocal Encouragement and Protection of Investment (entered into force 20 October 1994):

between an interference with investments not amounting to an expropriation and an indirect expropriation is difficult to decide and has been a disputed issue for many years. The impact of the PCIJ on decisions of investment tribunals in this area of investment law is limited. Only very sporadically have investment tribunals referred to the PCIJ in this context and relied on the *German Interests in Polish Upper Silesia* case or the *Oscar Chinn* case.

In the *German Interests in Polish Upper Silesia* case[53] the PCIJ did not distinguish between a direct and an indirect expropriation as far as the legal consequences and effects of the interference were concerned. It found that the taking of the factory was at the same time an indirect expropriation of the patents and licences to which the Bayerische had a right. The PCIJ said:

> Moreover it is clear that the rights of the Bayerische to the exploitation of the factory and to the remuneration fixed by the contract for the management of the exploitation and for the use of its patents, licences, experiments, etc., have been directly prejudiced by the taking over of that factory by Poland. As these rights related to the Chorzów factory and were, so to speak, concentrated in that factory, the prohibition contained in the last sentence of Article 6 of the Geneva Convention [adopted to implement the Treaty of Versailles] applies in respect of them … and the attitude of Poland in regard to the Bayrische has therefore … been contrary to Article 6 and the following articles of the Geneva Convention.[54]

The Tribunal in *CME Czech Republic BV* v *Czech Republic*[55] relied on the *German Interests in Polish Upper Silesia* case to justify its finding of an

---

Article IV

1. Investments shall not be expropriated or nationalized either directly or indirectly through measures tantamount to expropriation or nationalization ('expropriation-) except for a public purpose; in a non-discriminatory manner; upon payment of prompt, adequate and effective compensation; and in accordance with due process of law and the general principles of treatment provided for in Article II (2) Compensation shall be equivalent to the fair market value of the expropriated investment immediately before the expropriatory action was taken or became known, whichever is earlier; be paid without delay; include interest at a commercially reasonable rate from the date of expropriation; be fully realizable; and be freely transferable at the prevailing market rate of exchange on the date of expropriation.

Available at <http://www.unctad.org/sections/dite/iia/docs/bits/argentina_us.pdf>.

53 *Certain German Interests in Polish Upper Silesia* (n 1).

54 Ibid 44.

55 *CME Czech Republic BV* v *Czech Republic* (Partial Award and Separate Opinion, 13 September 2001) 9 ICSID Reports [121].

indirect expropriation of CME's rights. *CME* complained about interference in its contract rights by a regulatory authority, the Media Council. The interference had created a legal situation that enabled the investor's local partner to terminate the contract on which the investment depended. The Tribunal relied on the *German Interests in Polish Upper Silesia* case only in a very indirect way. It referred to Sacerdoti and mentioned the fact that he in turn had relied on the *German Interests* case:

> 604. The expropriation claim is sustained despite the fact that the Media Council did not expropriate CME by express measures of expropriation. De facto expropriations or indirect expropriations, i.e. measures that do not involve an overt taking but that effectively neutralize the benefit of the property of the foreign owner, are subject to expropriation claims. This is undisputed under international law (G. Sacerdoti page 382 as cited above, referring to numerous precedents such as the German Interests In Polish Upper Silesia case, 1926, PCIJ, Series A, No. 7, reprinted in M. Hudson, ed., I World Court Reports 475 (1934); see also Southern Pacific Properties (Middle East) Ltd. v. Egypt, ICSID Case No. ARB/84/3 (1992), 32 I.L.M. 993, 1993, dealing also with the expropriation of contractual rights of the operating company).[56]

The Tribunal in *Generation Ukraine* v *Ukraine*[57] only mentioned the *German Interests in Polish Upper Silesia* case. The *Generation Ukraine* case concerned a construction project for an office building. The main complaint was the failure by the Kyiv City State Administration to issue the necessary lease agreements. The Claimant contended that this refusal was the culmination of a series of other prejudicial acts amounting to a creeping expropriation.[58] The Tribunal discussed the phenomenon of creeping expropriation. In doing so it referred to the *German Interests in Polish Upper Silesia* case as one of many examples for an indirect expropriation which took place by a single act and which therefore did not present the characteristics of a creeping expropriation:

> 20.22 Creeping expropriation is a form of indirect expropriation with a distinctive temporal quality in the sense that it encapsulates the situation whereby a series of acts attributable to the State *over a period of time* culminate in the expropriatory taking of such property. The case of *German Interests in Polish Upper Silesia* is one of many examples of an indirect expropriation without a "creeping" element—the seizure of a factory and its machinery by the Polish Government was held by the PCIJ to constitute an indirect taking of the patents and contracts belonging to the management

56 Ibid [604].

57 *Generation Ukraine Inc* v *Ukraine* (Award, 16 September 2003) ICSID Case No ARB/00/9.

58 Ibid [20.21].

> company of the factory because they were so closely interrelated with the factory itself. But although international precedents on indirect expropriation are plentiful, it is difficult to find many cases that fall squarely into the more specific paradigm of creeping expropriation.[59]

The Tribunal in *Generation Ukraine* rejected the claim of a creeping expropriation because the investment had not yet existed at the relevant time and hence could not be expropriated. In addition, the Tribunal came to the conclusion that the conduct of the administration did not come close to creating a 'persistent or irreparable obstacle to the Claimant's use enjoyment or disposal of its investment.'[60]

Apart from the *CME* case investment tribunals have not relied on the *German Interests in Polish Upper Silesia* case when deciding on the existence of an indirect expropriation. Therefore, the impact of this judgment on the case law of investment tribunals on indirect expropriation is limited.

The *Oscar Chinn* case[61] concerned a British national, Oscar Chinn who established a shipping business on the Congo River in Belgian Congo in 1929. Chinn's main competitor was a company controlled by the Belgian State, Unatra. In the economic crisis in the 1930s the Belgian government ordered State controlled businesses to significantly reduce the carriage charges and promised to reimburse the State controlled companies for losses so sustained. This measure severely interfered with the competition in the shipping business on the river. Oscar Chinn had to wind up his business before the reimbursement offer was extended to Unatra's competitors. The British government exercised diplomatic protection on his behalf. At the centre of the case was the interpretation of a free trade and equal treatment clauses in the Convention of Saint-Germain-en-Laye.[62] However, the British government had also argued that the Belgian measure deprived Mr Chinn indirectly 'of any prospect of carrying on his business profitably' and that this 'constituted a breach of general principles of international law, and in particular of respect for vested rights.'[63]

The PCIJ dealt with this issue only very briefly. It dismissed the argument stating that favourable business conditions and good will are subject to inevitable changes and that no vested rights had been violated by Belgium:

---

[59] Ibid [20.22] emphasis in original (footnotes suppressed). Referencing *Certain German Interests in Polish Upper Silesia* (n 1).

[60] Ibid [20.26], [20.27], [20.32].

[61] *Oscar Chinn* (n 1).

[62] Ibid 79.

[63] Ibid 87.

> No enterprise… can escape from the chances and hazards resulting from general economic conditions. Some industries may be able to make large profits during a period of general prosperity, or else by taking advantages of a treaty of commerce or of an alteration in customs duties; but they are also exposed to the danger of ruin or extinction if circumstances change. Where this is the case, no vested rights are violated by the State.[64]

Only the tribunal in *LG&E* v *Argentina*[65] explicitly relied on the *Oscar Chinn* case to dismiss the existence of an indirect expropriation. *LG&E* v *Argentina* arose from the attractive framework of laws and regulations for foreign investors in the field of gas transportation that the Argentinean government had created to entice foreign investors. These guarantees were subsequently revoked by the Argentinian government.

After quoting the *Oscar Chinn* case the *LG&E* Tribunal concluded that Argentina had adopted severe measures that had an impact on the Claimant's investment. Nevertheless, it found that these measures did not deprive the investor of the right to enjoy the investment. The Tribunal justified this result with the fact that the investors did not lose control over their shares and licenses even though the value of the shares may have fluctuated and the day-to-day operations may have been affected by the Argentinian measures:

> 197. As was stated in the *Oscar Chinn* affair of 1934, adopted by the Permanent Court of International Justice:
>
> "No enterprise… can escape from the chances and hazards resulting from general economic conditions. Some industries may be able to make large profits during a period of general prosperity, or else by taking advantages of a treaty of commerce or of an alteration in customs duties; but they are also exposed to the danger of ruin or extinction if circumstances change. Where this is the case, no vested rights are violated by the State."
>
> 3. Tribunal's Conclusion
>
> 198. In the circumstances of this case, although the State adopted severe measures that had a certain impact on Claimants' investment, especially regarding the earnings that the Claimants expected, such measures did not deprive the investors of the right to enjoy their investment. As in *Pope & Talbot*, the true interests at stake here are the investment's asset base, the value of which has rebounded since the economic crisis of December 2001 and 2002.
>
> 199. Further, it cannot be said that Claimants lost control over their shares in the licensees, even though the value of the shares may have fluctuated

---

64 Ibid 88.

65 *LG&E* v *Argentina* (Decision on Liability, 3 October 2006) ICSID Case No ARB/02/1.

> during the economic crisis, or that they were unable to direct the day-to-day operations of the licensees in a manner different than before the measures were implemented.
>
> 200. Thus, the effect of the Argentine State's actions has not been permanent on the value of the Claimants' shares', and Claimants' investment has not ceased to exist. Without a permanent, severe deprivation of LG&E's rights with regard to its investment, or almost complete deprivation of the value of LG&E's investment, the Tribunal concludes that these circumstances do not constitute expropriation.[66]

Apart from this case only respondents in *CME* v *Czech Republic*[67] and *National Grid* v *Argentina*[68] seem to have relied on the *Oscar Chinn* case. The Tribunals in these cases did not discuss the *Oscar Chinn* case in any way. The impact of the case on the case law of investment tribunals is therefore limited.

Therefore, the PCIJ left important traces in investment law as far as the issue of expropriation of contractual rights is concerned. However, its impact in modern investment law on the questions surrounding the issue of indirect expropriation is limited.

IV. The Standard of Reparation for Treaty Violations

The PCIJ issued its famous principle on the question of reparations in *Factory at Chorzów*.[69] This is probably the PCIJ's judgment most frequently referred to in investment arbitration. No fewer than forty-eight decision and awards refer to *Chorzów*. Most of them quote *Chorzów* for its statement on reparations. The case concerned the interpretation of the Convention (Geneva Convention) between Germany and Poland relating to Upper Silesia concluded under the auspices of the League of Nations. Germany claimed that the liquidation of the factory at Chorzów by Poland was a violation of this Convention. The PCIJ found the liquidation of the factory to be an illegal expropriation. In the context of the assessment of the damages due the PCIJ made its famous dictum on reparations that is quoted in many awards of investment tribunals.

Investment treaties typically do not offer any guidance for the reparation due in case of a breach of the investment treaty. They only contain a norm that describes the just compensation due in case of a legal

---

66 Ibid. Referencing *Oscar Chinn* (n 1) at 88.

67 *CME Czech Republic BV* v *Czech Republic* (n 55) [324].

68 *National Grid PLC* v *Argentina* (Award, 3 November 2008) [139].

69 *Case Concerning the Factory at Chorzów* (Indemnity) (Germany v Poland), [1927] PCIJ Ser A No 13 (Judgment) and [1928] PCIJ Ser A No 17 at 47 (Order).

expropriation, which is typically fair market value. Therefore, tribunals dealing with reparation for illegal acts regularly turn to customary international law. They have frequently stated that they 'will resort to the relevant principles of customary international law and in particular to the principle set out by the Permanent Court of Justice in the Chorzów Factory case.'[70] This principle is encapsulated in the following well-known quote: 'reparation must, as far as possible wipe out all the consequences of the illegal act and re-establish the situation which would, in all probability, have existed if that act had not been committed.'[71]

According to the PCIJ, restitution in kind is the preferred remedy for an internationally wrongful act; but where it cannot be achieved, equivalent monetary compensation can be awarded. Two things are remarkable in this context:

First, while paying lip service to *Chorzów*, restitution is not the preferred remedy in international investment arbitration.[72] Some treaties such as NAFTA,[73] DR-CAFTA,[74] the ACIA,[75] the Energy Charter Treaty[76] and a number of BITs and free trade agreements (FTAs)

---

[70] *Saipem SpA* v *Bangladesh* (Award, 30 June 2009) ICSID Case No ARB/05/7 201; see also e.g. *Metalclad* v *Mexico* (Award, 30 August 2000) ICSID Case No ARB(AF)/97/1 [122]; *MTD Equity Sdn Bhd and MTD Chile SA* v *Chile* (Award, 25 May 2004) ICSID Case No ARB/01/7 at 238; *MTD Equity Sdn Bhd and MTD Chile SA* v *Chile* (Decision on Annulment, 21 March 2007) ICSID Case No ARB/01/7 [41]; *Petrobart* v *Kyrgyzstan* (Award, 29 March 2005) [144]; *ADC Affiliate Ltd and ADC & ADMC Management Ltd* v *Hungary* (Final Award on Jurisdiction, Merits and Damages, 2 October 2006) ICSID Case No ARB/03/16 [480], [493]; (n 48) [531]-[353]; *Enron Corporation and Ponderosa Assets* v *Argentina* (Award, 22 May 2007) ICSID Case No ARB/01/3 [359]; *Compañía de Aguas del Aconquija SA and Vivendi Universal SA* v *Argentina* (Award, 20 August 2007) ICSID Case No ARB/97/3 [8.2.4.]; *BG Group* v *Argentina* (Award, 24 December 2007) [423]-[427]; *Biwater Gauff* v *Tanzania* (Award, 24 July 2008) ICSID Case No ARB/05/22 [776]; *LG&E* v *Argentina* (Award, 25 July 2007) ICSID Case No ARB/02/1 [31]; *Sempra* v *Argentina* (Award, 28 September 2007) ICSID ARB/02/16 [400]; *Rumeli Telekom AS and Telsim Mobil Telekomikasyon Hizmetleri AS* v *Kazakhstan* (29 July 2008) ICSID ARB/05/16 [792]; *Duke Energy Electroquil Partners and Electroquil SA* v *Ecuador* (Award, 18 August 2008) ICSID ARB/04/19 at 468; *Waguih Elie George Siag and Clorinda Vecchi* v *The Arab Republic of Egypt* (Award and Dissenting Opinion, 1 June 2009) ICSID ARB/05/15 [545].

[71] *Factory at Chorzów* (n 69) at 47.

[72] S Ripinsky and K Williams, *Damages in International Investment Law* (British Institute of International and Comparative Law, London 2008) 57; I Marboe, *Calculation of Compensation and Damages in International Investment Law* (OUP, Oxford/New York 2009) 28.

[73] North American Free Trade Agreement (17 December 1992) Canada-Mexico-US, 32 ILM. 605 (1993) ("NAFTA").

[74] Dominican Republic-Central America-United States Free Trade Agreement (5 August 2004) Hein's No KAV 7157.

[75] Asean Comprehensive Investment Agreement adopted in Thailand (26 February 2009).

[76] The Energy Charter Treaty (17 December 1994) 2080 UNTS 100, 34 ILM 360.

concluded by the US[77] and Canada[78] contain specific provisions on the available remedies (NAFTA,[79] DR-CAFTA[80] and ACIA[81]). Some allow for monetary damages or restitution leaving the choice to the State.

---

77 See e.g. Chile/US FTA, Article 10.25:

> 1. Where a tribunal makes a final award against a respondent, the tribunal may award, separately or in combination, only:
>
> (a) monetary damages and any applicable interest;
> (b) restitution of property, in which case the award shall provide that the respondent may pay monetary damages and any applicable interest in lieu of restitution.

78 See e.g. US/Peru FTA, Article 10.26:

> 1. Where a tribunal makes a final award against a respondent, the tribunal may award, separately or in combination, only:
>
> (a) monetary damages and any applicable interest; and
> (b) restitution of property, in which case the award shall provide that the respondent may pay monetary damages and any applicable interest in lieu of restitution.

Similarly, Canada/South Africa BIT (Article XIII):

> …
>
> (9) A tribunal may award, separately or in combination, only:
> (a) monetary damages and any applicable interest;
> (b) restitution of property, in which case the award shall provide that the disputing Contracting Party may pay monetary damages and any applicable interest in lieu of restitution.

79 Article 1135 NAFTA (Final Award):

> 1. Where a Tribunal makes a final award against a Party, the Tribunal may award, separately or in combination, only:
>
> (a) monetary damages and any applicable interest;
> (b) restitution of property, in which case the award shall provide that the disputing Party may pay monetary damages and any applicable interest in lieu of restitution.

80 Article 10.26 CAFTA (Awards):

> 1. Where a tribunal makes a final award against a respondent, the tribunal may award, separately or in combination, only:
>
> (a) monetary damages and any applicable interest;
> (b) restitution of property, in which case the award shall provide that the respondent may pay monetary damages and any applicable interest in lieu of restitution.

81 Article 41 ACIA (Awards):

The Energy Charter Treaty[82] apparently is based on the assumption that specific performance can be ordered in an award. In case of a sub-national government or authority the state may pay monetary damages instead of any other remedy granted. Therefore, treaties that do contain rules on the matter all provide the debtor State with a possibility to pay monetary damages instead of restitution. But most BITs do not address the matter. Even in the absence of any rule in investment protection treaties the vast majority of tribunals accede to the investors' request for monetary relief, if appropriate. They typically just award compensation without discussing other forms of reparation. In cases where investors seek only monetary damages it would be *ultra petita* for a Tribunal to order specific performances.

Second, although tribunals have nearly unanimously relied on Chorzów and stated that 'reparation must, as far as possible wipe out all the consequences of the illegal act' this says little about the approach the tribunals have adopted to the calculation of damages. There are considerable inconsistencies in the case law of arbitral tribunals concerning the calculation of the fair market value as well as the proper calculation of damages. Even in the application of the *Chorzów* principle the case law of investment tribunals is inconsistent. A number of tribunals have stated that fair market value is inapplicable as the measure of compensation in case of a violation of a treaty standard. They applied the *Chorzów* principle trying to award the actual loss incurred as a result of the wrongful act.[83] However, other tribunals after referring to *Chorzów* with approval

---

2. Where a Tribunal makes a final award against either of the disputing parties, the tribunal may award, separately or in combination, only:

(a) monetary damages and any applicable interest; and
(b) restitution of property, in which case the award shall provide that the disputing Member State may pay monetary damages and any applicable interest in lieu of restitution.

82 Article 26(8) Energy Charter Treaty (ECT):

(8) The awards of arbitration, which may include an award of interest, shall be final and binding upon the parties to the dispute. An award of arbitration concerning a measure of a sub-national government or authority of the disputing Contracting Party shall provide that the Contracting Party may pay monetary damages in lieu of any other remedy granted. Each Contracting Party shall carry out without delay any such award and shall make provision for the effective enforcement in its Area of such awards.

83 See e.g. n 65 (Award, 25 July 2007) [31], [41] seq.

appear to have simply deployed the standard for legal expropriations also in case of treaty violations. They granted reparation in the amount of the fair market value of the investment in question as the measure of damages both for claims of expropriation and breaches of other treaty standards.[84]

Therefore, although arbitral tribunals unanimously invoked the *Chorzów* principle and some even alluded 'to the vitality of this statement of damages standard under customary interntional law',[85] some did not follow it through to the end.

V. Provisional Measures

A number of cases before the PCIJ concerned the issue of interim or provisional measures.[86] Only in two of these cases did the PCIJ actually grant interim measures.[87] The last of these cases before the PCIJ was the *Electricity Company of Sofia and Bulgaria* case.[88] In this case the Belgian government filed a request for the indication of interim measure concerning legal proceedings before Bulgarian courts against the Electricity Company in July 1938. It withdrew this request under reservation and renewed the request in October 1939. The content of the second request was to order that Bulgaria should suspend the proceedings in the Sofia courts against the Electricity Company aimed at collecting amounts

---

[84] See e.g. *Enron Corporation and Ponderosa Assets* v *Argentina* (n 70) [360]-[363]; *Sempra* v *Argentina* (n 70) [400]-[405]; *Rumeli Telekom AS and Telsim Mobil Telekomikasyon Hizmetleri AS* v *Kazakhstan* (n 70) [793].

[85] *Compañía de Aguas del Aconquija SA and Vivendi Universal SA* v *Argentina* (n 70) [8.2.5.].

[86] *Denunciation of the Treaty of 2 November 1865 Between China and Belgium* (Order of 8 January) [1927] PCIJ Ser A No 8 at 6; *Factory at Chorzów* (n 1) at 7; *Legal Status of South-Eastern Territory of Greenland (Norway v. Denmark)* (Order of 3 August) [1932] PCIJ Ser A/B No 48 at 278; *Prince of Pless Administration (Germany v Poland)* (Order of 11 May) [1933] PCIJ Ser A/B No 54 at 5; *Polish Agrarian Reform and German Minority (Germany v Poland)* (Order of 29 July) [1933] PCIJ Ser A/B No 58 at 5; *Electricity Company of Sofia and Bulgaria (Belgium v Bulgaria)* (Order of 5 December) [1939] PCIJ Ser A/B No 79 at 199.

On these cases see: MO Hudson, *The Permanent Court of International Justice 1920–1942* (The Macmillan Company, New York 1943) 424 et seq; JB Elkind, *Interim Protection: a Functional Approach*, (Nijhoff, The Hague 1981) 88–98; Spiermann (n 15) 380 et seq; HWA Thirlway, 'The Indication of Provisional Measures in the International Court of Justice' in R Bernhardt (ed), *Interim Measures Indicated by International Courts* (Springer, Berlin 1994) 1, 7 et seq.

[87] *Denunciation of the Treaty of 2 November 1865* (n 86) 6; *Electricity Company of Sofia and Bulgaria* (n 86) at 199. See Hudson (n 86) 428–430.

[88] *Electricity Company of Sofia and Bulgaria* (n 86).

allegedly due until the PCIJ had delivered its judgment on the merits. The hearing was scheduled to be held on December 4, 1939. Bulgaria did not appear, on account of the outbreak of the War. The PCIJ held the hearing nonetheless and ordered interim measures of protection. It said:

> Whereas the above quoted provision of the Statute applies the principle universally accepted by international tribunals and likewise laid down in many conventions to which Bulgaria has been a party—to the effect that the parties to a case must abstain from any measure capable of exercising a prejudicial effect in regard to the execution of the decision to be given and, in general, not allow any step of any kind to be taken which might aggravate or extend the dispute;
>
> Whereas, in this case, present conditions and the successive postponements and resulting delays and, finally, the action as demandant above mentioned, justify in the view of the Court the indication of interim measures calculated to prevent, for the duration of the proceedings before the Court, the performance of acts likely to prejudice, for either of the Parties to the case or for the interests concerned, the respective rights which may result from the impending judgment;
>
> ...
>
> The Court, *indicates* as an interim measure, that pending the final judgment of the Court in the suit submitted by the Belgian Application on January 26th, 1938, the State of Bulgaria should ensure that no step of any kind is taken capable of prejudicing the rights claimed by the Belgian Government or of aggravating or extending the dispute submitted to the Court.[89]

The proceedings on the merits never took place due to World War II. What follows from this order is that the parties to the dispute have under certain circumstances a right to the preservation of the status quo. The PCIJ did not spell out the requirements but stated that the respective party has to abstain from any measures which are capable of leading to an aggravation or extension of the dispute.

Article 47 of the ICSID Convention, Rule 39 of the ICSID Arbitration Rules (as amended in 2006) as well as Article 26 of the UNCITRAL Arbitration rules (as amended in 2010) provide for the granting of interim relief in arbitral proceedings.[90] When ordering provisional measures some

---

89 Ibid 199.

90 See e.g. C Schreuer et al (n 2) 757 et seq; R Volterra, 'Provisional Measures (Interim Measures) and Investment Treaty Arbitration Under ICSID and UNCITRAL: Developments and Trends' in AK Bjorklund, IA Laird and S Ripinsky, *Investment Treaty Law, Current Issues III, Remedies in International Investment Law, Emerging Jurisprudence of International Investment Law* (British Institute of International and Comparative Law, London 2009) 17–27.

though by far not all of the investment tribunals dealing with requests for provisional measures have relied on the PCIJ's *Electricity Company of Sofia and Bulgaria* case.

In *City Oriente Ltd* v *Ecuador*[91] the company filed a request for arbitration against Ecuador and Petroecuador pursuant to an ICSID arbitration clause in their Hydrocarbons Production Share Contract. City Oriente claimed that Ecuador's enactment of Law 2006–42 and the demand for payment of the extra revenue not provided for in the Contract were attempts to unilaterally modify the Contract in conflict with express provisions thereof and the *pacta sunt servanda* principle.

In its first request for provisional measures City Oriente asked the Tribunal to order Ecuador to refrain from prosecuting the enforced collection of any amounts disputed in the arbitration and to refrain from initiating a proceeding for an administrative declaration of termination of the concession on account of non-payment of said moneys. The Tribunal made such an order on 16 October 2007 pending a decision on provisional measures and confirmed it on 19 November 2007 after a hearing on provisional measures. But Ecuador did not comply. Therefore, less than a week later (27 November 2007) City Oriente again asked for the adoption of provisional measures since Ecuador had failed to abide by the indicated provisional measures. Ecuador had filed criminal complaints against City Oriente executives on allegations of embezzlement and refusal to pay moneys under Law 2006–42. In February 2008 Ecuador filed a request for revocation of the provisional measures. The Tribunal examined whether the adoption of interim measures had been necessary to preserve petitioner's rights, whether their ordering had been urgent, and whether each party had been afforded an opportunity to raise observations. It said:

> 83. Consequently, the Tribunal has come to the conclusion that City Oriente's request for provisional measures must be granted, as it meets the requirements laid down in the Convention and the Centre's Arbitration Rules: the measures are necessary to preserve Claimant's rights, their passing is urgent and they are recommended once each party has been afforded sufficient opportunity to raise observations.

Thereafter it pointed to case law supporting its decision. It found that the *Electricity Company of Sofia and Bulgaria* case referred to by the claimant was pertinent because of the similarity of the facts:

---

[91] *City Oriente Ltd* v *Ecuador* (Decision on Revocation of Provisional Measures, 13 May 2008) ICSID Case No ARB/06/21.

> 'Claimant has brought up the early decision of the International Court of Justice in *The Electricity Company of Sofia—Belgium v. Bulgaria*. Both the facts and the decision are actually closely connected to the instant case.'[92] The Tribunal rejected the request for revocation of the provisional measures.

The Tribunal in *Perenco Ecuador Ltd* v *Ecuador*[93] also relied on the PCIJ's order in the *Electricity Company of Sofia and Bulgaria* case in its decision on provisional measures. Perenco filed for ICSID arbitration alleging that Ecuador had breached the France-Ecuador BIT by expropriating Perenco's participating interest in an oil tenement in the Amazon region of Ecuador. At the heart of the dispute is the alleged expropriatory effect of Law 42 on Perenco's rights under the Participation Contracts, as a matter of Ecuadorian Law and under the BIT.[94] Ecuador and Petroecuador commenced a coercive process to collect from Perenco approximately $327 million they claimed was due under Law 42. Claimant applied for provisional measures to prevent Petroecuador from conducting an announced auction of seized crude oil.

The Tribunal found that without provisional measures Perenco's business in Ecuador risked being severely targeted or even destroyed.[95] It therefore ordered Ecuador not to enforce Law 42 pending the determination of the case. It said:

> 50. It is pertinent to recall that in any ICSID arbitration one of the parties will be a sovereign State, and where provisional measures are granted against it the effect is necessarily to restrict the freedom of the State to act as it would wish. Interim measures may thus restrain a State from enforcing a law pending final resolution of the dispute on the merits, as in *City Oriente* and *Sergei Paushok v Mongolia*, Order of interim measures (UNCITRAL, 2 September 2008), or from enforcing or seeking a local judgment, as in *Electricity Company of Sofia & Bulgaria* (*Belgium v Bulgaria*), 1939 P.C.I.J. (ser A/B) No 79, 5 December 1939, and *Ceskoslovensko Obchodni Banka AS v The Republic of Slovakia* (ICSID Case No ARB/97/4), Procedural Order No 4, January 11, 1999. While the enactment of a law by a sovereign State, upheld as constitutional in that State, is a matter of importance, it cannot be conclusive or preclude the Tribunal from exercise of its power to grant provisional measures. ....
>
> ...

[92] Ibid (footnotes suppressed). Referencing *Electric Company of Sofia and Bulgaria* (n 86).

[93] *Perenco Ecuador Ltd* v *Ecuador* (Decision on Provisional Measures, 8 May 2009) ICSID Case No ARB/08/6.

[94] Ibid [50].

[95] Ibid [53].

> 54. In the judgment of the Tribunal, the grant of provisional measures in such circumstances is fully sanctioned by a long line of authority, laid down by the Permanent Court of International Justice, the International Court of Justice, ICSID Tribunals and at least one UNCITRAL Tribunal.
>
> 55. In its judgment of 5 December 1939 in the *Electricity Company of Sofia* case cited above, the Permanent Court of International Justice referred to
>
> "the principle universally accepted by international tribunals and likewise laid down in many conventions to which Bulgaria has been a party to the effect that the parties to a case must abstain from any measure capable of exercising a prejudicial effect in regard to the execution of the decision to be given and, in general, not allow any step of any kind to be taken, which might aggravate or extend the dispute".

The facts in *Burlington Resources Oriente Limited* v *Ecuador*[96] are similar to the ones in the *Perenco* case. The Tribunal first dealt with the standards applicable to provisional measures in general. Thereafter it reviewed each such standard: the existence of right, urgency and necessity or the need to avoid harm. In its discussion of the existence of a right to the preservation of the status quo it relied on a number of cases starting with the PCIJ's order in the *Electricity Company of Sofia and Bulgaria case*. It said:

> '62. The existence of the right to the preservation of the *status quo* and the non-aggravation of the dispute is well-established since the case of the *Electricity Company of Sofia and Bulgaria*.'[97]

The Tribunal decided that the seizure of the oil production decided in the national legal proceedings was bound to aggravate the dispute before it and found that the Claimant had 'shown the existence of a right to preservation of the *status quo* and the nonaggravation of the dispute'.[98] After having affirmed the existence of right, urgency, and necessity or the need to avoid harm the tribunal ordered: 'The Parties shall confer and make their best efforts to agree on the opening of an escrow account' fulfilling specific conditions.

Therefore, investment tribunals relied on the PCIJ's finding that the preservation of the status quo and the non-aggravation of a dispute is a right in situations where certain measures of a party would have prejudicial effect in regard to the execution of a future decision on the merits. However, the tribunals could not base themselves on the PCIJ's judgment

---

[96] *Burlington Resources Oriente Limited* v *Ecuador* (Procedural Order No 1 Request for Provisional Measures, 29 June 2009) ICSID Case No ARB/08/5.

[97] Ibid [62] (footnotes supressed). Referencing *Electricity Company of Sofia and Bulgaria* (n 86) at 199; also, *LaGrand Case* (Judgement) [2001] ICJ Rep 466 [103].

[98] Ibid [65]-[68].

as far as the requirements which have to be fulfilled to justify the adoption of provisional measures are concerned. These where not set out in the PCIJ's Order in the *Electricity Company of Sofia and Bulgaria* case.

VI. Interpretation Proceedings

Article 50 ICSID Convention provides a possibility for the parties to obtain an authoritative interpretation of the award by the Tribunal that rendered the award.[99] The first case where a decision on the interpretation of an award was rendered by an investment tribunal was *Wena Hotels Ltd* v *Egypt*.[100]

In *Wena Hotels Ltd* v *Egypt* the investor had been forcibly deprived by its business partner of the possession of the hotel which constituted the investment. The Egyptian authorities had not given appropriate assistance for its recovery. The tribunal found a violation of Egypt's obligations of 'fair and equitable treatment' as well as 'full protection and security' by virtue of a number of omissions.[101] Furthermore, it held that Egypt's failure to act which led to a deprivation of Wena's contractual rights constituted an expropriation.[102] Three and a half years after the arbitral award had been rendered, Wena made an application for interpretation of the award regarding two issues. First, it asked whether the expropriation was total and permanent and on which date its property was to be considered as expropriated.[103] The second question concerned the issue of whether, as a consequence of the expropriation, Wena was under the burden of further liabilities which existed in its relationship with the Egyptian General Company for Tourism and Hotels, EHC's successor.[104]

In its decision the Tribunal stated that despite the fact that this was the first request of its kind ever received by ICSID it was able to rely not only on the ICSID Convention and the arbitration rules but also on established case law of the PCIJ and of the ICJ.[105]

---

[99] See e.g. C Schreuer et al (n 2) 866 et seq.

[100] *Wena Hotels Ltd* v *Arab Republic of Egypt* (Decision on Interpretation, 31 October 2005) ICSID Case No ARB/98/4; see U Kriebaum, 'Wena v Egypt Case' in R Wolfrum (ed) *Max Planck Encyclopedia of Public International Law* (OUP 2007) online edition <www.mpepil.com>.

[101] *Wena Hotels Ltd* v *Arab Republic of Egypt* (n 47) [95].

[102] Ibid [90].

[103] *Wena Hotels Ltd* v *Arab Republic of Egypt* (n 100) [70].

[104] Ibid [127].

[105] See S Rosenne, *Interpretation, Revision and Other Recourse from International Judgments and Awards* (Martinus Nijhoff, Leiden/Boston 2007) 91 et seq; Hudson (n 86) 590–591.

The PCIJ had received two requests for the interpretation of judgments. One concerned the case concerning the *Interpretation of Paragraph 4 of the Annex following Article 179 of the Treaty of Neuilly*.[106] The second case concerned the *Certain German Interest in Polish Upper Silesia* cases.[107] Germany had asked for an interpretation of Judgments Nos 7 and 8.

The Tribunal in Wena relied on the *Interpretation of Judgments Nos 7 and 8* case. It identified two requirements for the admissibility of an application for interpretation:

1. a dispute between the original parties as to the meaning or scope of the award;
2. the purpose of the application must be to obtain an interpretation of the award.

It found support for this approach in the PCIJ's judgment:

> 77. These conditions concur with the requirements for the admissibility of interpretation proceedings established by the PCIJ in the *Chorzów Factory Case*. In this decision, the PCIJ relied on Article 60 of its Statute, which reads as follows:
>
> "The judgment is final and without appeal. In the event of dispute as to the meaning or scope of the judgment, the Court shall construe it upon the request of any Party."
>
> 78. In its judgment, the PCIJ stated:
>
> "From the article [60] it appears that these conditions are the following:
> (1) there must be a dispute as to the meaning and scope of a judgment of the Court;
> (2) the request should have for its object an interpretation of the judgment."[108]

Furthermore the Tribunal stressed that it was not possible to elaborate on questions which were outside the scope of the original award. It declared the first question admissible but dismissed the second, since the original tribunal had not decided on the consequences of the expropriation on the legal relationship between Wena and EHC.[109] Here the Tribunal relied again on the PCIJ which had established that the dispute had to relate to those parts of the judgment which had been decided with binding force:

[106] *Interpretation of Judgment No 3* (*Bulgaria* v *Greece*) [1925] PCIJ Ser A No 4.

[107] *Interpretation of Judgments Nos. 7 and 8* (*Factory at Chorzów*) [1927] PCIJ Ser A No 13.

[108] *Wena Hotels Ltd v Arab Republic of Egypt* (n 100) [77] (footnotes supressed). Referencing *Factory at Chorzów* (n 69) at 10.

[109] *Wena Hotels Ltd* v *Arab Republic of Egypt* (n 100) [133].

> 82. Furthermore, the dispute must relate to the meaning or scope of what has been decided with binding force, thus in principle to the award's operative section, a condition well adhered to by international practice and confirmed by opinions of scholars, as will be shown below. Thus, in the *Chorzów Factory Case*, the PCIJ stated that the request must relate to the operative part:
>
> "In order that a difference of opinion should become the subject of a request for interpretation under Article 60 of the Statute, there must therefore exist a difference of opinion between the Parties as to those points in the judgment in question which have been decided with binding force."
>
> The Court further explained:
>
> "A difference of opinion as to whether a particular point has or has not been decided with binding force also constitutes a case which comes within the terms of the provision in question, [...]."
>
> ...
>
> 105. In the *Chorzów Factory Case*, the PCIJ stated that interpretation must be understood as meaning to give a precise definition of the meaning or scope which the Court intended to give to the judgment in question. It added:
>
> "The interpretation adds nothing to the decision, which has acquired the force of res judicata and can only have binding force within the limits of what was decided in the judgment construed."[110]

Therefore, it limited its interpretation to the clarification of points which had been settled with binding force in the award, without deciding new points which go beyond the limits of the award. Regarding the first set of questions, the interpretation the tribunal inferred from the reasoning of the original tribunal and the amount of damages granted was that the expropriation had indeed been total and permanent.

This case is an example of a PCIJ judgment which shaped the approach of an investment tribunal confronted with similar questions as the PCIJ. The Tribunal applied the test established by the PCIJ regarding the scope and limits of interpretations of its judgments.

VII. Summary and Conclusion

The PCIJ's legacy in investment law is undeniable. It has left important traces in the jurisprudence of arbitral tribunals as far as fundamental

---

[110] Ibid (footnotes supressed). Referencing *Factory at Chorzów* (Indemnity) (n 69) at 11, 12, 21.

principles are concerned. This is true for matters of jurisdiction as well as substance. An example can be found in the PCIJ's dictum in the *Factory at Chorzów* case on the reparation due in case of a breach of a treaty. It is frequently quoted by investment tribunals; some of them however, did not follow through on the dictum but rather only paid lip service to *Chorzów*.

The PCIJ's definition of the term 'dispute' in the *Mavrommatis Palestine Concessions* case has also become widely accepted in the case law of investment tribunals. The same is true for the PCIJ's finding that contractual rights are protected against expropriation without compensation which is today uncontroversial in investment arbitration.

The PCIJ's approach with regard to the exercise of jurisdiction *ratione temporis* has been followed to a large extent. However it has not gone unquestioned and remains controversial. In cases where a dispute has arisen before a Treaty containing the instrument of consent entered into force, the approach of the PCIJ to exercise jurisdiction if the Treaty does not explicitly exclude pre-Treaty disputes and is not limited to breaches of Treaty standards, is to be preferred. However, it has not been followed unanimously by investment tribunals.

When deciding upon provisional measures a number of tribunals relied on the PCIJ jurisprudence concerning the fundamental principle that in certain situations there is a right to non-aggravation of the dispute and preservation of the status quo. However, the precise requirements which have to be fulfilled to justify the adoption of provisional measures have to be looked for elsewhere.

An even more limited number of investment tribunals have found guidance on how to determine the scope of consent to their jurisdiction in the case law of the PCIJ.

Regarding the phenomenon of indirect expropriations investment tribunals only occasionally refer to the PCIJ's judgments.

With regard to the issue of interpretation proceedings the PCIJ's approach was followed by the tribunal in *Wena*. The tribunal applied the test established by the PCIJ regarding the scope and limits of interpretation of its judgments.

In short, in many important respects the PCIJ has laid valuable foundations upon which investment tribunals build today. However, help with the tricky details which arise when implementing these great lines often has to be found elsewhere. Especially when it comes to issues of jurisdiction, the text of the relevant treaty is of paramount importance. Jurisdictional clauses differ considerably in detail even if at first sight investment treaties appear similar.

THE HERITAGE OF THE PERMANENT COURT OF INTERNATIONAL JUSTICE IN WTO JURISPRUDENCE

Joanna Gomula

I. Introductory Remarks

The World Trade Organization (WTO) was established over 70 years after the Permanent Court of International Justice (PCIJ), as a framework for a multilateral trade regime that replaced a limited and imperfect arrangement under the General Agreement on Tariffs and Trade of 1947 (GATT 1947). According to the Preamble to the WTO Agreement,[1] the relations of WTO Members 'should be conducted with a view to raising standards of living, ensuring full employment and a large and steadily growing volume of real income and effective demand, and expanding the production of and trade in goods and services, while allowing for the optimal use of the world's resources'. The purpose of the WTO, as set forth by its Preamble, is 'to develop an integrated, more viable and durable multilateral trading system', as compared to that of the GATT 1947, which should be directed 'to the substantial reduction of tariffs and other barriers to trade and to the elimination of discriminatory treatment in international trade relations'.

GATT/WTO law, as it stands today, covers a relatively narrow field of international relations: trade in goods, trade in services and certain aspects of intellectual property rights. The suggestion that the heritage of the PCIJ may have influenced a branch of international law where principles of public international law seem to play a relatively minor role could seem perplexing. Considering that WTO rules are predominantly technical and economic in nature and that they do not regulate issues that were traditionally in the realm of public international law, one may wonder, as many did at the time of the WTO's creation, whether public international law has any role *at all* to play in this legal regime.[2] Surprisingly, jurisprudence

[1] Marrakesh Agreement Establishing the World Trade Organization, signed on 15 April 1994 and entered into force on 1 January 1995 (the WTO Agreement).

[2] On the relationship between the WTO and public international law see, e.g., J Pauwelyn, *Conflict of Norms in Public in International Law* (CUP, Cambridge 2009) and JH Jackson, *Sovereignty, the WTO, and Changing Fundamentals of International Law* (CUP, Cambridge 2009).

to date has shown that this scepticism is unfounded. Although not in an overwhelming manner, but certainly to a substantial degree, the principles and institutions of public international law have become visible in the jurisprudence of the WTO.

In this respect, it is necessary to stress the effects of a seemingly modest provision, Article 3.2 of the WTO Dispute Settlement Understanding (DSU), which has proved to be a forceful tool in enhancing the principles developed by the PCIJ and International Court of Justice (ICJ). Placed among other provisions setting forth the general principles of WTO's dispute settlement procedures, Article 3.2 states expressly that the dispute settlement system is 'a central element in providing security and predictability to the multilateral trading system' and that it 'serves to preserve the rights and obligations of Members under the [WTO] agreements, and to clarify the existing provisions of those agreements in accordance with customary rules of interpretation of public international law'.

The Appellate Body,[3] the principal judicial organ of the WTO,[4] has relied on Article 3.2 not only in introducing the Vienna Convention on the Law of Treaties (VCTL) as the basis for interpretation of WTO rules,[5] but also—in a more subtle manner—in defining the relationship between GATT/WTO law and public international law. This was particularly important in the first years after the establishment of the WTO, which were the 'formative years' for the WTO legal system. Owing to the quality of the Appellate Body in those years, solid foundations were set for the application of public international law in the WTO legal system. Already in its first report, issued and adopted in 1996, the Appellate Body pointed out, rather cautiously, that the content of Article 3.2 'reflects a measure of recognition that the General Agreement [on Tariffs and Trade] is not to be

[3] WTO disputes are reviewed, in the first instance, by panels, consisting of three or five members and established on an *ad hoc* basis to review particular disputes. The Appellate Body is a standing organ, composed of seven persons, appointed for four-year terms, which hears appeals from rulings of panels. The findings of panels and the Appellate Body are set out in reports, which are adopted through 'reverse consensus': a report is adopted unless the WTO Dispute Settlement Body (an organ composed of all Members) decides by consensus *not* to adopt the report.

[4] Under Article 17.6 of the DSU the Appellate Body is vested with the power to review issues of law covered in panel reports and legal interpretations developed by panels. The Appellate Body does not have authority to decide factual questions.

[5] On treaty interpretation by WTO disputes settlement bodies in general see, e.g., I Van Damme, *Treaty Interpretation by the WTO Appellate Body* (OUP, Oxford 2009) and AD Mitchell, *Legal Principles in WTO Disputes*, (CUP, Cambridge 2008). For more on the PCIJ's legacy in treaty law S Wittich (in this volume).

read in clinical isolation from public international law'.[6] In subsequent reports, this statement was extended to WTO law in general. As a result, the new multilateral trade regime was opened to the application of principles of public international law derived from other jurisdictions.

The number of WTO dispute settlement decisions is impressive. Since 1996 until the end of February 2012 the number of adopted reports reached 272: 169 panel reports (142 standard reports and 27 compliance reports) and 103 Appellate Body reports (85 and 18, respectively).[7] PCIJ Judgments and Advisory Opinions were quoted or just 'noted' by panels or the Appellate Body in fewer than 10% of these reports. Although this percentage may seem insignificant, given the nature of the regime, the PCIJ has appeared in WTO jurisprudence relatively frequently.[8] Moreover, in an overwhelming number of cases WTO disputes settlement bodies have relied on principles developed or confirmed by the ICJ and PCIJ, without quoting the source of these principles.

II. The PCIJ in WTO Jurisprudence—General Observations

The scope of matters in which the PCIJ has been relied on is very broad, ranging from treaty interpretation to more specific, trade-related issues, such as attribution in the case of the formation of a customs union. The principles developed by the Court have been invoked in numerous anti-dumping disputes, intellectual property disputes, countermeasures, and disputes concerning violations of basic GATT principles.

An overview of WTO decisions where the PCIJ has been quoted merits at least two general observations.

First, the Appellate Body has invoked PCIJ decisions much less frequently than panels: in approximately one third of the respective cases. This may come as a surprise because, as mentioned above, it is the Appellate Body that under Article 17.6 of the DSU is charged with

[6] *United States—Standards for Reformulated and Conventional Gasoline* (WT/DS2), Appellate Body Report and Panel Report adopted on 20 May 1996, DSR 1996:I, 16.

[7] WorldTradeLawnet, <http://www.worldtradelaw.net/dsc/database/basicfigures.asp> (accessed 29 February 2012).

[8] Especially in comparison to GATT 1947 jurisprudence where there seems to have been only one reference to PCIJ jurisprudence, in a party's arguments. The then European Economic Community relied on the *Lotus* case in support of the principle 'that the liberty of subjects of international law was presumed to be unlimited, except by obligations stemming from international norms binding on them', *EC—Imposition of Anti-Dumping Duties on Imports of Cotton Yarn from Brazil* ADP/137, Panel Report adopted on 30 October 1995, para 43.

reviewing issues of law covered in panel reports and legal interpretations of panels. Of course, this does not mean that the Appellate Body is reluctant to apply the principles developed by the PCIJ; to the contrary, it often does so but without referring to the precise source. For example, in *EC—Bananas*,[9] the Appellate Body recalled the principle that when reviewing a claim a tribunal should consider that factual situation under the norm which most specifically addresses it but did not elaborate on this further. It was only the Panel in *US—1916 Act*[10] that later developed the Appellate Body's reasoning, providing references to ICJ and PCIJ decisions and in this manner supplementing the Appellate Body's report.[11]

The reason for the more frequent reliance on ICJ or PCIJ decisions by panels than the Appellate Body may be that panel members prepare their reports in awareness that their legal findings will be subject to scrutiny on appeal. Therefore, they are more inclined to point to judicial and other authority as the source of their conclusions.[12]

Second, with the exception of customary rules of interpretation, the Appellate Body seems reluctant to engage in discussions of whether a general rule of public international law is binding or applicable in the WTO system. For example, when addressing the European Communities'[13] defense in *EC—Hormones*[14] that the Agreement on Sanitary and Phytosanitary Measures (SPS Agreement) should be interpreted in light of the precautionary principle, the Appellate Body refused to take a definite stance on the status of this principle in WTO law. The Appellate Body did not reach this decision lightly. It considered a number of writings, as well as a judgment of the ICJ, ultimately finding that it would be 'unnecessary, and probably imprudent, for the Appellate Body in this appeal to take a

[9] *European Communities—Regime for the Importation, Sale and Distribution of Bananas* (WT/DS27), Appellate Body Report and Panel Report adopted on 25 September 1997, para 204.

[10] *United States – Anti-Dumping Act of 1916* (WT/DS136) (complaint by the European Communities), Appellate Body Report and Panel Report adopted on 26 September 2000; *United States – Anti-Dumping Act of 1916* (WT/DS136) (complaint by Japan), Appellate Body Report and Panel Report adopted on 26 September 2000 (*US – 1916 Act*). In this case two separate reports were issued by a panel of identical composition; the Appellate Body issued a joint report on appeal.

[11] See below, Section III(2).

[12] As has been admitted by some panels, e.g., by the Panel in *EC—Poultry*, see below, Section III(2).

[13] Although since 1 December 2009 the official name for the former European Communities is, for legal reasons, the European Union, this paper will refer to the old name because the disputes in question were initiated prior to that date and have been recorded accordingly.

[14] *European Communities—Measures Concerning Meat and Meat Products (Hormones)* (WT/DS26, 48), Appellate Body Report and Panel Report adopted on 13 February 1998.

position on this important, but abstract, question'.[15] There is a certain paradox in this approach because, as mentioned above, it was the Appellate Body that explicitly confirmed the need for the WTO legal system to be linked to public international law. The paradox may, however, be explained by the limitations placed on panels and the Appellate Body by the DSU: these organs cannot add to or diminish the rights and obligations provided for in the WTO agreements.[16] There would have been little to gain for the WTO legal system, and for the Appellate Body itself, if it were to argue in favour of the binding effect of certain principles of international law, if such principles are controversial.

However, with respect to well-established principles of customary international law, such as those guiding treaty interpretation, the Appellate Body has had no problems in asserting their applicability.

What follows is an overview of selected areas in which panels and the Appellate Body have invoked PCIJ decisions, sometimes even with the effect that PCIJ jurisprudence has been the main source for a legal finding. The overview is divided into two sections. The next section deals with issues that are of a general character, that is, issues not specific to the WTO system; these are issues relating mostly to treaty interpretation. The subsequent section presents three problems that may be described as WTO-specific: attribution in case of the formation of a customs union, standing in WTO disputes, and certain jurisdictional questions.

III. Treaty Interpretation in WTO Jurisprudence

PCIJ dicta have been most frequently invoked as 'subsidiary means for the determination of rules of law' with respect to treaty interpretation. In most cases this has been limited to basic principles of treaty interpretation and formation, and the application of municipal law by panels. A recent panel has raised the principle of sovereignty, as essential, in its opinion, for this interpretation of a general exception provision in the GATT 1994.

1. *Treaty Interpretation and Formation*

The most often quoted decision of the PCIJ in the context of treaty interpretation seems to be the first of the two PCIJ Advisory Opinions

15 Ibid, Appellate Body Report para 123.
16 See Articles 3.2 and 19.2 of the DSU.

regarding the *Competence of the International Labour Organization (ILO)* in agricultural matters.[17] In *Korea—Dairy Safeguards*[18] the Appellate Body discussed the principle of effectiveness in the interpretation of treaties (*ut res magis valeat quam pereat*), which requires tribunals to give meaning and effect to all terms of the treaty. Drawing attention to 'an important corollary of this principle', namely, that the treaty should be interpreted as a whole, the Appellate Body recalled that this had been 'clarified' by the PCIJ in this Advisory Opinion.[19]

In this case, the Appellate Body set out to 'give meaning' to a phrase in Article XIX of GATT 1994 (the 'safeguards clause'),[20] which had not been repeated in the more specific Agreement on Safeguards. The phrase used in Article XIX, allowing the imposition of safeguards measures 'if, as a result of unforeseen developments and of the effect of the obligations incurred by a Member under this Agreement' serious injury had occurred to the domestic industry, had not been listed among the *conditions* for the imposition of a safeguard measure in Article 2.1 of the Agreement on Safeguards. The respondent argued that the omission had been intentional and that therefore the phrase was without meaning. The Appellate Body disagreed. Unable to qualify the phrase as an additional 'condition', it recalled the PCIJ's dictum that 'a treaty must be read as a whole' and concluded that the phrase related to 'circumstances which must be demonstrated as a matter of fact'.[21] It thus opted for the preservation of the integrity of the WTO Agreement, although the result was the *de facto*

---

[17] *Competence of the ILO in Regard to International Regulation of the Conditions of the Labour of Persons Employed in Agriculture* (Advisory Opinion) [1922] PCIJ Ser B No 2.

[18] See *Korea—Definitive Safeguard Measures on Imports of Certain Dairy Products* (WT/DS98), Appellate Body Report and Panel Report adopted on 12 January 2000.

[19] The PCIJ had said: '[I]t is obvious that the Treaty must be read as a whole, and that its meaning is not to be determined merely upon particular phrases which, if detached from the context, may be interpreted in more than one sense'. (n 17) 23. Regrettably, the Appellate Body gave an inaccurate quotation of the Advisory Opinion, appearing to confuse two Advisory Opinions issued by the PCIJ on the same day. See *Korea—Dairy Safeguards* Appellate Body Report, para 81, note 44. The title '*Competence of the ILO to Regulate Agricultural Labour*' had been used by the PCIJ in its 1922 annual report to describe two Advisory Opinions regarding the ILO, which had been issued on the same date. However, although dealing with similar issues the two Advisory Opinions are found in separate documents. See S Wittich (in this volume), at 91–94.

[20] Article XIX of GATT 1994 sets out the general requirements for the imposition of safeguards measures in case of increased imports that cause serious injury to a WTO Member's domestic industry. As is the case with many other WTO agreements relating to trade in goods, the Agreement on Safeguards develops the provisions of the more general GATT Article XIX.

[21] *Korea—Dairy Safeguards* Appellate Body Report, para 85.

imposition of an additional requirement, of rather obscure legal qualification, on Members intending to apply safeguards measures.

In another dispute, *US—Cotton Yarn*,[22] the parties were in disagreement as to whether the Panel, when interpreting the term 'directly competitive products' in the Agreement on Textiles and Clothing, should take into account WTO jurisprudence relating to other WTO rules containing similar terms (in particular, Article III of GATT 1994). When considering the scope of 'context', within the meaning of Article 31.1 of the VCLT, the Panel found the first of the *Competence of the ILO* Advisory Opinions particularly instructive. It emphasized that 'the context is not merely the article or section of the treaty in which the term occurs, but the treaty as a whole'[23] and, consequently, concluded that WTO jurisprudence relating to Article III of GATT 1994 must also be relevant for the interpretation of the terms used in the Agreement on Textiles and Clothing.[24]

Similarly, the Panel in *India—Quantitative Restrictions*[25] invoked the *Competence of the ILO* Advisory Opinion, when determining the meaning of the phrase 'application of measures', as used in footnote 1 of the Understanding on the Balance-of-Payments Provisions of GATT 1994.[26] The Panel also sought guidance in another PCIJ decision, the judgment in *SS Lotus*,[27] this time to justify its refusal to examine the preparatory work and legislative history of footnote 1. The Panel followed the Court's view that 'there is no occasion to have regard to preparatory work if the text of a convention is sufficiently clear in itself'.[28] This is noteworthy because in the period of GATT 1947 panels would frequently have recourse to *travaux préparatoires*, oblivious to the above principle. Generally, in WTO jurisprudence the *Lotus* principle has been consistently applied.

Another problem of treaty interpretation appeared in *US—1916 Act*: what should be the proper order of analysis, if there are several claims of

---

[22] *United States—Transitional Safeguard Measure on Combed Cotton Yarn from Pakistan* (WT/DS192), Appellate Body Report and Panel Report adopted on 5 November 2001.

[23] Ibid, Panel Report para 7.46.

[24] It should be noted that although the Panel included a quote of the relevant passage from the Advisory Opinion in the main part of its report, it relied on an indirect source: the 1966 Yearbook of the International Law Commission. It appears that for some reason, neither the Appellate Body in *Korea—Dairy Safeguards*, nor the Panel in *US—Cotton Yarn*, had verified the original source.

[25] *India—Quantitative Restrictions on Imports of Agricultural, Textile and Industrial Products* (WT/DS90), Appellate Body Report and Panel Report adopted on 22 September 1999.

[26] Ibid, Panel Report para 5.59, note 299.

[27] *The Case of the SS Lotus* [1927] PCIJ Ser A No 10. For details on the *Lotus case* and its reception see generally P Pazartzis (in this volume), 319.

[28] Ibid, 16. See *India—Quantitative Restrictions* Panel Report, para 5.110, note 320.

violations relating to various WTO provisions? The WTO Agreement consists of a multitude of agreements, set out in four annexes to the main Agreement. The Panel in *US—1916 Act* was mostly troubled by the order of examination of claims under two provisions in the GATT 1994: Article III (national treatment) and Article VI (antidumping). These articles were independent of each other and regulated different, unrelated obligations.

The Panel invoked the general principle of international law, as recalled by the Appellate Body in *EC-Bananas*, that 'when applying a body of norms to a given factual situation, one should consider that factual situation under the norm which most specifically addresses it'.[29] On that occasion, the Appellate Body had simply stated the principle, without reference to any sources. The Panel elaborated on this reasoning, quoting, among others, from the PCIJ judgment on *Serbian Loans* that 'the special words, according to elementary principles of interpretation, control the general expressions'.[30] The Panel pointed out that the 1916 Antidumping Act, which it had been called upon to assess, dealt with transnational price discrimination and that in this respect the terms of Article III were 'less specific' than those of Article VI of GATT 1994. Therefore, the Panel opted for an examination of the challenge to the legislation first under Article VI:

> In application of the principle recalled by the Appellate Body in *European Communities—Bananas* and by the Permanent Court of International Justice in the *Serbian Loans* case, there seems to be reasons to reach the preliminary conclusion that we should review the applicability of Article VI to the 1916 Act first, as that article apparently applies to the facts at issue more specifically. This preliminary conclusion is based on our understanding of the arguments of the parties and on a preliminary review of the terms of Articles III:4 and VI.[31]

The Panel found that the 1916 Antidumping Act violated Article VI and therefore exercised judicial economy with respect to the claim under Article III. On appeal, the Appellate Body upheld all of the Panel's conclusions.

Another interesting example is provided by *EC—Hormones*, where the Appellate Body was requested to review the Panel's ruling that the term

[29] *EC—Bananas* Appellate Body Report, para 204.

[30] *Case concerning the Payment of Various Serbian Loans issued in France* (Judgment) [1929] PCIJ Ser A Nos 20/21, 30. The Panel misquoted the word 'expressions', see *US—1916 Act* (Complaint by the European Communities), Panel Report, para 6.76, note 344; and *US—1916 Act* (Complaint by Japan), Panel Report, para 6.75 and note 468.

[31] *US—1916 Act* (Complaint by the EC) ibid, para 6.79; *US—1916 Act* (Complaint by Japan) ibid, para 6.77 (footnote omitted).

'based on (international standards)', as used in Article 3.1 of the SPS Agreement, required sanitary and phytosanitary measures to 'conform to' such international standards. The Appellate Body was highly critical of the Panel's conclusion: 'We cannot lightly assume that sovereign states intended to impose upon themselves the more onerous, rather than less burdensome, obligation by mandating *conformity* or *compliance with* such standards, guidelines and recommendations'.[32] It invoked the principle of *in dubio mitius*, 'widely recognized in international law', explaining that it directed the interpreter to choose, in the case of an ambiguous meaning of a term, the meaning which was less onerous to the party assuming an obligation. On this occasion, the Appellate Body supported its statement by several sources, including the PCIJ's Advisory Opinion on *Access of Polish War Vessels to the Port of Danzig*.[33] Surprisingly, however, the Appellate Body did not invoke the Court's earlier Advisory Opinion on the *Frontier between Turkey and Iraq*,[34] which expressed the principle of *in dubio mitius* in much more explicit terms and which was also quoted in the edition of *Oppenheim's International Law*, to which the Appellate Body had referred in the relevant passage of its report.[35]

The PCIJ has been quoted in support of the principles enshrined in the VCLT also in other contexts. An interesting example is provided by the dispute in *Korea—Government Procurement*,[36] where the United States advanced a non-violation complaint under the Agreement on Government Procurement.[37] The challenge concerned certain bidding requirements and domestic procedures applied by Korea in relation to the construction of an international airport. The United States argued that Korea's

---

32 *EC—Hormones*, Appellate Body Report, para 165 (emphasis in original).

33 The PCIJ had stated: 'The port of Danzig is not Polish territory, and therefore the rights claimed by Poland would be established in derogation of the rights of the Free City. Such rights must therefore be established on a clear basis': see *Access to, or Anchorage in, the Port of Danzig of Polish War Vessels* [1931] PCIJ Ser A/B No 43, 142.

34 The PCIJ described an argument raised by Turkey as follows: 'This argument appears to rest on the following principle: if the wording of a treaty provision is not clear, in choosing between several admissible interpretations, the one which involves the minimum of obligations for the Parties should be adopted. This principle may be admitted to be sound'. However, the Court immediately added that in the case before it the argument was 'valueless' because the disputed provision was 'clear'. *Article 3, Paragraph 2, of the Treaty of Lausanne* (*Frontier between Turkey and Iraq*) [1925] PCIJ Ser B No 12, 25. See also *Port of Danzig* (n 33) 258.

35 See *EC—Hormones*, Appellate Body Report, para 165, note 154.

36 *Korea—Measures Affecting Government Procurement* (WT/DS163), Panel Report adopted on 19 June 2000.

37 Both the cause of action, and the legal basis of the claims, was unusual for WTO dispute settlement. A non-violation complaint may be brought where there has been no

measures, regardless of whether or not they constituted a breach, had nullified or impaired US benefits. Its argument was based on 'error in treaty formation' but, interestingly, such error did not concern concessions obtained through the Agreement on Government Procurement, but related to US expectations formed during *negotiations* of that Agreement.

The starting point in the Panel's analysis was the relationship between WTO law and general principles of customary international law. It remarked that 'to the extent there is no conflict or inconsistency, or an expression in a covered WTO agreement that implies differently, … customary rules of international law apply to the WTO treaties and to the process of treaty formation under the WTO'.[38] With respect to the merits of the argument, the Panel saw no obstacle to extend the concept of non-violation beyond the context of *pacta sunt servanda* and to apply it to negotiations of a treaty; finding justification for this in the good faith obligation to negotiate.[39] The Panel noted that the concept of 'error in treaty formation' was 'a concept that has developed in customary international law through the case law of the Permanent International Court of Justice and of the International Court of Justice'.[40] Of these, it found particular use in the PCIJ judgment in *Legal Status of Eastern Greenland*[41] (noting also the dissenting opinion of Judge Anzilotti). The Panel explained that '[a]lthough these cases are concerned primarily with the question in which circumstances of error *cannot* be advanced as a reason for invalidating a treaty, it is implicitly accepted that error can be a ground for invalidating (part) of a treaty'.[42]

Ultimately, the Panel found that the United States had not demonstrated error 'successfully', mainly because it had been put on notice of the error but had delayed to act, so the error, even if existing, was no longer 'excusable'. The Panel contrasted the US reaction with that of another

---

breach of WTO rules, but the complaining Member considers that its benefits have been nullified or impaired by the application of a measure. The Agreement on Government Procurement is one of the plurilateral trade agreements, the accession to which is optional.

38 *Korea—Government Procurement*, Panel Report, para 7.96.

39 'Parties have an obligation to negotiate in good faith just as they must implement the treaty in good faith': ibid, para 7.100.

40 Ibid, para 7.123. The Panel noted with respect to Article 48 of the VCLT: 'Since this article has been derived largely from case law of the relevant jurisdiction, the PCIJ and the ICJ, there can be little doubt that it presently represents customary international law and we will apply it to the facts of this case', ibid.

41 *Legal Status of Eastern Greenland* [1933] PCIJ Rep Ser A/B No 53.

42 *Korea—Government Procurement*, Panel Report, para 7.123, note 764 (emphasis in original).

party involved in the negotiations, the European Communities, which had taken steps in respect of Korea's offer. The Panel noted the significance of the actions of a third State in avoiding error, explaining that this had been a circumstance 'already considered important in the case on the *Legal Status of Eastern Greenland*',[43] another PCIJ case appearing in this report.

The principle of good faith—this time not to negotiate, but to comply with a WTO ruling—was at the focus of another dispute, *Canada - Continued Suspension*.[44] In this case (formally, two separate cases brought against the United States and Canada, respectively) the European Communities was seeking the termination of suspension of concessions, which the respondents had for many years maintained against its imports.[45] The European Communities asserted that it had fully implemented the original ruling in *EC—Hormones*. Despite this, Canada and the United States continued to apply the sanctions and refused to initiate implementation proceedings under Article 21.5 of the DSU,[46] which would have determined the extent of the European Communities' compliance with the original ruling.

The European Communities insisted that it should enjoy 'a presumption of good faith compliance', a version of good faith performance of a treaty, as expressed in Article 26 of the VCLT. The argument was rather enthusiastically accepted by the Panel, which acknowledged that the presumption of good faith could 'extend to compliance', and added: 'It is the understanding of the Panel that States benefit in their actions from the principle that a breach of the principle of good faith cannot be presumed and that any State alleging an abuse of right (*abus de droit*) or, more particularly, a breach of the principle of good faith, must prove it'.[47] The Panel invoked the PCIJ judgment in *Upper Silesia*, where the Court had found

[43] Ibid, para 7.125, note 768. In this context, the Panel noted 'the reaction of the US to the Danish request not to make any difficulties in the settlement of the Greenland question compared to the Norwegian reaction', ibid.

[44] *Canada—Continued Suspension in the* EC—Hormones *Dispute* (WT/DS321), Appellate Body Report and Panel Report adopted on 14 November 2008.

[45] Canada and the United States were authorized to suspend concessions following the ruling in *EC—Hormones*, where the Panel and the Appellate Body found that the European Communities had violated the SPS Agreement in maintaining a ban on imports of hormone-treated beef and beef products.

[46] These are proceedings applicable when there is disagreement as to the existence or consistency with a covered agreement of measures taken to comply with the recommendations and rulings of the Dispute Settlement Body.

[47] *Canada—Continued Suspension* Panel Report, para 7.320, note 464. Identically, *United States—Continued Suspension in the* EC—Hormones *Dispute* (WT/DS320), Appellate Body Report and Panel Report adopted on 14 November 2008, Panel Report, para 7.320, note 470.

that the 'misuse' of a sovereign right could not be presumed and that it was 'with the party who states that there has been such misuse to prove his statement'.[48]

The Panel's enthusiasm was not shared on appeal by the Appellate Body, which was mostly concerned with the systemic implications of such interpretation: 'To allow the suspension of concessions to expire as a result of the application of a presumption of good faith with respect to a unilateral declaration of compliance would create an imbalance between the rights and obligations of the complainants and the respondents enshrined in the DSU and would undermine the effectiveness of the dispute settlement mechanism in providing security and predictability'.[49] The Appellate Body underlined that the proper course of action in the circumstances of the case was recourse to implementation proceedings under Article 21.5 of the DSU.

2. *Municipal Law and Its Application*

PCIJ decisions have been invoked frequently in consideration of issues relating to the application of municipal law. An example is *India—Patents* (*US*)[50] one of the earlier WTO disputes under the TRIPS Agreement. Here, the Panel assessed the legal status of India's 'administrative practices' and found that they created a certain degree of legal insecurity, resulting in Indian officials ignoring the mandatory provisions of India's Patent Act and thus violating the TRIPS Agreement. On appeal, India argued that the Panel had erred in the treatment of India's municipal law, which was a fact that had to be established before an international tribunal by the party relying on it.

The Appellate Body took the opportunity to provide a relatively detailed analysis of the role of municipal law in the practice of international tribunals, an issue that certainly merited guidance also for subsequent panels. It emphasized that municipal law could serve not only as evidence of facts

---

[48] In the relevant passage, the PCIJ had stated: 'Germany undoubtedly retained until the actual transfer of sovereignty the right to dispose of her property, and only a misuse of this right could endow an act of alienation with the character of a breach of the Treaty; such misuse cannot be presumed, and it rests with the party who states that there has been such misuse to prove his statement', *Case concerning Certain German Interests in Polish Upper Silesia* [1926] PCIJ Ser A No 7, 30.

[49] *Canada - Continued Suspension*, Appellate Body Report, para 317; *US - Continued Suspension*, Appellate Body Report, para 317.

[50] *India—Patent Protection for Pharmaceutical and Agricultural Chemical Products* (Complaint by US) (WT/DS350), Appellate Body Report and Panel Report adopted on 16 January 1998.

and provide evidence of State practice, but could also constitute evidence of compliance or non-compliance with international obligations. To illustrate the latter point, the Appellate Body quoted the PCIJ in *Certain German Interests in Polish Upper Silesia*, where the PCIJ had elaborated on the relevance of Polish law.[51] Relying on the Court's statement, the Appellate Body defended the Panel's examination of the provisions of India's Patent Act relating to 'administrative instructions' as 'essential to determining whether India has complied with its obligations under Article 70.8(a) [of the TRIPS Agreement]'. It explained further:

> There was simply no way for the Panel to make this determination without engaging in an examination of Indian law. But, as in the case cited above before the Permanent Court of International Justice, in this case, the Panel was not interpreting Indian law "as such"; rather, the Panel was examining Indian law solely for the purpose of determining whether India had met its obligations under the TRIPS Agreement. To say that the Panel should have done otherwise would be to say that only India can assess whether Indian law is consistent with India's obligations under the *WTO Agreement*. This, clearly, cannot be so.[52]

The Appellate Body has confirmed this position in other cases, including in *US—Section 211*,[53] where it explained that an assessment of municipal law by a panel for the purpose of determining whether a Member has complied with its obligations under the WTO Agreement was a 'legal characterization', subject to appellate review.[54] This was duly noted by the Panel in *EC—Poultry*.[55] Having stated that municipal law is to be

---

51 The PCIJ had said (*Certain German Interests* [n 48] 19):

> It might be asked whether a difficulty does not arise from the fact that the Court would have to deal with the Polish law of July 14th, 1920. This, however, does not appear to be the case. From the standpoint of International Law and of the Court which is its organ, municipal laws are merely facts which express the will and constitute the activities of States, in the same manner as do legal decisions and administrative measures. The Court is certainly not called upon to interpret the Polish law as such; but there is nothing to prevent the Court's giving judgment on the question whether or not, in applying that law, Poland is acting in conformity with its obligations towards Germany under the Geneva Convention.

See *India—Patent Protection*, Appellate Body Report, para 66. On the topic of municipal law see generally J d'Aspremont (in this volume), 221 and S Wittich (in this volume), at 91, 116 and 119.

52 *India—Patent Protection*, Appellate Body Report, para 66.

53 *United States—Section 211 Omnibus Appropriations Act of 1998* (WT/DS176), Appellate Body Report and Panel Report adopted on 1 February 2002.

54 Ibid, para 105. The Appellate Body did not refer to the PCIJ.

55 *United States—Certain Measures Affecting Imports of Poultry from China* (WT/DS392), Panel Report adopted on 25 October 2010.

approached as a factual issue and after invoking the judgment in *Certain German Interests in Polish Upper Silesia*, the Panel added: 'The Panel is aware that the Appellate Body has explicitly stated that when a panel examines the municipal law of a WTO Member for purposes of determining whether the Member has complied with its WTO obligations, that determination is a legal characterization by a panel, and is therefore subject to appellate review under Article 17.6 of the DSU'.[56]

The Appellate Body's reasoning in *India—Patents* (*US*) has been invoked by many subsequent panels. In the above-mentioned *US—1916 Act*, where the Panel had to assess the 1916 Antidumping Act against the provisions of the WTO Antidumping Agreement, the Panel considered not only the relevant legislation, but also a number of Judgments passed under the Act by US courts since the 1970s. As the Panel explained, '[a] panel may analyse the operation of the domestic legislation and determine whether the description of the functioning of the law, as made by the respondent, is consistent with the legal structure of that Member. In this way, it will be able to determine whether or not the law as applied is 'in conformity with the obligations of the Member concerned under the WTO Agreement'.[57] The Panel invoked the ICJ in the *ELSI*[58] Judgment and the PCIJ in *Brazilian Loans*,[59] where the Courts had pointed to the necessity of weighing the jurisprudence of the municipal courts in determining a question of municipal law.[60]

Based on the above jurisprudence, the Panel took the stand that neither the text of the DSU, nor Appellate Body practice, prevented it from 'weighing the jurisprudence of municipal courts' if such jurisprudence were 'uncertain or divided'. As the Panel explained, '[t]his would not require us to develop our own independent interpretation of US law, but simply to

[56] Ibid, para 7.104, note 289 and para 7.381, note 614.

[57] *US—1916 Act* (Complaint by Japan), Panel Report, para 6.50.

[58] *Case concerning Elettronica Sicula SpA* (*ELSI*) [1989] ICJ Rep 15.

[59] *Case concerning the Payment in Gold of Brazilian Federal Loans Contracted in France* [1929] PCIJ Ser A No 21.

[60] See *US—1916 Act* (Complaint by Japan), Panel Report, para 6.52, note 456, where the Panel quoted the relevant PCIJ passage:

> It follows that the Court must pay the utmost regard to the decisions of the municipal courts of a country, for it is with the aid of their jurisprudence that it will be enabled to decide what are the rules which, in actual fact, are applied in the country the law of which is recognized as applicable in a given case. … Of course, the Court will endeavour to make appreciation of the jurisprudence of municipal courts. If this is uncertain or divided, it will rest with the Court to select the interpretation which it considers most in conformity with the law ([1929] PCIJ Ser A No 21, at 124).

select among the relevant Judgments the interpretation most in conformity with the US law, as necessary in order to resolve the matter before us'.[61] The Panel added that it would not be engaging in interpreting US law and that its approach was consistent with the reasoning of the PCIJ in *Brazilian Loans*.

The above principles were relied on also by the Panel in *US—Section 301*,[62] which examined the WTO-consistency of another piece of US legislation. Sections 301–310 of the US 1974 Trade Act permitted US authorities to make unilateral declarations as to the denial of US rights under trade agreements; the issue was whether this was contrary to Article 23 of the DSU.[63]

Quoting the Appellate Body's conclusions in *India—Patents (US)*, as well as the *Brazilian Loans* judgment referred to by its predecessor in *US—1916*, the Panel emphasized that its mandate was to examine Sections 301–310 'solely for the purpose of determining whether the US meets its WTO obligations' and that it was not required to interpret US law 'as such'. However, the Panel hastened to add that 'any Member can reasonably expect that considerable deference be given to its views on the meaning of its own law'.[64]

The legacy of the PCIJ became visible in *US—Section 301* also in another context: the legal effects of representations made in the course of the panel proceedings by US officials. The US representatives had assured the Panel that with respect to disputes under the WTO Agreement any decisions under Section 301–304 would be based only on adopted findings of the Dispute Settlement Body; that is, they would not precede final WTO rulings. The Panel, having reviewed international jurisprudence, including the PCIJ Judgment in *Legal Status of Eastern Greenland*,[65] concluded that the US statements 'express the unambiguous and official position of the

---

61 Ibid, para 6.52.

62 *United States—Sections 301–310 of the Trade Act of 1974* (WT/DS152), Panel Report adopted on 27 January 2000.

63 Article 23 of the DSU prohibits Members from making unilateral declarations to the effect that a violation of WTO rules has occurred, without previous recourse to WTO dispute settlement procedures.

64 *US—Section 301*, Panel Report, paras 7.18-7.19.

65 The Panel invoked it as an example of where 'a statement was found to have legal effects even though it was not made publicly but in the course of conversations with the Norwegian Foreign Minister': see *US—Section 301*, Panel Report, para 7.118, note 692. The Panel emphasized, however, that '[a]ttributing international legal significance to unilateral statements made by a State should not be done lightly and should be subject to strict conditions', ibid, para 7.118.

US representing, in a manner that can be relied upon by all Members, an undertaking that the discretion of the USTR has been limited so as to prevent a determination of inconsistency before exhaustion of DSU proceedings'.[66] The US legislation was thus deemed WTO-consistent.

Many other panels have relied on *India—Patents* (*US*) and the relevant decisions of the PCIJ. For example, a panel reviewing the WTO-consistency of a controversial practice of 'zeroing' in antidumping investigations recalled that 'WTO panels and the Appellate Body have applied the principle, articulated by the Permanent Court of International Justice, that municipal laws are facts before international tribunals'.[67] Another panel, which examined Japan's sanitary measures related to the protection of apples from fire blight, invoked the above principles in a determination whether so-called 'operational criteria', used by Japan in implementation of its legislation, constituted a 'fact'.[68] A number of panels have referred to *Certain German Interests* and *Brazilian Loans* when recalling the principle that for the purposes of adjudication national law is to be considered as a fact, or in the context of 'weighing' the jurisprudence of municipal courts.[69]

The list of disputes where the PCIJ's legacy was visible in respect of questions of municipal law would not be complete without a reference to *Argentina—Textiles*.[70] Here, Argentina defended its specific tariff system by arguing that any possible violations of Article II of GATT 1994 could be remedied through the importers' recourse to Argentina's domestic court system. It argued that the courts had to take into account Argentina's constitution, which gave priority to international law over domestic legislation. The Panel was unimpressed by this reasoning. It pointed out that '[t]he inevitable delay and uncertainty in such procedure are

---

[66] See *US—Section 301*, Panel Report, para 7.125.

[67] *United States—Laws, Regulations and Methodology for Calculating Dumping Margins* (*'Zeroing'*), Appellate Body Report and Panel Report adopted on 9 May 2006, Appellate Body Report, para 7.53.

[68] *Japan—Measures Affecting the Importation of Apples. Recourse to Article 21.5 DSU by the United States* (WT/DS45/RW), Panel Report adopted on 20 July 2005, para 8.19, note 162.

[69] *United States—Anti-Dumping Measures on Certain Hot-Rolled Steel Products from Japan* (WT/DS184), Appellate Body Report and Panel Report adopted on 23 August 2001, Panel Report, para 7.143 and note 106; *United States—Anti-Dumping and Countervailing Measures on Steel Plate from India*, Panel Report adopted on 29 July 2002, para 7.90, note 79; *United States—Countervailing Measures Concerning Certain Products from the European Communities* (WT/DS212), Appellate Body Report and Panel Report adopted on 8 January 2003, Panel Report, para 7.124, note 380; *Columbia—Indicative Prices and Restrictions on Ports of Entry*, Panel Report adopted on 20 May 2009, para 7.93, note 79.

[70] *Argentina—Measures Affecting Imports of Footwear, Textiles, Apparel and Other Items*, (WT/DS56), Appellate Body Report and Panel Report adopted on 22 April 1998.

fundamentally at variance with the WTO principles and the aim of GATT/WTO tariff bindings which are to provide predictability and security for international trade'.[71] The Panel invoked the general principles of international law in this respect, seeking guidance in the PCIJ judgment in *Free Zones of Upper Savoy*:[72]

> There is a general rule of international law that a state cannot plead provisions of its own law (or deficiencies in that law) as a defence to a claim against it for an alleged breach of its obligations under international law. Thus, in the *Free Zones of Upper Savoy and the District of Gex*, the Permanent Court of International Justice said: "It is certain that France cannot rely on her own legislation to limit the scope of her international obligations". (1932, PCIJ, Series A/B, case No.46, p.167). A WTO Member cannot offer as a defence to a claim of violation of a WTO agreement, that its internal system provides for a remedy to such violation to certain individuals, either national or foreign, and that no violation of WTO has therefore taken place.[73]

3. *The Principle of State Sovereignty*

Basic principles relating to treaty interpretation and the application of municipal law are a 'natural accompaniment' to the process of clarification of the WTO Agreement, by virtue of its being an international treaty. Thus reliance by panels and the Appellate Body on the VCLT and decisions of the ICJ and even the PCIJ, is not unexpected. By contrast, the invocation of PCIJ jurisprudence in a recent case may have been more unusual. The Court's authority was called upon in the analysis of a principle of international law of a more fundamental and general kind: the principle of state sovereignty; or, more specifically: the principle of state sovereignty over natural resources.

In *China—Raw Materials*[74] China defended certain export restrictions on raw materials as taken for the purpose of conservation of exhaustible natural resources, within the meaning of Article XX(g) of GATT 1994.[75] It was during this interpretative exercise that the Panel found it necessary to consider 'one of the fundamental principles of international law', that of

---

[71] Ibid, Panel Report, para 6.68.

[72] *Case of the Free Zones of Upper Savoy and the District of Gex* (Third Phase) [1932] PCIJ Ser A/B No 46.

[73] *Argentina—Textiles*, Panel Report, note 198.

[74] *China—Measures related to the Exportation of Raw Materials* (WT/DS 394, 395, 398), Appellate Body Report and Panel Report adopted on 22 February 2012.

[75] Article XX(g) allows Members to take measures 'relating to the conservation of exhaustible natural resources if such measures are made effective in conjunction with restrictions on domestic production or consumption'.

state sovereignty, 'denoting the equality of all states in competence and independence over their own territories and encompassing the right to make laws applicable within their own territories without intrusion from other sovereign states'.[76]

The Panel set out on a historical journey, tracing back the principle's origins to several PCIJ decisions. It stated that the principle was 'first established' by the Court in the *SS Wimbledon*[77] and 'further elaborated' in the Advisory Opinion on *Exchange of Greek and Turkish Populations*.[78] However, it was the Advisory Opinion on the *European Danube Commission*[79] that the Panel found 'especially instructive for [its] purposes',[80] in particular, the Court's statement that 'restrictions on the exercise of sovereign rights accepted by treaty by the State concerned cannot be considered as an infringement of sovereignty'.[81]

It is not entirely clear (apart from the fact that some of China's arguments revolved around its 'inherent and sovereign right to regulate trade') why the Panel engaged at such length in a discussion of the principle of sovereignty, to the point of asserting that 'Article XX(g) has been interpreted and applied in a manner that respects WTO Members' sovereign rights over their own resources'.[82] The Panel quoted a multitude of GATT and WTO disputes, in most of which neither Article XX(g), nor the principle of state sovereignty, seems to have been at issue.[83] However, the Panel concluded that the Chinese measures could not be justified by

---

[76] *China—Raw Materials*, Panel Report, para 7.378.

[77] *Case of the SS Wimbledon* [1923] PCIJ Ser A No 1. The Panel quoted part of the passage where the PCIJ had said:

> The Court declines to see in the conclusion of any Treaty by which a State undertakes to perform or refrain from performing a particular act an abandonment of its sovereignty. No doubt any convention creating an obligation of this kind places a restriction upon the exercise of the sovereign rights of the State, in the sense that it requires them to be exercised in a certain way. But the right of entering into international engagements is an attribute of State sovereignty (at 25).

[78] *Exchange of Greek and Turkish Populations* [1925] PCIJ Ser B No 10. The Panel stated that the principle was 'further elaborated' by the Court in that Advisory Opinion; however, the PCIJ's 'elaboration' seems to have been limited to a quote of the *Wimbledon* dictum on the 'right to entering into international engagements'. See *China—Raw Materials*, Panel Report, para 7.379.

[79] *Jurisdiction of the European Commission of the Danube between Galatz and Braila* [1927] PCIJ Ser B No 14.

[80] *China—Raw Materials*, Panel Report, para 7.379.

[81] *Jurisdiction of the European Commission of the Danube* (n 79) 36.

[82] The Appellate Body had never elaborated on the principle of sovereignty in its decisions involving Article XX(g).

[83] *China—Raw Materials*, Panel Report, para 7.381 and note 607.

the environmental exception. Although the Panel's findings, including those on Article XX(g), were appealed, the Appellate Body did not take up the Panel's discussion of the 'principle of sovereignty'.

IV. The PCIJ and Issues Specific to GATT/WTO Law

The PCIJ has left a mark also in resolving problems that could be described as GATT/WTO-specific. What follows is an overview of those.

1. *The Meaning of a Customs Union*

One of the early WTO disputes, *Turkey—Textiles*,[84] concerned quantitative restrictions imposed by Turkey on the importation of textiles from India. Turkey maintained that the measures were taken in implementation of an association agreement between Turkey and the European Communities (the 'Ankara Agreement') and that therefore they should be attributable to the customs union created thereby and not to Turkey.

In resolving this issue, the Panel relied almost exclusively on the PCIJ's Advisory Opinion in *Customs Regime between Germany and Austria*.[85] The Panel explained that 'the assessment whether any customs union (or another legal entity) has a legal personality distinct from that of its constituent countries is to be based on an examination of the treaty forming such customs union and the relevant circumstances'.[86] Accordingly, the Panel scrutinized the Ankara Agreement and focused on its Article 58, which envisaged the existence of 'discrepancies between Community and Turkish legislation'. This, in the Panel's view, was 'a recognition that each party to the customs union may adopt measures, to some extent different, and which may not be fully consistent with one another', providing 'confirmation of the ability of the parties to act independently and that Turkey

84 *Turkey – Restrictions on Imports of Textile and Clothing Products* (WT/DS34), Appellate Body Report and Panel Report adopted on 19 November 1999.

85 *Customs Regime between Germany and Austria* (Protocol of March 19th, 1931) [1931] PCIJ Ser A/B No 41. Paradoxically, this was an Advisory Opinion that in Spiermann's words, had 'significantly damaged the Permanent Court's reputation' and had 'generally been regarded as a misfortune for the Permanent Court': see O Spiermann, *International Legal Argument in the Permanent Court of International Justice. The Rise of the International Judiciary* (CUP, Cambridge 2005) 316 and 320.

86 *Turkey—Textiles*, Panel Report, para 9.40. As the Panel explained, the PCIJ had concluded that 'the wording of the customs union was determinant as to whether a member lost its sovereignty', ibid, note 272.

maintains that sovereign right'.[87] The Panel found 'no indication of a transfer of sovereignty of the member states either to an institution established under the customs union, nor to the EC'. It added: 'In WTO terms, unless a customs union is provided with distinct rights and obligations (and therefore some WTO legal personality, such as the European Communities) each party to the customs union remains accountable for measures it adopts for application on its specific territory'.[88] Therefore, in the Panel's opinion, the challenged measures, even if taken 'in the ambit of a customs union', had been 'implemented, applied and monitored by Turkey, for application in the Turkish territory only', and should therefore be attributed to Turkey.[89]

In its analysis, the Panel took little note of the WTO rules regulating customs unions and free-trade areas: Article XXIV of GATT 1994 and the Understanding on the Interpretation of Article XXIV of GATT 1994. Although the Panel's findings on attribution were not appealed, the Appellate Body was clearly unhappy with the Panel's approach. When analyzing the chapeau of Article XXIV.5 of GATT 1994, which it described as 'the key provision in resolving the issue', the Appellate Body criticized the Panel for referring to this provision 'only in a passing and perfunctory way'.[90] The Appellate Body confirmed that panels were competent to examine the consistency of a customs union with WTO law and should do so before considering a defense—such as Turkey's—based on this provision. There seemed, however, to have been little room in the Appellate Body's approach for the PCIJ's legacy on attribution, as it focused primarily on the consistency of the customs union with WTO requirements.

2. *Standing—No Requirement of Legal Interest*

The issue of 'standing' to initiate a dispute in the WTO is a peculiarity of the WTO dispute settlement system. Article XXIII of GATT 1994 confers on the parties the right to take action whenever they consider that any benefit accruing to them is being nullified or impaired due to a breach of a GATT obligation by another party, the application of any measure not constituting a breach, or the existence of any other situation. Article 3.8 of the DSU contains a rebuttable presumption that an infringement of a

---

87 Ibid.
88 Ibid.
89 Ibid, para 9.44.
90 *Turkey—Textiles*, Appellate Body Report, para 43.

WTO agreement is to be considered *prima facie* as constituting a case of nullification or impairment.[91] The DSU does not impose any further requirements on complainants with respect to the initiation of a dispute. This contrasts with the rules relating to third parties, which have to demonstrate 'a substantial interest in a matter before a panel' in order to participate in the proceedings.

In *EC—Bananas* the 'banana regime' of the European Communities, which favoured imports of these products from certain African, Caribbean and Pacific countries, was challenged by several Members. One of the complainants was the United States, itself not a significant producer of bananas. The European Communities argued that the latter's claims should be rejected because it had not suffered any nullification or impairment, nor did it have any 'legal right or interest' in the dispute.[92] The European Communities insisted that even in the absence of express provisions in the DSU, the United States had still been under an obligation to show legal interest in order to initiate the dispute.[93]

However, the Panel accepted the US claim. It pointed to 'the increased interdependence of the global economy', which had resulted in WTO Members' having 'a greater stake in enforcing WTO rules than in the past'. As a result, even a 'potential interest in trade in goods and services and [a Member's] interest in a determination of rights and obligations under the WTO agreement' were sufficient to pursue a claim in WTO proceedings. The Panel emphasized that this view was 'consistent with decisions of international tribunals',[94] among which it listed the PCIJ's judgment in *SS Wimbledon* (also invoked by the European Communities to support an opposite argument). The Panel pointed out that the Court had found that 'a state could raise a claim with respect to the Kiel Canal even though its fleet did not want to use it, suggesting that a potential interest was sufficient for a legal interest'.[95]

The Appellate Body upheld the Panel's conclusions, also relying strongly on ICJ and PCIJ jurisprudence:

---

[91] As Article 3.8 of the DSU explains: 'This means that there is normally a presumption that a breach of the rules has an adverse impact on other members parties to that covered agreement, and in such cases, it shall be up to the Member against whom the complaint has been brought to rebut the charge'.

[92] It invoked several decisions of the ICJ and PCIJ, including the *Mavrommatis Palestine Concessions Case* [1925] PCIJ Ser A No 2 and the *SS "Wimbledon" Case* [1923] PCIJ Ser A No 1.

[93] See *EC—Bananas* (*US*), Panel Report, para 7.47; Appellate Body Report, para 15.

[94] *EC—Bananas* (*US*), Panel Report, para 7.50.

[95] Ibid, para 7.50, note 34.

> We do not read any of these judgments as establishing a general rule that in all international litigation, a complaining party must have a "legal interest" in order to bring a case. Nor do these judgments deny the need to consider the question of standing under the dispute settlement provisions of any multilateral treaty, by referring to the terms of that treaty.[96]

Accordingly, the Appellate Body justified the right of the United States to bring a claim because its 'potential export interest' could not be excluded and because of the effect the 'banana regime' could have on the US market, in terms of world supplies and world prices of bananas.[97]

The ruling in *EC—Bananas* has opened the door to what are effectively unlimited claims of WTO Members in response to violations of WTO obligations. As a result, it is easier in the WTO to initiate a new dispute as a complaining party than to join an existing dispute as a third party, where the requirement of demonstrating 'substantial interest in the matter' limits—at least formally—the right of a Member to participate in a dispute in that capacity.

3. *WTO-Specific Jurisdictional Issues*

The jurisprudence of the PCIJ has been invoked with respect to a number of jurisdictional problems arising in the context of WTO dispute settlement. An interesting example is provided by two disputes relating to the WTO Anti-Dumping Agreement. In the first, *Guatemala—Cement (I)*,[98] Mexico complained about certain actions of the Guatemalan authorities relating to the initiation and conduct of an antidumping investigation. However, in its panel request Mexico had not identified any of the three antidumping measures listed in Article 17.4 of the Antidumping Agreement, a provision enjoying the status of a 'special or additional rule or procedure' for the purposes of dispute settlement.[99] Despite this the Panel took the view that the matter was properly before it.

The Appellate Body reversed the Panel's conclusion, insisting that Mexico had been obliged to identify one of the three antidumping

---

[96] *EC—Bananas (US)*, Appellate Body Report, para 133.

[97] Ibid, para 136.

[98] *Guatemala—Anti-Dumping Investigation Regarding Portland Cement from Mexico* (WT/DS60), Appellate Body Report and Panel Report adopted on 25 November 1998 (*Guatemala – Portland Cement*).

[99] Article 17.4 provides that an anti-dumping matter may be referred to WTO dispute settlement if one of three anti-dumping measures listed therein have been taken: definitive anti-dumping duties, price undertakings or provisional measures. According to Article 1.2 of the DSU, special or additional rules and procedures prevail over the general rules of the DSU in case of a conflict.

measures in Article 17.4, and that therefore the merits of Mexico's claim had not been properly before the Panel, nor were they properly before the Appellate Body.[100] What remained for the complainant was to initiate new dispute settlement proceedings.

This finding was invoked by the United States, acting as defendant in a subsequent dispute under the Antidumping Agreement, in *US—1916 Act*. Here, the complaint did not concern specific antidumping measures, but US legislation 'as such': the US 1916 Antidumping Act. The United States argued that, in light of *Guatemala—Cement (I)*, for the matter to be properly before the Panel the complainants should have referred in their panel requests to an antidumping measure listed in Article 17.4 of the Antidumping Agreement.

The jurisdictional challenge was brought by the United States only during the interim review stage, that is, after the substantial hearings before the Panel had been completed. An interim report, with the Panel's provisional findings and conclusions, had already been circulated to the parties. The European Communities requested that the US objections be rejected by the Appellate Body, as not having been raised in a timely manner. However, although the Appellate Body agreed that the interim review stage was not an 'appropriate time' to raise jurisdictional objections, it ruled them admissible, as 'the vesting of jurisdiction in a panel is a fundamental prerequisite for lawful panel proceedings'. It emphasized that 'some issues of jurisdiction may be of such nature that they have to be addressed by the Panel at any time'.[101]

In reaching its conclusion, the Appellate Body invoked the 'widely accepted rule that an international tribunal is entitled to consider the issue of its own jurisdiction on its own initiative, and to satisfy itself that it has jurisdiction in any case that comes before it'. Among the sources for this rule the Appellate Body quoted the PCIJ decision in *Prince von Pless*,[102] as well as Manley O. Hudson's book on the PCIJ.[103] It had no doubt that, even in the absence of express provisions in the DSU, panels had broad discretion to decide about the extent of their jurisdiction, at any time.

On substance, both the Panel and the Appellate Body dismissed the US objections, on the basis that GATT and WTO case law 'firmly establishes

---

[100] *Guatemala—Portland Cement*, Appellate Body Report, para 80.
[101] Ibid, para 54; see also *US—1916 Act*, Panel Report, para 5.17.
[102] *Case concerning the Administration of the Prince von Pless* (Preliminary Objection) [1933] PCIJ Ser A/B No 52.
[103] Ibid, at 15; see *US-1916*, Appellate Body Report, para 54, note 30. For more on the matter see CJ Tams (in this volume), 29–37.

that dispute settlement proceedings may be brought based on the alleged inconsistency of a Member's legislation as such with that Member's obligations'.[104]

While in *Guatemala—Portland Cement* Mexico had been interested in asserting the Panel's jurisdiction, it found itself in an opposite position a few years later, as defendant in another dispute, *Mexico—Taxes on Soft Drinks*.[105] The background was a long dispute with the United States, which concerned the extent of US obligations under NAFTA to open its market to Mexico's sugar industry. The United States had been blocking the establishment of a panel under Chapter 20 of NAFTA, preventing the resolution of the matter through the procedures offered by this regional agreement. In 2001 Mexico imposed a series of taxes on the use in soft drinks of sweeteners other than cane sugar (US producers used high-fructose-corn sugar and beet sugar), which constituted an obvious violation of its national treatment obligations under Article III of GATT 1994. Mexico described these restrictions as 'countermeasures', designed to force the United States to honour the latter's commitment under NAFTA.[106]

Mexico requested the Panel to decline to exercise jurisdiction in favour of an arbitral panel under Chapter 20 of NAFTA, arguing that that under the circumstances there was no 'applicability' of its WTO obligations towards the United States. It invoked the *Factory at Chorzów* dictum that 'one party cannot avail himself of the fact that the other has not fulfilled some obligation ... if the former party has ... prevented the latter ... from having recourse to the tribunal which would have been open to him'.[107]

The Panel declined Mexico's request. It did so on the grounds that a WTO panel had no discretion under the DSU whether or not to exercise jurisdiction in a case properly before it. Moreover, as the Panel underlined, neither the subject matter nor the respective positions of the parties were identical as between the respective WTO and NAFTA disputes.

---

104 *US—1916 Act*, Appellate Body Report, para 75.

105 *Mexico—Tax Measures on Soft Drinks and Other Beverages* (WT/DS 308), Appellate Body and Panel Reports adopted on 24 March 2006 (*Mexico—Taxes on Soft Drinks*).

106 In proceedings before the WTO panel, Mexico did not present rebuttal arguments against the US claims relating to Article III, focusing instead on the defence under Article XX of GATT 1994.

107 *Case concerning the Factory at Chorzów* (Jurisdiction) [1927] PCIJ Ser A No 9, 31. As the Appellate Body summarized Mexico's position on appeal: WTO obligations were not applicable 'as a result of the United States having prevented Mexico, by an illegal act (namely, the alleged refusal by the United States to nominate panelists to the NAFTA panel) from having recourse to the NAFTA dispute settlement mechanism to resolve a bilateral dispute between Mexico and the United States regarding trade in sweeteners': *Mexico—Taxes on Soft Drinks*, Appellate Body Report, para 55.

The Appellate Body upheld the Panel's conclusion but with some modifications. Most importantly, it seemed not as determined as the Panel to reject a scenario where a WTO panel could decline to exercise jurisdiction, implying that there were situations in which 'legal impediments' could exist. However, it affirmed that in this case no such legal impediments were present.

As to Mexico's arguments and its reliance on the *Factory at Chorzów* ruling, in the Appellate Body's opinion they were 'misplaced'. Refusing to take a firm stand on whether the *Factory at Chorzów* principle applied in WTO dispute settlement, the Appellate Body assumed '*arguendo*' that it did. It explained that in such case, the acceptance of Mexico's position would require a panel (or the Appellate Body) to determine whether the United States had acted consistently or inconsistently with its NAFTA obligations, for which there was no basis in the DSU:

> Article 3.2 of the DSU states that the WTO dispute settlement system "serves to preserve the rights and obligations of Members under the *covered agreements*, and to clarify the existing provisions of *those agreements*". (emphasis added) Accepting Mexico's interpretation would imply that the WTO dispute settlement system could be used to determine rights and obligations outside the covered agreements. In light of the above, we do not see how the PCIJ's ruling in *Factory at Chorzów* supports Mexico's position in this case.[108]

Given the Appellate Body's conclusions, it is difficult to imagine the circumstances in which the *Factory at Chorzów* principle could find its application in a WTO dispute. The rules of the DSU, characterized by a high degree of specificity with respect to the WTO dispute settlement procedure, place stringent limitations on the powers of WTO dispute settlement organs to consider non-WTO obligations and to take into account other international regimes or international court decisions, in any other context than in support of interpretation of WTO rules.

V. Concluding Remarks

As shown in the preceding overview, there have been numerous references to the PCIJ by panels and (less frequently) by the Appellate Body. But there is no discernible pattern in reliance on PCIJ jurisprudence, to the point of such references sometimes being erratic. Naturally, the quality of a panel's report and its use of international jurisprudence depend on

---

[108] Ibid, Appellate Body Report, para 56.

the panel's composition. If, as in *US—1916 Act*, among its members is an expert in international law,[109] the result can be a well-balanced, thoroughly researched legal argument. In other cases, even if the PCIJ is relied on, a panel's reasoning may be not as convincing.

However, in general, there is no doubt that principles of international law, developed by international tribunals—including the PCIJ—are an important source of WTO law. The PCIJ has influenced many legal findings, in a variety of issues, which may come as a surprise if one takes into account the subject-matter of WTO regulation. Despite the flow of time and the specific nature of the multilateral trade regime, the heritage of the PCIJ is still appreciable in the WTO legal regime.

---

109 One of the Panel's members was an an international lawyer, Professor Eugeniusz Piontek.

PART THREE

THE PCIJ AND OTHER FORA OF DISPUTE RESOLUTION

THE PERMANENT COURT OF INTERNATIONAL JUSTICE, ARBITRATION, AND CLAIMS COMMISSIONS OF THE INTER-WAR PERIOD

Iain Scobbie

I. Introduction

The Permanent Court of International Justice operated in a very different international judicial landscape than that currently facing the International Court of Justice, and yet the early decisions in which it mapped out the contours of the international judicial function remain relevant. The judges of the Permanent Court had to invent the role of an institutionalized international judiciary with little guidance, although it was expected that this should be different from the role of international arbiters. This influenced the Court's approach in various ways in charting its relationship with international arbitral tribunals and claims commissions (and other bodies which were empowered to make binding decisions). Not only did the Permanent Court give advice to specific bodies on the discharge of their functions, but it also took the opportunity to elaborate key aspects of the international judicial or arbitral process. In doing so, two issues were central to its activity—the need to remain loyal to the constraints imposed by its Statute, and the need to maintain the integrity of its judicial character.

II. The Permanent Court as a "Court of Justice", not a "Court of Arbitration"

Article 1 of the original Statute of the Permanent Court of International Justice,[1] annexed to the Protocol of Signature of 16 December 1920, provided:

---

[1] The original Statute, adopted in 1920, was revised by the 1929 Protocol relating to the Revision of the Statute which entered into force on 1 February 1936. The Revision Protocol is reproduced in [1940] 4th edn PCIJ Ser D No 1 at 9, and the revised Statute at 13. All documents of the Permanent Court cited are available on the website of the International Court of Justice—<www.icj-cij.org>.

> A Permanent Court of International Justice is hereby established, in accordance with Article 14 of the Covenant of the League of Nations. This Court shall be in addition to the Court of Arbitration organised by the Conventions of the Hague of 1899 and 1907, and to the special Tribunals of Arbitration to which States are always at liberty to submit their disputes for settlement.[2]

The Advisory Committee of Jurists which drafted the Court's Statute, pursuant to Article 14 of the League of Nations Covenant,[3] was clear that the Permanent Court should be an innovation in then-existing international judicial institutions as it would be a standing judicial body whose function, in part, would be to develop international law, and thus contribute to the replacement of force in international relations with the rule of law.[4] As Bourgeois, the representative of the League Council, stated during the first meeting of the Advisory Committee on 16 June 1920:

> A tribunal whose sentences should guarantee the maintenance of peace has only authority if that peace is founded on public right itself. Peace…is simply the stable existence of right…
>
> The Court of Justice must be a true Permanent Court. It is not simply a question of arbitrators chosen on a particular occasion, in the case of conflict, by the interested parties; it is a small number of judges sitting constantly and receiving a mandate the duration of which will enable the establishment of a real jurisprudence, who will administer justice. This permanence is a symbol. It will be a seat raised in the midst of the nations, where judges are always present, to whom can always be brought the appeal of the weak and to whom protests of the violation of right can be addressed…[5]

---

[2] [1926] 1st edn PCIJ Ser D No 1 at 7: the 1920 Protocol of Signature is reproduced at 5. The French text of Article 1 provided: 'Indépendamment de la Cour d'Arbitrage, organisée par les Conventions de la Haye de 1899 et 1907, et des Tribunaux spéciaux d'arbitres, auxquels les Etats demeurent toujours libres de confier la solution de leurs différents, it est institué, conformément à l'Article 14 du Pacte de la Société des Nations, une Cour permanente de Justice internationale'.

[3] Article 14 of the League Covenant provided: 'The Council shall formulate and submit to the Members of the League for adoption plans for the establishment of a Permanent Court of International Justice. The Court shall be competent to hear and determine any dispute of an international character which the parties thereto submit to it. The Court may also give an advisory opinion upon any dispute or question referred to it by the Council or by the Assembly'.

[4] On late C19th/early C20th expectations of international arbitration and adjudication see, e.g., M Pomerance, *The United States and the World Court as a 'Supreme Court of the Nations': Dreams, Illusions and Disillusion* (Martinus Nijhoff, The Hague 1996) 41–64.

[5] 'Speech delivered by M Léon Bourgeois', in League of Nations, *Procès-verbaux of the Committee* (*June 16th-July 24th 1920*) (1920) 5 at 6–7. This quotation is from the official English translation of the original French text, the first paragraph of which reads, 'Un tribunal dont les sentences doivent garatir le maintien de la paix n'a d'aurorité que si cette paix est fondée sur le droit lui - mêrne. La paix, avons-nous déjà dit, c'est la durée du droit'. The word 'droit', which is also employed in the final clause of the second paragraph

This view was reiterated in the deliberations of the Advisory Committee. Thus, when it discussed the sources of law the Court should apply, Loder commented:

> Rules recognised and respected by the whole world had been mentioned, rules which were, however, not yet of the nature of positive law, but it was precisely the Court's duty to develop law, to "ripen" customs and principles universally recognised, and to crystallise them into positive rules; in a word, to establish an international jurisprudence.[6]

The League Covenant had not envisaged that the Permanent Court of Arbitration should be abolished,[7] and the first draft of the Court's Statute submitted to the Advisory Committee of Jurists proposed that both institutions should function alongside one another, but this raised the question whether a distinction existed between international arbitration and international adjudication, as "The Permanent Court will not be…a Court of arbitration, but a Court of justice".[8]

In a League Secretariat memorandum prepared for the Advisory Committee, it was argued that three characteristics distinguished arbitration from adjudication in broad terms. The parties to a case nominated the arbiters, and they could also decide which substantive norms the tribunal should apply. Further, arbitration was dependent on the consent of the parties. The memorandum noted that the distinction between the two was not hard and fast, but that when all three characteristics were present, then the procedure was arbitral rather than judicial in a strict sense.[9]

('la protestation du droit violé'), could equally be translated as 'law', rather than 'right', which would reinforce the expectation that the Permanent Court should develop a consistent jurisprudence, and thus contribute to international peace. The documents of the Advisory Committee are also available on the ICJ website.

6 *Procès-verbaux* (n 5) 294 (13th meeting, 1 July 1920).

7 This is apparent from the terms of Article 13 of the Covenant, which provided in part:

> The Members of the League agree that whenever any dispute shall arise between them which they recognise to be suitable for submission to arbitration or judicial settlement and which cannot be satisfactorily settled by diplomacy, they will submit the whole subject-matter to arbitration or judicial settlement.
>
> …
>
> For the consideration of any such dispute, the court to which the case is referred shall be the Permanent Court of International Justice, established in accordance with Article 14, or any tribunal agreed on by the parties to the dispute or stipulated in any convention existing between them.

8 Bourgeois, *Speech* (n 5) 8.

9 See 'Note on the Nature of the New Permanent Court of International Justice' in League of Nations, *Documents Presented to the Committee Relating to Existing Plans for the Establishment of a Permanent Court of International Justice* (1920) 112 (French text),

It should be recalled that the initial proposals for the Permanent Court envisaged that its jurisdiction would be compulsory, rather than consensual, but this was rejected by both the Council and Assembly of the League,[10] thus confounding the expectation that:

> the Court would redress the differences of power between the weak and the strong which had just been institutionalised in the League Council. An international court with compulsory jurisdiction would provide them with a forum where they could take their grievances against the strong and where the outcome would not be decided by the number of guns or economic power of a State.[11]

III. The Constructive Task Facing the Permanent Court

Article 1 of the Statute makes it clear that the Permanent Court was to function not merely "in the midst of the nations" but also in the midst of other international tribunals, but neither the Statute nor the League Covenant mentioned, far less regulated, what relationship, if any, should exist between them. Like many matters, this was left to the Permanent Court itself to construct. Thus, for example, in the *Mavrommatis Palestine Concessions case* (*Preliminary Objections*) judgment the Court itself had to determine the procedure to be followed in cases where the respondent challenged its jurisdiction:

> Neither the Statute nor the Rules of Court contain any rule regarding the procedure to be followed in the event of an objection being taken *in limine litis* to the Court's jurisdiction. The Court therefore is at liberty to adopt the principle which it considers best calculated to ensure the administration of justice, most suited to procedure before an international tribunal and most in conformity with the fundamental principles of international law.[12]

---

113 (English text); and BS von Stauffenberg *Statut et Règlement de la Cour Permanente de Justice Internationale: Éléments d'Interprétation* (Carl Heymanns Verlag, Berlin 1934) 12–13.

[10] See CJ Tams (in this volume), at 16–21; and further L Lloyd, *Peace Through Law: Britain and the International Court in the 1920s* (Royal Historical Society/Boydell Press, Woodbridge, Suffolk 1997) 5–15; O Spiermann, 'Historical introduction' in A Zimmermann, C Tomuschat, and K Oellers-Frahm (eds), *The Statute of the International Court of Justice: a Commentary* (OUP, Oxford 2006) 39, 45–48 [11]-[17]; C Tomuschat, *Commentary to Article 36*, ibid 598, 593–595 [2]-[4]; and Stauffenberg, (*n 9*), 242–254.

[11] Lloyd (n 10) 12.

[12] *Mavrommatis Palestine Concessions Case* (Preliminary Objection) [1924] PCIJ Ser A No 2 at 16. See further CJ Tams (in this volume), at 29–31.

This resulted in the famous maxim that "The Court, whose jurisdiction is international, is not bound to attach to matters of form the same degree of importance which they might possess in municipal law. Even, therefore, if the application were premature because the Treaty of Lausanne had not yet been ratified, this circumstance would now be covered by the subsequent deposit of the necessary ratifications".[13]

In essence, and not only in *Mavrommatis*, the Permanent Court had to determine how it would discharge its judicial function, and had to do so more or less from scratch. There was little, if any, guidance as to how an institutionalised international court should work and so, for instance, the Court had to invent how it would discharge its advisory function. Severe misgivings were expressed by Judge Moore that this was incompatible with the judicial function because, formally, Advisory Opinions were not binding. He argued:

> A Court of Justice, whether national or international, is essentially a judicial body, whose function it is to end disputes by deciding them. The maintenance of the character, reputation and usefulness of such a Court is inextricably bound up with the obligatory force and the effective performance of its decisions or judgments.[14]

This echoed the view expressed by his compatriot, Elihu Root, during the proceedings of the Advisory Committee of Jurists.[15] Nevertheless, fairly rapidly, the elements of advisory procedure were laid down in the Rules,[16] and in the *Eastern Carelia* Advisory Opinion the Court publicly affirmed that:

> The Court, being a Court of Justice, cannot, even in giving advisory opinions, depart from the essential rules guiding their activity as a Court.[17]

---

13 *Mavrommatis* (n 12) at 34.

14 'The Question of Advisory Opinions: Memorandum by Mr Moore, February 18th, 1922,' PCIJ Ser D No 2 at 383; see also 'Comment by Mr Moore on the Constitution of the Court for the Election of its President and the Giving of Advisory Opinions,' ibid 509 at 512–513; and M Dunne, *The United States and the World Court, 1920–1935* (Pinter, London 1988) 102–104 and 142–145 (on the memorandum Moore wrote in connection with the 1926 US Senate debates regarding accession to the Court's Statute).

15 Root thought that giving an Advisory Opinion in relation to an existing dispute was 'a violation of all juridical principles'—see *Procès-verbaux* (n 5) 584; and also Dunne (n 14) 37–38.

16 See 1922 Rules 71–74, [1926] 1st edn PCIJ Ser D No 1 at 81; and Ser D No 2 at 159–166 and 219–221. For details see generally M Giles Samson and D Guilfoyle (in this volume), 41.

17 *Status of Eastern Carelia* (Advisory Opinion) [1923] PCIJ Ser B No 5 at 29.

Some theorists, such as Alan Paterson, would describe this process as one of role-negotiation. The basic idea is that a high status actor which has a degree of autonomy can determine how to fulfil the social role conferred upon it.[18] Obviously, the principal way in which the Permanent Court defined its role was through the drafting, amendment, and revision of the Rules of Court, as well by indicating its judicial expectations in its jurisprudence.

On various occasions, the Permanent Court had to construct its role in relation to the operation and awards of other international tribunals, as well as national courts, with very little to guide it apart from vague notions of general principles of procedural law such as *res judicata* or litispendence.[19] In determining its relationship with other international tribunals, however, the Permanent Court did not have to address the problems, particularly concerning the unity and fragmentation of international law,[20] which are perceived to arise from the contemporary proliferation of international tribunals.[21] In 2000, these caused Gilbert Guillaume, then

---

18 See AA Paterson, *The Law Lords* (MacMillan, London 1982), especially at 201–212; and compare L V Prott, *The Latent Power of Culture and the International Judge* (Professional Books, Abingdon 1979) Chapters one and two.

19 See, e.g., *Chorzów Factory Case* (Interpretation Judgment)[1927] PCIJ Ser A No 13 at 20–21, and the dissenting opinion of Judge Anzilotti at 23. This case arose from projected proceedings by Poland before the domestic District Court of Katowice regarding the ownership of the Chorzów factory which Germany claimed had been determined by the Permanent Court in its earlier judgments. Discussion of the relationship between the Permanent Court and domestic courts is beyond the bounds of this chapter; for details see generally J d'Aspremont (in this volume), 221.

20 For an overview of these issues, see Report of the Study Group of the International Law Commission (under the chairmanship of Martti Koskenniemi), *Fragmentation of International Law: Difficulties Arising from the Diversification and Expansion of International Law* (A/CN.4/L.682, 4 April 2006).

21 On the contemporary discussion of proliferation see, e.g., the articles forming the symposium published in (1998–1999) 31 NYU J of Intl L and Politics, namely G Abi-Saab, 'Fragmentation or Unification: Some Concluding Remarks', 919; JI Charney, 'The Impact on the International Legal System of the Proliferation of International Courts and Tribunals', 697; P-M Dupuy, 'The Danger of Fragmentation or Unification of the International Legal System and the International Court of Justice', 791; B Kingsbury, 'Foreword: Is the Proliferation of International Courts and Tribunals a Systemic Problem?', 679; CPR Romano, 'The Proliferation of International Judicial Bodies: the Pieces of the Puzzle', 709; T Treves, 'Conflicts Between the International Tribunal for the Law of the Sea and the International Court of Justice', 809; and also JE Alvarez, 'Three Responses to "Proliferating" Tribunals', (2008–2009) 41 NYU J of Intl L and Politics 991; G Guillaume, 'Advantages and Risks of Proliferation: a Blueprint for Action', (2004) 2 J of Intl Crim Justice 300 and his *The International Judicial Function*, paper delivered at *The Function of Law in the International Community: an Anniversary Symposium* (Lauterpacht Centre for International Law, University of Cambridge 2008) <http://www.lcil.cam.ac.uk/25th_anniversary/book.php>; S Linton and FK Tiba, 'The International Judge in an Age of Multiple International Courts

President of the International Court, to propose to the Sixth Committee of the General Assembly that:

> In order to reduce the risks of conflicting interpretations of international law, should we not encourage other international courts to seek the opinion of the [International Court of Justice] on doubtful or important points of general international law raised in cases before them?[22]

Not all judges of the International Court concur in this solution: for example, Judge Higgins expressly rejected it on the basis that this would be a retrogressive step. She sees the multiplication of specialised tribunals as a consequence of globalisation and the increasing complexity of international legal relations, and to try to position the International Court as a final arbiter at the apex of the international judicial system would simply be to ignore the factors which caused proliferation in the first place.[23]

At a fairly early stage, the Permanent Court indicated its view on one important aspect of its relationship with other international bodies, namely the question of competing jurisdiction.[24] In the *Rights of Minorities in Upper Silesia (Minority Schools) case*, it observed:

> The Court's position, in regard to jurisdiction, cannot be compared to the position of municipal courts, amongst which jurisdiction is apportioned by the State, either *ratione materiae*, or in accordance with a hierarchical system.

---

and Tribunals' (2008–2009) 9 Chinese J of Intl L 407 ; J Paulwelyn and LE Salles, 'Forum Shopping Before International Tribunals: (Real) Concerns, (Im)Possible Solutions' (2009) 42 Cornell Intl L J 77; A Reinisch, 'The Use and Limits of *Res Judicata* and *Lis Pendens* as Procedural Tools to Avoid Conflicting Dispute Settlement Outcomes'(2004) 3 Law and Practice of Intl Courts and Tribunals 37; CPR Romano, 'Can You Hear Me Now? The Case for Extending the International Judicial Network', (2009–2010) 10 Chinese J of Intl L 233; and WT Worster, 'Competition and Comity in the Fragmentation of International Law' (2008–2009) 34 Brooklyn J of Intl L 119.

22 *The Proliferation of International Judicial Bodies: the Outlook for the International Legal Order*, speech by HE Judge Gilbert Guillaume, President of the International Court of Justice, to the Sixth Committee of the General Assembly of the United Nations, (ICJ, 27 October 2000) <http://www.icj-cij.org/court/index.php?pr=85&pt=3&p1=1&p2=3&p3=1>. For an account of the International Court's attitude to international arbitration, including appeals from arbitral awards, see S Rosenne, 'The International Court of Justice and International Arbitration', in S Muller and W Mijs (eds), *The Flame Rekindled: New Hopes for International Arbitration* (Nijhoff, Dordrecht 1994) 99 (and also in (1993) 6 Leiden Journal of International Law 297).

23 R Higgins, 'Respecting Sovereign States and Running a Tight Courtroom'(2001) 50 ICLQ 121, 121–122.

24 For modern commentary on the competing jurisdiction of international tribunals see, e.g., AV Lowe, 'Overlapping Jurisdiction in International Tribunals' (1999) 20 Australian Ybk of Intl L 191; and Y Shany, *The Competing Jurisdictions of International Courts and Tribunals* (OUP, Oxford 2003).

It claimed, on the basis of Article 36.1 of the Statute—"The jurisdiction of the Court comprises all cases which the parties refer to it and all matters specially provided for in treaties and conventions in force"—that there was no dispute that the parties could not refer to it. Further:

> This principle only becomes inoperative in those exceptional cases in which the dispute which States might desire to refer to the Court would fall within the exclusive jurisdiction reserved to some other authority.[25]

While this ruling concerned a claim that the League Council was the body competent to deal with the issue disputed in the case, its terms indicate that it was meant to be of general application, and would apply to international tribunals claimed to possess jurisdiction which competed with that of the Permanent Court.

IV. The Permanent Court and Non-Arbitral Bodies Empowered to Take Binding Decisions

In approaching the question of the Permanent Court's relations with arbitration and claims commissions in the inter-war period, the notion of arbitral and claims commissions should perhaps be construed rather broadly. On several occasions, the Permanent Court became involved with the functioning of commissions and other bodies that were essentially non-judicial in their operation, but which had the power to make binding decisions following representations made by the interested States. This was simply because of the nature of the post-World War One peace settlements, which included provision for the reference of specific situations or disputes to the League Council, which in turn could request an Advisory Opinion from the Permanent Court on the legal issues involved. The Court was thus often placed in the position where it was asked to advise on the operation of, or acted as an appellate tribunal for, these non-judicial bodies, as well as in relation to international arbitration and claims commissions as such.

A clear example of the Permanent Court acting in review of non-judicial decisions is the *Jaworzina* Advisory Opinion. This concerned a border dispute in the Teschen, Orava and Spisz regions between the newly emergent States of Poland and Czechoslovakia. The parties agreed that the

---

[25] *Rights of Minorities in Upper Silesia (Minority Schools) Case* [1928] PCIJ Ser A No 15 at 23.

Principal Allied and Associated Powers, after hearing both, should take the necessary steps for the final settlement of the dispute. The Conference of Ambassadors of the Principal Allied and Associated Powers duly adopted a decision on 28 July 1920, which Poland subsequently claimed left the frontier undelimited in the Spisz (Jaworzina) area. The Court rejected this challenge, ruling:

> The decision taken on July 28th is therefore the fulfilment at once of a resolution of the Principal Allied Powers and of an agreement between the interested parties. It was taken in accordance with a common desire on the part of all concerned to arrive at a final settlement of the dispute between Poland and Czechoslovakia. In this respect it has much in common with arbitration.[26]

Another instance where it is legitimate to take an extended view of what is meant by arbitral or claims commissions is demonstrated by the *Interpretation of Article 3.2 of the Treaty of Lausanne* Advisory Opinion. In this opinion, the Court had to decide on the nature of the decision to be taken by the League Council in executing its function to delimit the frontier between Turkey and Iraq under Article 3.2 of the Treaty of Lausanne.[27] The Council had posed the questions:

1. What is the character of the decision to be taken by the Council in virtue of Article 3, paragraph 2, of the Treaty of Lausanne—is it an arbitral award, a recommendation or a simple mediation?

---

[26] *Question of Jaworzina (Polish-Czechoslovakian frontier)* (Advisory Opinion) [1924] PCIJ Ser B No 8 at 29: see also *Monastery of Saint-Naoum* (Advisory Opinion) [1924] PCIJ Ser B No 9. For commentary on both, see JHW Verzijl, 'The Jurisprudence of the Permanent Court of International Justice from 1922 to May 1926' in his *The Jurisprudence of the World Court: a Case by Case Commentary, Volume I: The Permanent Court of International Justice (1922–1940)* (Sijthoff, Leyden 1965) 1 at 36–39.

[27] Article 3 of the Treaty of Lausanne provided:

> From the Mediterranean to the frontier of Persia, the frontier of Turkey is laid down as follows:
>
> (1)…With Iraq:
>
> The frontier between Turkey and Iraq shall be laid down in friendly arrangement to be concluded between Turkey and Great Britain within nine months.
>
> In the event of no agreement being reached between the two Governments within the time mentioned, the dispute shall be referred to the Council of the League of Nations.
>
> The Turkish and British Governments reciprocally undertake that, pending the decision to be reached on the subject of the frontier, no military or other movement shall take place which might modify in any way the present state of the territories of which the final fate will depend upon that decision.

2. Must the decision be unanimous or may it be taken by a majority?
3. May the representatives of the interested Parties take part in the vote?

As Britain administered Iraq under a Class A Mandate, the States interested in the delimitation were, formally, Turkey and Britain. The Court was very clear that the Council would not, technically, be acting as an arbitral body in determining the frontier but it also ruled that this did not prevent the parties to a dispute from conferring on the Council the competence to give a "definitive and binding decision" even though, under Article 15 of the Covenant,[28] it generally only had the power to make recommendations.[29] This, in turn, had an impact on the method by which the Council should reach its decision. Article 5.1 of the Covenant provided that, in principle, both the League Assembly and Council proceeded on the basis of unanimity.[30] As the Court observed:

> Only if the decisions of the Council have the support of the unanimous consent of the Powers composing it, will they possess the degree of authority which they must have: the very prestige of the League might be imperilled if it were admitted, in the absence of an express provision to that effect, that decisions on important questions could be taken by a majority.[31]

---

28 Article 15 provides in part:

> If there should arise between Members of the League any dispute likely to lead to a rupture, which is not submitted to arbitration or judicial settlement in accordance with Article 13, the Members of the League agree that they will submit the matter to the Council...
>
> The Council shall endeavour to effect a settlement of the dispute, and if such efforts are successful, a statement shall be made public giving such facts and explanations regarding the dispute and the terms of settlement thereof as the Council may deem appropriate.
>
> If the dispute is not thus settled, the Council either unanimously or by a majority vote shall make and publish a report containing a statement of the facts of the dispute and the recommendations which are deemed just and proper in regard thereto.

29 *Interpretation of Article 3.2 of the Treaty of Lausanne* (Advisory Opinion) [1925] PCIJ Ser B No 12 at 26–27.

30 This provides: 'Except where otherwise expressly provided in this Covenant or by the terms of the present Treaty, decisions at any meeting of the Assembly or of the Council shall require the agreement of all the Members of the League represented at the meeting'. The League Covenant formed Part I of the principal post-World War One peace treaties, namely the Treaties of Versailles, Saint-Germain, Neuilly, and Trianon.

31 (n 29) at 29.

If unanimity were required for the adoption of a recommendation, however, the Court held that this was required *a fortiori* when a binding decision was in question. This, however, raised the practical problem that if the parties' representatives on the Council had to concur in the decision, then this would effectively have given them a power of veto—and this would hardly be in conformity with their intention to seek a binding decision under Article 3.2 of the Treaty of Lausanne. The way that the Court avoided this impasse was to rule that Britain and Turkey could vote when the League Council adopted its decision, but their votes would not be counted for the purposes of ascertaining unanimity.[32]

V. The Permanent Court and Other International Tribunals

The principal aspects of the Permanent Court's relationship with bodies which clearly were arbitral tribunals or claims commissions concern its use of arbitral awards in its pronouncements; its regulation of the operation of specific bodies; its rulings on issues which had a general normative importance for international adjudication and arbitration; and its role as an appellate tribunal.

Despite the inclusion in Article 38 of "judicial decisions" as a "subsidiary means for the determination of rules of law", the Permanent Court only made sparse reference to the jurisprudence of other international tribunals. It did so expressly in only two pronouncements. In the recitals preceding its submissions in *The Lotus*, France referred to the *Costa Rica Packet arbitration* as authority for the proposition that the nationality of the victim was a not sufficient ground to over-ride the exclusive jurisdiction of the flag State regarding crimes committed on vessels on the high seas.[33] The Permanent Court expressly distinguished this award on the ground that the vessel concerned was "adrift without flag or crew, and this circumstance certainly influenced, perhaps decisively, the conclusion

---

32 (n 29) at 31–32. For commentary, see Verzijl (n 26) 53–57; and for the reception of this Advisory Opinion by the League Council, see 1926 League of Nations Official Journal 120 (*League of Nations Council, 37th Session, 4th meeting, 8 December 1925*). Dunne argues that this Advisory Opinion determined subsequent US policy to the Permanent Court, although the doctrine of qualified unanimity it espoused had no practical effect on the League's requests for Advisory Opinions: Dunne (n 14) at 105, 113–115, and also Chapter Six. See also PM Brown, 'The Role of Unanimity and the Fifth Reservation to American Adherence to the Permanent Court', (1928) 22 American J of Intl L 599.

33 *The SS Lotus* [1927] PCIJ Ser A No 10 at 7.

arrived at by the arbitrator".[34] Perhaps more significantly, in the *Polish Postal Service in Danzig* Advisory Opinion, the Court endorsed the ruling of the Permanent Court of Arbitration in the *Pious Funds of the Californias* award regarding the use of the reasoning in an award to construct the scope of its *res judicata*.[35]

Occasionally, the Court made vague and general reference to arbitral practice in support of specific propositions. Probably the most well-known example is the Permanent Court's ruling in the *Chorzów Factory* (*Merits*) judgment that:

> The essential principle contained in the actual notion of an illegal act—a principle which seems to be established by international practice and in particular by the decisions of arbitral tribunals—is that reparation must, as far as possible, wipe out all the consequences of the illegal act and re-establish the situation which would, in all probability, have existed if that act had not been committed.[36]

As Lauterpacht comments, the nearest the Permanent Court ever came to identifying which arbitral tribunals it had in mind when making such a general reference was in the *Peter Pázmány University case* when it cited the practice of Mixed Arbitral Tribunals.[37] This is perhaps not surprising, as that case was an appeal from an award of the Hungaro-Czechoslovak Mixed Arbitral Tribunal.

One may wonder why the Permanent Court made such sparing use of the jurisprudence of international arbitral tribunals but, speculatively, this might reflect the clearly drawn distinction between arbitration and adjudication which informed the creation of the Court itself. Arbitration was seen as sporadic and subject to the influence of the litigants in the determination of the grounds of awards while, in contrast, the purpose of the Permanent Court was "to establish an international jurisprudence".[38] Perhaps it was thought that citing arbitral jurisprudence

---

34 Ibid at 26.

35 *Polish Postal Service in Danzig* (Advisory Opinion) [1925] PCIJ Ser B No 11 at 30.

36 *Chorzów Factory Case: Merits Judgment* [1928] PCIJ Ser A No 17 at 47.

37 H Lauterpacht, *The Development of International Law by the International Court* (Stevens, London 1958) 16, see 15–18 for an account of the cases in which the Court referred to the awards of other tribunals. The reference to the jurisprudence of Mixed Arbitral Tribunals occurred in *Appeal from a Judgment of the Hungaro-Czechoslovak Mixed Arbitral Tribunal* (*Peter Pázmány University v The State of Yugoslavia*) [1933] PCIJ Ser A/B No 61 at 243.

38 Loder, *Procès-verbaux* (n 5) 294 (Advisory Committee of Jurists, 13th meeting, 1 July 1920).

might detract from the intended objective authority of the Court's own pronouncements.

The Permanent Court, at times, gave advice to specific arbitral bodies. On the whole these proceedings dealt with the interpretation of the governing instrument of the commission in question—for example, in the *Exchange of Greek and Turkish populations* Advisory Opinion,[39] the Mixed Commission for the Exchange of Greek and Turkish Populations asked for an interpretation of Article 2 of the 1923 Lausanne Convention for the Exchange of Greek and Turkish Populations. This dealt with the meaning of "established" populations, and the opinion was requested so that the Commission had an authoritative interpretation on which it could base its work. The Permanent Court complied with this request, but as was symptomatic of a number of proceedings which dealt with commissions of one form or another, the substantive content of the Court's pronouncement did not have repercussions beyond the specific commission involved in the proceedings. Because the Court was asked to interpret the terms of a given commission's governing instrument, these decisions had a fairly restricted ambit.

On the other hand, some proceedings did have wider normative implications—either for the work of arbitral or claims commissions in general, or in terms of their relation with the Permanent Court. To a great extent, once the Permanent Court of International Justice was established, given the expectation that it should develop international law, it effectively had to forge the elements of international judicial practice and procedure not only for itself, but also in order to give guidance to other international tribunals.

There were at least two opinions of the Permanent Court which had, or have, what might be called a generic effect, namely, which had, or which were intended to have, an impact on the operation of international arbitration tribunals or commissions in general. The rulings in these opinions were not meant to be restricted to the operation of the body in issue in the proceedings. One, already mentioned, remains famous—namely, the Court's rulings on the nature and content of the doctrine of *res judicata* in the *Polish postal service in Danzig* Advisory Opinion. The Court expressly stated that:

> it is quite clear that the functions of the High Commissioner are of a judicial character and are limited to deciding questions submitted by one or other of

---

[39] [1925] PCIJ Ser B No 10. For commentary, see Verzijl (n 26) 36, and his 'Exchange of Greek and Turkish Populations' in *Jurisprudence of the World Court* (n 26) 66.

> the Parties. The High Commissioner, therefore had no authority to decide questions which the Parties had not submitted to him; and his decision should, if possible, be construed as being in conformity with the powers conferred upon him.[40]

There is more to the *Polish Postal Service* Advisory Opinion than a simple parsing of the High Commissioner's ruling on the postal service. It sets out the bones of doctrines central to the judicial or arbitral function—*res judicata, non ultra petita*—but it does so generically, as a matter of general guidance.[41]

An opinion which is less celebrated than *Polish Postal Service*, but which nevertheless delineates a fundamental aspect of a commission's competence is the *Interpretation of the Greco-Turkish Agreement* Advisory Opinion.[42] This also dealt with the operation of the Mixed Commission for the Exchange of Greek and Turkish Populations, and with the interpretation of its governing instruments but, unlike the earlier proceedings in 1925, in the 1928 opinion the Permanent Court enunciated a proposition which was meant to have generic effect. The treaty at the heart of this opinion was the bilateral 1926 Greco-Turkish Athens Agreement which had been adopted to facilitate the application of some provisions of the Treaty of Lausanne concerning the exchange of populations. The Final Protocol of the Athens Agreement provided that, under certain circumstances, questions of principle should be referred to the President of the Greco-Turkish Arbitral Tribunal for decision, and these decisions would be binding. There was disagreement on the conditions for referral. The substance of the Court's decision need not detain us: what is important is the generic ruling it made in reaching its decision—which was an express affirmation of the principle of *compétence de la compétence*. The Court ruled:

> it is clear—having regard amongst other things to the principle that, as a general rule, any body possessing jurisdictional powers has the right in the first place itself to determine the extent of its jurisdiction—that questions affecting the extent of the jurisdiction of the Mixed Commission must be settled by the Commission itself without action by any other body being necessary.[43]

---

[40] (n 35) at 26.

[41] See *Polish Postal Service in Danzig* (Advisory Opinion) [1925] PCIJ Ser B No 11 at 23–31; for commentary, see Verzijl (n 26) 39–41.

[42] [1928] PCIJ Ser B No 16.

[43] (n 42) at 20.

These examples show that the Court was, at least sometimes, aware of the implications its rulings could have for arbitral or claims commissions in general, but there is perhaps a more interesting aspect of the Court's work in relation to commissions in the inter-war period.

A twist to the Permanent Court's field of competence was added in its final decade by virtue of the adoption of the 1930 Paris Agreement II between the States of the Petite Entente and Hungary. The members of the Petite Entente were Czechoslovakia, Romania and Yugoslavia: its aim, roughly, was to prevent the resurgence of Hungary and the restoration of the Hapsburg monarchy. Article X of the Paris Agreement provided:

> Czechoslovakia, Yugoslavia and Romania, of the one part, and Hungary, of the other part, agree to recognise, without any special agreement, a right of appeal to the Permanent Court of International Justice from all judgments on questions of jurisdiction or merits which may be given henceforth by the Mixed Arbitral Tribunals...
>
> The right of appeal may be exercised by written application by either of the two Governments between which the Mixed Arbitral Tribunal is constituted, within three months from the notification to its Agent of the judgment of the said Tribunal.

The Mixed Arbitral Tribunals in question were between Hungary and each of the States of the Petite Entente, and essentially dealt with questions of agrarian reform. Three sets of proceedings arose from Article X: the *Appeals from Certain Judgments of the Hungaro-Czechoslovak Mixed Arbitral Tribunal case*;[44] the *Peter Pázmány University case*;[45] and the *Pajzs, Csáky and Esterházy case*.[46] The substance of the cases need not concern us: while *Peter Pázmány University* and *Pajzs, Csáky and Esterházy* went to merits, *Appeals from Certain Judgments* was discontinued. All these cases, however, came before the Court under its 1931 Rules of Procedure, which contained no provision regulating appeals to the Court from some other tribunal.[47]

There is an obvious problem with providing appellate recourse to the Permanent Court, or for that matter to the International Court, from an award of a mixed arbitral tribunal. The proceedings at first instance before

---

[44] Czechoslovakia v Hungary [1933] PCIJ Ser A/B No 56.

[45] Czechoslovakia v Hungary [1933] PCIJ Ser A No 61.

[46] Hungary v Yugoslavia [1936] PCIJ Ser A/B No 68.

[47] A provision regulating appeals, Rule 67, was first included in the 1936 Rules: for commentary on its adoption, see G Guyomar, *Commentaire du Règlement de la Cour Internationale de Justice Adopté le 14 Avril 1978: Interprétation et Pratique* (Pedone, Paris 1983) 557–559.

the Mixed Arbitral Tribunal in question in these cases were between a State and a non-State entity, but Article 34 of the Permanent Court's Statute provided that "only States or Members of the League of Nations can be Parties in cases before the Court". Consequently, proceedings before the Permanent Court, given the non-identity of the parties involved in the two sets of proceedings, could not therefore have disrupted or revised the *res judicata*[48] of the first-instance decision, and accordingly could not constitute an appeal as such.

This clear inconsistency between the *compromis* which sought to confer appellate jurisdiction on the Court with the terms of its Statute obviously presented a situation in which the Court would have to determine its role. The way it did so, in the *Appeals from certain judgments* and the *Peter Pázmány University* proceedings, was to direct the parties to present preliminary arguments on the question of the Court's competence.[49] Even though the *Appeals from Certain Judgments* proceedings were discontinued after Hungary filed preliminary objections,[50] the parties, Hungary and Czechoslovakia, did submit reasonably detailed arguments on the question of competence,[51] upon which they expanded in *Peter Pázmány University*.[52]

Both States agreed that the proceedings before the Permanent Court could only be international proceedings between States. Hungary, in particular, drew a clear divide between the first instance Mixed Arbitral Tribunal proceedings and the "appeal" before the Permanent Court, arguing that "the interests of the litigating individuals cannot guide the appellant State".[53] It also argued that there was no judicial hierarchy between the Permanent Court and the Mixed Arbitral Tribunal; that it could

48 In his dissenting opinion in the *Chorzów Factory Case* (Interpretation Judgment), Judge Anzilotti referred to 'three traditional elements for identification, *persona, petitum, causa petendi*' as the core content of *res judicata*—[1927] PCIJ Ser A No 13 at 23. On the doctrine of *res judicata* in international judicial or arbitral proceedings see, e.g., B Cheng, *General Principles of Law as Applied by International Courts and Tribunals* (Stevens, London 1953) 336–372; AV Lowe, '*Res Judicata* and the Rule of Law in International Arbitration' (1996) 8 Revue Africaine de Droit Intl et Comparé 38; Reinisch (n 21); and I Scobbie, '*Res Judicata*, Precedent and the International Court: a Preliminary Sketch' (1999) 20 Australian Ybk of Intl L 299.

49 See *Appeals from Certain Judgments* (Pleadings) PCIJ Ser C No 68 at 262; and *Peter Pázmány University* (Pleadings) PCIJ Ser C No 73 at 762.

50 *Appeals from Certain Judgments Case: Order of 12 May 1933* [1933] PCIJ SerA/B No 56.

51 See *Appeals from Certain Judgments* (Pleadings) (n 49) at 209 (Hungary) and at 221 (Czechoslovakia).

52 See *Peter Pázmány University* (Pleadings) (n 49) at 783 (Czechoslovakia) and at 796 and at 805 (Hungary).

53 *Appeals from Certain Judgments* (Pleadings) (n 49) at 213. See also *Peter Pázmány University* (Pleadings) (n 49) at 803–804 and 806–809.

not quash first instance awards; and that "appellate" decisions by the Permanent Court could only have persuasive value—it could not lay down decisions of principle which would decide cases pending or to be brought before the Mixed Arbitral Tribunal.[54] While Czechoslovakia agreed that only States could be parties to proceedings before the Permanent Court, it also claimed that its ruling would be definitive for all concerned, and that its decisions would be determinative for the Mixed Arbitral Tribunal.[55] Indeed, the reason why Czechoslovakia discontinued the *Appeals from Certain Judgments* proceedings was because Hungary filed preliminary objections, the effect of which was to defeat the motive behind the Czech claims. This delayed the proceedings before the Permanent Court, which meant that Czechoslovakia could not obtain in time the decisions on principle it sought for cases then pending before the Mixed Arbitral Tribunal.[56]

Nevertheless, in both *Peter Pázmány University*[57] and *Pajzs, Csáky and Esterházy*,[58] the Permanent Court proceeded to the merits, but the way in which it proceeded hardly amounted to exercising an appellate competence. Indeed, it might be said that the Court evaded the whole issue. In *Peter Pázmány University*, it stated:

> In the present case, the Court considers it unnecessary to go into the various problems connected with the question of the nature of the jurisdiction thus conferred upon it.

It continued that the fact that in the appealed judgment one of the parties was an individual did not prevent that judgment from forming the subject of a dispute between States which they could refer to the Court. The dispute in the instant proceedings was that Czechoslovakia claimed that the Mixed Arbitral Tribunal had wrongly asserted jurisdiction over the claim brought by the University, that in substance it was not well-founded, and thus Czechoslovakia was not bound to make restitution to it. Hungary disputed these assertions, and thus "there is a distinct point at issue between two States".[59]

---

[54] *Appeals from Certain Judgments* (Pleadings) (n 49) at 217–219; and also *Peter Pázmány University* (Pleadings) (n 49) at 800–804.

[55] *Appeals from Certain Judgments* (Pleadings) (n 49) at 223–224; and also *Peter Pázmány University* (Pleadings) (n 49) at 786 and 795–796.

[56] See the 8 April 1933 letter from the Czechoslovakian agent to the Registrar: *Appeals from Certain Judgments* (Pleadings) (n 49) at 278.

[57] For commentary on this case, see Verzijl, 'Administration of International Justice on Appeal' in *Jurisprudence of the World Court* (n 26) 347.

[58] For commentary on this case, see 'A Juridical Epilogue to the Drama of the Hungarian Optants', 438.

[59] *Peter Pázmány University* (n 37) at 221. On non-State actors see further CJ Tams (in this volume), 13–15 and A Tzanakopoulos (in this volume), 344–346.

While it accepted that there was a dispute between the States parties regarding the Mixed Arbitral Tribunal decision, the Court ruled that, under the Paris Agreement, it was only competent to examine "questions of jurisdiction or merits". In particular, this meant that the Court had no power to rule upon the way the Mixed Arbitral Tribunal functioned from a procedural point of view.[60] In both cases that went to merits, the Permanent Court upheld the Mixed Arbitral Tribunal decisions under appeal. It is, accordingly, difficult to draw wider conclusions from these proceedings.

***

The Permanent Court operated for less than 20 years, and its role in relation to arbitral tribunals and commissions was, to a great extent, instrumental—giving guidance to specific bodies on fairly specific issues. On the other hand, it also made important rulings which had a general application to any body exercising judicial or arbitral functions. Central to its general construction of its role was the need to safeguard its judicial nature and to operate in accordance with its Statute. These considerations were key to, for example, its performance in advisory competence as exemplified in as *Eastern Carelia*, but also evident in its attitude to acting as an appellate body. The constraints of the Statute took precedence over rustling up business. It is beyond doubt that the parameters of the international judicial function laid down by the Permanent Court have had a lasting impact on subsequent international courts and tribunals.

60 *Peter Pázmány University* (n 37) at 222.

THE PERMANENT COURT OF INTERNATIONAL JUSTICE AND DOMESTIC COURTS: A VARIATION IN ROLES

Jean d'Aspremont*

We often think of the first half of the 20th century as an epoch of limited institutionalization of the international society. It is true that—without underestimating the importance of the League of Nations in this respect—it was not until the creation of the United Nations (UN) as well as that of a multitude of regional organizations in the aftermath of the Second World War that international relations between States came to be subjected to a high degree of institutionalization.[1] Yet, this finding ought to be qualified as regards the development of adjudicative mechanisms. It is well-known that the first half of the 20th century witnessed the creation of a multitude of adjudicative bodies, whether permanent or not. Whilst the creation of the Permanent Court of International Justice (hereafter PCIJ) came to symbolize the emergence of an international judiciary,[2] other bodies empowered to adjudicate international disputes were plentiful. It suffices here to mention the numerous arbitral tribunals created under the auspices of the Permanent Court of Arbitration,[3] the Central American Court of Justice,[4] the American-Mexican Claims Commission[5]

---

* The author wishes to thank Robin Morris for his helpful comments.

[1] For some critical remarks on the ideological motives behind the early judicialization of the international Legal order, see M Koskenniemi, 'The Ideology of International Adjudication and the 1907 Hague Conference' in Y Daudet (ed), *Topicality of the 1907 Hague Conference, the Second Peace Conference*, (Martinus Nijhoff, Leiden, 2008) 127–152.

[2] See O Spiermann, *International Legal Argument in the Permanent Court of International Justice: The Rise of the International Judiciary* (CUP, Cambridge 2005).

[3] For a rundown of these cases, see MO Hudson, *The Permanent Court of International Justice 1920–1942: A Treatise* (Garland Publishing, New York/London 1972) 12–36. See also the contribution by A Quast Mertsch to this volume (at 243).

[4] See generally MO Hudson, 'The Central American Court of Justice', (1932) 26 AJIL 759–786.

[5] See the General Claims Convention, signed September 8, 1923, in Washington DC by the United States and Mexico. The convention, which took effect on March 1, 1924, was intended to improve relations between the countries by forming a commission to settle claims arising after July 4, 1868, "against one government by nationals of the other for losses or damages suffered by such nationals or their properties" and "for losses or damages originating from acts of officials or others acting for either government and resulting in injustice." Excluded from the jurisdiction of the General Claims Commission were cases

as well as other arbitral tribunals.[6] It is noteworthy that the PCIJ even acted on appeal of the decisions of some of them.[7] Whatever the state of the judicialization of the international society at that time, it is important to note that these international adjudicatory bodies—with the PCIJ at their centre—blanketed existing domestic courts and tribunals which were growingly called upon to apply international law. Indeed, by the turn of the century, international law gradually ceased to exclusively govern inter-State relations and grew more to regulate internal matters and issues affecting individuals.[8] Besides those rules regulating inter-State relations already requiring domestic implementation, new rules expressly necessitating domestic measures also came into existence. As a result, international law started to trickle down in domestic legal systems, thereby elevating domestic judges to a new class of international law judges. By virtue of other international adjudicatory bodies or the role of domestic courts, the PCIJ was thus far from being entrusted with any sort of monopoly on the application of international law. It is accordingly fair to say that the PCIJ operated in a multi-judiciary world made up of domestic and international judicial bodies equally dealing with questions of international law.

It is against that backdrop that this paper examines some of the dynamics of the multi-judiciary world of the first half of the 20th century. It particularly zeroes in on the interactions of the PCIJ with other judicial bodies, in particular domestic judges. The first section offers a brief overview of the PCIJ's claim that it is a court of the international legal order and its use of the case law of other international adjudicatory bodies (I).

---

stemming from events related to revolutions or disturbed conditions in Mexico. (The Special Claims Commission was formed to address claims arising from events which occurred between November 20, 1910, and May 31, 1920). For more information, see <http://www.lib.utexas.edu/taro/utlac/00024/lac-00024.html>.

6 See the contribution of I Scobbie to this volume (at 203).

7 See *Appeal from a Judgment of the Hungaro/Czecoslovak Mixed Arbitral Tribunal* (*The Peter Pázmány University v The State of Czechoslovakia*) [1933] PCIJ Ser A/B No 61 at 221.

8 According to Provost and Conforti, "The truly legal function of international law essentially is found in the internal legal system of States". See C Provost and B Conforti, *International Law and the Role of Domestic Legal Systems* (Martinus Nijhoff, Dordrecht 1993) 8; JHH Weiler, 'The Geology of International Law: Governance, Democracy and Legitimacy', (2004) 64 ZaöRV 547, 559; See also A von Bogdandy, 'Globalization and Europe: How to Square Democracy, Globalization and International Law' (2004) 15 EJIL 885, 889; M Kumm, 'The Legitimacy of International Law: A Constitutionalist Framework of Analysis' (2004) 15 EJIL 917, 917. See contra Arangio-Ruiz, 'Le domaine reservé. L'organisation internationale et le rapport entre le droit international et le droit interne'. Cours général de droit international public' (1990-VI) 225 Receuil des cours 29, especially at 435–479.

The second section examines in further detail the relationship between the PCIJ and domestic courts, contrasting it with the Court's self-proclaimed international character (II). It will in particular be shown that, while, on the surface, the Court stopped short of engaging with domestic courts, paying lip-service to their case law, the PCIJ was inclined to freely interpret domestic law and actually operate as a municipal court itself. Finally, a few concluding and critical remarks are formulated, drawing on some analogies with the current dynamics in the practice of the International Court of Justice (hereafter the ICJ) (III).

I. The PCIJ and Other International Adjudicatory Bodies

The PCIJ, as is well-know, was not the judicial organ of any international organization with universal membership and had limited institutional kinship with any institutional subject of the international legal order, in contrast to the current World Court.[9] Yet, as a treaty-based court primarily entrusted with the application of international law,[10] the PCIJ did not balk, in the case on *Certain German Interests in Polish Upper Silesia*, to elevate itself into an "organ of international law".[11] In the *Brazilian Loans* case, the Court similarly deemed it to be a "tribunal of international law".[12] It is also worthy of attention that, in the *Mavrommatis Palestine Concessions* case, the Court claimed that its "jurisdiction is international".[13] The contention made in the case on *Certain German Interests in Polish Upper Silesia* was meant to underpin its—equally famous—claim that "municipal laws are merely facts which express the will and constitute the activities of States, in the same manner as do legal decisions or administrative measures".[14] In the *Brazilian Loans* case, the reference to the international nature of the Court was intended to express a restrictive understanding of

---

[9] See e.g. Articles 13 (peaceful settlement of disputes) and 14 (project for the establishment of a Court) of the Covenant of the League of Nations. See also Articles 4–14 (elections of judges), 18 (dismissal of judges), 26 (labour cases), 32 (salaries), 33 (expenses of the Court), 34–35 (contentious cases), 37 (jurisdiction for treaty referring to a tribunal institutionalized by the League of Nations), 40 (notification of new cases), 65–67 (Advisory Opinions) of the Statute of the Permanent Court of International Justice.

[10] Cf section II(4) below.

[11] *Upper Silesia Case*, [1926] PCIJ Ser A No 7 at 19. This was also recalled by D Anzilotti (Individual Opinion) *Consistency of Certain Danzig Legislative Decrees with the Constitution of the Free City* [1935] PCIJ Ser A/B No 65 at 63.

[12] *Brazilian Loans* [1929] PCIJ Ser A No 21 at 124.

[13] *The Mavrommatis Palestine Concessions, Greece vs. Britain* [1924] PCIJ Ser A No 2 at 34.

[14] *Upper Silesia Case* (n 11) 19.

the famous adage *jura novit curia*[15] and to indicate that the Court was only supposed to know international law and was conversely not supposed to know the domestic statutes which could be applicable in a case brought before it.[16] In both cases, and albeit that it subsequently came to qualify such positions,[17] the PCIJ thus elevated itself to a court of international law to define its relationship with domestic law. In the *Mavrommatis Palestine Concessions* case, the international character of its jurisdiction was affirmed with a view to claim that it was not bound to attach to matters of form the same degree of importance which they might possess in municipal law, a contention which is still considered nowadays an authoritative statement in support of the more limited role of formalism in international judicial proceedings.[18]

It is not entirely clear whether the understanding of municipal law as a fact and whether the restrictive interpretation of *jura novit curia* in the finding that the Court is a "tribunal" or an "organ" of international law—a finding that can itself be contested—was most appropriate and strictly necessary. The same can be said of the affirmation of the international character of its jurisdiction. Indeed, in making such contentions, the PCIJ may have not realized that being a "tribunal" or an "organ" of international law carries negative implications as to the possibility to eschew the ascertainment of domestic law and its demotion to pure facts. For instance, the argument can be made that being a tribunal or an organ of international law simultaneously entails positive duties as well, especially the duty to pay heed to parallel judicial development within the international legal order. In other words, being a tribunal or an organ of international law does not provide such a body with the ability to function in total isolation from domestic law and may carry the duty to take into account other international judicial bodies.[19] If this is true, the Court may not have strictly

15 J Verhoeven, 'Jura Novit Curia et le juge international' in P-M Dupuy et al (eds), *Common Values in International Law. Essays in Honour of Christian Tomuschat* (Engel Verlag, Kehl 2006) 635.

16 This was also recalled by Anzilotti in his individual opinion (n 11) 61.

17 Cf section II(4) below.

18 (n 13) 34.

19 Interestingly, the same argument as been made in the context of the controversies regarding the decision of the Court of First Instance of the European Union in the *Yusuf and Kadi* cases (2005) where the CFI took the position of a Court of International Law. See Case T-306/01, *Yusuf and Al Barakaat International Foundation v Council and Commission* [2005] ECR II-3533; Case T-315/01, *Kadi v Council and Commission*[2005] ECR II-3649. See the decision by the ECJ in Joint Cases C-402/05 P and C-415/05 P, *Yassin Abdullah Kadi and Al Barakaat International Foundation v Council and Commission*, 3 September 2008, available at <http://curia.europa.eu>. See generally J d'Aspremont and Fr Dopagne, 'Two

lived up to all the implications of the aforementioned—controversial—contention as to its status as an organ or tribunal of international law. In fact, the attention it devoted to the work of other international judicial bodies has been rather symbolic and the few references found to their case law have rarely been conclusive in its decisions. It suffices here to mention the Advisory Opinion on the *Delimitation of the Polish-Czechoslovakian Frontier* (*Question of Jaworzina*) where it cited the *Meerauge* case decided by an Arbitral Tribunal,[20] the *Lotus* case where it referred to the *Costa Rica Packet* case decided by an Arbitral Tribunal,[21] the *Chorzów Factory* case where a vague reference to the jurisprudence of arbitral tribunals was made,[22] the *Polish Postal Service* Advisory Opinion, in which the award of the PCA tribunal in the *Pious Fund* case[23] was referred to and the *Eastern Greenland* case where it made reference to the *Palmas Island* case.[24] Given the, already significant, activity of other international tribunals in the first decades of the 20th century,[25] the few references listed above can look rather meager. In that sense, it may not be an exaggeration to say that the practice of the PCIJ manifested a tendency to deliberately ignore the work of other international tribunals.[26] It is true that, information about international case law was not as readily available as it is today. However, most of these decisions were the object of publication. Moreover, it would be false to claim that the PCIJ lacked the ability to be aware of such decisions.[27] All necessary material means to access international judicial practice were put at its disposal. Access to information is thus not a credible explanation for the scant attention paid by the PCIJ to decisions of other international judicial bodies. The reason must thus be found elsewhere. One could probably venture some considerations as to the need of the PCIJ to affirm itself as the keystone of the—emerging—international judiciary and not look overly dependent on the findings of other courts and judicial bodies. It can reasonably be posited that such

---

Constitutionalisms in Europe: Pursuing an Articulation of the European and International Legal Orders', (2008) 68 ZaöRV 939. See also the remarks of J Allain, 'The European Court of Justice as an International Court' (1999) 68 Nordic J of Intl L 249.

20 [1923] PCIJ Ser B No 8 at 42–3.

21 [1927] PCIJ Ser A No 10 at 26.

22 [1928] PCIJ Ser A No 17 at 57.

23 [1925] PCIJ Ser B No 11 at 30.

24 [1933] PCIJ Ser A/B No 53 at 45.

25 See the account made by Hudson (n 3) 12–70.

26 For more on the relationship between the PCIJ and other international bodies, specifically the Permanent Court of Arbitration (PCA), see the contribution of A Quast to this volume.

27 See Hudson (n 3).

self-proclaimed independence must have been deemed instrumental in the consolidation of its overall authority. Yet, short of any precise knowledge of the deliberations of the Court,[28] such considerations are bound to remain purely speculative. Be that as it may, whatever the motives, the impression remains that even if the PCIJ were to consider itself of a supreme nature in comparison to these other non-permanent bodies—which it probably did—its disregard for the decisions of other judicial bodies was disproportionate for an "organ of international law".

In the same vein, it is not entirely clear if the Court fully observed its self-proclaimed status as an "organ of international law" when it devised principles for the interpretation of international law. Indeed, it could be defended that, being a Court of an international character, it ought not to systematically favour the most restrictive interpretation of legal rules which preserves the leeway of those bound by them.[29] In that sense, the restrictive interpretation principle espoused and developed by the PCIJ over the years—as illustrated by the *Treaty of Lausanne of 1925* Advisory Opinion,[30] the *Wimbledon* case,[31] the *Right of access to the Danzig Harbour* Advisory Opinion,[32] the *Free Zones of Upper Savoy and the District of Gex* case,[33] and the *Interpretation of the Statute of Memel* case[34]—may not have been fully consistent with the claim that the Court is a organ of the international law.

There probably are other aspects of the case law of the PCIJ which could be reconciled with the—somewhat brazen and audacious—affirmation that it is an organ of international law. I ought not to dwell upon them all here, as it would by far exceed the ambit of this chapter. Only its implications for the Court's relationship with domestic courts should draw attention. This is the object of the following paragraphs.

II. The PCIJ and Domestic Courts

As stated in the introduction above, the PCIJ was not only surrounded by other international judicial bodies. It also had to share the arena with

[28] See however the illuminating research carried out by Spiermann (n 2).

[29] On this principle see generally L Crema, 'Disappearance and New Sightings of Restrictive Interpretation(s)' (2010) 21 EJIL 681–700.

[30] *Interpretation of Article 3, Paragraph 2, of the Treaty of Lausanne,* (Advisory Opinion) [1925] PCIJ Ser B No 12, 7 at 25.

[31] [1923] PCIJ Ser A No 1 at 24.

[32] (Advisory Opinion) [1931] PCIJ Ser A/B No. 43 at 142.

[33] [1932] PCIJ Ser A No 22 at 166.

[34] [1932] PCIJ Ser A/B No 49, 294 at 313–314.

domestic courts. The relationship between the PCIJ and domestic courts was multifold and manifested itself in very diverging forms. In the following sections, mention is first made of the significant number of judges serving on the bench who had previously held positions in the domestic judiciary. In that sense it is shown how the PCIJ developed an organic link with domestic courts (II.1). It is also noteworthy that in a few cases, interpretations of international law by domestic courts came to be referred to by the PCIJ, without such references being necessarily conducive to the final decision of the Court (II.2). The applicable law prescribed by the Statute, and in particular the elevation of the general principles of law to a source of applicable law, also brought the PCIJ, at least theoretically, to heed domestic judicial practices and a few considerations are provided (II.3). Eventually, it is noted that, in a few cases, the PCIJ backed away from its traditional conception of domestic law as a mere fact[35] and turned itself into a domestic court directly interpreting and applying domestic law, thereby taking all the trappings of a domestic court (II.4).

The following section sheds some light on a paradox. Indeed, the PCIJ, despite considering itself an organ of international law which could have theoretically overlooked judicial developments in domestic legal orders, did engage with domestic courts. In the last section of this chapter, such relationships will be confronted with the attitude of the current World Court in its relationship with other international and domestic courts.

1. *An Organic Relationship: Domestic Judges on the Bench of the PCIJ*

The most natural link between the Court and domestic judiciary was an organic one in that a significant number of judges—including deputy judges—either originated in or had a stint at the domestic judiciary—including prosecutor offices—before joining the Court.[36] It suffices here to mention judges Wang Ch'ung-hui,[37] Charles Evans Hughes,[38] Frank Billings Kellogg,[39] Epitácio da Silva Pessoa,[40] Bernard Loder,[41] Didrik

---

35 See section II(4) below.

36 Some biographical elements can be found in J B Moore, 'The Organization of the Permanent Court of International Justice' (1922) 22 Colombia LRev 497, esp 502–504. See also Spiermann (n 2) chapters 5–7.

37 He was Chief Justice of the Chinese Supreme Court in 1920.

38 He was Associate Justice of the Supreme Court of the United States. After his stint at the PCIJ he became Chief Justice of the United States.

39 He was a prosecutor in the US Justice Department.

40 He was Justice of the Supreme Federal Tribunal of Brazil.

41 He belonged to the High Council of the Netherlands (Hoogeraad).

Nyholm,[42] Michailo Yovanovitch,[43] and M Beichmann.[44] The institution of *ad hoc* judges, although the judge may not necessarily be of the nationality of the State appointing him or her, also allowed the participation of domestic judges.[45]

Since there is no record of the deliberations,[46] it is difficult to evaluate the manner in which the professional background of these members of the bench impacted on the substance of its decisions. Yet, according to some analysts, such a compositional feature was instrumental in the variations in the Court's general way of reasoning.[47] This chapter certainly is not the place to further investigate this—mostly sociological—question. The foregoing only meant to show that the PCIJ—probably more than the current World Court[48]—was organically linked with domestic courts.

2. *A Hermeneutic Relationship: The Use of Domestic Courts' Interpretations of International Law*

In his famous opinion appended to the decision in the *Lotus case*, Judge Moore expressed the self-evident absence of *res iudicata* in international adjudication when it comes to decisions of domestic courts on questions of international law. He contended that:

> [The] directions (provided by Article 38) merely conforms to the well-settled rule that international tribunals whether permanent or temporary are not to treat the judgments of the courts of one State on questions of

42 He was a judge on the Mixed Courts in Egypt.

43 He was President of the Court of Cassation of Serbia.

44 He was President of the Court of Appeals of Trondhjem in Norway.

45 Hudson (n 3). 359, 365. See also S Rosenne, *The Law and Practice of the International Court, 1920–1996, Volume III, Procedure* (Martinus Nijhoff, The Hague 1997) 1135 [III.267]. See also MG Samson and D Guilfoyle (in present volume p17) who discuss the role of *ad hoc* judges in Advisory Opinions.

46 An importance source of information is however the written account by Paul de Vineuil, the pseudonym used by Ake Hammarskjöld, the Registar of the Permanent Court of Justice. See e.g. P de Vineuil, 'The Permanent Court of International Justice and the Geneva "Peace Protocol"' (1925) 17 Rivista di diritto internazionale 145–168 or P de Vineuil, 'Les leçons du quatrième avis consultative de la Cour permanente de Justice internationale' (1923) 4 Collected Courses 291; P de Vineuil, 'Les Résultats de la troisième session de la Cour Permanente de Justice internationale' (1923) 4 Collected Courses (1923) 573. On the value of such an account, see Spiermann (n 2) 157 et seq. That however did not prevent Hammarskjöld from publishing articles on the PCIJ under his real name.

47 See Spiermann (n 2) who discusses the biographies of some of the judges and the possible implications of judges' backgrounds throughout chapters 5, 6, and 7.

48 The biographies of the current members of the ICJ are available at <http://www.icj-cij.org/court/index.php?p1=1&p2=2&p3=1>.

> international law as binding on other States, but, while giving to such judgments the weights due to judicial expression of the view taken in the particular country, are to follow them as authority only so far as they may be found in harmony with international law.[49]

While Judge Moore's affirmation remains unchallenged and continues to be of the utmost relevance today, it is noteworthy that the PCIJ still occasionally made use of the decisions of domestic judges. In several cases, the PCIJ referred to the decisions of domestic courts. Indeed, references to domestic courts were made in the *Chorzów* Case,[50] *Lotus* case,[51] the *Opinion on the Competence of the ILO Personal to Regulate Incidentally the Personal Work of Employer*,[52] the *Panevezys-Saldutiskis Railway* case,[53] *Serbian Loans*,[54] and *Brazilian Loans*.[55] However, such references did not prove to be of much significance and often boiled down to pure lip-service to domestic judicial decisions.

For the reasons mentioned above[56] it is close to impossible to gauge whether the (limited) extent of the use of domestic courts' interpretation of international law was in one way or another influenced by the (limited) presence on the bench of judges having had a stint in the judiciary of their country. However, the practice of the PCIJ clearly demonstrates its averseness to rely on domestic judicial interpretations of international law in a decisive manner, a practice that is not much different from that of the present World Court.[57] That said, it is interesting for the sake of the argument made here, that domestic case law, regardless of its non-decisive role, was present in the reasoning of the PCIJ, thereby further accentuating the relationship between the Court and its domestic counterparts.

3. *A Statutory Relationship: General Principles in the Case-Law of the PCIJ*

As is well evidenced by the the *travaux préparatoires* of Article 38 of the Statute of the PCIJ, general principles of law, as originally designed by Baron Descamps to prevent *non liquet*, were informed natural law

49 (n 21) 74.
50 [1927] PCIJ Series A, No. 9, p. 31.
51 (n 21) 28–30.
52 [1926] PCIJ Ser B No 13 at 20.
53 [1939] PCIJ Ser A/B No 76 at 19–21.
54 [1929] PCIJ Ser A No 20 at 47.
55 (n 12) 124–125.
56 Cf section II(1) above.
57 Cf section II(3) below.

principles.[58] That naturalistic understanding of general principles eventually gave ground to a compromise with the positivist position defended by Elihu Root.[59] As a result of that compromise, general principles were meant to be construed as a convergence of domestic legal traditions—although the difficulty of collecting representative data for domestic traditions theoretically made a return to the substantive law-ascertainment criteria almost inevitable.[60] There is little dispute that the reference to general principles in Article 38 of the Statute comes close to enshrining a clause empowering the PCIJ with law-making responsibility, for the Court is expressly allowed to unearth convergences in national law which no doubts leaves it with a extremely wide margin of appreciation.[61] Particularly interesting for the argument made here is the fact that domestic traditions, whose convergence is accordingly to be ascertained by the

---

58 See *Permanent Court of International Justice, Advisory Committee of Jurists, Procès-Verbaux of the Proceedings of the Committee, 16 June-24 July 1920*, (The Hague 1920) 322–325. On this debate see M Bos, *A Methodology of International Law*, (TMC Asser Instituut, Amsterdam/New York/Oxford 1984) 68–75. A Pellet, 'Article 38' in A Zimmermann, C. Tomuschat, K. Oellers-Frahm and CJ Tams (eds), *The Statute of the International Court of Justice* (2nd edn., OUP, Oxford/New York 2012) 832–834. See also the separate opinion of Judge Cançado Trindade in the case pertaining to the *Pulp Mills* (*Argentina v. Uruguay*) before the International Court of Justice, [2010] ICJ Rep 3–6. On the Procès-verbaux, see generally, J Kammerhofer, 'Introduction', in *Permanent Court of International Justice, Advisory Committee of Jurists, Procès-verbaux of the proceedings of the Committee June 16th-July 24th 1920* with Annexes (1920) (Reprint 2006).

59 *Procès-Verbaux* (n 58), 322–325.

60 In the same vein, see M Koskenniemi, 'The Pull of the Mainstream' (1990) 88 Michigan LRev 1946, 1950.

61 H Kelsen, 'La Théorie Pure dans la Pensée Juridique' in C Leben and R Kolb (eds), *Controverses sur la Théorie Pure du Droit* (LGDJ, Paris 2005) 173; HLA Hart, *The Concept of Law* (2nd edn, OUP, Oxford 1997) 136; See also Hart and AM Honore, *Causation in the Law* (OUP, Oxford 1985)5 or N Bobbio, *Essais de théorie du droit* (M. Guéret tr, Bruylant/LGDJ, Paris 1998) 10, 38; J Raz, *Authority of Law* (Clarendon Press, Oxford 1983) especially 41–52. As regards international law more specifically, See R Jennings, 'What is International Law and How do we tell it when we see it' (1981) 37 Annuaire Suisse de Droit international 77; H Thirlway, 'The Sources of International Law' in M Evans (ed), *International Law* (2nd ed, OUP, Oxford 2006) 129–130; H Lauterpacht, *The Development of International Law by the International Court* (2nd ed, Praeger, New York 1958); M Lachs, 'Some Reflections on the Contribution of the International Court of Justice to the Development of International Law' (1983) 10 Syracuse JIL and Commerce (1983) 239; R Higgins, *Problems and Process: International Law and How We Use It* (OUP, Oxford 1995) 202. A Boyle and C Chinkin, *The Making of International Law* (OUP, Oxford 2007) 266–269 and 310–311. See however the statement of the International Court of Justice in its Advisory Opinion on the *Legality of the Threat or Use of Nuclear Weapons*, [1996-I] ICJ Rep 226 [18] (according to which the Court "states the existing law and does not legislate" and this is so "even if, in stating and applying the law, the Court necessarily has to specify its scope and sometimes not is general trend"). Article 38 of the Statute of the International Court of Justice also seems to lend support to a strictly cognitivistic task of international courts.

PCIJ, undoubtedly include the domestic judicial practice, especially in common law countries. By virtue of its Statute and the concept of general principles, the PCIJ was thus enticed to engage with domestic judicial practices if it sought to make use of general principles of law.

It is interesting to note that, despite the extremely large leeway left to the PCIJ in the ascertainment of the law by virtue of the recognition of general principles of law as a source of applicable law, the Court hardly used it. Indeed, as noted by Hudson, "(w)hether from a sense of caution or because of the nature of the cases which have come before it, the Court has never professed to draw upon 'the general principles of law recognized by civilized nations' in its search for the applicable law".[62] In ascertaining the rules applicable to the cases brought before it, the Court often furtively stood behind vague formulations, refraining from expressly revealing the exact source of the rule concerned, whether customary international law or general principles of law. For instance, in the *Greco-Bulgarian Communities* case, the Court referred to the "generally accepted principle of international law that in the relations between Powers who are contracting Parties to a treaty, the provisions of municipal law cannot prevail over those of the treaty."[63]

The PCIJ's tepid use of general principles of law—and thus its apparent qualms towards a self-empowerment to unearth convergences in domestic traditions—indicates that it barely engaged with domestic judicial traditions in this way. It is thus fair to say that the statutory relationship with domestic courts remained limited. Because of the inconclusiveness of the organic relationship,[64] the non-decisive character of the hermeneutic relationship,[65] and the paucity of the statutory relationship,[66] the most important contribution of domestic courts to the work of the PCIJ is to be found elsewhere. This is the object of the following paragraphs.

4. *A Transmutative Relationship: The Application of Domestic Law by the PCIJ*

It is unsurprising that the PCIJ was first and foremost expected to apply international law to settle the disputes that were brought before it or to

62 Hudson (n 3) 611–612.
63 [1930] Ser B No 17 at 32.
64 Cf section II(1).
65 Cf section II(2).
66 Cf section II(3).

answer the requests for an Advisory Opinion that were submitted to it. This was prescribed by its statute.[67] This also is what the PCIJ confirmed, as far as its contentious jurisdiction is concerned, by contending that its "true function" boiled down to settling disputes between States "on the basis of international law".[68] Yet, the Court made it expressly clear that it could be seized of disputes "which do not require the application of international law",[69] thereby not ruling out the application of domestic law. The same is true in relation to Advisory Opinions.[70] The theoretical possibility of applying domestic law was not subject to much controversy and unsurprisingly, questions of domestic law inevitably did actually arise before the PCIJ.[71] Indeed, questions of domestic law primarily emerged when appraising whether a State had lived up to its international obligations as illustrated by the *Certain German Interests in Polish Upper Silesia* case;[72] or when ascertaining certain facts governed by municipal law as is shown by the *Serbian Loans* case.[73]

Being called upon to examine municipal law on occasions, the PCIJ was bound to determine the status which it granted to the applicable municipal rules. The PCIJ's understanding of the status of domestic law in international judicial proceedings is well-known. In its decision in the *Certain German Interests in Polish Upper Silesia* the Court famously stated:

> From the standpoint of International Law and of the Court which is its organ, municipal laws are merely facts which express the will and constitute the activities of States, in the same manner as do legal decisions or administrative measures. The Court is certainly not called upon to interpret the Polish law as such; but there is nothing to prevent the Court's giving judgment on the question whether or not, in applying that law, Poland is acting in conformity with its obligations towards Germany under the Geneva Convention.[74]

---

67 See Article 38 of the PCIJ and ICJ Statute.
68 (n 54) 19–20.
69 Ibid.
70 See the individual opinion of Anzilotti (n 11) 62–63.
71 Ibid. 63.
72 *Upper Silesia Case* (n 11).
73 (n 54). See also *Consistency of Certain Danzig Legislative Decrees with the Constitution of the Free City*, [1935] PCIJ Ser A/B No 65.
74 (n 11) 19.

Today, international judicial bodies still abide by that position[75] which is also referred to in international pleadings.[76] It is also widely shared in the international legal scholarship.[77] Construed as simple "facts", domestic rules were accordingly examined by the PCIJ in a number of cases, especially to appraise the extent of the obligations of the parties or to determine whether a State had abided by its obligations. It suffices here to mention the *Serbian Loans*[78] and *Brazilian Loans*[79] cases as well as the *German Settlers in Poland*,[80] *Exchange of Greek and Turkish Populations*,[81] *Greco-Bulgarian "Communities"*,[82] and *Treatment of Polish Nationals and Other Persons of Polish Origin or Speech in the Danzig Territory*[83] Advisory Opinions.

Although demoted to mere facts which the PCIJ could take into account, municipal rules had inextricably to be interpreted. More precisely, while municipal law could be relied on by the PCIJ as facts, it still needed to be interpreted. Hence the question arose whether the PCIJ could engage in its own interpretation or whether it was to be bound by the interpretation provided by the domestic courts where the municipal rule concerned had been adopted and primarily yielded its legal effects.

Confronted with that question in the *Brazilian Loans* case, the PCIJ took the following general position:

> Once the Court has arrived at the conclusion that it is necessary to apply the municipal law of a particular country, there seems no doubt that it must seek to apply it as it would be applied in that country. It would not be applying the municipal law of a country if it were to apply it in a manner different from that in which that law would be applied in the country in which it is in force.

---

75 See International Tribunal for the Law of the Sea, 'Saiga No 2' Judgement of 1 July,[1999] ITLOS [120].

76 *Accordance with International Law of the Unilateral Declaration of Independence in Respect of Kosovo* (Request for Advisory Opinion), Public sitting held on Friday 4 December 2009, CR 2009/28 at 28.

77 See G Gaja, 'Dualism – a Review' in J Nijman and A Nollkaemper (eds), *New Perspectives on the Divide between National and International Law* (OUP, Oxford 2007) 52,58–59; MN Shaw, *International Law*, (5th ed, CUP, Cambridge 2003) 127; D Anzilotti, *Corso di diritto internazionale private*, (Anthenaeum, Rome 1925) 57.

78 (n 54).

79 (n 12) 123–5.

80 [1923] PCIJ Ser B No 6.

81 [1925] PCIJ Ser B No 10 at 19–20.

82 (n 63) 32.

83 [1932] PCIJ Ser A/B No 44 at 24.

> It follows that the Court must pay the utmost regard to the decisions of the municipal courts of a country, for it is with the aid of their jurisprudence that it will be enabled to decide what are the rules which, in actual fact, are applied in the country the law of which is recognized as applicable in a given case. If the Court were obliged to disregard the decisions of municipal courts, the result would be that it might in certain circumstances apply rules other than those actually applied; this would seem to be contrary to the whole theory on which the application of municipal law is based.[84]

Interestingly, the special agreements on which the *Brazilian Loans* case was based provided that the Court could freely decide to disregard the interpretation of a domestic statute, provided by the domestic courts of a State, and engage in its own interpretation of that statute, in determining the national law of each country.[85] Yet, the aforementioned position of the PCIJ indicated a great reluctance to do so, even though expressly allowed by the agreement in which its jurisdiction was based. This led the Court to affirm that it cannot be "compelled" to disregard municipal jurisprudence.[86]

Despite affirming the necessity to abide by the interpretation of municipal law provided by domestic courts, the PCIJ formulated an important qualification for situations where the case law of domestic courts is either hazy or inconsistent. The PCIJ thus went on: "Of course, the Court will endeavor to make a just appreciation of the jurisprudence of municipal courts. If this is uncertain or divided, it will rest with the Court to select the interpretation which it considers most in conformity with the law".[87]

This self-granted authorization to overturn domestic interpretation of municipal law went almost unnoticed at that time, for it was formulated in a case where the PCIJ eventually refrained from using that possibility.

---

84 (n 12) 124.

85 Ibid at 123.

86 Cf (n 12) 124–125: "But to compel the Court to disregard that jurisprudence would not be in conformity with its function when applying municipal law. As the Court has already observed in the judgment in the case of the Serbian loans, it would be a most delicate matter to do so, in a case concerning public policy—a conception the definition of which in any particular country is largely dependent on the opinion prevailing at any given time in such country itself—and in a case where no relevant provisions directly relate to the question at issue. Such are the reasons according to which the Court considers that it must construe Article VI of the Special Agreement to mean that, while the Court is authorized to depart from the jurisprudence of the municipal courts, it remains entirely free to decide that there is no ground for attributing to the municipal law a meaning other than that attributed to it by that jurisprudence".

87 Ibid at 124.

However, the subsequent case law of the Court showed a growing disposition to provide its own interpretation of domestic law. Indeed, in three cases submitted to it, the PCIJ ventured in that direction, thereby bestowing upon itself the role of a domestic court and independently interpreting the applicable domestic law.

In the *Appeal from a Judgment of the Hungaro/Czecoslovak Mixed Arbitral Tribunal* (*The Peter Pázmány University*),[88] the PCIJ, acting as a court of appeal to a Hungarian/Czechoslovak Mixed Arbitral Tribunal, examined, interpreted, and applied Hungarian law in order to determine whether The Peter Pázmány University was endowed with legal personality and whether it was entitled under Hungarian law to file a claim before the mixed tribunal. The PCIJ concluded that the University had legal personality and had the capacity to act independently, therefore fulfilling the conditions necessary to submit a claim by virtue of Article 250 of the Treaty of Trianon.[89] In that case, although there was no municipal case law invoked, the PCIJ did not rely on the interpretation of Hungarian law made by domestic authorities and embarked on a free interpretation thereof.

A bit more than a year later, the PCIJ was asked by the Council of the League of Nations to appraise the consistency of two Danzig legislative decrees pertaining to criminal law and criminal procedure matters of 29 August 1935 with the Constitution of the Free City of Danzig.[90] Again, the PCIJ carried out an analysis of the meaning and scope of both the decrees and the Constitution of the Free City of Danzig as if it were a constitutional court. It concluded that the decrees were not consistent with the guarantees provided by the Danzig Constitution.[91] The Court operating as the constitutional court of Danzig is precisely what prompted Anzilotti to object that the Court should have declined to give an opinion on that matter.[92] It is interesting to note that Anzilotti also regretted that the PCIJ appears to have held that, in carrying out its task as a constitutional court, it ought not to concern itself with the jurisprudence of the courts of Danzig.[93]

---

88 (n 7) 228 et seq.
89 Ibid at 232.
90 [1934] PCIJ Ser A/B No 62 at 22–4.
91 Ibid at 57.
92 See the Individual opinion of Anzilotti (n 11) 61–63.
93 Ibid at 64.

In its judgment on the *Lighthouses case between France and Greece*,[94] the PCIJ was called upon to determine whether the 1913 contract concluded between the French firm Collas & Michel—known as the *Administration générale des Phares de l'Empire ottoman*—and the Ottoman Empire renewing the concession for the maintenance of the lighthouses on the coasts of the Ottoman Empire was duly entered into according to Ottoman law and thus operative as regards Greece in so far as the lighthouses situated on the territory subsequently assigned to Greece. This led the Court to carry out a thorough examination of the domestic law and the constitutional practice of the Ottoman Empire.[95] The Court concluded that such a contract was valid under Ottoman law and was therefore operative towards Greece.[96]

In the three cases mentioned here, the PCIJ did not shy away from freely interpreting municipal law and behaved as if it were a domestic (supreme) court of the legal system whose law it was interpreting. According to one observer, the greater inclination shown by the PCIJ, in the three aforementioned cases, to operate as a domestic court, by providing its own interpretation of municipal law, directly originated in the second general elections of judges which had produced a bench where judges thought as national lawyers.[97] Whatever the possible explanation for such a disposition, it suffices for the sake of the argument made here to point out that, while balking at engaging with domestic case law, the PCIJ had no qualms endorsing the role of domestic courts and independently acting as a domestic court. In other words, the inclination—singled out in this section—of the PCIJ to freely interpret municipal law and act as a municipal court sharply contrasts with the reluctance of the PCIJ—observed in the two previous sections—to engage with domestic courts and their judicial practice, either by virtue of the authority attached to their interpretation of international law[98] or by virtue of general principles of law.[99]

III. The PCIJ and Its Successor: Which Legacy?

The foregoing has shown that the PCIJ, despite considering itself a Court of the international legal order, hardly paid its due to the case law of other

---

94 (n 73) 50.
95 Ibid at 19–24.
96 Ibid at 28–29.
97 Spiermann (n 2), 349.
98 Cf section II(2) above.
99 Cf section II(3) above.

international tribunals. Indeed, as has been argued above,[100] even if the PCIJ were to consider itself of a supreme nature in comparison to these other non-permanent bodies—which it probably did—its pronounced disregard for other judicial bodies' decision was out of proportion for an "organ of international law". Paradoxically, the PCIJ, despite considering itself an organ of international law which could have theoretically overlooked judicial developments in domestic legal orders, experienced fewer qualms to engage with domestic courts. Notwithstanding the inconclusiveness of the organic relationship with domestic courts,[101] or the paucity of its statutory relationship with them,[102] the Court did take notice of domestic interpretations of international law[103] and, above all, came to apply domestic law itself as if it had the capacity and authority of a judicial body of the domestic legal order whose rules were at stake in the cases submitted to it.[104] If these findings are correct, it is not without interest to end this brief chapter by critically appraising the attitude of the PCIJ in its relationship with other tribunals in the light of the practice of the current World Court.

The legacy of the PCIJ is indubitable. In particular, it cannot be contested that the PCIJ case law has particularly marked the case law of its successor in The Hague on a wide array of substantive and procedural issues. It surely is not the place to dwell on them here. For the sake of the argument made in this chapter, it is noteworthy that the ICJ in its first contentious decision on the merits immediately endorsed the—somewhat controversial—claim made by its predecessor in the *Certain German Interests in Polish Upper Silesia*[105] and the *Brazilian Loans* case[106] that it constituted an organ or a tribunal of international law. Indeed, in the *Corfu Channel* case, the Court made the following statement:

> The Court recognizes that the Albanian Government's complete failure to carry any out its duties after the explosions, and the dilatory nature of its diplomatic notes, are extenuating circumstances for the action of the United Kingdom Government. But to ensure respect for international law, *of which*

---

100 Cf section I above.
101 Cf section II(1) above.
102 Cf section II(3) above.
103 Cf section II(2) above.
104 Cf section II(4).
105 *Upper Silesia Case* (n 11) 19. This was also recalled by Anzilotti (n 11) 63.
106 (n 12) 124.

> *it is the organ,* the Court must declare that the action of the British Navy constituted a violation of Albanian sovereignty.[107]

Interestingly, the argument could be made that the ICJ, probably more than the PCIJ, takes its self-proclaimed status as an organ of international law more seriously, albeit belatedly. It is indeed well-known that the current World Court does pay heed to the findings of other international tribunals, although sometimes reluctantly or simply as a matter of convenience, be it for interpretative[108] or evidentiary[109] purposes. It is true that, given the far more numerous international judicial bodies in the era of the ICJ, the inspiration taken from other courts and tribunals remains proportionally very limited. Yet, it seems that the ICJ has come to accept the authority of other judicial bodies' decisions, a step which the PCIJ never made.

Whist the ICJ may have shown itself more amenable to other international tribunals' positions than the PCIJ, it seems that the exact opposite conclusion can be reached when it comes to the engagement with domestic courts. Indeed, the tendency of the PCIJ to endorse the role of domestic courts and substitute its own interpretation to that of domestic authorities—and which has been depicted in the previous sections—is a trait which the ICJ seems not to have continued and perpetuated.

This surely is not to say that there are no instances where the ICJ examined and reviewed legal rules which are not strictly speaking rules of the international legal order. Actually, such situations are plentiful in the case law of the current World Court. For instance, the ICJ is regularly called upon to interpret the law of the UN. In doing so, the ICJ interprets the law of an autonomous legal order which is, strictly speaking and despite the international nature of its constitutive instrument, separate from the international legal order.[110] In this situation, however, its status of

---

107 *Corfu Channel* (*United Kingdom of Great Britain and Northern Ireland v. Albania*), [1949] ICJ Rep 4, at 35 (emphasis added).

108 *Ahmadou Sadio Diallo* (*Republic of Guinea v. Democratic Republic of the Congo*), Judgment of 30 November 2010 [67] et seq. (at www.icj-cij.org).

109 See ICJ, *Application of the Convention on the Prevention and Punishment of the Crime of Genocide* (Bosnia and Herzegovina v. Serbia and Montenegro), [2007] ICJ Rep 43 [202]–[230].

110 On this debate see generally C Ahlborn, 'The Rules of International Organizations and the Law of International Responsibility' (Forthcoming) International Organizations L Rev, Amsterdam Centre for International Law Research paper No 2011–03 and Amsterdam Law School Research Paper No 2011–04. See also the remarks by J d'Aspremont and Fr Dopagne, 'Kadi: the ECJ's Reminder of the Elementary Divide Between Legal Orders' (2008) 5 International Organizations L Rev 371–379.

principal judicial organ of the UN[111] suffices to justify that the ICJ ventures into the law of the UN. Leaving aside advisory procedures specifically addressing the law of the UN, it must be highlighted that the Court is called upon to review domestic law in a variety of situations. In frontier disputes for instance, the Court will often engage with the interpretation of national law—taking in its factual evidentiary virtues—to try to establish the frontier.[112] Likewise, in case of diplomatic protection, and especially when gauging the fulfillment of local remedies[113] or establishing the nationality of the victim,[114] the Court has been examining and interpreting domestic law. By the same token, in determining the possible wrongful character of the behavior of a State, the ICJ can be called upon to review and interpret domestic law with a view to determining whether the piece of domestic law at stake is not in itself illegal[115] or the source of a wrongful act,[116] or at least the preparatory act to the breach.[117] Furthermore, when seeking to determine the legal subject to which an act is attributable, the Court can—theoretically at least—also turn to domestic law despite the latter playing only an evidentiary role for the sake of attribution.[118] For example in the evaluation of the validity of a treaty, and especially in a situation where the consent to be bound by a treaty has been expressed in manifest violation of a provision of internal law regarding competence to conclude treaties which are of fundamental importance.[119]

---

111 Article 92 of the United Nations Charter.

112 See e.g. *Frontier Dispute (Benin v. Niger)*, [2005] ICJ Rep 90; *Frontier Dispute (Burkina Faso/Republic of Mali)*, [1986], ICJ Rep 1986 554 [30].

113 *Elettronica Sicula S.p.A. (ELSI) (United States of America v. Italy)*, [1989] ICJ Rep 15 [56] et seq.

114 *Nottebohm (Liechtenstein v. Guatemala)*, [1955] ICJ Rep 4, at 17 ff.

115 *Accordance with International Law of the Unilateral Declaration of Independence in Respect of Kosovo*, Advisory Opinion of 22 July 2010 [85]-[121], especially at para. 88 (at www.icj-cij.org). The same is true with respect to domestic case law. See e.g. *Certain Property (Liechtenstein v. Germany)*, [2005] ICJ Rep 6; and *Jurisdictional Immunities of the State (Germany v. Italy: Greece intervening)*, Application of 22 December 2008, available at http://www.icj-cij.org/docket/files/143/14923.pdf.

116 See *Diallo* (n 108) [72] et seq.; *Avena and Other Mexican Nationals (Mexico v. United States of America)* [2004] ICJ Rep 12 [63] and [112]-[113]; *LaGrand (Germany v. United States)*, [2001] ICJ Rep 466 [90]. See also Separate Opinion of Judge Lauterpacht, *Norwegian Loans* [1957] ICJ Rep at 37.

117 On the concept of preparatory act, see *Gabčíkovo-Nagymaros Project (Hungary/Slovakia)*, [1997] ICJ Rep 7 [79].

118 This possibility arises out of Article 4.2 of the Articles on the Responsibility of States for Internationally Wrongful Acts. See the 'Commentary of Article 4, Report of the International Law Commission on the work of its fifty-third session', *Yearbook of the International Law Commission* (vol II, Pt Two, 2001) 42.

119 *Land and Maritime Boundary between Cameroon and Nigeria (Cameroon v. Nigeria: Equatorial Guinea intervening)*, [2002] ICJ Rep 303 [258]-[268]; and further S Wittich in the present volume. 20 seq.

There thus exists a fair number of instances where the Court has been (or could be) called upon to interpret and review domestic law. Interestingly, in all these cases where the Court has actually engaged with domestic law, it has always refrained from substituting its own interpretation for that of a body which under domestic law would have had the authority to do so. In that sense, the ICJ has never shown the same inclination as the PCIJ to play the role of a domestic supreme Court. However, interestingly, the ICJ has invoked the PCIJ's jurisprudence in this respect and, especially, the abovementioned *Brazilian Loans* principle empowering the Court to set aside the interpretation of domestic courts. Such a precedent was mentioned, for instance, in its judgments in *ELSI*[120] and in *Diallo*.[121] Notwithstanding taking note of that possibility, the Court has always refused to make use of that prerogative in practice and has eschewed any direct engagement with domestic courts. More often than not, the question of the influence of other domestic interpretation of domestic law has been reduced to a mere question of proof.

The foregoing shows that the ICJ has never excluded the possibility of substituting itself for domestic authorities and cases where it could have done so are many. The ICJ has however shown much more self-restraint than its predecessor, thereby living up, more strictly, to the division of roles inherent in its similar self-proclaimed status of "organ of international law". If this is true, such a finding inevitably spawns the temptation to embark on a historical, political, and sociological analysis of the differences of mindset of the two courts in this respect. Certainly, historical, institutional, political, and sociological narratives would be very conducive to understand and decipher the greater inclination of the PCIJ, in comparison to its successor, to substitute itself for domestic courts. It suffices here to mention that the PCIJ felt it necessary to establish its authority in a community of States obsessively attached to their monopoly of power on their territory, and the perceived need not to leave domestic interpretation of national law to corrupt the international ambitions of the Court as a world player, or more simply the intricate and subtle character of the peace edifice built after World War I of which the Court was meant to be the guardian. More pragmatically, it could also be explained by virtue of a timely and case-by-case analysis of the case law of each court, the situations submitted to the ICJ having not required it to endorse

120 (n 113) [62].
121 (n 108) [70].

the role of a domestic supreme court, in contrast to those with which its predecessors had to grapple. Reasons for such a discrepancy in attitude are numerous. The task—highly speculative in nature—of unearthing them should surely not be taken on in the framework of this volume. Whatever the motives for such diverging approaches to the relationship between the World Court and domestic courts, the foregoing shows that the abundant case law of the PCIJ, more than sixty-five years since its dissolution, continues to provide insights into the dynamics of our contemporary multi-judiciary world.

THE RELATIONSHIP BETWEEN THE PERMANENT COURT OF ARBITRATION AND THE PERMANENT COURT OF INTERNATIONAL JUSTICE, AND ITS SIGNIFICANCE FOR INTERNATIONAL LAW

Anneliese Quast Mertsch

I. Introduction

When the relationship between the Permanent Court of International Justice (PCIJ) and the Permanent Court of Arbitration (PCA) is assessed, two points are often noted. First, that the PCA paved the way for the PCIJ. Second, that upon the establishment of the PCIJ, the PCA's caseload reduced drastically. From this, some draw the conclusion that the PCIJ overshadowed the PCA. This Chapter will revisit the relationship between the two Courts and provide a different analysis thereof. Its first part will look at the traditional perception of the relationship, focusing on how and why the PCA was overshadowed by the PCIJ, and conclude by offering an alternative perception of the PCA.

The second part will examine the contribution that this relationship, or the co-existence of these institutions at the beginning of the 20th century, has made, bringing with it the modern notion of arbitration and its delimitation from adjudication. Admittedly, this delimitation is a matter of form rather than substance. Nevertheless, against the background of the indeterminacy of legal rules and the element of choice that lies in their application, it will be submitted that the delimitation matters, that arbitral tribunals and permanent courts will be guided by different considerations when they make their choice in the application of legal rules. Thus, it will be submitted that the modern notion of arbitration and its delimitation from adjudication is a meaningful contribution both to the development of international law and the settlement of disputes in the international sphere. The Chapter will conclude by suggesting this contribution as an alternative, or additional, aspect under which the relationship between the PCA and the PCIJ can be seen, and by highlighting the relevance of an analysis of the relationship of these two Courts for present day international law.

II. Background to the PCA and the PCIJ

In order to introduce the individual components that form the relationship under consideration in the present Chapter, a brief background will be provided to the PCA and the PCIJ.

The Permanent Court of Arbitration is a mechanism facilitating dispute settlement by various means, including arbitration.[1] It consists of a standing secretariat that acts as registry, is governed by an administrative council in which the member States take executive decisions, and offers a list from which arbitrators can be chosen once States decide to submit a dispute to it. It is not a court in the sense the term is used today:[2] there are no judges, and no permanent bench. Instead the dispute settling body is constituted on each occasion that a dispute is referred to it (in an *ad hoc* manner).[3] The PCA is based on the 1899 and 1907 Conventions for the Pacific Settlement of International Disputes.[4] It was established in 1900, began operating in 1902 and still exists today.[5] Its heyday was in the years preceding the First World War.[6] In this period it decided sixteen disputes.[7] In the 1930s, it administered a mixed arbitration between a company, Radio Corporation of America, and China.[8] After a period of seeming demise,

[1] WE Butler 'The Hague Permanent Court of Arbitration' in MW Janis (ed) *International Courts for the Twenty-First Century* (Martinus Nijhoff, Dordrecht 1992) 44; and see the section 'History' on the ICJ website: www.icj-cij.org/court/index.php?p1=1&p2=1#Permanent.

[2] B Shifman, 'The Permanent Court of Arbitration' in PJ van Krieken and D McKay (eds) *The Hague: Legal Capital of the World* (TMC Asser Press, The Hague 2005) 129; Butler (n 1) 44; see also J Collier and V Lowe, *The Settlement of Disputes in International Law: Institutions and Procedures* (OUP, Oxford 1999) 35.

[3] Accordingly, the adjective 'permanent' in its name relates correctly more to the secretariat, which is a standing organ, and not to the organ that will decide a dispute (at best the list of arbitrators could be seen as providing some degree of permanency, in that it might facilitate an easier and quicker constitution of a tribunal).

[4] Convention for the Pacific Settlement of International Disputes, 29 July 1899, <http://www.pca-cpa.org/showfile.asp?fil_id=192> and Convention for the Pacific Settlement of International Disputes, 18 October 1907 <http://www.pca-cpa.org/showfile.asp?fil_id=193>.

[5] <http://www.icj-cij.org/court/index.php?p1=1&p2=1>.

[6] Collier and Lowe (n 2) 36; G Best, 'Peace Conferences and the Century of Total War: the 1899 Hague Conference and what Came After' (1999) 75 International Affairs 630; N Ando, 'Permanent Court of Arbitration (PCA)' in R Wolfrum (ed) *The Max Planck Encyclopedia of Public International Law* (OUP 2008) online edition <www.mpepil.com> [21].

[7] Ando (n 6) [21].

[8] International commercial disputes between States and private entities had since the 1920s been dealt with by the Arbitration Court of the International Chamber of Commerce in Paris, see H Jonkman, 'The Role of the Permanent Court of Arbitration in International Dispute Resolution: addresses on 6 and 27 July 1999, at the Hague Academy of International

linked to the establishment of the PCIJ,[9] the PCA is now experiencing a second spring, with at least twenty-four cases decided between 1998 and 2011, and at least nine cases registered with the PCA pending.[10] Its significance lies in being the first global dispute settlement mechanism;[11] and whilst in itself the PCA is not a true court, its existence has helped foster the international consensus that such a court is beneficial and necessary, and has thereby helped pave the way for the PCIJ.

The PCIJ was the first international permanent court with a standing adjudicative body. It had general jurisdiction, and was institutionally linked to the League of Nations.[12] Between 1922 and 1940, it decided twenty-seven cases and rendered eighteen Advisory Opinions.[13] Due to the outbreak of the Second World War and the German invasion of the Netherlands in 1940, the PCIJ ceased working.[14] After the war it was formally dissolved, preparing the ground for its successor—the ICJ.[15] Despite the apparent formal separation of the PCIJ and the ICJ, denoted in the different names, there is a substantive link between the two courts: The last President of the PCIJ became the first President of the ICJ,[16] the ICJ statute is based on the PCIJ statute,[17] and the ICJ builds on the PCIJ's body of case law.[18] Thus, the ICJ is largely seen as the substantive continuation

---

Law, Peace Palace, The Hague, on the occasion of the Centennial Celebration of the Permanent Court of Arbitration' (1999) 279 Recueil des Cours 27.

9 Ando (n 6) [23]; Jonkman (n 8) 26, see also 28.

10 <http://www.pca-cpa.org/showpage.asp?pag_id=1029>, the numbers of past and pending proceedings are limited to those in which the parties have agreed that information on the proceedings may be published by the PCA. It is worth mentioning that in these more recent disputes, the role of the PCA is different from that under disputes brought in the first decades of the 20th century: the PCA's more recent activity is *not* based on the Hague Conventions, but on jurisdiction derived from other instruments, notably *ad hoc* agreements.

11 T van den Hout, 'Resolution of International Disputes: The Role of the Permanent Court of Arbitration...' (2008) 21 Leiden JIL 643; see also R Mackenzie et al, *Manual on International Courts and Tribunals* (OUP, New York 2010) 102; <http://www.pca-cpa.org/showpage.asp?pag_id=1044>.

12 Cf. information on the PCIJ provided on the ICJ website: www.icj-cij.org/pcij/index.php?p1=9.

13 Ibid.

14 Ibid; and also 16th Annual Report of the PCIJ (June 1939—December 1945), Series E, at 9.

15 See S Rosenne, *The Law and Practice of the International Court, 1920–2005* (Nijhoff, Leiden/Boston 2006), vol. I, at 14–16.

16 Ibid.

17 Article 92 of the UN Charter.

18 CH Brower II, 'Arbitration' in R Wolfrum (ed) *The Max Planck Encyclopedia of Public International Law* (OUP 2008) online edition <www.mpepil.com>, [33].

of the PCIJ,[19] and in this many see the main significance of the PCIJ, aside from it being the true first (universal) permanent international court.

III. The Relationship between the PCA and the PCIJ

After this brief introduction to the individual institutions forming the relationship under consideration, the analysis of the relationship itself can commence, with a review of academic views and comments thereupon.

1. *Review of Academic Writings*

Little has been written that would offer an in-depth analysis on the relationship between the two dispute settlement institutions that coexisted in the first half of the 20th century.[20] This is possibly so because the PCA and the PCIJ are seen not so much as coexistent but rather in a successive order; as (though not in strict terms) predecessor and successor. Indeed, the two comments most frequently made of the two institutions are, first, that the PCA paved the way for the PCIJ,[21] in that the discussions and work of the Hague Peace Conferences, and the experience with the PCA, served as material sources for the drafting of the PCIJ Statute; second, that once the PCIJ was established, recourse to the PCA became much less frequent, so much so that the PCA fell into relative disuse.[22]

Some add to this an interpretative assessment of the relationship. They suggest that with the less frequent recourse to the PCA, its importance as a dispute settlement institution diminished, and that it was overshadowed by the PCIJ.[23] An illustration of this can be seen in the fact that the PCA's

---

19 I Brownlie, *Principles of Public International Law* (7th edn, OUP, New York 2008) 707.

20 With the exception of e.g., O Spiermann 'Historical Introduction' in A Zimmermann, C Tomuschat, K Oellers-Frahm and CJ Tams (eds), *The Statute of the International Court of Justice: A Commentary* (2nd edn., OUP, Oxford 2012) 49–52; see also O Spiermann, *International Legal Argument in the Permanent Court of International Justice* (CUP, Cambridge 2005) 3 et seq.

21 DD Caron, 'War and International Adjudication: Reflections on the 1899 Peace Conference' (2000) 94 AJIL 24; Jonkman (n 8) 26; Brownlie (n 19) 707; G de Magyary *La Juridiction de la Cour Permanente de Justice Internationale* (Les Editions Internationales, Paris 1931) 43.

22 Jonkman (n 8) 26; Ando (n 6) [23]; MO Hudson, *The Permanent Court of International Justice, 1920–1942* (The Macmillan Company, New York 1943) 32; Brower II [n 18) [35]; Butler (n 1) 43; Collier and Lowe (n 2) 36.

23 Hudson (n 22) 32; Caron (n 21) 24; Brower II (n 18) [35]–[36]. O'Connell notes that the PCIJ 'substantially usurped' the functions of the PCA, [*International Law* (vol 2, 2nd edn, Stevens & Sons, London 1970) 1070].

significance by some is seen to lie not in itself but in preparing the ground for further developments in legal dispute settlement, including the establishment of the PCIJ.[24] Underlying this approach would appear to be the view that, what the PCA did with regard to one of its designated tasks—the facilitation and promotion of arbitration, including the awards it rendered—is not worth mentioning. A similar sense of indifference seems to be tangible in textbooks today when for instance Brownlie in his assessment of the PCA does not stop after saying that it has had a useful existence, but instead feels the need to specify that the existence was "useful but hardly spectacular".[25] In earlier textbooks this indifference seems to be yet more tangible. O'Connell for instance seems to adopt a slightly dismissive tone when dealing with the PCA: "It was a court only in name, since it consisted of little more than a panel from which arbitrators could be selected and a Bureau to provide the machinery. [...] [T]he deficiencies of the PCA are substantial."[26]

2. *Criticism of the PCA and its Effect on the Relationship with the PCIJ*

In light of the above, the following section will examine the criticism and perception of the PCA, assess its validity, and reflect upon how the criticism possibly affected the relationship between the PCA and the PCIJ.

a) *Criticism of the PCA*

The starting point is the criticism voiced only seven years into the PCA's existence, at the second Hague Peace Conference. The PCA received severe criticism, including that of its own drafters. It was generally accepted that all was not as it should be.[27] In the words of Martens: "We are agreed upon one essential and indispensable fact, namely that the Present Court is not organized as it should be."[28] The main point of

---

[24] 'In retrospect, its [the PCA's] historical importance was to serve as a point of departure for more ambitious projects of international justice that aimed at adjudication, as opposed to arbitration': Spiermann, *International Legal Argument* (n 20) 4; and cf. de Magyary (n 21) 43.

[25] Brownlie (n 19) 703.

[26] O'Connell (n 23) 1069.

[27] *The Second International Peace Conference: Acts and Documents* (vol 2, National Printing Office, The Hague 1907) Bieberstein 597; Asser 232. JB Scott (ed), *The Proceedings of the Hague: The Conference of 1907* (OUP, New York 1920), Annex A 'Project Relative to the Creation of a Court of Arbitral Justice', Report to the Conference, 341, Martens 347; Choate 344.

[28] JB Scott (ed) *The Proceedings of the Hague: The Conference of 1907* (Oxford University Press New York 1920), Annex A 'Project Relative to the Creation of a Court of Arbitral Justice', Report to the Conference, 341, Martens 347.

criticism was the lack of permanency of the dispute settling body, which created a distance not only between the arbitrators, but also between the institution and its member States, making it not readily accessible, even seemingly 'intangible': "What then is this court, whose members do not even know one another? The Court of 1899 is but an idea which occasionally assumes shape and then again disappears."[29]

The lack of permanency was the source of several follow-up problems. For instance it meant, as already mentioned, that the PCA was not readily and easily accessible for States' convenience. On the contrary, once States decided to submit a dispute to it, the tribunal first needed to be constituted. This was a time-consuming and at times complicated procedure, requiring close cooperation and agreement between the parties when their relations were strained due to the ongoing dispute. In addition to the problems of access and inconvenience, the procedure was rather costly.[30] A further consequence of the lack of institutional permanency was that the cases were decided in isolation from one another; accordingly, the case law emanating from the various tribunals was not necessarily coherent, and did not make the desired contribution to the establishment and further development of international law.[31]

Asser summarized all the above by describing the PCA as a "heavy moving organism": "It is difficult, it is long and costly to put in motion."[32] Thus, clearly, in the eyes of the diplomats at the Second Hague Peace Conference all was not as it should be with the PCA. So much so, that the remedy chosen to fix the situation was not to make changes to the PCA, but rather to draw up another dispute settlement institution—this time with a permanent dispute settlement body.[33] Thus, both the criticism and remedy seem

---

29 *The Second International Peace Conference* (n 27) Martens 327; Asser at 234: 'Instead of a permanent court, the Convention of 1899 gave but the phantom of a court, an impalpable spectre, or to be more precise, it gave us a recorder with a list.'

30 *The Second International Peace Conference* (n 27) Bieberstein: '... Everyone realizes that the Court is too costly'. *The Proceedings of the Hague* (n 27), Report to the Conference, 341, Choate 343.

31 *The Second International Peace Conference* (n 27), Choate 596:'The present Permanent court has not gone far in the direction of establishing and developing international law. Each case is isolated, lacking both continuity and connection with the other...'

32 *The Second International Peace Conference* (n 27), Asser 597, see also Bieberstein 597.

33 Hudson (n 22) 75. The Court of Arbitral Justice, see e.g. S Rosenne, 'Permanent Court of International Justice(PCIJ)' in R Wolfrum (ed), *The Max Planck Encyclopedia of Public International Law* (OUP 2008) online edition <www.mpepil.com> [2]. The constituent instrument of that Court never entered into force due to a disagreement on the number of judges on the Court 'some representatives requiring as many judges as there were states member of the Court', see Brownlie (n 19) 707.

to indicate that the problem was less the PCA itself (its actions or inactions), but rather the way it had been set up. Somehow, the PCA was not what its drafters had hoped for. Or as *Caron* put it: the PCA did not fully meet the vision of those who sought it.[34]

b) *Validity of the Criticism of the PCA*

Therefore, the following section will examine the reasons underlying the discontentment with the PCA and assess whether and to what extent the resulting criticism was justified.

c) *The PCA as a Compromise*

One explanation for the delegates' profound discontentment with their own creation might be that the PCA, when set up at the first Hague Peace Conference, was a compromise.[35] The aim of the majority at the conference was to establish a prestigious institution managed by a Secretariat that would even have had a limited right of intervention in case of serious disputes threatening the peace, since it would have been entitled to encourage States parties to have recourse to the PCA in order to settle such ongoing disputes peacefully.[36] Furthermore, the majority was in favour of a relatively short list of the most prominent potential arbitrators, aiming at providing the tribunal with (concentrated and thus) great authority,[37] and the majority was, in principle, even in favour of compulsory arbitration in some specified categories of disputes—broadly those disputes

---

[34] Caron (n 21) 5; and see also DE Khan, 'Max Huber as Arbitrator: The Palmas (Miangas) Case and Other Arbitrations' (2007) 18 EJIL 148.

[35] Jonkman (n 8) 17–22; Shifman (n 2) 129–130; see also JH Ralston, 'Some Suggestions as to the Permanent Court of Arbitration' (1907) 1 AJIL 321.

[36] The draft provision put forward to this effect reads as follows:

> 'The signatory Powers, considering it a duty, in case a sharp dispute threatens to break out between two or more of them, to call the attention of the disputants to the fact that the Permanent Court is open to them, hereby authorize the secretary general of the Bureau, when occasion arises, to place himself at the service of each of the interested parties, by writing to their representatives in the Netherlands. The exercise of this authority shall not be considered an unfriendly act.'

See 'Report to the Conference from the Third Commission on Pacific Settlement of International Disputes', in S Rosenne (ed), *The Hague Peace Conferences of 1899 and 1907 and International Arbitration – Reports and Documents* (TMC Asser, The Hague 2001) 59. See at 51–52 for the reasoning underlying this French proposal for a limited power of the Bureau to trigger proceedings.

[37] See the discussion surrounding the number of arbitrators at the Fifth Meeting of the Third Commission (17 July 1899) in *The International Peace Conference* (Martinus Nijhoff, The Hague 1907) 607.

not involving vital interests.[38] Yet, the minority was set against the establishment of any international dispute settlement institution. If any institution was to be established, this minority wanted States to retain as much power as possible, and the institution to be as weak as possible; preventing, for instance, the Secretariat from having the power to "remind" the parties of the PCA in case of serious disputes threatening peace.[39] It furthermore rejected any kind of compulsory arbitration, and preferred a long list of potential arbitrators, representing a blend of lawyers and technical experts. A long list of potential arbitrators can be seen to dilute the 'institutional' character of the mechanism, indeed making it more of a list (or reference point): the longer the list, the less concrete and tangible the institution would be, since it was less likely that the institution would come to be associated with certain names or faces.

The majority made great concessions to the minority, for both political and technical reasons. One political reason was that Germany, then one of the Great Powers and rather influential, formed part of the minority.[40] Its strong opposition to any dispute settlement institution led to severe crises at the conference. Yet, the Third Commission, which was in charge of dispute settlement at the First Hague Peace Conference, seemed determined to try to keep Germany on board. This was so much the worse for a technical reason, namely the fact that the unanimity principle then applied to decisions being taken on the international plane, including discussions at international conferences.[41] Thus, to keep Germany on board, its delegates needed to agree to every single provision of the draft Convention. In the end, Germany's adherence to the Court was won but not without the cost of renouncing any form of compulsory arbitration, nor the heavy remodelling of the 'right of intervention' regarding serious disputes threatening the peace (Article 27), and the general weakness of the institution's organs. Against this background, one may understand the comment made in retrospect by one of the conference negotiators, according to whom "[g]ood will was not lacking; but circumstances did not then permit of realizing the idea".[42]

---

38 Jonkman (n 8) 22.

39 Jonkman (n 8) 22 and 18.

40 Jonkman (n 8) 18; as well as Brower II (n 18) [33].

41 S Rosenne, 'Introduction' in S Rosenne (ed), *The Hague Peace Conferences of 1899 and 1907 and International Arbitration – Reports and Documents* (TMC Asser, The Hague 2001) xvii; and further R Sabel, 'Conferences and Congresses, International' in R Wolfrum (ed), *The Max Planck Encyclopedia of Public International Law* (OUP 2008) online edition <www.mpepil.com> [46].

42 *The Second International Peace Conference* (n 27) Asser 234.

In conclusion, it is understandable that the majority of States after the first conference, having made such concessions, were left with a sense of disappointment and the feeling that all was not as it should be. As we have seen above, much of the criticism was focused on the PCA and what it was not or had failed to be: its dispute settlement body was not permanent, hence it was not easily and readily accessible; recourse to it was costly, and so on. Ultimately, the criticism linked back to the PCA's constitution and the structural features that the negotiating States had agreed therein. This is a point that should be borne in mind and one to which we shall return later in the assessment of the validity of the criticism.

d) *Shifting Negotiating Priorities*

Yet, not all points of criticism of the PCA were a result of the struggle for compromise. Some also were a matter of gaining practical experience of the functioning of such an institution, which led to a shift in negotiating priorities between the first and the second conference. In this way, matters that received broad support at the first Hague Peace Conference, eight years later at the second Conference attracted heavy criticism. A case in point is the lack of permanency of the PCA's dispute settlement body. At the first conference, the institution was often referred to as 'permanent'—whilst simultaneously accommodating the States' power to choose the arbitrators on each occasion from a long list. This apparent inconsistency was seen as a way of asserting sovereignty in the face of a mechanism that would facilitate legally binding dispute settlement by a neutral third party—and many, including the Four Great Powers, placed great emphasis on it. From this retention of State power it follows that 'permanency' as understood at the First Conference did not relate to the composition and availability of the dispute settlement body as such, but rather to the facilitating mechanisms, ie the secretariat and the list of arbitrators; both of which could possibly create the impression of the mechanism's general availability and disposition. At the Second Hague Conference, however, this seemed to have changed. As suggested earlier, much of the criticism clearly aimed at the lack of permanency of the dispute settlement body itself. To some extent, this criticism uncovers a logical tension: if as in 1899 it was decided that arbitrators were to be chosen *on each occasion* from a long list, then this necessarily meant that in the following years disputes would not be decided by a *permanent* bench of judges, ie a bench to whose composition one would have agreed only *once*, in advance, and for a certain period of time.[43] This shows how between the first and the second conference some negotiating priorities shifted.[44] Thus, if the PCA did not fully meet the vision of those who sought it, this was, in part, due to the struggle for compromise; but it was also a matter of the shifting priorities, possibly a result of the practical experience gained through the actual functioning of the institution after the First Hague Peace Conference.

Similarly, the PCA has been criticized for dealing with each case in an isolated manner, thereby not contributing greatly to the establishment and further development of international law. It may be difficult to assess whether or to what extent the arbitrators in each case could have done more to achieve this aim. Yet, what is clear is that law making would not appear to have been a priority in the design of the PCA. In fact, several institutional features would seem to be more harmful than beneficial to such a function: first, having a choice of arbitrators rather than a permanent bench of judges inevitably diminished any sense of shared responsibility for the formation of a coherent body of case law. This had disadvantages, since the greater the number of arbitrators from which the tribunal can be chosen, the greater the possibilities for divergence in decisions on similar questions. Finally, the 1899 and 1907 Conventions did not provide for the systematic publication and distribution of awards by the arbitral tribunals formed under the PCA.[45] Again, this hampered the creation of a shared sense of responsibility to contribute towards the formation of a coherent body of case law; and for those arbitrators who did aim to create such a thing, the failure to adopt systematic publication stood as a barrier to the easy access to and knowledge of the case law of previous

---

43 Indeed, it would appear difficult to reconcile the power to choose the arbitrators *ad hoc* from a long list with a permanent dispute settlement body. One attempt at reconciling a permanent bench with a 'right' to choose its composition (at least in practice) would appear to be the ICJ chamber system: the parties can indicate that certain names of Judges would be acceptable, and the Court would then be virtually certain to elect these Judges, see H Thirlway, 'The International Court of Justice' in MD Evans *International Law* (3rd edn, OUP, Oxford 2010) 590.

44 See delegate Bourgeois' comment: "If there are at present no judges at The Hague [the PCA], it is because the Conference of 1899 [...] intended to leave to the parties the duty of choosing their judges"; in *The Proceedings of the Hague* (n 27), Report to the Conference, 341, 342. Choate at 343 mentions that the work of the First Conference "has not proved entirely complete and adequate to meet the *progressive* demands of the nations" (emphasis added). See also H Kelsen who emphasizes, that the purpose of the Convention was, as Article 41 expressly states, to facilitate an immediate recourse to arbitration of international differences, not to establish directly a working tribunal, [*Principles of International Law* (2nd edn, Holt Rinehart and Winston, New York 1966) 531].

45 Hudson (n 22) 31.

tribunals. Accordingly, factors that may have furthered the formation of a coherent body of case law were not put in place by the contracting States. Such factors clearly represent structural deficiencies, possibly due to shifting priorities or lack of practical experience of the functioning of such an institution.

e) *The PCA as Failed Adjudicative Institution, Overshadowed by a 'True Permanent International Court'*

The relevance of these factors being structural deficiencies is as follows. States create international organisations.[46] They set out their tasks, their organs, and the rights and duties they have in order to perform those tasks. The organisation has its (own) sphere of competence, which is, loosely put, everything conferred onto it by the treaty.[47] But the treaty itself, in terms of its negotiation, amendment and termination, is outside that sphere of competence. States are the Masters of the Treaty, and remain so. As a result, structural criticism of an institution should be addressed to the Member States and not the institution. Yet, often such criticism is focused on the organisation alone.[48] This may be merely a convenient shortcut, since it is the organisation that is or acts a certain way. Nevertheless, it is a simplification, an analysis that remains at the surface and looks at symptoms rather than causes. The PCA may have been not easily accessible, intangible, and costly—not because that is what it chose to be, but rather because that is how its member States had (in part involuntarily) set it up. Thus to criticize the institution rather than the member States creates a partial story and may well have ultimately contributed to the sense of failure that, often in the past and at times still today, resonates when the PCA is mentioned.

---

[46] M Shaw, *International Law* (CUP, Cambridge 2008) 1303.

[47] This terminology is intended to cover both powers expressly conferred onto the organization as well as implied powers. See e.g. D Akande, 'International Organizations' in MD Evans *International Law* (3rd edn, OUP, Oxford 2010) 264ff and *Reparations for Injuries Suffered in the Service of the United Nations (Advisory Opinion)* [1949] ICJ Rep 174, 182 et seq.

[48] The most frequent example of this is news coverage of the UN's repeated 'failure' to act in a given crisis on the basis of a State exercising its veto power in the Security Council. Either such a power is granted in the constituent treaty, or it is not granted. This is a structural decision of the Member States. Once the power is granted, and unless the conduct in question is ultra vires, it is *not* a *failure* of the *organization* when this power is exercised. All the organization does in such a moment, is to function in accordance with its constituent instrument, in the way the member States shaped and structured its powers. If it is felt, by the public, that such a veto power should be abolished, then civil society and other actors should enter a dialogue with the UN Member States (and especially those having a veto power) on UN Security Council reform.

In part this criticism is about the elements of the PCA system which made it impractical or inconvenient to use; such as the cost of bringing a case or the lengthy procedure. Yet, some of the criticism also attaches to features which today form part of the dividing line between international 'arbitration' and 'adjudication': the right to choose the arbitrators on an *ad hoc* basis[49] versus a pre-constituted permanent bench; the case law emanating from the latter is expected to have, and often does have, a higher degree of coherence and continuity. This observation can be seen to go to the very nature of the mechanism: the PCA in part was criticised for being an arbitral dispute settling body, when what many States really wanted (certainly at the Second Conference, but some also already at the First one) was an adjudicative institution.[50] Thus, in part the criticism relates to the PCA 'not being a *real* court'.

Based on the above, it could be said that some did not see the PCA for what it was and what it did, but for what it was not (it was 'not a true international permanent Court') and accordingly what it was not able to deliver (the 'confirmation and further establishment of international law'). To this extent, and even prior to the PCIJ's existence, the PCA was overshadowed by the idea and desire to establish a true international court, comparable to those existing in the domestic sphere of law.[51]

Perhaps then, the criticism of the PCA was driven by the, in certain quarters, relatively strong desire to establish a proper international permanent court.[52] The desire was based on the expectation that peace could be sustained through international adjudication and law, and more precisely, that an international court with obligatory jurisdiction could do

---

49 The frequent *ad hoc* character of arbitration tribunals, or their frequent lack of permanence, is, however, not a categorical feature of arbitration, see LB Sohn, 'The Function of International Arbitration Today' (1963) 108 Recueil des Cours 22; H von Mangoldt, *Die Schiedsgerichtsbarkeit als Mittel Internationaler Streitschlichtung* (Springer Verlag, Berlin 1974) 16.

50 Hudson e.g. speaks of the PCA's "inadequacy as a judicial institution" (n 22) 75.

51 Moore summarized this view in the following way: "It is said that heretofore we have had arbitration, but that arbitration has failed, and that now we are to have 'judicial settlement' of international disputes." JB Moore (ed), *International Adjudications Ancient and Modern: History and Documents* (OUP, New York 1929) xxxvi. The then quest for judicial settlement of disputes can be encountered when reading e.g. JH Ralston, 'Some Suggestions as to the Permanent Court of Arbitration' (1907) 1 AJIL 321. See also DD Caron, 'Towards a Political Theory of International Courts and Tribunal' (2006) 24 Berkeley JIL 403.

52 "... a popular belief circulated at the end of the century that the establishment of a permanent international court would be an important step toward a world free of war. Ad hoc arbitration, as distinct from adjudication by such a permanent court, was not the same and by itself, not enough": Caron (n 21) 4.

this.[53] Today, with the benefit of hindsight this may seem an exorbitant or even naïve expectation concerning the influence of international courts on the peaceful settlement of disputes and the avoidance of war, considering that the past century has witnessed two World Wars and innumerable other armed conflicts 'despite' the existence of the PCIJ, the ICJ and others. At the beginning of the 20th century, however, there was a growing and genuine hope that peace may be achieved through compulsory adjudication. This belief at first probably benefited and backed the drafting inter alia of the Hague Convention, but then possibly turned against the PCA, highlighting its 'shortcomings' compared to a true permanent international court.

f) *The PCA as Successful Arbitral Institution*

The point has been made above that the PCA was overshadowed by the idea and desire to establish a true permanent international court. The focus seemed to be on its failings as an adjudicative institution; its performance as an arbitral institution seemed to be less important. The following section will assess the PCA's performance as an arbitral institution and show that there are good grounds to see the PCA as quite a successful arbitral institution.

Today, it is acknowledged that cases decided under the auspices of the PCA have contributed significantly to the development of substantive international law, in areas such as territorial sovereignty and territorial rights, state responsibility, and the law of treaties.[54] Back then, some criticism surrounded the case law emanating from the tribunals, concerning its coherence and consistency, but also its grounding in international law[55]—some went as far as submitting that the awards were decided *ex aequo et bono*.[56] According to authorities such as John Bassett Moore and

---

53 An address expressing this belief, delivered (by Senator Cosme de la Torriente before the Cuban Society of International Law at Havana) on 1 March 1922, is reprinted in GA Finch, 'Proposed Amendments to the Covenant of the League of Nations' (1922) 16 AJIL 268 (end of penultimate paragraph). Spiermann, *International Legal Argument* (n 20) 3; Caron (n 21) 23–24; see also WM Reisman, 'The Supervisory Jurisdiction of the International Court of Justice: International Arbitration and International Adjudication' (1996) 258 Recueil des Cours 42.

54 Shifman (n 2) 135–37.

55 Hudson (n 22) 31.

56 H Wehberg and CG Fenwick (tr) *The Problem of an International Court of Justice* (Clarendon Press, Oxford 1918) 29 et seq. For a summary of the criticism see Note of Baron Descamps, Annex 6, PCIJ Advisory Committee of Jurists, Proces Verbaux of the Proceedings of the Committee The Hague 1920, 47–50 (at www.icj-cij.org/pcij/serie_D/D_proceedings_of_committee_annexes_16june_24july_1920.pdf).

others the latter criticism was not justified.[57] Be that as it may, the present author is inclined to agree with Hudson when he said that the awards "achieved with considerable satisfaction the object of international arbitration, as set out in the Hague Conventions, namely the settlement of disputes between states on the respect of law".[58] Indeed, the overall recourse to the institution would suggest that, despite the severe criticism, the institution must have met a real need at the beginning of the century:[59] States worldwide trusted the PCA and referred disputes to its tribunals. These were not only the European (Great) Powers, but also the US, several Latin-American States (Venezuela, Peru, Mexico), an Asian State (Japan), a Middle-Eastern State (Turkey), and Russia.[60] Furthermore, recourse to arbitration under the PCA was quite regular. Leaving aside the period of inactivity of the First World War, the PCA on average dealt with roughly one case per year.[61] To compare this with the PCIJ: the PCA managed roughly 60% of what would later be the (contentious) caseload of the PCIJ.[62] Given that the PCIJ was especially designed to make recourse to it easier, less expensive etc than recourse to the PCA, this is quite a respectable comparison for the PCA.

Thus, the frequent, regular and widespread recourse to the PCA shows that its perception as a failed adjudicative institution was not shared by all and does not do it justice. Finally, on the basis of the above, the PCA can be seen as significant not only as an institution that paved the way for further developments in the international dispute settlement system, but also in itself, for being the first global mechanism for the settlement of disputes between States,[63] and for being quite successful at that.

g) *Conclusion*

The assessment of the criticism of the PCA at the beginning of the Chapter shows that the PCA did not fully meet the vision of its drafters and

---

57 Moore (n 51) xxxvi; RY Hedges 'The Juridical Basis of Arbitration' (1926) 7 British Yearbook of International Law 116.

58 Hudson (n 22) 31.

59 Rosenne (n 41) xxiv; see also van den Hout (n 11) 660.

60 For an overview of all cases submitted to PCA tribunals, and the parties thereto, see Ando (n 6) [21].

61 Between 1900 and 1921 the PCA was active for seventeen years (deducting the period of inactivity in the First World War), in which it decided sixteen cases, see Ando (n 6) [21].

62 Between 1922 and 1940, the PCIJ dealt with 29 cases: cf information provided at www.icj-cij.org/pcij/index.php?p1=9.

63 PCA website <http://www.pca-cpa.org/showpage.asp?pag_id=1044>; R Mackenzie et al, *Manual on International Courts and Tribunals* (2nd edn, OUP, New York 2010) 102.

promoters, for a variety of reasons. First, a compromise had to be struck at the First Hague Peace Conference, in order to overcome the strong opposition to the establishment of a dispute settlement institution. Second, influenced by the practical experience gained since the PCA had come into existence, negotiating priorities shifted: what had been at the top of the list of institutional features at the First Conference was severely criticised at the Second Conference. Finally, and in a similar vein to the second point, the PCA was an arbitral and not an adjudicative institution, and some delegations clearly had come to favour the latter over the former. As has been seen, much of this criticism would be more appropriately addressed to the PCA's Member States, the masters of the Hague Conventions, rather than the PCA itself; that notwithstanding, many simply criticised the institution, and some of the criticism, apparently, stuck. The sense of failure that underlay the perception of the PCA meant that it was not objectively assessed, and its successes as an arbitral institution were to some extent overlooked. History cannot be rewritten, and it is a matter of speculation whether a more objective assessment of the PCA would have led to a coexistence of the two institutions similar to that today between the ICJ and the PCA rather than the seeming demise of the PCA that occurred back then. But it is quite probable that the perception of the PCA hastened its apparent decline once the PCIJ had been established, and determined that today the relationship between the two institutions is seen mostly as one of predecessor and successor.

3. *The Coexistence of the PCA and PCIJ, and Its Contribution to International Law*

Having discussed the traditional perception of the relationship between the PCA and the PCIJ, which broadly conceives the two as predecessor and successor, this section will try to offer another perspective on their relationship. The emphasis will be on the coexistence of the two institutions and its contribution to international law.

a) *Coexistence of the PCA and the PCIJ*

It has already been mentioned that the PCA went into relative disuse once the PCIJ had been established. In terms of the theoretical conception of the relationship between the two institutions, the abolition of the PCA had been considered during the drafting of the PCIJ Statute but was rejected unanimously in the relevant subcommittee.[64] It was rejected on technical grounds, since the (future) parties to the PCIJ Statute were unable to terminate the Hague Peace Convention to which some third States were also a party (*pacta tertiis* rule).[65] Moreover, it was argued that the PCA still had a role to play regarding disputes that lent themselves more easily to an arbitral decision rather than an award based on strict rules of law. Accordingly, the PCIJ Statute stipulated that the PCIJ should be "in addition to" the PCA, as the second sentence of Article 1 shows:

> A Permanent Court of International Justice is hereby established, in accordance with Article 14 of the Covenant of the League of Nations. This Court shall be in addition to the Court of Arbitration organized by the Conventions of The Hague of 1899 and 1907, and to the special Tribunals of Arbitration to which States are always at liberty to submit their disputes for settlement.[66]

Thus, while recourse to the PCA dwindled after the early 1920s, it coexisted with the PCIJ for more than 20 years, until the dissolution of the latter in 1946.[67]

b) *Delimitation of 'Arbitration' and 'Adjudication' in the International Sphere*

The coexistence of two Permanent International Courts raised the question of a delimitation of spheres of competence. Prior to the adoption of the PCIJ Statute, the establishment of a "Permanent Court of International Justice" had been envisaged in Article 14 of the Covenant of the League of Nations.[68] Since that Article made mention of a 'Court of Justice', the question arose whether the spheres of competence could be delimited along the lines of a potential distinction between a 'Court of Arbitration' and a

64 See League of Nations, 'Documents concerning the action taken by the Council of the League of Nations under Article 14 of the Covenant and the adoption by the Assembly of the Statute of the Permanent Court, 1921' no 48 (206) (at www.icj-cij.org/pcij/serie_D/D_documents_conseil_de_la_societe_des_nations.pdf).

65 Ibid, nos 48 (206) and 44 (137).

66 See Article 1 of the PCIJ Statute, e.g. in PCIJ, Series D No 1 (1926).

67 See also de Magyary (n 21) 44; Rosenne (n 33) [8].

68 See Article 14 of the Covenant of the League of Nations: "The Council shall formulate and submit to the Members of the League for adoption plans for the establishment of a Permanent Court of International Justice. The Court shall be competent to hear and determine any dispute of an international character which the parties thereto submit to it. The Court may also give an advisory opinion upon any dispute or question referred to it by the Council of the Assembly."

'Court of Justice', ie between arbitration and adjudication.[69] It should be added that 'arbitration' at the beginning of the 20th century had at least two meanings both of which differ from today's understanding of the notion.

First, arbitration had a broad meaning and was used as a generic term for *legal* dispute settlement.[70] This is probably so because arbitration was the first,[71] and, in the time preceding international adjudication, the *only* legal dispute settlement mechanism in the international sphere. Accordingly, in that time, the term 'arbitration' equalled 'legal dispute settlement' in general, and both could be used synonymously.[72] Thus, 'arbitration' so understood was the general term used in distinction to diplomatic means of dispute settlement. Examples of this broad meaning of 'arbitration' are for instance Articles 12, 13 and 15 of the 1919 Covenant of the League of Nations, setting out the dispute settlement system under the League and referring to 'arbitration' as legal dispute settlement in general.

Of course, academics and diplomats also employed terms such as 'adjudication' and 'court of justice'.[73] Yet, when the broad meaning of 'arbitration' was used, these terms were not categorically distinguished from it, but rather used interchangeably. This indiscriminating use of words can for instance be seen in the name of the Court, that the Second Hague Peace Conference wished to see established alongside the PCA, the (today unthinkable) "Court of Arbitral Justice". Pieces published in the British Yearbook of International Law were entitled "the juridical basis of arbitration"[74] and the eminent JB Moore, in his historical and legal notes on arbitration, wrote about the "adjudications of the PCA" and the "judicial" 'conduct' or 'decisions' of 'international arbitrators'.[75] Thus, at the beginning of the 20th century, arbitration in the international

---

69 Berthold Schenk Graf von Stauffenberg, Article Premier in *Statut et Règlement de la Cour Permanente de Justice Internationale: Eléments d'Interprétation* (Carl Heymanns Verlag, Berlin 1934).

70 'Arbitrage A. sense large' in *Dictionnaire de la Terminologie du Droit International* (Sirey, Paris 1960) 50–51, see also 'C.' 52.

71 Wehberg and Fenwick (n 56) 144; Reisman (n 53) 41.

72 J Ray, *Commentaire du Pacte de la Société des Nations selon la Politique et la Jurisprudence des Organes de la Société* (Librairie du Recueil Sirey, Paris 1930) 397; 'Arbitrage A. sense large' (n 70).

73 See e.g. JB Scott, *The Status of the International Court of Justice* (OUP, New York 1916); Wehberg and Fenwick (n 56).

74 Hedges (n 57) 110ff.

75 Moore (n 51) xxxv, xxxviii, and xc.

sphere had a broad meaning and so understood was not distinct from adjudication.

The second meaning of 'arbitration' was narrower than the first and was based on a categorical distinction between 'arbitration' and 'adjudication'. According to this understanding, arbitration referred to dispute settlement *ex aequo et bono* (ie not as a result of a strict application of rules of law), whereas adjudication was dispute settlement in accordance with international law.[76] In part, this understanding underlay at least some of the criticism analysed earlier, according to which the PCA was not a 'proper' court. An example of this meaning of arbitration is the following statement, where arbitration is taken to mean 'a decision according to equity' and the above-mentioned broad understanding of arbitration, as a generic term for legal dispute settlement, is rejected: "... the mistake has often been made of confusing arbitration (a decision according to equity) with judicial settlement (a decision according to strict law) as practical institutions of present international law, and of joining them together under the common name of 'international arbitration'.[77]

Thus, these were two meanings 'arbitration' had at the beginning of the 20th century. It is the coexistence of the PCA with the PCIJ that led to a new enquiry into the meaning of the institution and notion of arbitration in the international sphere, as well as that of adjudication, in order to clarify their delimitation.[78] The change of meaning can be traced in international instruments adopted at that time. Therein, 'arbitration' progressed from being a notion with a broad meaning (synonymous with legal dispute settlement) to one with a narrow meaning (one type of legal dispute settlement) that could be distinguished from the other type of legal dispute settlement, adjudication. One example of this can be found in the League of Nations Covenant's provisions on dispute settlement. In the 1919 version of the Covenant, Articles 12, 13 and 15 used 'arbitration' in its broad meaning, as a generic term for legal dispute settlement. Thus, Article 12 distinguished arbitration from diplomatic dispute settlement ("inquiry"), and Article 13(2) provided a non-exhaustive list of disputes suitable for arbitration, including "disputes as to the interpretation of a treaty, as to any question of international law, as to the existence of any fact which if

[76] Wehberg and Fenwick (n 56) 13 and 144 ; see also Scott (n 73) 25.

[77] Wehberg and Fenwick (n 56) 13.

[78] Berthold Schenk Graf von Stauffenberg (n 69) ; P Barandon, *Die Vereinten Nationen und der Völkerbund in Ihrem Rechtsgeschichtlichen Zusammenhang* (Rechts- und Staatswissenschaftlicher Verlag, Hamburg 1948) 152; see also Wehberg and Fenwick (n 56) 144.

established would constitute a breach of any international obligation, or as to the extent and nature of reparation to be made for any such breach"—clearly outlining matters suitable for legal dispute settlement. Once the PCIJ had come into existence, as envisaged in Article 14 of the Covenant, Articles 12, 13 and 15 were adjusted to reflect the new notion of arbitration and the delimitation of spheres of competence, by adding 'adjudication' or 'judicial settlement' anytime that 'arbitration' was mentioned within those articles.[79] With this, the modern distinction between arbitration and adjudication had been drawn.

There are some references in academic writings to the effect that the coexistence of the two institutions led to a new enquiry into the meaning of the terms, and ultimately to the described change. The most explicit statement to this effect is to be found in Stauffenberg's commentary to the PCIJ Statute, Article 1, where the delimitation of competences between the two institutions is approached by enquiring whether it could be done along the lines of a potential distinction between 'arbitration' and 'adjudication':

> Le fait que le Pacte prévoyait la création d'une 'Cour de Justice', tandis que la vieille Cour portait le nom 'Cour d'Arbitrage', soulevait la question de savoir de quelle manière la compétence de la nouvelle Cour serait délimitée par rapport a l'ancienne Cour. *Dans cet ordre d'idées* se posait la question de savoir si une distinction pouvait être établie entre l'Arbitrage international et la Justice internationale.[80]

A few other authors make similar[81] if less explicit statements,[82] for instance implying that the coexistence of the institutions affected the understanding of the notion of arbitration. Especially in more recent writings, there is at best reference to the change in the notion of arbitration over time but often without linking it back to the coexistence of the two institutions.[83] Therefore, it is part of the purpose of this Chapter to serve as a reminder that the relationship between the institutions can be viewed

[79] Ray (n 72) 396–97; GA Finch, 'Proposed Amendments to the Covenant of the League of Nations' (1922) 16 AJIL 263–266; BCJ Loder, 'La Différence entre l'Arbitrage International et la Justice Internationale' (1923) IX Bulletin de l'Institut Intermédiaire International 269. Cf the assertion by the League of Nations Assembly that the amendments to Articles 12, 13 and 15 were 'une affaire de pure rédaction', as mentioned by Loder (ibid, at 270).

[80] Berthold Schenk Graf von Stauffenberg (n 69) (Emphasis added). Cf 'Arbitrage: A. sense large' (n 70) 52–53.

[81] P Barandon (n 78) 152.

[82] See e.g. Reisman (n 53) 49; Brower II (n 18) [34]; Rosenne (n 33) [8].

[83] See e.g. Brownlie (n 19) 702.

under several aspects. Emphasis can be placed either on their (perceived) temporal succession (predecessor and successor) or on their coexistence. With regard to the latter, the relationship should be credited for making a contribution to international law, namely for shaping the modern notion of arbitration and its delimitation to adjudication. Whether one thinks this is a meaningful distinction and accordingly useful contribution to international law, is a matter of opinion and will be examined in the next section.

c) *Significance of this Contribution to International Law*

The new notion of arbitration and its delimitation to adjudication gave new impetus to the debate in academic writings as to the distinguishing criteria between the two and the significance of the distinction.

It could be said that the new notion of arbitration, coined and defined on the international plane, was in itself a valuable contribution. Due to the decentralised nature of the international legal system, more often than not the starting point of analysis is to admit that there is disagreement or at least uncertainty as to the meaning of a certain term or concept, be it 'sustainable development', 'self-defence', or 'soft law'. Thus, to have clarity as to the meaning of a certain notion is valuable because it contributes to the building and maturation of the international legal system.

As regards the delimitation of arbitration from adjudication, it is agreed that the difference between the two now is one of degree rather than category. It is a formal difference,[84] lying in the character of the legal dispute-settling body, rather than a difference of substance. From this it could be deduced that the difference is insubstantial, or of little actual significance, but this would not necessarily be convincing in light of dispute settlement practice. It is clear that States have regular recourse to both arbitration and adjudication, which may indicate that the difference matters to them. Furthermore, it has been said that: "Law is law, but lawyers who have the option of 'forum-shopping' appreciate that changes in venue may change outcomes."[85] The fact that changes in venue—such as the choice between an arbitral and a judicial institution—may change the outcome of legal proceedings, is linked, amongst other things, to the flexibility that lies in

[84] Brower II (n 18) [5]; Brownlie (n 19) 702; Sohn (n 49) 22.
[85] Reisman (n 53) 49.

the application of legal rules and principles, ie a flexibility that arises also for dispute settlement bodies.

d) *Indeterminacy of Legal Rules and the Element of Choice in Their Application*

The indeterminacy of legal rules and the discretion that arises as a result thereof in their application is not exclusive to international law and its lack of a central and institutionalized law-making process. The problem is one of legal rules generally, resulting inter alia from "the open texture" of language,[86] in that there is a limit to the guidance which general language, as used in general legal rules, can provide.[87] The problem can be addressed by providing examples and other concretizations as to how a term is to be understood, for instance in relevant case law or a commentary, clarifying whether the general rule should apply to particular instances or fact patterns. Yet, the problem cannot be entirely overcome, due to the fact that nature and human invention continually generate new fact situations.[88] Examples of the latter would be e.g. the invention of electricity, cars, the Internet—any development in society and daily life, which requires new regulation.[89]

Thus, the open texture of language, in combination with the inability of any lawmaker to foresee all possible future fact patterns and combinations of circumstances, means that legal rules to a certain extent are indeterminate. As a result, it is a basic and frequently recurring question in any lawyer's mind, when applying the law to the facts (subsumption), "whether the present case resembles 'sufficiently' and in 'relevant' aspects the one that was agreed to fall under the law".[90] This element of choice, and the

---

86 On this and the following in general see HLA Hart, *The Concept of Law* (2nd edn, Clarendon Press, Oxford 1994) 124 et seq.; C Lim and O Elias, 'The Role of Treaties in the Contemporary International Legal Order' (1997) 66 Nordic JIL 1, 7 et seq.; see also Moore (n 51) xc.

87 "... where verbally formulated general rules are used, uncertainties as to the form of behavior required by them may break out in particular concrete cases." Hart (n 86) 126.

88 Hart (n 86) 126.

89 An example of the lawmaker not being able to foresee all fact patterns and inventions: In RGSt 32, 165, the then German *Reichsgericht* found a person not guilty of theft in a matter involving the tapping of electricity wires since electricity was not a movable matter but 'bodiless', and therefore, according to the Court, not covered by the then definition of theft.

90 Hart (n 86) 127. Judge McNair described the problem in the following way: "Whereas I may have thought, as a teacher or as the author of a book or an article, that I had adequately examined some particular rule of law, I have constantly found that, when I have been confronted with the same rule of law in the course of writing a professional opinion

risks it involves for the equality before the law and the rule of law more generally,[91] is acknowledged in domestic legal systems by the introduction of factors into court systems designed to act as counterbalance. One such factor is the centralised and hierarchical organisation of domestic court systems, providing for an appeal system.[92] If there are divergent interpretations of the same concept or legal provision, then this system guarantees that there is a higher court (and eventually the highest court) that decides the matter, and the other courts are obliged to follow.[93] Thus, there clearly is an "exercise of choice in the application of general rules to particular cases"[94] and it poses certain risks to the equality before the law and the rule of law more generally.

e) *Effect of Choice on Individual Cases of Arbitral and Adjudicative Bodies*

Against this background of the indeterminacy of legal rules and the resulting discretion or element of choice in their application, it can be shown that the difference between arbitration and adjudication has a profound effect on the way in which individual cases are decided on the international plane.

In adjudication, there is a permanent court and a permanent bench, set up by a multilateral treaty and linked to an international organisation.[95] The judges are elected in regular intervals by all the States parties to the treaty. The permanency of the institution means that there is an *esprit de corps* ensuring strong emphasis on coherence and continuity in the case

---

or of contributing to a judgment, I have been struck by the different appearance that the rule of law may assume when it is being examined for the purpose of its application in practice to a set of ascertained facts." [*The Development of International Justice: Two Lectures Delivered at the Law Center of New York University in December, 1953* (N Y UP, New York 1954) 16–7.

[91] On these notions see S Chesterman, 'Rule of Law' in R Wolfrum (ed) *The Max Planck Encyclopedia of Public International Law* (OUP 2008) online edition <www.mpepil.com> [43] et seq. Regarding equality before the law in the international sphere, Chesterman makes the point that this would require a "more general and consistent application of international law to States…" (Ibid, at [45]).

[92] H Thirlway, 'The Proliferation of International Judicial Organs: Institutional and Substantive Questions' in NM Blokker and HG Schermers, *Proliferation of International Organizations* (Kluwer Law International, The Hague 2001) 262.

[93] Preliminary reference systems permitting or requiring lower courts to put questions to a higher court constitute a variation: see e.g. A Reinisch, 'The Issues Raised by Parallel Proceedings and Possible Solutions' in M Waibel et al (eds), *The Backlash against Investment Arbitration: Perceptions and Reality* (Kluwer Law International, Alphen aan den Rijn 2010) 118–119.

[94] Hart (n 86) 129.

[95] Brower II (n 18) [4].

law.[96] To practically ensure the continuity of the case law, elections to the bench at the ICJ are staggered.[97] Since the ICJ is the only international universal tribunal of general jurisdiction, there is also a strong sense of responsibility as regards the further development of international law. For the decision of a particular case this means that the following factors are taken into account: the near-term aim of solving the dispute, but also the long-term interests of ensuring the highest degree of coherence and consistency in the application and interpretation of the—Court's own—case law, and to bear in mind or prepare the ground for any future developments of the law.[98] Thus, any particular case will always be set against the background of international law in general, and will be solved by looking at the picture as a whole.

By contrast, arbitration is frequently[99] *ad hoc*, and the right of the parties to choose the arbitrators means that change in the composition of arbitral tribunals is a permanent feature.[100] This makes coherence and consistency in the case law of arbitral tribunals more difficult to achieve.[101] It also means that there is a lesser degree of an *esprit de corps*, and accordingly more freedom to divert from previous case law if felt desirable or necessary. Also, since there are many different arbitral tribunals, the potential of each individual tribunal significantly to affect the future development of the law is smaller than that of the ICJ,[102] thus this factor, too, is less important in arbitral decisions. Finally, the fact that the parties choose the arbitrators (or are involved in their selection) can impact on the arbitrator's decision-making process and the application of general legal rules in several ways. First, it means that there is (or is expected to be) a certain affinity of the party-nominated arbitrators towards their party's approach to the case—otherwise they would not be chosen.[103] Second, there may be the arbitrator's ambition to be nominated again in the future. All these factors further contribute to the motivation of arbitral tribunals

[96] H Steinberger, 'Judicial Settlement of International Disputes' in R Bernhardt (ed), *Encyclopedia of Public International Law* (Elsevier, Amsterdam 1997) vol III, 53.

[97] DW Bowett, *The Law of International Institutions* (3rd edn, Stevens & Sons, London 1975) 239.

[98] RY Jennings, 'The Role of the International Court of Justice in the Development of International Environmental Protection Law' (1992) 1 Revue of the European Community & International Environmental Law 240–44.

[99] But cf. the references in (n 49).

[100] Reinisch (n 93) 115.

[101] Å Hammarskjöld, *Juridiction Internationale* (AW Sijthoff, Leiden 1938) 91.

[102] See also von Mangoldt (n 49) 18.

[103] Scott (n 73) 24.

to arriving at an overall satisfactory outcome to the dispute in question. In other words, the primary focus of arbitral decisions is the dispute at hand.[104] Coherence with earlier case law, or a responsibility for the development of international law, therefore may be less important than in ICJ decisions.

Thus, the formal difference in the longevity of the bench and the process of its composition have far-reaching and substantial consequences regarding the factors that are taken into account in rule-application and decision-making by the different legal dispute settlement mechanisms. While of course individual decisions of both types of institutions will divert from this broad-stroke analysis, it is thought that these generalisations by and large reflect the main differences between them, and are taken into account by the parties when deciding on the forum for their legal settlement of a specific dispute.

f) *Effect of Choice on Case Law of Arbitral and Adjudicative Bodies*

The above difference not only affects decisions in individual cases but also the body of case law that emanates from these institutions over time. Broadly speaking, adjudication ensures more continuity, coherence, and consistency in the case law; whereas arbitration achieves these to a lesser degree, due to the emphasis on the individual case. Accordingly, in arbitration the risk of diverting decisions on similar concepts or legal issues is increased,[105] ultimately posing a risk to the equality before the law and to this extent the rule of law more generally. Finally, this also affects the role the case law can play as a subsidiary means in the determination of rules of law, Article 38(1)(d) ICJ Statute.

IV. Conclusion

This Chapter has looked at the relationship between the PCA and the PCIJ. Today, this relationship is often seen under an aspect of temporal sequence: the PCA paved the way for the PCIJ and went into seeming demise once the PCIJ had been established. The purpose of this Chapter has been to serve as a reminder of another aspect under which this relationship can be viewed: the coexistence of the two institutions. This coexistence raised the matter of a delimitation of spheres of competence between the two

104 Brower II (n 18) [5].
105 Reinisch (n 93) 114–15.

permanent international courts, along the lines of a potential distinction between a 'Court of Arbitration' and a 'Court of Justice', ie between arbitration and adjudication. This way, the modern notion of arbitration was coined, as well as its delimitation from adjudication. Ever since then, both have existed as separate legal dispute settlement institutions.[106] Thus, the coexistence of the PCA and PCIJ made a contribution to both international law and the dispute settlement system in the international sphere.

The delimitation of arbitration from adjudication since then has been based on formal distinguishing criteria such as the longevity of the bench and the process of its composition. Thus in theory, it has become a matter of form rather than substance. Nevertheless, this affects the issues that come to bear in the decision-making process of the legal dispute settling body. For arbitral tribunals the main focus is on the resolution of the dispute before them, whereas the ICJ will be guided by at least two additional considerations, namely coherence with its earlier case law and the future development of international law. Accordingly, the formal difference affects how individual cases are decided, and leads to certain characteristic features of the case law that these institutions build. Thus, whilst the distinction appears to be merely formal, it does make a difference in practice.[107]

By looking back at the relationship of the PCA and PCIJ the aim is to remind us that the international community reacted to their coexistence by delimiting their spheres of competence, leading overall to a clarification and evolution of dispute settlement in the international sphere. In times where a proliferation of international courts and tribunals has been noted, similar action might be called for, concerning the organisation of the system as a whole; action to avoid fragmentation, ensure equality before the law, and strengthen the rule of law more generally; so as to support the well-rounded overall development of the international system of administration of justice.

---

106 Rosenne (n 33) [8].
107 Reisman (n 53) 51–55.

PART FOUR

METHOD AND SOURCES

THE DOCTRINE OF SOURCES IN THE DISCOURSE OF THE PERMANENT COURT OF INTERNATIONAL JUSTICE

Akbar Rasulov*

I. Introduction

As Thomas Skouteris points out in a recent monograph, in modern international law the term 'doctrine' is typically used in three different senses.[1] In the first place, and most traditionally, it refers to what in other contexts would be called the writings of the most qualified publicists, or, as the more critically minded observer might put it, the discourse of the disciplinary mainstream. The idea of doctrinal analysis and the concept of doctrinal consensus offer a good illustration of what one would normally have in mind when using the term in this way. This usage does not, on the whole, seem to be particularly widespread today among Anglo-American scholars, but Francophone writers certainly seem to be rather fond of it and the diffuse quasi-corporatist reasoning it tends to imply.[2]

In the second place, the term 'doctrine' in modern international law is also frequently used to describe various programmes and sets of policies proposed by powerful international players, typically as part of some broader hegemonic enterprise, aimed at changing the existing state of affairs in international law. A classic illustration of this kind of usage would be the infamous Bush doctrine or, to use a slightly more traditional example, the so-called Monroe doctrine. A common pattern of presumption here seems to be that, all things considered, each such doctrine ultimately represents everything that is potentially wrong with the idea of structuring international law as a horizontal legal order: self-legislation, abuse of power, regional fragmentation, relativity of legal obligation, the blurring of the boundary between *lex lata* and *lex ferenda*, and so on and so forth.

* The writing of this essay has benefited from conversations with Christian J. Tams, Duncan Kennedy, and Arnulf Becker Lorca. All errors and misinterpretations are mine alone.

[1] T Skouteris, *The Notion of Progress in International Law Discourse* (2010) 94.

[2] For further discussion of, see P Jestaz and C Jamin, 'The Entity of French Doctrine: Some Thoughts on the Community of French Legal Writers' (1998) 18 Legal Studies 415, 416 (in normal usage 'doctrine' describes a 'collection of works', but behind every 'totality of works' one ultimately finds the 'totality of those who write them').

The third meaning which is usually given to the term 'doctrine' among international lawyers has a somewhat more 'technical' orientation. One almost feels tempted to describe it as one last echo of the great nineteenth-century project of (German) legal science, since the central idea behind it essentially seems to be to give a name to those relatively stable clusters of international legal rules, analytical categories, and policy presumptions that allegedly appear in the mind of the legal practitioner to operate as analytically distinct normative blocks existing at a level above that occupied by individual legal rules but below that of a fully systematized 'legal field' (branch of law). A standard illustration for this sort of normative phenomena would be something like the doctrine of the permanent sovereignty over natural resources, the Calvo doctrine, or the doctrine of the responsibility to protect.

The idea of the doctrine of sources referenced in the title of this essay belongs in this third category of 'technical' concepts. As traditionally understood, it refers to what appears, at root, to be a *set of commonly agreed rules and presumptions* the application of which, according to the conventional disciplinary protocols of reasoning, is supposed to 'determine [the] two essential aspects of the normativity of international law rules: law-creation (how is international law made) and law-ascertainment (how do we distinguish between legally binding and non-binding norms).'[3]

For the most part of the last one hundred years, the ideational object produced by the belief in the essential identifiability of this set of rules and presumptions seems to have provided one of the most important elements in the imaginational structure of the international legal discourse. For some international law scholars, it supplied what they took to be the discipline's 'principal intellectual instrument' for determining the limits of its own reach.[4] For others, it served as the main guarantee of that 'solid bedrock' on which a genuinely effective international legal order would eventually have to be built.[5] In this essay, I am not going to explore the logical implications of either one of these two basically opposing analytical positions. What I am going to attempt instead is a critical excavation of an imaginational orientation that, according to the received wisdom, is meant to have tried to incorporate both of them. My question in the pages ahead is going to be: how was the doctrine of sources conceptualized in

3 Skouteris (n 1) 94–5.

4 O Schachter, *International Law in Theory and Practice* (1991) 35.

5 JF Williams, *Aspects of Modern International Law* (1939) 38.

the discourse of the Permanent Court of International Justice? What shape was it given? What content was inscribed into it? In what exact configuration was it articulated?

II. First Impression

When I first started to think about this essay, I must confess my initial impression was that there really was not that much I could say about my topic. How did the Court approach the subject of international law's sources? As I surveyed the relevant literature, it appeared to me that, all things considered, there were ultimately only *two* questions that had to be explored as part of this problematic.

The first question was exceedingly obvious: how did the Court conceptualize the logic of the relationship between the principle of State sovereignty and the idea of international law? Considering that, like every other international tribunal in modern times, the Court essentially operated *only* within the framework of the classical positivist tradition and given also that within the positivist tradition every inquiry into the question of legal sources sooner or later inevitably translates into an inquiry into the structural relationship between 'law' and 'sovereignty', it seemed to me quite self-evident that any attempt to establish how the Court may or may not have constructed its understanding of the doctrine of sources rather unavoidably would have to begin with a fairly close examination of what it said, suggested, or otherwise implied about the way in which the idea of international law could be reconciled with the idea of State sovereignty.

As I seemed to recall, the Court's first notable contribution to that debate may have happened already as far back as the *Wimbledon* case, where it famously proposed that 'entering into international engagements' should not be considered a 'limitation' but rather 'an attribute of State sovereignty'.[6] It also seemed to have explored the same theme, albeit only in passing, in the *Mavrommatis*[7] judgment, as well as in the *Eastern Carelia* opinion[8] and, quite possibly, also in the *Nationalities Decrees* opinion.[9]

---

[6] *SS Wimbledon* [1923] PCIJ Ser A No 1 at 25.

[7] *The Mavrommatis Palestine Concessions* [1924] PCIJ Ser A No 2 at 24 ('in a sense, it may be said that the whole body of international law has been accepted by States'). See also ibid at 12, 23.

[8] *Status of Eastern Carelia* [1923] PCIJ Ser B No 5 at 27 (State sovereignty is a fundamental principle of international law which means all international legal obligations have to be freely undertaken).

[9] *Nationality Decrees Issued in Tunis and Morocco* [1923] PCIJ Ser B No 4. See the discussion at 24 and 28.

But its most important pronouncement on the subject, as far as I could tell, surely must have been the *Customs Regime* case,[10] where, as I understood it, its basic argument line went more or less according to this formula:[11]

(i) the concept of sovereignty in international law has the same legal meaning as the concept of independence;
(ii) only those States that are formally placed under the authority of other States can be considered not to be independent for the purposes of international law;
(iii) the independence of a State cannot be diminished by the fact of its subordination to the rules of international law;
(iv) thus, no matter how extensive or burdensome the weight of restrictions upon a State's liberty arising out of its international legal obligations may become, this does not in the least affect its sovereign status.[12]

Needless to say, the logical structure behind the proposed sequence was far from perfect—everything else apart, there was a great deal of analytical slippage between steps (iii) and (iv)—and the unsightly ghost of Henry Maine eagerly haunted its every stage, but the Court clearly did not seem to mind any of this, and neither, for that matter, did most of its contemporaries.[13] And that, as far as I could tell, was all one really needed to know about it as a legal historian.

---

10 *Customs Regime Between Germany and Austria* [1931] PCIJ Ser A/B No 41.

11 Strictly speaking, in its full form this argument sequence only appears in the individual opinion of Judge Anzilotti (ibid at 57–8). From reading the text of the main opinion, however, it seems beyond doubt that the majority of the Court shared Anzilotti's views on this particular question.

12 'It follows that the legal conception of independence has nothing to do with a State's subordination to international law … It also follows that the restrictions upon a State's liberty whether arising out of ordinary international law or contractual engagements, do not as such in the least affect its independence.' (Ibid at 58.)

13 As the following comment by Thomas Baty indicates, the essential validity of the Anzilottian argument derives from the classical 19th century distinction (which has since lost all its theoretical currency) between 'status' and 'contract': 'It is necessary, however, carefully to distinguish between the position of a State which has resigned certain functions of sovereignty, and that of one which has contracted not to exercise them. It is the vital difference between status and contract. It may be most clearly expressed by saying that in the one case, if the State in question attempts to exercise the given function, it cannot do so, whilst in the other case, it will do wrong to do so.' T Baty, *The Canons of International Law* (1930) 19. The same pattern of reasoning can also be found in the written submissions made by the German government in the *Customs Regime Case* [PCIJ] Ser C No 53, 46 at 58): 'Du cas de l'aliénation [de l'indépendance] doit être distingué celui de l'obligation assumée par un Etat de faire ou de ne pas faire quelque chose. La simple

The second main question that I thought the terms of my inquiry required me to address lay in a very similar direction. It appeared to me, after considerable reflection, that any attempt to understand how the Court went about constructing its conceptualisation of the doctrine of sources at some point or another inevitably would have to address that legendary passage in the *Lotus* judgment, where, as the received wisdom strongly seems to suggest, it openly endorsed what to all intents and purposes looked like an essentially *contractualist paradigm* of international lawmaking:

> International law governs relations between independent States. The rules of law binding upon States therefore *emanate* from their own *free will* as *expressed in conventions or usages* generally accepted as expressing principles of law and established in order to regulate the relations between these co-existing independent communities or with a view to the achievement of common aims. Restrictions upon the independence of States cannot therefore be presumed.[14]

Now, most commentaries that deal with this part of the *Lotus* judgment typically would tend to focus on the last sentence of this passage. To my mind, however, it was quite obviously in the second sentence that the Court had made its most significant legal-theoretical claim. Consider the essential import behind the phrase: 'emanate from their own free will as expressed in conventions or usages'. The idea that an international treaty can be regarded as the formal expression of its parties' underlying wills, i.e. as a juridical embodiment of their collective political decision, is, of course, to this day still regarded as essentially rather uncontroversial from

obligation laisse intact le droit d'indépendance; elle est seulement une restriction à l'exercice de ce droit.' (For further elaboration, see also the oral pleadings by Professor Bruns in the same case, ibid at 210, at 229–37.) The main difficulty with this view, of course, is that as elegant as it may sound in the abstract, in practice it does not seem to be possible to distinguish between those legal engagements which can lead to the renunciation of 'status' and those which will merely result in the assumption of 'simple' contractual restrictions. For the most famous statement of the status-versus-contract theory, see H Maine, *Ancient Law* (1861). For Maine's influence on the evolution of the early 20th-century international legal thought, see generally C Landauer, 'From Status to Treaty: Henry Summer Maine's International Law' (2002) 15 Canadian J of L & Jurisprudence 219.

14 *SS Lotus* [1927] PCIJ Ser A No 10 at 18 (emphasis added). By way of comparison, the French version of the text reads: 'Le droit international régit les rapports entre des Etats indépendants. Les règles de droit liant les Etats procèdent donc de la volonté de ceux-ci, *volonté manifestée dans des conventions ou dans des* usages acceptés généralement comme consacrant des principes de droit et établis en vue de regler la co-existence de ces communautés indépendantes ou en vue de la poursuite de buts communs. Les limitations de l'indépendance des Etats ne se présument donc pas.'

the point of view of the general doctrinal consensus. Whether one looks at the official judicial pronouncements or at scholarly writings, the most important feature of international conventional law for most international lawyers even today appears to be the idea that 'treaties epitomize the principle of consent'.[15] But notion that the same assumption could also be extended to international customs,[16] the claim, in other words, that 'usages generally accepted as expressing principles of law' should *also* be seen as 'emanations' of the participating States' 'own free wills' and embodiments of their collective decisions—however fragmented the terms of the scholarly debate on customary international law may have become in recent years, this argument, it seems safe to conclude, would almost certainly find no support in the modern doctrinal consciousness.

In fact, to the extent to which it can be said to exist at all, the standard doctrinal position today would much more likely, it seems, tend to incline towards the view that the fundamental mechanics of norm-creation underpinning the two formal processes, rather than being governed by the same single logic of 'will emanation', must actually follow entirely dissimilar operative patterns. For, indeed, at least since the days of the *North Sea Continental Shelf* judgment,[17] the common view within the profession has been that the processes of customary norm-production must be ultimately grounded in the logic of *belief* and *perception* (or what has been described elsewhere as diffuse consensus of opinion)[18] rather than any kind of *tacit consent* or *deliberate choice*.[19] What is more, given the terms of the

15 L Henkin, 'International Law: Politics, Values and Functions' (1989/IV) 216 RCADI 9, 47.

16 In the *Lotus* file, this presumption can be perhaps most explicitly found in Judge Nyholm's dissenting opinion (n 14 at 60): '[T]he foundation of a custom must be the *united will* [volonté commune] of several and even of many states constituting *a union of wills* [unité des volontés] or a general consensus of opinion among the countries which have adopted the European system of civilization, or a manifestation of international legal ethics which takes place through the continual recurrence of events with an innate consciousness of their being necessary. These [requirements] give a general idea of the necessary conditions for the existence of an international law.' (emphasis added)

17 See *North Sea Continental Shelf Cases* [1969] ICJ Rep 3, 44–5 [77]-[78].

18 See M Byers, *Custom, Power and the Power of Rules* (1999) 19.

19 While it would not be perhaps correct to say that logic of the general test for 'proving custom' established in the *Shelf* judgement leaves no scope for the possibility that a customary international regime could be deliberately engineered *ex nihilo* (which is what the theory of *pactum tacitum* would necessarily require), it would be very difficult to argue convincingly otherwise. (A slightly more charitable interpretation might be that the logic of the *Shelf* test does leave some scope for the idea of deliberate intentionality but that its role is nevertheless severely restricted in the sense that it includes no possibility of direct manipulation of custom at its productive stage but rather presumes that any willed action

contemporary debate, one might even argue that under the current rhetorical protocols almost *any* attempt to demonstrate the presence of some form of tacit intentionality behind a given pattern of international behaviour will far more probably push the resulting conversation in the direction of treaty law theory than a debate about custom. The more convincing, in other words, the evidence in support of the argument of tacit consent is going to look in any given case, the more likely it will be that the established factual record will then be interpreted as evidencing the creation of some form of informal treaty-like arrangement rather than a standard-grade international custom.[20]

Now, the word 'likely', of course, remains the key operative word here: the tendency for that sort of characterisation would almost certainly not arise automatically.[21] But—and this is what really needs to be emphasized here—in the days of the *Lotus* judgment there would not even be any room for this tendency to emerge, at least not in the context of the

---

by the subjects of the customary norm vis-à-vis that norm itself will occur only *after* the respective custom has already formed.) For evidence of explicit rejection of the *pactum tacitum* theory in modern doctrine, see, among others, M Mendelson and R Mullerson, 'Final Report of the Committee on the Formation of Customary (General) International Law', in (2001) International Law Association: Report of the 69th Conference 712, 740–53; M Akehurst, 'Custom as a Source of International Law' (1975) 47 British Ybk Intl L 1, 31–42; HWA Thirlway, *International Customary Law and Codification* (1972) 47–60; J Kunz, 'The Nature of Customary International Law' (1953) 47 AJIL 662. But see also, rather ambiguously, K Wolfke, *Custom in Present International Law* (2nd edn, 1993) 44–51 (arguing that the general doctrinal view agrees with the idea that *opinio juris* equals consent but proving this point by reference to statements arguing that opinio juris equals recognition). More generally for a sense of how the modern doctrinal consensus constructs the psychological element in custom, see, among others, J Combacau and S Sur, *Droit International Public* (9th edn, 2010) 54–70; V Lowe, *International Law* (2007) 36–58; H Koh, 'Remarks on Contemporary Conceptions of Customary International Law' (1998) 92 ASIL Proc 37; R Higgins, *Problems & Process: International Law and How We Use It* (1995) 13–22; P Hulsroj, 'Three Sources—No River' (1999) 54 Zeitschrift fur Offentliches Recht 219. For the standard doctrinal argument about the difficulty of taking the idea of tacit consent seriously (and the practical impossibility of separating tacit consent from perception), see also O Schachter, 'Towards a Theory of International Obligation' (1968) 8 Virginia J Intl L 300, 312–3.

[20] Though such kind of reasoning has been typically associated with the work of international relations scholars, there exists no reason to refuse this conclusion as a matter of international legal analysis. For a standard illustration of a typical international relations argument about 'tacit agreements', see C Lipson, 'Why Are Some International Agreements Informal?' (1991) 45 Intl Organization 495, 527–32. Cf A Aust, 'The Theory and Practice of Informal International Instruments' (1986) 35 ICLQ 787.

[21] The basic inertia of interpretative practices would still make it highly unlikely that any talk of a treaty-like arrangement would succeed in practice without the demonstration of a considerable measure of procedural formalism.

standard doctrinal debate,[22] which means, quite possibly, that it is precisely here, in that second sentence in the above-quoted passage from *Lotus*, that one should start looking for the traces of whatever it is that ultimately distinguishes the logic of the Court's conceptualisation of the doctrine of sources from that which seems to have been adopted in today's usage.

And if there should be any doubts as to how momentous that part of the *Lotus* argument may have been in its time consider now also this fact: by elevating the will-emanation thesis to the position of the master-theory of international lawmaking, the Court not only managed in one fell swoop to resolve one of the most pressing theoretical questions confronting the discipline of international law but also worked out a remarkably effective solution to one of its most significant ideological challenges. Look at that passage again. In the space of less than half-a-dozen lines, through an argument spread over a mere three sentences, the Court not only finds a way to put to rest every possible doubt about international law's credentials as a 'positive science' but also establishes a virtually irrefutable logical equation whereby so long as one grants its initial premise every increase in the size, density, and reach of the international legal regime *necessarily* has to be considered a resounding revalidation of the principle of State sovereignty. One only needs to agree with the idea that the rules of international law 'emanate from the [States'] own free will': everything else follows as a matter of straight logical deduction. If all legal rules that bind the community of States are indeed a projection of their own sovereign wills, then none of the liberties traditionally associated with the idea of sovereign freedom can even in principle be infringed by the growth, expansion, intensification, etc. of the international legal order. What is more, since it is only the States that can participate in international legal relations, one could also argue, by flipping the formula backwards, that the heavier and more diversified the burden of obligations arising out of international legal rules applicable to the given State tends to become, the more clearly this will establish the reality of its sovereign status. Or, which is essentially

22 Notably, as Jan Klabbers points out, the sway which the logic of practical formalism had over the structures of doctrinal imagination has been so much higher in the interwar period that even the (currently entirely uncontroversial) idea that a treaty could be created through an exchange of documents, let alone through a procedure that does not involve the production of any formalized written instruments, was considered sufficiently contentious for various doctrinal sources to insist on rejecting it outright, or at the very least creating a whole separate category of 'irregular' treaties to accommodate this regrettable possibility. See J Klabbers, *The Concept of Treaty in International Law* (1996) 45–6.

the same thing, the more effectively the given State finds its hands tied by international law, the more convincingly it thus reaffirms its sovereignty:[23]

> The Court declines to see in the conclusion of any Treaty by which a State undertakes to perform or refrain from performing a particular act an abandonment of its sovereignty. No doubt any convention creating an obligation of this kind places a restriction upon the exercise of the sovereign rights of the State, in the sense that it requires them to be exercised in a certain way. But the right of entering into international engagements is an attribute of State sovereignty.[24]

***

And thus in two simple steps I thought I was going to complete this investigative exercise. Everything that needed to be said about the Court's theory of sources would be uncovered, explained, and conveniently illustrated through a simple exegesis of three landmark cases. The resulting summary would run for no more than half-a-dozen sentences but what an elegant logical structure it would project:

1. All rules of international law are created through a *positive lawmaking process*.
2. This does not mean that international law has no respect for the *principle of sovereignty*; quite on the contrary: every rule of international law is grounded solely in the *free agreement* of its subjects—which fact can be easily proven by tracing its presence either in the respective set of treaties or in the respective set of international customary practices.
3. In those cases where this cannot be done, i.e. in those cases where neither the treaty law nor customary international law has anything to say about the given subject matter, the basic rule proposed by the Court in line with the principle of sovereignty holds that no binding obligations will be found to exist between the States in question—that is to say, it will be inadmissible to presume that any 'restrictions upon [their]

---

23 It is interesting to note that once it is articulated in its full form this argument seems to be remarkably similar to the so-called theory of 'new sovereignty' as well as, perhaps more notably, Thorstein Veblen's theory of 'conspicuous consumption'. See further A Chayes and A Handler Chayes, *The New Sovereignty* (1994) 26–7; T Veblen, *Theory of the Leisure Class* (1994 [1899]) 46–60.

24 *Wimbledon* (n 6).

> independence' have been created[25]—which in Hohfeldian terms means that the States will have been placed in the position of *privilege*, that is to say, they will enjoy a legally protected *license* to exercise their sovereign prerogatives vis-à-vis one another howsoever they please.[26]

And that, in a nutshell, I thought, was all that there ever was to say about the Court's concept of the doctrine of sources.

But then the following complication suddenly caught my attention.

For the argument sequence that I have just outlined above to hold true—for the idea, in other words, that the increase in the quantity of international legal engagements should be automatically considered evidence of one's sovereign status to qualify as logically valid—it would necessarily have to be assumed that the *only* way in which international legal obligations could be created in practice would be through the exercise of the principle of sovereign consent, that is to say, through the performance of an operative dynamic premised *exclusively* on the idea of a perfectly voluntary interactive process occurring between mutually equal juridical subjects.

Now, as anyone who has ever studied this topic would immediately recognize, the most obvious problem with proposing this kind of assumption is that it is, quite simply, entirely and incontestably false. As far as the available historical evidence seems to indicate, at no relevant point during the interwar period did the actual processes by which international legal obligations arose and spread across the international legal arena ever seem to reflect, follow, or imply this sort of operative dynamics.[27] What is more, neither the States themselves, through their law-creating and

---

25 This proposition, commonly known as the principle of the least restrictive interpretation, can also be found in a number of other judgments produced by the Court during that period. See, for example, *The Free Zones of Upper Savoy and the District of Gex (Second Phase)* [1930] PCIJ Ser A No 24 at 12; *Territorial Jurisdiction of the International Commission of the River Oder* [1929] PCIJ Ser A No 23 at 26.

26 For a general overview of Hohfeldian categories, see A Corbin, 'Legal Analysis and Terminology' (1919) 29 Yale L J 163. Specifically on the logic of Hohfeldian privileges, see also JR Commons, *Legal Foundations of Capitalism* (1924) 94–100.

27 Any number of recent and not so recent studies can be cited in support of this conclusion. See, among others, A Anghie, *Imperialism, Sovereignty and the Making of International Law* (2004) 115–95; N Berman, 'Modernism, Nationalism, and the Rhetoric of Reconstruction' (1992) 4 Yale J of L & the Humanities 351; David Kennedy, 'The Move to Institutions' (1987) 8 Cardozo L Rev 841; M Koskenniemi, The *Gentle Civilizer of Nations* (2002) 236–65, 302–69; Skouteris (n 1) 93–157; R Parfitt, 'Empire des Negres Blancs: The Hybridity of International Personality and the Abyssinia Crisis of 1935–36' (2011) 24 Leiden J Intl L 849; M Fakhri, 'The 1937 International Sugar Agreement: Neo-Colonial Cuba and Economic Aspects of the League of Nations' (2011) 24 Leiden J Intl L 899.

law-confirming conduct, nor the broader community of international lawyers who worked with them, through their rhetorical and theoretical work, appear to have either enacted or internalized as part of their standard discursive protocols the kind of operative analytical formulae that this sort of juridical orientation would require. Indeed, if anything, the most common presumption that can be detected within the general disciplinary consciousness during that period appears to have been the view that such kind of theoretical approach offered, in fact, an entirely 'inadequate account of the system as it can be seen in actual operation',[28] since both as a matter of the available historical evidence and as a matter of the basic ontological argument it was excruciatingly obvious that international law comprised 'something more than the rules which result from treaties, conventions or other voluntary agreements, or from custom'.[29]

And so inevitably the question arises: how should one understand, against this background, the meaning of the Court's argument in the two excerpted passages? Is it possible that the Court might somehow have erred in its presentation of the general operative dynamics of the international legal system? Could it be perhaps that in drawing so eagerly on the

28 JL Brierly, *The Law of Nations* (4th edn, 1949) 52–3.

29 JF Williams, *Current International Law and the League of Nations* (1929) 11–8. For a more comprehensive sense of where the interwar disciplinary consensus stood on the question of how international legal obligations arise in general, see further H Kelsen, *Introduction to the Problems of Legal Theory* (trans Bonnie Litschewski Paulson and Stanley Paulson, 1992 [1934]) (offering an explanation grounded in a mixture of interpretivism and 'logical positivism'); A Verdross, 'Les Principes Généraux du Droit dans la Jurisprudence Internationale' (1935/II) 52 RCADI 195 (offering an explanation derived from a mixture of natural law and light-touch sociological jurisprudence); H Lauterpacht, *The Function of Law in the International Community* (1933) (offering an explanation grounded in a loose combination of functionalist sociological theory and proto-Dworkinean interpretivism); G Scelle, *Precis de Droit des Gens* (Vols 1 and 2, 1932–4) (offering an explanation derived from a mixture of solidarism, objectivist sociological jurisprudence, and socio-theoretical monism); L Le Fur, *Guerre Juste et Juste Paix* (1920) (offering an explanation grounded in a mixture of organic solidarism and quasi-religious natural law). See also, in a similar vein, the oral pleadings by E Kaufmann in *Customs Regime* (n 13)259 at 276: 'l'indépendance des Etats est, d'une part, la base sur laquelle repose le droit international en ce sens particulier que les Etats indépendants sont en même temps les sujets créateurs des règles écrites et coutumières de ce droit, et les sujets soumis aux règles du droit international. Mais, d'autre part, le droit international repose sur le fait de l'interdépendance des Etats qui se trouvent dans des relations de dépendance mutuelle, soit d'ordre général et découlant de la solidarité et des interdépendances générales qui unissent tous les Etats, soit d'ordre particulier et découlant des solidarités et interdépendances qui unissent d'une façon particulière certains Etats—des groupes d'Etats, si l'on veut user de ce terme—de la communaute internationale.' But see also PE Corbett, 'The Consent of States and the Sources of the Law of Nations' (1925) 6 British Ybk Intl L 20; L Oppenheim, *International Law* (Vol 1, 3rd edn, 1920).

imagery of the contractualist model it ended up losing sight of the basic distinction between metaphors and reality? Or was it rather the case that what it had to say about this matter was simply ignored by the rest of the international law community?

Could it be that the Court might have actually been perfectly aware that the will emanation thesis was ultimately entirely bogus but that for some obscure reason it nevertheless still decided to pay lip service to it? Could it be that it never really was 'into' voluntarist positivism? Or that it is not actually in those three particular judgments that the key to what it 'really believed' should be sought? Could it be that all these much-celebrated dicta that one typically turns to were, in fact, nothing more than an elaborate smokescreen? It would certainly not be unreasonable to advance this hypothesis, considering the argument that was just made, though it would obviously be quite difficult to know how one would then go about verifying it, especially given how strongly the force of the conventional wisdom would oppose it.

Then again, one might also say, in some basic sense none of this would be really important: one may question as much as one pleases to what extent the Court did or did not believe that the contractualist metaphor offered an entirely inaccurate picture of the international legal process, but in the context of an inquiry such as this one what matters the most, ultimately, is not how the Court *had actually thought* the contemporary international legal system was like in practice but rather what it *aspired* it to become in principle. And, as the received wisdom appears to suggest, what it aspired it to become, in the end, was a perfectly horizontal legal order constructed on the basis of an essentially contractualist model of lawmaking, at the root of which lay the will emanation theory, the principle of sovereign consent, and the concomitant axiom that every State, ultimately, is the master of all its obligations.

****

Now, what I would like to propose in this essay, essentially, is this: both of these last two propositions—the idea that what matters the most in an inquiry such as this one is what the Court aspired to articulate rather than what it believed to be true, and that what it aspired to articulate when it came to formulating its concept of the doctrine of sources, ultimately, was a vision built around the logic of the contractualist model—are, in fact, completely and fundamentally incorrect. Firstly, there exists no plausible theory that can allow us to separate the cognitive from the normative dynamics in this context, i.e. what the Court 'thought' the international legal process was like in practice from what it 'aspired' it to become in principle. The one inexorably collapses and morphs into the other and vice versa. Secondly, if we look at the actual evidence supplied by the Court's own discursive record, we will see that it very often seemed to draw no principled distinction between describing and aspiring. Partly it seems this happened because most of the judges who sat on the Court appeared to take the classical liberal concept of the separation of powers quite seriously. But mainly I think it was due to the fact that, one or two slightly uncharacteristic moments aside, most of the judges sincerely believed also in the virtues of gradual, 'organic' change and felt quite apprehensive about any type of revolutionary programmes. For that sort of vision to remain effective, it seems inevitable that a judge must aspire to keep the doctrine of sources as he finds it.

Thirdly, even if we leave all this aside, it seems rather incontrovertible from reading the Court's own discourse that the Court's basic position on the subject of sources has been a lot more complex, ambivalent, and contradictory than what it would have to be in order to sustain the contractualist vision argument. Inasmuch as the received memory of the Court's legacy tends to support that argument, it follows, it must be rejected as fundamentally specious and unwarranted.

In the pages ahead I am going to throw light on one particular set of these typically ignored complexities, ambivalences, and contradictions in the Court's broader discursive legacy. I will do this by subjecting a number of fairly characteristic formal pronouncements taken from the Court's own caselaw to a relatively close critical reading informed by a series of symptomatological insights derived to some extent from the groundbreaking legal-historical studies of Duncan Kennedy and Morton Horwitz,[30] but mainly from Grant Gilmore's landmark work *The Death of Contract*.[31] My idea of symptomatological reading is borrowed from Louis Althusser.[32] My concept of distinctly *legal-historical* symptomatology derives from those used in the early NAIL scholarship.[33] More specifically, my central methodological assumption here is going to be this: by turning Gilmore, Horwitz, and Kennedy's arguments about the general trajectory at the

---

30 See *infra* (n42), (n 46).

31 G Gilmore, The Death of Contract (1974).

32 See L Athusser, 'From *Capital* to Marx's Philosophy', in L Althusser and E Balibar, *Reading Capital* (trans. Ben Brewster; 1969) 11, 14–30.

33 See, in particular, David Kennedy, *International Legal Structures* (1987) and Berman (n 27).

heart of the internal history of US contract law into a legal-historiographic model, it should be possible to develop a critical legal-discourse-theoretic analytic the application of which in the present context ought to enable us, firstly, to obtain a far better understanding of how exactly the Court may or may not have understood the essential logic of international law-making to operate, and, secondly, to figure out just how much of a contractualist mindset it had ultimately brought into its discourse.

III. Contract(ualism): The Basic Structure of a Sensibility

1. *The Three Ages of Contract(ualism): The General Argument*

In the thirty odd years that have passed since its first publication, *The Death of Contract* has been hailed variously as a 'clarion call',[34] a 'remarkably imaginative and provocative book',[35] a 'poetic polemic [with a] somewhat unreliable description of the facts',[36] 'one of those few books that deserve our most careful thought and attention',[37] 'more an escapade than a serious endeavour',[38] an argument that 'transforms the mundane into high drama',[39] a 'very curious performance',[40] and 'a work of perverse dictum'.[41] Whichever view one takes of it, one thing seems to be certain, the argument Gilmore offered in *The Death of Contract* most definitely was not devoid of controversy.[42]

---

34 R Collins, 'Foreword', in Gilmore (n 31) vii, xviii.

35 RJ Mooney, 'The Rise and Fall of Classical Contract Law: a Response to Professor Gilmore' (1976) 55 Oregon L Rev 155, 156.

36 C Yablon, 'Grant Gilmore, Holmes, and the Anxiety of Influence' (1995) 90 Northwestern U L Rev 236, 252.

37 Collins (n 34) xvii (citing Richard Epstein).

38 AJ Waters, 'For Grant Gilmore' (1983) 42 Md L Rev 865, 869.

39 R Hillman, 'The Triumph of Gilmore's The Death of Contract' (1995) 90 Northwestern U L Rev 32, 43.

40 R Gordon, 'Book Review' (1974) Wisconsin L Rev 1216, 1218.

41 Collins (n 34) xxiv (quoting Robert Braucher).

42 For all its unquestionable originality, *The Death of Contract* did not, of course, spring out of the proverbial vacuum. Published for the first time in 1974, it arrived on the scene as part of a much broader pattern of intellectual transformation in Anglo-American legal historiography, whose driving impulse can be traced in principle as far back at the realist age, if not earlier. See in this vein, among others, L Friedman, *Contract Law in America* (1965); M Horwitz, 'The Historical Foundations of Modern Contract Law' (1974) 87 Harvard L Rev 917; Duncan Kennedy, *The Rise and Fall of Classical Legal Thought* (2006 [1975]); PS Atiyah, *The Rise and Fall of Freedom of Contract* (1979). The basic narrative about the evolution of the Western private legal tradition that emerged as a result of this transformation to this day forms an essential part of the disciplinary canon not only in the Anglo-American world but also outside it. What makes this narrative interesting for our

Its opening statement captures its most fundamental thesis: in the US, the law of contract, as traditionally understood, is 'dead'.[43] Indeed, all things considered, it is a point that seems hardly 'worth arguing anymore',[44] for even if the law of contract had ever been alive in the past, those days now seem so distant that one can hardly even work out the journey that the US legal system has made since.[45] Still, every journey follows a certain trajectory. The one that Gilmore tried to sketch out in *The Death of Contract* can be summarized thus:[46]

At some point in the late 19th century a remarkable transition took place in the structure of the Western private law consciousness.[47] As a result of this transition, the classical subjectivist paradigm that had crystallized in US contract law practice over the course of the previous several decades, and at the heart of which lay the so-called 'will theory of contract' that essentially defined contract as a 'meeting of the minds', quickly gave way to an entirely new way of thinking about the law of contract built around what the later generations of legal historians came to describe as the 'objectivist approach'.[48] Driven in part by the legal profession's desire to turn law into a positive science, the objectivist paradigm insisted on formulating a theory of contractual regulation organized entirely around the idea that it was only the externally verifiable actions of the contracting parties, not their actual wills or intentions, that should matter in the eyes of the law.[49] The launcher of this new creed among American lawyers was the legendary Christopher Columbus Langdell. Its main theoretician and

purposes, however, is not the actual degree of its scholarly acceptance but rather the specific methodological contribution which Gilmore's work makes to its internal logic.

43 Gilmore (n 31) 1.

44 Ibid.

45 Ibid 2.

46 As stated earlier, my understanding of this trajectory is derived not only from Gilmore's own account, but also, more generally, from Kennedy and Horwitz's works. See further in this connection Duncan Kennedy, 'From the Will Theory to the Principle of Private Autonomy: Lon Fuller's "Consideration and Form"' (2000) 100 Columbia L Rev 94 and M Horwitz, *The Transformation of American Law 1870–1960: The Crisis of Legal Orthodoxy* (1992) 9–63. See also B Mensch, 'Freedom of Contract as Ideology' (1981) 33 Stanford L Rev (1981) 753 as well as the sources cited in (n 42).

47 Because Gilmore, Kennedy, and Horwitz wrote about American law, most of the discussion below focuses on US sources. Nevertheless, it has to be noted that the broader paradigmatic shifts each of them describes do not just characterize the evolution of US contract law but can also be traced across the rest of the Western legal tradition. See further in this respect F Wieacker, *A History of Private Law in Europe* (trans Tony Weir, 1995) 410–1, 417–8; as well as Atiyah (n 42).

48 See, however, Kennedy (n 42) 214 (the memory of the subjectivist age may very well have been invented in the twilight years of the objectivist period).

49 Horwitz (n 46) 35.

doctrinal architect, however, was none other than Justice Oliver Wendell Holmes.[50]

No sooner had the new objectivist approach taken root, however, than its various logical contradictions rapidly began to emerge. As the doctrine set out to find its way around these contradictions, its intellectual coherence progressively diminished, until by the mid-1920s it became obvious that an entirely new disciplinary paradigm began to take shape. What distinguished this new paradigm from either of its predecessors, among other things, was the fact that rather than trying to formulate some grand overarching *essentialist* concept of contract it simply put forward a loosely assembled set of what in effect were nothing more than public policy propositions. One of the most immediate consequences of such a transformation, as one might expect, was the swift dissolution at the level of the practical legal discourse of all traditional doctrinal categories. Everything that was solid melted into air and all the differences that had previously been said to separate the volitional law of contractual relations from the non-volitional law of unjustified enrichment and tort increasingly came to be seen as entirely illusory. As the conceptual structure of contract law rules started to develop the same analytical signature which had hitherto been associated with the standard duty-of-care paradigm, the whole concept of contractualism as a *distinct regulatory model* ran itself into the sand. By the early 1960s, the only thing that seemed pertinent to say in characterizing the law of contract was that, really, it was just another instrument of public governance primarily designed to support the operation of the 'free market' institution in a mixed capitalist economy.[51] The writing was on the wall:

> Speaking descriptively, we might say that what is happening is that "contract" is being reabsorbed into the mainstream of "tort". Until the general theory of contract was hurriedly run up late in the nineteenth century, tort had always been our residual category of civil liability. As the contract rules dissolve, it is becoming so again. ... [T]he two fields, which had been artificially set apart, are gradually merging and becoming one.[52]

2. *Doctrinal Symptomatology*

Now, to what extent the history of American contract law has really followed this general pattern remains to this day, admittedly, somewhat

---

[50] Gilmore (n 31) 15.

[51] S Macaulay, 'Justice Traynor and the Law of Contracts' (1961) 13 Stanford L Rev 812, 813–7.

[52] Gilmore (n 31) 95–6.

unclear.[53] For the purposes of the present inquiry, however, I do not think this fact should have any relevance. Whatever doubts may have been raised about Gilmore's account over the years, the three-ages-of-contract (ualism) narrative sketched out above clearly seems to enjoy enough support among private law historians to be considered sufficiently reliable as a matter of descriptive accuracy. At the same time, inasmuch as this essay is not meant to be a study in the history of US contract law, its principal interest in Gilmore's work is not determined by the latter's success in depicting the 'exact truth' of what may or may not have happened in the history of US contract law. Rather, it is only what Gilmore has to say *as a matter of legal-theoretic contention* about the general way in which the rise and fall of the objectivist paradigm has manifested itself *at the level of the respective doctrinal-discursive patterns*—his basic take, in other words, on the *essential juridical symptomatology* of contractualism as a distinct mode of legal consciousness—that motivates the present excursion into *The Death of Contract*, not anything else.

Looking at Gilmore's argument from this point of view, consequently, the one single most important insight that one ought to be able to take away from it as a student of international legal history has to be, I think, the following idea:

The spectacular demise of contractualism as a distinct mode of legal consciousness was in many ways the result of its own internal contradictoriness. When the objectivist approach first entered the American legal mainstream in the third quarter of the 19th century, a number of radically new epistemological assumptions were added to the general theoretical framework of the US contract law discourse. Some of the new analytical protocols inspired by these assumptions openly conflicted with the general epistemic setup left over from the subjectivist period. In an ideal scenario, each such conflict would have been immediately noted and expressly resolved in favour of the new analytical patterns. In the actual event, the paradigmatic transition did not proceed nearly as seamlessly. In the absence of a coherent top-down 'de-contradictization' programme,

---

53 It is not impossible, for example, as some scholars have pointed out, that what really stood behind those transformational patterns which Gilmore, Kennedy, and Horwitz describe should be seen in terms of some kind of cyclical development pattern, rather than as a strict linear progression. See in this connection, among others, J Perillo, 'The Origins of the Objective Theory of Contract Formation and Interpretation' (2000) 69 Fordham L R 427, 428. For further discussion of the various shortcomings of Gilmore's argument and summaries of the main criticisms directed against it, see also Hillman (n 39) 38–41; C Knapp, 'Rescuing Reliance: The Perils of Promissory Estoppel' (1998) 49 Hastings L J 1191.

the legal system, as it always does in such cases, started experimenting at the level of substantive doctrinal argument, searching intuitively for a way to defuse the mounting epistemic crisis. Some of these experiments yielded relatively positive results. Others, however, ended up having the exact opposite effect. It is the latter that Gilmore's argument in *The Death of Contract* is primarily focused on, and it is this argument that the students of international legal history can most benefit from analysing closely.

As part of its blind intuitive search for epistemic coherence, at some unspecified point in the late 19th century American contract law suddenly took note of two hitherto relatively neglected doctrines that it had seemingly kept in its arsenal for the better part of the preceding half-century without ever so much as acknowledging, let alone fully exploring, their theoretical potential.

The first doctrine centred around the concept of *promissory estoppel*, i.e. the idea, essentially, that recovery in contractual disputes ought to be made available even to those plaintiffs who suffered a material detriment from the defendant's breach of promise *in the absence of a formal contract*, so long as the detriment was suffered in reliance on the defendant's assurances and was sufficiently substantial.[54] The second doctrine built on the old Roman law concept of *quasi-contracts*. The difference between the two in many ways was essentially semantic:

> As a matter of usage it came to be felt that [the concept of] quasi-contract [offered] a better way of talking about the situation where plaintiff was seeking reimbursement for some benefit he had conferred on the defendant, while promissory estoppel was better for the situation where plaintiff was seeking recovery for loss or damage suffered as the result of reliance on the defendant's promises or representations. [A]s a matter of jurisprudential economy, [of course] both situations could have been dealt with under either slogan but the legal mind has always preferred multiplication to division.[55]

New practices breed new theories. The steady popularization of the two new doctrines in contractual practice quickly precipitated the formation of an entirely new set of analytical protocols, which after a very short period of time triggered a complete theoretical breakdown of the classical doctrine of consideration. The latter, as traditionally defined, stated that, as a matter of principle, recovery and enforcement in contractual disputes should be awarded only with regard to those benefits and detriments

---

54 Gilmore (n 31) 70.

55 Ibid 97.

which the contracting parties had explicitly bargained for in advance. Without this sort of limitation, assumed the majority of the late 19th-century writers, it would be simply impossible to formulate a sufficiently feasible theory of contract that did not slip back into the subjectivist tropology of the 'meeting of the minds' theory; much more importantly, it was also felt, it would also be impossible to sustain a viable distinction between the idea of contractual liability and liability in tort.[56] In the event, as subsequent experience showed, even if the former belief turned out to be without basis, the latter presumption was entirely justified.

As the requirement that only those benefits and detriments which had been explicitly 'bargained-for' deserved to be enforced under the rubric of contract lost its traction, so did unavoidably the idea that 'liability in contract' could not be imposed unless the legally stipulated formalities of offer and acceptance had been duly completed. Once that assumption went out of the window, however, there was no longer any way to maintain convincingly that the law of contract was in any conceivable sense designed to protect the freedom of consent.[57]

The original objectivist challenge, recall, began with two main innovations.[58] The first was the idea that (i) the old subjectivist hypothesis that contracts must be upheld inasmuch as they embodied the meetings of their parties' minds created an entirely practically inoperable doctrinal test; and so (ii) it made a lot more sense to insist instead that the only factor which mattered in deciding whether or not a given private agreement should merit public enforcement was the actual words and deeds of the contracting parties, i.e. their externally observable conduct as opposed to their internal psychological processes.[59]

The second was the presumption that the key to the evaluation of this external conduct had to be sought in the opinion of that redoubtable bedrock of Victorian morality, the 'reasonable man'.[60]

---

56 Ibid 96.

57 For further discussion, see Horwitz (n 46) 35–7.

58 For further background, see Kennedy, (n 42) 210–28; Horwitz (n 46) 33–63.

59 For a classical expression of this sentiment, see F Pollock, *Principles of Contract* (1876) 30 ('not intention in the abstract, but the communicated intention, is what we have to look to in all questions of the formation of contracts').

60 For a typical illustration of this sort of reasoning, see *Smith v Hughes* [1871] LR 6 QB 597 (per Blackburn J): 'If, whatever a man's real intention may be, he so conducts himself that a reasonable man would believe that he was assenting to the terms proposed by the other party, and that other party upon that belief enters into a contract with him, the man thus conducting himself would be equally bound as if he had intended to agree to the other party's terms.'

The law, argued the objectivist theory, had no business 'tak[ing] account of the infinite varieties of temperament, intellect, and education which make the internal character of a given act so different in different men': 'the standards of the law are standards of general application' and it is thus that they are meant to be used. Whatever may have been the original justification for the classical subjectivist approach, the *real* task of every legal inquiry was to address itself only to those 'external phenomena [and] manifest acts and omissions' which can be positively established and verified, while at the same time remaining 'wholly indifferent to the internal phenomena of conscience', replacing them wherever necessary with an empirically derived standard of what 'the man of ordinary intelligence and prudence' would typically do in the normal course of business.[61]

What came after such kind of theoretical reorientation should not be too difficult to work out. In its standard Anglo-American configuration, the objectivist theory articulated a vision of contract law centred around, on the one hand, a decidedly textualist interpretative approach[62] and, on the other, a fundamentally fetishistic conception of contractuality expressed in a tri-partite formula of offer, acceptance, and consideration. Looking through this prism, a legally valid contract, it followed, could only come into existence when one duly formalized procedural act (offer) was met with another duly formalized procedural act (acceptance), the performance of a third such act (the assumption of an explicitly agreed detriment by each party in return for the same by the other) being treated as the metonymic stand-in for what in the subjectivist theory was understood as the 'meeting of the minds' moment. Any attempt to determine whether or not the given private agreement should qualify for legal protection, on this view of things, consequently, would have to involve nothing more than a fairly straightforward exercise of verifying the available factual record against this tripartite checklist, the former being interpreted solely on the basis of the actual words and deeds of the respective parties as interpreted from the point of view of the 'reasonable man'.

For a while, the new theory seemed to work rather well. But the seeds of its irreversible disintegration had already taken root.

---

61 OW Holmes, *The Common Law* (1881) 308–10.

62 The ultimate pinnacle of which became the so-called parole evidence rule, which stated that 'where a contract has been reduced to writing, neither party can rely on extrinsic evidence of terms alleged to have been agreed, i.e. on evidence not contained in the document'. (C Mitchell, *Interpretation of Contracts* (2007) 34 (quoting from Treitel).)

The rise of the solidarist mentality at the end of the 19th century[63] translated into the growing conviction felt across different segments of the profession that legal protection, at least in principle, should be made available not only to those plaintiffs who fully complied with all their contractual obligations but also to those who, even though they performed their obligations only in part, in doing so proceeded to change their relative position in reliance on the defendants' promise to perform their part of the bargain. Under the classical objectivist theory, the standard solution in such situations would have been to declare that the defendants had no duty to compensate the plaintiffs inasmuch as no valid contractual relationship had been concluded between them. Under the pressure of the new ideological consensus, the legal practice, however, soon began to revisit that assumption by insisting on awarding recovery in such cases not just in the measure traditional for decisions 'in equity' but at the same level as would be the case had there been a duly formulated express contract between the two parties. What enabled this revisitation, as Gilmore's argument reveals, to a very large degree was the analytical structure of the objectivist paradigm itself.

Once it had been accepted, contrary to the old subjectivist claim, that what made a given set of private transactions into a legally valid contract was not the actual attainment of the 'meeting of the minds' but only the completion of a certain set of formal rituals meant to present an irrefutable evidence of such an attainment, the argument logically followed that the creation of a valid contractual relation could be recognized in practice even in those situations where the parties in question did not, objectively speaking, enter into any kind of practically meaningful communication with one another—as would be the case, for example, with contracts concluded 'through telephone operators who fail to repeat messages properly'[64] as well as with almost all varieties of standard-form contracts where the parties, typically, would not even need to become aware of one another's immediate identities to be able to enter into a legally valid contractual relation. Since without communication there can be no expression of consent, it followed at this point that, despite everything that was said at the level of official theory, at the level of its actual analytical protocols the law of contract discourse did not really 'care' that much about the principle of

---

[63] For background on which, see, inter alia, Koskenniemi (n 27) 268–9, 288–90, 297–301.

[64] G Costigan, 'Implied-in-fact Contracts and Mutual Assent' (1919) 33 Harvard L Rev 376, 379.

consent.[65] As soon as that idea began to sink in, it was only a matter of time before it started to become obvious that none of those formal rituals whose completion was initially identified as probatively crucial was, in fact, at all necessary for the formation of a valid contractual relation. If it was true indeed that 'the making of a contract does not depend on the state of the parties' minds, it depends on their overt acts'[66] and that a direct logical implication of this idea was that in practice 'a person is bound not by his real but by his manifested intention, [so that, in effect] contracts [can] often arise where there has been no mutual assent, no meeting of the minds of the parties, in fact',[67] then as a matter of principle it would seem to follow that it must be as right for the legal system, ultimately, to seek to compensate those plaintiffs who enjoyed the protection of a formally concluded contractual agreement as it was to compensate those who did not. The moment this realisation emerged, the entire objectivist model was done for.

The only factor, recall, that originally warranted the introduction of the tri-partite formula offer-acceptance-consideration was the assumption that it was the accumulation of these particular elements that would best evidence in practice the attainment of that all-important 'meeting of the minds'. If, as it became now clear, it was not really the 'meetings of the minds' that the law actually cared about, what justification could there be found for the continued retention of this formula? Put differently, if it was true indeed that what made a private agreement into a contract was *only* its capacity to satisfy a certain set of pre-determined externally verifiable criteria and not its capacity to embody a particular psychological state, then there existed no cogent reason why these criteria would necessarily have to be defined in reference to such specific phenomena as offer, acceptance, or consideration. On the contrary, it would seem a lot more logical to presume at this point that what the legal system would *really* be inclined

---

65 '[The] shift from a subjective to an objective theory [of contract] was part of a broader tendency to create formal, general theories that would provide uniformity, certainty, and predictability of legal arrangements. ... In the process of formalizing and generalizing the system of contract law, the legal rules came to bear a more and more tenuous relationship to the actual intent of the parties. What once could be defended and justified as simply a more efficacious way of carrying out the parties' intentions came eventually to be perceived as a system that subordinated and overruled the parties' will. ... Objectivism could not be reconciled with individual autonomy or voluntary agreement.' Horwitz (n 46) 35–6.

66 Holmes (n 61) 307.

67 WW Cook, 'Agency by Estoppel' (1905) 5 Columbia L Rev 36, 40.

to do in this situation was dispense with that sort of assumptions altogether and simply posit instead, without limiting itself in any formalistic manner, a general set of basic social values and policies which it considered worthy of its attention and try to fix its definitional criteria in such a way as to give these values and policies the force of the law. And if this set of values and policies would then come to include, say, some kind of reliance interest principle or a prohibition against unjust enrichment, then so be it—there existed no obvious reason why the juridical definition of contract could not be reformulated accordingly.[68]

A highly characteristic illustration of this moment of complete paradigmatic disintegration can be found in Arthur Corbin's ground-breaking essay 'Offer and Acceptance, and Some of the Resulting Legal Relations', published in Yale Law Journal in January 1917.[69] 'The rule generally laid down', begins Corbin his argument in the last section of the article, has traditionally implied

> that the acts of offer and acceptance must be expressions of assent. This has long been the theory upon which contractual obligations have been enforced. The test question usually put is, what was the intention of the parties? It must not be supposed from this, however, that no contractual relation can exist unless the parties both foresaw and intended it. If two parties have gone through the form of offering and accepting, the law determines the legal relations that follow. Frequently these come with surprise and shock to the parties themselves.[70]

The standard explanation for this proceeds from the assumption that the parties will be 'bound by the reasonable meaning of what they said and not by what they thought' since this enables the courts to 'carry out the intentions of the parties in the great majority of cases'. The actual reality of legal practice, however, does not seem to offer much support for this conclusion:

> The legal relations consequent upon offer and acceptance are not wholly dependent even upon the reasonable meaning of the words and acts of the parties. The law determines these relations in the light of subsequent circumstances, these often being totally unforeseen by the parties. In such cases it is sometimes said that the law will create that relation which the parties would have intended had they foreseen [it]. *The fact is, however, that*

---

[68] See L Fuller and W Perdue, 'The Reliance Interest in Contract Damages' (1936) 46 Yale L J 52; (1937) 46 Yale L J 373.

[69] Cf G Gilmore, *The Ages of American Law* (1977) 80.

[70] AL Corbin, 'Offer and Acceptance, and Some of the Resulting Legal Relations' (1917) 26 Yale L J 169, 204–5.

> *the decision will depend* [*solely*] *upon the notions of the court as to policy, welfare, justice, right and wrong, such notions often being inarticulate and subconscious.*[71]

From the 'intention of the parties' to the 'reasonable meaning of words' to the 'notions of the court as to policy, welfare, justice and morality'—two pages of text, half a century of legal progress, an epic journey from a fully integrated structure of crystal-clear ontological presumptions to a constantly shifting assemblage of loosely fragmented insights about the apparent workings of knowledge and evidentiary presumptions. The decline and fall of contractualism initiated and completed within the space of three analytical transformations.

3. *General Conclusion*

The story of the progressive breakdown of the objectivist paradigm related above, as the attentive reader will notice, exudes a rather strong Hegelian air. To what extent this recognition should alert us to the possibility that the narrative thus depicted may, in fact, be more of a reverse-engineered projection than an actual representation of 'how things really happened' presents, of course, a very relevant consideration, but one that is such only from the standpoint of the general historiography of US contract law. In the context of the present inquiry, considering the specific investigative needs of the particular exercise which this narrative is intended to serve, it would seem to remain essentially irrelevant. What matters for our present purposes, what determines the value of Gilmore, Kennedy, and Horwitz's contribution to this study, is not their grand-theoretic sense of legal history but rather their 'practical' insights into the sequences of logical entailment, that is to say, their explanation of the basic analytical architectures of each of those three paradigms of contract law thinking that have been detailed above.

This explanation, schematically, can be summarized as follows:

1. As soon as the view that the law should only care about the actual words and deeds of the parties and not the 'internal phenomena of conscience' was accepted, the dissolution of the principle of consent as an analytically operative concept of contract law became by and large unavoidable.

---

71 Ibid 206 (emphasis added).

2. The rise of the *doctrine of quasi-contract*, which was built around the idea that contractual remedies could be provided, in some circumstances, for any benefit conferred by the plaintiff on the defendant that had not been reimbursed to the former, effectively implied that the formation of contractual relations did not, in law, require any prior exchange of offer and acceptance. The rise of the *doctrine of promissory estoppel*, which was built around the idea that contractual remedies could similarly be provided to reimburse any detriment which the plaintiff reasonably suffered as the result of his reliance on the defendant's assurances, confirmed further that at least in some cases an offer, once duly extended, could become effectively irrevocable.[72] In both cases, the essential message, once the surface complexities of the substance-procedure interplay were distilled, was that the creation of a legally valid contract did not, strictly speaking, depend on any kind of consensual dynamics.
3. The immediate logical implication of all this at the micro-level was the progressive relaxation of the *classical regime of privity*, and in particular the *rule of pacta tertiis*, wherefrom it was only a short logical step to the complete *decoupling of the general dynamics of opposability from the principle of strict textualist interpretation*.

Collect all the italicized passages and what comes out at the end is the basic *doctrinal symptomatology* of the demise of objectivism, that is to say, the end of contractualism as a distinct mode of legal consciousness. Or, which is essentially the same thing: the basic telltale signs of the use of the non-contractualist modality in contract law discourse.

IV. Further Methodological Observations

The next step in the argument should not be hard to predict, but before we go any further with this, let us pause briefly to consider what, against all this background, the argument presented above actually does and does not say, imply, or presuppose.

1. The death-of-contract thesis does not imply the idea that contract law is 'finished' as a field of academic inquiry or a body of law. Gilmore's argument only covers the 'objective dynamics' of analytical patterns or

[72] See B Markesinis et al, *The German Law of Contract* (2nd edn, 2006) 65.

'ways of thinking'.[73] That is to say, it concerns the idea that a certain pattern of conceptualizing the structure of private law—a pattern whose operative mechanics was built around the idea that a particular type of remedies could only be awarded where the formal requisites of offer, acceptance, and consideration were duly completed—ceased being followed in legal practice so clearly that it would not be unreasonable to say that 'its time was over'.

2. The death-of-contract thesis, to put it differently, is not, thus, a story about the 'death' of the eponymous legal instrument, or the respective body of legal materials regulating its use, or the corresponding academic subject. It is a story about an imaginational shift that was triggered by a series of very particular evolutions occurring at the micro-level of practical doctrinal argument which led to a very specific kind of theoretical disintegration of a very specific discursive formation, at the heart of which lay a deeply ingrained belief in the reality of the categorical dichotomy between consensual and non-consensual legal relations and, accordingly, the analytical operability of the idea of voluntary choice in the analysis of horizontally functional legal relations.

3. The death-of-contract thesis does not presuppose any essentialist concept of contract law—or, for that matter, the law of tort. On the contrary, if we look at it closely, Gilmore's account rather consistently eschews in its description of what should be included under these labels any type of essentialist language, which not only makes the resulting argument a lot more nuanced and complicated but also eminently more suitable for analytical appropriation in the context of the present study.

By way of illustration, consider how a typical anti-contractualist argument would have unfolded if it were constructed along essentialist lines.

'As a matter of logic, it should of course be obvious that in the field of private law the need for some kind of tort-law-like regime will be insurmountable. The law of contract, for all its undeniable flexibility, has a very limited practical functionality as an instrument of regulatory action. This is so not least because due to the way a typical contractual transaction is organized the law of contract simply cannot reach and cover every potential scenario that requires the attention of the private legal regime.

Consider, for instance, the case of accidents. The whole point about accidents, of course, is that one cannot negotiate all the relevant rules that will govern the resolution of one's disputes in advance for the obvious

[73] For further elaboration of this idea, see R Collins, 'Gilmore's Grant (Or the Life & Afterlife of Grant Gilmore and His Death' (1995) 90 Northwestern U L Rev 7, 18–20.

reason that, accidents being accidents, one simply does not know who one would have to negotiate with before the relevant accident happens. Hence, to avoid the dangers of a potential *non liquet,* there will always have to be posited some form of a background system of catch-all default rules to take care of such situations.

What holds true for non-bargained-for accidents holds true also for any other class of practical situations that fall into the proverbial gaps in incompletely specified contractual arrangements—and all real-life contracts, of course, are incompletely specified contracts. Hence, the argument follows, even in those areas of private legal intercourse that are otherwise subsumed under a web of interlocking contractual regimes, there will always still remain present a certain residue of background rules that, without, strictly speaking, being of public legal provenance, will not at the same time be of contractual origin either.'

Now, the crucial point here, of course, is not to what extent an argument made along such lines would make sense in the context of international law. It seems rather obvious that it would not, since the only way in which one could hold every element of this reasoning sequence together would be by projecting a deeply reified, institutionally fetishized conception of tort law,[74] i.e. by presenting what in effect is a historically conditioned state of affairs whose achievement depends on the maintenance of a highly specific (and not at all self-evident) set of institutional structures of governance—the so-called municipal legal order—as though it were somehow an emanation of some innate transcendental essence.

The crucial point here, rather, is that even though one certainly could have made that argument, Gilmore quite emphatically did *not* make it.

4. As Gilmore presents it, the death-of-contract scenario became a historical inevitability as soon as—and because—the 'meeting of the minds' doctrine stopped being treated as *analytically operative,* having been replaced by the assumption that it was 'the words and acts of the parties [that were] themselves the basis of contractual liability', not the metaphysical convergence of their psychological wills that they were meant to represent.[75] Once that idea had sunk in, it was only a matter of time before something like the doctrine of promissory estoppel or quasi-contract

[74] 'Institutional fetishism is the imagined identification of highly detailed and largely accidental institutional arrangements with comprehensive and vague [concepts].' R Unger, *Social Theory: Its Situation and Its Task* (1987) 200.

[75] S Williston, 'Mutual Assent in the Formation of Contracts' (1919–20) 14 Illinois L R 85, 87 (1919–20).

would begin to be recognized as a legitimate basis for the award of contractual remedies. As soon as that happened, however, the whole argument that in contract, unlike in tort, the parties always remain the 'masters of their obligations'[76] immediately lost its practical relevance, as did also the traditional rule of contractual privity, the principle of *pacta tertiis*, and the classical liberal notion of *autonomie de la volonté*. Whatever was left thereafter could still, of course, be called *a* law of contract—in the modernist universe everything is nominalist to a certain degree—but it would take a very hypocritical attitude not to admit that there would be something seriously inappropriate about that.

5. One only needs to take a few steps back now to make out the basic contours of Gilmore's implied ontological argument.

a. Each of the three paradigms of contract law thinking detailed above—subjectivism, objectivism, and modernism—has to be understood ultimately only as an embodiment of a certain regime of analytical predispositions and nothing else. Each of them finds its expression not in any specific collection of substantive legal rules or principles, let alone a specific political or moral creed, but in a certain structure of reasoning patterns, or, if one is willing to use this metaphor, a certain *mode of discursive production*.[77]
b. Seen in this light, the exercise of investigating the use of the contractualist model in the discourse of the Permanent Court of International Justice becomes effectively an exercise in tracing out the general analytical protocols at the heart of the Court's practice of knowledge concerning, on the one hand, the *determination of the contents of international law* and, on the other, the *production of formally valid international legal 'conclusions'*, that is to say, a study whose principal driving question is: which particular sets of metaphors, operative fictions, and rhetorical tropes did the Court's pronouncements on the subjects of *international lawmaking* and *international legal interpretation* tend to rely on and have sought to operationalize as a matter of regular analytical practice?

---

[76] See G Cheshire et al, *Law of Contract* (13th edn, 1996) 29 ('A contracting party, unlike a tortfeasor, is bound because he has agreed to be bound.')

[77] There seems to be a strong resemblance between the idea of the paradigm as used in this context and the concept of the *mode of legal consciousness* proposed by Duncan Kennedy. See Duncan Kennedy, *Legal Reasoning: Collected Essays* (2008) 201.

c. Considered from this perspective, the two main defining characteristics of the subjectivist paradigm could accordingly be identified as, firstly, the unquestioned presumption that the doctrine of the 'meeting of the minds' could be used as an analytically operative heuristic and, secondly, the resulting link-up between the discourse on enforcement and the quasi-psychologistic inquiry into the internal reality of the contracting parties' individual intentions.
d. The principal defining traits of the objectivist paradigm in its standard configuration, by contrast, could be detected in its strong predilection for linking the decision to enforce to procedural formalism and the resulting insistence on centring every inquiry into the facticity of contractual relations around textualism and apparently empirical examinations of externally traceable events, the operative yardstick for the measurement of which it would find in the ordinary-meaning-of-words approach underpinned by a deductively posited abstraction about 'what reasonable people in this context would do'.
e. Finally, the general symptomatology of the modernist paradigm could be defined in terms of its progressive dissipation of any concern for the idea of verifying consent and the concomitant foregrounding of 'equitabilizing' reasoning patterns driven by the aspiration to connect the logic of contract regulation with the logic of public policy consideration.

V. The Place of the Contractualist Paradigm in the Court's Discourse

I think it should be quite obvious where this argument is going to go next. If sufficient account is taken of the foregoing observations, the conclusion that most readily suggests itself, once the full record of the Court's official discourse is duly examined, is that through its various pronouncements concerning the twin logics by which international legal obligations arise and invite themselves for interpretation, the Court, contrary to what the received wisdom would tend to suggest, has, in fact, quite eagerly contributed, if not necessarily to a full-scale demise of the contractualist model of international, then at least to its fundamental delegitimation as an analytical metaphor.

In the *Eastern Greenland* case, for instance, it introduced a reasoning pattern premised directly on the operative logic of promissory estoppel.[78] In *Mavrommatis*[79] and in the *Chorzów Factory* (*Interpretation of Judgments*)[80] case, it did the same for the doctrine of quasi-contract,[81] and in the *Jurisdiction of the Danube Commission* opinion,[82] for the theory of contracts-implied-in-fact.[83] In the *Free Zones* case, it struck out, even if not in the open, against the principle of *pacta tertiis*;[84] in the *Borchgrave* affaire,[85] against the logic of textualist interpretation (and the restrictive principle).[86]

---

[78] *Legal Status of Eastern Greenland* [1933] PCIJ Ser A/B No 53 at 71: 'What Denmark desired to obtain from Norway was that the latter should do nothing to obstruct the Danish plans in regard to Greenland. The declaration which the [Norwegian] Minister for Foreign Affairs gave ... was definitely affirmative: "I told the Danish Minister to-day that the Norwegian Government would not make any difficulty in the settlement of this question." The Court considers it beyond all dispute that a reply of this nature ... is binding upon [Norway].'

[79] (n 7).

[80] *Interpretation of Judgments Nos 7 and 8* [1927] PCIJ Ser A No 13.

[81] The common argument in both cases was that where this would serve the advancement of a widely recognized public policy the failure by the parties to complete the procedural formalities established under the respective compromissory instruments correctly could not prevent the award of the benefits of that compromissory agreement to the applicant State. Thus, in the former case, having observed that the application was filed under a treaty that had not yet entered into force, the Court reasoned that since it was easy to repair this defect, it was going to disregard this fact, as it was 'not bound to attach to matters of form the same degree of importance which they might possess in municipal law' (n 7 at 34). In the latter case, having first pointed out that the German application for interpretative judgment did not meet the formal criteria, the Court immediately went on to conclude that it was entirely appropriate that within reasonable limits it would disregard such defects of form on the grounds that doing so would serve the end of encouraging the use of international adjudication, making the judicial settlement of disputes more effective. (*Interpretation of Judgments* (n 80) at 16.)

[82] *Jurisdiction of the European Commission of the Danube between Galatz and Braila* [1927] PCIJ Ser B No 14.

[83] Ibid at 23: 'as all the Governments concerned in the present dispute have signed and ratified both the Treaty of Versailles and the Definitive Statute [of the Danube signed at the Paris Conference, on 23 July 1921] they cannot, as between themselves, contend that some of [the latter's] provisions are [not part of the legal regime created] under Article 349 of the Treaty of Versailles.'

[84] *Case of the Free Zones of Upper Savoy and the District of Gex* (*First Phase*) [1929] PCIJ Ser A No 22.

[85] *The Borchgrave Case* (*Belgium v Spain*) (Preliminary Objections) [1937] PCIJ Ser A/B No 72.

[86] Despite the fact that the terms of the compromissory agreement concluded between Belgium and Spain only referred to the question of the parties' dispute with regard to Spain's responsibility incurred in connection with the death of Baron de Borchgrave and not to the question of her responsibility incurred with regard to the alleged denial of justice produced as the result of showing a manifest lack of diligence in investigating the Baron's death, the Court opted for a differing interpretation on the grounds that the

In the *Oscar Chinn*[87] and the *Chorzów Factory* (*Merits*)[88] judgments, the reasoning protocols it deployed suggested a complete break not just with the contractualist metaphor as such but with the entire positivist tradition *tout court*. In both of these cases the basic thrust of its argument evoked what to all intents and purposes seemed to be an 18th-century-style natural law aesthetic. As if to prove that this was not a mere fluke, the Court then went on to confirm in the *Serbian Loans* case[89] that, at least as far as its understanding of its institutional mandate was concerned, there existed, in fact, two entirely different normative orders both of which were part of 'international law' but only one of which derived from positively enacted international legal structures. In the *Chorzów Factory* (*Jurisdiction*) judgment, as an extension of the same logic, it further reasoned that a particular rule of international law would have to be considered in force, even though it had not been included in any sources listed under Article 38, on the grounds that to hold otherwise would actually be 'contrary to the *fundamental conceptions* by which the movement in favour of general arbitration has been characterized.'[90]

Some of these moves—and the troublesome implications they spelled for the classical positivist paradigm—were spotted almost as soon as the Court made them. The fact, for example, that in the *Free Zones* case, in spite of declaring that it did not need to 'decide as to the extent to which international law takes cognizance of the principle of stipulations in favour of third parties', the Court nevertheless did precisely that,[91] thus adding a considerable wrinkle to the principle of lawmaking-by-consent, was certainly not lost even on the most conservative among its contemporary observers.[92]

preceding history of the controversy between the parties supported that conclusion. (See ibid at 13–4, 168.)

87 *Oscar Chinn Case* [1934] PCIJ Ser A/B No 63.

88 *Case concerning the Factory at Chorzów* (Merits) [1928] PCIJ Ser A No 17.

89 *Case concerning the Payment of Various Serbian Loans Issued in France* [1929] PCIJ Ser A Nos 20/21.

90 *Case concerning the Factory at Chorzów* (Jurisdiction) [1927] PCIJ Ser A No 9 at 22.

91 *Free Zones* (n 84) at 20.

92 'In spite of these cautious words, it seems that the Court's decision as regards the Gex Zone is based upon the recognition of a stipulation in favour of a third party, Switzerland, contained in a treaty between the Powers, as creating a right in Switzerland on which Switzerland could insist and which the Powers ... could not thereafter terminate without Swiss consent, by agreement between themselves. The Court must have held, therefore, that international law does—in some circumstances—take cognizance of the principle of stipulations in favour of third parties. Indeed in the case of the Gex Zone the Court seems to give the fullest possible effect to the principle. [The recognition that] a treaty provision

Most of these blips (if one may call them that), however, went by and large unnoticed and thus, effectively, untheorized.

Thus, there seems to have been no attention given, for example, to the rather obvious contradiction in the *International Commission of the River Oder* case between the argument that, on the one hand, however convincing the contention made by the six governments with regard to the meaning of a given treaty provision might be as a matter of the ordinary-meaning-of-words analysis, logic alone would not be sufficient to justify imputing to the contracting parties an intention the existence of which could not otherwise be demonstrated,[93] and the presumption, on the other hand, that 'arguments, drawn from [an in-depth examination of the *travaux préparatoires*] cannot modify the conclusions which [the Court] has reached by means of a direct interpretation of the [applicable] provisions'.[94]

Nor does it seem there has been any considerable discussion of what sort of implications would have to follow from such statements as: 'The Court cannot as a general rule be compelled to choose between constructions determined [and submitted to it by the parties] none of which may correspond to the opinion at which it may arrive [but is] entirely free to interpret [the respective treaty provisions] without restrictions.'[95] (Under the logic of the will-emanation theory and the principle of restrictive interpretation, the ground rule in such situations, of course, would have to be that, quite to the contrary, it was always the States themselves that, being the owners of their consent, should have the last word on how their relations and the instruments on which they were based would have to be interpreted unless this privilege was expressly discarded by them in each given case.)

To be sure, it definitely helped to advance the project of judicial independence if everyone agreed that the rules of international law, once established, were no longer 'controlled' by their authors even in the limited sense of the 'original intent' doctrine—or, as Judge Huber put it in the *Danzig ILO* case, 'the Treaty of Versailles, and therefore the system established by that Treaty, is final and independent of the will of the

may be held to create a right for a third party to insist on its observance ... is of considerable interest.' WE Beckett, 'Decisions of the Permanent Court of International Justice on Points of Law and Procedure of General Application' (1930) 11 British Ybk Intl L. 1, 14–5.

93 *Territorial Jurisdiction of the International Commission of the River Oder* (n 25) at 20.

94 Ibid at 30.

95 *Free Zones* (n 84) 15.

Parties'[96]—but whatever did that do to the operative status of the principle of consent, the idea of sovereign will, and the metaphor of the 'meeting of the minds'?

Or take the fundamentally bizarre conception of the basic ontology of international law given in the *Serbian Loans* case. Consider the movement of the argument between the following two statements which the Court makes about halfway through the judgment: (i) 'it would be scarcely accurate to say that only questions of international law may form the subject of a decision of the Court'; and (ii) the reason for this is that, as §2 of Article 36 of the Court's Statute explains, the Court also may obtain jurisdiction 'in legal disputes concerning "the existence of any fact which, if established, would constitute a breach of an international obligation.'[97] Now, the actual language in (ii) comes, of course, directly from the League Covenant: the phrase 'the existence of any fact which, if established, would constitute a breach of an international obligation' is lifted directly from Article 13.[98] Given the nature of the Court's relationship with the Covenant and its own Statute, it certainly was not within the Court's authority to second-guess the correctness of that formula. Even then, none of it explains why it decided to assert (i) and (ii) simultaneously.

For, indeed, how can the logic of (i) be reconciled with the logic of (ii)? Two possible hypotheses seem to suggest themselves. Either it must be the case that what the Court understood by 'international law' in (ii) was not the same as what it understood by that concept in (i)—which means that what we have here is a classic example of conceptual slippage—or it must be the case that the Court actually believed that 'a breach of an international obligation' could be committed in such a manner that the resulting dispute over it would become a 'legal dispute' but not one that concerned a 'question of international law'—whereupon the question inevitably arises: so what would then be the exact legal basis for the corresponding international obligation? Given that it would be highly uncharitable to conclude that whoever wrote those parts of the judgment had no idea what they were saying, the only logical conclusion would have to be that either the Court believed that it had jurisdiction over what in effect are matters of natural law or that in its mind there a great deal of international legal rules were of a distinctly non-positive origin.

---

[96] *Case Concerning the Free City of Danzig and the International Labour Organization* [1930] PCIJ Ser B No. 18 at 29.

[97] *Serbian Loans* (n 89) at 19.

[98] Covenant of the League of Nations, 1919 UKTS 4 (Cmd 153).

One could go on citing other examples, but the basic point should be rather clear by now. While the received wisdom suggests that the reception of the contractualist paradigm into the Court's analytical protocols had been an essentially fairly straightforward and uncomplicated affair, a close scrutiny of the Court's own discourse paints a far more ambivalent picture. Without necessarily becoming conscious of this fact, it seems, the Court had, in fact, tried to do everything in its power to prevent the incorporation of the contractualist metaphor into the contemporary doctrine of sources debate.

At which point, the question inevitably arises: if all this is true, why did the Court then go on to endorse the contractualist model as enthusiastically as it did in that passage in *Lotus*?

***

Or did it indeed?

It has long been noted in the scholarly literature that the one defining characteristic of the Court's position on the question of customary international law had always been its rather manifest failure to develop any kind of coherent view on the matter of evidencing *opinio juris*.[99] Indeed, if anything, the only generalisation that it would seem to be possible to make on this front is that the Court somehow appears to have never given much consideration to the idea that, according to the traditional doctrinal test, to prove the existence of any rule of customary international law the presence of some empirically concretized *opinio juris* required to be demonstrated.

Now, from the general doctrinal point of view, this kind of omission, of course, might seem deeply frustrating and perhaps even irresponsible. But from the point of view of legal-historiographic symptomatology, if one considers it against the backdrop of some of the more general observations made above, this trend, in fact, would seem to make a lot of sense.

If one recalls that in terms of the official theory of *opinio juris* the standard split between the constitutive and the declaratory doctrines of customary international law—that is to say, between the theory of *opinio juris* as consent and the theory of *opinio juris* as belief—maps rather neatly onto the basic Gilmorean dichotomy between the subjectivist paradigm with its will-centred analytical protocols and the objectivist paradigm with its external facts-focused approach, the refusal to get drawn into

99 See, e.g., L Kopelmanas, 'Custom as a Means of the Creation of International Law' (1937) 18 British Ybk Intl L 127, 145–6.

working out a general methodology for either 'proving belief' or exploring the logic of the relationship between *opinio individualis juris individuali* and *opinio generalis juris generali* appears to be perfectly consistent with what one might assume to be the typical epistemic pattern of a relentlessly *modernist juristic sensibility*—that is to say, the same sensibility which in Gilmore's account arises at the end of the objectivist period. A sensibility which, while it would be perfectly happy to continue to pay generous homage to the principle of consent as a matter of official hypocrisy, would at the same time no less eagerly turn to progressively loosening every doctrinal test establishing the formalities of consent-expression, grounding this enterprise in a characteristically 'unprincipled' fashion in whatever justification would most readily present itself at that moment: promissory estoppel, contracts-implied-in-fact, unjust enrichment, the principle of legitimate expectations, or, indeed, if need be, natural law-style equity.

For, indeed, the spectre of natural law reasoning quite certainly did not just haunt the *Serbian Loans* judgment. Consider the basic argument sequence behind one of the most oft-cited passages in the *Chorzów Factory* (*Merits*) decision:

> The essential principle contained in the actual notion of an illegal act—a principle which seems to be established by international practice and in particular by the decisions of arbitral tribunals—is that reparation must, as far as possible, wipe out all the consequences of the illegal act and re-establish the situation which would, in all probability, have existed if that act had not been committed. Restitution in kind, or, if this is not possible, payment of a sum corresponding to the value which a restitution in kind would bear; the award, if need be, of damages for loss sustained which would not be covered by restitution in kind or payment in place of it—such are the principles which should serve to determine the amount of compensation due for an act contrary to international law.[100]

Leave aside the decidedly indeterminate reference to 'international practice' and 'the decisions of arbitral tribunals'. (It would be quite impossible to take it seriously anyway: the idea that the decisions of arbitral tribunals could be assigned any probative value in the context in which the Court invokes it is at best rather ridiculous;[101] and in any event, even if the principle of reparation were to be established as part of customary

100 *Chorzow Factory* (n 88) at 47.

101 As anyone who has even the slightest familiarity with the rules of inductive logic will recognize, the exercise of asking what arbitral tribunals, i.e. those institutions which ultimately exist only because the parties that establish them share the belief that breaches of

international law, the argument in support of that claim would have to provide a great deal more specific evidence than the simple invocation of the phrase 'international practice' can supply.)

Consider instead what the Court's reasoning in the quoted passage seems to suggest in terms of its implied theory of law: not only does the 'actual notion of an illegal act', as the Court sees it, inexorably presuppose the adoption of the *expectation damages* rule[102] (i.e. a very specific regime of remedial action), it also seems to dictate that the application of this rule in the international arena should automatically entail a very particular procedural sequence whereby the breaching party would be encumbered at first with the duty to provide an in-kind restitution and, only where the performance of that duty should prove impossible, would it also accrue the duty of monetary compensation. To put the matter in a slightly different way: not only does the Court seem to be suggesting here that *every legal system* which recognizes the concept of a legal breach should solely because of that fact alone *necessarily* adopt the regime of expectation damages, but it also seems to be arguing that in practice there exists only one, entirely self-evident algorithm according to which this regime can be made operational.

It is worth pausing a short moment to dwell on the sheer strangeness of this argument.

In the past, historians of legal thought used to have a name for this kind of reasoning. They called it conceptualism.[103] The first two things, they argued, every student of law had to learn about conceptualism were that, firstly, every one of its underlying theoretical assumptions was completely and fundamentally invalid; and, secondly, the more time one spent working within the conceptualist framework, the more it damaged and destroyed one's intellectual abilities. Put crudely, conceptualism, the story went, blunted the legal mind: it encouraged sloppy thinking habits, inculcated delusional beliefs, and progressively degraded the analytical

legal rights should be repaired, think about the idea that breaches of legal rights should be repaired, smacks of a certain kind of charlatanry.

102 '[The rule of] expectations damages awards the breached-against party an amount of money that puts him in the same position he would have been in had the contract been completed. [By contrast, the rule of] reliance damages awards an amount of money that places the breached-against party in the position he would have been in had he never entered into the contract initially.' A Mitchell Polinsky, *An Introduction to Law and Economics* (2nd edn, 1989) 28.

103 L Kalman, *Legal Realism at Yale* (1986) 14.

skills of all those involved on every side of the respective discursive performances.[104]

What was the logic behind these claims? In its basic contours the history of the anti-conceptualist challenge can be summarized more or less as follows:

1. For most of the 19th century, the vast majority of all legal-discursive exercises conducted in the Western legal tradition drew in one way or another on the operative logic of the conceptualist paradigm. The principal theoretical claim at the heart of this paradigm derived from the presumption that every abstract legal concept had at its core a certain intrinsic essence that was fixed, determinate, and fundamentally objective. Inasmuch as the meaning of every legal idea could thus be considered to be fundamentally self-consistent, i.e. independent of anyone's interpretative commitments, ideological agendas, prejudices, and so on, it followed that as a matter of principle it should be possible not only to develop an entirely neutral and impartial protocol of juridical reasoning but also to use it to determine what would be the 'right legal answer' to every given legal question.

2. At some point around the turn of the 20th century, all three of these assumptions increasingly began to be viewed as fundamentally indefensible. The presented critique unfolded for the most part across two fronts.[105] In the first place, as countless jurists from Jhering[106] onward have noted, the use of conceptualist protocols seemed to encourage what a logician would call a culture of the 'abuse of deduction'. In the second place, as Justice Holmes so vividly pointed out in his epochal dissent in *Lochner v. New York*,[107] the use of the conceptualist protocols also made the practice of legal argument excessively vulnerable to politicization. Since every legal concept—as it turned out, thanks to the insights lifted from analytical philosophy and modern linguistics—was inherently indeterminate in the sense that any well-trained thinker could always be

---

104 For an example of the most comprehensive attack on conceptualism in modern times, see P Schlag, *The Enchantment of Reason* (1998). For the *locus classicus* of the genre, see F Cohen, 'Transcendental Nonsense and the Functional Approach' (1935) 35 Columbia L Rev 809.

105 For typical example of these early critical efforts, see F Geny, *Méthode d'Interpretation et Sources en Droit Privé Positif* (2nd edn, 1919); R Demogue, 'Analysis of Fundamental Notions' in A Fouilée et al, *Modern French Legal Philosophy* (1916) 347; OW Holmes, *Collected Legal Papers* (1920) 310.

106 See, e.g., R von Jhering, 'In the Heaven of Legal Concepts', in M Cohen and F Cohen (eds), *Readings in Jurisprudence and Legal Philosophy* (1951) 678.

107 *Lochner v New York*, 198 US 45 (1905) at 74–76.

expected to develop more than one valid interpretation for it in any given situation, it followed that as a matter of elementary logic one simply could not rely on the conceptualist approach to generate the kind of definitive objective answers that it promised it could help obtain. Whenever such kind of answers were, consequently, seen to be supplied, it followed inevitably that the reasoning process that was used to produce them must have been 'contaminated' by some unacknowledged external influences.

3. Where the earlier critics of conceptualism may have been inclined for the most part to view it as a relatively 'innocent' mistake born from the illusion that meaning was an inherent attribute of words and that the right answer to every legal problem could therefore be produced by simply deducing in a quasi-mathematical fashion the objective logical conclusions that flowed from the correct application of the appropriate legal concepts, the generation that came after World War I took a much bleaker view of the problem.[108] For them, conceptualism was not only a fundamentally delusional theory but also a deeply reactionary ideology. Presenting a completely false image of the mechanics of legal reasoning, conceptualism, they argued, consistently blocked its followers' cognitive processes, obfuscated the full extent of the rampant politicisation of the judicial process, suppressed progress, and surreptitiously strengthened the ideological case not only for political conservatism but also for the vilest form of *laissez-faire* economics.[109]

Now, the reason why all of this should be relevant to mention in the present context is, of course, that, firstly, as even the briefest scrutiny of its case-law can confirm, the Court throughout its twenty-year career remained a very committed practitioner of conceptualist reasoning. In judgment after judgment, from *Mavrommatis* to *Workers Delegate Designation*[110] to *Oscar Chinn*, it repeatedly made use of the same basic pattern of argument: (i) start with some vague general concept, such as

[108] For typical illustrations, see Cohen (n 104); R L Hale, 'The "Fair Value" Merry Go-Round, 1898 to 1938: A Forty-Year Journey from Rates-Based-on-Value to Value-Based-on-Rents' (1939) 33 Illinois L Rev 517; T Arnold, 'The Role of Substantive Law and Procedure in the Legal Process' (1932) 45 Harvard L Rev 617.

[109] For further discussion, see Kalman (n 103) 11–13.

[110] *Designation of the Workers' Delegate for the Netherlands at the Third Session of the International Labour Conference* [1922] PCIJ Ser B No 1. The central issue in this case was the meaning of the phrase 'most representative workers' organisations' as used in Article 389 of the Treaty of Versailles. (The treaty itself did not specify what meaning had to be given to this concept.) Rather than looking at the *travaux* or the subsequent practice under the treaty, the Court decided to settle this question as follows: 'The most representative organisations ... are, of course, those organisations which best represent the employers and the

'freedom of trade' or 'legal breach'; (ii) identify its purported objective meaning; (iii) extract from this meaning a fully specified legal principle; (iv) deduce from this principle by way of 'objective' legal reasoning an entire juridical regime with numerous details and complicated normative and remedial structures; (v) claim that this regime is part of international law. Secondly, given what has just been noted about the terms of the contemporary scholarly debate, it also seems to be very unlikely that the Court, packed as it was with intellectual luminaries of the highest calibre, many of them with a strong interest in academic work, might have somehow remained 'unaware' of the various theoretical and ideological deficiencies of conceptualism. Whatever role the jurisprudence of ignorance[111] may have played in its work in other contexts, the decision to utilize the conceptualist paradigm, it seems safe to conclude, was a fundamentally deliberate one. Thirdly, given that the analytical protocols of conceptualism are essentially indistinguishable from those of natural-law reasoning, a jurisprudential legacy that appears to be so deeply—and so rather deliberately—embedded in a conceptualist approach, it seems obvious, can hardly be considered indicative of an aspiration to conceive the logic of the international legal order after *any kind of positivist paradigm*, let alone one based around the idea of sovereign will emanation.

But how essential, in the end, was this conceptualist turn to the development of the Court's jurisprudential legacy? As David Kennedy points out, as a pattern of intellectual practice the use of the conceptualist approach in many ways can be considered one of the most important constants of international legal history. One can find traces of it as far back as Vitoria's *De Indis et de Jure Belli* (1557) and Gentili's *De Legationibus Libri Tres* (1582), but it obviously has also had quite a notable influence on the work of Hans Kelsen, Myres McDougal, Grigoriy Tunkin, Hersch Lauterpacht as well as, closer to our times, Ian Brownlie, Harold Koh, Anne-Marie Slaughter, and any number of their apprentices and collaborators.[112] In the end, though, it seems, there was only that much use a conceptualist aesthetics could give to an international *court*. Pushed to its

workers respectively. … Numbers are not the only test of the representative character of the organisations, but they are an important factor … If, therefore, in a particular country there exist several industrial organisations representing the working classes, the Government must take all of them into consideration when it is proceeding to the nomination of the workers' delegate and his technical advisers. Only by acting in this way can the Government succeed [in discharging its obligations under Article 389]' (ibid at 21–3.)

[111] For the idea of a jurisprudence of ignorance, see further Gilmore (n 31) 63.

[112] For Kennedy's discussion of the classics, see David Kennedy, 'Primitive Legal Scholarship' (1986) 27 Harvard Intl L J 1. For his discussion and characterization of 20th

logical conclusion, a conceptualist paradigm simply seems incapable of articulating any concept of legal sources—and for a good reason too: in an ideal conceptualist universe, all things considered, there ultimately would not be any need for that sort of intellectual instrument just as there would not be any room for a theory of normative conflict.

A paradigm that imagines that the bindingness of any given proposition is determined in the final analysis by its logical connectability to some pre-established objective juridical meaning will simply never be able to conceive how two normative propositions could ever enter into a conflict: the inexorable power of logic and the norms themselves would make sure this would never happen. The more powerful norms would simply turn out to be more powerful because the concepts in which they are grounded would be *self-evidently* of a higher ranking (and to an educated observer there could never be any doubt as to how these rankings were organized), or because they would say so themselves.[113]

A mind steeped in such kind of reasoning protocols, it follows then, would never be able to perceive the need to work out any kind of methodology for how to choose between two or more equally valid conflicting normative propositions, which means by implication that it would also never be able to work out any kind of theory of adjudication—or, which is essentially the same thing, a conceptual understanding of the 'essential' difference between lawmaking, law-ascertainment by the subject, and third-party legal interpretation. And where there exists no scope for a coherent concept of third-party interpretation, one cannot, in a secular cultural environment, find any justification for the creation of a *permanent* judicial function.[114]

VI. In Lieu of a Conclusion (Part 1): An Argument about Judgeship

It would be tempting—and not at all unjustifiable—to imagine there must have been some kind of latent strategic project behind all of this: the

century writers, see generally David Kennedy, 'The Disciplines of International Law and Policy' (1999) 12 Leiden J of Intl L 9; David Kennedy, 'A New World Order: Yesterday, Today, and Tomorrow' (1994) 4 Transnational L & Contemporary Probs 329. On Kelsen, Lauterpacht, and McDougal, see also Chapters 3, 5, and 6 in Koskenniemi (n 27).

113 David Kennedy, 'The Sources of International Law' (1987) 2 American U J Intl L & Policy 1, 90.

114 Though one can still find plenty of scope for the idea of impartial mediation and ad-hoc arbitration.

Court 'felt' it had no other choice but to declare its allegiance to the contractualist metaphor and through that to confirm the descriptive and normative validity of the voluntarist-positivist dogma, since if it had not done that it would have severely undermined its own position and also, quite possibly, retarded the whole enterprise of the international rule of law. If the contractualist theory had not been declared to be true, the whole voluntarist-positivist argument would have fallen apart. To obtain a logically coherent theory of international obligation one would then either have to turn back to some form of natural law reasoning, which would be both politically unsustainable and jurisprudentially displeasing, or summarily dispense with the entire idea of international law being a horizontal legal system, which would then raise all kinds of unacceptable ideological implications. Absent the contractualist presumption, thus, the only way forward for the Court would have been either to endorse a profoundly suspect political philosophy or to dignify with the title of law what in effect would be a textbook example of imperialist governance.

I am not sure one should necessarily resist such kind of legal-historical readings. But it seems to me that to propose this particular reading in the present case would be to credit the Court's 'ideological leadership' with far too much strategic talent and political acumen and to reinforce thereby an altogether unrealistic view of judicial practice—or, as the old Marxists used to put it, 'the role of the person in history'—that seems to be so characteristic of modern-day conservative legal historiography. And I do not just have in mind here the kind of argument that Ole Spiermann makes about the dangers of postulating a single voice where in reality one had a majority voting system and a collective writing exercise.[115]

The cheap metaphor often depicts international adjudication as 'the continuation of multilateral diplomacy by other means'. A much more accurate characterisation, to my mind, would be: multilateral diplomacy minus any institutional back-up, the right to manoeuvre, and the benefit of operational secrecy.

Whether we take the Permanent Court itself or any other comparable institution, it seems to me it would be far more helpful to view the working conditions of a typical international judge as an institutionalized exercise in Beckettian stress: 'can't go on, must go on'. Consider the basic terms of their labour process. Not only is it the case that almost everything that they do involves typically the duty to defuse highly charged antagonistic

---

[115] See, generally, O Spiermann, *International Legal Argument in the Permanent Court of International Justice* (2004).

situations by *recasting* the underlying real-world conflicts in the form of abstract conceptual contradictions that are somehow meant to be endowed with some sort of *innate logical resolvability*—and this in a cultural environment over-saturated with first-hand awareness of the essential indeterminacy of formal logic—but they also have to perform all of these magical feats practically all by themselves.

To borrow an observation made in a similar context by Pierre Schlag:

> What little help they have in terms of actual human contact, apart from their clerks, typically takes the form of two or more advocates whose entire *raison d'être* is to persuade, coax, and manipulate the judge into reaching a predetermined outcome—one which often instantiates or exemplifies only the most tenuous positive connection to the rhetoric of social purpose, legal doctrine, and moral value deployed by the advocates.[116]

Add to this now Spiermann's argument and the whole idea of assuming that such a group of people—people whose everyday existence unfolds in that proverbial 'field of pain and death'[117] but whose composition at the same time, remains no more stable than summer weather in northern Scotland—should on top of everything else they were dealing with have set for themselves the task also of articulating, without ever findings a formally appropriate occasion for that, an internally coherent, fully integrated series of mutually reinforcing statements on a subject as academically abstract as the theory of international law sources, one must admit, begins to take on the air of a somewhat unjustifiable fantasy.

VII. In Lieu of a Conclusion (Part 2): An Argument about Scholarship

It has long been one of the main defining features of the European international legal tradition (though perhaps more so on the continent than in Britain) to assume that there ultimately exists some kind of fundamental distinction between a civil-law approach and a common-law approach to thinking about international law. While the former is typically seen to be defined by its strong emphasis on deductivism and systematicity and its predilection for assuming an essentially organic relationship between international law and 'international life', the latter is widely presumed to have no time for any variety of grand-scale philosophizing: thanks to its

---

116 P Schlag, 'Clerks in the Maze' (1993) 91 Michigan L Rev 2053, 2053.

117 R Cover, 'Violence and the Word' (1986) 95 Yale L J 1601.

deeply held attachment to empiricism the common-law mind only cares about the study of cases, decisions, and precedents.

The reason why this assumption deserves to be mentioned in these pages is essentially threefold. Firstly, the issues it touches on are very closely related to the subject of the present inquiry. Secondly, the list of this volume's contributors includes scholars who come both from the civil-law background and from the common-law background, and yet the volume's central subject matter, quite clearly, is the study of the historical impact of a *judicial* institution. Thirdly, and most significantly, this view of the international legal discourse, while being extremely popular, I think is also entirely without foundation: what the conventional wisdom depicts as an exclusively Anglo-Saxon creed is, in fact, a perfectly 'global' habit of thought shared by the vast majority of international lawyers around the world today.

This does not seem to be the best occasion for delving too far into such kind of 'comparativist' studies. And yet I think it should be rather obvious to any informed observer that over the last several decades there has developed within the international legal discipline a rather strong sense of epistemological commitment that has long since come to be shared across all conceivable national, regional, and cultural divides. What lies at the heart of this commitment is the assumption that the essential material of international legal history should be *conceptualized* ultimately as nothing more than a loosely arranged sequence of randomly interconnected textual events. Some of these events, to be sure, are going to look completely different from others: a typical treaty will usually be contained in a relatively easily identifiable singular document; a typical international custom, on the other hand, will normally be spread across a much wider range of distinct communicative acts. No matter the difference, however: both the ones and the others, in the final analysis, will still reflect in the same manner the latent content of the international legal order and thus will both mark and direct the historical movement of its evolution.

Now, one can find, of course, all sorts of reasons for why this sort of fiction may make good sense from the disciplinarily *pragmatic* point of view, but in the present context I think what needs to be highlighted at this point is this: the moment one accepts this set of assumptions as one's guiding analytical orientation, it becomes only a matter of straight logical deduction before one inevitably arrives at the conclusion that from the point of view of international legal study there can be, ultimately, no more privileged object of investigation than the decisions of permanent international courts.

Where the dominant mode of cultural knowledge production is conditioned by the imaginational economy of liberal thought—which in the field of international legal discourse certainly seems today to be the case—in a system of causational assumptions whose chief defining structure is the principle of reducing processes to events and events to texts, the most obvious logical option will always be to elevate above all other symptomatological instruments the discourse of judicial institutions. For, indeed, it is only in that context alone that the basic disciplinary mandate of the legal profession can be consistently presumed to coincide with the essential institutional loyalty of the respective discursive agents, since neither the treaty form nor 'multilateral diplomatic practice', both of which are operated and dominated by 'politicians', can be expected to connect to the inner core of 'the law' in an equally reliable manner.

But, of course, like all others texts, judicial decisions never exist in a social vacuum—and not just in that banal sense that 'courts are always surrounded by politics' or 'all judges are human and no man is an island'. Every body of texts, no matter how analytically self-referential, be it a series of judicial decisions or a collection of epic poems, exists, ultimately, from the broader historical point of view only as an *object-effect* created within a certain system of cultural diffusion—a system that, in the final instance, is determined, among other things, by the respective mode of epistemological selection, that is to say, a conventionally established structure of discursive pathways internalized by the participating cultural agents whose practical implementation gives the respective intersubjective interactive contexts their essential sense of order, coherence, and intelligibility. A different way to express this last point would be to reformulate it as a conceptual combination of the classical Foucauldian thesis that the logic of the general relationship between discourse and politics is not only that the former provides the enabling medium for the latter but that it also provides a site in which the latter can be pursued, with the standard Frankfurt-School thesis that the situation of any practically implementable discourse always presumes a certain intrinsic inequality of participation. No discursive system ever puts all speakers on an equal footing—some interlocutors are always elevated above others.

Framed in such terms, the argument outlined above inexorably seems to lead to the conclusion that the principled opposition between the pure textual reflectivity of judicial pronouncements and the complex worldly embeddedness of treaties and diplomatic incidents not only must be rejected as 'bad jurisprudence' but that it also makes no sense in ontological terms. Think of this, if you will, as international law's equivalent of

Heisenberg's uncertainty principle:[118] every time an international tribunal sets out to pronounce what the essential content of the respective treaty or the relevant pattern of State practice might be, by the very act of this pronouncement it automatically interferes with the 'objective composition' of that content.

Every time the Permanent Court of International Justice set out to detect what might have been the configuration of that factuality which it had to examine in order to determine the content of international law, it thereby inevitably contributed to the practical re-constitution of that factuality: what 'made up' State practice in such circumstances became systemically indeterminable without taking into account the formative role of this act of detection. When as the students of the Court's work we go on to identify such pronouncements as an accurate representation of those aspects of the international legal order, we thus automatically side with the Court's re-constitutive agenda—that is to say, by *identifying* the 'what' we also *identify-with* the 'who'.

Now, the implications of this last point may not seem immediately obvious, but the following observation should go some way towards elucidating them. At the root of all behavioural structures that underpin the social field of the legal profession, explains Pierre Bourdieu, lies ultimately the struggle 'for the control of access to the legal resources inherited from the past'.[119] This struggle, importantly, not only has a very strongly pronounced external dimension—the struggle between the 'lay people' and the 'legal professionals' has long attracted the attention of critical legal scholarship—but also a clearly detectable internal aspect (inasmuch as it extends also into the internal horizon of the legal profession).

The crucial difference between the two dimensions lies in the distribution of the agonistic momentum. Even though both in its external and in its internal contexts the competitive struggle always proceeds by means of the same kind of language game—a game whose ultimate objective is to prove the inherent superiority of one's interpretative protocols vis-à-vis those deployed by the other party—in its internal phase the struggle tends to be conducted almost exclusively within the internal discourse of one party.

---

118 For an introductory-level overview of which, see J Gribbin, *In Search of Schrodinger's Cat: Quantum Physics and Reality* (1984) 156–7; R Feynman, *Six Easy Pieces* (1998 [1995]) 127–38.

119 P Bourdieu, 'The Force of Law: Toward a Sociology of the Juridical Field' (1987) 38 Hastings L J 814, 817.

Outside a few highly exceptional situations, the 'judicial' segment of the profession neither seem to care nor feel it possible to admit that they might, about asserting their interpretative superiority vis-à-vis the 'academic' segment. Why exactly things have come to be this way is not clear. The more conservative explanation would probably be that in the eyes of a typical judge the internal phase of the struggle has long since lost its importance because of the evolution in the intra-disciplinary practices of knowledge transmission.[120] A somewhat more radical approach, by contrast, would be to emphasize instead the more socio-psychological aspect of the situation, perhaps by revisiting some of the arguments proposed by Paul Kahn[121] or Pierre Schlag.[122] Whichever view one finds more convincing, it certainly seems rather remarkable that while a typical international judge will almost never seek to self-identify with the persona of an international legal academic, the business tends to be a lot livelier on the other side.

My own sense of all this, for what it is worth, is that, like with all other types of ideological phenomena, the key to all patterns of intra-disciplinary self-identification, at the end of the day, must be sought in the respective economic processes. And as Veblen showed, of course, the sphere of economic exchange, like that of consumption, covers ultimately a far greater scope of events than those which are directly related to the material foundations of subsistence.[123] The sense of professional importance and purpose derived by international law academics from their pretend competition with the judicial segment of the profession surely belongs in the domain of the intra-disciplinary economy as much as anything else.

---

[120] In the international legal context this argument would run more or less as follows: At some point in the past, when there were fewer treaties and digests of State practice, the opinions of the learned academic authors mattered a lot. Those days are now over. The inherent worth of an academic opinion in the eyes of an international legal practitioner today is generally quite insignificant. One only needs to consult the recent jurisprudence of the International Court of Justice to see how easy it has become for an active international judicial organ these days to churn out any number of highly sophisticated reasoning patterns about the contents and implications of various international legal regimes without ever drawing on any academic works. For a typical illustration of this sort of reasoning, see C Parry, *The Sources and Evidences of International Law* (1965) 103–5. See also, more generally, R Posner, 'Law, Knowledge, and the Academy: Legal Scholarship Today' (2002) 115 Harvard L Rev 1314.

[121] See, in particular, PW Kahn, *The Cultural Study of Law* (1999) 18–29.

[122] See, in particular, P Schlag, 'Writing for Judges' (1992) 63 U of Colorado L Rev 419 and P Schlag, 'Authorizing Interpretation' (1998) 20 Connecticut L Rev 1065. See also (n 116).

[123] See, generally, Veblen (n 23).

The beginning of all genuine knowledge about the social world, writes Bourdieu at the start of *The Logic of Practice*, lies in the act of the self-objectification of the objectifying gaze: the key at all times is to recall that beyond 'every theoretical analysis' lies the fact of 'the theorist's subjective relation to the social world and the objective (social) relation presupposed by this subjective relation.'[124] To become able to approach the object of one's study in a genuinely critical manner, one must understand the stakes of one's investigative exercise not only as they may be experienced from within that exercise itself but also as they (most probably) play out in the context of one's immediate social existence as an investigator of that object.[125]

[124] P Bourdieu, *The Logic of Practice* (trans Richard Nice, 1990) 29.

[125] 'Knowledge does not only depend, as an elementary relativism suggests, on the particular viewpoint that a "situated and dated" observer takes up vis-à-vis the object. A much more fundamental alteration—and a much more pernicious one, because, being constitutive of the operation of knowing, it inevitably remains unnoticed—is performed … by sheer fact of taking a "viewpoint" on [the studied object] and so constituting it as an object (of observation and analysis). … This critical reflexion on the limits of theoretical understanding is not intended to discredit theoretical knowledge in one or another of its forms and, as is often attempted, to set in its place a more or less idealized practical knowledge; but rather to give it a solid basis by freeing it from the distortions arising from the epistemological and social conditions of its production' (ibid 27.)

JUDICIAL ACTIVISM AND JUDICIAL SELF-RESTRAINT: THE PCIJ'S *LOTUS* CASE

Photini Pazartzis

I. Introduction

The creation of the Permanent Court of International Justice (PCIJ) is considered to be the point of departure in the institutionalization of international justice and the emergence of a permanent international judiciary. Over the course of two decades, the PCIJ rendered thirty-two judgments in contentious cases and twenty-seven opinions in advisory proceedings. While many of these decisions involved questions of treaty interpretation, they have been seen as "standing out for their quality and for the unprecedented accumulation of practice by an international tribunal".[1] Indeed, the PCIJ represented a decisive advance by producing a jurisprudence that for the first time marked case law as a significant factor in the development of substantive international law.[2] The generally satisfactory track record of the PCIJ ensured that it emerged from World War II with its reputation largely intact. Consequently, it came as no surprise that the Charter's drafters, despite the formal inauguration of the International Court of Justice as a new Court, and a principal organ of the United Nations, sought to preserve continuity with the PCIJ at a functional level, so that the new Court appeared as a continuation of its predecessor. From that time on, the International Court of Justice has to a large extent maintained a continuous jurisprudence, without this signifying that its 'judicial policy' has remained unchanged.[3]

---

[1] CH Brower, 'The Functions and Limits of Arbitration and Judicial Settlement under Private and Public International Law' (2007–2008) 18 Duke J of Comparative and IntlL 259, 286. Also, MO Hudson, *International Tribunals: Past and Future*, (Carnegie Edowment for International Peace and Brookings Institution, Washington DC 1944) 11.

[2] H Lauterpacht, *The Development of International Law by the International Court*, (Grotius, Cambridge 1958) 5.

[3] G Abi-Saab, 'De l'évolution de la Cour internationale. Réflexions sur quelques tendances récentes' (1992/2) 96 RGDIP 273, 275. See also J d'Aspremont (in this volume), at 17. and for an understanding of the impact of contentious jurisdiction on the continuation of jurisprudence see generally CJ Tams (in this volume), 11.

The role and record of the two Courts has naturally attracted the attention of international law scholars and practitioners, who, at regular intervals, have identified and assessed a variety of issues, such as the fluctuations of their respective rate of judicial activity, the decline, crisis, or revival of the Court's activity, or the continuity or change regarding the categories (or number) of disputes that have in fact been brought before the two Courts for judicial scrutiny, the 'champ opératoire' of judicial settlement of disputes identified by Michel Virally in his empirical study of the activity of the two Courts.[4]

It is true that there are many perspectives through which one could approach the PCIJ and its lasting legacy to modern international law, as the various contributions in this volume show. And indeed, it is probably through this 'kaleidoscopical' approach that, at the end of the day, some conclusions could be advanced on the impact of the PCIJ on modern international law and on the international judiciary.

To these various approaches, a further perspective stems from the expectations of the international community as to the role of the World Court.[5] In this regard, there are two approaches which have been advanced in international legal theory, of the function of an international judge.[6] The Court can be seen as a 'dispute settler',[7] deciding a case at hand through the application of the relevant rules; or its role can be conceived as transcending this narrow parameter and making general pronouncements of law or principle which may enrich or develop the law. This is a

---

[4] M Virally, 'Le champ opératoire du règlement judiciaire international' (1982) RGDIP 281. The author identifies the *ratione materiae* sphere of activity of the Court, that is, the categories of disputes that have in fact been brought before the two Courts (up to 1982). What is interesting is that Virally brings them down into one category, the "rights of jurisdiction of the State", which covers almost the whole of international law and constitutes its "noyau dur" (309).

[5] Judge P Kooijmans, 'The ICJ in the 21st Century: Judicial Restraint, Judicial Activism, or Proactive Judicial Policy' (2007) 56 ICLQ 741, 742.

[6] The starting point is, of course, is the famous passage in the seminal article by G Fitzmaurice, 'Hersch Lauterpacht—The Scholar as Judge', (1961) 37 BYIL 1, 14–15: "There are broadly two main possible approaches to the task of a judge, whether in the international sphere or elsewhere. There is the approach which conceives it to be the primary, if not the sole duty of the judge to decide the case in hand, with the minimum of verbiage necessary for this purpose, and to confine himself to that. The other approach conceives it to be the proper function of the judge, while duly deciding the case in hand, with the necessary supporting reasoning, and while not unduly straying outside the four corners of the case, to utilize those aspects of it which have a wider interest or connotation, in order to make a general pronouncement of law and principle that may enrich and develop the law."

[7] JE Alvarez, 'The New Dispute Settlers: (Half) Truths and Consequences' (2003) 38 Texas IL J 405.

question which continues to be discussed and to which there is no definitive answer.[8]

This contribution seeks to address these underlying issues through the PCIJ's *Lotus* case,[9] a case which has "attracted more attention among international lawyers than any other decision of the 1920s, at that time and ever since".[10] This choice is not dictated by a belief this is the most significant case to be adjudicated by the Permanent Court.[11] But the Court's pronouncements in this case (one, at least, and an *obiter* at that) spurred much discussion and debate on international law and its structure and, 85 years after the judgment was issued, continue to do so. What stands out, in particular, is a perception, a vision of the Court on "the very nature and existing conditions of international law".[12] The judgment can be viewed under a minimalist reading, or, alternatively, as a pronouncement of a more general import. The following sections examine *Lotus* from this perspective. An initial inquiry will focus on the judgment, in particular the *Lotus dictum* and its meaning (II), before discussing whether and to what extent this *dictum* has had an influence on the post-PCIJ era (III).

II. *Lotus* Through the PCIJ's Prism

The decision of the PCIJ in the case of *The SS Lotus* and the question of its influence on international law, or on the perception of the international judiciary, brings to the fore a number of paradoxes. Firstly, in what was a relatively factually simple case, the PCIJ came to deal with questions of general international law as opposed to issues of treaty interpretation.[13]

---

[8] For a discussion, see Kooijmans (n 5); H Thirlway, 'Judicial Activism and the International Court of Justice' in N Ando, E McWhinney and R Wolfrum (eds), *Liber Amicorum Judge Shigeru Oda* (Kluwer Law International, The Hague 2002) 75–105; E McWhinney, 'The International Court of Justice and International Law-Making: The Judicial Activism/Self-Restraint Antinomy' (2006) 5 Chinese JIL 3–13. Also, CJ Tams & A Tzanakopoulos, '*Barcelona Traction* at 40: The ICJ as an Agent of Legal Development' (2010/4) 23 Leiden J Intl L 781–800 (with a discussion and bibliography on 'judicial law-making').

[9] *The Case of the SS Lotus*, [1927] PCIJ Ser A No 10 at 5.

[10] O Spiermann, *International Legal Argument in the Permanent Court of International Justice: The Rise of the International Judiciary* (CUP, Cambridge 2005) 247.

[11] Indeed, other cases of the PCIJ have had a greater impact on the shaping of the law, such as, for example, the *Mavrommatis* case (and its classical definition of a dispute, or its lasting formulation of the principle of diplomatic protection) or the *Chorzów Factory* case (and its pronouncement on reparation).

[12] *Lotus* (n 9) 18.

[13] O Spiermann, 'Judge Max Huber at the Permanent Court of International Justice' (2007) 18 EJIL 115, 129.

Secondly, the decision itself (as to the merits) was subsequently overruled by international treaty law.[14] Thirdly, the judgment has been referred to as a 'mine of valuable material upon the subject of jurisdiction', and even 'one of the landmarks of twentieth century jurisprudence', while at the same time, it has been linked to the theory of positivism, "from which most theorists spent the twentieth century trying to distance themselves",[15] or has been seen as the expression of a "spirit of the times" which has since been replaced by a "more objective conception of international law".[16] All these paradoxes, and maybe many others, have contributed to generating such a persistent interest in the judgment itself and, through it, the role of the international judiciary.

For some, the 1927 judgment was hailed as the first decision of the Court on a question of general international law.[17] It could, however, be noted that since its first steps in its adjudicatory function, the Court had already been afforded the occasion to address points of general international law or procedure, and this heralded the development towards an international judiciary advancing authoritative pronouncements on international law.[18]

The Court had already had the opportunity to address general issues, as, for example, the 'sovereignty dilemma' in the *Wimbledon* case, the first contentious case brought before it.[19] Furthermore, the 'permissive theory' of international law had already been touched upon in the case concerning *Tunis-Morocco Nationality Decrees*,[20] where the Court was asked to provide an Advisory Opinion on whether or not the issuing of nationality

---

14 Which changed the principle of concurrent jurisdiction for collisions on the high seas laid down by the PCIJ; see the 1952 Brussels Collision Convention (Article 1), the 1958 Geneva Convention on the High Seas (Article 11), and the 1982 United Nations Convention on the Law of the Seas (Article 97).

15 (n 10) 249.

16 See the Declaration of Judge Bedjaoui in the Advisory Opinion on the *Threat or Use of Nuclear Weapons*: "No doubt this decision expressed *the spirit of the times*, the spirit of an international society which as yet had few institutions and was governed by an international law of strict co-existence, itself a reflection of the vigour of the principle of State sovereignty…The resolutely positivist, voluntarist approach of international law still current at the beginning of the century…has been replaced by an objective conception of international law, a law more readily seeking to reflect a collective juridical conscience and respond to the social necessities of States organized as a community", [1996] ICJ Rep, 270–271.

17 See the Note "The Case of the *Lotus*", (1928) 9 *BYIL* 181.

18 M Shahabuddeen, *Precedent in the World Court* (CUP, Cambridge 1996) 21.

19 On the sovereignty dilemma, J Klabbers, 'Clinching the Concept of Sovereignty: Wimbledon Redux' (1998/3) 3 Austrian Rev of Intl and Eur L 345–367.

20 *Nationality Decrees Issued in Tunis and Morocco*, (Advisory Opinion) [1923] PCIJ Ser B No 4.

decrees fell solely within the domestic jurisdiction of States. In this case, France contended that the right to legislate on nationality within the limits of one's own territory stemmed directly from a State's sovereignty and could only be set aside by a formal rule of international law. While not directly addressing the issue posed by France, the Court stated:

> For the purpose of the present opinion, it is enough to observe that it may well happen that, in a matter which, like that of nationality, is not, in principle, regulated by international law, the right of a state to use its discretion is nevertheless restricted by obligations which it may have undertaken towards other states. In such a case, jurisdiction which, in principle belongs solely to the state, is limited by rules of international law.[21]

In this context, a few years later, the Court was asked to pronounce on another issue of jurisdiction, this time, the criminal jurisdiction of States. The dispute giving rise to the Permanent Court's *Lotus* judgment was quite straightforward: in 1926, the SS Lotus, a French steamship, collided on the high seas with the Boz Kourt, a Turkish vessel, causing the loss of eight lives. The French ship then sailed into Constantinople, where the French officer on watch at the time of the collision was arrested and subsequently prosecuted and sentenced before the Turkish courts. The French government protested the arrest and the conviction, and, following negotiations, the two governments agreed to submit by special agreement to the Permanent Court the question whether Turkey had "acted in conflict with the principles of international law—and if so, what principles—by instituting proceedings in pursuance of Turkish law against Mr. Demons…"[22] France contended that the Turkish courts, in order to have jurisdiction, should be able to point to some specific entitlement to jurisdiction recognized by international law in favor of Turkey. Turkey, on the other hand, claimed that it had jurisdiction unless it was forbidden by international law.

The Court ultimately ruled, with the casting vote of President Huber, that trying Demons was not an exercise of power on the territory of another State, further that the Court could deduce no rule or principle of international law preventing Turkey from exercising jurisdiction, and that, under the circumstances, France and Turkey had concurrent jurisdiction. The Court's decision in favor of Turkey, was in fact premised on a

---

[21] Ibid at 24. For an analysis of the inter-play between domestic and international law in the context of the PCIJ see generally J d'Aspremont (in this volume), 221.

[22] *Lotus* (n 9) 5.

traditional, if erroneous ground (by assuming the 'territoriality' of a ship), namely that the act in question could be said to have had its effect on the Turkish vessel and on thus what might be deemed to be Turkish territory and that, for this reason, the assumption and exercise of criminal jurisdiction was supported by the traditional principle of territoriality.[23]

But the importance of the judgment lies not so much in the ruling, as in the, since often-quoted, *dictum* of the Court on the permissive or prohibitive nature of international law:[24]

> International law governs relations between independent States. The rules of law binding upon states therefore emanate from their own free will as expressed in conventions or by usages generally accepted as expressing principles of law and established in order to regulate relations between these co-existing independent communities or with a view to the achievement of common aims. Restrictions upon the independence of States cannot therefore be presumed.[25]

This pronouncement has caused much debate and discussion, while there have been a range of interpretations advanced, sometimes diametrically opposed.[26] The view presented by the majority of the Court has been considered the classical articulation of the positivist school of thought[27] and has since been evoked either as a sound ground on which to found the positivist theory, or as a sounding board for criticism against this school of thought.[28]

In the view of many, the *Lotus dictum* enshrined the strictest view of State sovereignty unfettered in all circumstances except those in which specific prohibitions exist, proclaiming a presumptive freedom of State action, where limitations are always self-imposed.[29] The Court's judgment appeared to give considerable support for this reading when it spoke of a principle of freedom. Even at that time, several dissenting judges who

---

23 See the discussion by FA Mann, 'The Doctrine of Jurisdiction in International Law' (1964-I) RCADI 33 seq.

24 A *dictum* which, according to H Lauterpacht, could have been omitted without affecting the judgment of the Court, (n 2) 361.

25 *Lotus* (n 9) 18.

26 For a compilation of a bibliography generated by the judgment in the years right after its issuance, see [1935] PCIJ Rep, vol 2 at 21–22.

27 Or "l'un des axiomes du positivisme classique", P-M Dupuy, *Droit international public* (9ème éd. Dalloz, Paris 2008) 16.

28 See A Pellet, '*Lotus* que de sottises on profère en ton nom! Remarques sur le concept de souveraineté dans la jurisprudence de la Cour mondiale', in F Alabrune, *L'État souverain dans le monde d'aujourd'hui. Mélanges en l'honneur de J.-P. Puissochet* (Pedone, Paris 2008) 215–230.

29 Notably JL Brierly, 'The *Lotus* Case' (1928) 44 LQ Rev 154.

interpreted the judgment in this way, expressed doubts that this view was consonant with accepted principles of international law.[30] It has been remarked that the dissenters in this case transformed the *dictum* into a principle, the *Lotus principle*,[31] reading it as an attempt by the Court to articulate a general principle of law that governs whenever no applicable law constraining State behavior can be discerned.[32] Thus Judge Nyholm read in the majority view that, "over and above positive international law, there is a kind of international law which amounts to this: that the absence of a rule prohibiting an action suffices to render that action permissible…"[33]

It has been equally argued, however, that the majority did not intend to promulgate such a sweeping rule of absolute sovereignty and that this *dictum* is to be interpreted in a more limited way.[34] Ole Spiermann has questioned the attribution of strict positivism to the judgment, observing that "such a presumption in favor of sovereignty and against international law…would have been a singularly astonishing proposition on the part of a newly established international court, which had moreover discarded principles of restrictive treaty interpretation and other arguments based on national sovereignty in favor of an international lawyer's approach".[35] Accordingly, he contends that the *Lotus* case should be read not as an attempt to create a presumption against the limitation of State sovereignty, but as an effort to articulate a residual principle, one that would

---

30 Thus in his dissenting opinion, Judge Loder criticized Turkey's defence as being based on the contention that, "…every door is open unless it is closed by treaty or by established custom", *Lotus* (n 9), at 34.

31 Or the *Lotus* presumption, see J Crawford, *The Creation of States in International Law* (2nd edn, OUP, Oxford 2006) 41–42. According to Crawford, this presumption, rebuttable in any case, while having declined in importance, is "still part of the hidden grammar of international legal language".

32 See H Handeyside, 'The *Lotus* Principle in the ICJ Jurisprudence: Was the Ship Ever Afloat?' (2007–2008) 29 Michigan J of Intl L 71, 76.

33 *Lotus* (n 9), Diss Op Nyholm, at 63.

34 See the developments by Lauterpacht according to whom, "[o]n closer investigation, however, the principle enunciated by the Court is less dogmatic and more flexible than a first reading makes it appear", (n 2) 359 et seq. The extreme positivist approach (or the interpretation as such) of the *Lotus* principle, suggesting that the legal order is thus closed or complete, has been criticized by many authors, see for example, G Fitzmaurice, 'The Problem of *Non Liquet*: Prolegomena to a Restatement' *Mélanges offerts à Charles Rousseau* (Pedone, Paris 1974) 89–112; H Lauterpacht, 'Some Observations on the Prohibition of *Non Liquet* and the Completeness of the Law' in *Symbolae Verzijl* (Martinus Nijhoff, The Hague 1958) 196–221. For a discussion, I Scobbie, 'The Theorist as Judge: Hersch Lauterpacht's Concept of the International Judicial Function' (1997) 2 EJIL 264–298.

35 Spiermann (n 13) 130.

make room for deference to State sovereignty in all cases where the jurisdiction being asserted does not violate well-established rules of international law.[36]

Indeed, the Court did refer to international law in terms of 'co-existing independent communities' and 'common aims', language that does not in itself support an 'absolutist' conception of the freedom of States.[37] Moreover, after declaring that "restrictions upon the independence of states cannot be presumed", the Court immediately proceeded to qualify one important restriction:

> Now the first and foremost restriction imposed by international law upon a State is that—failing the existence of a permissive rule to the contrary- it may not exercise its power in any form on the territory of another State. In this sense jurisdiction is certainly territorial; it cannot be exercised by a State outside its territory except by virtue of a permissive rule derived from international custom or from a convention.[38]

This proposition asserts that States' jurisdiction is in principle confined to the State's territory and indeed a State's jurisdiction within its territory is extensive. Outside its territory, the situation is different: the reference to international law suggests that an expansive principle of absolute and unfettered sovereignty of States was not what the Court intended to propound.[39] The reference to limits placed by international law on extraterritorial jurisdiction would not have been necessary if the Court had taken the presumption of freedom literally.

In a similar vein, Sir Gerald Fitzmaurice questioned the *Lotus* presumption, turning to the phrase 'not in conflict with the principles of international law' used in the *Compromis*, which the Court was bound to

---

[36] Thus, "[l]iterally, the *Lotus* statement did not give expression to a presumption of freedom: it rejected a presumption against freedom. The general principle, which was clearly expressed elsewhere in the judgment, was the residual principle of state freedom… not a presumption", Spiermann (n 10) 254.

[37] See Pellet (n 28) 216 et seq.

[38] *Lotus* (n 9) 18–19.

[39] See the remarks by FA Mann: "But even of the footing of the actual words used by the Court there is room for the suggestion that they are not as far reaching as has sometimes been feared…The Court had stated that in determining the extent of its jurisdiction a State had 'a wide measure of discretion'. The Court ended by referring to 'the limits which international law places upon its jurisdiction' and which 'it should not overstep'. Perhaps it is the true explanation of the Court's statements that it intended, not to deny the existence of restraints upon a State's jurisdiction, but to reject the test of the strict territoriality of criminal jurisdiction which, according to the Court.., 'is not an absolute principle of international law..', and to adopt a more flexible rule", (n 23) 35–36.

apply strictly. In his view, this precluded the presumption from being considered as

> an abstract and independent rule of law. The Court can be regarded as applying the criterion of non-conflict with the principles of international law because the *Compromis* directed it to do so, rather than because this criterion had any abstract validity...Had the Court been asked to determine whether the Turkish action was in conformity with international law, the decision would almost certainly have been the other way, in view of the very narrow, even nominal majority.[40]

According to the reading one takes, Lotus either enshrines the strictest view of the interpretation of international law with the Court showing a deference towards State sovereignty, or on the other hand, a more moderate or 'international lawyer's approach', whereby the Court assesses international law as it stands at a given point of time. Despite the generality of the Court's pronouncements, extreme interpretations favouring either a minimalist or a very expansive reading of the judgment have been abandoned.[41] As Iain Scobbie remarks, while judicial and doctrinal opinion inclines towards the position that the *Lotus* presumption is discredited, "it is nevertheless the case that the presumption expresses an analytical axiom...as a matter of legal system structure rather than one of the weight to be accorded to an ageing precedent or of the existence of a substantive rule of international law".[42]

The Court apparently endorsed the contractual model of international law; a model in tune with a legal system deferential to State sovereignty, and in so doing can be regarded as acting within the confines of judicial restraint. However, it is submitted that, if one views the *Lotus principle* in its more moderate form, as one applying within the limits placed by international law, then the Court can be seen as stepping into its role of an international court upholding the rule of international law, albeit very cautiously, at a time when international law was not yet fully developed.

---

[40] GG Fitzmaurice, 'The Law and Procedure of the International Court of Justice, 1951–54: General Principles and Sources of Law' (1953) 30 BYIL 16–17. In fact, the way a question is phrased, or re-interpreted by the Court, can be 'outcome determinative', see the discussion below in the context of the Advisory Opinions on the *Legality of the Threat or Use of Nuclear Weapons* and *Kosovo*.

[41] L Reydams, *Universal Jurisdiction. International and Municipal Legal Perspectives* (OUP, Oxford 2003) 16.

[42] Scobbie (n 34) 294.

III. *Lotus* Revisited

Whatever reading one takes of the Permanent Court's judgment, it remains that the "cogency of the Lotus presumption in modern law has been doubted".[43] The reversal of the ruling by conventional law suggests that the impact of the Court's contribution on the issues before it was limited. To a great extent, its more general pronouncements, in particular the *Lotus* presumption, found a small echo in the later jurisprudence of the World Court.[44]

The reticence of the Court to address the *Lotus* statement directly in its judicial reasoning, when having an opportunity to do so, has been understood as a sign of judicial restraint on its part: directly addressing *Lotus* would involve delving into broader issues of State sovereignty and freedom of action, areas that still warrant caution in judicial decision-making.[45]

The underlying principle has been discussed in the Advisory Opinion on the *Legality of the Threat or Use of Nuclear Weapons*,[46] in the *Arrest Warrant* case,[47] and most recently in the *Kosovo* Advisory Opinion.[48] It is mainly through separate or dissenting opinions of its judges, who have revisited the PCIJ's pronouncements, that the *Lotus* statement has on occasion reappeared, and its reception has been quite ambiguous.[49]

The Court avoided addressing the issue in the *Arrest Warrant* case, a case very similar to *Lotus*, since it involved the question of a State's extra-territorial jurisdiction. The parties, in particular Belgium, had given the issue a great deal of attention in their pleadings. The Court ruled against Belgium on the merits, without specifically addressing the *Lotus* statement; it refused to address the issue of universal jurisdiction despite having explicitly stated that the *non ultra petita* rule "cannot preclude the

---

[43] Crawford (n 31) 42.

[44] For an analysis of relevant case-law see Handeyside (n 32) 80 et seq.

[45] Ibid at 81. According to Alain Pellet, even on the rare occasions where a 'voluntarist' approach can be identified in the Court's practice, "il s'agit d'exceptions limitées cadrant mal avec l'approche générale beaucoup plus ouverte et 'moderne' de la souveraineté véhiculée par la jurisprudence dominante, qui, d'une manière générale, s'abstient d'exhalter la souveraineté de l'Etat au détriment de la supériorité du droit international", (n 28) 223.

[46] *Legality of the Threat or Use of Nuclear Weapons*, [1996] ICJ Rep at 226.

[47] *Case Concerning the Arrest Warrant of 11 April 2000 (DRC v. Belgium)*, Judgment, [2002] ICJ Rep 3.

[48] *Accordance with International Law of the Unilateral Declaration of Independence in Respect of Kosovo*, Advisory Opinion of 22 July 2010 (at www.icj-cij.org).

[49] Pellet (n 28).

Court from addressing certain legal points in its reasoning".[50] Thus the Court did not avail itself of the opportunity to give clarification on the matter of universal jurisdiction which continues to be highly controversial. The opinions of the judges, who did address the issue, were diverse. Some viewed *Lotus* favourably, at the very least as an expression of sovereignty in its absolute form within the territory of the State.[51] On the other hand, in a joint separate opinion, Judges Higgins, Kooijmans, and Buergenthal noted that, while the PCIJ's pronouncements on international criminal jurisdiction retained value, the Lotus *dictum* "represents the high water mark of laissez-faire in international relations, and an era that has been significantly overtaken by other tendencies."[52]

In contrast, the *Lotus* statement was more thoroughly addressed, in particular during the proceedings and through the opinions of the judges in the two Advisory Opinions issued by the ICJ. One can discern a similarity of themes underpinning both opinions, and the reactions thereto, in particular as regards the question of prohibition/permission.

In the *Nuclear Weapons* opinion, the *Lotus* statement was addressed by the Court directly, but very briefly, because it had been raised in the course of the pleading by some States.[53] The formulation of the question posed to the Court: 'is the threat or use of nuclear weapons in any circumstance permitted under international law?' left room for divergent interpretations. For some States, this wording implied that the threat or use of nuclear weapons was unlawful, absent a permissive rule to the contrary. Others, in particular nuclear-weapon States, argued for the applicability of *Lotus*, contending that that the use of nuclear weapons was lawful, unless it was established that international law contained a prohibitory rule. In a brief passage, the Court acknowledged the *Lotus dictum*,[54] but disposed of

---

50 *Arrest Warrant* (n 47) [43]. On this point, see Kooijmans (n 5) 751.

51 See the Individual Opinions of Judges Ranjeva, Rezek and Guillaume. In particular, the latter's view seems to be more mitigated, as compared to his remarks in the *Nuclear Weapons* opinion: "In particular, classic international law does not exclude a state's power in some cases to exercise its judicial jurisdiction over offenses committed abroad. But, as the Permanent Court stated, once again in the *"Lotus"* case, the exercise of that jurisdiction is not without its limits..": *Arrest Warrant* (n 47), Sep Op Guillaume, at 37.

52 *Arrest Warrant* (n 47), Joint Sep Op, at 78, [50]-[51].

53 For a discussion of the opinion, inter alia, L Boisson de Chazournes and P Sands (eds), *International Law, the International Court of Justice and Nuclear Weapons* (CUP, Cambridge 1999).

54 The relevant passage reads: "Support for this contention was found in dicta of the Permanent Court of International Justice in the *Lotus* case that 'restrictions upon the independence of States cannot be ...presumed' and that international law leaves to States 'a wide measure of discretion which is only limited in certain cases by prohibitive

the arguments as "without particular significance" since nuclear-weapon States had accepted that their independence to act was limited by international law.[55]

The separate and dissenting opinions reveal the contrasting views of the bench: apart from the separate opinion of Judge Guillaume, asserting that States remain free to act in the absence of a prohibition,[56] many other Judges directly repudiated the *Lotus* statement as outdated,[57] inapplicable,[58] or simply unacceptable.[59]

In his declaration, Judge Bedjaoui distinguished the opinion from the decision of the Permanent Court, stating that the Court was far more circumspect than its predecessor in the *Lotus* case in asserting that what is not expressly prohibited by international law is therefore not authorized. For Bedjaoui, the Court did not infer any freedom to take a position from the uncertainties surrounding the law and facts.[60]

Judge Shahabuddeen's remarks are very instructive on the reading of *Lotus* in favour of an international-law oriented approach:

> There is not any convincing ground for the view that the *"Lotus"* Court moved off on a supposition that States have an absolute sovereignty which would entitle them to do anything however horrid or repugnant to the sense of the international community, provided that the doing of it could not be shown to be prohibited under international law. The idea of internal supremacy associated with the concept of sovereignty in municipal law is not neatly applicable when that concept is transposed to the international plane. The existence of a number of sovereignties side by side places limits on the freedom of States to act as if the others did not exist. These limits define an objective, structural framework within which sovereignty must necessarily

rules'...Reliance was also placed on the *dictum* of the present Court in the case concerning *Military and Paramilitary Activities in and against Nicaragua* (*Nicaragua v. United States of America*) that: 'in international law there are no rules, other than such rules as may be accepted by the State concerned, by treaty or otherwise, whereby the level of armaments of a sovereign State can be limited'...": *Nucelar Weapons* (n 46) at 238–239 [21] [references have been omitted].

55 Ibid [22].

56 *Nuclear Weapons* (n 46), at 291.

57 See the passage of Judge Bedjaoui's Declaration, cited above (n 16).

58 *Nuclear Weapons* (n 46), Diss Op Shahabuddeen, at 389–390.

59 Dissenting Opinion of Judge Weeramantry, who discussed the presumption at length, to conclude that: "It would be an interpretation totally out of context that the *Lotus* decision formulated a theory, equally applicable in peace and war, to the effect that a State could do whatever it pleased so long as it had not bound itself to the contrary. Such an interpretation of *Lotus* would cast a baneful spell on the progressive development of international law": *Nuclear Weapons* (n 46) at 495–496.

60 *Nuclear Weapons* (n 46), Declaration Bedjaoui, at 271 [15].

> exist...the framework and its defining limits, are implicit in the reference in "Lotus" to 'co-existing independent communities'...It is difficult for the Court to uphold a position that, absent a prohibition, a state has a right in law to act in ways which could deprive the sovereignty of all other States of meaning.[61]

The overall impression from the various opinions shows that there was an unwillingness of the majority to endorse an extensive interpretation, and application in the case, of the *Lotus* presumption.

The same could be said when one turns to the Court's *dispositif*. By a wide majority, the Court did not find a specific rule authorizing or prohibiting the threat or use of force. The absence of a specific prohibition was not an obstacle for the Court to declare that the threat or use of nuclear weapons would "generally be contrary to the rules of international law applicable in armed conflict". But, in the absence of any relevant treaty or customary rules, it declined to "conclude definitively whether the threat or use of nuclear weapons would be lawful or unlawful in an extreme circumstance of self-defence, in which the very survival of a State would be at stake".[62] This conclusion has been interpreted as a *non liquet*.[63] However, despite the Court's finding that international law did not provide a definitive answer to the question, the Court's reasoning indicates that it preferred to adopt a position of "legal neutrality".[64] This approach was foreshadowed in the Court's perceived conception of its judicial function, expressed in the first stages of its opinion:

> [The Court's] task is to engage in its normal judicial function of ascertaining the existence or otherwise of legal rules and principles applicable to the threat or use of nuclear weapons ... An entirely different question is whether the Court, under the constraints placed upon it as a judicial organ, will be able to give a complete answer to the question asked of it. However, that is a different matter from a refusal to answer at all.[65]

---

[61] *Nuclear Weapons* (n 46), Diss Op Shahabuddeen, at 393–394.

[62] *Nuclear Weapons* (n 46), at [105].

[63] For a discussion, see D Bodansky, '*Non Liquet* and the Incompleteness of International Law' in (n 53) 153–170; J Salmon, 'Le problème des lacunes à la lumière de l'avis 'Liceité de la menace ou de l'emploi d'armes nucléaires' rendu le 18 juillet 1996 par la CIJ' in *Mélanges en l'honneur de Nicolas Valticos: droit et justice* (Pedone, Paris 1999) 197–232; J Kammerhofer, 'Gaps, the *Nuclear Weapons* Advisory Opinion and the Structure of International Legal Argument Between Theory and Practice' (2009) BYIL 333–360.

[64] In the words of President Bedjaoui, the Court felt unable to give either the green light of authorization, or the red light of prohibition: see *Nuclear Weapons* (n 46), Declaration Bedjaoui, at [14].

[65] *Nuclear Weapons* (n 46), at [18]-[19].

The Court's finding that international law did not provide a definitive answer to the question is surprising, in particular in view of the panoramic analysis of the 'great corpus of general international law'. This analysis indicates that broader principles embedded within various fields of international law, could serve as a basis for deciding the question. The Court's failure to arrive at a definitive conclusion, in the extreme case where the survival of a State would be at risk, is disappointing.[66] In refusing to give an answer, the Court did not discharge itself fully of its judicial function.[67] Interpreting and applying international norms requires a degree of creativity, which is not always to be conflated with judicial activism.[68]

On the other hand, while failing to arrive at a definitive conclusion, the Court did not imply that there was presumption of freedom of States in the matter or an underlying assumption that States were absolutely unrestrained in the matter. In so doing, the Court seems, at least implicitly, to have rejected an application of a *Lotus*-type freedom of States, either as a residual rule or as a gap-filler.[69]

In its Advisory Opinion on the *Accordance with International Law of the Unilateral Declaration of Independence in Respect of Kosovo*,[70] the Court

---

66 See L Condorelli, 'Nuclear Weapons: A Weighty Matter for the ICJ—*Jura Non Novit Curia?*' (1997) 316 Intl Rev of the Red Cross 9; M Kohen, 'L'avis consultatif de la CIJ sur la *Liceité de la menace ou de l'emploi d'armes nucléaires* et la fonction judiciaire' (1997) 2 EJIL 336–362.

67 The Court's *non liquet* was regretted by Judge Higgins, who saw it as a failure by the Court to discharge itself of its judicial function, which is "to take principles of general application, to elaborate their meaning and to apply them to specific situations": *Nuclear Weapons* (n 46), Diss Op Higgins, at 591 [32].

68 As Daniel Bodansky remarks: "If law is simply a system of rules, then some degree of judicial creativity is unavoidable, since often rules do not yield determinate answers and must be interpreted. Allowing judges only to apply the law, not to engage in any creative work, would make *non liquets* the rule rather than the exception. But recognizing the need for judicial creativity in interpreting and applying an existing legal norm does not mean that we must concede that judges should be able to legislate an entirely new norm to fill a gap in the law. The two cases lie along a continuum and differ in degree—but as we approach the two ends of the spectrum, the difference in *degree* becomes a difference in *kind* between *applying* the law and *creating* it": see "*Non Liquet* and the Incompleteness of International Law", in Boisson de Chazournes and Sands (n 53), at 168.

69 As Jean Salmon remarks: "en tout état de cause, puisque la Cour a admis en fin de compte *nollens volens* l'existence d'une lacune, elle doit etre considérée comme n'ayant pas admis que celle-ci pouvait être comblée par un prétendu principe que tout ce qui n'est pas interdit est permis…Admettre que l'on se trouve dans une situation de neutralité juridique, c'est-à-dire d'un comportement ni permis ni interdit…signifie que la Cour adopte un positivisme juridique relativisé, limité par les contradictions profondes qui divisent la société interétatique", (n 63) 208, 213.

70 Advisory Opinion, 22 July 2010 (at www.icj-cij.org). For commentaries, see, among others, the symposia 'Kosovo in the International Court of Justice: The Case' (2010/8) 11

took a position that some understood as a reaffirmation of the *Lotus principle*. This was traced to the fact that the Court read the question posed to it by the General Assembly whether the declaration was 'in accordance with international law' as 'whether or not the declaration of independence was adopted in violation of international law'. In other words, the Court adopted a narrow view of the question framing it not in terms of entitlement, but in terms of the existence of a prohibition.[71] During the proceedings, there was considerable discussion about the *Lotus principle*. States supporting the independence of Kosovo cited this principle in their arguments, while Serbia contended that the principle had no room in the case. The Court itself did not refer to the *Lotus* judgment.

In his Declaration to the Advisory Opinion, Judge Bruno Simma suggests that the Court endorsed the *Lotus principle*, the request, in his opinion, deserving a more comprehensive answer, assessing both permissive and prohibitive rules of international law:

> The underlying rationale of the Court's approach reflects an old, tired view of international law, which takes the adage, famously expressed in the '*Lotus*' judgment, according to which restrictions on the independence cannot be presumed because of the consensual nature of the international legal order … As the Permanent Court did in that case … the Court has concluded in the present Opinion that, in relation to a specific act, it is not necessary to demonstrate a permissive rule so long as there is no prohibition …"[72]

However, as it has been suggested, the Court's ultimate conclusion that the unilateral declaration of independence was not in violation of international law, cannot be considered as a 'blanket endorsement' of the *Lotus* presumption.[73] This is mainly because in its rationale, the principle is

---

German LJ <www.germanlawjournal.com>; 'The International Court of Justice on Kosovo: Opinion or Non-Opinion?' (28 September 2010) Hague Justice Portal <www.haguejusticeportal.net>; 'Kosovo Symposium' (2011/1) 24 Leiden J of Intl L 71.

71 It followed that: "The Court is not required by the question it has been asked to take a position on whether international law conferred a positive entitlement on Kosovo unilaterally to declare its independence, or, a fortiori, whether international law generally confers an entitlement on entities situated within a state unilaterally to break away from it. Indeed, it is entirely possible for a particular act—such as a unilateral declaration of independence- not to be in violation of international law without constituting the exercise of a right conferred by it. The Court has been asked for an opinion on the first point, not the second", *Kosovo* Opinion (n 70) [56].

72 *Kosovo* Opinion (n 70), Declaration of Judge Simma, at [2].

73 On this, M Weller, 'Modesty Can Be a Virtue: Judicial Economy in the ICJ *Kosovo* Opinion?' (2011/1) 24 Leiden J of Intl L 127, 134–135; A Peters, 'Does Kosovo Lie in the *Lotus*-Land of Freedom?' ibid 95, 100–101; T Christakis, 'The ICJ Advisory Opinion on Kosovo: Has International Law Something to Say about Secession?' ibid 73; JA Frowein, 'Kosovo and

confined to inter-State relations, encapsulating a presumption of State freedom. Applying this principle to the authors of the declaration of independence would work against the State, actually reversing the *Lotus* postulate.[74] Rather, the Court's conclusion is the judicial affirmation of the (present) neutrality of international law on the issue of a possible right to secession or external self-determination.[75] Thus, more importantly than whether the Court endorsed or not a *Lotus*-like approach (and which one),[76] the question is whether the Court based its conclusions on an in-depth and comprehensive analysis of the existing law and its trends. In this sense, Judge Simma's remarks on the 'minimalist', 'mechanical approach' of the Court and his call for Advisory Opinions 'with greater relevance as regards the international legal order' make a forceful point.[77]

IV. Conclusion

The *Lotus* case is considered a jurisprudential classic, in that it encapsulates "a whole conception of international law".[78] At the same time, the *Lotus dictum* has generated much debate, and, while its underlying assumption has been surpassed to a large extent by the development of international law, it is still remembered from time to time and evoked in its 'infinite variety'. Whichever interpretation one adopts, *Lotus* remains one of the leading cases to be turned to when assessing the PCIJ's influence in the development of the theory of international law-making.

The case also shows the difficulties one faces in seeking to extract generalizations concerning the influence of jurisprudence, or the judicial function in international law.[79] The contribution of a particular case, a particular ruling to the development, or change of international law occurs over a period of time. Rather than being viewed from a perspective

---

Lotus' in *From Bilateralism to Community Interest: Essays in Honour of Bruno Simma* (OUP, Oxford 2011) 923–931.

74 Peters (n 73) 100; Christakis (n 73) 79.

75 Christakis (n 73).

76 Anne Peters considers that the Court actually reversed the *Lotus principle*; according to the author, "the Court's implicit and upside-down *Lotus* approach does not take sides with the traditional idea that secession happens in an international law-free zone…The *Kosovo AO* can be read both ways: either secession is outside international law in the sense that international law is simply neutral vis-à-vis secession, or international law allows secession….*Lotus* is not the key to Kosovo": Peters (n 73) 101.

77 *Kosovo* Opinion (n 70), Declaration Simma, at [7], [9]-[10].

78 Dupuy (n 27) 349.

79 For some 'rules of thumb', Tams & Tzanakopoulos (n 8) 781–800.

of economy or activism on the part a judicial body, the impact of a pronouncement in a specific case can also be that it initiates a spark that lights up a discussion, develops into a flame paving the way for change in the law, or just fades away with the first breath of air. Seen from this viewpoint, the *Lotus obiter*, whatever its cogency in modern international law, has contributed to the discussion—and why not, the change—on the nature of international law itself.

PART FIVE

CONSTITUTIONAL INTERNATIONAL LAW

THE PERMANENT COURT OF INTERNATIONAL JUSTICE AND THE 'INTERNATIONAL COMMUNITY'

Antonios Tzanakopoulos*

I. (De-)Construction

The purpose of this brief study is to gauge what the Permanent Court of International Justice might have had to say about the 'international community', as the Court administering the law of that community,[1] but also developing it, thereby contributing to the stabilization and further integration of that community.[2] No such attempt can be undertaken, however, without some preliminary understanding of this rather nebulous term—'international community'. One must at least have an idea of what one is looking for.

Ubi societas ibi jus,[3] goes the Latin maxim: where there exists a society, there is law. Or is it maybe the other way around? Is it the existence of a society that necessitates the creation of a legal framework, or is it the development of a legal framework that integrates and thus 'constitutes' the relevant society?[4] Perhaps it is indeed futile to ask which comes first.[5]

---

* Many thanks to Professors Vaughan Lowe QC and Christian Tams, and to Drs Akbar Rasulov and Gleider Hernández, for helping me deal with the *prothysteron* that this brief study entails (see further at the end of section I, below). The usual disclaimer applies.

[1] H Lauterpacht, *The Development of International Law by the Permanent Court of International Justice* (Longmans, Green and Co, London 1934) 1, though, to be pedantic, Lauterpacht consistently referes to 'international society'. So he does also in the work cited at n 15, despite the title. See further in this section.

[2] Idem, *The Development of International Law by the International Court* (Stevens & Sons, London 1958) (reprint: Grotius, Cambridge 1982) 7.

[3] Cicero, *De legibus* 1,42; cf J Crawford, 'Responsibility for Breaches of Communitarian Norms: An Appraisal of Article 48 of the ILC Articles on Responsibility of States for Internationally Wrongful Acts' in U Fastenrath et al (eds), *From Bilateralism to Community Interest—Essays in Honour of Bruno Simma* (OUP, Oxford 2011) 224; PS Rao, 'The Concept of International Community in International Law: Theory and Reality' in I Buffard et al (eds), *Festschrift Gerhard Hafner* (Martinus Nijhoff, Leiden 2008) 85, 86.

[4] Taking a similar line of inquiry, constitutional lawyers debate whether only an already existing political community can make a constitution, or whether the community is but the result of a constitutional process. See B Fassbender, *The United Nations Charter as the Constitution of the International Community* (Martinus Nijhoff, The Hague 2009) 64–5.

[5] Ibid at 65. And cf the understanding of the term 'community' by the PCIJ in *Greco-Bulgarian 'Communities'* (Advisory Opinion) [1930] PCIJ Ser B No 17 (a question of fact that may receive legal recognition) with that by Bulgaria (a legal fiction, which exists only by virtue of law).

Any organized interaction between entities requires basic rules on which to function, and the establishment of a legal framework for coexistence and interaction necessarily 'constitutes' a legal community.[6] In this sense, law primarily reflects (and conserves to a large extent) social conditions, changes as they change, and to some (limited) degree also shapes social conditions in its image.[7] States (themselves communities under law[8]) and other entities are active on the international level, and their interactions are regulated by law—there must thus exist something like an international society, at once a mirror and an aspiration,with international law as its transcendental expression.[9]

But already the terms used (society, community, legal community) create more questions than they answer: while 'society' (*Gesellschaft*), for example, seems to hint at a lesser degree of cohesion than 'community' (*Gemeinschaft*) does,[10] the terms have also been used 'the other way around'. The term 'legal community' on the other hand denotes the existence of a community merely on the basis that the various members are united into such a community by the recognition that they are bound by some common rules,[11] and at that is rather circular.

---

[6] Cf J Basdevant 'Règles générales du droit de la paix' (1936) 58 RdC 508–20. Jenks observes that '[n]either the State as we know it nor the community of States can be regarded as antecedent to the other; they are products of the same process of historical growth': CW Jenks, 'The Will of the World Community as the Basis of Obligation in International Law' in *Hommage d'une génération de juristes au Président Basdevant* (Pedone, Paris 1960) 280, 281. Similarly neither law nor society can be regarded as antecedent to one another. The two emerge simultaneously.

[7] See e.g. M Koskenniemi, *From Apology to Utopia—The Structure of International Legal Argument* (re-issue: CUP, Cambridge 2006) 474.

[8] See, for the recognition of this by the Permanent Court itself in *SS 'Lotus'*, the quote at n 25 below.

[9] P Reuter, 'Confédération et fédération: "vetera et nova"' in *Mélanges offerts à Charles Rousseau* (Pedone, Paris 1974) 199, 213: '...le droit international, expression transcendantale de la société internationale'.

[10] See generally F Tönnies, *Gemeinschaft und Gesellschaft—Grundbegriffe der reinen Soziologie* (3d edn, Wissenschaftliche Buchgesellschaft, Darmstadt 1991); cf among many others S Villalpando, *L'emergence de la communauté internationale dans la responsabilité des États* (PUF, Paris 2005) 18 et seq; G Abi-Saab, 'Wither the International Community' (1998) 9 EJIL 248, 249.

[11] See generally H Mosler, 'The International Society as a Legal Community' (1974) 140 RdC 1, 17 et seq; cf G Danilenko, *Law-Making in the International Community* (Martinus Nijhoff, Dordrecht 1993) 13. To borrow Koskenniemi's words in another context '[an] artificial communit[y] ... linked principally by the existence of a ... decision-procedure which makes it possible for [the members] to participate in the conduct of their common affairs ...': M Koskenniemi, 'National Self-Determination Today: Problems of Legal Theory and Practice' (1994) 43 ICLQ 241, 249.

Perhaps these definitional problems could be avoided by substituting the League of Nations for the international community, at least for the period in question: indeed, the international community may have been oscillating for a very long time 'between myth and history',[12] but the creation of the first 'global' international organizations in the interwar period, most notably the League of Nations, could be seen to signify the progressive institutionalization of the amorphous concept of the international community,[13] referred to by jurists since the days of Grotius and Suárez.[14]

For those who believed that law was not necessarily the hallmark of a community at all (or vice versa), but who thought rather that it was the existence of a judge competent to decide upon disputed rights and to command peace that constituted the decisive test,[15] the interwar period brought the establishment of the Permanent Court of International Justice, further evidence towards the consolidation of a still primitive international community under primitive law.[16] Accepting this would have a salutary effect for present purposes, as it would make the need for any more nuanced understanding of the 'international community' redundant.

It would be premature, however, to characterize the League of Nations as the 'embodiment' of the international community. For one, if anything, the organization by its (French) name refers to a 'society' of nations (*Société des Nations*), and by its German one to an 'association' or even '(con-)federation' of peoples (*Völkerbund*), thereby further adding to the terminological mess. For another, the constitutive treaty of an international organization, even a quasi-global one, does not but—in the first instance—create a 'partial community', to use Riccardo Monaco's words.[17]

---

[12] See the seminal work of R-J Dupuy, *La communauté internationale: entre le mythe et l'histoire* (Economica, Paris 1986).

[13] Or, for some, the progressive 'constitutionalization' of the decentralized, non-organized international community on the basis of a contractual, written constitution: K Ginther, 'Die Verfassung der Völkerrechtsgemeinschaft im Lichte der Entscheidungen des Internationalen Gerichtshofes im sogennanten Südwestafrika-Streit' in R Marcic et al (eds), *Internationale Festschrift für Alfred Verdross zum 80. Geburtstag* (Wilhelm Fink, München 1971) 91, 92–3. See also Lauterpacht (n 1) 1, and cf idem (n 2) 4.

[14] See I Feichtner, 'Community Interest' in R Wolfrum (ed), *Max Planck Encyclopedia of Public International Law* (OUP, Oxford 2012) [8].

[15] See H Lauterpacht, *The Function of Law in the International Community* (Clarendon Press, Oxford 1933) 432–4. But see n 71 below for his recognition of the League of Nations Covenant as an 'instrument in the process of political integration of mankind'.

[16] Ibid at 439–42.

[17] R Monaco, 'Le caractère constitutionnel des actes institutifs d'organisations internationales' in *Mélanges Rousseau* (n 9) 153, 157: 'traites destinés à instituer des *communautés partielles*' (emphasis added).

For yet another, the Covenant refers predominantly to the 'Members of the League' rather than to the League itself—Article 11 thus reading more like the odd one out.[18] The League was seemingly more a 'they' than an 'it'.

This brief exposé should have made it clear that any further attempt at defining the term 'international community' is likely to yield diminishing results. It is suggested rather to 'reverse-engineer' the jurisprudence of the PCIJ, seeking to canvass how the Court understood the international community and how it would have wanted it to evolve.[19] This could be done by looking, in the Court's case law, for what are commonly accepted as the 'hallmarks' of an (international) community, or at least for those features commonly associated with the idea: the make-up of the community; the concept of obligations and action in the 'general' interest—as distinct from any individual interest of a member, even if that happens to coincide with the individual interests of other members (which constitutes a 'common' or 'shared'—but not a general—interest);[20] and the existence of institutions providing protection of the community interest.[21] This may be seen as a *prothysteron*, in the sense that these 'hallmarks' of an 'international community' much postdate the Permanent Court of International Justice. But in the attempt to 'reverse-engineer' the jurisprudence of the Court, this *prothysteron* will have to be excused.

---

18 Art 11 provided in part: 'Any war or threat of war, whether immediately affecting any of the Members of the League or not, is hereby declared *a matter of concern to the whole League*, and *the League shall take any action* that may be deemed wise and effectual to safeguard the peace of nations' (emphasis added).

19 Koskenniemi (n 7) 474.

20 A 'common' or 'collective' interest is shared between community members, but it is not a community or general interest, above and beyond the individual interests of community members, or even entailing their (partial) sacrifice. In its commentary to Article 48 of the Articles on the Responsibility of States for Internationally Wrongful Acts ('ASR'), the International Law Commission discusses the concept of a 'common' or 'collective' interest in the context of Article 48(1)(a) referring to obligations *erga omnes partes*. The common or collective interest is one 'over and above any of the interests of the States concerned individually', but it is not an interest of 'the ... community as a whole' (ie a community interest), which falls to be discussed under Article 48(1)(b), and which is defined as an interest of 'the international community *as such*' (emphasis added): UN Doc A/56/10 (2001); (2001) II(2) YILC 31, 126–7 [6]–[10]. Cf B Simma, 'From Bilateralism to Community Interest in International Law' (1994) 250 RdC 217, 233: 'a consensus according to which the respect for certain fundamental values is not to be left to the free disposition of States individually or *inter se*, but is recognized and sanctioned by international law as a matter of concern to all States'. See finally Villalpando (n 10) 26–8.

21 Cf the list of positive manifestations of the concept of an international community through law in Villalpando (n 10) 75; a similar list is found, among others, in Rao (n 3) and V Gowlland-Debbas, 'Judicial Insights into Fundamental Values and Interests of the International Community' in AS Muller et al (eds), *The International Court of Justice—Its Future Role after Fifty Years* (Martinus Nijhoff, The Hague 1997) 327.

II. The International Community and Its Membership

The Permanent Court was actually requested to render an Advisory Opinion in which to determine, inter alia, the meaning of the term 'community'. This was in the context of the Greco-Bulgarian Convention of 1919 concerning the mutual migration of Greek and Bulgarian populations (in effect, an exchange), and thus not in general terms. The Court opted for the 'traditional' interpretation of the term, which held that a 'community' was 'a group of persons living in a given country or locality, having a race, religion, language and traditions of their own and united by this identity of race, religion, and traditions in a sentiment of solidarity, with a view to preserving their traditions, maintaining their form of worship, ensuring instruction and upbringing of their children in accordance with the spirit and traditions of their race and rendering mutual assistance to each other.'[22] In its view then the existence of a 'community' is a question of fact rather than law, even if this existence may receive some recognition in law.[23]

One might argue that little is to be made of this construction of the Court, which equated the concept of a 'community' under the treaty with that of a 'nation' rather than dealing with the term in abstracto. However, the definition is helpful if one accepts that

> [t]here is hardly any possible root for the notion of an international community other than one's conception of a national community, and perhaps various sub-communities, those being the legally relevant communities known. The notion of an international community is a reflection of the conception of the (world) state as a national sovereign.[24]

Further, the statement is suitably general to convey the Court's understanding of some of the crucial properties of a community beyond the concept of a nation. These are the existence of a group of entities that have certain common characteristics, that are united by these characteristics in a sentiment of solidarity, and that have a common purpose or interest. The Permanent Court further conceded that if in fact some community has

22 *Greco-Bulgarian 'Communities'* (n 5) 21.

23 Ibid at 23 et seq.

24 O Spiermann, *International Legal Argument in the Permanent Court of International Justice—The Rise of the International Judiciary* (CUP, Cambridge 2005) 118; cf A Paulus, 'The Influence of the United States on the Concept of the "International Community"' in M Byers and G Nolte (eds), *United States Hegemony and the Foundations of International Law* (CUP, Cambridge 2003) 57, 86.

been established, then legal recognition of that existence may follow. It seems that the Court may have relied on the elements of this definition, even if unconsciously, in shaping its understanding of the 'international community', in particular with respect to its membership.

The Permanent Court did use the term 'international community' on occasion, even though mostly to dress up its decisions rather than to necessarily make a normative statement or to draw from the existence of such a community any specific conclusions as to the state of the law. In *SS 'Lotus'*, for example, the Permanent Court referred to international law as applying to all States making up the 'communauté internationale',[25] without any further elaboration. And yet, this statement allows a glimpse into what the Court understood to be the membership of that 'international community'. At the time—if expectedly—this seemed limited to States:[26] they were entities united by certain common characteristics. Individual judges further limited the membership of the community, arguably opting for stricter criteria of 'commonality' of characteristics, to 'civilized' States,[27] which was, at the time, to some extent supported by the wording of Art 38(1)(c) of the Court's Statute; and even to 'countries which have adopted the European system of civilization',[28] which presumably should not—even at that time—have been the sole necessary condition for being considered 'civilized'. (And yet this type of thinking continues to have traction almost a century later—after all Margaret Thatcher unabashedly wrote in her memoirs with respect to the UN-authorized intervention in Iraq in 1991 that this was undertaken by 'the West or, as we tactfully prefer to describe it, "the international community"'.[29])

It appears then that there was some question as to who would count as a member of the community, even from among States, during the early years of the Court's life. Perhaps the implicit extension by the Court of membership in the international community to States 'other than the civilized ones' (as some judges would have it) can explain the replacement of up-to-that-point rather usual term 'family of nations'[30] by the less

---

[25] [1927] PCIJ Ser A No 10 at 16–17. The English version refers to 'international law as it is applied to between all nations belonging to the community of States.'

[26] See also ibid at 44 (diss op Weiss) (referring to 'all nations constituting the international community').

[27] Ibid at 34 (diss op Loder) (referring to 'civilized States, members of the great community of nations', translated from the original French 'membres de la grande famille des nations').

[28] Ibid at 60 (diss op Nyholm).

[29] M Thatcher, *The Path to Power* (HarperCollins, London 1995) 508.

[30] Cf Loder at n 27 above.

intimate one that is the 'international community'. Still, the Court was to make further leaps in its understanding of membership in the international community, even if only implicitly.

In *Jurisdiction of the Courts of Danzig*, in what can only be described as a groundbreaking decision, the Permanent Court found that international agreements may actually create rights and obligations which are enforceable in national courts, if that intention on the part of the parties is evident from the terms of the agreement.[31] While this does not directly admit individuals to membership in the 'international community' on an equal footing with States—far from it—it concedes and recognizes their existence as beneficiaries of community regulation and as participants in the operation of the community legal system: they can seek direct application and enforcement of law produced by the 'international' community within their different 'sub-communities'. Similarly, the 1922 German-Polish treaty on Upper Silesia was found by the Permanent Court to 'bestow ... rights' upon every national of Poland.[32]

When seen against the background of the strict rules of diplomatic protection depriving the individual of any claim to existence at the international level and reiterated by the Court in a number of cases,[33] the dicta in *Danzig* becomes all the more striking. The Permanent Court established the principle that States may grant a (smaller or larger) 'measure of international legal personality'[34] to entities other than themselves, through (explicit or implicit) agreement: this laid the groundwork and lies at the basis of the recognition of international legal personality of international organizations,[35] the possibility for States to circumvent, through agreement, the traditional rules of diplomatic protection (and the fiction of injury to the State) by acknowledging not just rights of individuals under international law, but also a capacity in them to bring claims for their violation in their own name,[36] and even—if remotely—the eventual move

---

[31] [1928] PCIJ Ser B No 15 at 17–18. For further discussion of the nuanced relationship between the PCIJ and domestic courts see generally J d'Aspremont to (in this volume), 221.

[32] *Rights of Minorities in Upper Silesia* (*Minority Schools*) [1928] PCIJ Ser A No 15 at 46, [2] of the *dispositif.* Cf I Scobbie (in this volume), at 218–220 and CJ Tams (in this volume), at 13–15.

[33] Most notably in *Mavrommatis Palestine Concessions* (Preliminary Objection) [1924] PCIJ Ser A No 2.

[34] As the successor court, the ICJ, was to state in *Reparation for Injuries Suffered in the Service of the United Nations* (Advisory Opinion) [1949] ICJ Rep 174, 179.

[35] Ibid.

[36] See, e.g., *Ahmadou Sadio Diallo* (*Republic of Guinea v DRC*) (Preliminary Objections) [2007] ICJ Rep [88]: The Court is bound to note that, in contemporary international law,

from 'the international community of States as a whole' (as in Article 53 of the Vienna Convention on the Law of Treaties[37]) to the 'international community as a whole' (as in *Barcelona Traction*[38] and in Article 48 ASR). Even if the ILC justifies the move on the basis that the former expression is meant merely to 'stress the paramountcy that States have over the making of international law',[39] the fact remains that the change in terminology is significant when it comes to the membership of the international community: this is no longer absolutely limited to States—even if it doesn't quite establish Scelle's position that, like all societies, the international society is made up of individuals, and that the predominance of States is but a historical accident as the means of choice in the realization of the solidarity of individuals.[40]

III. The Individual as the Link between Membership and General Interest

Beyond the first timid moves towards extending the membership of the international community beyond States, individuals also featured in another aspect of the Permanent Court's jurisprudence, long before the dawn of internationally protected human rights. The minorities regime under the auspices of the League of Nations and the establishment of the International Labour Organization were the precursors of such international protection, which was only properly and comprehensively to be established and to flourish after the second World War. During the interwar period, at any rate, the two regimes—minority and labour rights—gave the Permanent Court the opportunity to explore the 'humanitarian' aspect of the then contemporary positive international law, even if indirectly.

This expression by States, through positive international law, of certain 'humanitarian' sensibilities, their assumption of obligations beyond

the protection of the rights of companies and the rights of their shareholders, and the settlement of the associated disputes, are essentially governed by bilateral or multilateral agreements for the protection of foreign investments ... In that context, the role of diplomatic protection somewhat faded, as in practice recourse is only made to it in rare cases where treaty régimes do not exist or have proved inoperative.'

[37] 1155 UNTS 331 ('VCLT').

[38] *Barcelona Traction, Light and Power Company, Limited (New Application: 1962) (Belgium v Spain) (Second Phase)* [1970] ICJ Rep 3, 32 [33].

[39] Commentary to Article 25 ASR (n 20) 84 [18].

[40] See M Koskenniemi, *The Gentle Civilizer of Nations* (CUP, Cambridge 2002) 330–3; cf generally G Scelle, 'Essai de systématique du droit international (Plan d'un cours de droit international public)' (1923) 30 RGDIP 116.

strictly reciprocal engagements seeking to enable or achieve mutually beneficial transactions, denotes perhaps the first emergence of an interest that was not just 'common' in the sense of benefiting all parties to the transaction, but rather 'general' or 'community' interest, in the sense that rules were established that were not directly benefiting any State in any way, but were rather meant to safeguard what was considered as the 'general interest' in protecting certain vulnerable groups of individuals. No doubt, less noble intentions may have also played a significant part in the motivations for the establishment of the minority protection system, for example, which was also by and large imposed on States wishing to secure international recognition or consolidate territorial gains after World War I, rather than freely agreed to. And yet the humanitarian sensibilities that at least partly underpin the project cannot be overlooked.

The Permanent Court was called upon regularly to help implement the regimes,[41] and in the process it offered *dicta* that would evolve into *loci classici* in human rights law beyond the strict confines of minority protection, such as the definition of equality and the distinction between formal and genuine equality, or equality in law and equality in fact, in *German Settlers in Poland*,[42] and *Minority Schools in Albania*,[43] as well the human rights implications of nationality links in *Acquisition of Polish Nationality*.[44] The PCIJ's legacy with respect to rights of groups and individuals is treated more fully elsewhere,[45] but it does indicate the recognition by States of interests above and beyond their individual or shared interests. It is with respect to the elucidation of such general or community interest that the next section now turns.

IV. The Concept of a General Interest

The term 'general interest' is a notion that resists definition in abstracto, especially since cognate concepts, such as that of a 'common' or 'shared' interest, tend to further muddy the waters. A beautiful generic definition,

---

[41] See further under section V.2 below, and cf *Rights of Minorities in Upper Silesia*, mentioned in the text at n 32 above.

[42] *Certain Questions relating to Settlers of German Origin in the Territory Ceded by Germany to Poland* [1923] PCIJ Ser B No 6 at 23–4 and 36–7.

[43] [1935] PCIJ Ser A/B No 64 at 19.

[44] [1923] PCIJ Ser B No 7.

[45] See generally C Brölmann (in this volume), 123; see also, for a brief account, D Guilfoyle and M Giles Samson (in this volume), at 63.

which is arguably brought out in the jurisprudence of the PCIJ to some extent, is that by Reeves in his Hague lectures in 1924: he argues that, a 'measure' being a choice of means to achieve certain aims, and no two States ever having adopted all identical 'measures', one must seek those measures that are similar and distinguish them from those measures that isolate States.[46] The former are those which bring States together, and represent a mutual recognition of their common interests.[47] But, as argued above,[48] a general (community) interest is not the same as a common (collective) interest. Does the Permanent Court's jurisprudence offer any help in understanding these concepts?

In *Nationality Decrees*,[49] the Court directly juxtaposes community interest in the preservation of the peace, institutionalized through the League of Nations, with individual State interest, in construing and therefore delimiting the jurisdiction of the League to make recommendations. The power of the League to act in the general interest stops where the *domaine réservé* of a State, ie its domestic jurisdiction, begins.[50] The Permanent Court concedes that the question is relative, and depends upon the development of international relations,[51] read: international law. Those areas of domestic jurisdiction where a State has accepted limitations under international law no longer remain within the reserved domain.[52] In effect then the Court admits that (part of) international law is laid not just in the *common*, but also in the *general* interest: States may reciprocally grant each other rights under international law, bilaterally or multilaterally, or create non-reciprocally-structured regimes,[53] this being in their common interest; but this then brings the matter so regulated within the general interest, in the sense that, should there be a dispute over the matter so regulated that may endanger peace, then intervention by an international organ is admitted, in the general interest of keeping the peace.

---

46 JS Reeves, 'La communauté internationale' (1923) 3 RdC 1, 12.

47 Ibid.

48 See the attempt to distinguish between a common/collective interest and a community/general interest in section I, above.

49 *Nationality Decrees Issued in Tunis and Morocco* [1923] PCIJ Ser B No 4.

50 Ibid at 25.

51 Ibid at 24.

52 Ibid.

53 The dissents by Judges van Eysinga and Schücking in *Oscar Chinn* [1934] PCIJ Ser A/B No 63 contain some of the first indications of the potential existence of 'objective regimes'; and cf *SS 'Wimbledon'* [1923] PCIJ Ser A No 1 at 23; *Territorial Jurisdiction of the International Commission of the River Oder* [1929] PCIJ Ser A No 23 at 19–22, accepting in principle the possibility of a treaty being opposable to non-parties under certain circumstances.

But does the Court take a position on the extent of the *domaine réservé*, ie on the part of regulation that escapes any consideration in the general interest? The case of the *SS 'Lotus'*[54] is generally considered as demonstrating a preference of the Permanent Court (and by implication of international law, which the Court interprets and applies under Article 38(1) of its Statute) for autonomy of States over community interest: '[r]estrictions upon the independence of States cannot … be presumed'.[55] One should approach this statement with caution, however. The crucial question is not whether the Permanent Court, by starting out from the point of freedom of action of States, prefers 'autonomy' over 'community'. This is not only because the presumption adopted by the Court could easily be argued to support both the concept of autonomy and that of community;[56] it is because the Court purports to state the law as it is, to adopt a presumption embedded in the *lex lata*.[57] Indeed the Court establishes that States, through freely expressing their will, move parts of regulation out of the reserved domain and into the purview of international law.[58] The matter then becomes one where intervention by organs of the international community may be justified in the protection of the general interest, as per the construction of *Nationality Decrees*, above. Such a finding is further corroborated by the Permanent Court's Advisory Opinion in the *Exchange of Greek and Turkish Populations*,[59] where the Court established that international obligations may make it incumbent upon a State to bring its domestic law 'into harmony' with international law, ie introduce changes required under international law.[60] The assumption of an international

54 For further discussion of the importance of the *Lotus Case* see generally P Pazartzis (in this volume), 319.

55 *SS 'Lotus'* (n 25) 18.

56 Koskenniemi (n 7) ch 7 and *passim*.

57 Cf *Accordance with International Law of the Unilateral Declaration of Independence in Respect of Kosovo* (Advisory Opinion) [2010] ICJ Rep [84]: '… the Court considers that general international law contains no applicable prohibition of declarations of independence. Accordingly, it concludes that the declaration of independence of 17 February 2008 did not violate general international law.' Cf the declaration of Judge Simma appended to the Advisory Opinion, especially [2]–[3] and [8] et seq.

58 *SS 'Lotus'* (n 25) 18: 'The rules of law binding upon States therefore emanate from their own free will as expressed in conventions or by usages generally accepted as expressing principles of law and established in order to regulate the relations between these co-existing independent communities or with a view to the achievement of common aims'.

59 [1925] PCIJ Ser B No 10.

60 Ibid at 20–1. In many cases the Permanent Court had to consider and even interpret domestic law to ascertain whether it was in compliance with a State's international obligations: see, e.g., *Appeal from a Judgment of the Hungaro-Czechoslovak Mixed Arbitral Tribunal*

obligation on a specific matter removes it from the reserved domain and allows international organs to review domestic law for compliance with international law.[61]

Is all this supposed to mean that there is an area of 'sovereignty' or 'autonomy' that is clearly juxtaposed to the concept of an 'international community', whose regulation in the general interest, as it expands, leads to the diminution of sovereign power? A number of pronouncements of the Permanent Court aim at dispelling any idea that the international community and its law is whatever is left after the scope of the various 'sovereign' or 'reserved' domains are determined—rather, the Permanent Court establishes that the purview of international law may expand without the sovereign domains 'contracting' or 'diminishing' in any way. This is because, as it states in *SS 'Wimbledon'*,[62] and in the *Exchange of Greek and Turkish Populations*,[63] and as Judge Anzilotti makes clear in his dissent in *Customs Union*,[64] the assumption of international obligations is in and of itself an exercise of sovereignty. In effect, the Permanent Court may be seen as removing the contradiction between 'autonomy' and 'community', by conceptualizing the assumption of international obligations as autonomous expression of the wish and will to participate, co-exist, even co-operate in an (international) community. The tension between autonomy and community can be seen then as merely a tension inherent in the

(*The Peter Pázmány University v The State of Czechoslovakia*) [1933] PCIJ Ser A/B No 61; *Lighthouses Case between France and Greece* [1934] PCIJ Ser A/B No 62.

[61] Cf generally *Arrest Warrant of 11 April 2000* (*Democratic Republic of the Congo v Belgium*) [2002] ICJ Rep 3, and the subsequent changes in Belgian 'universal jurisdiction law'; and *Avena and Other Mexican Nationals* (*Mexico v US*) [2004] ICJ Rep 12, 56–7 [111]–[112].

[62] (n 53) 25: 'The Court declines to see in the conclusion of any Treaty by which a State undertakes to perform or refrain from performing a particular act an abandonment of its sovereignty. No doubt any convention creating an obligation of this kind places a restriction upon the exercise of the sovereign rights of the State, in the sense that it requires them to be exercised in a certain way. But *the right of entering into international engagements is an attribute of State sovereignty*' (emphasis added).

[63] (n 59) 21.

[64] *Customs Régime between Germany and Austria* [1931] PCIJ Ser A/B No 41 at 58 (ind op Anzilotti) ('*Customs Union*'): '… the legal conception of independence has nothing to do with a State's subordination to international law or with the numerous and constantly increasing states of *de facto* dependence which characterize the relation of one country to other countries.

It also follows that the restrictions upon a State's liberty, whether arising out of ordinary international law or contractual engagements, do not as such in the least affect its independence. As long as these restrictions do not place the State under the legal authority of another State, the former remains an independent State however extensive and burdensome those obligations may be.'

international society, as it is in every society: a tension at once inherent in and constitutive of a society.[65]

But this has the effect of integrating a community with interests that are separate and distinct from those of its members, ie with interests that are general, and in certain cases call for or allow intervention for the purpose of their preservation. What are these cases, and who shall be allowed to intervene in the general interest? It is to this issue that the next section now turns.

V. Emanation and Legal Expression of a General Interest

The emergence of a common interest, or a general interest, or shared values—call them as one will—require some recognition in law, even if they can be cast as a mere fact to be ascertained from the (normative) conduct of States. This is the case when the legal order acknowledges some limits to the bilateral structure of relationships within any given community, limits which cannot be overcome by the sheer will of the parties to derogate from the law.[66] And it is so even more when the legal order of the community establishes institutions for the protection of the general interest, and when it vests its members with the authority to take (legal) action in the general interest.

1. *Peremptory Law (Hierarchy)*

The most important rules in any given legal order are given peremptory character. Unlike most other norms, that are of the dispositive variety, peremptory norms cannot be derogated from: subjects may not vary them through agreement. By logical necessity, agreements to derogate from peremptory norms will not produce legal effect, and this introduces an element of verticality, of hierarchy of norms: those of lesser importance are subject to those of greater importance. The 'importance' can be determined by reference to the values or the interests that the relevant rules protect, and rules that protect community values or the general interest are an obvious candidate for the hierarchically supreme status. This criterion of importance by reference to values or interests, however, is hopelessly subjective: importance of values and interests protected lies in the

---

[65] Cf K Τσουκαλάς, *Η επινόηση της ετερότητας* (Εστία, Αθήνα 2010) 11 [K Tsoukalas, *The Invention of Otherness* (Estia, Athens 2010) 11].

[66] Cf Gowlland-Debbas (n 21) 328–9.

eye of the beholder. For this reason, in domestic legal orders, importance is usually determined by reference to an objective criterion: the source of the rules. Those contained in the Constitution are considered to be the most important. No similarly 'preferred' source exists in international law, and so the existence of peremptory norms, if logical, is in the first instance anything but obvious.

The individual opinion of Judge Schücking in the *Oscar Chinn* case[67] is probably the first reference to peremptory norms of international law, and their hierarchically supreme status, uttered in an international judicial capacity. Judge Schücking wrote that

> [he] can hardly believe that the League of Nations would have already embarked on the codification of international law if it were not possible, even to-day, to create a *jus cogens*, the effect of which would be that, once States have agreed on certain rules of law, and have also given an undertaking that these rules may not be altered by some only of their number, any act adopted in contravention of that undertaking would be automatically void.[68]

Even though Judge Schücking was referring specifically to whether some parties to the Congo Act were able to vary the terms of the Congo Act *inter se* by agreement, he seems to deduce the concept of peremptory law from legal logic. But he also identifies the Covenant of the League of Nations, 'and more particularly its Article 20, in which the Members undertake not to enter into obligations or understandings *inter se* inconsistent with its provisions' as part of peremptory, hierarchically supreme law, in that 'treaties concluded in violation of that undertaking were to be regarded as absolutely null and void'.[69]

This is an obvious precursor of the concept of *jus cogens* as it appears in Article 53 VCLT, but also of the understanding by part of the scholarship

---

[67] (n 53) 148 et seq.

[68] Ibid at 149.

[69] Ibid. Judge van Eysinga referred to *jus cogens* by implication, arguing that the Congo Act 'does not constitute *jus dispositivum*': ibid at 134. Finally, perhaps the dissent of Judge Altamira in *SS 'Lotus'* (n 25) 95 can be seen as putting forward a similar argument in favour of peremptory law, this time drawn from the importance of a rule pure and simple: he argued that, while 'it is certain that amongst the most widely recognized principles of international law are the principles that the jurisdiction of a State is territorial in character and that in respect of its nationals a State has preferential, if not sole jurisdiction ... exceptions to these principles ... have only been recognized in extreme cases where it has been absolutely necessary or inevitable. This applies for instance to *the case of a general need of mankind or of a common danger* (the slave trade, piracy, etc.)' (emphasis added). The choice of examples, one dare say, is strikingly familiar. For more on the constitutional perspective of the PCIJ's legacy see generally of R Kwiecien (in this volume), 361.

of Article 103 of the UN Charter as a provision that evidences the hierarchical superiority of the Charter over the rest of international law and the 'constitutional character' of the instrument as a whole.[70] The problem is that there is no obvious or explicit connection between the quality of certain law as peremptory and its protection of the 'general' or 'community' interest; but this can be deduced through the same exercise of 'legal logic' that Judge Schücking seems to be indulging in: if certain law is made so as not to allow any derogation by agreement, this must be because it protects a very important value or interest of the entire group (of States) establishing it.[71] A community interest, that is.

But who is the guardian of that community interest? Is there an organ or institution that may vindicate the interests of the international community, or is every member of the community empowered to do so?

2. *Institutionalization (Centralization): Defence by Community Organs*

In the first instance, defence of community or general interest requires some community organs to defend it, lest such defence were left to decentralised action of community members, with all the dangers as to uniformity and objectivity that this would entail. But the members of the international community of States were never particularly happy to centralize powers to international organs, even if the interwar period marked the first revolution in international organization. The Permanent Court had to straddle this uncomfortable period of nascent institutionalization of the international community (and what a very long gestation period this would turn out to be—if anything, it is still not completed).

In *Customs Union*, Judge Anzilotti claims in his dissent that the international legal requirement that Austria remain independent and not undertake any action that may endanger that independence without the consent of the League of Nations, as established in the Treaty of Versailles and further elaborated upon in the Treaty of St Germain, was adopted 'in the interests of Europe as a whole'.[72] This (partial?) general interest is put

[70] See, among many others, TM Franck, 'Is the UN Charter a Constitution?' in JA Frowein et al (eds), *Vehandeln für den Frieden*—Liber Amicorum *Tono Eitel* (Springer, Berlin 2003) 95.

[71] On the other hand, Lauterpacht deduces such superiority exclusively from substance: '[T]he substance of [the League of Nations Covenant's] law *differs so radically* from other international conventions in its scope *and significance* as a *purposeful instrument in the process of political integration of mankind* as to deserve the designation of A "higher law"': 'The Covenant as the "Higher Law"' (1936) 17 BYIL 54, 64–5 (emphasis added).

[72] *Customs Union* (n 64) 57 (indiv op Anzilotti).

under the protection of the Council of the League of Nations, as 'the sovereign judge of political situations and of the requirements of peace'.[73] Judge Anzilotti draws the conclusion that the relevant requirement is established in the general interest *from the fact that* any diversion from the requirement is subject to the 'sovereign judgment' of the League Council. This indicates (apart from the fact that the interest is probably not just 'European', but universal, judging from the Council's membership) an understanding that the existence of institutions that operate as the guardians of the general interest is conclusive proof of the existence itself of a general interest.

The institutionalization and representation of the general interest, even if to some extent entrusted to the League of Nations, remains, according to the Permanent Court, subject to cumbersome decision-making: in its Advisory Opinion on the *Interpretation of Article 3(2) of the Treaty of Lausanne*,[74] the Permanent Court gives a rather far-reaching justification of the requirement of unanimity for the League Council's decisions: this requirement is '*naturally* and even *necessarily* indicated', since

> only if the decisions of the Council have the support of the unanimous consent of the Powers composing it, *will they possess the degree of authority which they must have*: the very prestige of the League might be imperilled if it were admitted, in the absence of an express provision to that effect, that decisions on important questions could be taken by a majority. Moreover, *it is hardly conceivable that resolutions on questions affecting the peace of the world could be adopted against the will of those amongst the Members of the Council who, although in a minority, would, by reason of their political position, have to bear the larger share of the responsibilities and consequences ensuing therefrom.*[75]

Two points should be raised here: the first is the PCIJ's clear and almost cynical (if pragmatic) justification of the future privileged position of the 'Permanent Five', which reads almost like dramatic irony in an ancient Greek drama.[76] More importantly, the passage demonstrates the reluctance to allow centralization of the power to defend the general interest in

---

73 Ibid.

74 *Article 3, Paragraph 2, of the Treaty of Lausanne* (*Frontier between Turkey and Iraq*) [1925] PCIJ Ser B No 12.

75 Ibid at 29 (emphasis added).

76 'Dramatic irony' (*τραγική ειρωνεία*) is a means employed by ancient Greek dramatic poets for dramatic effect, notably invoking empathy in the audience: unbeknownst to the character, he or she says or does something that the audience already knows will bring about his or her tragic end.

an international organ: even to the extent that this is done, the actions of the organ must still reflect the 'unanimous consent', if not of all States, then of the select not-so-few (at that time) who comprise it. This effectively leaves defence of the general interest in the hands of States acting individually. And even that is not that easy (even though probably easier than it is today) as the next section will demonstrate.

3. *Standing for Decentralized Defence: General Interest as a Legal Interest*

The Permanent Court of International Justice operated under rules that today are the accepted orthodoxy and treated as self-evident, but do not cease to be quite striking: it had no compulsory jurisdiction over legal disputes, its jurisdiction being based on consent. Even if such consent was present, however, not everyone had standing before the Court. Most obviously, standing was limited to States, but even then more was needed to justify standing. The question of *jus* or *locus standi* before an international court in order to sue in the general interest is still a vexing one; the *South-West Africa* cases[77] and the *Barcelona Traction* practically inconsequential (if doctrinally important) *volte face* of the ICJ[78] still command scholarly interest, and have led to important developments in international law—such as, e.g., Article 48 ASR. The question of standing in the general interest—or the existence of an *actio popularis*, when standing is limited to the lodging of a claim before an international instance[79]—is still outstanding. One could not have expected the Permanent Court to have resolved such a—still extremely divisive—issue; but the Permanent Court had the occasion to make important pronouncements in the periphery of the question of standing in the general interest, due to the existence of peculiar treaty regimes in the interwar period, especially in the context of protection of minorities.

The regime of minority protection established after World War I and put under the auspices of the League of Nations had the peculiar characteristic of allowing any or specific members of the League (or League Council) to bring any infraction or danger of infraction to the League

[77] *South West Africa Cases* (*Ethiopia v South Africa*) (*Liberia v South Africa*) (Preliminary Objections) [1962] ICJ Rep 319; cf (*Second Phase*) [1966] ICJ Rep 6, 28 [32].

[78] (n 38) 32 [33].

[79] For the broader notion of standing, which includes the power to take countermeasures, and which is adopted here in principle, even if only claims before the PCIJ are discussed, see CJ Tams, *Enforcing Obligations* Erga Omnes *in International Law* (CUP, Cambridge 2005) 25 et seq.

Council, upon which relevant disputes between a Council member and the State under minority protection obligations could be brought before the PCIJ.[80] Further, the League Council was given the power to request Advisory Opinions on relevant matters. Here one could again claim the existence of a general interest being subject to the protection of an international institution (finally, the Permanent Court, the 'custodian of international law'[81]); but the power to initiate proceedings for such protection was awarded to either another international institution (the League Council) or to individual States acting as representatives of the general interest.

A similar set up was said by the Court to have been established by the Treaty of Versailles with respect to passage through the Kiel Canal. To cut a long story very short, in *SS 'Wimbledon'*[82] the Permanent Court 'interpreted a vaguely formulated jurisdictional clause in the broadest possible terms',[83] effectively admitting standing in the general interest. Indeed, if the US and France could be construed as exercising diplomatic protection over the SS 'Wimbledon' (who was refused entry to the Kiel canal by Germany allegedly in violation of the relevant provisions of the Treaty of Versailles), as the flag State and the State of incorporation of the firm that had chartered the vessel, there was no obvious basis for the standing of Italy and Japan, save their general interest in seeing an international treaty complied with.[84] But the Permanent Court did note that the general interest protected was not simply that of compliance with an international treaty: it read the relevant Article 380 of the Treaty of Versailles as having 'intended to provide under treaty guarantee easier access to the Baltic *for the benefit of all nations of the world*'.[85] The treaty thus established itself a general interest, which was merely complemented by a standing provision that, if vague, was justifiably interpreted broadly. A similar situation where States were considered as having standing in the general interest of seeing

[80] See, e.g., *Rights of Minorities in Upper Silesia* (n 32) 17 et seq. Note that many relevant provisions on standing in minorities treaties were closely modeled on Art 26 of the ILO Constitution 1919, which is a remarkably broad provision on standing (even if not before an international tribunal of a permanent nature): see Tams (n 79) 72–4 with further references.

[81] *Oscar Chinn* (n 53) 149 (indiv op Schücking).

[82] (n 53).

[83] Tams (n 79) 77.

[84] See ibid 78–9.

[85] *SS 'Wimbledon'* (n 53) 22 (emphasis added). See also further at 28, where the Permanent Court refers to an 'artificial waterway ... permanently dedicated to the use of *the whole world*' (emphasis added).

a convention complied with was the *Memel Statute* case[86]—the applicants claimed but such a general interest,[87] and the Court did not consider this in any way problematic.[88] Notably, also here was the relevant treaty establishing a particular status (of a territory rather than a canal) in the general interest.[89]

Effectively, in view of the lack of any centralized defence of the general interest, the Court showed itself as willing to admit standing of individual States in the general interest. While it may have been able to base itself on clear provisions allowing such standing, such as in *Memel* and in minorities cases, it did not hesitate to adopt broad interpretations of vague standing provisions, as in *SS 'Wimbledon'*, in order to accept standing. This is in marked contrast to the generally circumscribed way in which the ICJ has dealt with standing in the general interest, despite existing in a similarly thinly institutionalized international legal order.

VI. The 'Missing' Aspects?

One will not fail to notice that, for all the aspects today commonly associated with the notion of an international community that the Permanent Court touches upon—or breaks new ground in first articulating and even consolidating—there are crucial aspects of the notion that are nowhere to be found. But these seem rather limited to concepts of enforcement of international law through criminal sanctions: the lack of a concept of universal jurisdiction, for example, or the lack of any notion of international criminal responsibility of individuals. Even these, as well as other aspects commonly associated today with the existence of an international community with distinct 'general' interest, may be said to be merely the evolutionary product of the basic tenets of an international community present in the jurisprudence of the Permanent Court: the recognition of the role of the individual (even if subject to the will of the States), the development of human rights protection, the emergence of a 'common heritage of mankind' or of an aggravated regime of responsibility for violation of non-derogable rules, all can be traced back (if, sometimes, only remotely or with some degree of creativity) to the basic ideas of wide membership of

---

[86] *Interpretation of the Statute of the Memel Territory* (Preliminary Objection) [1932] PCIJ Ser A/B No 47; (Merits) [1932] PCIJ Ser A/B No 49.

[87] See argument in [1932] PCIJ Ser C No 59 at 173 and 190.

[88] See Tams (n 79) 75–6 with further references.

[89] Cf *Memel Statute* (Preliminary Objection) (n 86) 247 and 249.

the international community and the notion of a general interest explored in the decisions of the first permanent international jurisdiction.

VII. Deduction and (Re-)Construction

The provisional conclusion that one may draw from this brief survey of some of the Permanent Court's decisions as regards the concept of an 'international community' is that the concept was at once presumed to exist (if only in its undefined use as a rhetorical or ornamental device), deduced to some extent from positive international law, and at the same time constructed by the Permanent Court and by its judges in their individual opinions. The term was used to decorate decisions, it was implied in the construction of positive provisions, and it was constructed through the sometimes unqualified presumption of its existence. And it could not have been any other way, one might venture: the judges, like all international lawyers, first trained as domestic jurists, brought their own sensibilities to the bench, and at once presumed the existence of a community regulated by law, and constructed a community on the basis of (its) existing law. They, individually and as a bench, through the different periods of the Permanent Court's life,[90] planted the seeds of what are today considered the hallmarks of the 'international community', the elements that have moved international law from a predominantly bilateralist structure to a legal order which recognizes the existence of at least a degree of community interest.[91]

But it would be unfair to attribute the existence of the concept of an international community merely to the creativity or the (perhaps to some degree unconscious) preconceptions of the judges on the Permanent Court. The Court did not merely conjure the concept out of thin air: some elements were deduced from positive international law. And while the Court's presence may have, in and of itself, altered the exact content of the positive law through its interpretation, by perceiving it through its own unique lens, at the same time the States that were creating the law were bringing in their own sensibilities, from their own domestic legal orders, which at once constructed and served as the foundation of their own local communities (in the final analysis States only really act through natural

---

[90] For detailed discussion of the periods of the Permanent Court's life, and the impact of the make-up of the bench see generally Spiermann (n 24) chs 5–7.

[91] Cf the title of Simma's Hague lectures (n 20).

persons, and these are anything but immune from such sensibilities and unquestioned premises, whether consciously or less so). And States made much of their law transactional, but they also infused it to some extent with humanitarianism, with an underlying acceptance of the existence of some common interest among themselves—if not for any other reason, than because otherwise co-existence, interaction, and—finally—co-operation would simply be impossible. In that, yet another society was auto-institutionalized,[92] however inchoately. Whether this reduces the concept of an international community to the bare minimum—and whether it does so 'rightly'—is a question for another day.

92 See generally C Castoriadis, *L'institution imaginaire de la société* (Seuil, Paris 1975).

THE PERMANENT COURT OF INTERNATIONAL JUSTICE AND THE CONSTITUTIONAL DIMENSION OF INTERNATIONAL LAW: FROM EXPECTATIONS TO REALITY

Roman Kwiecień

I. Introduction

In the modern discipline of international law, one of the most prominent issues is that of constitutionalization of the international legal order. The broad framework of the current debate aims to answer the question of whether and to what extent the Permanent Court of International Justice's judicature allows for a constitutional 'reading' of international law; and indeed whether the Court's legacy can contribute something important to this debate.

The first World Court established to address international issues is today recognized as one among "many previous attempts at international pseudo-constitutionalism".[1] The question of the PCIJ's contribution to the current constitutional debate is made all the more interesting because the Court declared itself to be a body responsible for the knowledge of international law. In the *Brazilian Federal Loans* case it stated: "[T]he Court, which is a tribunal of international law, ... in this capacity, is deemed to know what this law is...".[2] The position of the Hague Court may be understood both as a statement of fact, ie the Court's knowledge of law with reference to the specific cases it tried, but beyond the Court's duty to adjudicate on specific legal obligations that the Court had competence for the very nature of international law as a whole. In the latter case, it would be, thus, capable of taking an authoritative stance on the constitutional interpretation of international law.

In none of its decisions, except the separate opinions by a few judges, did the PCIJ use the concept 'constitution' with reference to the international legal order. However this omission is not in itself decisive. Such a factor is, in turn, the nature of international law as a system of law.

[1] P Allott, *The Health of Nations. Society and Law Beyond the State* (CUP, Cambridge 2002) 250.

[2] *Case Concerning the Payment in Gold of Brazilian Federal Loans Contracted in France* [1929] PCIJ Ser A No 21, at 124.

Indeed, it is by reconstructing the PCIJ's approach regarding the nature of international law that will allow to us to determine to what extent the Court's judicial decisions justify the constitutional reading of international law. This reconstruction will be conducted in the first part of the article in the context of two issues that seem to be of key significance to the problem of the nature of international law: 1) the basis of obligations in international law; 2) the significance of State sovereignty in and for international law. In the next part of the article, an attempt will be made to present, in the light of the PCIJ's decisions, the position that is held in international relations by the idea of the Rule of Law, which seems to be fundamental for the issue of constitutionalization. The following problems are particularly significant here, namely, the existence of a common *lex superior* in the law of the interwar international society, and the relationship between the Rule of Law and the principle of sovereignty (independence) of States that was frequently emphasized by the PCIJ. The analysis of the above issues will be preceded by a few remarks on the importance of the idea of constitution in the law of international society.

II. International Law and the Idea of Constitution (An Outline of the Problem)

The political and legal changes following World War I resulted in new expectations regarding the role and function of international law: guided by the hope of instilling the Rule of Law in international relations. The establishment of key new international organizations and institutions such as the League of Nations and the PCIJ justified the recognition of the post-War situation as a real 'constitutional moment' for the international society; constituting a specific historical situation which offered favourable conditions for introducing significant changes in the political, legal, and organizational structure of society.[3] Not accidentally, it was then that the theory of international constitutionalism was formed. The views that are typical of the theory are the ones presented by Georges Scelle, Borys

[3] Such opinion was presented in the interwar period and is still expressed in today's doctrine. See MO Hudson, *Progress in International Organization* (Rothman, Littleton,Colorado 1932) 6, 23, 42, 45; CEJ Schwöbel, *Global Constitutionalism in International Legal Perspective* (Martinus Nijhoff, Leiden,Boston 2011) 81; C Walter, 'Progress in International Organization: A Constitutionalist Reading' in RA Miller and RM Bratspies (eds), *Progress in International Law* (Martinus Nijhoff, Leiden, Boston 2008) 133, 136. On the concept 'constitutional moment' see B Ackerman, 'Constitutional Politics/Constitutional Law' (1989) 99 Yale L J 453, 489.

Mirkine-Guetzévitch, as well the representatives of the Vienna school of law: Hans Kelsen and Alfred Verdross.

All these scholars were representatives of the so-called monistic doctrine. As is well known, this doctrine was not uniform in explaining the bases of the relationship between international law and domestic legal orders. The mentioned scholars also represented differing views regarding the understanding and the role of constitution in international law, or even the meanings given to the term 'international constitutional law'.

To Kelsen, constitution, whose function was served by hypothetical *Grundnorm*, was a logical and, in this sense, necessary consequence of thinking about the system of law. Without it—according to Kelsen—the basis of the binding force of law and legal obligations cannot be justified.[4] Verdross represented a different approach. What he recognized as the constitutional underpinnings of international law were meta-principles that indicate the sources of international law, its subjects, and determine the division and exercise of authority between States.[5] Yet another approach on the position of constitution in international law was given by Georges Scelle. The core of his construction was a then unique thesis on the reference of all legal norms, irrespective of their sources, to individuals as the only legal subjects (theory of *dédoublement fonctionnel*). What Scelle understood as 'international constitutional law' (*droit constitutionnel international*) were customary rules that served three functions in international relations: legislative, administrative and judicial. International constitutional law determines the scopes of operations of such branches of international law as administrative law, contract law, or criminal law. According to Scelle, constitutional rules do not have to be clearly defined norms. They may seem, thus, as "*incertaine et irregulière*". Nevertheless, they are of fundamental significance to the international society, as without them, it would lack the normative core. To the international society, constitutional law is its "*droit constructif*".[6]

---

[4] See H Kelsen, *Reine Rechtslehre. Einleitung in die Rechtswissenschaftliche Problematik* (Deuticke, Leipzig 1934) 115–119, 147–154.

[5] See A Verdross, *Die Verfassung der Völkerrechtsgemeinschaft* (Springer, Wien 1926) v. Surprisingly enough, Christine Schwöbel states that Verdross's interwar "vision of global constitutionalism can almost be regarded as utopian ...". Schwöbel(n 3) 8. Verdross's vision was not utopian. It was just an attempt to point out systemic basis of international law. More controversial seems to be Verdross's the post-War view recognizing the Charter of the United Nations as a constitution of the international society. See A Verdross, *Völkerrecht*, (5 Aufl, Springer-Verlag, Wien 1964) 135–136; A Verdross and B Simma, *Universelles Völkerrecht. Theorie und Praxis* (3 Aufl, Duncker & Humblot, Berlin 1984) vii-viii, 72, 221.

[6] See G Scelle, *Le Pacte des Nations et sa Liaison avec le Traité de Paix* (Recueil Sirey, Paris 1919) 101–107; idem, *Précis de Droit des Gens. Principes et Systématique* (*Droit Constitutionnel*

The author who greatly contributed to the spread of the term 'international constitutional law' (*droit constitutionnel international*) in the twenty-year interwar period was a then well-known scholar examining the relationship between international law and States' constitutional law, Borys Mirkine-Guetzévitch. He would, however, give it a different meaning than Verdross, or even Scelle. Mirkine-Guetzévitch viewed international constitutional law as a new branch of public law that was formed as a result of the contents of domestic constitutions being saturated with the international legal issues. The result of the opening of domestic constitutions to international relations was the formation of 'the unity of public law' (*l'unité du droit public*).[7] International constitutional law was, thus, not so much part of international law, as a manifestation of close, monistic relations between international law and domestic legal orders.

There is no need here for a broader comparison and assessment of interwar doctrinal concepts of international constitutionalism. It is worth emphasizing, though, that all of the thinkers above shared faith in the idea of constitution as a manifestation of the Rule of Law in international relations. Referring to the idea of constitution in international law, both then and today, signifies rejecting the choice between realism (supremacy of power over law) and hegemonial liberalism. The constitutional reading of international law offers, among other things, a promise of spreading the Rule of Law over international relations, and thus refusing the political claims and usurpations of States. From this perspective, constitution is supposed to establish a strong legitimization of international legal order.[8]

There arises a question as to what extent the doctrine of international constitutionalism attempts to explain the new normative quality in the law of international society, and to what extent it is only a hermeneutic, that is exactly constitutional, interpretation of international law. In the latter case, it would provide not so much a description of legal reality, as

---

International) (t 2, Recueil Sirey, Paris 1934) 7–11; idem, *Essai de Systematique de Droit International* (*Plan d'un Cours de Droit International Public*) (1923) 30 RGDIP 116, 124–141. Let us mention in passing an apt criticism of Scelle's views, which shows that his theory postulating to be based on social facts would, indeed, deny them. Scelle would, for instance, recognize the politically-motivated actions of States as the execution of constitutional functions by States. Cf T Opsahl, 'An "International Constitutional Law"?' (1961) 10 ICLQ 760, 766; M Koskenniemi, *The Gentle Civilizer of Nations. The Rise and Fall of International Law 1870–1960* (CUP, Cambridge 2002) 333–338.

[7] See B Mirkine-Guetzévitch, 'Droit International et Droit Costitutionnel' (1931/IV) 38 RCADI 307, 319–324; idem, *Droit Costitutionnel International* (Recueil Sirey, Paris 1933) 7–8.

[8] See M Kumm, 'The Legitimacy of International Law: A Constitutionalist Framework of Analysis' (2004) 15, EJIL 907 ff; Schwöbel (n 3) 103–104, 143–145.

an expression of the belief in the causative force of the idea of constitution, and its ability to influence the practice of international law. Such an approach is frequently seen in the contemporary debate on the constitutionalization of international law.[9] It was also largely shared by the aforementioned interwar doctrine of international constitutionalism. But, it is an open issue whether the first World Court supported this approach.

The chosen meaning of the concept of constitutionalism has a necessarily broad impact on the extent of expectations of and promises offered by constitutionalism. Meanwhile, this concept is not unambiguous. There are two essential meanings of the concept of constitution. It may be defined in the descriptive ('weak' meaning of constitution) or normative ('strong' meaning of constitution) senses.[10] In the former sense, constitution is an act of universal scope which regulates the execution of the political authority within a given society, and obliging the society members to obey the law created by the authority. In this sense, however, constitution does not guarantee complete subordination of the authority's activities to a Rule of Law. This requirement is met by the constitution in the 'strong' meaning, which is a manifestation of the Enlightenment ideal of the Rule of Law over the arbitrary rule of man. Understood as such, constitution plays an important integrating role in society.[11]

While referring to such a constitutional ideal, one needs to reject the possibility of recognizing as a constitution of international society, at least

---

[9] See e.g. Allott (n 1) 342–379; S Besson, 'Whose Constitution(s)? International Law, Constitutionalism, and Democracy' in JL Dunoff and JP Trachtman (eds), *Ruling the World? Constitutionalism, International Law, and Global Governance* (CUP, Cambridge 2009) 381 ff; A von Bogdandy, 'Constitutionalism in International Law: Comment on a Proposal from Germany' (2006) 47, 1 Harvard Intl L Journal 223 ff; B Fassbender, 'The United Nations Charter as Constitution of the International Community' (1998) 36 Columbia J of Transnational L 529 ff; T Giegerich: 'The Is and the Ought of International Constitutionalism: How Far We Come on Habermas's Road to a "Well-Considered Constitutionalisation of International Law"?' (2009) 10, 1 German L J (2009) 31 ff; J Klabbers, A Peters, and G Ulfstein, *The Constitutionalization of International Law* (OUP, Oxford 2011) 37–44, 153–157; AL Paulus, 'The International Legal System as a Constitution' in JL Dunoff, JP Trachtman (eds) *supra* 69 ff; Schwöbel (n 3) 133–165; E de Wet, 'The International Constitutional Order' (2006) 55 ICLQ 55 ff; C Walter, 'Constitutionalising (Inter)national Governance—Possibilities for and Limits to the Development of an International Constitutional Law' (2001) 44 German Ybk Intl L 192 ff.

[10] Cf J Crawford, 'Multilateral Rights and Obligations in International Law' (2006/I) 319 RCADI 325, 372–383; P-M Dupuy, 'The Constitutional Dimension of the Charter of the United Nations Revisited' in in JA Frowein, R Wolfrum and CE Philipp (eds), *Max Planck Yearbook of United Nations Law 1* (Martinus Nijhoff, The Hague 1997) 1, 3; Giegerich (n 9) 42–46; Walter (n 3) 138–142.

[11] See extensively D Grimm, *Integration durch Verfassung*, Walter Hallstein-Institut für Europäisches Verfassungsrecht, Vortrag an der Humboldt-Universität zu Berlin am 12 Juli 2004 (FCE 6/04), available at <http://whi-berlin.de/documents/grimm.pdf>.

in the 'strong' sense, the acts and/or principles that do not cement the identity of this society; the acts and/or principles that do not concern the authority and do not determine the boundaries of its exercise, and do not determine the institutional and procedural framework of settling disputes within the society. The only acts and/or principles that may aspire to the rank of constitution are the ones that provide stable bases of the legal system, thus being the main point of reference in the relations between the subjects of the legal order. Such acts and/or principles *ipso facto* legitimize the legal order. However, there still remains an open question whether the legitimization by means of constitution is the only, and necessary in this sense, form of legitimization of the legal order, the international legal order in particular. The establishment of the Permanent Court, in the specific post-War situation, created hopes for introducing great improvements within international society and did offer the possibility of a new approach to the underpinnings of international law. That is why the legacy of the PCIJ can serve in the attempt to resolve, firstly, the issue of aptness of presenting of international law within the framework of a constitutional pattern, and, secondly, the need of using such pattern at all.

The examination of the PCIJ's legacy shows that, on the one hand, the Court 'only' applied international law, and thus referred the concrete interpretation of the law to 'the present case' exclusively. On the other hand, however, the understanding of international law as manifested in concrete judgments and Advisory Opinions determined the Court's future approach, and consequently resulted in setting quasi-precedents. In this way, the Court's decisions, being primarily evidence of the existing principles and norms of international law, to some extent became the sources of this law as well. The absence of a clear boundary between the application and the creation of law was explained by Hersch Lauterpacht in the following way: "The imperceptible process in which the judicial decision ceases to be an application of existing law and becomes a source of law for the future is almost a religious mystery into which it is unseemly to pry".[12] Such a double-track approach to international law as represented by the PCIJ must have undoubtedly contributed to the development of international law.[13] In this sense Manley O Hudson was right in stating

[12] H Lauterpacht, *The Development of International Law by the International Court* (Stevens & Sons, London 1958) 21. Lauterpacht is known to have recognized one of the functions of the PCIJ and the ICJ known as 'judicial legislation' as an important factor shaping international law. See ibid 155–157.

[13] Cf e.g. V Bruns, 'La Cour Permanente de Justice Internationale. Son Organisation et sa Compétence' (1937/IV) 62 RCADI 547, 557; MA Caloyanni, 'L'organisation de la Cour

that the PCIJ gave more than had justified the expectations of its founders.[14]

There is another reason for the importance of the PCIJ's legacy for the international constitutionalizm. If such qualities of legal order as completeness, coherence and unity are to be significant for its constitutional interpretation, then the PCIJ's activity is particularly crucial because, as Andreas L Paulus argues, the "unity of the international legal system was never as great as in the interwar years, when the PCIJ provided some systemic coherence".[15] However, this in itself does not mean that the Hague Court viewed international law as a legal system based on a constitution. Thus, the issue of constitutional 'reading' of international law by the Court is still open.

III. The Nature of International Law

1. *The Basis of Obligation in International Law*

Referring to the judicial decisions in order to support specific statements carries the risk of generalization of the Courts' views which are, in their essence, limited to the context of concrete cases. The practice of quoting excerpts from courts' decisions in isolation of their context results in a

Permanente de Justice et son Avenir' (1931/IV) 33 RCADI 651, 662; JP Fockema Andreae, *An Important Chapter from the History of Legal Interpretation. The Jurisdiction of the First Permanent Court of International Justice (1922–1940)* (Sijthoff, Leyden 1948) 70–71, 140–142; H Lauterpacht (n 12) 42; TD Gill, *Rosenne's the World Court. What It Is and How It Works*, (6th rev ed,Martinus Nijhoff, Leiden, Boston 2003) 13–14. It needs to be stressed that the influence of the PCIJ's decisions on the development of international law was different in particular periods of its activity. This is well shown by Ole Spiermann in his *International Legal Argument in the Permanent Court of International Justice. The Rise of the International Judiciary* (CUP, Cambridge 2005). It is not unfounded that Spiermann most appreciates the PCIJ's decisions at the time of Max Huber's presidency [1924–1931] (132–133). A similar opinion was expressed, when the PCIJ still existed, by its long-time secretary, and then a judge in the final period of the court's activity, Åke Hammarskjöld. He wrote: "During the first years of its existence, the Court displayed a tendency to discuss and to give its views on most of the important questions of principle which arose in the cases submitted to it because it held that to contribute in this way to the restatement of international law was not the least important of its tasks. Subsequently, however, and, curiously enough, more particularly after 1930 ... the tendency has rather been, following the example of municipal tribunals, to avoid pronouncing upon questions the solution of which does not appear to be indispensable for the decision of the case". Å Hammarskjöld, 'The Permanent Court of International Justice and the Development of International Law' (1935) 14 International Affairs 799.

[14] MO Hudson, *The World Court 1921–1938. A Handbook of the Permanent Court of International Justice* (5th ed, World Peace Foundation, Boston 1938) 8.

[15] Paulus (n 9) 75.

situation when—as Robert Jennings wrote—any thesis may be supported by the authority of a court's standpoint.[16] The danger involved in assessing the PCIJ's decisions was noted by Åke Hammarskjöld a long time ago:

> [T]he *dicta* of the Court are almost always carefully limited to particular situations arising in concrete cases; and if one takes these *dicta* as a basis in estimating the Court's contribution to positive international law, there is always the risk of generalizations which may only correspond remotely to the Court's past and present views, to say nothing of the opinions it may adopt in the future.[17]

Another of Hammarskjöld's remarks on this topic deserves to be cited:

> [H]aving regard to the limited number of cases so far decided by the Court, it has only in exceptional cases had an opportunity of affirming a given principle or rule. Often there exists only one *dictum* on a given point. It is always difficult to judge whether such a *dictum* should or should not be deemed to represent a more general tendency.[18]

Today, we are in a better situation than Åke Hammarskjöld, as the PCIJ's activity is already a thing of the past. However, the danger he notes in the second quote may remain, namely whether the limited number of cases decided by the Court should or should not be deemed to be representative of more general tendencies in the PCIJ's legacy.

The judgments and Advisory Opinions of the Court are not uniform in their character. Some of them actually refer to concrete cases and their circumstances. In some PCIJ decisions, however, we do come across statements that go beyond the context of concrete cases decided by the Court. These are present in cases of differing content and gravity. They, thus, set some permanent trends in the Court's judicature, and serve as specific landmarks in the panorama of international law; and as such, they indicate the PCIJ's reasoning of the nature of this law. Their general character makes it possible to avoid the risk of generalization of individual *dicta*. Therefore, they are going to be the focus of our analysis.

One such statement is to be found in a famous excerpt from the judgment given in the *Lotus* case:

> International law governs relations between independent States. The rules of law binding upon States therefore emanate from their own free will as expressed in conventions or by usages generally accepted as expressing

16 RY Jennings, 'Role of the International Court' (1997) 58 British Ybk of Intl L 1, 41–42.
17 Hammarskjöld (n 13) 797.
18 Ibid, 797. See also Spiermann (n 13) 27–29.

> principles of law and established in order to regulate the relations between these co-existing independent communities or with a view to the achievement of common aims.[19]

Although the PCIJ's position met with almost immediate criticism, due to being recognized as an extreme manifestation of legal positivism,[20] in its later decisions, the Court would consistently confirm the *dictum* expressed in the above judgment. In the light of this *dictum*, international law is basically a law which operates in the horizontal dimension exclusively, and regulates the relationship between independent entities. It is, as a matter of fact, interstate law.

The voluntaristic and at the same time State-centric perception of the nature of international law was confirmed by the PCIJ's view of its own jurisdiction being determined by the will of States (see below) and the view presenting the operations of States' institutions regarding the protection of their citizens as the States' powers stemming from international law.[21] The State-centric character of international law was also reinforced by the Court's view on the secondary character of the legal subjectivity of international organizations. Within this view, the PCIJ would emphasize that international organizations, despite remaining autonomous in the scope of their competence, derive their existence and right to operate from the founding treaties made between States.[22]

These views clearly influenced the dualistic perception of the relationship between international law and domestic legal orders. The PCIJ recognized international conventions and customs as sources of 'true international law governing the relations between States',[23] and, at the same time, it denied such character both to contracts in which States were

---

19 *The Case of the SS "Lotus"* [1927] PCIJ Ser A No 10 at 18.

20 See e.g. JL Brierly, *The "Lotus" Case* in JL Brierly, H Lauterpacht, and CHM Waldock, (eds), *The Basis of Obligation in International Law and Other Papers* (Clarendon Press, Oxford 1958) 142, 143–144; L Cavaré, 'L'arrêt du 'Lotus' et le Positivisme Juridique' (1930) 10 Travaux Jurudiques et Economiques de l'Université de Rennes 144, 148; A Steiner, 'Fundamental Conceptions of International Law in the Jurisprudence of the Permanent Court of International Justice' (1936) 30 AJIL 414, 416.

21 See *Case Concerning the Factory at Chorzów* (*Claim for indemnity*) (Merits) [1928] PCIJ Ser A No 17 at 28; *Case Concerning the Payment of Various Serbian Loans Issued in France* [1929] PCIJ Ser A Nos 20/21 at 17–18; *The Panevezys-Saldutiskis Railway Case* [1939] PCIJ Ser A/B No 76 at 16.

22 See *Competence of the International Labour Organization to Regulate, Incidentally, the Personal Work of the Employer* (Advisory Opinion) [1926] PCIJ Ser B No 13 at 20; *Jurisdiction of the European Commission of the Danube between Galatz and Braila* (Advisory Opinion) [1927] PCIJ Ser B No 14 at 63–64.

23 *Serbian Loans* (n 21) at 41.

not international law entities, as well as agreements between States and private persons.[24] It had a clear influence on the frontiers of international law as determined by the Court, particularly by recognizing relations between States and private persons as "relations which are, in themselves, within the domain of municipal law".[25] The dualism of the Hague Court is additionally emphasized by its reluctance to interpret national law,[26] and its determination of national law as"merely facts".[27]

There is, however, the other side of the relationship between international and national laws in the PCIJ's activity. These are the decisions that point to the direct effect that treaties have for individuals, among which the most well-known is, naturally, the Advisory Opinion on *Jurisdiction of the Courts of Danzig*. The PCIJ emphasized here the significance of "well established principle of international law according to an international agreement, cannot, as such, create direct rights and obligations for private individuals". However, it added:

> But it cannot be disputed that the very object of an international agreement, according to the intention of the contracting Parties, may be the adoption by the Parties of some definite rules creating individual rights and obligations and enforceable by the national courts ... The intention of the Parties, which is to be ascertained from the contents of the Agreement has been applied, is decisive.[28]

For the PCIJ, the consequence of the direct applicability of the treaties' provisions in domestic legal order was the obligation of the States being the parties to the treaties to respect the decisions of domestic courts that directly apply their provisions, and thus the supremacy of the treaties' provisions over domestic law.[29] There are four conclusions stemming from

---

24 *Serbian Loans* (n 21) at 40–41; *Interpretation of the Greco-Bulgarian Agreement of December 9th, 1927* (Advisory Opinion) [1932] PCIJ Ser A/B No 45 at 86. For more on the PCIJ's legacy for individual rights see the contribution from Catherine Brölmann in the present volume.

25 *Serbian Loans* (n 21) at 18.

26 See *Case Concerning the Payment in Gold of Brazilian Federal Loans Contracted in France* (n 2) 124–125.

27 *Case Concerning certain German Interests in Polish Upper Silesia* (The Merits) [1926] PCIJ Ser A No 7 at 19;. *Serbian Loans* (n 21) at 46; *Phosphates in Morocco* [1938] PCIJ Ser A/B No 74 at 26. For a further discussion of the place of municipal law in the PCIJ's jurisprudence see the contribution of J d'Aspremont to the present volume (at 221).

28 *Jurisdiction of the Courts of Danzig* (Advisory Opinion) [1928] PCIJ Ser B No 15 at 17–18.

29 Ibid at 25, 26–27. See also *Treatment of Polish Nationals and Other Persons of Polish Origin or Speech in the Danzig Territory* (Advisory Opinion) [1932] PCIJ Series A/B No 44 at 24–25.

such a position of the Court: 1) both States and private individuals may be the direct beneficiaries of international legal norms; 2) a treaty may be a source of domestic law; 3) every State is obliged to respect the decisions of domestic courts based on treaties; 4) the primacy of international law over national law.

The first World Court's acceptance of the common area of operation of international and national laws is particularly well evinced in its decisions concerning national minorities.[30] It is primarily in these decisions that the Court emphasized the priority of international law over national law. Let us remember here a well-known excerpt from the Advisory Opinion on *The Greco-Bulgarian "Communities"*, it reads as follows: "[I]t is a generally accepted principle of international law that in the relations between Powers who are contracting Parties to a treaty, the provisions of municipal law cannot prevail over those of the treaty".[31] In the Advisory Opinion on *Exchange of Greek and Turkish Populations*, the Court recalled the "self-evident principle" according to which "a State which has contracted valid international obligations is bound to make in its legislation such modifications as may be necessary to ensure the fulfillment of the obligations undertaken".[32] And although it refused, as previously mentioned, to interpret national law, it nevertheless recognized its competence to assess whether the State did or did not violate its international obligations while applying its own law.[33]

The comparison of this approach to the *dictum* of *Lotus* case, results in the need to pose two questions: what did the international society actually mean to the PCIJ, and what was the character of the legal relations that established it? The question then arises whether, according to the World Court, the society had a normative core serving a constitutional integrating function within its boundaries.

In its own decisions, the PCIJ did not use the concept of 'international society', surprisingly enough. Yet, in a few decisions it used the concept of 'community', both with reference to internal and international context.[34]

---

[30] See *Certain Questions Relating to Settlers of German Origin in the Territory Ceded by Germany to Poland* (Advisory Opinion) [1923] PCIJ Ser B No 6 at 37; *Acquisition of Polish Nationality* (Advisory Opinion) PCIJ Ser B No 7 at 15–16; *The Greco-Bulgarian "Communities"* (Advisory Opinion) [1930] PCIJ Ser B No 17 at 28.

[31] *The Greco-Bulgarian "Communities"* ibid at 32.

[32] *Exchange of Greek and Turkish Populations* (Advisory Opinion) [1925] PCIJ Ser B No 10 at 20.

[33] *Certain German Interests in Polish Upper Silesia* (n 27) at 19.

[34] For more on the concept of international society/community see the contribution by Antonios Tznakopoulos in the present volume (at 339).

In the Advisory Opinion on *The Greco-Bulgarian "Communities"*, the Court emphasized that a community is not a "legal fiction" existing by virtue of a given State's legal regulations, and that its existence is a question of facts and not law. "[T]he very nature of a community shows—the Court said–that [the] relations are bonds of solidarity uniting the individuals who are members of the community and involving mutual rights and obligations for these individuals".[35] To what extent did the PCIJ extend this concept of community to international relations? Now, it did not speak about an 'international community', but merely a 'community of States'. In the *Lotus* case defining the 'principles of international law' the Court stated that these words "can only mean international law as it is applied between all nations belonging to the community of States".[36] In *The Territorial Jurisdiction of the International Commission of the River Oder* case, the Court introduced the term 'community of interests of States', which creates, according to the Court, "the basis of a common legal right".[37] What stems from the above analysis is that the PCIJ applied the community dimension of legal relations to interstate relations exclusively, and it related them to the definition of international law as a law governing relations between independent States, as formed in the *Lotus* case. Such a grasp of international law determined a narrow concept of international community in which there was no place not only for individuals but for international organizations as well.

In the excerpt of *The Greco-Bulgarian "Communities"* Advisory Opinion mentioned above, the PCIJ saw "bonds of solidarity uniting the members of the community" as the nature of community relations. At the same time, the PCIJ perceived international law, which is so clearly shown by the *Lotus* case, in the prospect of States' sovereignty. The Court considered sovereignty not only as a necessary element defining international law, but also as a basic principle of this law. In the Advisory Opinion on *Status of Eastern Carelia*, the PCIJ recognized the principle of the independence of States as a "fundamental principle of international law".[38] Does sovereignty—a constitutive element of Statehood and the basis of

35 *The Greco-Bulgarian "Communities"* (n 30) at 25. The same meaning of community was repeated by the PCIJ in *Minority Schools in Albania* (Advisory Opinion) [1935] PCIJ Series A/B No 64 at 11.

36 *SS "Lotus"* (n 19) at 16.

37 *Case Relating to the Territorial Jurisdiction of the International Commission of the River Oder* [1929] PCIJ Ser A No 23 at 27.

38 *Status of Eastern Carelia* (Advisory Opinion) [1923] PCIJ Ser B No 5 at 27. Cf also Hammarskjöld (n 13) 805.

international relations—allow for the existence of bonds of solidarity between States? Is sovereignty, in other words, capable of being a uniting factor, or at least one that does not disintegrate the actual and legal relations? To put it yet another way, can a community of States as a legal community, be reconciled with the model of international legal argument that is present in the PCIJ's decisions, which was—as Ole Spiermann broadly argues—based on the concept of the State as a national sovereign.[39] Consequently, we face the necessity of deciding the question of whether sovereignty is or is not the feature of international law that *ipso facto* excludes its constitutionalization.

2. *The Meaning and Importance of State Sovereignty in and for International Law*

Already in its first judgment, the PCIJ presented an attempt to explain State sovereignty. In the *Wimbledon* case one can find that:

> The Court declines to see in the conclusion of any treaty by which a State undertakes to perform or refrain from performing a particular act an abandonment of its sovereignty. No doubt any convention creating an obligation of this kind places a restriction upon the exercise of the sovereign rights of the State, in the sense that it requires them to be exercised in a certain way. But the right of entering into international engagements is an attribute of State sovereignty.[40]

On the one hand, the PCIJ's position defends sovereignty as the basis of modern international relations, yet on the other hand, it shows a different, little known at that time, face. It emphasizes, namely, that a sovereign State does not curtails its legal subjectivity as a result of contracting international obligations. What is more, the ability to undertake them is the essence of sovereignty. As a result, a sovereign State is not above international law, yet quite contrary—this law determines its position in the community of States.

In its later decisions, the PCIJ referred *expressis verbis* to the interpretation of sovereignty presented in the *Wimbledon* case.[41] Moreover, the

---

[39] Spiermann himself criticizes the term 'international community', as, according to him, it is based on unauthorized analogies to national law. Such a practice results, according to Spiermann, in presenting international community in the role of national sovereign, which, consequently, deprives international law of its autonomous juridical character. Spiermann (n 13) 116–125.

[40] *Case of the SS "Wimbledon"* [1923] PCIJ Ser A No 1 at 25.

[41] See *Exchange of Greek and Turkish Populations* (n 32) at 21; *Jurisdiction of the European Commission of the Danube between Galatz and Braila* (n 22) at 36.

restrictive interpretation of the limitations of rights of sovereign State that was frequently emphasized by the PCIJ, confirms the well-established character of the *dictum* of the *Wimbledon* case in the Court's activity. Already in the *Wimbledon* case, the World Court set clear boundaries of such an interpretation. With reference to Germany's obligations within the scope of navigation on the Kiel Canal as set by the Treaty of Versailles, the Court remarked:

> [T]he fact remains that Germany has to submit to an important limitation of the exercise of the sovereign rights which no one disputes that she possesses over the Kiel Canal. This fact constitutes a sufficient reason for the restrictive interpretation, in case of doubt, of the clause which produces such a limitation. But the Court feels obliged to stop at the point where so-called restrictive interpretation would be contrary to the plain terms of the article and would destroy what has been clearly granted.[42]

The restrictive interpretation of limitations of the exercise of rights of the sovereign State cannot thus, according to the Court, influence the scope of State's international obligations, and thus curtail the rights of other parties and third subjects protected by the treaty. The boundary of the restrictive interpretation of limitations of States' freedom of action is determined, in other words, by the inviolability of the 'substance' of contracted international obligations. Already prior to the decision in the *Wimbledon* case, the PCIJ, in its Advisory Opinion on *Nationality Decrees Issued in Tunis and Morocco*, presented interesting and influential, to this day, arguments concerning the relation between State sovereignty and international obligations. The essence of the arguments concerned the issue of the so-called reserved domain (domestic jurisdiction). The arguments clearly expressed that it is international law and not States themselves that determine the boundaries of reserved domain. Contrary to the doctrine of State auto-limitation, which was widely spread at the turn of the nineteenth and twentieth centuries, especially in the German theory of law, the PCIJ opted for the priority of international law over domestic law; hence it did not consider that disputes about the existence if international obligations could be part of the reserved domain (domestic jurisdiction) of States. In its interpretation of Article 15(8) of the Covenant of the League of Nations, it remarked that the phrase "solely within the domestic jurisdiction" signified only the issues that were, as a principle, not regulated by international law. And it is only with reference to these issues that

42 *SS "Wimbledon"* (n 40) at 24–25.

the State remains a "sole judge".[43] The appraisal of the Permanent Court that still remains valid is as follows: "The question whether a certain matter is or is not solely within the jurisdiction of a State is an essentially relative question; it depends upon the development of international relations".[44]

Although the PCIJ recognized the reserved domain of States as a relevant element in the protection of their sovereignty, it did not, however, see it as a threat to the international legal order, as the reserved domain is an international law institution, the scope of which is determined by this law. The reserved domain cannot, thus, justify the non-fulfillment of international obligations. Each issue concerning the existence and scope of State's international obligations is, according to the Court, a "question of international law". Therefore, the PCIJ, in its Advisory Opinion on *Exchange of Greek and Turkish Populations*, refused to recognize the disputes concerning the interpretation and application of international agreements in States' internal relations as issues coming within the reserved domain (domestic jurisdiction). Consequently, the Court emphasized that "a State which has contracted valid international obligations is bound to make in its legislation such modifications as may be necessary to ensure the fulfillment of the obligation undertaken".[45]

In view of the foregoing, it would be difficult to support the thesis that in the light of the PCIJ's decisions, sovereignty, being the main determinant of the legal status of States is a destructive factor in the community of States. The Court did not see a discrepancy between sovereignty and law. According to the Court, a sovereign State may be a law-abiding subject of the international legal order.[46]

Returning to the PCIJ's position concerning the interpretation of the limitations of States' rights, let us recall the famous *dictum* of the *Lotus* case: "International law governs relations between independent States. The rules of law binding upon States ... emanate from their own free will..." The doctrine of the *Lotus* case sees States as international legislators, as it recognizes sovereignty as a constitutive element of international law.

---

[43] *Nationality Decrees Issued in Tunis and Morocco* (Advisory Opinion) [1923] PCIJ Ser B No 4 at 23–24.

[44] Ibid at 24. Cf. the Resolution of Institut de Droit International of 29 April 1954, *La determination du domaine reserve et ses effets*, Article 1, "Annuaire de L'Institut de Droit International" (vol 45, 1954) 292–293, 299–300.

[45] *Exchange of Greek and Turkish Populations* (n 32) 17, 20.

[46] Part of the doctrine of the time, naturally, saw it differently. See especially H Lauterpacht, *infra* note 57.

Thus, any limitations of sovereignty, as the PCIJ emphasized, cannot be presumed.[47] In essence the *Lotus* case boils down to establishing the bases of the exercise of jurisdiction outside States. On the one hand, the Court assumed that States cannot, within the scope of jurisdiction, cross the boundaries defined by international law. Within these boundaries, the State's entitlement to exercise jurisdiction stems from its sovereignty. On the other hand, however, it recognized that the States' freedom of action outside their borders can only be restricted by concrete prohibitive norms, those that are "generally accepted international law". Consequently, it rejected the view of the State's obligation to present the norm authorizing it to act.[48]

The *Lotus* doctrine was strongly criticized by a part of the scholarship of international law. However, the PCIJ's position does not seem to have had destructive effects on international law. The Court only rejected the presumption of States' consent to prohibitive norms. Such consent needs to be explicit, ie it must stem from States' will that is embodied in treaties and/or international customs. The lack of explicit consent results in a contrary presumption, namely the presumption of States' freedom of action. Thus, the core of the *Lotus* doctrine comes down to the standpoint that international law leaves to States a wide measure of discretion which is only limited in certain cases by prohibitive rules. It is noteworthy that this standpoint is also supported by some the ICJ's judgments and Advisory Opinions.[49]

This position is directly connected with the restrictive interpretation of the limitations of States' rights applied by the Court in the interpretation of treaties. In the Advisory Opinion on *Polish Postal Service in Danzig*, the PCIJ remarked that the party's rights could not be restrictively interpreted in the absence of any explicit reservations or restrictions in the treaty.[50] Similarly, in *The Territorial Jurisdiction of the International Commission of the River Oder* case, the Court recognized that in a case where the intention of the parties to the treaty was uncertain, "that interpretation should

47 *SS "Lotus"* (n 19) at 18.

48 Ibid at 19, 20.

49 See *Fisheries Case* (*United Kingdom v Norway*) [1951] ICJ Rep at 116; *Military and Paramilitary Activities in and Against Nicaragua* (*Nicaragua v United States of America*) (Merits, Judgment) [1986] ICJ Rep at 135 [269]; *Legality of the Threat or Use of Nuclear Weapons* (Advisory Opinion) [1996] ICJ Rep at 238–239, 247 [21]-[22], [52]; *Accordance with International Law of the Unilateral Declaration of Independence in Respect to Kosovo* (Advisory Opinion) ICJ Rep [56] available at <http://www.icj-cij.org/docket/files/141/15987.pdf>.

50 *Polish Postal Service in Danizg* (Advisory Opinion) [1925] PCIJ Ser B No 11 at 37–38.

be adopted which is most favorable to the freedom of States".[51] Any limitations of the State's freedom or rights must, according to the Court, have a clear legal basis and cannot be merely presumed. The PCIJ would particularly emphasize it with reference to the restrictions of States' territorial power (territorial sovereignty).[52]

It is worth considering the broader nature of the PCIJ's position on sovereignty, and its significance to the constitutional interpretation of international law. The PCIJ was not always consistent in the terms it applied. Most frequently, it would use the term sovereignty (*soveraineté*), although, sometimes, it would also interchangeably use the term independence (*indépendance*). It was only in one decision—namely, the *Customs Régime Between Germany and Austria* Advisory Opinion—that it attempted to directly explain what State sovereignty is. It recognized that a sovereign State was the one that exercised "sovereign control over its own independence".[53] It is hard, however, to consider this attempt to define 'sovereignty' as a successful one. It can even be accused of an *ignotum per ignotus* mistake, as the *definiens* that is applied in the definition, ie 'sovereign control', remains unclear. Moreover, what the explanation of what 'independence' is also problematic. The Court presented it with reference to the legal position of Austria.

> [T]he independence of Austria, according to Article 88 of the Treaty of Saint-Germain, must be understood to mean the continued existence of Austria within her present frontiers as a separate State with sole right of decision in all matters economic, political, financial or other with the result that that independence is violated, as soon as there is any violation thereof, either in the economic, political, or any other field, these different aspects of independence being in practice one and indivisible.[54]

This definition was created in order to determine the specific status of Austria after World War I. Nevertheless, the relation of sovereignty to independence, as expressed by the PCIJ, and particularly the question whether sovereignty is something more than independence, remains unclear.

---

[51] *Case Relating to the Territorial Jurisdiction of the International Commission of the River Oder* (n 37) at 26. See also *Minority Schools in Albania* (n 35) at 15.

[52] See *Access to, or Anchorage in the Port of Danzig, of Polish War Vessels* (Advisory Opinion) [1931] PCIJ Series A/B No 43 at 142; *Case of the Free Zones of Upper Savoy and the District of Gex* [1932] PCIJ Ser A/B No 46 at 166–167; *Interpretation of the Statute of the Memel Territory* [1932] PCIJ Ser A/B No 49 at 314, 316; *Lighthouses in Crete and Samos* [1937] PCIJ Ser A/B No 71 at 103.

[53] *Customs Régime Between Germany and Austria* (Advisory Opinion) [1931] PCIJ Ser A/B No 41 at 45.

[54] Ibid at 45.

In the *Custom Régime* Opinion, the PCIJ actually deprives sovereignty of the quality of being a characteristic of the State's legal status, and reduces it to the sphere of facts and politics. Pursuant to the Court's view, the conclusion of virtually any treaty would violate sovereignty and independence, as it would reduce the scope of sovereign control. Such a position leads to a contradiction with the approach to sovereignty as presented in the *Wimbledon* case, and as such seems to detract from the PCIJ's other decisions concerning sovereignty. Not without reason, thus, the *Customs Régime* Opinion is recognized as a "decline in the standard of the Permanent Court's legal reasoning".[55]

Nevertheless the totality of the PCIJ's decisions allows us to claim that it recognized sovereignty as the main characteristic of the State in international law. From sovereignty stems the States' ability to establish international legal norms, and freedom of action, which can only be limited by explicit prohibitive norms. Therefore, entering into international obligations does not violate sovereignty, although it may restrict its exercise by curtailing States' freedom of action. Permanent limitations of sovereignty are, according to the Court, exceptional, and stem from treaty regulations. The occasion for the formulation of the view by the Court was provided by the numerous motions for Advisory Opinions concerning various aspects of the legal status of the Free City of Danzig.[56]

The most important and, at the same time, the most controversial side of the PCIJ's views on sovereignty, concerns the Court's questioning of the presumption of limitations of States' freedom of action stemming from sovereignty. Such limitations must have a clear legal basis, ie must stem, as the doctrine of *Lotus* has it, from the "free will of States". Such a view of the Court was subject to fierce criticism by the opponents of legal positivism. It was Hersch Lauterpacht that particularly excelled at it. He would consistently criticize the principles of States' consent and presumptive freedom of action as a basis of international legal obligations.[57] Lauterpacht would

---

55 Spiermann (n 13) 316.

56 See especially *Free City of Danzig and International Labour Organization* (Advisory Opinion) [1930] PCIJ Ser B No 18 at 11; *Treatment of Polish Nationals and Other Persons of Polish Origin or Speech in the Danzig Territory* (n 29) at 23–24. The PCIJ treated Free City of Danzig as a State sui generis. In *Treatment of Polish Nationals* opinion it stated that "the fact that the legal status of Danzig is *sui generis* does not authorize it to depart from the ordinary rules governing relations between States and to establish new rules for the relations between Poland and Danzig" (at 23).

57 See H Lauterpacht, *Private Law Sources and Analogies of International Law (with Special Reference toInternational Arbitration)* (Archon Books, Hamden, Connecticut [1927] 1970) part 1, 43 ff; idem, *The Function of Law in the International Community* (Clarendon

accuse the positivistic approach represented by the PCIJ of undermining the completeness of international law, and thus justifying the presence of 'gaps' in this law, which consequently leads to the strengthening of the *non-liquet* rule in international judiciary. Lauterpacht criticized the presumptive freedom of action primarily due to the dependence of the binding force of international law on the wills of sovereign States. From this perspective and according to Lauterpacht, international law,"proves to be nothing but a delusion", and therefore he viewed the positivistic doctrine of sovereignty as an "aberration of logic".[58]

Hersch Lauterpacht's approach to the PCIJ's decisions may be seen as a manifestation of a tendency that is diagnosed by Ole Spiermann, who writes: "[U]nderstanding of some of the Permanent Court's key decisions says more about the preconceived ideas, or hidden agendas, of readers and of international legal theory than about the attitudes of the judges themselves".[59] In fact, Lauterpacht saw the PCIJ's decisions through the prism of his own, non-positivistic theory of law, within the framework of which he would primarily accentuate the expectations that ought to be met by international law, and therefore he would attach less importance to the actual motives behind the Court's arguments. Nonetheless, Lauterpacht would rightly draw attention to two issues. Firstly, the PCIJ was actually an advocate of the positivistic approach, which presented international law as a horizontal legal order. Secondly, a possible, though not necessary, consequence of basing the binding force of international law on States' will, is the limitation of the completeness of a legal order. The lack of completeness, in turn, makes a constitutional interpretation of international law doubtful, as it sets clear boundaries for the Rule of Law in international relations. A question may, thus, be posed whether the establishment of common principles as a permanent and unquestionable point of reference for the whole community of States, is possible in the law whose rules stem from the wills of particular sovereign States? Another question is: which of the sources of law could play the role of the most

---

Press, Oxford 1933) 94–96; idem, *The Development of International Law by the International Court*(n 12) 359–361; idem, *Brierly's Contribution to International Law* in Brierly, Lauterpacht, and Waldock (eds) *The Basis of Obligation in International Law and Other Papers* (n 20) XVI-XVIII.

58 Lauterpacht, *Brierly's Contribution to International Law* (n 57) XXII, XXIV. For a different approach to an issue of 'gaps' in international law and connected with it the so-called 'doctrine of non-justiciable disputes' see e.g. C De Visscher, *Théories et Réalités en Droit International Public* (3 éd, Éditions A Pedone, Paris 1960) 446–453.

59 Spiermann (n 13) 28.

important source, ie constitution, in this legal system? These questions will be returned to later.

IV. The PCIJ and the Rule of Law within International Society

1. *Preliminary Issues*

The Rule of Law is universally recognized as a fundamental value of legal order. But there is not universal agreement about what it means. As Francis G Jacobs says there are two main aspects of the Rule of Law: formal and substantive.[60] Formally, argues Jacobs, the principle requires that the exercise of power—and thus all acts of the public authorities—is subject to review by the courts to ensure that the exercise was authorized by law, which is known as the principle of legality.[61] As such the Rule of Law may be viewed as the precondition for constitution in the 'strong' meaning. In substantive terms, the Rule of Law embodies certain fundamental values to a given community.

From the foregoing it follows that the Rule of Law is not a concrete legal norm, but an ideal expressing the primacy of law over force. It includes the institutions applying law, common values manifested by a given community, and, primarily, the sources of law of a universal scope of application in a given community. The universal scope of their application guarantees the completeness of the legal order, ie its capability of offering legal solutions to all real contentious situations. Hence, the implementation of the Rule of Law in a given community allows for talk about the constitutionalization of its legal order.

In the Advisory Opinion concerning *Consistency of Certain Danzig Legislative Decrees with the Constitution of the Free City*, the PCIJ directly referred to the twin ideas of the Rule of Law and the notion of *Rechtsstaat*. It defined *Rechtsstaat* as "a State governed by the rule of law".[62] Although the PCIJ did not directly consider the idea of the Rule of Law in the context of international relations, it may analogously be referred to that context, and a question may be posed as to within what scope the international relations were, according to the Court, subjected to the control by law and its institutions. The question posed will be considered in two aspects.

60 FG Jacobs, *The Sovereignty of Law: The European Way* (CUP, Cambridge 2007) 7.

61 Ibid.

62 *Consistency of Certain Danzig Legislative Decrees with the Constitution of the Free City* (Advisory Opinion) [1935] PCIJ Ser A/B No 65 at 54.

Firstly, what is the potential constitutional status of sources of law in the law of the interwar international society? In the light of the Court's decisions treaties could aspire to such a status, including that most special post-World War I treaty ie the Covenant of the League of Nations. A consititutional case could, on the basis of the Court's decisions, also be made for 'general law', ie general principles of law and principles of international law. Secondly, for international law what are the consequences of State sovereignty on the Rule of Law? Special attention here will be drawn to the formal aspect of the Rule of Law, ie to what extent the exercising of political power in international relations was subjected to review by the Court.

Before we discuss these issues it is worth elucidating, as a point of reference, what constitutional interpretation of international law judges Jonkher Van Eysinga and Walter Schücking presented in their separate opinions in the *Oscar Chinn* case.

2. *"Constitutional Nicety of the Treaty"—Constitutional Underpinnings of International Law According to Judges Van Eysinga and Schücking*

The key concern of the *Oscar Chinn* case was to uncover the basis of treaty obligations of the parties to the proceedings. It was significant in this regard for the Court to determine whether the signatory States of the Convention of Saint-Germain were entitled to consider the General Act of Berlin of February 26th 1885 (except for the stipulations of its first Article, which were embodied in Article I of the Convention of Saint-Germain), and the Declaration of Brussels of July 2nd 1890, as abolished *inter se*, and to replace these instruments *inter se* by the articles of the Convention of Saint-Germain.

According to Judge Van Eysinga, the Berlin Act presented a case in which a large number of States, which were territorially or otherwise interested in a vast region, endowed it with a "highly internationalized statute, or rather a constitution established by treaty", by means of which the interests of peace, those of "all nations" as well as those of the natives, appeared to be most satisfactorily guaranteed.[63] The General Act of Berlin, in Van Eysinga's view, was not an ordinary treaty, that is a treaty establishing a number of contractual relations between a number of States, instead "it provides the Congo Basin with a régime, a statute, a constitution". Such a treaty created an "indivisible whole" and could be modified only by the

---

[63] *Oscar Chinn Case* (Separate Opinion of Jonkheer Van Eysinga) [1934] PCIJ Series A/B No 63 (1934) at 132–133.

consent of all contracting Parties.[64] Therefore, the *inter se* modification of the General Act of Berlin introduced by the Convention of Saint-Germain was, according to Van Eysinga, a faulty modification. The States that introduced it acted contrary not only to an essential principle of international law, but also to Article 36 of the General Act of Berlin. What is characteristic is that Van Eysinga emphasized the PCIJ's obligation to serve the constitutional function in the international society. The unauthorized change in the General Act of Geneva, Van Eysinga stated, was a "legal situation of such importance that a tribunal should reckon with it *ex officio*".[65]

Judge Schücking, in his separate opinion, essentially shared Van Eysinga's standpoint. What Schücking recognized as particularly invalid was that the treaty had been concluded as a result of the *inter se* modification of the Berlin Act. "It remains null and void [Schücking emphasized] because it transgresses the bounds which the authors of the Berlin Act established for themselves when they subscribed to that Act". Schücking used the term 'absolutely null and void', which he thought was legitimate due to the meaning of Article 20 of the Covenant of the League of Nations. This article, according to him, "would possess little value unless treaties concluded in violation of that undertaking were to be regarded as absolutely null and void, that is to say, as being automatically void".[66] Judge Schücking also introduced the term *jus cogens*, the effect of which would be that, "once States have agreed on certain rules of law, and have also given an undertaking that these rules may not be altered by some only of their number, any act adopted in contravention of that undertaking would be automatically void".[67] Thus the Court should not apply such an act. Like Van Eysinga, Schücking also recognized the constitutional function of the Court. He stated: "Our Court has been set up by the Covenant as the custodian of international law".[68] Therefore, according to Schücking, the Court's task was to apply a holistic approach to the international legal order, including the assessment of the validity of its legal acts. In particular, the Court must not apply invalid acts, even if the parties to the dispute base the Court's jurisdiction on them. The PCIJ should also examine the validity of legal acts not only in their relation to other acts, but also as regards the aspect of 'public morality'. The Court's approach, as Schücking added,

64 Ibid, 133–134.
65 Ibid, 135.
66 *Oscar Chinn Case* (Separate Opinion of M Schücking) (n 63) 149.
67 Ibid, 149.
68 Ibid, 149.

should be governed not only by the will of the parties to the proceedings, but by "international public policy" as well.[69]

The arguments offered in these two separate opinions introduced important elements of constitutional interpretation of international law, namely: the concept of a treaty as a constitution; the hierarchy of legal norms by introducing their division into *jus cogens* and *jus dispositivum*; the invalidity of treaties that are contrary to *jus cogens*; the idea of "international public policy"; and, finally, the constitutional function of the Permanent Court thus recognized as the "custodian of international law".

These separate opinions aside in the *Oscar Chinn* case the PCIJ presented a different interpretation of international law. It was a manifestation of a broader trend that was present in its decisions after 1930, "to avoid pronouncing upon questions the solution of which does not appear to be indispensable for the decision of the case".[70] Within this trend, the Court viewed international law as a legal order of an exclusively horizontal dimension of action, ie an order whose authors and main subjects were sovereign States. States' legal relations remain to be based on the obligations stemming from the norms they explicitly adopted. The PCIJ did not distinguish between the obligations of States towards the "international community as a whole", and those owed to other (individual) States, which is today strongly supported by the ICJ.[71] Consequently, the legal relations within the international community are, as follows *inter alia* from *Oscar Chinn* case, made of a number of contractual relations between a number of independent States. These relations may be replaced, as regards some of these States, by other contractual relations.

3. *The Role of the Covenant of the League of Nations in International Society*

The notion of 'constitutional nicety of the treaty' is useful in considering the importance of the Covenant of the League of Nations to the interwar

69 Ibid, 150.

70 Hammarskjöld (n 13) 799.

71 See *Case Concerning Barcelona Traction, Light and Power Company, Limited* (*Belgium v Spain*) (Second Phase, Judgment) [1970] ICJ Rep at 32 [33]; *Case Concerning East Timor* (*Portugal v Australia*) [1995] ICJ Rep at 102 [29]; *Case Concerning Application of the Convention on the Prevention and Punishment of the Crime of Genocide* (*Bosnia and Herzegovina v Yugoslavia*) (Preliminary Objections, Judgment) [1996] ICJ Rep at 615–616 [31]; *Legal Consequences of the Construction of a Wall in the Occupied Palestinian Territory* (Advisory Opinion) [2004] ICJ Rep at 199 [155]; *Case Concerning Armed Activities on the Territory of the Congo New Application: 2002* (*Democratic Republic of the Congo v Rwanda*) (Jurisdiction and Admissibility, Judgment) [2006] ICJ Rep at 31–32 [64].

international society. Firstly, the Covenant instituted an institutional structure for this society. Secondly, by limiting the possibility of going to wars and reinforcing peaceful ways of settling international disputes, it gave grounds for establishing a system of collective security. Thirdly, it included a norm derogating the League of Nations members' obligations and agreements that were contrary to it, and at the same time prohibiting them to undertake similar obligations in the future (Article 20). These characteristics of the Covenant offer an image with huge constitutional potential. It is worth mentioning in this context that one of the eminent scholars of the time recognized the Covenant as "higher law" on account of its primacy over other sources of international law.[72]

The PCIJ's first judgment anticipated this important role of the Covenant. In the *Wimbledon* case, the Court recognized a provision of a general character contained in Article 380 as "peremptory" and "categorical".[73] The hierarchy of international legal norms and obligations as outlined in these arguments was not, however, maintained in the Court's decisions. The PCIJ did not attribute to the Covenant such a role as was indicated by its potential. What is particularly characteristic is that the Court made seldom reference to the Covenant's regulations.[74] Admittedly, the Court occasionally recognized the significance of some of the Covenant's regulations for the development of international law,[75] yet its practice was too accidental and selective to become a permanent trend in the Court's jurisprudence.

As regards the League of Nations's significance in the interwar international society, the PCIJ's avoidance of making a systemic attempt to determine the position of its statute in international law is indicative. As compared to the numerous references to the United Nations Charter in the contemporary constitutional debate, the role attributed to the Covenant by the Court seems, indeed, quite modest. The PCIJ would, basically, treat the obligations contained in the Covenant on a par with the obligations present in other international agreements. The fact that the Court did not derive from the Covenant the arguments serving the systemic interpretation of international law is characteristic of its attitude

---

72 H Lauterpacht, 'The Covenant as the Higher Law' (1936) 17 British Ybk of Intl L 54, 55.

73 *SS "Wimbledon."* (n 40) at 21, 22.

74 Cf Fockema Andreae (n 13) 61–69.

75 For example, it recognized Article 13 of the Covenant as a "step forward towards the realization of compulsory arbitration". *Factory at Chorzów* (Jurisdiction) [1927] PCIJ Ser A No 9 at 22–23.

towards a constitutional reading of the Covenant. It also opted against imposing on States concrete obligations from the Covenant's general provisions.[76] Thus, it downplayed the significance of Article 20 of the Covenant.

In light of the above, it is difficult to find in the PCIJ's decisions the arguments for the thesis of the constitutional status of the Covenant of the League of Nations in the law of the interwar international society. As shown by the *Oscar Chinn* case, the Court did not see other treaties in the role of an international constitution, either. Similarly, it did not attribute the constitutional functions to the peremptory norms, the conception of which did not become established in its activity.

4. *General Principles of Law and General Principles of International Law as Applied by the Permanent Court*

Hersch Lauterpacht, in his well-known interpretation of the World Court's decisions and their significance to the development of international law, assigned a special place to the general principles of law. Lauterpacht attributed two basic functions to them.[77] The first of them relies on judicial legislation through application of general principles of law. It amounts not to a change of the law, but to the fulfillment of its purpose. Consequently, as Lauterpacht wrote, "the border line between judicial legislation and the application of the existing law may be less rigid than appears at first sight".[78] The second function of general principles of law consists in protecting the completeness of international law, that is safeguarding against the possibility of a *non liquet*. Thus, it is the gap-filling function. Lauterpacht himself and authors of some contemporary treatises on international law emphasize the importance of this function.[79] It is also strongly supported in the EU law.[80]

---

[76] See *Railway Traffic Between Lithuania and Poland* (*Railway Sector Landwarów-Kaisiadorys*) (Advisory Opinion) [1931] PCIJ Ser A/B No 42 at 119. The Court stated: "[I]t is impossible to deduce from the general rule contained in Article 23 (e) of the Covenant an obligation for Lithuania to open the Landwarów-Kaisiadorys railway sector for international traffic, or for part of such traffic; such obligation could only result from a special agreement". Different Opinion on this subject was given by Judge Anzilotti (ibid, 123).

[77] See Lauterpacht (n 12) 158–172.

[78] Ibid, 161.

[79] See e.g. R Jennings and A Watts (eds), *Oppenheim's International Law* Vol I: *Peace* (9th ed, Longman, London-New York 1992) 12–13; J Combacau and S Sur, *Droit International Public* (4e éd, Montchrestein, Paris 1999) 105; M Shaw, *International Law* (6th ed, CUP, Cambridge 2008) 99.

[80] See T Tridimas, *The General Principles of EU Law* (2nd ed, OUP, Oxford 2006) 17–19.

The significance of the general principles of law goes beyond the functions served by the sources of law which are the source of positive rights and obligations of legal subjects. Indeed, the general principles of law also serve a systemic interpretation of international law, and are a link between law and other normative systems, ethics in particular. As Lauterpacht put it: "Like law as a whole, so 'general principles of law' are, in substance, an expression of what has been described as socially realizable morality. In legal history, courts—as distinguished from formal legislation—have been mainly responsible for the infusion of morals into law".[81]

The Court would apply various terms to signify the general principles of law. It described them as a "generally accepted principle",[82] "the well-known rule",[83] "almost universal opinion and practice",[84] "an established principle",[85] "a principle generally accepted in the jurisprudence of international arbitration, as well as by municipal courts",[86] or "a general conception of law".[87]

The general principles of law were viewed by the PCIJ as a source of positive rights and obligations of the parties to the proceedings. Their autonomous legislative effect was, however, restricted by their subsidiary character in relation to customs, and particularly treaties that were the Court's main basis for passing judgments. The general principles of law were also applied by the Court for the purposes of a systemic interpretation of international law. In this context, they served as important elements of the legal argumentation showing the mutual relations between

81 H Lauterpacht (n 12) 172.

82 *Case Concerning the Payment in Gold of Brazilian Federal Loans Contracted in France* (n 2) 122. The PCIJ spoke of the principle according to which a "State is entitled to regulate its own currency". See also *Serbian Loans* (n 21) at 44.

83 *Article 3, paragraph 2, of the Treaty of Lausanne* (*Frontier between Turkey and Iraq*) (Advisory Opinion), [1925] PCIJ Ser B No 12 at 32. According to the Court the "well-known rule" is that "no one can be judge in his own suit".

84 *Certain Questions Relating to Settlers of German Origin in the Territory Ceded by Germany to Poland* (n 30) at 36. The Court recognized as conformable with "almost universal opinion and practice" that "private rights acquired under existing law do not cease on a change of sovereignty".

85 *Question of Jaworzina* (*Polish-Czechoslovakian Frontier*) (Advisory Opinion) [1923] PCIJ Ser B No 8 at 37. For the Court it is an "established principle that the right of giving an authoritative interpretation of a legal rule belongs solely to the person or body who has power to modify or suppress it".

86 *Factory at Chorzów* (n 75) at 31. As such the Court recognized the principle *nemo auditur propriam turpitudinem allegans*.

87 *Factory at Chorzów* (n 21) at 29. The PCIJ stated: "[I]t is a principle of international law, and even a general conception of law, that any breach of an engagement involves an obligation to make reparation".

concrete rights and obligations of the parties to the proceedings, and their position within the structure of international law.

These functions of the general principles of law should not, however, be overestimated. In the light of the judgments and Advisory Opinions of the PCIJ, their importance in international law is clearly not as great as in national law. The effectiveness of the general principles of law as a source of international law was primarily diminished due to the fact that they were not frequently referred to by the Court. This was admitted even by Hersch Lauterpacht. He was aware that the importance of general principles of law as a safeguard against the possibility of a *non liquet* remained unaffected by "the relative infrequency of or lack of articulation in their use. Experience has shown that the main function of 'general principles of law' has been that of a safety-value to be kept in reserve rather than a source of law of frequent application".[88] This view, incidentally, seems to be supported not only by the PCIJ's approach, but also today by the ambiguous decisions of the ICJ.[89]

In the light of the PCIJ's activity, the second source of 'general international law', that is, the general principles of international law were of greater legislative importance. This part of international law also shows a constitutional potential due to its general scope of application. In the *Lotus* case, the PCIJ stated:

> [T]he words 'principles of international law', as ordinary used, can only mean international law as it is applied between all nations belonging to the community of States... [I]t is impossible—except in pursuance of a definite stipulation—to construe the expression 'principles of international law' otherwise than as meaning the principles which are in force between all independent nations and which therefore apply equally to all the contracting Parties.[90]

What stems from the above is that the general principles of international law are *lex generali* in the law of the international society. A question arises, however, whether they are at the same time *lex superior* in relation to concrete treaties and customs, and how they relate to general principles of law. The answers to these questions are relevant for the assessment of their function in the international society.

---

88 H Lauterpacht (n 12) 166.

89 See on the one hand *Barcelona Traction* (n 71) at 38 [52] and on the other hand *Legality of the Threat or Use of Nuclear Weapons* (n 49) at 247 [52].

90 *SS "Lotus"* (n 19) at 16, 17.

It is worthwhile to point to the rules of law that were recognized by the Court as the general principles of international law. In the *Status of Eastern Carelia* Advisory Opinion, the PCIJ recognized as a fundamental principle of international law "the principle of the independence of States".[91] In *Certain German interests in Polish Upper Silesia* case, the Court described the principle of "respect for vested rights" as "generally accepted international law".[92] In the *Factory of Chorzów* cases, it stated that "the breach of an engagement involves an obligation to make reparation in an adequate form", and as such was the principle of "positive international law".[93] In the *Lotus* case, the Court underlined that the contention that a State must in each case be able to cite a rule of international law authorizing it to exercise jurisdiction was "opposed to the generally accepted international law". It recognized as a principle of international law the "principle of freedom", by virtue of which each State may act outside its territory, provided that in so doing it does not come in conflict with a restriction imposed by international law.[94] In *Jurisdiction of the Courts of Danzig* Advisory Opinion, it stated that it was a "well established principle of international law that an international agreement cannot create direct rights and obligations for private individuals".[95] In the *Greco-Bulgarian "Communities"* Advisory Opinion, it emphasized that "it is a generally accepted principle of international law that in the relations between Powers who are contracting Parties to a treaty, the provisions of municipal law cannot prevail over those of the treaty".[96]

The aforementioned principles are of varying 'specific gravity'. Their relation to the general principles of law is different, as well. Some of them are identical to the general principles of law, which proves that under Article 38(1)(c) of the Statute of the PCIJ, the general principles of law are not only sources of international law, but a part of the positive international law as well. The principle of respect for vested rights and the principle establishing an obligation to make reparation in case of the breach of an engagement, were *expressis verbis* considered as a "positive international law" by the PCIJ.[97] This is not, however, what is most relevant for the

[91] *Status of Eastern Carelia* (n 38) at 27. According to the Court, this principle is the source of the prohibition to settle international disputes within the available political and legal procedures without the consent of the State concerned.

[92] *Certain German Interests in Polish Upper Silesia* (n 27) at 42.

[93] *Factory at Chorzów* (n 75) at 21; *Factory at Chorzów* (n 21) at 29.

[94] *SS "Lotus"* (n 19) at 19, 20.

[95] *Jurisdiction of the Courts of Danzig* (n 28) at 17.

[96] *The Greco-Bulgarian "Communities"* (n 30) at 32.

[97] See n 92 and n 93.

constitutional significance of these principles. What is most relevant is their relation to States' concrete obligations contained in treaties and international customs. It is primarily about whether the general principles of international law and the general principles of law are *lex superior* in relation to treaties and customs, and whether States' concrete obligations ought to be interpreted in their light. This problem may be expressed in yet another way, namely by posing a question of whether the general principles of international law play the role of 'power conferring rules', using Herbert Hart's terminology, and thus serve the function of constructive elements of the international legal order.

The PCIJ's decisions do not provide an unambiguous answer to the questions posed, as in their light the general principles of international law do not have a uniform normative status. A few of them, indeed, play the role of 'power conferring rules', as they determine the direction of the Court's argumentation concerning the existence and interpretation of concrete rights and obligations of the parties to the proceedings. In this sense, they play a key role in the systemic structure of international law. They include the following: the principle of independence of States, the principle of freedom of States' action, and the principle of the primacy of international law over national law. The status of the next two general principles of international law, the source of which are the general principles of law, namely, the principle of respect for vested rights and the principle to make reparation in case of the breach of an engagement, is different. They are a direct source of rights and obligations of legal subjects, although they exist outside of concrete treaty and customary obligations. In the *Factory of Chorzów* case, the Court stated: "Reparation ... is the indispensable complement of a failure to apply a convention and there is no necessity for this to be stated in the convention itself".[98] They also serve as a significant factor in interpreting treaty obligations of the parties to the proceedings.[99]

There are, however, also such general principles of international law that are of relative character, ie may be overruled by the will of the parties to a treaty (*lex specialis derogat legi generali*). The PCIJ directly emphasized this, as already mentioned, with reference to the principle that a treaty, as such, could not create direct rights and obligations for private persons. It stated that "according to the intention of the contracting Parties

---

98 *Factory of Chorzów* (n 75) at 21.

99 See *Certain German Interests in Polish Upper Silesia* (n 27) at 22; *Factory at Chorzów* (n 75) at 27; *Interpretation of Judgements Nos 7 and 8 (The Chorzów Factory)* [1927] PCIJ Ser A No 13 at 19.

every treaty can create direct individual rights and obligations and enforceable by the national courts".[100] In several decisions, the Court simply omitted the general principles of international law and emphasized the priority of the will of the parties expressed in the binding agreement over them. In the *Mavrommatis Jeruzalem Concessions* case, interpreting the Protocol relating to certain concessions granted in the Ottoman Empire (Protocol XII), the Court stated: "[P]rotocol XII is complete in itself, for a principle taken from general international law cannot be regarded as constituting an obligation contracted by the Mandatory except in so far as it has been expressly or implicitly incorporated in the Protocol".[101] The approach to the position of the general principles of law or the principles of international law, based on the rule *lex specialis derogat legi generali*, was also presented by the PCIJ in the *Lighthouses Case Between France and Greece*,[102] the *Oscar Chinn* case[103] and in the *Diversion of Water from the Meuse* case.[104]

The principles of international law that are not of *lex superior* character, cannot play a constitutional role in it, as they do not serve the function of a stable normative point of reference for the entities creating and applying this law. Thus, they do not serve the integrative function within the international society. Among the aforementioned general principles of international law, a permanent position in the PCIJ's decisions, in explaining both the nature of international law and concrete legal obligations, is held by two mutually complementary principles: independence of States and freedom of States' action. Do, however, these principles pointing to the States' will as the basis of the binding force of international law, allow for a constitutional reading of international law? The main doubt concerns the question whether the States, which are the *spiritus movens* of international law in the light of these principles, are capable of establishing a legal order in which a significant role may be played by the Rule of Law.

5. *The Principles of Independence and Freedom of States' Action and the Rule of Law—An Issue of the Court's Jurisdiction*

What the Court derived from the principle of the independence of States was the lack of obligatory jurisdiction of tribunals and other bodies within

---

100 *Jurisdiction of the Courts of Danzig* (n 28) at 17–18.

101 *The Mavrommatis Jerusalem Concessions* [1925] PCIJ Ser A No 5 at 27. Cf also Fockema Andreae (n 13) at 69.

102 *Lighthouses Case Between France and Greece* [1934] PCIJ Ser A/B No 62 at 19, 25.

103 *Oscar Chinn Case* (n 63) 79, 81.

104 *The Diversion of Water from the Meuse* [1937] PCIJ Ser A/B No 70 at 16.

the scope of peaceful settlement of international disputes. Although, according to the Court, there are no disputes that the States could not submit to the Court for consideration,[105] the jurisdiction of the bodies settling disputes must be based on the States' consent.[106] Thus, the objective of the Court examining the question of jurisdiction is "always to ascertain whether an intention on the part of the Parties exists to confer jurisdiction upon it".[107] A manifestation of the Court's great caution as regards the examination of the bases of own jurisdiction, is the *Status of Eastern Carelia* Advisory Opinion, in which the Court refused to pass an Opinion, as it recognized it as "substantially equivalent to deciding the dispute between the parties".[108]

In the face of the Court's approach in *Eastern Carelia* the scope of operation of the Rule of Law in international relations obviously remains dependent on the will of States. The Court itself went even further as regards the limitation of the significance of the Rule of Law, as it recognized that "its judgments must be limited to questions of law and other matters cannot be controlled by it".[109] In the light of Article 38(1) of its Statute, the Court's view in this regard does not seem right, since the Court's task was not only to decide disputes limited to legal issues, but to settle all disputes submitted to it "in accordance with international law". The PCIJ's approach led to the division of international disputes into legal disputes and political ones,[110] and thus to the determination of the competence boundaries of the political organs of the League of Nations and judicial bodies. According to the Court, the main duty of the Council of the League of Nations was to "dissipate or settle political disputes".[111] The Council of the League of Nations did not, in turn, deal with legal issues, the settlement of which was within the Court's competence. The competences

---

105 *Rights of Minorities Schools in Upper Silesia (Minority Schools)* [1928] PCIJ Ser A No 15 at 22; *Factory at Chorzów (Claim for Indemnity)* (Merits) (n 21) at 37.

106 *Status of Eastern Carelia* (n 38) at 27. The Court stated: "It is well established in international law that no State can, without its consent, be compelled to submit its disputes with other States either to mediation or to arbitration, or to any other kind of pacific settlement".

107 *Factory at Chorzów* (n 75) at 32.

108 *Status of Eastern Carelia* (n 38) at 28–29.

109 *Case of the Free Zones of Upper Savoy and the District of Gex* (n 52) at 162. In this case the Court stated that economic interests of States could not be controlled by an outside organ.

110 For more on this issue see the contribution of Giles Samson and Guilfoyle to the present volume (at 56–57).

111 *Article 3, Paragraph 2, of the Treaty of Lausanne (Frontier between Turkey and Iraq)* (n 83) at 27.

of these bodies, being "different in character", were separate and independent. The consequence of this attitude was the lack of the PCIJ's competence within the scope of controlling the Council's decisions.[112]

The change of the character of the jurisdiction of political and judicial bodies was, however, possible as a result of the will of the parties to the dispute. According to the PCIJ there was "nothing to prevent the Parties from accepting obligations and from conferring on the Council the powers wider than those resulting from the strict terms of Article 15 and in particular from substituting for the Council's power to make a mere recommendation, the power to give a decision which, by virtue of their previous consent, compulsorily settles the dispute".[113] Thus, it was the consent of the parties to the proceedings, a result of their will, which was a factor deciding whether and within what scope the dispute in question would be legally settled. This leads to a hardly optimistic conclusion that in the state of affairs where the activities of States and political bodies were excluded from the compulsory judicial, that is, legal appraisal, talking about the Rule of Law is groundless. Thereby, the basic principles of international law, in the light of the Permanent Court's approach, do not completely regulate the execution of the political authority within the international society and, at the same time, they do not guarantee subordination of States' activity to law. Naturally, this prevents a constitutional reading of international law.

V. Concluding Remarks

What emerges from the PCIJ's decisions is an image of international law as a legal order based on consensual grounds, ie the State's will. The pillars of this order are the principles of independence and (presumptive) freedom of States' action. Therefore, the Court would, on the one hand, frequently emphasize the prohibition to presume the limitations of States' rights, and on the other hand, would indicate that only explicit prohibitive norms are competent to limit the freedom of the States' actions. It would, at the same

---

112 See Minority Schools (n 105) at 29–30. At the same time, however, the Court emphasized its own competence to assess whether the political bodies of the League of Nations used their competence of settling a dispute which they were vested by the Covenant of the League of Nations. See *Question of the Monastery of Saint-Naoum* (*Albanian Frontier*) (Advisory Opinion) [1924] PCIJ Ser B No 9 at 12 et seq.

113 *Article 3, Paragraph 2, of the Treaty of Lausanne* (*Frontier between Turkey and Iraq*) (n 83) at 27.

time, also stress the dependence of the judicial control of the States' actions on their consent. Moreover, the Court rejected the hierarchy of legal norms. Consequently, it interpreted the relations between the norms of international law based on the collision rules: *lex specialis derogat legi generali* and *lex posterior derogat legi priori*. These characteristics of international law do not allow for a convincing defense of the thesis of the Rule of Law being rooted in the law of international society. Furthermore, they do not allow us to talk about the constitutional dimension of international law in the light of the PCIJ's decisions.

The critics of the interwar international law saw the positivistic dogma of State sovereignty as its main drawback.[114] According to them, State sovereignty weakens the systemic bases of international law as a true legal order. Today, such opinions are even more frequent than at the time of the PCIJ. The question whether international law without the guiding idea of sovereignty would be a better legal order, remains a disputable, and perhaps not highly significant, issue; the most fundamental question is the one whether, without sovereignty, this law would be international law, or perhaps would be merely some form of transnational law similar to the legal order of the medieval *reipublicae christianitatis*. It seems that what we call State sovereignty secures the normative autonomy of international law. In this sense, sovereignty of States is its constitutive idea. Such idea simply does not allow international law to be presented within the framework of a constitutional pattern.

The question remains of what contribution the PCIJ's decisions make to the contemporary broad debate on the constitutionalization of international law. Perhaps their greatest significance consists in warning against the hasty search for analogies between international and national laws within the scope of their systemic underpinnings. The constitutional interpretive schema, which aptly describes and explains national law, rather fails with reference to international law and easily risks the accusation of 'wishful thinking'. What stems from the comparison of international and national laws in the context of a constitutional ideal is the conclusion that international law is a lesser and imperfect law. Due to its primarily horizontal dimension of action, it is not capable of meeting the requirements imposed by this constitutional ideal. Therefore, presumably, the PCIJ did not compare international law to national law. It did not

114 See especially JL Brierly, *The Shortcomings of International Law*, in JL Brierly (n 20) 75 et seq.; H Lauterpacht (n 57) *passim*.

estimate them either. Within the scope of systemic bases, according to the PCIJ, these legal orders are different and largely incommensurate to each other.

A constitution as a form of legitimacy of the legal order only exists within a true community, ie such a community where relations are based on stable principles, around which the identity of a community is formed. A constitution in the community is what unites it. As such, it is a counterweight to the atomization of social ties. In the light of the PCIJ's decisions, such a uniting factor does not exist in the international society. The main constitutive characteristic of international law is, indeed, sovereignty. The restrictive interpretation of the limitations of the freedom of States' actions that stems from it, supports rather better the protection of States' individual interests, over so-called 'community interests'. This essentially remains true in contemporary international law. Although we may speak about 'community interests' that are clearly being formed, their enforcement and protection are largely conditioned by the protection of the individual interests of States.[115] These individual interests often remain outside of the judicial control, which emphasizes the inadequacy of a constitutional schema of international law. The reading of the jurisprudence of the Permanent Court above seems to suggest that the international legal order has few of the constitutional features comparable to those found in national law. In this sense international law is beyond constitutionalization.

And yet, this state of affairs has another, more optimistic, side to it. It shows the autonomous character of international law and its normative independence from national law. The PCIJ did not, naturally, question the mutual relations between them. What is more, it did emphasize the primacy of international law over national law. However, it did not identify them with each other in the context of their normative systemic

115 Cf recently AL Paulus, 'International Adjudication' in S Besson and J Tasioulas (eds) *The Philosophy of International Law* (OUP, Oxford-New York 2010) 207, 210–212; S Villalpando, 'The Legal Dimension of the International Community: How Community Interests Are Protected in International Law' (2010) 21, 2 EJIL 387 ff. Cf also O Spiermann, 'Twentieth Century Internationalism in Law'(2007) 18, 5 EJIL 785, 812–814 and especially a direct contribution to constitutional discussion by J Dunoff and J Trachtman, 'The Lotus Eaters' in J Klabbers, A Peters, and G Ulfstein (n 9) 369–373. Generally see B Simma, *From Bilateralism to Community Interests in International Law* (1994/IV) 250 RCADI 217 ff; CJ Tams, *Enforcing Obligations Erga Omnes in International Law* (CUP, Cambridge 2005), *passim*; K Zemanek, 'New Trends in the Enforcement of Erga Omnes Obligations' in A von Bogdandy, R Wolfrum, and CE Philipp (eds) *Max Planck Yearbook of United Nations Law 4* (Martinus Nijhoff, The Hague 2000) 1 ff.

underpinnings. The ups and downs of the PCIJ's decisions were conditioned, as shown by Ole Spiermann,[116] by judges' capability (or lack thereof) to approach an international law that was independent of national law and, in this sense, autonomous. That is what the development of international legal argument in the Court's decisions depended on. An independent approach to international law allows for it to be seen as a legal order that is not so much primitive, as simply different from national law. And perhaps this autonomy of international law is of greater value than the striving for its constitutional interpretation that makes this law rather artificially similar to the national constitutional ideal. This legacy, it seems, is the Permanent Court's most vital contribution to the present day's debate on the constitutionalization of international law.

116 Spiermann (n 13).

CONCLUSIONS

THE LEGACY OF THE PERMANENT COURT OF INTERNATIONAL JUSTICE—ON JUDGES AND SCHOLARS, AND ALSO ON BISHOPS AND CLOWNS

Ole Spiermann

I. Introduction

This volume is a token to the legacy of the Permanent Court of International Justice. It was the first significant Court of Justice at the international level. It brought the Peace Palace at The Hague to life, and it was partly due to its legacy that, since the Second World War, we have witnessed not only an International Court of Justice but also several other successful international institutions devoted to dispute resolution.

Obscure cases decided by the Permanent Court are household names, familiar to present generations of international lawyers, because they were, by chance, the first place for authoritative expression of various principles of general international law. Such statements of principle have found wide use far beyond their original context. As such they have little to do with the actual life of the Permanent Court, except for confirming the ambition on the part of the Permanent Court to take an active role in the development of international law, at least in the 1920s.

"The Development of International Law by the Permanent Court of International Justice" was the title of Hersch Lauterpacht's celebrated lectures published in 1934. At the time, they formed one of the most influential scholarly accounts of the work of the Permanent Court, yet they were inherently paradoxical. On the one hand, Lauterpacht saw two main threads running through the decisions, "judicial caution" and "judicial legislation", and he subordinated caution to legislation,[1] which in turn he translated into a principle of effectiveness.[2] On the other hand, Lauterpacht

[1] H Lauterpacht, *The Development of International Law by the Permanent Court of International Justice* (London 1934) 43–44.

[2] Ibid, 50, 69–70 and 84. For more on the use of the 'principle of effectiveness' see generally S Wittich (in this volume), at 16–21 and in relation to WTO jurisprudence see J Gomula (in this volume), at 180.

tailored decisions of the Permanent Court to fit his own theoretical agenda. Lauterpacht concluded that "the work of the Court can to a large extent be conceived in terms of a restrictive interpretation of claims of State sovereignty".[3] And this was his theoretical agenda, witnessing the relative simplicity of international law in practice at the time, to refute sovereignty-based arguments and dogmas. What Lauterpacht had originally described as the Permanent Court's genuine contribution to international law, "[j]udicial legislation, conceived as a process of changing the existing law",[4] was in the end treated as a necessity, "a matter of judicial duty".[5]

Today, many years later, the Permanent Court still has the potential to provide more than just general statements used to cloak and ornament preconceived legal theories and arguments. The work of the Permanent Court and subsequent international courts has not merely contributed "case law" as a new "source" of international law. It has changed the way in which international law is approached. It has brought not only the Peace Palace but also international law to life. There is more to international law in practice than what is conventionally accounted for in, to take an example, Article 38 of the Statute of the International Court of Justice. Max Sørensen's doctoral thesis from 1946, *Les Sources du Droit International: Etude sur la Jurisprudence de la Cour Permanente de Justice Internationale*, showed that when one categorizes *dicta* of the Permanent Court along the lines of Article 38 and sources theory in general, one is not using the theory to describe the decisions but the decisions to describe the theory.[6]

The following is an attempt to indicate what roles were offered to international lawyers consequent to the establishment of the Permanent Court. The role as titular judge was new. These stand as pioneers, the achievements and experiences of whom subsequent international tribunals have been inspired by and continue to draw on. But also the role as reader was new. Academics and diplomats read and had to live with the decisions of the Permanent Court.

---

3 Ibid, 89, 104.

4 Ibid, 45 and also 68.

5 Ibid, 105, 107; see also ibid, 50.

6 M Sørensen, *Les sources du Droit International: Etude sur la Jurisprudence de la Cour Permanente de Justice Internationale* (Copenhagen 1946).

II. The Role as Judge

Sir Cecil Hurst, the legal adviser to the Foreign Office, wrote about the result of the first general election to the Permanent Court in 1921:

> The Court only contains three men who have had judicial experience. It is made up of three judges, three legal advisers and five professors. I think I can safely prophesy that it will be completely dominated by Lord Finlay and Loder, assisted by a vast fund of information which Moore will provide, and troubled with a certain amount of narrow obstructiveness from Anzilotti and Huber. I doubt if the rest will count.[7]

There was a Danish judge, DG Nyholm, of the Mixed Courts at Cairo. It was said in the British Foreign Office that according to the French, "having been some years in Egypt, he would be an adequate representative for the Mussulman".[8] The British Government had pressed for more direct representation, but the French Government had opposed this in order not to increase British influence. Those were the times.

There are many ways to exemplify the unprecedented situation in which, at the inaugural meeting on 15 February 1922, the judges of the Permanent Court found themselves. One of the less abstract examples had to do with their physical appearance. It was decided that they should wear robes—after prolonged discussions and by six votes to five.[9] There were also the caps ordered by the President; in Judge Moore's view, they were "something like a miter, with gold bands around them, making us look like a cross between bishops and clowns".[10] They were abolished, however. As for the specially designed presidential gown President Loder preferred the gown he had been wearing as a member of the Dutch Supreme Court. Whether the judges would, figuratively speaking, dress as international, as opposed to national, lawyers in the years to come and so treat international law as a legal system detached in various ways from the specific national legal systems, from which they came, was to be of critical importance.

In the beginning, the decisions of the new Permanent Court did not attract much commentary, to put it mildly, but perhaps for this very reason

---

[7] L Lloyd, *Peace Through Law: Britain and the International Court in the 1920s* (Boydell Press, Suffolk 1997) 19.

[8] O Spiermann, 'A Permanent Court of International Justice' (2003) 72 Nordic J of Intl L 399, 404.

[9] [1922] PCIJ Ser D No 2 at 2, 8, 144, 234.

[10] Spiermann, (n 8) 399, 402.

a blunt note in the American Journal of International Law earned historical significance as it caused much ill feeling on the bench. Referring to the lengthy arguments in the Nationality Decrees case, which I will come back to shortly, the author—Charles Noble Gregory—wrote that "the judges showed both their disapproval and their aptness for judicial functions by falling fast asleep".[11] The author also noted that the judges had "little in common, except access to the same fund by way of compensation". This provoked a bold reaction by some of the judges. Professor Manley O Hudson, one of the few true friends of the Permanent Court in the US, was encouraged to take make a reply.[12] What is more, Åke Hammarskjöld, the industrious Registrar of the Permanent Court, disclosed a semi-official analysis—which we shall also come back to.

The instrument most often addressed by the Permanent Court was, of course, its own Statute and the underlying Article 14 of the Covenant of the League of Nations.

The question of compulsory jurisdiction loomed large in the preparations of the Statute of the Permanent Court and its early years. According to the first draft of the Statute of the Permanent Court prepared by an Advisory Committee of Jurists, legal disputes could be brought before the Permanent Court against any State that had become a party to the Statute, thus investing the Permanent Court with "compulsory" jurisdiction similar to national systems of justice.[13] However, it was found subsequently by the Council of the League of Nations to be contrary to the Covenant and thus omitted.[14] Consequently, a case could only be brought against a State if it gave its consent to the specific proceedings, or the case came under a jurisdictional clause to which the respondent had agreed in advance. In the end, such a clause was inserted in the Statute, but it was optional, each ratifying State being free not to adhere to "the Optional Clause" (or if adhering, to make reservations). Dionisio Anzilotti had assisted the Council in cleaning the draft Statute of compulsory jurisdiction, a noteworthy effort bearing in mind that Anzilotti had been responsible for and assisted the work of the Advisory Committee of Jurists. As a judge of the

11 CN Gregory, 'An Important Decision by the Permanent Court of International Justice' (1923) 17 AJIL298, 306.

12 MO Hudson, 'The Second Year of the Permanent Court of International Justice', (1924) 18 AJIL 1, 6 and 30, fn 114.

13 See Advisory Committee of Jurists, *Procès-verbaux of the Proceedings of the Committee, June 16th – July 24th 1920, with Annexes* (The Hague, 1920) 693–749.

14 See C J Tams (in this volume), at 13, 16–17, and 19–21.

Permanent Court, Anzilotti became the main exponent of a purely consensual test to jurisdiction. The omission of compulsory jurisdiction was regretted by quite a few. In 1920, from the floor of the Assembly of the League of Nations, Loder—who became the first President of the Permanent Court—had told the opponents of compulsory jurisdiction:

> You are fighting against time; you will do so in vain ... Ensure the present for yourselves; the future will be ours ... We recognise no greatness which is raised above justice, even when it wears the mantle of sovereignty.[15]

Compulsory jurisdiction formed a hot topic in the early years of the Permanent Court, until judges had learned to distance themselves from the inherent logic of national systems of justice and abide by the consensual test.

In the *Nationality Decrees* opinion, the question before the Permanent Court was whether the Council of the League could entertain a dispute between France and Great Britain on the occasion of nationality decrees issued by the French Government, bearing in mind that under Article 15(8) of the Covenant the Council could not entertain a dispute if it arose "out of a matter which by international law is solely within the domestic jurisdiction". In its well-known opinion, the Permanent Court held:

> The question whether a certain matter is or is not solely within the jurisdiction of a State is an essentially relative question; it depends upon the development of international relations.[16]

Two further steps taken by the Permanent Court require immediate attention. Firstly, treaty obligations brought the matter outside domestic jurisdiction. Secondly, it did not have to be shown that treaty obligations actually applied; a "provisional conclusion" as to their relevance to the matter in question was sufficient. It followed, in the view of the Permanent Court, that the specific dispute was not covered by Article 15(8).

The judges taking part in the majority had not agreed on the reasoning, and substantial parts of the draft prepared by Judge Huber in collaboration with Judge Anzilotti and Deputy-Judge Beichmann had been omitted.[17] Thus, the *motifs* did not address the exact reason why a provisional

---

15 *League of Nations Records of the Assembly: Plenary Meetings* 1920, 445.

16 *Nationality Decrees in Tunis and Morocco*, [1923] PCIJ Ser B No 4 at 24. For more on the Courts dealings with municipal jurisdiction see generally J d'Aspremont (in this volume), 221.

17 M Huber, *Denkwürdigkeiten, 1907–1924* (Orell Füssli, Zurich 1974) 276.

conclusion as to the applicability of a treaty provision was seen as sufficient to exempt an issue from domestic jurisdiction.

Lauterpacht took the view that the "provisional" conclusion had to be an opinion on the merits. For if the "provisional" conclusion proved wrong, Lauterpacht wrote, "that would mean that the matter is within the domestic jurisdiction of the defendant State, and that the relevancy, as provisionally assumed, did not in fact exist".[18] This was misconceived, but then insiders to the decision provided the reasoning omitted by the Permanent Court—as a response to Charles Noble Gregory and his blunt note in the American Journal. The analysis submitted by Hammarskjöld explained why a provisional conclusion was sufficient for purposes of Article 15(8).[19] Firstly, a stricter test would amount to a decision on the merits. Secondly, as Article 15(8) linked domestic jurisdiction to international law, a stricter test would be equivalent to compulsory jurisdiction, which had been found to be contrary to the Covenant of the League of Nations when preparing the Statute of the Permanent Court. In 1920, this finding had attracted widespread criticism and now the *Nationality Decrees* opinion was cleared of references to the point due to disagreement on a bench partly influenced by misplaced analogies taken from national legal systems.

The question of compulsory jurisdiction came up again in the next Advisory Opinion, the *Eastern Carelia* opinion, delivered later in 1923. The request for the opinion arose out of a dispute between Finland and Russia. However, Russia was not at the time a member of the League of Nations, and the Permanent Court held—*ex officio*, demonstrating its independence of the Council—that under the Covenant of the League of Nations the Council was not competent to undertake the dispute and so, by implication, nor was it competent to request an Advisory Opinion on the subject:

> This rule ... only accepts and applies a principle which is a fundamental principle of international law, namely, the principle of the independence of States. It is well established in international law that no State can, without its consent, be compelled to submit its disputes with other States either to mediation or to arbitration, or to any other kind of pacific settlement.[20]

---

[18] H Lauterpacht, *The Function of Law in the International Community* (Clarendon Press, Oxford, 1933) 362–363.

[19] Paul de Vineuil, 'Les Leçons du Quatrième Avis Consultatif de la Cour Permanente de Justice Internationale' (1923) 4 Revue de Droit International et de Legislation Comparée 291, 299.

[20] *Status of Eastern Carelia*, [1923] PCIJ Ser B No 5 at 27.

The Permanent Court indicated that this principle might also apply to the Permanent Court to the effect that in a specific case a State had to consent not only to the Council entertaining the dispute, but also to the Permanent Court exercising advisory jurisdiction.

As strongly recommended by Judge Moore,[21] the Permanent Court assimilated its advisory jurisdiction to its contentious jurisdiction. Its advisory jurisdiction would not be a back-door version of compulsory jurisdiction. Perhaps needless to say, some members of the Council were not pleased with the result, a criticism which in turn prompted Judge Moore to take an active role in stiffening American conditions for possible adherence to the Court Protocol, constructing the infamous fifth reservation according to which the Permanent Court could not, "without the consent of the United States, entertain any request for an advisory opinion touching any dispute or question in which the United States has or claims an interest".[22]

This brings us to the *Mavrommatis* case, which for the first time saw a responding State objecting to the contentious jurisdiction of the Permanent Court. The jurisdictional question was whether a jurisdictional clause in the Mandate for Palestine extended to international obligations outside the Mandate because generally referred to in a provision of the Mandate. Relevant obligations were found in an external protocol containing no jurisdictional clause on its own.

A narrow majority of the Permanent Court, following an absolutely chaotic process of drafting, opted for an extensive interpretation and dismissed the objection, although only in part.[23] A first draft of the motifs, to which President Loder had no doubt contributed, was modelled on notions familiar to civil law and national systems of justice, which in turn Huber and Anzilotti sought to remove in a second draft. In the final motifs, the absence in the Statute and Rules of Court of provisions regarding preliminary objections led the Permanent Court to infer that it was "at liberty to adopt the principle which it considers best calculated to ensure the administration of justice, most suited to procedure before an international tribunal and most in conformity with the fundamental principles of international law".[24] This sentence neatly summarised divisions on the bench:

---

21 [1922] PCIJ Ser D No 2 at 383–98.

22 See DF Fleming, *The United States and the World Court, 1920–1966* (2nd edn, Russell & Russell, New York 1968) 60–64 and M Dunne, *The United States and the World Court, 1920–1935* (Pinter, London 1988) 139–47.

23 Huber (n 17) 282–283.

24 *Mavrommatis*, [1924] PCIJ Ser A No 2 at 16.

- "ensure the administration of justice"—this seems to have reflected President Loder's appetite for compulsory jurisdiction and analogies from national systems of justice, even if contrary to the Statute.
- "most suited to procedure before an international tribunal"—possibly a test reflecting concerns on the part of Max Huber about adjudication disturbing coexistence between States.
- "most in conformity with the fundamental principles of international law" seems to reflect the consensual test advocated by Anzilotti, "the principle of the independence of States", as the Permanent Court had it in the *Eastern Carelia* opinion.

This division into three principles testifies to the importance of the judge being conscious of his or her role as international lawyer. In particular, President Loder was seen as too much a national lawyer, and dissatisfaction with how he had filled his position during the deliberations in the *Mavrommatis* case resulted in his not being re-elected as President of the Permanent Court. Instead, first Max Huber and then Anzilotti served as presidents. Under their influence, the Permanent Court delivered a number of decisions reflecting thinking as international lawyers, as opposed to national lawyers.

President Huber soon changed the deliberations procedure to a format familiar to succeeding generations (written notes prepared by each judge, the detailed questionnaire produced by the President, and the President's *ex officio* membership of the drafting committee).

Judge Huber's presidency between 1925 and 1927 saw the Permanent Court's approach to treaty interpretation maturing, with one important context being contentious jurisdiction in a series of decisions involving Mavrommatis' claims and Polish Upper Silesia (in particular a factory at Chorzów). In rejecting principles of restrictive interpretation and the like, the Permanent Court eschewed arguments attractive to national lawyers and moulded an international lawyer's approach to international legal argument. In respect of contentious jurisdiction, consent came to overshadow other considerations, an important implication being the *forum prorogatum*.[25] A principle of effective treaty interpretation made the Permanent Court broaden its jurisdiction to "incidental" or "preliminary"

---

[25] *Mavrommatis*, [1925] PCIJ Ser A No 5 at 27–28 and *Rights of Minorities in Upper Silesia (Minority Schools)* [1928] PCIJ Ser A No 15 at 23–24. For more on the role of the PCIJ in shaping modern treaty interpretation see generally S Wittich (in this volume), 89.

issues,[26] whereas considerations bearing on compulsory jurisdiction were confined to the question of how to characterise the power of the Permanent Court to construe "the meaning or scope" of prior judgments.[27] In its last judgment arising out of Mavrommatis' claims, and in which the Permanent Court for the first time declined jurisdiction in a contentious case, the Court stated that

> [t]he Court sees no reason to depart from a construction which clearly flows from the previous judgements the reasoning of which it still regards as sound, more especially seeing that the two Parties have shown a disposition to accept the point of view accepted by the Court.[28]

This statement may not excite writers on precedent in the International Court and its predecessor, yet it expressed a not-so-unusual reservation at the time as to the precedential value of former rulings, at least in the field of jurisdiction.

Sovereignty-based arguments were discarded out of hand. Instead, treaties were given an "objective" interpretation based on the texts and, more importantly, their aim and purpose. Provisions regulating the Permanent Court's jurisdiction were interpreted in the same way as other treaties. Gone were aspirations for compulsory jurisdiction cherished by judges too much influenced by national legal reasoning. In short, these years saw the bench being moulded into international judges and the crystallisation of an international lawyer's approach to international legal argument, answering the questions referred from national law independently of particular national legal systems.

III. The Role as Reader

It took *The Lotus* to attract the interest of scholars in the activities of the Permanent Court.[29] Unlike many of the other decisions, *The Lotus* was almost exclusively concerned general international law, as opposed to treaty interpretation. And so it involved questions that international legal theory had been troubling with for centuries; answers to which were

---

[26] *Case concerning Certain German Interests in Polish Upper Silesia*, [1925] PCIJ Ser A No 6 at 18 and *Case concerning the Factory at Chorzów*,[1927] PCIJ Ser A No 9 at 24–25.

[27] *Interpretation of Judgments Nos. 7 and 8*, PCIJ Series A No. 13 (1927).

[28] *Mavrommatis*, [1927] PCIJ Ser A No 11 at 18.

[29] *The Case of the SS Lotus*, [1927] PCIJ Ser A No 10. For further discussion of this case see generally P Pazartzis (in this volume), 319.

almost bound to be controversial. This was at the time when Judge Moore objected to "the popular impression of some restful sea voyages and refreshing care-free summers on the North Sea, marred only by occasional presence at the reading of a judgment or opinion that came out of the air."[30]

At the opening of the ordinary session in 1927, President Huber welcomed the new tendency among scholars to subject the decisions of the Permanent Court to intense analysis. Using a metaphor that had a clear bearing on *The Lotus*, President Huber compared "our decisions to ships which are intended to be launched on the high seas of international criticism".[31] *The Lotus* attracted much analysis and made it less easy in international legal theory to neglect the Permanent Court. But theory got it wrong. The *motifs* were misrepresented, as Hammarskjöld and also Huber subsequently tried to correct.[32]

Establishing an international lawyer's approach to international legal argument in the context of an international court required it being articulated by judges. But it also had to be appreciated by lawyers reading and commenting on the decisions. In 1927, the leading members of the Permanent Court were ahead of their contemporaries. Some of those openly disagreeing with the Permanent Court, among them Hersch Lauterpacht, imported the conception of *obiter dictum* in order not to feel to restrained by *The Lotus*.[33] The distinction between *ratio decidendi* and *obiter dicta* is known to systems investing court decisions with a binding force, the *ratio decidendi* being the grounds on which the decision are actually based and thus binding, while the *obiter dicta* are comments not strictly necessary for the *dispositif* and so not binding. In what Verzijl later referred to as "a curious instance of opposition by the community of States against a pronouncement of the International Court", treaties were

---

[30] O Spiermann, *International Legal Argument in the Permanent Court of International Justice* (CUP, Cambridge 2005) 275.

[31] Ibid, 247–248.

[32] See M de la Grotte, 'Les Affaires Traitées par la Cour Permanente de Justice Internationale Pendant la Periode 1926–1928' (1929) 10 Revue de Droit International et de Legislation Comparée 387, 387 and Max Huber in (1931) 36-I Annuaire de l'Institut de Droit International 79.

[33] See JF Williams, 'L'affaire du "Lotus"', (1928) 35 Revue Générale de Droit International Public 361, 364; cf, WE Beckett, 'Les Questions d'Intérêt Général au Point de Vue Juridique dans la Jurisprudence de la Cour Permanente de Justice Internationale', (1932) 39 *Recueil des Cours* 135, 144 and Lauterpacht, (n 1) 23–24 and 104.

adopted that modified the principle of concurrent jurisdiction laid down by the Permanent Court.[34]

The facts of the case were simple. In 1926 a Turkish steamship suffered a collision on the high seas causing loss of life. The ship had collided with the SS Lotus, a mail steamer flying the French flag, which then sailed into a Turkish port to land the survivors and obtain repairs. Here the French officer on watch at the time of the collision was arrested and was subsequently prosecuted and sentenced before the Turkish courts. The French Government protested the action taken against the officer and as a result the French and Turkish Governments signed a Special Agreement submitting to the Permanent Court the question whether Turkey had acted in conflict with international law by exercising criminal jurisdiction.

One question was whether general international law imposed restraints upon such jurisdiction, or to phrase it differently, whether Turkey legislating over a French subject on French territory was an issue as for which lawyers recognised that not only Turkey but also France had a significant interest. Six members of the Permanent Court took this view and found a breach of the principle of territorial jurisdiction, while six other members, including President Huber exercising the casting vote, took the opposite view. That being said, it could still be that Turkey had undertaken treaty obligations restricting its jurisdiction to legislate. This alternative angle was the underpinning theme of the *motifs*, which owed much to President Huber and Judge Anzilotti. It was pointed to in this oft-quoted paragraph:

> International law governs relations between independent States. The rules of law binding upon States therefore emanate from their own free will as expressed in conventions or by usages generally accepted as expressing principles of law and established in order to regulate the relations between these co-existing independent communities or with a view to the achievement of common aims. Restrictions upon the independence of States cannot therefore be presumed.[35]

The last sentence, "[r]estrictions upon the independence of States cannot therefore be presumed", has been taken to imply that the Permanent Court saw no need for international law, that each State was sovereign and self-contained, and that it supported a presumption against international

[34] JHW Verzjil, *International Law in Historical Perspective* (vol 4, Sijthoff, Leiden 1971) 53; and see Art 1 of the International Convention for the Unification of Certain Rules relating to Penal Jurisdiction in Matters of Collision or other Incidents of Navigation from 1952 and also Art. 11 of the Geneva Convention on the High Seas and Art. 97 of the United Nations Convention on the Law of the Sea.

[35] (n 29) 18.

law—not exactly intuitive thinking, and nor was this the intended meaning. What the majority had in mind was possible treaty obligations on the part of Turkey. The sentence about restrictions that could not be presumed was a restatement of the principle of independence articulated in the *Eastern Carelia* opinion. It merely meant that if a State had not entered into a contract, the issue had not become international in form and the State could not simply be presumed to be bound (as the French Government was taken to assume). The persistent tradition of criticising *The Lotus* suggests that the international lawyer's approach underpinning the judgment has not been that easily disseminated.

Decisions of the Permanent Court quite clearly made an impact not only upon scholars but also diplomats. In 1928, when the negotiations on the revision of the Statute of the Permanent Court were upcoming, Sir Cecil Hurst made the following observations, echoing his views on the result produced by the first general election of judges in 1921:

> I have been surprised at the frequency with which during the last few years I have heard criticisms made upon the Court on the ground that it contains too many professors. The criticisms are well-founded. Professors make bad judges. What is required is people who have had practical experience and not professorial experience. At the same time, it would be undesirable to make any change in the wording of the Statute on this point; but the adoption of a delicately worded recommendation advocating the choice as candidates of persons who have had practical or judicial experience of the application of international law would be free from objection.[36]

Despite criticism echoing the misgivings dating back to 1920 about such a recommendation throwing the Permanent Court open to diplomats, first the Committee of Jurists, then the Conference of Signatories and finally the Tenth Assembly of the League of Nations adopted resolutions to the effect that "in accordance with the spirit of Articles 2 and 39 of the Statute of the Court, the candidates nominated by the national groups should possess recognised practical experience in international law".[37]

On 25 September 1930, the second general election of judges to the Permanent Court was held. In accordance with the Statute this was a

---

[36] Spiermann (n 30) 308–309.

[37] *League of Nations Records of the Assembly: Plenary Meetings* 1929, 119–21; the sentence continued: "and that they should be at least able to read both the official languages of the Court and to speak one of them; it also considers it desirable that to the nominations there should be attached a statement of the careers of the candidates justifying their candidature".

general election comprising all members, the number having been increased to 15. In 1920, Sir Cecil Hurst had been critical of the result of the first general election, there being too few national judges and too many professors. Experience had shown that some of the former professors had taken the lead; their achievements had been significant, developing an international lawyer's approach to international legal argument. In 1929, Sir Cecil had been elected to the Permanent Court, filling the vacancy left by the death of Lord Finlay. In 1930 he was re-elected. So was his French counterpart, Henri Fromageot. They had been full-time legal advisers to, respectively, the Foreign Office and the Quai d'Orsay. Their overarching conceptions of the Permanent Court's proper functioning were similar, and they regarded the *motifs* of many of the past decisions as being too long and too theoretical.

The second general election brought in a new, numerous breed who were neither former national judges, nor professors in international law, but former diplomats, also in addition to Hurst and Fromageot. In Hammarskjöld's words, the new Court contained, "if I remember correctly, three ex-members of the Council and five ex-legal advisers to members of the Council".[38] Anzilotti stayed—at the cost of becoming "the great dissenter". Characteristically, Hammarskjöld changed the aim of his articles reviewing the Permanent Court's work. While originally intended to correct misrepresentations on the part of commentators, the new articles written in a more secretive style took the form of correcting the Permanent Court.

It was perhaps bad luck that, in 1931, the Permanent Court in its new composition was requested to advise on the legality of a planned customs union between Germany and Austria. It was the most politically sensitive dispute to be referred to the Permanent Court and a watershed in its history as the Advisory Opinion, carried by a narrow majority, was accused of having turned a legal question into a political one. Criticism was fuelled by the combination of the obscurity of the *motifs*, Judge Anzilotti's boldness in his concurring opinion and the dissenters' scarcely veiled accusations. The majority found that the planned customs union would be in breach of Austria's treaty obligations not to "compromise" or "threaten" its "independence" (without the consent of the Council, which had requested the opinion).[39]

---

38 Spiermann (n 30) 311.
39 *Customs Régime*, [1931] PCIJ Ser A/B No 41.

The 1930s saw a disappointing, though perhaps not surprising, backsliding in many cases to a national lawyer's approach to international law. Of course, times had already changed and the decay was well underway. Yet most decisions were shot through with formalism and self-restraint. Occasionally the new Court appeared even to apply national law as if there were no difference before an international court between national and international law. There were no grand statements as in the 1920s, much less food for thought, much less to quote for future generations. Just to take an example, the standard quotation from the Customs Union opinion on the definition of independence is not from the reasoning of the majority but from the individual opinion of Anzilotti.

IV. Concluding Reflections

As an institution, and a project of international justice, the Permanent Court was a success, being the framework within which the world first experienced the development of an international judiciary. During the negotiations of the Charter of the United Nations, there was little doubt that an International Court should be part of the institutional arrangement, and that it would be closely modelled on its predecessor. Despite the significant political changes in the world since 1945, many of which have been given legal form, there has been no decline in the international judiciary, and no change in the basic framework laid down after 1921 for the Court. Today, there are several active international courts in existence in addition to the principal judicial organ of the United Nations.

Many of the decisions of the Permanent Court concerned the interpretation of treaties that are now obsolete; most of them had emerged out of the conclusion of the First World War and most did not survive yet another upheaval of the world. Many decades later, there are often more recent and less eccentric precedents to cite. Yet, and as demonstrated by this volume, there is more to the decisions of the Permanent Court than history. The structures of international legal argument then used were not a result of the *interbellum*, its political or other circumstances; they take part in a conceptual deep structure ingrained in internationalism at all times. The Permanent Court saw the development of an international lawyer's approach to international law, as well as the risks underpinning it, and it provides a context in which to study international legal argument that may well be second to none even today.

The Permanent Court of the 1920s founded an international lawyer's approach to international legal argument, which stands as an example to admire and be inspired by, partly because it is a continuing task of international lawyers to dress internationally, as it were, as opposed to nationally.